Introduction to

LEGAL STUDIES

THIRD EDITION

edited by

THE CARLETON DEPARTMENT OF LAW CASEBOOK GROUP

Logan Atkinson
Jane Dickson-Gilmore
Mary-Anne Nixon
Neil Sargent
Peter Swan
Barry Wright

CANADIAN LEGAL STUDIES SERIES

Captus Press

Canadian Legal Studies Series
Introduction to Legal Studies, Third Edition

Copyright © 1990–2001 by the editors and Captus Press Inc.

First Captus Press edition, 1990
Revised edition, 1991
Second edition, 1995
Third edition, 2001

All rights reserved. No part of this publication may be reproduced, stored in a retrieval system, or transmitted, in any form or by any means, electronic, mechanical, photocopying, recording, or otherwise, without written permission of the editor and Captus Press Inc.

Care has been taken to trace ownership of copyright materials contained in this book. The publisher will gladly take any information that will enable the rectification of any reference or credit in subsequent editions.

Canada *We acknowledge the financial support of the Government of Canada through the Book Publishing Industry Development Program (BPIDP) for our publishing activities.*

Canadian Cataloguing in Publication Data

Main entry under title:

Introduction to legal Studies

(Canadian legal studies series)
3rd ed.
Includes bibliographical references and index.

ISBN 1-55322-958-4

1. Law — Canada.   2. Sociological jurisprudence. I. Atkinson, Logan, 1954–   II. Carleton University. Dept. of Law. Casebook Group. III. Series.

KE442.I57 2001   349.71   C2001-902255-7

Captus Press Inc.
Units 14 & 15
1600 Steeles Avenue West
Concord, Ontario
L4K 4M2, Canada
Telephone: (416) 736-5537
Fax: (416) 736-5793
Email: Info@captus.com
Internet: http://www.captus.com

0 9 8 7 6 5 4 3
Printed and bound in Canada

Table of Contents

Note to Students xi

1   **The Legal Terrain** 1

      A. Law in Social Life

        (i)   The Functions of Law
             Edward Adamson Hoebel 1

        (ii)   The Cheyenne Way
             Karl N. Llewellyn and E. Adamson Hoebel 4

        (iii)   Conflicts as Property
             Nils Christie 6

        (iv)   People to People, Nation to Nation
             The Report of the Royal Commission on Aboriginal Peoples 9

      B. Law, The State and The Constitution

        (i)   The Rule of Law: Its Nature and General Applications
             A.V. Dicey 11

        (ii)   The Environment of Canada's Judicial System
             Peter H. Russell 13

        (iii)   *Reference re Secession of Quebec* 18

      C. Canadian Legal Culture in Global Context

        (i)   The 'Meech Generation'
             Colin Grey 23

        (ii)   Canada's 18 Years of Human Rights Case Law Are Sure
             to Be Mined Heavily by Our Judges
             Clare Dyer 25

        (iii)   Globalization
             David Held and Anthony McGrew
             with David Goldblatt and Jonathan Perraton 28

        (iv)   Threat of NAFTA Case Kills Canada's MMT Ban: Challenge
             over gasoline additive could have cost Ottawa millions
             Shawn McCarthy 31

Table of Contents

2 Law and Morality 35

(i) Tragic Choices
Patrick J. Fitzgerald.. 35
(ii) *R. v. Dudley & Stephens* 39
(iii) Law and Morality
Lord Patrick Devlin 42
(iv) *R. v. Butler* 46

3 Legal Reasoning and Legal Method.................... 55

A. Sources of Law and Legal Reasoning
(i) Precedents, Statutes and Legal Reasoning
F.L. Morton... 55
(ii) Legal Reasoning
John Farrar and A. Dugdale 58
(iii) The Doctrine of Precedent
Patrick Atiyah... 60
(iv) This Case System: Precedent
Karl Llewellyn.. 62

B. Standpoint and "Truth" in Legal Method
(i) The Maleness of Legal Language
Karen Busby... 64
(ii) Native Culture on Trial
Louise Mandell.. 72
(iii) *Delgamuukw v. B.C.* 76

C. Connecting Law and Society
(i) Legal System and Society
Lawrence Friedman and Stewart Macaulay...... 79
(ii) The New Legal Scholarship: Problems and Prospects
John Hagan... 80
(iii) The Pedagogic Challenge
Neil C. Sargent.. 82

4 Citizenship and Human Rights......................... 85

A. Citizenship
(i) *Henrietta Muir Edwards et al. v. Canada (A.G.)* 85
(ii) Citizenship and Social Class
T.H. Marshall... 89

Table of Contents

- (iii) Return of the Citizen: A Survey of Recent Work on Citizenship Theory
  Will Kymlicka and Wayne Norman 95
- (iv) Left and Rights
  Stuart Hall and David Held 101

B. The Charter of Rights

- (i) The Legalisation of Politics in Advanced Capitalism: The Canadian Charter of Rights and Freedoms
  Harry J. Glasbeek and Michael Mandel 109
- (ii) The Concept of Human Dignity
  Trudeau, Pierre Elliott 115
- (iii) Judging and Equality: For Whom Does the Charter Toll?
  A. Wayne Mackay 116
- (iv) Popular Rights In (and Out of) the Constitution
  Gail Starr 121
- (v) Aboriginal Peoples and the Canadian Charter of Rights and Freedoms: Contradictions and Challenges
  Aki-Kwe/Mary Ellen Turpel 126

5 Law, Crime and Social Order 135

- (i) The Treason Trial of David Maclane
  R. DeSalaberry 135
- (ii) Law, State, and Class Struggle
  Alan Hunt 138
- (iii) Police Under Fire
  Chris Wood et al. 147
- (iv) The [Nova Scotia] Royal Commission on the Donald Marshall Jr., Prosecution 151
- (v) Understanding Over-representation 153
- (vi) Is There a Place for the Victim in the Prosecution Process?
  Patricia Clarke 159
- (vii) Restorative Justice and Mediation: Is the Public Interested?
  Mark S. Umbreit 167

6 Law, Economy and Society 175

A. Formal Legal Regulation

- (i) Max Weber on Law and the Rise of Capitalism
  David M. Trubek 175
- (ii) *Donoghue* v. *Stevenson* 178

(iii) *Lloyds Bank Ltd. v. Bundy* *181*
(iv) Harvard Presses Claim for Patent on Mouse: Genetically engineered rodent designed to develop cancer easily
Tom Spears.................. *185*
(v) Regulability of the Cyberspace
Lawrence Lessig.................. *186*

B. Informal Modes of Regulation
(i) Non-Contractual Relationships in Business: A Preliminary Study
Stewart Macaulay.................. *187*
(ii) Bargaining in the Shadow of the Law: The Case of Divorce
Robert H. Mnookin.................. *193*
(iii) Profiting from Pollution: Canada promotes U.S.-style emissions sales to ease pain of cutting greenhouse gases
Andrew Duffy.................. *200*

7 Dispute Resolution **203**

A. The Disputes Resolution Spectrum
(i) The Mediator and the Judge
Torstein Eckhoff.................. *203*
(ii) Alternative Dispute Resolution and the Ontario Civil Justice System
Allan Stitt, Francis Handy and Peter A. Simm.................. *208*

B. Adjudication
(i) The Judge and the Adversary System
Neil Brooks.................. *212*
(ii) 'Fight' Theory vs. 'Truth' Theory
Judge Jerome Frank.................. *225*
(iii) The Family Court
Peter H. Russell.................. *228*

C. The Debate Over Use of Settlement-Based Dispute Resolution Processes
(i) Against Settlement
Owen M. Fiss.................. *230*
(ii) For Reconciliation
Andrew Wolfe McThenia and Thomas L. Shaffer.................. *235*
(iii) Unpacking the 'Rational Alternative': A Critical Review of Family Mediation Movement Claims
Martha J. Bailey.................. *238*

Table of Contents

(iv) The ADR Explosion — The Implications of Rhetoric in Legal Reform
Laura Nader 245

(v) Water Disputes in Ontario: Environmental Dispute Resolution and the Public Interest
Dianne Saxe. 249

(vi) Understanding the Critiques of Mediation: What Is All the Fuss About?
Neil Sargent. 255

8 People in the Legal Process: Access to "Justice" 259

A. Who Uses the Law and Why?

(i) Why the "Haves" Come Out Ahead: Speculation on the Limits of Legal Change
Marc Galanter 259

(ii) Legal Victory Still Leaves Rosa Becker Out in Cold
William Marsden 277

(iii) Access to the Courts
G. Brodsky and S. Day 279

(iv) Naken, The Supreme Court and What Are Our Courts For?
W.A. Bogart. 286

(v) Class Actions Seen Ideal in Handling Mass-termination Claims
Randall Scott Echlin. 289

B. Access to Justice for the Poor

(i) Legal Services and the Poor
R.J. Gathercole. 290

(ii) Small Claims Courts: A Review
Iain Ramsay. 297

(iii) The Development of Prepaid Legal Services in Canada
C.J. Wydrzynski. 301

(iv) Paralegals Fill Gaps in Legal Service Delivery Ontario Task Force Discussion Paper Argues
Don Brillinger. 304

9 The Personnel of Law 307

A. Lawyers: Education and Training

(i) Legal Education as Training for Hierarchy
Duncan Kennedy 307

(ii) Task Force Reports on Women in the Courts: The Challenge for Legal Education
Elizabeth M. Schneider. 311

B. Control over Access to the Profession

(i) Rogue Lawyer Runs Out of Arguments: Bruce Clark's in-your-face fight for native rights has led the once-acclaimed legal mind to be found guilty of conduct unbecoming of a solicitor
Paul Mckay 314

(ii) *Regina* v. *Lawrie and POINTTS Ltd.* 316

(iii) Debate Heating Up over Paralegals' Role
Margot Gibb-Clark 320

(iv) Franchising Paralegals
Ian McGugan 322

C. The Organization of Legal Practice

(i) Specialization and the Legal Profession
Alvin Esau 324

(ii) Styles of Legal Work
Edwin M. Schur 332

(iii) Law Firm Mergers: A Case of Greed or Survival?
Kirk Makin 335

(iv) Societies Keep Legal Ads' Volume Turned Low
Margot Gibb-Clark 337

(v) Turning Lawyers into Gamblers Is a Bad Bet
Alan Hutchinson 339

D. Juries

(i) Justice and the Jury
W. Neil Brooks and Anthony N. Doob 340

(ii) *Morgentaler, Smoling and Scott* v. *The Queen* 346

(iii) Are Selection Experts Stacking Juries?
Michael Crawford 347

(iv) *R.* v. *Williams* 350

E. The Judges

(i) The Meaning and Scope of Judicial Independence
Bora Laskin 355

(ii) Judicial Inquiries
Stephen Bindman 358

(iii) Stupid Judge Tricks
Sandra Martin 360

(iv) Will Women Judges Really Make a Difference?
Justice Bertha Wilson 362

(v) *R.* v. *S. (R.D.)* 368

(vi) Antonio Lamer: Should Judges Hold Their Tongues? —
The Chief Justice worries that, by keeping silent, judges
are helping misconceptions to spread
Antonio Lamer *374*

(vii) Gavels, Microphones Don't Mix: Judicial decisions may be
political, but judges don't need to act like politicians *375*

10 Law and Social Transformation 377

(i) Doing Justice to "British Justice":
Law, Ideology and Canadian Historiography
Greg Marquis *377*

(ii) Interest Group Litigation and Canadian Democracy
Gregory Hein *379*

(iii) Social Control, State Autonomy and Legal Reform:
The Law Reform Commission of Canada
Ross Hastings and R.P. Saunders *384*

(iv) The Role of Law in Social Transformation:
Is a Jurisprudence of Insurgency Possible?
Stephen Brickey and Elizabeth Comack *387*

(v) Structure: The Mosaic of Dominion
Samuel Bowles and Herbert Gintis *395*

(vi) Toward a Political Economy of Law
Amy Bartholomew and Susan Boyd *398*

(vii) The Statistical Protection of Minorities:
Affirmative Action Policy in Canada
Rainer Knopff *400*

(viii) Sex Equality Litigation
Gwen Brodsky and Shelagh Day *402*

(ix) Ardour in the Court: The Charter has done less to
enhance your rights than to increase the policy-making
power of judges
Rainer Knopff and F.L. Morton *409*

(x) The Case for a Strong Court: The judiciary is accountable
to the public interest, not public opinion
Judge Rosalie Abella *411*

Note to Students

We thank the authors and publishers who gave permission to reproduce their works herein. Please note that the reproduced excerpts do not all contain the original footnotes, endnotes, references or footnote and endnote numbering. For brevity's sake, they have been edited out of the articles included in this book. Some of these articles may have very useful references in the footnotes for students writing research papers. To obtain these references students should look for original copies of the articles. The full citation for each article or case (the publishing information) is given at the bottom of the page at the beginning of each article or case excerpt.

1 The Legal Terrain

A. Law in Social Life

(i) The Functions of Law

Edward Adamson Hoebel

Law performs certain functions essential to the maintenance of all but the most simple societies.

The first is to define relationships among the members of a society, to assert what activities are permitted and what are ruled out, so as to maintain at least minimal integration between the activities of individuals and groups within the society.

The second is derived from the necessity of taming naked force and directing force to the maintenance of order. It is the allocation of authority and the determination of who may exercise physical coercion as a socially recognized privilege-right, along with the selection of the most effective forms of physical sanction to achieve the social ends that the law serves.

The third is the disposition of trouble cases as they arise.

The fourth is to redefine relations between individuals and groups as the conditions of life change. It is to maintain adaptability.

Purposive definition of personal relations is the primary law-job. Other aspects of culture likewise work to this end, and, indeed, the law derives its working principles (jural postulates) from postulates previously developed in the nonlegal spheres of action. However, the law's important contribution to the basic organization of society as a whole is that the law specifically and explicitly defines relations. It sets the expectancies of man to man and group to group so that each knows the focus and the limitations of its demand-rights on others, its duties to others, its privilege-rights and powers as against others, and its immunities and liabilities to the contemplated or attempted acts of others. This is the "bare-bones job", as Karl Llewellyn likes to call it. It is the ordering of the fundamentals of living together.

No culture has a specific starting point in time; yet in the operation of the first function it is as though men were getting together and saying to each other. "Look here! Let's have a little organization here or we'll never get anywhere with this mess! Let's have a clear understanding of who's who, what we are to do, and how we are going to do it!" In its essence it is what the social-contract theorists recognized as the foundation of social order.

The second function of the law — the allocation of authority to exercise coercive physical force — is something almost peculiar to things legal.

Custom has regularity, and so does law. Custom defines relationships, and so does law. Custom is sanctioned, and so is law. But the sanctions of law may involve physical coercion. Law is distinguished from mere customs in that it endows certain selected

---

Reproduced by permission of the publisher from "The Functions of Law," pp. 275–84, 287 in *The Law of Primitive Man* by Edward Adamson Hoebel. Notes omitted. Cambridge, Mass.: Harvard University Press. Copyright © 1954 by the President and Fellows of Harvard College.

individuals with the privilege-right of applying the sanction of physical coercion, if need be. The legal, let it be repeated, has teeth that can bite. But the biting, if it is to be legal and not mere gangsterism, can be done only by those persons to whom the law has allocated the privilege-right for the affair at hand.

We have seen that in primitive law authority is a shifting, temporary thing. Authority to enforce a norm resides (for private wrongs) with the wronged individual and his immediate kinsmen — but only for the duration of time necessary to follow through the procedural steps that lead to redress or punishment of the culprit. In primitive law the tendency is to allocate authority to the party who is directly injured. This is done in part out of convenience, for it is easier to let the wronged party assume the responsibility of legal action. It is also done because the primitive kinship group, having a more vital sense of entity, is naturally charged with a heavier emotional effect. In any event, when the community qua community acknowledges the exercise of force by a wronged person or his kinship group as correct and proper in a given situation, and so restrains the wrongdoer from striking back, then law prevails and order triumphs over violence.

We have also found in our studies of primitive societies that in a limited number of situations authority is directly exercised by the community on its own behalf. It takes the form of lynch law in some instances where clear procedures have not been set up in advance, as in the Comanche treatment of excessive sorcery and Shoshone treatment of cannibalism. Lynch law among primitives, however, is not a backsliding from, or detouring around, established formal law as it is with us. It is a first fitful step toward the emergence of criminal law in a situation in which the exercise of legal power has not yet been refined and allocated to specific persons. It is a blunt crude tool wielded by the gang hand of an outraged public.

Yet lynch law is rare among primitives. Even the simplest of them have crystallized standards as to what constitutes criminal behaviour, and the exercise of public authority is delegated to official functionaries — the chieftain, the council of chiefs, and the council of elders.

Power may sometimes be personal, as is the power of the bully in the society of small boys, and as was to some extent the power of William the Conqueror. But personal tyranny is a rare thing among primitives. Brute force of the individual does not prevail. Chiefs must have followers. Followers always impose limitations on their leaders. Enduring power is always institutionalized power. It is *transpersonalized*. It resides in the office, in the social status, rather than in the man. The constitutional structures of the several tribes examined in this book have all clearly revealed how political and legal authority are in each instance delimited and circumscribed.

This point is emphasized only to dispel any residue of the hoary political philosophies that assumed without basis in fact that primitive societies existed under the rule of fang and claw.

However, the personal still obtrudes. An "office" although culturally defined is, after all, exercised by an individual. And who that individual is at any moment certainly makes a difference. There is leeway in the exercise or non-exercise of power just as there are limits. A man may be skilled in finding the evidence and the truth in the cases he must judge and in formulating the norms to fit the case in hand — or he may be all thumbs. He may be one who thirsts for power and who will wield all he can while grasping for more. Or he may shrink from it. Power defined through allocation of legal authority is by its nature trans-personalized, yet by the nature of men it can never be wholly depersonalized. A Franklin Roosevelt is not a Warren Harding....

The third function of law calls for little additional comment.... Some trouble cases pose absolutely new problems for solution. In these cases the first and second functions may predominate. Yet this is not the situation in the instance of most legal clashes in which the problem is not the formulation of law to cover a new situation but rather the application of pre-existing law. These cases are disposed of in accordance with legal norms already set before the issue in question arises. The job is to clean the case up, to suppress or penalize the illegal behaviour and to bring the relations of the disputants back into balance, so that life may resume its normal course. This type of law-work has frequently been compared to work of the medical practitioner. It is family doctor stuff, essential to keeping the social body on its feet. In more homely terms, Llewellyn has called it, "garage-repair work on the general order of the group when that general order misses fire, or grinds gears, or even threatens a total breakdown." It is not ordinarily concerned with grand design, as is the first law-job. Nor is it concerned with redesign as is the fourth. It works to clean up all the little social messes (and the occasional big ones) that recurrently arise between the members of the society from day to day.

Most of the trouble cases do not, in a civilized society, of themselves loom large on the social scene, although in a small community even one can lead

(i) The Functions of Law

directly to a social explosion if not successfully cleaned up. Indeed, in a primitive society the individual case always holds the threat of a little civil war if procedure breaks down, for from its inception it sets kin group against kin group — and if it comes to fighting, the number of kinsmen who will be involved is almost always immediately enlarged. The fight may engulf a large part of the tribe in internecine throat-cutting. Relatively speaking, each run-of-the-mill trouble case in primitive law imposes a more pressing demand for settlement upon the legal system than is the case with us.

While system and integration are essential, flexibility and constant revision are no less so. Law is a dynamic process in which few solutions can be permanent. Hence, the fourth function of law: the redefinition of relations and the reorientation of expectancies.

Initiative with scope to work means new problems for the law. New inventions, new ideas, new behaviours keep creeping in. Especially do new behaviours creep in, nay, sweep in, when two unlike societies come newly into close contact. Then the law is called upon to decide what principles shall be applied to conflicts of claims rooted in disparate cultures. Do the new claims fit comfortably to the old postulates? Must the new realized ways of behaving be wholly rejected and legally suppressed because they are out of harmony with the old values? Or can they be modified here and altered there to gain legal acceptance? Or can the more difficult operations of altering or even junking old postulates to accommodate a new way be faced? Or can fictions be framed that can lull the mind into acceptance of the disparate new without the wrench of acknowledged junking of the old? What *is* that is wanted? The known and habitual, or the promise of the new and untested? Men may neglect to turn [to] the law to the answer of such questions. But they do not for long. Trouble cases generated by the new keep marching in. And the fourth law-job presses for attention.

Recapitulation of just one Cheyenne case will throw the process into focus. The acquisition of horses greatly altered all Plains Indian cultures. One important Cheyenne basic postulate ran, "Except for land and tribal fetishes, all material goods are private property, but they should be generously shared with others." When it came to horses, this led some men to expect that they could freely borrow horses without even the courtesy of asking. For horse owners this got to the point of becoming a serious nuisance, as in the cases of Pawnee and Wolf Lies Down. Wolf Lies Down put his trouble case to the members of the Elk Soldier Society. They got his horse back for him with a handsome free-will offering of additional "damages" from the defendant to boot. The trouble case was neatly disposed of. But the Elk Soldiers did not stop there. There was some preventive channeling of future behaviour to be done. Hence the "Now we shall make a new rule. There shall be no more borrowing of horses without asking. If any man takes another's goods without asking, we will go over and get them back for him. More than that, if the taker tries to keep them, we will give him a whipping." Here was the fourth function of law being performed. The lines for future conduct re horses were made clear.

Work under Function IV represents social planning brought into focus by the case of the instant and with an eye to the future.

The problem of reorienting conduct and redirecting it through the law when new issues emerge is always tied to the bare-bones demand of basic organization and the minimal maintenance of order and regularity. It may also shade over into work colored by a greater or lesser desire to achieve more than a minimum of smoothness in social relations. When this becomes an important aspect of law-work, a special aspect of law-ways activity may be recognized: the creation of techniques that efficiently and effectively solve the problems posed to all the other law-jobs so that the basic values of the society are realized through the law and not frustrated by it.

The doing of it has been called by Llewellyn "Juristic Method". It is the method not only of getting the law-jobs done but doing them with a sure touch for the net effect that results in smoothness in the doing and a harmonious wedding of what is aspired to by men and what is achieved through the law. It is the work not just of the craftsman but of the master craftsman....

. . . .

The very fact that the bulk of the substance and procedure of primitive law emerges through case action involving claim and counterclaim, pleading and counterpleading, tends to keep legal behaviour relatively close to the prevailing social values. Which way a new issue will go will depend not alone upon the facts but also upon the skill of the litigants in framing the issue and arguing the relevance of their respective positions to the prevailing social ideas of right conduct and group well-being — or upon persuasiveness in argument that a new orientation of values is in order to meet changed conditions, even though the tough man and his kinsman, though "wrong," may sometimes make his position stick with naked force. Thus, the wise claimant argues his case not in terms of "this is good for me" but rather by maintaining "this is what we all want and should do". If he is a primitive advocate, it is more likely than not that he will also insist, if he can, that this is the way it has been from time immemorial. But the past certainly has no inflexible grip on primitive law.

Fiction is one of the great devices of juristic method by means of which men fit new legal norms into old principles so as to reorient conduct without the need to junk long-standing postulates. Except for the universal practice of adoption, whereby outsiders are identified as *if* they are actually kinsmen, primitive men do not have to rely too heavily on the subterfuge of fiction to achieve legal change. Nevertheless, when the need is there many tribes have had recourse to its use.

An outstanding example may be found in adoptive marriage among the patrilineal groups of Indonesia. The important value for these people is to maintain the unbroken continuity of the paternal lineage. To do this, a family without sons adopts their daughter's husband as a "son" with the effect that her children remain within their clan and their inheritance will remain within their line. ...

. . . .

When the law-jobs get done, these norms inevitably become the common denominator of legal culture. But the functions of law, whatever the norms they may give rise to in any particular society, are what constitute the crucial universal elements of the law. Any one or half-hundred societies may select one rule of law and not another — the range is wide — but none can ignore the law-jobs. In the last analysis, that the law-jobs get done is more important than how they are done. Their minimal doing is an imperative of social existence. Their doing with juristic finesse is an achievement of high skill.

(ii) The Cheyenne Way

Karl N. Llewellyn and E. Adamson Hoebel

A war party of eight Cheyennes, on its way south to take horses from the Kiowas, Comanches, or Apaches, was stopping at a large Arapaho camp. At the same time some Apaches came to visit Bull, an Arapaho leader. The Apaches told their host that the Kiowas and Comanches were seeking peace with the Arapahoes and Cheyennes. Bull took the opportunity to bring the eight Cheyennes together with the Apaches in his tipi; he filled his pipe and offered the smoke. The Cheyennes declined, Seven Bulls, the leader of the war party saying, "Friend, you know that we are not chiefs. We cannot smoke with these men, nor make peace with them. We have no authority; we can only carry the message. I have listened to what you say and tomorrow with my party I will start back [He has authority to call off his own raid.] to our Cheyenne village, and I will carry this word to the chiefs. It is for them to decide what must be done. We are young men and cannot say anything, but we will take your message back to the chiefs."

When Seven Bulls reached the Cheyenne camp with his companions, he told of the Kiowa-Comanche proposition. That night a crier went about the camp calling for the chiefs to convene the next day. The big double-sized chiefs' lodge was pitched and early the next morning the chiefs all gathered there. Seven Bulls and his companions were sent for to deliver their message officially. The proposal was then on the floor.

After the first speakers had sat down, it was evident that there was no ready agreement at hand within the Council, so the proposition was made and accepted that the Dog Soldier Society should be asked to render a decision to the Council on the question.

High Backed Wolf, who was the directing head chief of the Council, sent one of the door-

---

From *The Cheyenne Way: Conflict and Case Law in Primitive Jurisprudence*, pp. 91–94, 127–28, by Karl N. Llewellyn & E. Adamson Hoebel. Notes omitted. Oklahoma: University of Oklahoma Press. Copyright © 1941 by the University of Oklahoma Press. All rights reserved.

servants to bring in White Antelope and Little Old Man, the bravest chiefs of the Dog Soldier Society. When these two had been greeted in the chiefs' lodge, High Backed Wolf told them about the order of business, describing to them the state of opinion in the Council. "Now, my friends," he concluded, "you go and assemble your Dog Soldiers. Tell them about this matter and talk it over among them. Let us know what you think of it. Tell us what you think is best to be done."

When the Dog Soldiers had assembled, White Antelope laid the problem before them. "The chiefs are leaving this matter to us," he told his followers, "because we are the strongest of the military groups. It is my own thought that our chiefs are in favor of making peace. What do you all think about it?"

Said another of the Dog Soldier chiefs, "I think it best to leave the decision to you two, White Antelope and Little Old Man. Whatever you say will please us all." All the Dogs agreed to this with one assent.

The two men accepted it and declared for peace. Leaving their troop, they went back to where the Council was waiting for them, to tell the Council that they would make peace with the enemies. The chiefs all stood up at this and gladly said, "Thank you, thank you, Dog Soldiers."

The procedure which has just been described is a typical handling of an important situation in the Cheyenne manner. The proposition, the reader will realize, was no simple one. The Cheyenne had become dependent upon the horse, and any warrior's path to glory and wealth lay most easily and quickly in raids upon the rich horse herders of the south, these same Kiowas and Comanches. Acceptance of the proposal meant that the young men would be blocked in one of their main and favorite avenues of activity. Hostility with the Kiowas and Comanches had been unceasing for at least half a century. The alternative values to the Cheyennes are not clear to us, unless they lay in some scheme for trading horses, on which we lack information. The soldier interest in the case is obvious; no less obvious is the fact that it had the favorable aspect of coinciding with the interests of the whole Cheyenne tribe. In the light of this one understands the diplomatic reluctance of the Council of Forty-Four to reach a decision by themselves. So smooth a delegation of an important decision, inverting the pyramid without any bickering, yet with the machinery at all points for the sensing of opinion in widening representative groups, is an act of social beauty. From the Council to the Dog Men, from the Dog Men to their two most outstanding warriors, to a momentous decision binding on the entire tribe! Nevertheless, the Council at no time gave up its authority; the decision, be it noted, was reported for announcement back to the Council, which then discharged the Dog Soldiers with thanks. This is also a superb face-producing, as well as face-saving, procedure. The actual announcement of the decision for peace was made to the camp at large by the head priest-chief himself.

Such interaction between the Council and the military societies was not unusual; rather, whenever there was an important problem of tribal policy (new policy in general or in particular) to be decided, it was the ordinary thing to see the chiefs' and the soldiers' messengers moving back and forth between the meeting lodges, sensing, reporting, and subtly influencing the state of both "expert" and "lay" opinion until the decision was accomplished. In this way, the legislative knot was cut without resort to dictatorship or friction.

But what happened when there was an irreconcilable opposition within the body politic? Then the governmental authority could act with force. It acted also with tact. It moved sometimes in involution. Power was present, form was not always achieved. Note, however, the Cheyenne drive for form, if repetition of situation makes it possible, if time serves, if dramatic urge finds — even for a sole occasion — an inventive voice. Seven Bulls was called on for an "official" presentation of a proposal the camp had buzzed with for a night. Little Wolf was "required" to be present. Compare the careful staging of Pawnee's rehabilitation. It is not too much to argue that *drama* is a vital *line* of reconciliation hit on by the Cheyennes, between their urge toward form (pattern, ritual) and their urge toward individualizing self-glorification. If this be sound, it suggests a relation between aesthetic balance and soundness of working institution, or of the individual's work in and with an institution, which deserves inquiry.

. . . .

While Wolf Lies Down was away, a friend took one of his horses to ride to war. This man had brought his bow and arrow and left them in the lodge of the horse's owner. When Wolf Lies Down returned, he knew by this token security who had his horse, so he said nothing.

A year passed without the horse's return, and then Wolf Lies Down invited the Elk Soldier chiefs to his lodge, because he was in their society. "There is this thing," he told them. "My friend borrowed my horse, leaving his bow and arrow; there they are yet. Now I want to know what to do. I want you to tell me the right thing. Will you go over and ask him his intentions?"

The borrower was in another camp well distant, yet the chiefs agreed. "We'll send a man to bring him in, get his word, or receive his presents," they promised.

The camp moved while the messenger was gone, but he knew of course where it would be on his return. The soldier returned with the borrower, who was leading two horses, "one spotted, one ear-tipped." He called for the four Elk chiefs on his arrival. The chiefs laid before him the story told by Wolf Lies Down.

"That is true," the man assented. "My friend is right. I left my bow and arrow here. I intended to return his horse, but I was gone longer than I expected. I have had good luck with that horse, though. I have treated it better than my own. However, when I got back to camp I found my folks there. Our camps were far apart and I just could not get away. I was waiting for his camp and mine to come together. Now, I always intended to do the right thing. I have brought two good horses with me. My friend can have his choice. In addition I give his own horse back, and further, I am leaving my bow and arrow."

Then up spoke Wolf Lies Down, "I am glad to hear my friend say these things. Now I feel better. I shall take one of those horses, but I am giving him that one he borrowed to keep. From now on we shall be bosom friends."

The chiefs declared, "Now we have settled this thing. Our man is a bosom friend of this man. Let it be that way among all of us. Our society and his shall be comrades. Whenever one of us has a present to give, we shall give it to a member of his soldier society.

"Now we shall make a new rule. There shall be no more borrowing of horses without asking. If any man takes another's goods without asking, we will go over and get them back for him. More than that, if the taker tries to keep them, we will give him a whipping."

Thus was a situation fraught with possible friction brought to an amicable close through the good offices of the chiefs of the society of an aggrieved member.

Far more important, however, was the crystallization of a new social policy, the formulation of a law making it a crime henceforth to borrow an owner's horse without his expressed permission. The old custom of free utilization of another's goods, providing one left an identifying "security," was apparently creating friction as it came to be applied to horses. What between good friends could develop into a tense situation — as evidenced here by the resort to soldier chiefs as spokesmen of inquiry — could become immediately and actively disruptive if the concept "friend" were loosely interpreted by a borrower, or the horse not cared for, or if the unnotified borrowing broke in upon the owner's plans, or one owner became the recipient of too many such evidences of friendship. Pawnee's case of horse "borrowing" and its punishment (CASE 2) shows the degree of social irresponsibility which the older practice, left unguarded, could engender. Black Wolf stated that the soldiers, and even the tribal chiefs, had been for some time talking about means of putting a stop to the practice. The Elk Soldier chiefs on this occasion took the opportunity to make the step. After declaring the case at hand settled, they moved into general policy. They did not mix the two. Note also, as a soldier society moves into the very unfamiliar matter of legislation, their sound technical attention to what they shall do, if....

(iii) Conflicts as Property

Nils Christie

Abstract

Conflicts are seen as important elements in society. Highly industrialised societies do not have too much internal conflict, they have too little. We have to organise social systems so that conflicts are both nurtured and made visible, and also see to it that professionals do not monopolize the handling of

---

Originally appeared in The British Journal of Criminology, January 1977, vol. 17 at 1–5. Reproduced by permission of Oxford University Press and the author. References omitted.

them. Victims of crime have in particular lost their rights to participate. A court procedure that restores the participants' rights to their own conflicts is outlined.

Introduction

Maybe we should not have any criminology. Maybe we should rather abolish institutes, not open them. Maybe the social consequences of criminology are more dubious than we like to think.

I think they are. And I think this relates to my topic. Conflicts as property. My suspicion is that criminology to some extent has amplified a process where conflicts have been taken away from the directly involved parties and thereby either disappeared or have become other people's property. In both cases a deplorable outcome. Conflicts ought to be used, not only left in erosion. And they ought to be used, and become useful, for those originally involved in the conflict. Conflicts *might* hurt individuals as well as social systems. That is what we learn in school. That is why we have officials. Without them, private vengeance and vendettas will blossom. We have learned this so solidly that we have lost track of the other side of the coin: our industrialised large-scale society is not one with too many internal conflicts. It is one with too little. Conflict might kill, but too little of it might paralyze. I will use this occasion to give a sketch of this situation. It can't be more than a sketch. This paper represents the beginning of the development of some ideas, not the polished end product.

On Happenings and Non-Happenings

Let us take our point of departure far away. Let us move to Tanzania. Let us approach our problem from the sunny hillside of the Arusha province. Here, inside a relatively large house in a very small village, a sort of happening took place. The house was overcrowded. Most grown-ups from the village and several from adjoining ones were there. It was a happy happening; fast talking, jokes, smiles, eager attention, not a sentence was to be lost. It was circus, it was drama. It was a court case.

The conflict this time was between a man and a woman. They had been engaged. He had invested a lot in the relationship through a long period, until she broke it off. Now he wanted it back. Gold and silver and money were easily decided on, but what about utilities already worn, and what about general expenses?

The outcome is of no interest in our context. But the framework for conflict solution is. Five elements ought to be particularly mentioned:

1. The parties, the former lovers, were in *the centre* of the room and in the centre of everyone's attention. They talked often and were eagerly listened to.
2. Close to them were relatives and friends who also took part. But they did not *take over*.
3. There was also participation from the general audience with short questions, information, or jokes.
4. The judges, three local party secretaries, were extremely inactive. They were obviously ignorant with regard to village matters. All the other people in the room were experts. They were experts on norms as well as actions. And they crystallized norms and clarified what had happened through participation in the procedure.
5. No reporters attended. They were all there.

My personal knowledge when it comes to British courts is limited indeed. I have some vague memories of juvenile courts, where I counted some 15 to 20 persons present, mostly social workers using the room for preparatory work or small conferences. A child or a young person must have attended, but except for the judge, or maybe it was the clerk, nobody seemed to pay any particular attention. The child or young person was most probably utterly confused as to who was who and for what, a fact confirmed in a small study by Peter Scott (1959). In the USA, Martha Baum (1968) has made similar observations. Recently, Bottoms and McClean (1976) have added another important observation: "There is one truth which is seldom revealed in the literature of the law or in studies of the administration of criminal justice. It is a truth which was made evident to all those involved in this research project as they sat through the cases which made up our sample. The truth is that, for the most part, the business of the criminal courts is dull, commonplace, ordinary and after a while downright tedious."

But let me keep quiet about your system, and instead concentrate on my own. And let me assure you: what goes on is no happening. It is all a negation of the Tanzanian case. What is striking in nearly all the Scandinavian cases is the greyness, the dullness, and the lack of any important audience. Courts are not central elements in the daily life of our citizens, but peripheral in four major ways:

1. They are situated in the administrative centre of the towns, outside the territories of ordinary people.
2. Within these centres they are often centralised within one or two large buildings of considerable complexity. Lawyers often complain that they need months to find their way within these buildings. It does not demand much fantasy to imagine the situation of parties or public when they are trapped within these structures. A comparative study of court architecture might become equally relevant for the sociology of law as Oscar Newman's (1972) study of defensible space is for criminology. But even without any study, I feel it safe to say that both physical situation and architectural design are strong indicators that courts in Scandinavia belong to the administrators of law.
3. This impression is strengthened when you enter the courtroom itself — if you are lucky enough to find your way to it. Here again, the periphery of the parties is the striking observation. The parties are represented, and it is these representatives and the judge or judges who express the little activity that is activated within these rooms. Honoré Daumier's famous drawings from the courts are as representative for Scandinavia as they are for France.

    There are variations. In the small cities, or in the countryside, the courts are more easily reached than in the larger towns. And at the very lowest end of the court system — the so-called arbitration boards — the parties are sometimes less heavily represented through experts in law. But the symbol of the whole system is the Supreme Court where the directly involved parties do not even attend their own court cases.
4. I have not yet made any distinction between civil and criminal conflicts. But it was not by chance that the Tanzania case was a civil one. Full participation in your own conflict presupposes elements of civil law. The key element in a criminal proceeding is that the proceeding is converted from something between the concrete parties and into a conflict between one of the parties and the State. So, in a modern criminal trial, two important things have happened. First: the parties are being *represented*. Secondly: the one party that is represented by the State, namely the victim, is so thoroughly represented that she or he for most of the proceedings is pushed completely out of the arena, reduced to the triggerer-off of the whole thing. She or he is a sort of double loser. First vis-à-vis the offender, but secondly and often more cripplingly by being denied rights to full participation in what might have been one of the more important ritual encounters in life. The victim has lost its case to the State.

Professional Thieves

As we all know, there are many honourable as well as dishonourable reasons behind this development. The honourable ones have to do with the State's need for conflict reduction and certainly also its wishes for the protection of the victim. It is rather obvious. So is also the less honourable temptation for the State, or Emperor, or whoever is in power, to use the criminal case for personal gain. Offenders might pay for their sins. Authorities have back in time shown considerable willingness in representing the victim as receivers of the money or other property from the offender. Those days are gone. The crime control system is not run by profit. But they are also not gone. There are, in all banality, many interests at stake here, most of them related to professionalisation.

Lawyers are particularly good at stealing conflicts. They are trained for it. They are trained to prevent and solve conflicts. They are socialised into a sub-culture with a surprisingly high agreement concerning interpretation of norms, and regarding what sort of information can be accepted as relevant in each case. Many among us have, as laymen, experienced the sad moments of truth when our lawyers tell us that our best arguments in our fight against our neighbour are without any legal relevance whatsoever and that we for God's sake ought to keep quiet about them in court. Instead they pick out arguments we might find irrelevant or even wrong to use. My favourite example took place just after the war. One of my country's absolutely top defenders told with pride how he had just rescued a poor client. The client had collaborated with the Germans. The prosecutor claimed that the client had been one of the key people in the organisation of the Nazi movement. He had been one of the master-minds behind it all. The defender, however, saved his client. He saved him by pointing out to the jury how weak, how lacking in ability, how obviously deficient his client was, socially as well as organisationally. His client could simply not have been one of the organisers among the collaborators. He was without talents. And he won his case. His client got a very minor sentence as a very minor figure. The defender ended his story by telling me — with some indignation — that neither the accused, nor his wife, had ever thanked him, they had not even talked to him afterwards.

Conflicts become the property of lawyers. But lawyers don't hide that it is conflicts they handle. And the organisational framework of the courts underlines this point. The opposing parties, the judge, the ban against privileged communication within the court system, the lack of encouragement for specialisation — specialists cannot be internally controlled — it all underlines that this is an organisation for the handling of conflicts. *Treatment personnel* are in another position. They are more interested in *converting the image of the case from one of conflict into one of non-conflict*. The basic model of healers is not one of opposing parties, but one where one party has to be helped in the direction of one generally accepted goal: the preservation or restoration of health. They are not trained into a system where it is important that parties can control each other. There is, in the ideal case, nothing to control, because there is only one goal. Specialisation is encouraged. It increases the amount of available knowledge, and the loss of internal control is of no relevance. A conflict perspective creates unpleasant doubts with regard to the healer's suitability for the job. A non-conflict perspective is a precondition for defining crime as a legitimate target for treatment.

One way of reducing attention to the conflict is reduced attention given to the victim. Another is concentrated attention given to those attributes in the criminal's background which the healer is particularly trained to handle. Biological defects are perfect. So are also personality defects when they are established far back in time — far away from the recent conflict. And so are also the whole row of explanatory variables that criminology might offer. We have, in criminology, to a large extent functioned as an auxiliary science for the professionals within the crime control system. We have focused on the offender, made her or him into an object for study, manipulation and control. We have added to all those forces that have reduced the victim to a non-entity and the offender to a thing. And this critique is perhaps not only relevant for the old criminology, but also for the new criminology. While the old one explained crime from personal defects or social handicaps, the new criminology explains crime as the result of broad economic conflicts. The old criminology loses the conflicts, the new one converts them from interpersonal conflicts to class conflicts. And they are. They are class conflicts — also. But by stressing this, the conflicts are again taken away from the directly involved parties. So, as a preliminary statements: Criminal conflicts have either become *other people's property* — primarily the property of lawyers — or it has been in other people's interests to *define conflicts away*.

(iv) People to People, Nation to Nation

The Report of the Royal Commission on Aboriginal Peoples

2. AN HISTORICAL FRAMEWORK

> Some of the old people ... talk about the water ... and it is really nice to hear them talk about the whole cycle of water, where it all starts and where it all ends up.
>
> Chief Albert Saddleman
> Okanagan Band
> Kelowna, British Columbia, 16 June 1993

Aboriginal and non-Aboriginal people have had sustained contact in the part of North America that has become known as Canada for some 500 years, at least in some areas. To summarize and interpret the nature of so complex, fluid and interdependent a relationship ("where it all starts and where it all ends up") is a formidable assignment. This is especially the case when one considers the sheer diversity in the nature of the relationship in different areas of the country, populated by different Aboriginal peoples and settled at different periods by people of diverse non-Aboriginal origins.

From *The Report of the Royal Commission on Aboriginal Peoples*, Vol. 1 at 36–39. Source of Information: Privy Council Office. Reproduced with the permission of the Minister of Public Works and Government Services Canada, 2000.

In the Atlantic region, for instance, a sustained non-Aboriginal presence among the Mi'kmaq and Maliseet peoples has been a fact for nearly 500 years, but it most parts of the far north, Inuit have been in sustained contact with non-Aboriginal people only in recent times. In Quebec and southern and central Ontario, the relationship is of almost the same duration as that in the Atlantic region, while in northern Ontario and the Prairies, sustained contact and the development of formal treaty relationships has occurred only within the last 150 years. In parts of the Pacific coast, the nature of the relationship has yet to be formalized in treaties, even though interaction between Aboriginal and non-Aboriginal people has taken place for some 200 years.

In approaching the task of summarizing and interpreting the relationship between Aboriginal and non-Aboriginal people, the Commission has found it useful to divide its own account of the historical relationship into four stages, as illustrated in Figure 3.3 and as described in the next four chapters. The stages follow each other with some regularity, but they overlap and occur at different times in different regions.

2.1 Stage 1: Separate Worlds

In the period before 1500, Aboriginal and non-Aboriginal societies developed in isolation from each other. Differences in physical and social environments inevitably meant differences in culture and forms of social organization. On both sides of the Atlantic, however, national groups with long traditions of governing themselves emerged, organizing themselves into different social and political forms according to their traditions and the needs imposed by their environments.

In this first stage, the two societies — Aboriginal and non-Aboriginal — were physically separated by a wide ocean. From an Aboriginal philosophical perspective, the separation between the two distinct worlds could also be expressed as having been established by the acts of creation. Accordingly, the Creator gave each people its distinct place and role to perform in the harmonious operation of nature and in a manner and under circumstances appropriate to each people. Aboriginal creation stories are thus not only the repository of a people's distinct national history, but also an expression of the divine gift and caretaking responsibility given to each people by the Creator.

By the end of Stage 1 (see Chapter 4), the physical and cultural distance between Aboriginal and non-Aboriginal societies narrowed drastically as Europeans moved across the ocean and began to settle in North America.

2.2 Stage 2: Contact and Co-operation

The beginning of Stage 2 (see Chapter 5) was marked by increasingly regular contact between European and Aboriginal societies and by the need to establish the terms by which they would live together. It was a period when Aboriginal people provided assistance to the newcomers to help them survive in the unfamiliar environment; this stage also saw the establishment of trading and military alliances, as well as intermarriage and mutual cultural adaptation. This stage was also marked by incidents of conflict, by growth in the number of non-Aboriginal immigrants, and by the steep decline in Aboriginal populations following the ravages of diseases to which they had no natural immunity.

Although there were exceptions, there were many instances of mutual tolerance and respect during this long period. In these cases, social distance was maintained — that is, the social, cultural and political differences between the two societies were respected by and large. Each was regarded as distinct and autonomous, left to govern its own internal affairs but co-operating in areas of mutual interest and, occasionally and increasingly, linked in various trading relationships and other forms of nation-to-nation alliances.

2.3 Stage 3: Displacement and Assimilation

In Stage 3 (see Chapter 6), non-Aboriginal society was for the most part no longer willing to respect the distinctiveness of Aboriginal societies. Non-Aboriginal society made repeated attempts to recast Aboriginal people and their distinct forms of social organization so they would conform to the expectations of what had become the mainstream. In this period, interventions in Aboriginal societies reached their peak, taking the form of relocations, residential schools, the outlawing of Aboriginal cultural practices, and various other interventionist measures of the type found in the Indian Acts of the late 1800s and early 1900s.

These interventions did not succeed in undermining Aboriginal social values or their sense of distinctiveness, however. Neither did they change the determination of Aboriginal societies to conduct their relations with the dominant society in the manner Aboriginal people considered desirable and appropriate, in line with the parameters established in the initial contact period. (Hence the continuation of the horizontal line in dotted form in Figure 3.3.)

Non-Aboriginal society began to recognize the failure of these policies toward the end of this period, particularly after the federal government's ill-fated 1969 white paper, which would have ended the special constitutional, legal and political status of Aboriginal peoples within Confederation.

2.4 Stage 4: Negotiation and Renewal

This stage in the relationship between Aboriginal and non-Aboriginal societies, which takes us to the present day, is characterized by non-Aboriginal society's admission of the manifest failure of its interventionist and assimilationist approach. This acknowledgement is pushed by domestic and also by international forces. Campaigns by national Aboriginal social and political organizations, court decisions on Aboriginal rights, sympathetic public opinion, developments in international law, and the worldwide political mobilization of Indigenous peoples under the auspices of the United Nations have all played a role during this stage in the relationship.

As a result, non-Aboriginal society is haltingly beginning the search for change in the relationship. A period of dialogue, consultation and negotiation ensues, in which a range of options, centring on the concept of full Aboriginal self-government and restoration of the original partnership of the contact and co-operation period, is considered. From the perspective of Aboriginal groups, the primary objective is to gain more control over their own affairs by reducing unilateral interventions by non-Aboriginal society and regaining a relationship of mutual recognition and respect for differences. However, Aboriginal people also appear to realize that, at the same time, they must take steps to re-establish their own societies and to heal wounds caused by the many years of dominance by non-Aboriginal people.

It is clear that any attempt to reduce so long and complex a history of interrelationship into four stages is necessarily a simplification of reality. It is as though we have taken many different river systems, each in a different part of the country, each viewed from many different vantages, and tried to channel them into one stream of characteristics that would be most typical of the river as it has flowed through Canada.

We have attempted to retain a sense of the diversity of the historical experience by presenting numerous snapshots or slices of history. Instead of providing a linear, chronological overview, we have chosen particular societies, particular events or particular turning points in history to illustrate each of the stages and to give the flavour of the historical experience in at least some of its complexity.

It is difficult to place each stage within a precise time frame. In part this is because of the considerable overlap between the stages. They flow easily and almost indiscernibly into each other, with the transition from one to the other becoming apparent only after the next stage is fully under way. Nor is the time frame for each period the same in all parts of the country; Aboriginal groups in eastern and central Canada generally experienced contact with non-Aboriginal societies earlier than groups in more northern or western locations.

B. Law, The State and The Constitution

(i) The Rule of Law: Its Nature and General Applications

A.V. Dicey

Two features have at all times since the Norman Conquest characterised the political institutions of England.

The first of these features is the omnipotence or undisputed supremacy throughout the whole country of the central government. This authority of the state

---

From *Introduction to the Study of the Law of the Constitution*, 10th ed. (New York: St. Martin's Press, 1965) at 183–84, 187–88, 193, 195–96, 202–203. Notes omitted. Copyright © 1965, Macmillan Press Ltd. Reproduced by permission of Macmillan Press Ltd., Hampshire, U.K.

1. The Legal Terrain — B. Law, The State and The Constitution

or the nation was during the earlier periods of our history represented by the power of the Crown. The King was the source of law and the maintainer of order. The maxim of the courts, *tout fuit in luy et vient de lui al commencement*, was originally the expression of an actual and undoubted fact. This royal supremacy has now passed into that sovereignty of Parliament which has formed the main subject of the foregoing chapters.

The second of these features, which is closely connected with the first, is the rule or supremacy of law. This peculiarity of our polity is well expressed in the old saw of the courts, "*La ley est le plus haute inheritance, que le roy ad; car par la ley il meme et toutes ses sujets sont rules, et si la ley ne fuit, nul roi, et nul inheritance sera.*"

This supremacy of the law, or the security given under the English constitution to the rights of individuals looked at from various points of view, forms the subject of this part of this treatise.

. . . .

When we say that the supremacy or the rule of law is a characteristic of the English constitution, we generally include under one expression at least three distinct though kindred conceptions.

We mean, in the first place, that no man is punishable or can be lawfully made to suffer in body or goods except for a distinct breach of law established in the ordinary legal manner before the ordinary courts of the land. In this sense the rule of law is contrasted with every system of government based on the exercise by persons in authority of wide, arbitrary, or discretionary powers of constraint.

. . . .

We mean in the second place, when we speak of the "rule of law" as a characteristic of our country, not only that with us no man is above the law, but (what is a different thing) that here every man, whatever be his rank or condition, is subject to the ordinary law of the realm and amenable to the jurisdiction of the ordinary tribunals.

. . . .

There remains yet a third and a different sense in which the "rule of law" or the predominance of the legal spirit may be described as a special attribute of English institutions. We may say that the constitution is pervaded by the rule of law on the ground that the general principles of the constitution (as for example the right to personal liberty, or the right of public meeting) are with us the result of judicial decisions determining the rights of private persons in particular cases brought before the courts whereas under many foreign constitutions the security (such as it is) given to the rights of individuals results, or appears to result, from the general principles of the constitution.

This is one portion at least of the fact vaguely hinted at in the current but misguiding statement that "the constitution has not been made but has grown." This *dictum*, if taken literally, is absurd.

> Political institutions (however the proposition may be at times ignored) are the work of men, owe their origin and their whole existence to human will. Men did not wake up on a summer morning and find them sprung up. Neither do they resemble trees, which, once planted, are 'aye growing' while men 'are sleeping.' In every stage of their existence they are made what they are by human voluntary agency.

Yet, though this is so, the dogma that the form of a government is a sort of spontaneous growth so closely bound up with the life of a people that we can hardly treat it as a product of human will and energy, does, though in a loose and inaccurate fashion, bring into view the fact that some polities, and among them the English constitution, have not been created at one stroke, and far from being the result of legislation, in the ordinary sense of that term, are the fruit of contests carried on in the courts on behalf of the rights of individuals. Our constitution, in short, is a judge-made constitution, and it bears on its face all the features, good and bad, of judge-made law.

. . . .

That "rule of law," then, which forms a fundamental principle of the constitution, has three meanings, or may be regarded from three different points of view.

It means, in the first place, the absolute supremacy or predominance of regular law as opposed to the influence of arbitrary power, and excludes the existence of arbitrariness, of prerogative, or even of wide discretionary authority on the part of the government. Englishmen are ruled by the law, and by the law alone; a man may with us be punished for a breach of law, but he can be punished for nothing else.

It means, again, equality before the law, or the equal subjection of all classes to the ordinary law of the land administered by the ordinary law courts and "rule of law" in this sense excludes the idea of any exemption of officials or others from the duty of obedience to the law which governs the citizens or from the jurisdiction of the ordinary tribunals; there can be with us nothing really corresponding to the "administrative law" (*droit administratif*) or the "administrative tribunals" (*tribunaux administratifs*) of France. The notion which lies at the bottom of the "administrative law" known to foreign countries is, that affairs or disputes in which the government or its servants are concerned are beyond the sphere of the civil courts and must be dealt with by special and more or less official bodies. This idea is utterly unknown to the law of England, and indeed is fundamentally inconsistent with our traditions and customs.

The "rule of law," lastly, may be used as a formula for expressing the fact that with us the law of the constitution, the rules which in foreign countries naturally form part of a constitutional code, are not the source but the consequence of the rights of individuals, as defined and enforced by the courts; that, in short, the principles of private law have with us been by the action of the courts and Parliament so extended as to determine the position of the Crown and of its servants; thus the constitution is the result of the ordinary law of the land.

(ii) The Environment of Canada's Judicial System

Peter H. Russell

Social and Economic Development

As an industrialized and urbanized society, Canada has experienced, to a relatively high degree, what the political sociologists refer to as "modernization." This modernization has been accompanied by increased complexity in Canadian law and increased professionalization of Canada's legal institutions. For the judicial system this has meant, among other things, an increased insistence on the possession of professional legal credentials by those adjudicating disputes about the law. Thus in Canada we have witnessed nearly a complete repudiation of the lay person as judge and a tendency to regard juries as technically too incompetent to be reliable fact-finders. Growing professionalism has also been felt, although in a much more delayed fashion, in the administration of Canadian courts, where there is increasing recognition of the merit of applying specialized administrative skills and the techniques of the computer age to managing court case flows.

But the effects of the modernization of Canadian society on its judicial system have been more pervasive and profound than a tendency to specialization. As industrialization and urbanization weaken traditional social bonds of family and community, basic social attitudes and relations are altered. We become a society of strangers relying increasingly, each of us, on formal positive law to define our rights and obligations; as a consequence, we turn increasingly to formal adjudication to settle our differences. This transformation of social relations from those based on custom and informal sources of authority to a system depending much more on legally defined rights and duties tends to expand the role of adjudicative agencies. This can be seen in fields as far apart as family law and federalism: as squabbling spouses and government turn to positive law as a guide to good conduct, they resort increasingly to courts to adjudicate conflict. Another facet of the social alienation accompanying modernity is increased reliance on enforcement of the criminal law rather than more informal communal sanctions as a means of maintaining social order. This, too, places increased burdens on Canadian courts, not so much to adjudicate disputes (few criminal charges produce not guilty pleas and formal court adjudication) but to provide a judicial presence in the processing of those selected by the police for criminal prosecution.

From *The Judiciary in Canada* (Whitby, Ontario: McGraw-Hill Ryerson Limited, 1987) at 31–39. Notes omitted. Reproduced by permission of the author.

Socio-economic development does not affect the business of courts in industrialized societies in a uniform way. The impact is considerably influenced by the litigiousness of a people — that is to say, their general propensity to settle disputes by pressing claims to formal adjudication rather than negotiating settlements more informally. A litigious tendency may be present in a society quite independently of its level of modernization. Among modern industrialized countries, England, New Zealand, and the United States have much higher civil case loads per capita than Italy, Japan, or Spain. The preference of the Japanese for mediation and conciliation over adjudication is reflected in the small size of their legal profession: 1 lawyer for each 10,000 of population compared with a ratio of 1 to 400 in the United States. No systematic research has been done on the litigiousness of Canadians, but the fact that on a per capita basis the Canadian judiciary and legal profession are roughly comparable in size to their American counterparts suggests that Canada is one of the more litigious of the industrialized and urbanized countries, perhaps only slightly less so than the United States. Canadian patterns may have been brought closer to American ones by the rapid expansion of the legal profession and legal aid programs over the past decade or so. These developments, while not necessarily altering the general disposition of Canadians to litigate, have made the option of taking disputes to court more available to people of limited means.

Increases in the number and complexity of laws, in the number of lawyers, and even in the litigiousness of the population, do not necessarily lead to a mushrooming of court business and expansion of the courts. Much depends on the relative attractiveness of judicial institutions as dispute-settling mechanisms and the availability of alternatives. The evidence in Canada suggests that very little of the increased need for adjudicative services generated by social change and industrial development has been taken care of by the general jurisdiction trial courts (i.e., the superior, district, and county courts of the provinces), which at the time of Confederation were regarded as the most important of Canada's judicial institutions. These provincial courts, staffed by federally appointed judges — the original linchpins of Canada's judicial system — have scarcely expanded at all. Whereas the number of judges serving at this level was 2.52 per 100,000 of population in 1867, by 1975 the ratio had actually declined to 2.23 per 100,000. Some of this increased demand for adjudication, especially in the field of criminal justice, has been met by the provincially appointed judges in the so-called lower courts of the provinces, and a little, on the civil side, by the major federally established trial court, the Federal Court of Canada. But probably a great deal more has been taken care of outside the formal court system through private arbitration and administrative tribunals. Improvements in the administration of courts may begin to reverse this trend by reducing some of the delay and inconvenience which in the past drove business away from the courts. Another factor working in the same direction is the Canadian version of what in the United States is referred to as the "public law explosion." On the one hand, the expanded use of the criminal sanction by the state; on the other hand, the expanded range of statutory and even constitutional rights that can be claimed by the individual or corporation against the state generate disputes which in our society must finally be settled by the courts.

Political Beliefs and Ideology

Here we encounter the second environmental influence on the judicial system: political beliefs and ideology. An increase in the degree of independence enjoyed by Canadian courts and their added capacity to serve as vehicles for challenging government has been closely related to a strengthening of support of liberalism in Canada's political culture. This growth in respect for liberal values — for the rights of individuals and the value of preventing excessive and illegal exercises of governmental authority — has not, to be sure, developed to the point of extinguishing strong conservative tendencies in Canada's political culture. Canada was founded by counter-revolutionaries suspicious of the excesses of American democracy. The continued popularity of the national police force, the RCMP (despite the exposure of its infringements of the legal rights of Canadians and its intolerance of political dissent), as well as popular support for the invocation of the *War Measures Act* in the 1970 October crisis, point to the survival of this conservative strain. But liberal critics of these recent manifestations of Canadians' respect for authority and fear of disorder often fail to mark the liberalization of political attitudes that has been occurring in Canada. Manifestations of moral outrage and the favourable treatment it receives in the popular media are, in themselves, an indication of this change.

A growing egalitarianism in Canadian society has fostered the extension of liberal values to all classes in society. This tendency has had important consequences for the functioning of the courts. Legal aid (the provision of publicly funded legal counsel to indi-

(ii) The Environment of Canada's Judicial System

gent persons) is, as we have noted, a leading example of this trend. Another is reform of the criminal justice system which has taken place over the last century. The reduction of close ties between the criminal courts and the police, bail reform, and an upgrading of the qualifications of the judges who preside over the country's busiest criminal courts are part of this movement. These reforms are relatively modest; none goes as far as critics of the system might wish. But the direction of change is clearly liberal.

A further illustration of this liberalization of attitudes and its effect on the judicial system is the change which has taken place in the appeal system in criminal cases. Up until 1892 there was no right of appeal in criminal cases. When a right of appeal was included in the *Criminal Code*, it was typical of the mixture of values in Canadian society that not only was the accused given a right to appeal his conviction but the crown was also given a right to appeal the accused's acquittal, even if the verdict was rendered by a jury. The review of trial court decisions in criminal cases has become an increasingly important function of Canada's courts of appeal. We can get some idea of how much Canadian attitudes have changed by noting that in 1975 when the crown successfully appealed a jury's acquittal of Dr. Morgentaler, a Montreal physician who ran an abortion clinic, there was a sufficient public outcry to bring about an amendment of the *Criminal Code* removing the power of appeal courts to substitute a guilty verdict for an acquittal in a case heard by judge and jury.

An egalitarian extension of legal rights has also affected the work of courts in non-criminal areas. New legal rights have been established for classes of persons whose bargaining position was relatively weak: for example, wives in relation to husbands, children in relation to parents, employees in relation to employers, students and professors in relation to university officials. The establishment of these rights means that disputes which might have been settled informally are now often litigated and go to court. Dispute settlement through informal negotiation becomes less acceptable when social and economic "underdogs" believe their interests will be better protected by claiming rights in court rather than counting on the benevolence of those in positions of power.

A similar reduction of trust in those exercising political authority has made Canadians more interested in the liberal notion of building checks and balances into their system of government. Canadians may continue to believe that the purpose of government is as much to provide for peace, order and good government as it is to protect the rights and liberties of the individual, but they have become increasingly apprehensive about the problems of controlling the governmental leviathan. Several generations of experience under big government have generated scepticism about the inherent good sense and self-restraint of those who govern. The nineteenth-century achievement of responsible government has proved to be no panacea for ensuring that government is accountable to the people. The decline of the legislature's significance in law-making and in its capacity for monitoring government operations has been evident for many years. Cabinet government concentrates enormous power in the hands of a very few politicians and officials. There may be some dim recognition that the vitality of the division of powers and competition between federal and provincial governments in Canada by dispersing power enhances political liberty. Still, both provincial and federal governments are recognized as centres of power against whose arbitrary and unlawful activities citizens need further institutional protection.

Increasingly this liberal impulse looks to the judiciary for such protection. Where there is fear that government will abuse newly acquired powers, the judiciary is brought in to guard against this danger. A good example is the inclusion of a requirement for judicial warrants in the legislation that legalized electronic eavesdropping by the police. More recently, in the debate over a federal *Access to Information Act*, distrust of the government forced the inclusion of a provision giving the courts, in most instances, the final word in deciding whether government refusals to provide information fall within statutory criteria.

This tendency in the Canadian political system to rely on the judicial process as a means of preventing abuse of power and protecting rights may now be at a turning point. Canada's new constitutional *Charter of Rights and Freedoms* significantly expands expectations about the judiciary's capacity and inclination to check government. The apparent popularity of increasing the power of judges at the expense of the power of politicians and officials demonstrates the extent to which Canadians, at this point in their history, regard their judges as less tied to the interests of government; they are seen in a fundamental sense as being less political and more trustworthy than those holding executive and legislative positions. But, again, it is important to point out that this perception of the judiciary as the politically neutered branch of government may well be undermined by the political nature of the judiciary's responsibilities under the new Charter.

Canada's Legal Culture

The third and most direct of the environmental influences on the judicial system is a country's legal culture. The basic character of Canada's legal system, and hence of its judicial system, might be expected to reflect the legal cultures of the two European peoples, the English and the French, who founded Canada. But this expectation is not borne out by the facts. So dominant has the English common law system been that it is misleading to think of Canada's legal culture as fundamentally dualistic. This is especially true of its judicial system, which has been even more thoroughly anglicized than the substantive law. As far as the legal culture of Canada's original inhabitants is concerned, it was totally ignored and for all practical purposes obliterated by the European settlers. Thus, in legal terms, Canada today belongs essentially to the common law world although as with all the common law countries, there are some distinctive wrinkles stemming from the country's particular circumstances.

There is a strong element of legal dualism in Quebec's history. Soon after the British conquest of New France, through the *Quebec Act* of 1774, the laws of the French Canadians were made the basis of the colony's civil law, while its criminal law was to be British. Despite this original dualism, French civil law was subjected to powerful common law influences. The principal vehicle for this process of anglicization was the judicial system. British governors selected the judges and for the most part they chose persons whose legal knowledge, if it existed at all, was based process on English experience. Most importantly, the appeal was dominated by English Canadians and British judges. Consequently the judicial method in both civil and criminal law became the common law method, with its emphasis on judicial precedent. These common law techniques were so firmly embedded by the time a *Civil Code* was adopted in Quebec that English-style judicial precedents rather than French civilian doctrine became the dominant force in interpreting the code. The anglicization of Quebec's civil law system is a testament to the quiet way in which power can flow through a judicial system, especially one with a powerful appeals hierarchy.

An essential part of the Confederation settlement in 1867 was that Quebec, as the province in which the French Canadians could maintain a majority, would be able to preserve the distinctive language, religion, and laws of the French-Canadian people. Section 92(13) of the *British North America Act* gave all the provinces jurisdiction over "property and civil rights" — a concept that embraces most of the subjects included in Quebec's *Civil Code* and *Code of Procedure*. Thus Quebec has retained legislative jurisdiction over those matters which are central to the French civil law tradition. On particular points of substantive law and civil procedure Quebec civil law differs from the laws of the common law provinces, although under the impact of secularization and modern commerce these differences have narrowed and may not be more significant than differences that exist in some areas of statutory law among the common law provinces. Since Confederation the highest court of appeal, whose opinions interpreting Quebec's civil law bind Quebec judges, has been, first, an imperial court, the Judicial Committee of the Privy Council, and then the Supreme Court of Canada. Although Quebec judges have always been in a minority position on the latter court, more often than not they have been the dominant influence on the panels hearing civil law cases from Quebec.

For our purposes here the most important point is that the judicial institutions of Quebec, despite any residue of French civil law and procedure that survives, bear the essential features of English common law courts. A lawyer from English-speaking Canada, or for that matter from virtually any other part of the English-speaking world, who wished to practise in Quebec, would not have to adapt to an alien judicial system. It is only in very recent years that Quebec court reformers have begun to look to continental French institutions for inspiration — for instance, to the idea of a career judiciary based on a special legal education for judges. So far, this application of Quebec nationalism to judicial institutions has not borne fruit in any concrete changes.

Some of the features of the common law tradition that have important consequences for the role of the judiciary in Canada (for example, the use of juries and the adversary system) have already been mentioned and will be referred to later in the text. In this introductory discussion of judicial power there are two features of common law systems that deserve special emphasis: the central importance of the judges, and the power of the legal profession.

In any legal system based on the common law tradition, the judge has a preeminent position as compared with other legal functionaries. Common law is indeed judge-made law. On many subjects of contemporary legislative interest, common law rules are dwarfed in importance by statutes enacted by the legislature, by delegated legislation or regulations enacted by the executive, and in Canada by the written Constitution. Long ago common law judges

(ii) The Environment of Canada's Judicial System

accepted their subordination to Parliament as a sovereign law maker, and in Canada they must accept the Constitution of Canada as the highest source of law. Even so, judicial decisions applying and interpreting regulations, statutes, and the Constitution, as we have already stressed, can have a tremendous influence on the policies that are actually effected and the rights that are actually established through these other sources of law. It is true that the difference between the legislative role of the judge in the common law system as compared with the civil law system has been exaggerated. Modern scholarship on civil law systems has revealed the important role that judicial interpretation and judicial opinions play in applying civil law codes, despite the civil law system's theoretical denial of their importance. Nevertheless the fact remains that it is the common law system that openly accepts the judicial opinion with all its potential for law development as an integral part of the system.

The pre-eminence of the judge in the common law system extends beyond the judge's law-making role. It is also manifest in the social and political status of the judge. In continental Europe the legal scholar has a high, if not a higher, status than the judge. This is certainly not the case in Canada. The lustre of the judicial position in Canada is reflected in the practice, already commented upon, of assigning judges major extra-judicial responsibilities, notably on royal commissions and commissions of inquiry, on matters of great public interest. A symbolic indication of the high status of the judicial office in Canada is that the chief justice of the country's highest court, the Supreme Court of Canada, in the absence or incapacity of the governor general, represents the head of state. Whether or not there is validity in the generalization that Canadian judges are self-restrained or uncreative in the exercise of their judicial powers, the high status accorded them in the Canadian legal and political systems continues to be a significant political resource for the Canadian judiciary.

The prestige and power of judges in the common law system is closely related to the strength of the legal profession. It might even be said that the pre-eminent position of the bench within common law legal systems largely derives from the pre-eminent position of the bar within common law societies. Going back to the roots of the common law judicial system in England, it was the ability of a small guild of private legal practitioners centred in the Inns of Court in London — first the sergeants, then the barristers — to monopolize appointments to the Royal Courts of Justice that was decisive in ensuring that the common law judiciary would not develop in the continental fashion as a career branch of government service. Instead, judicial positions in the higher courts would be awarded to persons who had distinguished themselves in private legal practice. The bench in Canada, even at its lowest levels, is recruited almost exclusively from the bar. Thus, in studying the forces that shape the Canadian judiciary it is essential to take into account the nature of the Canadian legal profession. Access to that profession, its education system, and the characteristics of private practice will have a great deal to do with determining what kinds of men and women become judges in Canada.

In Canada the bar is considerably less elitist than in England. Instead of the English division between a small group of barristers who plead cases in court and a great mass of solicitors advising clients and transacting legal business out of court, or France's four or five separate legal professions (advocates, avoues, notaries, and judges), Canada has a fused and unified legal profession. There are specializations within this profession, but all Canadian lawyers belong to a single profession. Further, the Canadian bar is not concentrated in a single metropolitan centre but is dispersed across the country; there are centres of professional activity in every Canadian province. Thus the professional pool from which Canadian judges are recruited is much larger and more diverse than the tiny coterie of London-based barristers from which English judges are drawn. As a social interest group, geographical dispersal is more than compensated for by professional unity. The Canadian bar's ability to assert itself as a unified profession has few parallels in other countries.

Some lawyers might object to the suggestion that they belong to a private interest group. Formally, as members of the bar, they are "officers of the court," and in that sense belong to a public institution. Nevertheless, the profession has emphasized the need to maintain its independence of government. It has insisted, successfully, on its own self-government, on controlling the standards of professional education and in most provinces, on keeping private legal practitioners, rather than salaried lawyers, as the mainstay of publicly funded legal aid programs. The rationale for this commitment to the profession's independence has been fundamentally ideological: recognition of the value in a liberal state under the rule of law of ensuring that individuals and groups have access to legal counsel not controlled by the government.

If the press can be referred to as the fourth estate, the legal profession as a private organization providing an essential public service might be thought of as a fifth estate in Canada. The power of this fifth estate is exercised through its professional activities and advocacy, and also through the participation of so many of its members at the highest levels of the political branches of government. The private practice of law provides exceptional opportunities for those who wish to take their chances in electoral competition. No other profession or occupational group has been so well represented in legislatures and cabinets at both the federal and provincial levels. Among other things, the political prominence of the profession means that the views of professional lawyers are paramount in shaping policies with regard to judicial institutions and judicial reform. No major changes in the structure or functioning of Canada's courts can take place without the approval of leaders of the bar.

It would be a mistake, however, to think of the bar as an unchanging monolithic force. The winds of change which affect all other important social institutions are beginning to bring about significant changes in the size and shape of Canada's legal profession. The last decade has seen a major transformation. The ranks of the profession have expanded so that on a per capita basis it approximates the size of the American profession. The dominant position of males and the charter ethnic groups has declined. Most significantly, the political diversity of the profession would appear to have increased with the formation of radical breakaway organizations outside of the professional establishment. In the long run, all of this is likely to have profoundly important effects on the social and political orientation of the Canadian judiciary.

(iii) *Reference re Secession of Quebec*

THE COURT —

I. INTRODUCTION

This Reference requires us to consider momentous questions that go to the heart of our system of constitutional government. The observation we made more than a decade ago in *Reference re Manitoba Language Rights*, [1985] 1 S.C.R. 721 (*Manitoba Language Rights Reference*), at p. 728, applies with equal force here: as in that case, the present one "combines legal and constitutional questions of the utmost subtlety and complexity with political questions of great sensitivity". In our view, it is not possible to answer the questions that have been put to us without a consideration of a number of underlying principles. An exploration of the meaning and nature of these underlying principles is not merely of academic interest. On the contrary, such an exploration is of immense utility. Only once those underlying principles have been examined and delineated may a considered response to the questions we are required to answer emerge.

. . . .

III. REFERENCE QUESTIONS
A. Question 1

Under the Constitution of Canada, can the National Assembly, legislature or government of Quebec effect the secession of Quebec from Canada unilaterally?

(1) Introduction

As we confirmed in *Reference re Objection by Quebec to a Resolution to Amend the Constitution*, [1982] 2 S.C.R. 793, at p. 806, "The *Constitution Act, 1982* is now in force. Its legality is neither challenged nor assailable." The "Constitution of Canada" certainly includes the constitutional texts enumerated in s. 52(2) of the *Constitution Act, 1982*. Although these

[1998] 2 S.C.R. 217.

texts have a primary place in determining constitutional rules, they are not exhaustive. The Constitution also "embraces unwritten, as well as written rules", as we recently observed in the *Provincial Judges Reference, supra*, at para. 92. Finally, as was said in the *Patriation Reference, supra*, at p. 874, the Constitution of Canada includes

> the global system of rules and principles which govern the exercise of constitutional authority in the whole and in every part of the Canadian state.

These supporting principles and rules, which include constitutional conventions and the workings of Parliament, are a necessary part of our Constitution because problems or situations may arise which are not expressly dealt with by the text of the Constitution. In order to endure over time, a constitution must contain a comprehensive set of rules and principles which are capable of providing an exhaustive legal framework for our system of government. Such principles and rules emerge from an understanding of the constitutional text itself, the historical context, and previous judicial interpretations of constitutional meaning. In our view, there are four fundamental and organizing principles of the Constitution which are relevant to addressing the question before us (although this enumeration is by no means exhaustive): federalism; democracy; constitutionalism and the rule of law; and respect for minorities. The foundation and substance of these principles are addressed in the following paragraphs. We will then turn to their specific application to the first reference question before us.

. . . .

(A) NATURE OF THE PRINCIPLES

What are those underlying principles? Our Constitution is primarily a written one, the product of 131 years of evolution. Behind the written word is an historical lineage stretching back through the ages, which aids in the consideration of the underlying constitutional principles. These principles inform and sustain the constitutional text: they are the vital unstated assumptions upon which the text is based. The following discussion addresses the four foundational constitutional principles that are most germane for resolution of this Reference: federalism, democracy, constitutionalism and the rule of law, and respect for minority rights. These defining principles function in symbiosis. No single principle can be defined in isolation from the others, nor does any one principle trump or exclude the operation of any other.

. . . .

Although these underlying principles are not explicitly made part of the Constitution by any written provision, other than in some respects by the oblique reference in the preamble to the *Constitution Act, 1867*, it would be impossible to conceive of our constitutional structure without them. The principles dictate major elements of the architecture of the Constitution itself and are as such its lifeblood.

The principles assist in the interpretation of the text and the delineation of spheres of jurisdiction, the scope of rights and obligations, and the role of our political institutions. Equally important, observance of and respect for these principles is essential to the ongoing process of constitutional development and evolution of our Constitution as a "living tree", to invoke the famous description in *Edwards v. Attorney-General for Canada*, [1930] A.C. 123 (P.C.), at p. 136. As this Court indicated in *New Brunswick Broadcasting Co. v. Nova Scotia (Speaker of the House of Assembly)*, [1993] 1 S.C.R. 319, Canadians have long recognized the existence and importance of unwritten constitutional principles in our system of government.

(B) FEDERALISM

Federalism was a legal response to the underlying political and cultural realities that existed at Confederation and continue to exist today. At Confederation, political leaders told their respective communities that the Canadian union would be able to reconcile diversity with unity. It is pertinent, in the context of the present Reference, to mention the words of George-Etienne Cartier (cited in J. C. Bonenfant, "Les Canadiens francais et la naissance de la Confédération", [1952] C.H.A.R. 39, at p. 42):

> [TRANSLATION] When we are united, he said, we shall form a political nationality independent of the national origin or the religion of any individual. There are some who regretted that there was diversity of races and who expressed the hope that this distinctive character would disappear. The idea of unity of races is a utopia; it is an impossibility. A distinction of this nature will always exist, just as dissimilarity seems to be in the order of the physical, moral and political worlds. As to the objection based on this fact, that a large nation cannot be formed because Lower Canada is largely French and Catholic and Upper Canada is English and Protestant and the interior provinces are mixed, it constitutes, in

my view, reasoning that is futile in the extreme.... In our own federation, we will have Catholics and Protestants, English, French, Irish and Scots and everyone, through his efforts and successes, will add to the prosperity and glory of the new confederation. We are of different races, not so that we can wage war on one another, but in order to work together for our well-being.

The federal-provincial division of powers was a legal recognition of the diversity that existed among the initial members of Confederation, and manifested a concern to accommodate that diversity within a single nation by granting significant powers to provincial governments. The *Constitution Act, 1867* was an act of nation-building. It was the first step in the transition from colonies separately dependent on the Imperial Parliament for their governance to a unified and independent political state in which different peoples could resolve their disagreements and work together toward common goals and a common interest. Federalism was the political mechanism by which diversity could be reconciled with unity.

. . . .

The principle of federalism facilitates the pursuit of collective goals by cultural and linguistic minorities which form the majority within a particular province. This is the case in Quebec, where the majority of the population is French-speaking, and which possesses a distinct culture. This is not merely the result of chance. The social and demographic reality of Quebec explains the existence of the province of Quebec as a political unit and indeed, was one of the essential reasons for establishing a federal structure for the Canadian union in 1867. The experience of both Canada East and Canada West under the *Union Act, 1840* (U.K.), 3-4 Vict., c. 35, had not been satisfactory. The federal structure adopted at Confederation enabled French-speaking Canadians to form a numerical majority in the province of Quebec, and so exercise the considerable provincial powers conferred by the *Constitution Act, 1867* in such a way as to promote their language and culture. It also made provision for certain guaranteed representation within the federal Parliament itself.

. . . .

(C) DEMOCRACY

Democracy is a fundamental value in our constitutional law and political culture. While it has both an institutional and an individual aspect, the democratic principle was also argued before us in the sense of the supremacy of the sovereign will of a people, in this case potentially to be expressed by Quebecers in support of unilateral secession. It is useful to explore in a summary way these different aspects of the democratic principle.

. . . .

Democracy is commonly understood as being a political system of majority rule. It is essential to be clear what this means. The evolution of our democratic tradition can be traced back to the *Magna Carta* (1215) and before, through the long struggle for Parliamentary supremacy which culminated in the English *Bill of Rights* in 1688–89, the emergence of representative political institutions in the colonial era, the development of responsible government in the 19th century, and eventually, the achievement of Confederation itself in 1867. "[T]he Canadian tradition", the majority of this Court held in *Reference re Provincial Electoral Boundaries (Sask.)*, [1991] 2 S.C.R. 158, at p. 186, is "one of evolutionary democracy moving in uneven steps toward the goal of universal suffrage and more effective representation". Since Confederation, efforts to extend the franchise to those unjustly excluded from participation in our political system — such as women, minorities, and aboriginal peoples — have continued, with some success, to the present day.

Democracy is not simply concerned with the process of government. On the contrary, as suggested in *Switzman v. Elbling*, supra, at p. 306, democracy is fundamentally connected to substantive goals, most importantly, the promotion of self-government. Democracy accommodates cultural and group identities: *Reference re Provincial Electoral Boundaries*, at p. 188. Put another way, a sovereign people exercises its right to self-government through the democratic process. In considering the scope and purpose of the *Charter*, the Court in *R. v. Oakes*, [1986] 1 S.C.R. 103, articulated some of the values inherent in the notion of democracy (at p. 136):

> The Court must be guided by the values and principles essential to a free and democratic society which I believe to embody, to name but a few, respect for the inherent dignity of the human person, commitment to social justice and equality, accommodation of a wide variety of beliefs, respect for cultural and group identity, and faith in social and political institutions which enhance the participation of individuals and groups in society.

. . . .

(iii) Reference re Secession of Quebec

It is, of course, true that democracy expresses the sovereign will of the people. Yet this expression, too, must be taken in the context of the other institutional values we have identified as pertinent to this Reference. The relationship between democracy and federalism means, for example, that in Canada there may be different and equally legitimate majorities in different provinces and territories and at the federal level. No one majority is more or less "legitimate" than the others as an expression of democratic opinion, although, of course, the consequences will vary with the subject matter. A federal system of government enables different provinces to pursue policies responsive to the particular concerns and interests of people in that province. At the same time, Canada as a whole is also a democratic community in which citizens construct and achieve goals on a national scale through a federal government acting within the limits of its jurisdiction. The function of federalism is to enable citizens to participate concurrently in different collectivities and to pursue goals at both a provincial and a federal level.

. . . .

Finally, we highlight that a functioning democracy requires a continuous process of discussion. The Constitution mandates government by democratic legislatures, and an executive accountable to them, "resting ultimately on public opinion reached by discussion and the interplay of ideas" (*Saumur v. City of Quebec*, supra, at p. 330). At both the federal and provincial level, by its very nature, the need to build majorities necessitates compromise, negotiation, and deliberation. No one has a monopoly on truth, and our system is predicated on the faith that in the marketplace of ideas, the best solutions to public problems will rise to the top. Inevitably, there will be dissenting voices. A democratic system of government is committed to considering those dissenting voices, and seeking to acknowledge and address those voices in the laws by which all in the community must live.

. . . .

(D) CONSTITUTIONALISM AND THE RULE OF LAW

The principles of constitutionalism and the rule of law lie at the root of our system of government. The rule of law, as observed in *Roncarelli v. Duplessis*, [1959] S.C.R. 121, at p. 142, is "a fundamental postulate of our constitutional structure."

As we noted in the *Patriation Reference, supra*, at pp. 805–6, "[t]he 'rule of law' is a highly textured expression, importing many things which are beyond the need of these reasons to explore but conveying, for example, a sense of orderliness, of subjection to known legal rules and of executive accountability to legal authority". At its most basic level, the rule of law vouchsafes to the citizens and residents of the country a stable, predictable and ordered society in which to conduct their affairs. It provides a shield for individuals from arbitrary state action.

. . . .

The constitutionalism principle bears considerable similarity to the rule of law, although they are not identical. The essence of constitutionalism in Canada is embodied in s. 52(1) of the *Constitution Act, 1982*, which provides that "[t]he Constitution of Canada is the supreme law of Canada, and any law that is inconsistent with the provisions of the Constitution is, to the extent of the inconsistency, of no force or effect." Simply put, the constitutionalism principle requires that all government action comply with the Constitution. The rule of law principle requires that all government action must comply with the law, including the Constitution. This Court has noted on several occasions that with the adoption of the *Charter*, the Canadian system of government was transformed to a significant extent from a system of Parliamentary supremacy to one of constitutional supremacy. The Constitution binds all governments, both federal and provincial, including the executive branch (*Operation Dismantle Inc. v. The Queen*, [1985] 1 S.C.R. 441, at p. 455). They may not transgress its provisions: indeed, their sole claim to exercise lawful authority rests in the powers allocated to them under the Constitution, and can come from no other source.

. . . .

Canadians have never accepted that ours is a system of simple majority rule. Our principle of democracy, taken in conjunction with the other constitutional principles discussed here, is richer. Constitutional government is necessarily predicated on the idea that the political representatives of the people of a province have the capacity and the power to commit the province to be bound into the future by the constitutional rules being adopted. These rules are "binding" not in the sense of frustrating the will of a majority of a province, but as defining the majority which must be consulted in order to alter the fundamental balances of political power (including the spheres of autonomy guaranteed by the principle of federalism), individual rights, and minority rights in our society. Of course, those constitutional rules are themselves amenable to amendment, but only through a process of negotiation which ensures that there is an opportunity for the constitutionally defined rights of all the parties to be respected and reconciled.

In this way, our belief in democracy may be harmonized with our belief in constitutionalism. Constitutional amendment often requires some form of substantial consensus precisely because the content of the underlying principles of our Constitution demand it. By requiring broad support in the form of an "enhanced majority" to achieve constitutional change, the Constitution ensures that minority interests must be addressed before proposed changes which would affect them may be enacted.

. . . .

(E) PROTECTION OF MINORITIES

The fourth underlying constitutional principle we address here concerns the protection of minorities. There are a number of specific constitutional provisions protecting minority language, religion and education rights. Some of those provisions are, as we have recognized on a number of occasions, the product of historical compromises. As this Court observed in *Reference re Bill 30, An Act to Amend the Education Act (Ont.)* [1987] 1 S.C.R. 1148, at p. 1173, and in *Reference re Education Act (Que.)*, [1993] 2 S.C.R. 511, at pp. 529–30, the protection of minority religious education rights was a central consideration in the negotiations leading to Confederation. In the absence of such protection, it was felt that the minorities in what was then Canada East and Canada West would be submerged and assimilated. See also *Greater Montreal Protestant School Board v. Quebec (Attorney General)*, [1989] 1 S.C.R. 377, at pp. 401-2, and *Adler v. Ontario*, [1996] 3 S.C.R. 609. Similar concerns animated the provisions protecting minority language rights, as noted in *Société des Acadiens du Nouveau-Brunswick Inc. v. Association of Parents for Fairness in Education*, [1986] 1 S.C.R. 549, at p. 564.

. . . .

The concern of our courts and governments to protect minorities has been prominent in recent years, particularly following the enactment of the *Charter*. Undoubtedly, one of the key considerations motivating the enactment of the *Charter*, and the process of constitutional judicial review that it entails, is the protection of minorities. However, it should not be forgotten that the protection of minority rights had a long history before the enactment of the *Charter*. Indeed, the protection of minority rights was clearly an essential consideration in the design of our constitutional structure even at the time of Confederation: *Senate Reference, supra*, at p. 71. Although Canada's record of upholding the rights of minorities is not a spotless one, that goal is one towards which Canadians have been striving since Confederation, and the process has not been without successes. The principle of protecting minority rights continues to exercise influence in the operation and interpretation of our Constitution.

Consistent with this long tradition of respect for minorities, which is at least as old as Canada itself, the framers of the *Constitution Act, 1982* included in s. 35 explicit protection for existing aboriginal and treaty rights, and in s. 25, a non-derogation clause in favour of the rights of aboriginal peoples. The "promise" of s. 35, as it was termed in *R. v. Sparrow*, [1990] 1 S.C.R. 1075, at p. 1983, recognized not only the ancient occupation of land by aboriginal peoples, but their contribution to the building of Canada, and the special commitments made to them by successive governments. The protection of these rights, so recently and arduously achieved, whether looked at in their own right or as part of the larger concern with minorities, reflects an important underlying constitutional value.

C. Canadian Legal Culture in Global Context

(i) The 'Meech Generation'

Colin Grey

Canada's constitutional battles spawned a cadre of political thinkers who now find their groundbreaking work on democracy, nationalism and minority rights in demand around the globe. **Colin Grey** reports.

The constitutional debates of a decade ago may have left Canadians fed up and exasperated, but they also spawned an academic movement — a "Meech Lake generation" of political philosophers — that has shot to the forefront of international debates.

The group, dubbed the "Canadian school" of political philosophy, has grown influential in a way not seen among Canadian scholars since Marshall McLuhan made his mark on communications theory in the 1960s.

"Suddenly, we turn out to be ahead of the pack," said Charles Taylor, a philosophy professor at McGill University, "as opposed to being some odd neurotic that can't get it together and ought to be quiet about it."

The peaking of the Canadian scholars' reputations has grown almost directly out of Meech Lake's demise. The story of the collapse of the constitutional pact on June 23, 1990, contained an underlying theoretical drama — the issue of what distinct powers or rights a minority group should enjoy in a Western democracy.

While hardly identical in their arguments, the most prominent members of the school generally endorse some form of minority rights, rather than give primacy to individual rights that don't provide special status for groups.

Canadian writings on topics such as citizenship, multiculturalism and nationalism possess an immediacy that has captured the attention of a world in which more and more countries are rethinking how to cope with their minorities.

Thinkers in India enthuse that "the most lively debates on citizenship are in fact Canadian debates," according to the introduction to an anthology on Canadian political philosophy to be published in the fall.

In another new book, French philosopher Alain Dieckhoff praises "the prodigious vitality of philosophy and political science in Canada, either in French or English."

American academic superstar Michael Walzer has extolled the vitality of Canadian thinking on issues of justice, federalism and group rights.

And governments and universities around the world have begun seeking out some of the group's preeminent members, like 68-year-old Mr. Taylor — the grandfather of the school — and Will Kymlicka of Queen's University who, at 37, is both its baby and most renowned younger member.

"I've just been very fortunate that I've picked a topic that no one was talking about," said Mr. Kymlicka, who writes on reconciling classic models of liberal democratic rights with minority rights.

"And then things kind of exploded. Partly in Canada because of Meech Lake, but internationally with all the ethnic conflict after the fall of the Berlin wall. By 1989, just when my first book appeared, this was sort of the topic, and I was, if you like, one step ahead of everyone else in discussing these issues."

While not exactly a cohesive group, members of the Canadian school are united in the way their Canadian political experience inspires their work, even indirectly.

Guy Laforest of Quebec City's Université de Laval coined the term "Meech Lake generation" to describe himself and his peers who say they had to think through Canadian problems largely on their own. "They came to their professional identity as scholars, as political theorists, as political scientists, during or immediately after the Meech Lake accord," Mr. Laforest said, "and they wrote directly on some of the major issues involved in Meech Lake."

From *The Sunday Observer* (London, England: The Observer Ltd.) (11 June 2000) A14. Guardian Unlimited © Guardian Newspaper Limited 2000. Reproduced with permission.

Apart from Mr. Kymlicka and Mr. Laforest, the group includes people such as Intergovernmental Affairs Minister Stéphane Dion, a political scientist; Joseph Carens and Jennifer Nedelsky, married expatriate Americans at the University of Toronto; and Daniel Weinstock from Université de Montréal, among many others.

Depending on your definition, the group also might include older scholars responsible for training the new generation, such as Mr. Taylor and his contemporary, the University of Victoria's James Tully.

"This phrase, the Canadian school, is one I'm not sure I've ever heard in Canada," said Wayne Norman, co-editor of the new anthology. "But it's one that I've heard from many different countries. People sort of ask me, you know, 'What's going on with this Canadian school of political philosophy?'"

Far and away the most noted work is that of Mr. Kymlicka, who writes on how liberal democracies can accommodate minority-rights claims.

"A comprehensive theory of justice in a multicultural state will include both universal rights, assigned to individuals regardless of group membership, and certain group-differentiated rights or 'special status' for minority cultures," he writes in his most influential book, *Multicultural Citizenship*.

His books have been translated into 18 languages, and he has become one of the most cited scholars in the world. "There is almost never a work in any of the fields of political philosophy on which Kymlicka works that does not cite him," Mr. Norman said.

He has also been called on to dispense his wisdom in the farthest corners of the world.

He has advised the government of Estonia on how to deal with its ethnic Russian population and been called on in Spain to advise on minority rights for the Catalan population. The Flemish Party in Belgium, a country split between its Flemish and French populations, has also reached out to him for counsel.

"What I try to do is identify policies that worked well in the West and which I think would work well if adopted, say, in Estonia," Mr. Kymlicka said. "It's more a matter of confirming and supporting certain trends or certain forces that were already at play in these countries, and I'm just trying to buttress them a bit."

What is seared in most Canadians memories are the politics: then-prime minister Brian Mulroney's boast that he had "rolled the dice" with constitutional negotiations; Pierre Trudeau's ominous warnings that granting Quebec distinct-society status would spell the end of the country; Elijah Harper holding up the vote on the deal in the Manitoba legislature; or Clyde Wells' refusal to hold a vote on the deal in Newfoundland.

But underlying the debate were issues now seen as critical: What is the best way to organize a federal state? Or, how do you reconcile classic ideas of individual rights and liberal democracy with the kinds of group rights demanded by Quebecers and aboriginal groups?

Just as Canadians wiped their hands of Meech Lake, the debates on these issues heated up around the world, Mr. Laforest said.

He argues in a new paper that the fall of the Berlin Wall in 1989 represented a watershed moment for political philosophy, marking the shift of debate from the rivalry between communism and liberalism, to an intramural debate about what form liberal democracies should take.

At the same time, Western democracies, even ones with strong individualistic traditions such as France, have had to deal with unprecedented numbers of immigrants and demands for group rights. In addition, Eastern European countries eager to establish their liberal credentials had to figure out how to build democracies despite tense relationships with Russian minorities who had migrated since the end of the Second World War.

"That's why I think one could argue in terms of history of ideas that the Meech Lake debate was very important," Mr. Laforest said. "Since those issues were in a sense front and centre in the Canadian debate kind of before they became dominant in much of the advanced Western democracies ... it gave us a kind of edge, a comparative advantage."

Behind the renaissance looms the considerable shadow of Pierre Trudeau.

Mr. Trudeau's patriation of the Constitution in 1982 without the Quebec government's signature created the circumstances that prompted Mr. Mulroney to bring the province back into the country's fold.

Mr. Trudeau's arguments for individual rights without special status for any minority groups were pivotal in shaping the 1982 Constitution, and in his successful campaign to defeat the Meech deal.

When the Meech Lake Accord fell through, many saw it as a victory for Mr. Trudeau and his vision of a country with equal rights for all, and no special distinctions.

But most of the Canadian school have begun to argue for the kinds of group-rights claims that Mr. Trudeau has consistently rejected as incompatible with those rights — even if his 1982 Constitution nonetheless contained certain concessions to them, like the granting of treaty rights to aboriginals.

Many of the current school see Mr. Trudeau's ideas as going against Canadian history, an attempt to impose American or French ideas of democracy on the country.

"Trudeau is a bit of an aberration," said Mr. Weinstock of Université de Montréal. "He tried to import an understanding of what the country was about — one nation from coast to coast, rather than two nations in a kind of a compact, and an equalization or an equality of all citizens irrespective of their culture.

"It's a powerful vision that has moved people to take up arms and everything, but one that, for deep sociological and historical reasons, the Canadian body politic never really fully took to," he added.

Mr. Trudeau's views have lost some of their lustre in foreign academic circles as well, according to Mr. Taylor. The problems now faced by other countries need to be solved by turning to more complex solutions that simply identical treatment for all citizens.

"Similar intractable problems are beginning to create similar opening out of possibilities," said Mr. Taylor, long considered something of an intellectual foil to the former prime minister.

"So the very rigid intellectual structure in which Pierre Trudeau thought of all this is, I think, if not discredited, it's lost a lot a of its credibility. In the rest of the world, people are facing intractable problems of, roughly speaking, multiculturalism and so on, which require a much greater deal of flexibility and can't all be derived from a single principle," Mr. Taylor added.

Neither are solutions modelled on the United States as widely applicable.

Joseph Carens at the University of Toronto came to Canada from the United States 15 years ago with his wife, Jennifer Nedelsky.

He said the couple, both scholars, felt their outlook beginning to change simply because they were living in Canada and following debates on such issues as Quebec and aboriginal rights.

In the United States, debates on the women's and civil-rights movements focus on individual liberties, and debates on multiculturalism usually mean discussions of school curriculum or affirmative action.

In contrast, Canada has always reserved a place for thinking about special status for groups, providing "the sense that one has, or at least that I have, that you can't ignore these things. You can't do justice and ignore these things," Mr. Carens said. "People disagree (about) what justice requires, but you can't ignore it."

What they haven't been able to turn to, however, are theoretical models based on the American experience. The American model — where individual freedom is paramount and where national minorities such as aboriginals or Puerto Ricans have only a fraction of the types of powers granted in Canada — is seen as less applicable to many countries.

"There's a recognition that there's a set of issues that Canada has been dealing with that are relevant now to the European experience around multiculturalism," Mr. Carens said.

(ii) Canada's 18 Years of Human Rights Case Law Are Sure to Be Mined Heavily by Our Judges

Clare Dyer

[In this article journalist Clare Dyer discusses the potential impact of Canadian Charter jurisprudence on judicial interpretation of the new Human Rights Act in the United Kingdom.]

Beverley McLachlin is Canada's first woman chief justice. But thanks to the impending Rights Act, her court could have a significant influence on English law. **Clare Dyer** reports

---

From the "Guardian Law Column," *The [Manchester] Guardian* (19 June 2000) 8. Guardian Unlimited © Guardian Newspaper Limited 2000. Reproduced with permission.

The chances are you've never heard of Beverley McLachlin. But her pronouncements and those of her colleagues are about to have a profound influence on the way our law develops.

McLachlin is the newly installed Chief Justice of Canada, the first woman to hold this powerful and influential post. She heads the nine-judge supreme court of Canada, the country's highest court. But why should the rulings of a court thousands of miles away in a foreign country affect what happens here?

For the answer, see Margaret Brown v Procurator Fiscal. That was the Scottish case that caused a furore last February when the appeal court ruled that 30-year-old Brown's admission that she was driving while over the alcohol limit could not be used against her. Since that was a key piece of evidence, the case had to be dropped.

The Human Rights Act, which comes into force in October, will bring the European Convention on Human Rights into English law. The convention has been part of Scottish law for more than a year as a result of the act which brought in devolution. Since 1982, Canada has had a charter of rights and freedoms modelled on the European convention. As the judgments in Brown's case and others in the last year show, Canada's 18 years of case law are certain to be mined heavily by our judges when cases with human rights points come before our courts.

The judgment in Brown's case is peppered with dicta from McLachlin and other Canadian supreme court judges. Our courts will have to take account of judgments from the European court in Strasbourg in deciding cases that come before them, but the Brown judgment draws even [more] extensively on case law from Canada, where the laws and values are similar to Britain's.

The Scottish judges quote McLachlin's pronouncement in a 1990 case: "The protection conferred by a legal system which grants the accused immunity from incriminating himself at trial but offers no protection with respect to pre-trial statements would be illusory." And: "A person in the power of the state in the course of the criminal process has the right to choose whether to speak to the police or remain silent."

Interpreted by a generation of activist judges, the Canadian charter has had a revolutionary effect, little anticipated back in 1982. The supreme court's rulings have been controversial, much criticised in academic journals, newspaper leaders and news magazines. The judges, critics say, have usurped the role of parliament. Constitutional experts and court watchers predict that the Human Rights Act will similarly politicise British judges.

So when Lord Woolf met the press this month for the first time in his new role as Lord Chief Justice of England, I was in Ottawa, following a Mountie through the corridors of Canada's supreme court building to the chief justice's wood-panelled office. I was greeted not by a 67-year-old man but by a young-looking woman of 56. However similar the two countries' laws and institutions, Canada's senior judges are much more representative of the people they serve.

Even the titles in Britain assume that women will never hold them: Lord Chief Justice, Lords of Appeal in Ordinary (the full title of the law lords). No woman in Britain has ever held one of the two highest posts, Lord Chief Justice or Master of the Rolls, or sat in our highest court, the House of Lords. (In Britain the Lord Chief Justice is the senior judge but does not sit in the highest court — he heads the court of appeal's criminal division; in Canada the chief justice heads the supreme court, a role more akin to the [sic] that of the senior law lord in Britain — a post just taken up by Lord Bingham, who was till this month Lord Chief Justice.)

While McLachlin is the first woman to occupy Canada's highest judicial office, the supreme court has had women members for nearly 20 years. Of the nine judges, three are currently women — including Louise Arbour, formerly chief prosecutor at the UN war crimes tribunal for the former Yugoslavia and Rwanda.

Unlike Britain's senior judiciary, dominated by the products of elite public schools, McLachlin, like most Canadian judges, was state-educated. She grew up as one of five children in the small farming community of Pincher Creek, Alberta. "We didn't have much money. We struggled," she told guests at her swearing-in ceremony. "What you could do mattered more than where you came from."

Her parents both had German roots. The Scottish surname came from her first husband, Rory, who died young, when their son was 12. Rory encouraged her to go to law school: "Without his infusions of confidence I would never have believed I could have succeeded in the male-dominated legal profession."

Eleven years ago, after seven years as a judge in British Columbia, she got the call to the nation's supreme court in Ottawa. Her son, Angus, who had to leave his friends in Vancouver, told her: "Go for it, Mom." She married her second husband, a lawyer, eight years ago.

Thirty years ago, women were as scarce in the law schools of Canada as they were in Britain's law

(ii) Canada's 18 Years of Human Rights Case Law Are Sure to Be Mined Heavily by Our Judges

faculties. Yet in Canada they have made it to the top of the system as they have not here. "I do think that because women sometimes have had different experiences in life they may bring perspectives that are important to the discussion table," says McLachlin. "You can have a richer, fuller discussion and one that better reflects the real values and concerns of society."

Critics of the court's activism counter that it is for the people's elected representatives in parliament to fashion the law to reflect the values and concerns of society, and not for the judges. The view that the judges have grown too powerful is a widespread theme in the Canadian media. Typical is a leader in the Montreal Gazette: "The supreme court has become a political institution. Its power should be checked."

The court, indeed, has the power to strike down statutes passed by parliament and provincial legislatures, and it is a power it uses freely. In Britain, judges will not be able to strike down a statute; there will be a fast-track procedure for parliament to amend any law found to breach human rights. McLachlin believes, however, that the difference may be more apparent than real.

Between 1982 and 1998 the Canadian supreme court struck down 58 statutes. Last year, in a controversial ruling hailed as a victory for gay rights, it outlawed any provisions in a statute which define a spouse as "a member of the opposite sex". That one judgment will mean rewriting up to 1,000 federal and provincial statutes. Conrad Black's National Post took issue with the ruling, claiming "public opinion is too divided on gay rights for judges to take sides". But McLachlin points to a survey last month showing strong public support for the charter.

In 1991 she delivered the majority judgment striking down rape shield laws protecting alleged rape victims from questioning about their sexual history. In a powerfully reasoned judgment, she argued that the accused's right to a fair trial should not be sacrificed. Citing the Birmingham Six and other cases of wrongful conviction, she insisted: "The price is too great."

Another woman judge, Claire l'Heureux-Dubé, delivered an equally eloquent dissent. The rape shield laws were rewritten but have come before the court again in a case awaiting judgment. Other current issues concern gun-control laws, child pornography and whether Canadians charged with murder in the US should be extradited to face the death penalty, which is outlawed in Canada.

A new book, The Charter Revolution and the Court Party, by political scientists FL Morton and Rainer Knopf, accuses the court of allowing itself to be hijacked by women's organisations, civil liberties bodies and other interest groups permitted to intervene in cases. Even the Italian senate, campaigning globally against the death penalty, was allowed to intervene in the extradition case. British courts, which have so far been sparing in allowing interveners — Amnesty International's role in the Pinochet case was an example — will have to hear more when the Human Rights Act comes into force, according to Robert Hazell, professor of government and the constitution at University College London. McLachlin insists: "This court is not hijacked by any interest groups or anyone else. We listen to all the arguments and make our decisions accordingly, I think, in a very independent way."

Most Canadians were unprepared for the revolution the charter has brought. But, she says, the supreme court signalled from the outset "that they were going to take these rights and freedoms very seriously, that they were going to give a generous, purposive approach to them, that they were going to interpret them in the world context of human rights issues and human rights law". There's little doubt that British judges will do the same.

(iii) Globalization

*David Held and Anthony McGrew
with David Goldblatt and Jonathan Perraton*

Globalization: n. a process (or set of processes) that embodies a transformation in the spatial organization of social relations and transactions, generating transcontinental or interregional flows and networks of activity, interaction, and power.

Although everybody talks about globalization, few people have a clear understanding of it. The "big idea" of the late twentieth century is in danger of turning into the cliché of our times. Can we give it precise meaning and content, or should globalization be consigned to the dustbin of history?

The reason there is so much talk about globalization is that everyone knows that something extraordinary is happening to our world. We can send e-mail across the planet in seconds; we hear that our jobs depend on economic decisions in far-off places; we enjoy films, food, and fashion from all over the world; we worry about an influx of drugs and how we can save the ozone layer. These growing global connections affect all aspects of our lives — but it is still not clear what globalization really means.

There has been a heated debate about whether globalization is occurring at all. The debate rages between those who claim that globalization marks the end of the nation-state and the death of politics and those who dismiss the globalization hype and say that we have seen it all before. This debate has continued for a decade, leading to ever more confusion. It is not that these positions are wholly mistaken. In fact, both capture elements of a complex reality. But it is the wrong debate to have when there is no common ground about what globalization is. Until we know what globalization actually means, we will not be able to understand how it affects our lives, our identities, and our politics.

In this essay, we try to go beyond the rhetoric of entrenched positions and produce a richer account of what globalization is, how the world is changing, and what we can do about it. So what does globalization mean? We show that globalization is made up of the accumulation of links across the world's major regions and across many domains of activity.

It is not a single process but involves four distinct types of change:

- It stretches social, political, and economic activities across political frontiers, regions, and continents.
- It intensifies our dependence on each other, as flows of trade, investment, finance, migration, and culture increase.
- It speeds up the world. New systems of transport and communication mean that ideas, goods, information, capital, and people move more quickly.
- It means that distant events have a deeper impact on our lives. Even the most local developments may come to have enormous global consequences. The boundaries between domestic matters and global affairs can become increasingly blurred.

In short, globalization is about the connections between different regions of the world — from the cultural to the criminal, the financial to the environmental — and the ways in which they change and increase over time.

. . . .

The Fate of National Cultures

When people move, they take their cultures with them. So, the globalization of culture has a long history. The great world religions showed how ideas and beliefs can cross the continents and transform societies. No less important were the great premodern empires that, in the absence of direct military and political control, held their domains together through a common culture of the ruling classes. For long periods of human history, there have been only these global cultures and a vast array of fragmented local cultures. Little stood between the court and the village until the invention of nation-states in the eighteenth century created a powerful new cultural identity that lay between these two extremes.

(1999) 5 Global Governance 483 at 483–84, 486–89, 494–96. Boulder, CO: Lynne Rienner Publishers. © David Held et al. Reproduced with permission of David Held.

(iii) Globalization

This rise of nation-states and nationalist projects truncated the process of cultural globalization. Nation-states sought to control education, language, and systems of communication, like the post and the telephone. But as European empires became entrenched in the nineteenth century, new forms of cultural globalization emerged with innovations in transport and communications, notably regularized mechanical transport, and the telegraph. These technological advances helped the West to expand and enabled the new ideas that emerged — especially science, liberalism, and socialism — to travel and transform the ruling cultures of almost every society on the planet.

Contemporary popular cultures have certainly not yet had a social impact to match this, but the sheer scale, intensity, speed, and volume of global cultural communications today is unsurpassed. The accelerating diffusion of radio, television, the Internet, and satellite and digital technologies has made instant communication possible. Many national controls over information have become ineffective. Through radio, film, television, and the Internet, people everywhere are exposed to the values of other cultures as never before. Nothing, not even the fact that we all speak different languages, can stop the flow of ideas and cultures. The English language is becoming so dominant that it provides a linguistic infrastructure as powerful as any technological system for transmitting ideas and cultures.

Beyond its scale, what is striking about today's cultural globalization is that it is driven by companies, not countries. Corporations have replaced states and theocracies as the central producers and distributors of cultural globalization. Private international institutions are not new, but their mass impact is. News agencies and publishing houses in previous eras had a much more limited impact on local and national cultures than the consumer goods and cultural products of global corporations today.

Although the vast majority of these cultural products come from the United States, this is not a simple case of "cultural imperialism." One of the surprising features of our global age is how robust national and local cultures have proved to be. National institutions remain central to public life, and national audiences constantly reinterpret foreign products in novel ways.

These new communication technologies threaten states that pursue rigid closed-door policies on information and culture. For example, China sought to restrict access to the Internet but found this extremely difficult to achieve. In addition, it is likely that the conduct of economic life everywhere will be transformed by the new technologies. The central question is the future impact of cultural flows on our sense of personal identity and national identity. Two competing forces are in evidence: the growth of multicultural politics almost everywhere and, in part as a reaction to this, the assertion of fundamentalist identities (religious, nationalist, and ethnic). Although the balance between these two forces remains highly uncertain, it is clear that only a more open, cosmopolitan outlook can ultimately accommodate itself to a more global era.

The Territorial State and Global Politics

One thousand years ago, a modern political map of the world would have been incomprehensible. It is not just that much of the world was still to be "discovered." People simply did not think of political power as something divided by clear-cut boundaries and unambiguous color patches. But our contemporary maps do not just misrepresent the past. By suggesting that territorial areas contain indivisible, illimitable, and exclusive sovereign states, they may also prove a poor metaphor for the shape of the politics of the future.

Modern politics emerged with and was shaped by the development of political communities tied to a piece of land, the nation-state. This saw the centralization of political power within Europe, the creation of state structures, and the emergence of a sense of order between states. Forms of democracy were developed within certain states, while at the same time the creation of empires saw this accountability denied to others.

Today, we are living through another political transformation, which could be as important as the creation of the nation-state: the exclusive link between geography and political power has now been broken.

Our new era has seen layers of governance spread within and across political boundaries. New Institutions have both linked sovereign states together and pooled sovereignty beyond the nation-state. We have developed a body of regional and international law that underpins an emerging system of global governance, both formal and informal, with many layers.

Our policymakers experience a seemingly endless merry-go-round of international summits. Two or three congresses a year convened 150 years ago. Today more than four thousand convene each year. They include summits of the UN, the Group of Seven, the International Monetary Fund, the World

Trade Organization, the European Union (EU), the Asia-Pacific Economic Cooperation bloc, the regional forum of the Association of Southeast Asian Nations, and Mercado Común del Sur (Mercosur). These summits and many other official and unofficial meetings lock governments into global, regional, and multilayered systems of governance that they can barely monitor, let alone control.

Attention has tended to focus on the failure of global institutions to live up to the vast hopes that their birth created. But they have significant achievements to their credit. Although the UN remains a creature of the interstate system with well-documented shortcomings, it does deliver significant international public goods. These range from air traffic control and the management of telecommunications to the control of contagious diseases, humanitarian relief for refugees, and measures to protect our oceans and atmosphere.

However, it is regional institutions that have done most to transform the global political landscape. The EU has transformed Europe from postwar disarray to a situation where member states can pool sovereignty to tackle common problems. Despite the fact that many people still debate its very right to exist, the view from 1945 would be of astonishment at how far the EU has come so quickly. Although regionalism elsewhere is very different from the European model, its acceleration in the Americas, in the Asian Pacific, and (somewhat less) in Africa has had significant consequences for political power. Despite fears of Fortress Europe and protectionist blocs, regionalism has been a midwife to political globalization rather than a barrier to it. In fact, many global standards have resulted from negotiations involving regional groupings.

Another feature of the new era is the strengthening and broadening of international law. States no longer have the right to treat their citizens as they think fit. An emerging framework of "cosmopolitan law" — governing war, crimes against humanity, environmental issues, and human rights — has made major inroads into state sovereignty. Even the many states that violate these standards in practice accept general duties to protect their citizens, to provide a basic standard of living, and to respect human rights.

These international standards are monitored and vociferously lobbied for by a growing number of international agencies. In 1996, there were nearly 260 intergovernmental organizations and nearly 5,500 international nongovernmental organizations. In 1909, the former numbered just 37 and the latter a mere 176. There has also been a vast increase in the number of international treaties and regimes, such as the nuclear nonproliferation regime.

The momentum for international cooperation shows no sign of slowing, despite the many vociferous complaints often heard about it. The stuff of global politics already goes far beyond traditional geopolitical concerns and will increase whenever effective action requires international cooperation. Drug smugglers, capital flows, acid rain, and the activities of pedophiles, terrorists, and illegal immigrants do not recognize borders; neither can the policies for their effective resolution.

This transformation of international politics does not mean that the nation-state is dead. The multilateral revolution, rather than replacing the familiar world of nation-states, overlays and complicates it. Many familiar political distinctions and assumptions have been called into question. The context of national politics has been transformed by the diffusion of political authority and the growth of multilayered governance (which we discuss further in the section on governing globalization). But it is not entirely clear which factors will determine how far old institutions can adapt and whether new institutions can be invested with legitimacy.

. . . .

Governing Globalization

Contemporary globalization represents the beginning of a new epoch in human affairs. In transforming societies and world order, it is having as profound an impact as the Industrial Revolution and the global empires of the nineteenth century. We have seen that globalization is transforming our world, but in complex, multifaceted, and uneven ways. Although globalization has a long history, it is today genuinely different both in scale and in form from what has gone before. Every new epoch creates new winners and losers. This one will be no different. Globalization to date has already both widened the gap between the richest and poorest countries and further increased divisions within and across societies. It has inevitably become increasingly contested and politicized.

National governments — sandwiched between global forces and local demands — must now reconsider their roles and functions. But to say simply that states have lost power distorts what is happening, as does any suggestion that nothing much has changed. The real picture is much more complex. States today are at least as powerful, if not more so, than their predecessors on many fundamental measures of power — from the capacity to raise taxes to the ability to hurl force at enemies. But the demands on states have grown very rapidly as well. They must often work together to pursue the public good — to prevent recession or to protect the environment. And transnational agreements, for example dealing with acid rain, will often force national governments to adopt major changes in domestic policy.

So state power and political authority are shifting. States now deploy their sovereignty and autonomy as bargaining chips in multilateral and transnational negotiations, as they collaborate and coordinate actions in shifting regional and global networks. The right of most states to rule within circumscribed territories — their sovereignty — is not on the edge of collapse, although the practical nature of this entitlement — the actual capacity of states to rule — is changing its shape. The emerging shape of governance means that we need to stop thinking of state power as something that is indivisible and territorially exclusive. It makes more sense to speak about the transformation of state power than the end of the state; the range of government strategies stimulated by globalization [is], in many fundamental respects, producing the potential for a more activist state.

But the exercise of political and economic power now frequently escapes effective mechanisms of democratic control. And it will continue to do so while democracy remains rooted in a fixed and bounded territorial conception of political community. Globalization has disrupted the neat correspondence between national territory, sovereignty, political space, and the democratic political community. It allows power to flow across, around, and over territorial boundaries. And so the challenge of globalization today is ultimately political. Just as the Industrial Revolution created new types of class politics, globalization demands that we re-form our existing territorially defined democratic institutions and practices so that politics can continue to address human aspirations and needs.

This means rethinking politics. We need to take our established ideas about political equality, social justice, and liberty and refashion these into a coherent political project robust enough for a world where power is exercised on a transnational scale and where risks are shared by peoples across the world. And we need to think about what institutions will allow us to tackle these global problems while responding to the aspirations of the people they are meant to serve.

This is not a time for pessimism. We are caught between nostalgia for causes defeated and ideas lost, and excitement at the new possibilities that we face. We need to think in new ways. Globalization is not bringing about the death of politics. It is reilluminating and reinvigorating the contemporary political terrain.

(iv) Threat of NAFTA Case Kills Canada's MMT Ban: Challenge over gasoline additive could have cost Ottawa millions

Shawn McCarthy

The Liberal government is beating an embarrassing retreat on its year-old ban of the gasoline additive MMT, despite new evidence that the manganese used in the octane enhancer can cause nervous-system problems.

Sources say government officials have reached a tentative deal with MMT-maker Ethyl Corp., of Richmond, Va., to avoid a potentially devastating legal challenge under the North American free-trade agreement.

From *The [Toronto] Globe and Mail* (20 July 1998) A1. Reproduced with permission from The Globe and Mail.

Federal lawyers had warned the Liberal cabinet that Ethyl would be likely to win that NAFTA case, a ruling that could cost taxpayers hundreds of millions of dollars and hand a potent weapon to critics of the free-trade pact.

Sources said the negotiators for the two sides have agreed that Ottawa would drop its ban on MMT and pay the company an estimated $10-million for legal costs and lost profits. The government will also issue a statement to the effect that the manganese-based additive is neither an environmental nor a health risk.

In return, Ethyl would drop its NAFTA challenge and its claim for $250-million (U.S.) in damages.

However, Prime Minister Jean Chrétien must still approve the agreement.

The Liberal government legislated the ban on the cross-border sale of MMT last year, claiming the substance interferes with automobile emission controls and is therefore an environmental hazard. The legislation prohibited the importation or interprovincial sale of the additive.

The acrimonious debate pitted Ethyl and gasoline refiners, who wanted access to the inexpensive additive, against environmentalists and auto makers, who insisted the use of the substance ran counter to the goal of lower emissions.

Trade Pact's Clout Batters Fears about Gasoline Additive

Former environment ministers Sheila Copps and Sergio Marchi both argued that they couldn't ban MMT directly because Health Canada had found there was not sufficient evidence that it was toxic at low levels. So they resorted to the trade ban.

Federal lawyers had warned the government when the legislation was being debated that the importation ban would not likely withstand a NAFTA challenge. But Mr. Marchi, now International Trade Minister, has consistently vowed the government would defend its bill.

"We have a sovereign right to not only speak about alternate and cleaner fuels, but to do something about it." Mr. Marchi said last summer when he was named International Trade Minister.

Ethyl's NAFTA challenge has become a cause célèbre for critics of the trade deal, who see it as proof that such liberalizing agreements restrict governments' ability to pass the environmental and health legislation that might hurt corporate interests.

But the government's resolve to fight that challenge has crumbled.

Senior ministers worry that the auto industry has failed to provide solid evidence that MMT does in fact interfere with emission-control hardware, undercutting Ottawa's case. As well, a panel ruled last month that the prohibition on interprovincial trade in MMT contravenes a four-year-old agreement on internal trade.

Still, the Liberals' reversal comes as new studies indicate the low-level exposure to manganese can cause memory impairment and tremors similar to those experienced by victims of Parkinson's Disease.

Elizabeth May, executive director of the Sierra Club of Canada, said the government should have prohibited the use of MMT because it was a health risk rather than relied on the indirect ban on trade.

"It should be banned because of its risk to public health. We are against MMT in gas for health and environmental grounds," she said.

Donna Mergler, a neurotoxicologist at the University of Quebec at Montreal, is conducting one study of 306 people in southwestern Quebec that correlates manganese blood levels with neurological problems.

Her work, which is supported by the U.S. Environmental Protection Agency, is not complete, but preliminary findings presented to a conference in Little Rock, Ark., last October suggested that even low levels of manganese in the blood can have health effects, particularly in children and the elderly.

"We know that in large concentrations, airborne manganese does pose a risk to human health," Ms. Mergler said in an interview. What we don't know is at what level does it not pose a risk.

"There remain a lot of questions about manganese and we should know a lot more about it before we use it."

Ethyl has responded with its own study in which 1,000 people in Toronto wore air-monitoring devices over a year. The Ethyl research done by Research Triangle Institute of North Carolina found that manganese levels in the air were mere fractions of the safe levels set by both Health Canada and the U.S. EPA.

(MMT has been used by Canadian refiners to boost octane since 1977, when lead was banned on the ground that it caused neurological problems in children. MMT is still used by Ontario refiners who had stockpiled it before the cross-border ban came into effect last year, though supplies are running out in other provinces.)

Ethyl says that only a small drop of MMT is added to a litre of gasoline and that only a small fraction of the manganese becomes airborne after combustion.

(iv) Threat of NAFTA Case Kills Canada's MMT Ban

"The exposures are very, very low," said Ethyl vice-president Don Lynam. "They are far below levels set by Health Canada in its risk assessment."

However, critics question whether those levels, set by the Health Department in 1994, are appropriate in light of new evidence of low-level effects.

Meanwhile, the debate over MMT's impact on auto-emission controls continues.

Alain Perez, president of the Canadian Petroleum Products Institute, said the car makers have failed to prove their case and have used MMT as a scapegoat for their own inability to meet emission standards.

He noted that the U.S. environmental agency was forced to back off its ban of MMT in 1995 after a federal court found there was no basis for making the additive illegal.

If the Canadian ban was upheld, refiners say, they would be forced to spend up to $2-billion to retool their operations or use less efficient additives.

However, spokesmen for the auto industry insist that the manganese additive does do damage and will make it difficult for them to meet lower emission standards set by government.

Mark Nantais of the Canadian Motor Vehicle Manufacturers Association said 80 per cent of the manganese in MMT stays in the catalytic converter and "gums up the system."

While car makers are being pushed to improve controls on vehicle emissions, "nothing is happening on the fuel side," he said. "We can't get there from here with this poison in the gasoline. It's garbage in, garbage out."

2 Law and Morality

(i) Tragic Choices

Patrick J. Fitzgerald

You can't win 'em all," we say to console ourselves when things go wrong. What if they go so wrong that winning is impossible? What if life really puts us on the spot and confronts us with a tragic choice? Let's look at the following examples.

A pilot named Marten Hartwell crashed in the Northwest Territories in the early 70's. He was the only survivor. To stay alive until he was rescued he had to eat. His only source of food was the dead body of his companion, a young nurse. What should he have done — become a cannibal or starved to death? He chose to live.

In another case, some years ago, an international expedition set out to climb Mount Everest. One of the team, a man called Harsh, slipped and fell. He came to rest suspended upside down over an icefield. To get to him his companions would have had to venture across the extremely dangerous ice; and when they reached him there was no guarantee that they could bring him back alive. What should they have done — risked their lives with little hope of saving Harsh, or let him die? They let him die.

There are even worse situations. Two mountaineers were climbing in the Alps, roped together. On an isolated peak, one slipped and fell. Unable to move, he lay dangling at the end of the rope. The other climber couldn't lift his companion back up, nor could he himself move on without cutting the rope. What should he have done — cut the rope and sent his companion to his death, or stayed where he was till both died of exposure? He cut the rope.

1. What would you have done in Hartwell's place?
2. Do you think the Everest climbers ought to have risked their lives to save Harsh?
3. If you had been the climber in the Alps, would you have cut the rope?
4. Which would you put first — self-preservation or the maintenance of another human life?
5. Do you think the law should have the answers to these questions?

THE ONLY WAY

Sometimes the law is forced to deal with these tragic choices, as it did in the following nineteenth century English case. The case concerned three shipwrecked sailors and a cabin boy. The story was a grisly one. The facts were not in dispute. The only question was: had the law been broken? To answer this, the judges had to decide what the law was. And their decision, given almost a hundred years ago in England, still contains the law for Canada today.

For over twenty days three sailors and a cabin boy had drifted in an open boat a thousand miles from land. Their only food was two tins of turnips and a turtle they had caught, their only drink the rain collected in their oilskin capes. When this gave out, they stayed seven days without food and five without water. They couldn't have lived many more days unless they took the only course remaining. That course, said one of them, Captain Dudley, was

From *This Law of Ours* (Scarborough, ON: Prentice-Hall of Canada, 1977) at 40–47, 49. Reproduced by permission of the author.

to sacrifice one life to save the rest — kill one for the other three to eat.

Which one? The captain, who proposed this course? The sailor, Stephens, who agreed with him? The other sailor, Brooks, who disagreed? Or the seventeen-year-old cabin boy, prostrate from famine and drinking seawater? Which one should be the sacrificial victim?

1. Even if there is only one course, would they be right to take it?
2. If so, who should be the victim?
3. And how should they decide on the victim?

The Agony and the Argument

"If no help comes," said Dudley and Stephens, "We'll have to sacrifice one to save the rest." Brooks knew they meant the boy and didn't agree.

"Let's do it this way," said the captain the next day; "let's all draw lots to see which one to kill." It was the twentieth day when he made this suggestion to Brooks and Stephens. He never made it to the boy himself. But Brooks would not agree and lots were never drawn.

"We have families," said Dudley and Stephens, "and the boy has no one dependent on him. Better to kill him to save the rest of us. If no help comes tomorrow, we'll have to kill the boy."

Next day no help came. No ship appeared. The captain motioned to Stephens and to Brooks that they had better kill the boy, who lay helpless at the bottom of the boat. He would have died anyway before the other three. Once again Brooks would have no part of it.

1. Three possibilities of setting the question emerge from what the captain said. What are they?
2. Which is the best?
3. Who should decide?

The Ultimate Solution

The captain, a religious man, offered a prayer. He asked forgiveness for them all. Then he and Stephens told the boy his time had come. They put a knife to his throat and killed him.

For four days afterwards the three men fed upon his body and his blood. Had they not done so, they would all have died. On the fourth day a passing ship picked them up. All three were in the lowest state of prostration. Their rescuers brought them home to England, where the law took over.

The authorities investigated the incident and then launched a murder prosecution against two of the survivors — Dudley and Stephens. Brooks was never charged, but was a witness at the trial.

The trial took place before a jury which gave a special verdict. Instead of pronouncing the defendants guilty or not guilty, they merely decided what had happened. They decided that Dudley and Stephens had killed the boy, and that they had had no other chance of survival. They left it to the judge to say whether this was murder or not.

1. Do you think the sailors were justified in killing the cabin boy?
2. Can you think of any circumstances where killing is justified?
3. Do you think the case should have come to trial at all?
4. Was it fair that Brooks wasn't charged?
5. Only very exceptionally does a jury refuse to say "guilty" or "not guilty." Why do you think they did so in this case?
6. If you had been on the jury, would you have wanted to refuse to give a verdict?

The Judges' Verdict

Was the act of Dudley and Stephens justified? The jury left it to the judges to determine. This is what the judges said:

There remains to be considered the real question in the case — whether killing under the circumstances set forth in the verdict be or be not murder.

Now except for the purpose of testing how far the conservation of a man's own life is in all cases and under all circumstances, an absolute, unqualified, and paramount duty, we exclude from our consideration all the incidents of war. We are dealing with a case of private homicide, not one imposed upon men in the service of their Sovereign and in the defence of the country. Now it is admitted that the deliberate killing of this unoffending and unresisting boy was clearly murder, unless the killing can be justified by some well-recognized excuse admitted by the law. It is further admitted that there was in this case no such excuse, unless the killing was justified by what has been called "necessity." But the temptation to the act which existed here was not what the law has ever called necessity. Nor is this to be regretted. Though law and morality are not the same, and many things may be immoral which are not necessarily illegal, yet the absolute divorce of law from morality would be of fatal consequence; and such divorce would follow if the temptation to murder in this case were to be held by law an absolute defense of it. It is not so. To preserve one's life is generally speaking a duty, but it may be the plainest and the highest duty to sacrifice it. War is full of instances in which it is a man's duty not to live, but to die. The duty, in case of shipwreck, of a captain to his crew, of the crew to the passengers, of soldiers to women and children, these duties impose on men and moral necessity, not of the preservation, but of the sacrifice of their lives for others, from which in no country, least of all, it is to be hoped, in England, will men ever shrink, as indeed they have not shrunk. It is not correct, therefore, to say that there is any absolute or unqualified necessity to preserve one's life.

It is not needful to point out the awful danger of admitting the principle which has been contended for. Who is to be the judge of this sort of necessity? By what measure is the comparative value of lives to be measured? Is it to be strength, or intellect, or what? It is plain that the principle leaves to him who is to profit by it to determine the necessity which will justify him in deliberately taking another's life to save his own. In this case the weakest, the youngest, the most unresisting, was chosen. Was it more necessary to kill him than one of the grown men? The answer must be "No."

It is not suggested that in this particular case the deeds were "devilish," but it is quite plain that such a principle once admitted might be made the legal cloak for unbridled passion and atrocious crime. There is no safe path for judges to tread but to ascertain the law to the best of their ability and to declare it according to their judgment; and if in any case the law appears to be too severe on individuals, to leave it to the Sovereign to exercise that prerogative of mercy which the Constitution has entrusted to the hands fittest to dispense it.

It must not be supposed that in refusing to admit temptation to be an excuse for crime it is forgotten how terrible that temptation was; how awful the suffering; how hard in such trials to keep the judgment straight and the conduct pure. We are often compelled to set up standards we cannot reach ourselves, and to lay down rules which we could not ourselves satisfy. But a man has no right to declare temptation to be an excuse, though he might himself have yielded to it, nor allow compassion for the criminal to change or weaken in any manner the legal definition of the crime. It is therefore our duty to declare that the prisoners' act in this case was wilful murder, that the facts as stated in the verdict are no legal justification of the homicide; and to say that in our unanimous opinion the prisoners are upon this special verdict guilty of murder.

(*R. v. Dudley & Stephens*, 1884)

1. What is the argument put forward by the defence?
2. Why did the judges say it wasn't necessary to kill the cabin boy? Do you agree with them?
3. What did the judges say would be the consequences of accepting the argument put forward by the defence? Do you agree?
4. Do you think it was easier for the judges than it was for the jury to decide whether Dudley and Stephens were guilty? If so, why?
5. What do you think the consequence would have been if the judges, like the jury, had been unable to decide?

The Sentence of the Court

What Dudley and Stephens did was murder, said the judges. And murder was a capital offence in England at that time. The Lord Chief Justice sentenced them as follows:

The sentence of the court upon you is that you be taken from this place to a lawful prison and thence to a place of execution, and that you there suffer death by hanging; and that your body be afterwards buried within the precincts of the prison in which you shall have been confined before your execution. And may the Lord have mercy on your souls.

(*R. v. Dudley & Stephens*, 1884)

1. Was the death penalty justified in this case?
2. Is it ever justified? Does this alter your views on the sanctity of human life?
3. If they had had to decide, do you think the jury would have decided any differently than the judges did?

The Punishment

Dudley and Stephens were sentenced to death, but they were given a reprieve: the *royal prerogative of mercy* was exercised in their favor and the death sentence was commuted to one of life imprisonment. But this was not the end of it. The authorities exercised their discretion and released the prisoners after six months.

1. Should there be a royal prerogative of mercy? Why or why not?
2. Should the government be able to alter the sentences passed by the judges?

3. Should the law fix the sentence the judges must pass (as it does in murder cases)? Why not leave sentencing to the judges' discretion?
4. Do you think it was their knowledge of the penalty for murder that prevented the jury from saying Dudley and Stephens were guilty? If so, do you think the jury should have allowed that knowledge to prevent them?

THE MORAL DILEMMA

Murder, says the law, is intentionally killing a person without lawful justification. This is common sense, because in general we believe it is wrong to kill. However, we think it is justified in exceptional cases. When is it justified? The difficulty of this question can be seen from the following example, well known to legal textbook writers.

Two sailors, X and Y, are shipwrecked. Neither can swim. X reaches a floating plank and climbs onto it. Y reaches the plank and tries to climb onto it. The plank will hold only one person, so X prevents Y from getting onto it and Y drowns.

1. Is this situation exceptional enough to make X's act morally justified?
2. Suppose Y had climbed onto the plank and pushed X off, would Y's act have been morally justified?
3. Suppose the survivor in 1 or 2 had been charged in front of Dudley's and Stephens's judges with murder. What verdict do you think would have been given?
4. Suppose Y climbed onto the plank and X remained on it, and they both drowned. Would each have been justified in staying on the plank?

JETTISONING THE CARGO

"Necessity knows no law," it is often said. In other words, you can't be held legally liable for an act you had to do. From this point of view Dudley and Stephens would not be guilty of the murder of the cabin boy because their act was one which was necessary for their survival. But the judges in their case rejected the defendants' plea of necessity. As a result, it has been said that there is no defence of necessity in common law.

This is not true. Necessity can be a good defence, as in the 1608 *Mouse's* case.

A ship carrying a cargo of goods was overtaken by a storm. The captain feared that it would sink and that all aboard would be drowned, because it was already dangerously low in the water. To stop it from sinking further he ordered the crew to throw the cargo overboard. This lightened the vessel and enabled her to keep afloat, survive the storm, and come to safety.

The captain, so the court held at this trial, was within his rights in throwing the cargo overboard. He had to sacrifice the cargo for the greater good of saving human life.

1. Suppose the cargo had been a human one. Would the captain's act have been justified?
2. Suppose the open boat with the three men and the cabin boy had been sinking. Would Captain Dudley have been entitled to throw one of the passengers overboard to save the rest? If so, which one? If not, can you think of any circumstances where a captain might be morally justified in throwing a passenger overboard?
3. Saving human life is obviously more important than saving cargo. In Dudley's and Stephens's case was it equally obvious that saving the lives of the three sailors was more important than saving the cabin boy's life?
4. In such a case do three lives have three times the importance of one life?
5. Because the cabin boy would have died before they were rescued, was it more important to save the sailors' lives?
6. Do you think Dudley and Stephens would have been well-advised to put forward such arguments? Would they have answered the judges' points?
7. What light does this case throw on the notion of necessity? What do we mean by saying it was necessary for the captain to throw the cargo overboard? What did Dudley mean by saying it was necessary to kill the cabin boy?
8. There is a well-known story about Oscar Wilde in which a beggar, trying to convince Wilde to give him some money, says, "Man must live." Wilde answers, "I don't see the necessity." What point is Wilde making? Strictly speaking, is anything ever really necessary?

. . . . .

ENEMIES IN WAR

. . . .

During the Second World War a British bomber pilot was shot down over Germany and taken prisoner. He escaped and on his way through Germany to neutral territory, he carried on his own private war effort: each day he killed one German soldier. Back in England, he resumed his flying duties and ended the war with high rank and honors.

1. Do you think such killings are justified?
2. Are there any moral limits to the right to kill the enemy in war?
3. If Dudley and Stephens had been survivors of a warship torpedoed by the enemy, and the boy a survivor of the enemy submarine, would they have been justified in killing him simply as an enemy?
4. Would they have been justified in killing him for food?

THE ROMAN SOLDIER'S WAY OUT

So far we've discussed the taking of other people's lives. What about taking one's own life? Suicide has often been seen as an honorable way out. The Roman solider, if defeated, preferred death to dishonor. Rather than surrender and allow himself to be captured he would fall upon his sword and kill himself. We see this in the story of Brutus.

(ii) R. v. Dudley & Stephens

Indictment for the murder of Richard Parker on the high seas within the jurisdiction of the Admiralty.

At the trial before Huddleston, B., at the Devon and Cornwall Winter Assizes, November 7, 1884, the jury at the suggestion of the learned judge, found the facts of the case in a special verdict which stated "that on July 5, 1884, the prisoners, Thomas Dudley and Edward Stephens, with one Brooks, all able-bodied English seamen, and the deceased also an English boy, between seventeen and eighteen years of age, the crew of an English yacht, a registered English vessel, were cast away in a storm on the high seas 1,600 miles from the Cape of Good Hope, and were compelled to put into an open boat belonging to the said yacht. That in this boat they had no supply of water and no supply of food, except two 1 lb. tins of turnips, and for three days they had nothing else to subsist upon. That on the fourth day they caught a small turtle, upon which they subsisted for a few days, and this was the only food they had up to the twentieth day when the act now in question was committed. That on the twelfth day the remains of the turtle were entirely consumed, and for the next eight days they had nothing to eat. That they had no fresh water, except such rain as they from time to time caught in their oilskin capes. That the boat was drifting on the ocean, and was probably more than 1000 miles away from land. That on the eighteenth day, when they had been seven days without food and five without water, the prisoners spoke to Brooks as to what should be done if no succour came, and suggested that some one should be sacrificed to save the rest, but Brooks dissented, and the boy, to whom they were understood to refer, was not consulted. That on the 24th of July, the day before the act now in question, the prisoner Dudley proposed to Stephens and Brooks that lots should be cast who should be put to death to save the rest, but Brooks refused to consent, and it was not put to the boy, and in point of fact there was no drawing of lots. That on that day the prisoners spoke of their having families, and suggested it would be better to kill the boy that their lives should be saved, and Dudley proposed that if there was no vessel in sight by the morrow morning the boy should be killed. That next day, the 25th of July, no vessel appearing, Dudley told Brooks that he had better go and have a sleep, and made signs to Stephens and Brooks that the boy had better be killed. The prisoner Stephens agreed to the act, but Brooks dissented from it. That the boy was then lying at the bottom of the boat quite helpless, and extremely weakened by famine

---

(1884), 14 Q.B.D. 273; 54 L.J.M.C. 32; 52 L.T. 107; 1 T.L.R. 118; 15 Cox C.C. 624; 49 J.P. 69; 33 W.R. 347. Queen's Bench.

and by drinking sea water, and unable to make any resistance nor did he ever assent to his being killed. The prisoner Dudley offered a prayer asking forgiveness for them all if either of them should be tempted to commit a rash act, and that their souls might be saved. That Dudley, with the assent of Stephens, went to the boy, and telling him that his time was come, put a knife into his throat and killed him then and there; that the three men fed upon the body and blood of the boy for four days; that on the fourth day after the act had been committed the boat was picked up by a passing vessel, and the prisoners were rescued, still alive, but in the lowest state of prostration. That they were carried to the port of Falmouth, and committed for trial at Exeter. That if the men had not fed upon the body of the boy they would probably not have survived to be so picked up and rescued, but would within the four days have died of famine. That the boy, being in a much weaker condition, was likely to have died before them. That at the time of the act in question there was no sail in sight, nor any reasonable prospect of relief. That under these circumstances there appeared to the prisoners every probability that unless they then fed or very soon fed upon the boy or one of themselves they would die of starvation. That there was no appreciable chance of saving life except by killing some one for the others to eat. That assuming any necessity to kill anybody, there was no greater necessity for killing the boy than any of the other three men. But whether upon the whole matter by the jurors found the killing of Richard Parker by Dudley and Stephens be felony and murder the jurors are ignorant, and pray the advice of the Court thereupon, and if upon the whole matter the Court shall be of opinion that the killing of Richard Parker be felony and murder, then the jurors say that Dudley and Stephens were each guilty of felony and murder as alleged in the indictment."

[LORD COLERIDGE C.J.:

. . . .

...From these facts, stated with the cold precision of a special verdict, it appears sufficiently that the prisoners were subject to terrible temptation, to sufferings which might break down the bodily power of the strongest man, and try the conscience of the best. Other details yet more harrowing, facts still more loathsome and appalling, were presented to the jury, and are to be found recorded in my learned Brother's notes. But nevertheless this is clear, that the prisoners put to death a weak and unoffending boy upon the chance of preserving their own lives by feeding upon his flesh and blood after he was killed, and with the certainty of depriving *him* of any possible chance of survival. The verdict finds in terms that "if the men had not fed upon the body of the boy they would *probably* not have survived," and that "the boy being in a much weaker condition was *likely* to have died before them." They might possibly have been picked up next day by a passing ship; they might possibly not have been picked up at all; in either case it is obvious that the killing of the boy would have been an unnecessary and profitless act. It is found by the verdict that the boy was incapable of resistance, and, in fact, made none; and it is not even suggested that his death was due to any violence on his part attempted against, or even so much as feared by, those who killed him. Under these circumstances the jury say that they are ignorant whether those who killed him were guilty of murder, and have referred it to this Court to determine what is the legal consequence which follows from the facts which they have found.

. . . .

There remains to be considered the real question in the case—whether killing under the circumstances set forth in the verdict be or be not murder. The contention that it could be anything else was, to the minds of us all, both new and strange, and we stopped the Attorney General in his negative argument in order that we might hear what could be said in support of a proposition which appeared to us to be at once dangerous, immoral, and opposed to all legal principle and analogy. All, no doubt, that can be said has been urged before us, and we are now to consider and determine what it amounts to. First it is said that it follows from various definitions of murder in books of authority, which definitions imply, if they do not state, the doctrine that in order to save your own life you may lawfully take away the life of another, when that other is neither attempting nor threatening yours, nor is guilty of any illegal act whatever towards you or any one else. But if these definitions be looked at they will not be found to sustain this contention. The earliest in point of date is the passage cited to us from Bracton, who lived in the reign of Henry III. ... But in the very passage as to necessity, on which reliance has been placed, it is clear that Bracton is speaking of necessity in the ordinary sense—the repelling by violence, violence justified so far as it was necessary for the object, any illegal violence used towards oneself....

(ii) R. v. Dudley & Stephens

It is, if possible, yet clearer that the doctrine contended for receives no support from the great authority of Lord Hale....

... For in the chapter in which he deals with the exemption created by compulsion or necessity he thus expresses himself: — "If a man be desperately assaulted and in peril of death, and cannot otherwise escape unless, to satisfy his assailant's fury, he will kill an innocent person then present, the fear and factual force will not acquit him of the crime and punishment of murder, if he commit the fact, for he ought rather to die himself than kill an innocent; but if he cannot otherwise save his own life the law permits him in his own defence to kill the assailant, for by the violence of the assault, and the offence committed upon him by the assailant himself, the law of nature, and necessity, hath made him his own protector *cum debito moderamino inculpatae tutelae*." (*Hale's Pleas of the Crown*, vol. 1, 51.)

But, further still, Lord Hale in the following chapter deals with the position asserted by the casuists, and sanctioned, as he says, by Grotius and Puffendorf, that in a case of extreme necessity, either of hunger or clothing; "theft is no theft, or at least not punishable as theft, as some even of our own lawyers have asserted the same." "But," says Lord Hale, "I take it that here in England, that rule, at least by the laws of England, is false; and therefore, if a person being under necessity for want of victuals or clothes, shall upon that account clandestinely and *anima furandi* steal another man's goods, it is felony, and a crime by the laws of England punishable with death." (*Hale, Please of the Crown*, i, 54). If, therefore, Lord Hale is clear — as he is — that extreme necessity of hunger does not justify larceny, what would he have said to the doctrine that it justified murder?

. . . .

Is there, then, any authority for the proposition which has been presented to us? Decided cases there are none. ... The American case cited by my Brother Stephen in his Digest, from Wharton on Homicide, in which it was decided, correctly indeed, that sailors had no right to throw passengers overboard to save themselves, but on the somewhat strange ground that the proper mode of determining who was to be sacrificed was to vote upon the subject by ballot, can hardly, as my Brother Stephen says, be an authority satisfactory to a court in this country....

The one real authority of former time is Lord Bacon, who, in his commentary on the maxim, "*necessitas inducit privilegium quoad jura privata*," lays down the law as follows: — "Necessity carrieth a privilege in itself. Necessity is of three sorts — necessity of conservation of life, necessity of obedience, and necessity of the act of God or of a stranger. First of conservation of life, if a man steal viands to satisfy his present hunger, this is no felony nor larceny. So if divers be in danger of drowning by the casting away of some boat or barge, and one of them get to some plank, or on the boat's side to keep himself above water, and another to save his life thrust him from it, whereby he is drowned, this is neither *se defendendo* nor by misadventure, but justifiable." On this it is to be observed that Lord Bacon's proposition that stealing to satisfy hunger is no larceny is hardly supported by Staundforde, whom he cites for it, and is expressly contradicted by Lord Hale in the passage already cited. And for the proposition as to the plank or boat, it is said to be derived from the canonists. At any rate he cites no authority for it, and it must stand upon his own. Lord Bacon was great even as a lawyer; but it is permissible to much smaller men, relying upon principle and on the authority of others, the equals and even the superiors of Lord Bacon as lawyers, to question the soundness of his dictum. There are many conceivable states of things in which it might possibly be true, but if Lord Bacon meant to lay down the broad proposition that a man may save his life by killing, if necessary, an innocent and unoffending neighbour, it certainly is not law at the present day.

. . . .

Now, except for the purpose of testing how far the conservation of a man's own life is in all cases and under all circumstances, an absolute, unqualified, and paramount duty, we exclude from our consideration all the incidents of war. We are dealing with a case of private homicide, not one imposed upon men in the service of their Sovereign and in the defence of their country. Now it is admitted that the deliberate killing of this unoffending and unresisting boy was clearly murder, unless the killing can be justified by some well-recognised excuse admitted by the law. It is further admitted that there was in this case no such excuse, unless the killing was justified by what has been called "necessity." But the temptation to the act which existed here was not what the law has ever called necessity. Nor is this to be regretted. Though law and morality are not the same, and many things may be immoral which are not necessarily illegal, yet the absolute divorce of law from morality would be of fatal consequence; and such divorce would follow if the temptation to murder in this case were to be held by law an absolute defence of it. It is not so. To preserve one's life is generally speaking a duty, but it may be the plainest and the highest duty to sacrifice it. War is full of instances in which it is a man's duty not to live, but to die. The duty in case of shipwreck, of a captain to his crew, of the crew to the passengers, of soldiers to women and children, as in the noble case of the *Birkenhead*; these duties impose on men and moral necessity, not of the preservation, but of the sacrifice of their lives for others, from which in no country, least of all, it is to be hoped, in England, will men ever shrink, as indeed, they have not shrunk. It is not correct, therefore, to say that there is any absolute or unqualified necessity to preserve one's life. *"Necesse est ut cam, no at vivam,"* is a saying of a Roman officer quoted by Lord Bacon himself with high eulogy in the very chapter on necessity to which so much reference has been made. It would be a very easy and cheap display of commonplace learning to quote from Greek and Latin authors, from Horace, from Juvenal, from Cicero, from Euripides, passage after passage, in which the duty of dying for others has been laid down in glowing and emphatic language as resulting from the principles of heathen ethics; it is enough in a Christian country to remind ourselves of the Great Example whom we profess to follow. It is not needful to point out the awful danger of admitting the principle which has been contended for. Who is to be the judge of this sort of necessity? By what measure is the comparative value of lives to be measured? Is it to be strength, or intellect, or what? It is plain that the principle leaves to him who is to profit by it to determine the necessity which will justify him in deliberately taking another's life to save his own. In this case the weakest, the youngest, the most unresisting, was chosen. Was it more necessary to kill him than one of the grown men? The answer must be "No"—

> So spake the Fiend, and with necessity,
> The tyrant's plea, excused his devilish deeds.

It is not suggested that in this particular case the deeds were "devilish," but it is quite plain that such a principle once admitted might be made the legal cloak for unbridled passion and atrocious crime. There is no safe path for judges to tread but to ascertain the law to the best of their ability and to declare it according to their judgment; and if in any case the law appears to be too severe on individuals, to leave it to the Sovereign to exercise that prerogative of mercy which the Constitution has intrusted to the hands fittest to dispense it.

It must not be supposed that in refusing to admit temptation to be an excuse for crime it is forgotten how terrible the temptation was; how awful the suffering; how hard in such trials to keep the judgment straight and the conduct pure. We are often compelled to set up standards we cannot reach ourselves, and to lay down rules which we could not ourselves satisfy. But a man has no right to declare temptation to be an excuse, though he might himself have yielded to it, nor allow compassion for the criminal to change or weaken in any manner the legal definition of the crime. It is therefore our duty to declare that the prisoners' act in this case was wilful murder, that the facts as stated in the verdict are no legal justification of the homicide; and to say that in our unanimous opinion the prisoners are upon this special verdict guilty of murder.

The Court then proceeded to pass sentence of death upon the prisoners.

[NOTE: This sentence was afterwards commuted by the Crown to six months' imprisonment.]

(iii) Law and Morality

Lord Patrick Devlin

The relationship between law and morals has recently, in England and in the United States and also in Canada, received quite a considerable degree of interest. Of course, if one wants to go back to the

---

(1964) 3 *Manitoba Law School Journal* 243 at 243, 248–54. Notes omitted. © Oxford University Press 1965. Reproduced from *The Enforcement of Morals* by Patrick Devlin (1965) by permission of Oxford University Press.

(iii) Law and Morality

very beginning, one must begin with John Stuart Mill in 1859 and the publication of his essay *On Liberty*, and his announcement of the famous principle which should govern, in his view, all law-making in relation to all subjects. That principle is, he said:

> ...the sole end for which mankind are warranted, individually or collectively, in interfering in the liberty of action of any of their number, is self-protection. That the only purpose for which power can be rightfully exercised over any member of a civilized community, against his will, is to prevent harm to others. His own good, either physical or moral, is not a sufficient warrant. He cannot rightfully be compelled to do or forbear because it will be better for him to do so, because it will make him happier, because in the opinions of others, to do so would be wise, or even right.

This principle was attacked by Mr. Justice Stephen in the celebrated book, *Liberty, Equality, Fraternity*, which he wrote in the 1870's. I think it is fair to say that the principle never got beyond academic discussion; nor had it ever been translated into practice. However, it was resurrected and translated into practice in 1957 in the report of the committee that was presided over by Sir John Wolfenden on the amendment of the laws on homosexuality and prostitution. There the principle was stated in this way:

> There must remain a realm of private morality and immorality which is, in brief and crude terms, not the law's business.

. . . .

The attraction of the doctrine, for undoubtedly it is attractive, to me lies in this: that it seems to be a logical extension from freedom of religion. We have now achieved, not without a great struggle, the sort of society in which a man's religion is his own affair. Ought not his morals to be his own affair too? Is there any greater need, we may ask ourselves, for a common morality than there is for a common religion? However, there is a distinction. The ordinary free thinker has no religion. He can doubt the existence of God as he does the existence of the Devil, and if society can accommodate people who have no personal religion and yet reckon them as good citizens, as so many of them are, then there is no need for a common religion. But it is one thing to doubt the existence of God and the Devil and another thing to doubt the existence of good and evil. God and the Devil is what religion is about; good and evil is what morals are about. Whether good and evil are properly personified in God and the Devil is a theological question upon which the man of faith, and the free thinker, can disagree, but there will be no disagreement, and can be no disagreement about whether good and evil exist.

Thus, while Mill, in common with most free thinkers, both of his century and of the present one, had no personal religion, and would deny the need for a common religion, he had a personal morality and he accepted the need for a common morality. Indeed, his opinion of what was virtuous did not substantially differ from that of his contemporaries, but no one, he felt, could be sure. In a free society, full scope must be given to individuality as one of the elements of well-being, and the individual must be free to question, to challenge, and to experiment. "The liberty of the individual", he wrote:

> must be thus far limited; he must not make himself a nuisance to other people. But if he refrains from molesting others in what concerns them, and merely acts according to his own inclination and judgment in things which concern himself, the same reasons which show that opinion should be free, prove also that he should be allowed, without molestation, to carry his opinions into practice at his own cost. That mankind is not infallible; that his truths, for the most part, are only half-truths; that unity of opinion, unless resulting from the fullest and freest comparison of opposite opinions, is not desirable, and diversity not an evil, but a good; until mankind is much more capable than at present of recognizing all sides of the truth, are principles applicable to men's modes of action, not less than to their opinions. As it is useful that while mankind is imperfect there should be different opinions, so it is that there should be different experiments of living; that free scope should be given to varieties of character, short of injury to others; and that the worth of different modes of life should be proved practically, when anyone thinks fit to try them.

You see, it is with freedom of opinion and discussion that Mill is primarily concerned. Freedom of action follows naturally on that. Men must be allowed to do what they are allowed to talk about doing. Evidently, what Mill visualizes is a number of people doing things he himself would disapprove of but doing them earnestly and openly after thought and discussion in an endeavour to find a way of life best suited to them as individuals.

This seems to me on the whole to be an idealistic picture. It has happened to some extent, say in the last couple of generations in the growth of free love outside marriage. Although for many it is just the indulgence of the flesh, for some it is a serious decision to break the constraint of chastity outside marriage. But in the area of morals that is touched by the law I find it difficult to think of any other example of high-mindedness. A man does not, as a rule, commit bigamy because he wants to experiment with two wives instead of one. He does not, as a rule, lie with his daughter or sister because he thinks that an incestuous relationship can be a good one, but because he finds in it a way of satisfying his lust in the home. He does not keep a brothel so as to prove the value of promiscuity, but so as to make money. There must be some homosexuals who believe theirs to be a good way of life, but many more who would like to get free of it if only they could. And certainly no one in his senses can think that habitual drunkenness or drugging leads to any good at all. But Mill believed, you see, that diversity in morals and the removal of restraint on what was traditionally held to be immorality (and held by him to be immorality) would liberate men to prove what they thought to be good. He would have been the last man to have advocated the removal of restraint so as to permit self-indulgence. He conceived of old morality being replaced by a new and perhaps better morality. He would not have approved of those who did not care whether there is any morality at all, but he never really grappled with the fact that along the paths that depart from traditional morals, pimps leading the weak astray far outnumber spiritual explorers at the head of the strong.

But let me return to the distinction I was drawing between freedom of religion and freedom in morals. The abolition of established religion is a relatively recent development. It is a feature of modern thought. It came with the Reformation, which is comparatively late in the history of civilization. Before that it would have been thought that a society could not exist without a common religion. The pluralist society in which we now live was not achieved without the complete destruction of medieval thought, and it involved a change of civilization which was comparable with the triumphs of Christianity over paganism. Mill records how the Emperor Marcus Aurelius, whom he considered to be one of the greatest of world rulers — tender, enlightened and humane — persecuted Christianity because existing society, as he saw it, was held together by belief in and reverence of the received divinities. The struggle more recently between received religion and freedom of conscience was of the same order, and entailed as much suffering.

But the removal of religion from the structure of society does not mean that a society can exist without faith. There is faith in moral belief as well as in religious belief, and although it is less precise and less demanding, moral belief is not necessarily less intense. In our society we believe in the advance of man towards a goal, and this belief is the mainspring of our morals. We believe that at some time in the history of mankind, whether on a sudden by divine stroke, or imperceptibly in evolutionary millennia, there was extracted from the chaos of the primeval mind, concepts of justice, benevolence, mercy, continence and others, that we call virtues. The distinction between virtue and vice, between good and evil as it affects our actions, is what morals is about. A common religious faith means that there is common agreement about the end of man; a common moral faith means that there is common agreement about the way he should go. A band of travellers can go forward together without knowing what they will find at the end of the journey, but they cannot keep in company if they do not journey in the same direction.

Keeping in company is what society is about.

Diversity in moral belief and practice would be no more injurious to a society which had no common morality than the like diversity in religious matters is to a society without a common religion. However, as I have said, Mill and his disciples do not conceive of a society without a common morality. If they did, if they wanted a society in which morality is as free as religion, they would indeed be faint-hearted in what they preached. They could not then sensibly permit the law, as they do, to punish the corruption of youth or public acts of indecency. Where there is freedom of religion the conversion of a youth is not thought of as corruption. Men would have thought of it as that in the Middle Ages, just as we now think of the introduction of a youth to homosexual practices as corruption and not as conversion. Where there is true freedom of religion it would be thought intolerant to object to a religious ceremony in a public place on the ground that it was offensive to have brought to one's attention the exhibition of a faith which one thought false and pernicious. Why, then, do we object to the public exhibition of a false morality and call it indecency? If we thought that unrestricted indulgence in the sexual passions was as good a life as any other for those who liked it we should find nothing indecent in the practice of it either in public or in private. It would become no more indecent than kissing in public. Decency as an objective depends on the belief in continence as a virtue, a virtue which requires sexual activity to be kept within prescribed bounds.

(iii) Law and Morality

These reflections show the gulf which separates the religious toleration we have achieved from the moral toleration that Mill wanted. The former is practicable, because while each man believes that his own religion, or the lack of it, is the truth or nearest to the truth, he looks upon the alternatives as lesser good and not as evil. What Mill demands is that we must tolerate what we know to be evil and what no one asserts to be good. He does not ask that in particular cases we should extend tolerance out of pity. He demands that we should cede it forever as a right. Because it is evil we can protect youth from corruption by it, but save for that we must allow it to spread unhindered by the law and infect the minds of those who are not strong enough to resist it. Why do ninety-nine of us have to grant this license to the other one? Because, the answer is, we are fallible; are all quite convinced that what we call vice is evil, but we may be mistaken. True it is that if the waters of toleration are poured upon the muck, bad men will wallow in the bog, but it may be (how can we tell otherwise?) that it is only in such a bog that seed may flourish that some day some good man may bring to fruit, and that otherwise the world would lose and be the poorer for it. That is the kernel of Mill's freedom; that is why we must not suppress vice. It is not because it is not evil; Mill thought that it was. It is not because legal suppression would be futile; some of Mill's followers advanced this argument, but he did not. Nor is it because Mill thought that virtue would be bound to triumph over vice without the aid of the law; in some cogent passages he refuted that argument. When all this is stripped away, the kernel of Mill is just this: that he beseeches us to think it possible that we may be mistaken. Because of this possibility he demands almost absolute freedom for the individual to go his own way, the only function of society being to provide for him an ordered framework within which he might experiment in thought, and in action, secure from physical harm.

There is here, I believe, a flaw. Even assuming that we accept Mill's ideal, it is unacceptable to the lawmaker as a basis for action because it fails to distinguish sufficiently between freedom of thought and freedom of action. It may be a good thing for the man to keep an open mind about all his beliefs so that he will never claim for them absolute certainty and never dismiss entirely from his mind the thought that he may be wrong. But where there is a call for action he must act on what he believes to be true. The lawyer, who in this respect stands somewhere midway between the philosopher and the man of action, requires to be satisfied beyond a reasonable doubt. If he is so satisfied, he would then think it right to punish a man for breach of the law while acknowledging the possibility that he may be mistaken. Is there any difference, so far as the freedom of the individual is concerned, between punishing a man for an act which admittedly he did, and which we believe, perhaps erroneously, to be wrong, he denying that it is wrong; and punishing him for an act that is admittedly wrong, and which we honestly but perhaps erroneously believe that he did, he denying that he did it? Suppose you prosecute a man for bigamy. His defence might be, "I honestly believed that my first wife was dead". If that defense is rejected, it is rejected because there is no reasonable doubt in the minds of the jury that he did not honestly believe it. And yet they must say, "We might be mistaken; we are not required to have absolute certainty, but we must act on what we reasonably believe to be true". Well, then, if his defence were simply that: "I admit I married a second time but I honestly believe that bigamy is a good thing", must we not act in the same way? We must say, "Well, we have no reasonable doubt that bigamy is a bad thing; we can't be certain, we may be mistaken, but we must act upon our belief". Philosophers, after all, may philosophize under the shadow of perpetual doubt, but the governors of society cannot do their duty if they are not permitted to act upon what they believe.

I might now usefully return to what Mill said about Marcus Aurelius. He cited him as an example of the fallibility of even the best and wisest of men. Marcus Aurelius thought Christianity wholly unbelievable, and could see in it only a force that would cause the society he governed to fall into pieces. Mill certainly did not regard Christianity as an unmixed blessing, but it might have been a different thing, he thought, if it had been adopted under Marcus Aurelius instead of under Constantine. So, Mill urged, unless a man flatters himself that he is wiser than Marcus Aurelius, let him abstain from that assumption of joint infallibility of himself and the multitude which the great man made with such unfortunate results. The example is a perfectly fair one on the point of fallibility. If we were to be confronted with the creed today which taught that constraint was the only vice and the unlimited indulgence of the appetites of all sorts the only virtue worth cultivating, we should look at it without any comprehension at all. But I dare say that our contempt would not be greater than that of Marcus Aurelius for Christianity, or that of a medieval philosopher for the notion that heresy was something to be tolerated. The example is also a fair one on the point I am making. What else, one may ask, did Mill expect Marcus Aurelius to do? It is idle to lament that he did not forestall Constantine in accepting Christianity, for he could not accept what he disbelieved. In Mill's view, and probably in that of most of his disciples, Marcus Aurelius was right in rejecting the claims of Christianity. On this view the Emperor's mistake lay in his failure to realize that if he permitted the destruction of his society through the agency of a religion which he rightly concluded to be false, the successor civilization would be an improvement upon him. To put Mill's question again in another context, can any man, putting himself in the position of the great Emperor, flatter himself that he would have acted more wisely?

It is not feasible to require of any society that it should permit its own destruction by that which, whether rightly or wrongly, it honestly believes to be in error in case it may be mistaken. To admit that we are not infallible is not to admit that we are always wrong. What we believe to be evil may indeed be evil, and we cannot forever condemn ourselves to inactivity against evil because of the chance that we may by mistake destroy good.

For better or for worse, the lawmaker must act according to his lights, and he cannot, therefore, accept Mill's doctrine as practicable even if, as an ideal, he thought it desirable. But I must say that for my part I do not accept it even as an ideal. I accept it as an inspiration. What Mill taught about the value of freedom of inquiry and the dangers of intolerance has placed all free men forever in his debt. His admonitions were addressed to a society that was secure and strong and hidebound. Their repetition today is to a society much less solid. As a tract of the times, what Mill wrote was superb, but as dogma it has lost much of its appeal. I say dogma, for Mill's doctrine is just as dogmatic as any of those he repudiates. It is dogmatic to say that if only we were allowed to behave just as we liked so long as we did not injure each other the world would become a better place for all of us. There is no more evidence for this sort of utopia than there is evidence of the existence of heaven, and there is nothing to show that the one is any more easily attained than the other. We must not be bemused by words. If we are not entitled to call our society free unless we pursue freedom to an extremity that would make society intolerable for most of us, then let us stop short of the extreme and be content with some other name. The result may not be freedom unalloyed, but there are alloys which strengthen without corrupting.

(iv) *R.* v. *Butler*

SOPINKA J.: This appeal calls into question the constitutionality of the obscenity provisions of the Criminal Code, R.S.C., 1985, c. C-46, s. 163. They are attacked on the ground that they contravene s. 2(b) of the Canadian Charter of Rights and Freedoms. The case requires the Court to address one of the most difficult and controversial of contemporary issues, that of determining whether, and to what extent, Parliament may legitimately criminalize obscenity. I propose to begin with a review of the facts which gave rise to this appeal, as well of the proceedings in the lower courts.

1. FACTS AND PROCEEDINGS

In August 1987, the appellant, Donald Victor Butler, opened the Avenue Video Boutique located in Winnipeg, Manitoba. The shop sells and rents "hard core" videotapes and magazines as well as sexual paraphernalia. Outside the store is a sign which reads:

> Avenue Video Boutique; a private members only adult video/visual club.
>
> Notice: if sex oriented material offends you, please do not enter.
>
> No admittance to persons under 18 years.

[1992] 1 S.C.R. 452, 89 D.L.R. (4th) 449.

(iv) R. v. Butler

On August 21, 1987, the City of Winnipeg Police entered the appellant's store with a search warrant and seized all the inventory. The appellant was charged with 173 counts in the first indictment: three counts of selling obscene material contrary to s. 159(2)(a) of the Criminal Code, R.S.C. 1970, c. C-34 (now s. 163(2)(a)), 41 counts of possessing obscene material for the purpose of distribution contrary to s. 159(1)(a) (now s. 163(1)(a)) of the Criminal Code, 128 counts of possessing obscene material for the purpose of sale contrary to s. 159(2)(a) of the Criminal Code and one count of exposing obscene material to public view contrary to s. 159(2)(a) of the Criminal Code.

. . . .

The trial judge convicted the appellant on eight counts relating to eight films. Convictions were entered against the co-accused McCord with respect to two counts relating to two of the films. Fines of $1,000 per offence were imposed on the appellant. Acquittals were entered on the remaining charges.

The Crown appealed the 242 acquittals with respect to the appellant and the appellant cross-appealed the convictions. The majority of the Manitoba Court of Appeal allowed the appeal of the Crown and entered convictions for the appellant with respect to all of the counts, Twaddle and Helper JJ.A. dissenting.

. . . .

2. RELEVANT LEGISLATION

Criminal Code, R.S.C., 1985, c. C-46

163.(1) Every one commits an offence who,
(a) makes, prints, publishes, distributes, circulates, or has in his possession for the purpose of publication, distribution or circulation any obscene written matter, picture, model, phonograph record or other thing whatever; or
(b) makes, prints, publishes, distributes, sells or has in his possession for the purpose of publication, distribution or circulation a crime comic.

(2) Every one commits an offence who knowingly, without lawful justification or excuse,
(a) sells, exposes to public view or has in his possession for such a purpose any obscene written matter, picture, model, phonograph record or other thing whatever;
(b) publicly exhibits a disgusting object or an indecent show;
(c) offers to sell, advertises or publishes an advertisement of, or has for sale or disposal, any means, instructions, medicine, drug or article intended or represented as a method of causing abortion or miscarriage; or
(d) advertises or publishes an advertisement of any means, instructions, medicine, drug or article intended or represented as a method for restoring sexual virility or curing venereal diseases or diseases of the generative organs.

(3) No person shall be convicted of an offence under this section if he establishes that the public good was served by the acts that are alleged to constitute the offence and that the acts alleged did not extend beyond what served the public good.

(4) For the purposes of this section, it is a question of law whether an act served the public good and whether there is evidence that the act alleged went beyond what served the public good, bur it is a question of fact whether the acts did or did not extend beyond what served the public good.

(5) For the purposes of this section, the motives of an accused are irrelevant.

(6) Where an accused is charged with an offence under subsection (1), the fact that the accused was ignorant of the nature or presence of the matter, picture, model, phonograph record, crime comic or other thing by means of or in relation to which the offence was committed is not a defence to the charge.

(7) In this section, "crime comic" means a magazine, periodical or book that exclusively or substantially comprises matter depicting pictorially
(a) the commission of crimes, real or fictitious; or
(b) events connected with the commission of crimes, real or fictitious, whether occurring before or after the commission of the crime.

(8) For the purposes of this Act, any publication a dominant characteristic of which is the undue exploitation of sex, or of sex and any one or more of the following subjects, namely, crime, horror, cruelty and violence, shall be deemed to be obscene.

3. ISSUES

The following constitutional questions are raised by this appeal:

1. Does s. 163 of the Criminal Code of Canada, R.S.C., 1985, c. C-46, violate s. 2(b) of the Canadian Charter of Rights and Freedoms?
2. If s. 163 of the Criminal Code of Canada, R.S.C., 1985, c. C-46, violates s. 2(b) of the Canadian Charter of Rights and Freedoms, can s. 163 of the Criminal Code of Canada be demonstrably justified under s. 1 of the Canadian Charter of Rights and Freedoms as a reasonable limit prescribed by law?

4. ANALYSIS

The constitutional questions, as stated, bring under scrutiny the entirety of s. 163. However, both lower courts as well as the parties have focused almost exclusively on the definition of obscenity found in s. 163(8). Other portions of the impugned provision, such as the reverse onus provision envisaged in s. 163(3) as well as the absolute liability offence created by s. 163(6), raise substantial Charter issues which should be left to be dealt with in proceedings specifically directed to these issues. In my view, in the circumstances, this appeal should be confined to the examination of the constitutional validity of s. 163(8) only.

. . . .

(i) "Community Standard of Tolerance" Test

In Brodie, Judson J. accepted the view espoused notably by the Australian and New Zealand courts that obscenity is to be measured against "community standards". He cited, at pp. 705–6, the following passage in the judgment of Fullager J. in *R.* v. *Close*, [1948] V.L.R. 445, at p. 465:

> There does exist in any community at all times — however the standard may vary from time to time — a general instinctive sense of what is decent and what is indecent, of what is clean and what is dirty, and when the distinction has to be drawn, I do not know that today there is any better tribunal than a jury to draw it ... I am very far from attempting to lay down a model direction, but a judge might perhaps, in the case of a novel, say something like this: "It would not be true to say that any publication dealing with sexual relations is obscene. The relations of the sexes are, of course, legitimate matters for discussion everywhere ... There are certain standards of decency which prevail in the community, and you are really called upon to try this case because you are regarded as representing, and capable of justly applying, those standards. What is obscene is something which offends against those standards."

The community standards test has been the subject of extensive judicial analysis. It is the standards of the community as a whole which must be considered and not the standards of a small segment of that community such as the university community where a film was shown (*R.* v. *Goldberg*, [1971] 3 O.R. 323 (C.A.)) or a city where a picture was exposed (*R.* v. *Kiverago* (1973), 11 C.C.C. (2d) 463 (Ont. C.A.)). The standard to be applied is a national one (*R.* v. *Cameron* (1966), 58 D.L.R. (2d) 486 (Ont. C.A.); *R.* v. *Duthie Books Ltd.* (1966), 58 D.L.R. (2d) 274 (B.C.C.A.); *R.* v. *Ariadne Developments Ltd.* (1974), 19 C.C.C. (2d) 49 (N.S.S.C., App. Div.), at p. 59). With respect to expert evidence, it is not necessary and is not a fact which the Crown is obliged to prove as part of its case (*R.* v. *Sudbury News Service Ltd.* (1978), 18 O.R. (2d) 428 (C.A.); *R.* v. *Prairie Schooner News Ltd.* (1970), 75 W.W.R. 585 (Man. C.A.); *R.* v. *Great West News Ltd.*, [1970] 4 C.C.C. 307 (Man. C.A.)). In *R.* v. *Dominion News & Gifts (1962) Ltd.*, [1963] 2 C.C.C. 103 (Man. C.A.), Freedman J.A. (dissenting) emphasized that the community standards test must necessarily respond to changing mores (at pp. 116–17):

> Community standards must be contemporary. Times change, and ideas change with them. Compared to the Victorian era this is a liberal age in which we live. One manifestation of it is the relative freedom with which the whole question of sex is discussed. In books, magazines, movies, television, and sometimes even in parlour conversation, various aspects of sex are made the subject of comment, with a candour that in an earlier day would have been regarded as indecent and intolerable. We cannot and should not ignore these present-day attitudes when we face the question whether [the subject materials] are obscene according to our criminal law.

Our Court was called upon to elaborate the community standards test in *Towne Cinema Theatres Ltd.* v. *The Queen*, [1985] 1 S.C.R. 494. Dickson C.J. reviewed the case law and found (at pp. 508–9):

> The cases all emphasize that it is a standard of tolerance, not taste, that is relevant. What matters is not what Canadians think is right for themselves to see. What matters is what Canadians would not abide other Canadians seeing because it would be beyond the contemporary Canadian standard of tolerance to allow them to see it.

(iv) R. v. Butler

Since the standard is tolerance, I think the audience to which the allegedly obscene material is targeted must be relevant. The operative standards are those of the Canadian community as a whole, but since what matters is what other people may see, it is quite conceivable that the Canadian community would tolerate varying degrees of explicitness depending upon the audience and the circumstances. [Emphasis in original.]

Therefore, the community standards test is concerned not with what Canadians would not tolerate being exposed to themselves, but what they would not tolerate other Canadians being exposed to. The minority view was that the tolerance level will vary depending on the manner, time and place in which the material is presented as well as the audience to whom it is directed. The majority opinion on this point was expressed by Wilson J. in the following passage, at p. 521:

It is not, in my opinion, open to the courts under s. 159(8) of the Criminal Code to characterize a movie as obscene if shown to one constituency but not if shown to another.... In my view, a movie is either obscene under the Code based on a national community standard of tolerance or it is not. If it is not, it may still be the subject of provincial regulatory control.

(ii) "Degradation or Dehumanization" Test

There has been a growing recognition in recent cases that material which may be said to exploit sex in a "degrading or dehumanizing" manner will necessarily fail the community standards test....

. . . .

Among other things, degrading or dehumanizing materials place women (and sometimes men) in positions of subordination, servile submission or humiliation. They run against the principles of equality and dignity of all human beings. In the appreciation of whether material is degrading or dehumanizing, the appearance of consent is not necessarily determinative. Consent cannot save materials that otherwise contain degrading or dehumanizing scenes. Sometimes the very appearance of consent makes the depicted acts even more degrading or dehumanizing.

This type of material would, apparently, fail the community standards test not because it offends against morals but because it is perceived by public opinion to be harmful to society, particularly to women....

. . . .

(iv) The relationship of the tests to each other

. . . .

Pornography can be usefully divided into three categories: (1) explicit sex with violence, (2) explicit sex without violence but which subjects people to treatment that is degrading or dehumanizing, and (3) explicit sex without violence that is neither degrading nor dehumanizing. Violence in this context includes both actual physical violence and threats of physical violence. Relating these three categories to the terms of s. 163(8) of the Code, the first, explicit sex coupled with violence, is expressly mentioned. Sex coupled with crime, horror or cruelty will sometimes involve violence. Cruelty, for instance, will usually do so. But, even in the absence of violence, sex coupled with crime, horror or cruelty may fall within the second category. As for category (3), subject to the exception referred to below, it is not covered.

Some segments of society would consider that all three categories of pornography cause harm to society because they tend to undermine its moral fibre. Others would contend that none of the categories cause harm. Furthermore there is a range of opinion as to what is degrading or dehumanizing. See *Pornography and Prostitution in Canada: Report of the Special Committee on Pornography and Prostitution* (1985) (the Fraser Report), vol. 1, at p. 51. Because this is not a matter that is susceptible of proof in the traditional way and because we do not wish to leave it to the individual tastes of judges, we must have a norm that will serve as an arbiter in determining what amounts to an undue exploitation of sex. That arbiter is the community as a whole.

The courts must determine as best they can what the community would tolerate others being exposed to on the basis of the degree of harm that may flow from such exposure. Harm in this context means that it predisposes persons to act in an anti-social manner as, for example, the physical or mental mistreatment of women by men, or, what is perhaps debatable, the reverse. Anti-social conduct for this purpose is conduct which society formally recognizes as incompatible with its proper functioning. The stronger the inference of a risk of harm the lesser the likelihood of tolerance. The inference may be drawn from the material itself or from the material and other evidence. Similarly evidence as to the community standards is desirable but not essential.

In making this determination with respect to the three categories of pornography referred to above, the portrayal of sex coupled with violence will almost always constitute the undue exploitation of sex. Explicit sex which is degrading or dehumanizing may be undue if the risk of harm is substantial. Finally, explicit sex that is not violent and neither degrading nor dehumanizing is generally tolerated in our society and will not qualify as the undue exploitation of sex unless it employs children in its production.

If material is not obscene under this framework, it does not become so by reason of the person to whom it is or may be shown or exposed nor by reason of the place or manner in which it is shown. The availability of sexually explicit materials in theatres and other public places is subject to regulation by competent provincial legislation. Typically such legislation imposes restrictions on the material available to children. See *Nova Scotia Board of Censors* v. *McNeil*, [1978] 2 S.C.R. 662.

The foregoing deals with the interrelationship of the "community standards test" and "the degrading or dehumanizing" test. How does the "internal necessities" test fit into this scheme? The need to apply this test only arises if a work contains sexually explicit material that by itself would constitute the undue exploitation of sex. The portrayal of sex must then be viewed in context to determine whether that is the dominant theme of the work as a whole. Put another way, is undue exploitation of sex the main object of the work or is this portrayal of sex essential to a wider artistic, literary, or other similar purpose? Since the threshold determination must be made on the basis of community standards, that is, whether the sexually explicit aspect is undue, its impact when considered in context must be determined on the same basis. The court must determine whether the sexually explicit material when viewed in the context of the whole work would be tolerated by the community as a whole. Artistic expression rests at the heart of freedom of expression values and any doubt in this regard must be resolved in favour of freedom of expression.

. . . .

(a) Is s. 163 a Limit Prescribed by Law?

The appellant argues that the provision is so vague that it is impossible to apply it. Vagueness must be considered in relation to two issues in this appeal: (1) is the law so vague that it does not qualify as "a limit prescribed by law"; and (2) is it so imprecise that it is not a reasonable limit....

. . . .

Standards which escape precise technical definition, such as "undue", are an inevitable part of the law. The Criminal Code contains other such standards. Without commenting on their constitutional validity, I note that the terms "indecent", "immoral" or "scurrilous", found in ss. 167, 168, 173 and 175, are nowhere defined in the Code. It is within the role of the judiciary to attempt to interpret these terms. If such interpretation yields an intelligible standard, the threshold test for the application of s. 1 is met. In my opinion, the interpretation of s. 163(8) in prior judgments which I have reviewed, as supplemented by these reasons, provides an intelligible standard.

(b) Objective

The respondent argues that there are several pressing and substantial objectives which justify overriding the freedom to distribute obscene materials. Essentially, these objectives are the avoidance of harm resulting from antisocial attitudinal changes that exposure to obscene material causes and the public interest in maintaining a "decent society". On the other hand, the appellant argues that the objective of s. 163 is to have the state act as "moral custodian" in sexual matters and to impose subjective standards of morality.

. . . .

...To impose a certain standard of public and sexual morality, solely because it reflects the conventions of a given community, is inimical to the exercise and enjoyment of individual freedoms, which form the basis of our social contract. D. Dyzenhaus, "Obscenity and the Charter: Autonomy and Equality" (1991), 1 C.R. (4th) 367, at p. 370, refers to this as "legal moralism", of a majority deciding what values should inform individual lives and then coercively imposing those values on minorities. The prevention of "dirt for dirt's sake" is not a legitimate objective which would justify the violation of one of the most fundamental freedoms enshrined in the Charter.

On the other hand, I cannot agree with the suggestion of the appellant that Parliament does not have the right to legislate on the basis of some fun-

(iv) R. v. Butler

damental conception of morality for the purposes of safeguarding the values which are integral to a free and democratic society. As *Dyzenhaus, supra*, at p. 376, writes:

> Moral disapprobation is recognized as an appropriate response when it has its basis in Charter values.

As the respondent and many of the interveners have pointed out, much of the criminal law is based on moral conceptions of right and wrong and the mere fact that a law is grounded in morality does not automatically render it illegitimate. In this regard, criminalizing the proliferation of materials which undermine another basic Charter right may indeed be a legitimate objective.

In my view, however, the overriding objective of s. 163 is not moral disapprobation but the avoidance of harm to society. In Towne Cinema, Dickson C.J. stated, at p. 507:

> It is harm to society from undue exploitation that is aimed at by the section, not simply lapses in propriety or good taste.

The harm was described in the following way in the Report on Pornography by the Standing Committee on Justice and Legal Affairs (MacGuigan Report) (1978), at p. 18:4:

> The clear and unquestionable danger of this type of material is that it reinforces some unhealthy tendencies in Canadian society. The effect of this type of material is to reinforce male-female stereotypes to the detriment of both sexes. It attempts to make degradation, humiliation, victimization, and violence in human relationships appear normal and acceptable. A society which holds that egalitarianism, non-violence, consensualism, and mutuality are basic to any human interaction, whether sexual or other, is clearly justified in controlling and prohibiting any medium of depiction, description or advocacy which violates these principles.

. . . .

This Court has thus recognized that the harm caused by the proliferation of materials which seriously offend the values fundamental to our society is a substantial concern which justifies restricting the otherwise full exercise of the freedom of expression. In my view, the harm sought to be avoided in the case of the dissemination of obscene materials is similar. In the words of Nemetz C.J.B.C. in *R. v. Red Hot Video Ltd.* (1985), 45 C.R. (3d) 36 (B.C.C.A.), there is a growing concern that the exploitation of women and children, depicted in publications and films, can, in certain circumstances, lead to "abject and servile victimization" (at pp. 43–44). As Anderson J.A. also noted in that same case, if true equality between male and female persons is to be achieved, we cannot ignore the threat to equality resulting from exposure to audiences of certain types of violent and degrading material. Materials portraying women as a class as objects for sexual exploitation and abuse have a negative impact on "the individual's sense of self-worth and acceptance".

. . . .

...I would therefore conclude that the objective of avoiding the harm associated with the dissemination of pornography in this case is sufficiently pressing and substantial to warrant some restriction on full exercise of the right to freedom of expression. The analysis of whether the measure is proportional to the objective must, in my view, be undertaken in light of the conclusion that the objective of the impugned section is valid only in so far as it relates to the harm to society associated with obscene materials. Indeed, the section as interpreted in previous decisions and in these reasons is fully consistent with that objective. The objective of maintaining conventional standards of propriety, independently of any harm to society, is no longer justified in light of the values of individual liberty which underlie the Charter. This, then, being the objective of s. 163, which I have found to be pressing and substantial, I must now determine whether the section is rationally connected and proportional to this objective....

. . . .

The values which underlie the protection of freedom of expression relate to the search for truth, participation in the political process, and individual self-fulfilment. The Attorney General for Ontario argues that of these, only "individual self-fulfilment", and only in its most base aspect, that of physical arousal, is engaged by pornography. On the other hand, the civil liberties groups argue that pornography forces us to question conventional notions of sexuality and thereby launches us into an inherently political discourse. In their factum, the B.C. Civil Liberties Association adopts a passage from R. West, "The Feminist-Conservative Anti-Pornography Alliance and the 1986 Attorney General's Commission on Pornography Report" (1987), 4 Am. Bar Found. Res. Jo. 681, at p. 696:

Good pornography has value because it validates women's will to pleasure. It celebrates female nature. It validates a range of female sexuality that is wider and truer than that legitimated by the non-pornographic culture. Pornography (when it is good) celebrates both female pleasure and male rationality.

A proper application of the test should not suppress what West refers to as "good pornography". The objective of the impugned provision is not to inhibit the celebration of human sexuality. However, it cannot be ignored that the realities of the pornography industry are far from the picture which the B.C. Civil Liberties Association would have us paint. Shannon J., in *R.* v. *Wagner, supra,* described the materials more accurately when he observed, at p. 331:

> Women, particularly, are deprived of unique human character or identity and are depicted as sexual playthings, hysterically and instantly responsive to male sexual demands. They worship male genitals and their own value depends upon the quality of their genitals and breasts.

In my view, the kind of expression which is sought to be advanced does not stand on an equal footing with other kinds of expression which directly engage the "core" of the freedom of expression values.

This conclusion is further buttressed by the fact that the targeted material is expression which is motivated, in the overwhelming majority of cases, by economic profit. This Court held in *Rocket* v. *Royal College of Dental Surgeons of Ontario,* [1990] 2 S.C.R. 232, at p. 247, that an economic motive for expression means that restrictions on the expression might "be easier to justify than other infringements".

. . . .

I am in agreement with Twaddle J.A. who expressed the view that Parliament was entitled to have a "reasoned apprehension of harm" resulting from the desensitization of individuals exposed to materials which depict violence, cruelty, and dehumanization in sexual relations.

Accordingly, I am of the view that there is a sufficiently rational link between the criminal sanction, which demonstrates our community's disapproval of the dissemination of materials which potentially victimize women and which restricts the negative influence which such materials have on changes in attitudes and behaviour, and the objective.

. . . .

There are several factors which contribute to the finding that the provision minimally impairs the freedom which is infringed.

First, the impugned provision does not proscribe sexually explicit erotica without violence that is not degrading or dehumanizing. It is designed to catch material that creates a risk of harm to society. It might be suggested that proof of actual harm should be required. It is apparent from what I have said above that it is sufficient in this regard for Parliament to have a reasonable basis for concluding that harm will result and this requirement does not demand actual proof of harm.

Second, materials which have scientific, artistic or literary merit are not captured by the provision. As discussed above, the court must be generous in its application of the "artistic defence". For example, in certain cases, materials such as photographs, prints, books and films which may undoubtedly be produced with some motive for economic profit, may nonetheless claim the protection of the Charter in so far as their defining characteristic is that of aesthetic expression, and thus represent the artist's attempt at individual fulfilment. The existence of an accompanying economic motive does not, of itself, deprive a work of significance as an example of individual artistic or self-fulfilment.

Third, in considering whether the provision minimally impairs the freedom in question, it is legitimate for the court to take into account Parliament's past abortive attempts to replace the definition with one that is more explicit. In Irwin Toy, our Court recognized that it is legitimate to take into account the fact that earlier laws and proposed alternatives were thought to be less effective than the legislation that is presently being challenged. The attempt to provide exhaustive instances of obscenity has been shown to be destined to fail (Bill C-54, 2nd Sess., 33rd Parl.). It seems that the only practicable alternative is to strive towards a more abstract definition of obscenity which is contextually sensitive and responsive to progress in the knowledge and understanding of the phenomenon to which the legislation is directed. In my view, the standard of "undue exploitation" is therefore appropriate. The intractable nature of the problem and the impossibility of precisely defining a notion which is inherently elusive makes the possibility of a more explicit provision remote. In this light, it is appropriate to question whether, and at what cost, greater legislative precision can be demanded.

(iv) R. v. Butler

Fourth, while the discussion in this appeal has been limited to the definition portion of s. 163, I would note that the impugned section, with the possible exception of subs. 1, which is not in issue here, has been held by this Court not to extend its reach to the private use or viewing of obscene materials....

3. Legal Reasoning and Legal Method

A. Sources of Law and Legal Reasoning

(i) Precedents, Statutes and Legal Reasoning

F.L. Morton

One of the most distinctive characteristics of the judicial process is its formalized method of reasoning. Because their authority flows from the public perception that they are "merely" applying pre-existing rules to resolve new disputes, judges are not permitted the broad prerogative enjoyed by the legislative and the executive branches. Unlike the latter, courts are not supposed to create new policies to deal with new problems. In their oral or written judgments, judges must explain where and how they derived the "rule" used to settle a case. There are three principal sources for these "rules": a written constitution, legislative statutes (including administrative regulations), and prior judicial decisions, known as precedents. Constitutional interpretation is the subject of the following two chapters. This chapter is concerned with the role of precedent and statutory interpretation in judicial reasoning.

Until the middle of the nineteenth century, most internal or domestic law in English-speaking societies was common law. Common law originated in the judicial recognition and enforcement of traditional usages and customs of the Anglo-Saxon and later Norman peoples in the British Isles. As these judicial decisions were made, they in turn became part of the common law. The common law in contemporary Canadian society consists of all previous judicial decisions by Canadian and British courts, as they are recorded in the case reports of these nations. The common law system is distinguished from the civil law system by its basis in precedent rather than legislative enactment. The civil law system originated in ancient Roman law, developed on the European continent, and was imported into Quebec by the French. It is based on a single, comprehensive code, enacted by the legislature.

The law of precedent, or *stare decisis*, is a self-imposed judicial rule that "like cases be decided alike." As Gordon Post explains, the law of precedent is essentially a formalization of the common sense use of past experience as a guide to present conduct. The value of judicial adherence to *stare decisis* is two-fold. First, continuity and certainty in the law is a prerequisite of civilized human activity. If there is no reasonable guarantee that what is valid law today will still be valid law tomorrow, personal, economic, and political intercourse would grind to a halt. In each of these spheres of human activity, present-day decisions and activities are predicated on expectations about the future. Ensuring a high degree of predictability and continuity between the present and the future is one of the primary

---

From *Law, Politics and the Judicial Process in Canada* (Calgary: University of Calgary Press, 1984) at 185–89. Notes and references omitted. Reproduced by permission of the author.

purposes of a political regime. As the institutions charged with interpreting and adapting the laws over time, the courts are responsible for maintaining continuity and certainty. As Dicey said, "A law which was not certain would in reality be no law at all." Adherence to the rule of precedent — "deciding like cases alike" — is the mechanism that provides this certainty.

The rule of precedent also contributes to guaranteeing the "rule of law, not of men." One of the ideals of the Western tradition's conception of justice is that the laws be applied equally and impartially to all persons. This ideal precludes any *ad hoc* application of the laws, and demands instead that laws be applied uniformly, or that any deviation from the rule be justified on principle — that is, by another rule. The idiosyncrasies or personal preferences of a judge are not permissible grounds for judicial decisions. This would re-introduce the "rule of men" rather than the "rule of law." By minimizing the discretion or freedom of individual judges, *stare decisis* preserves the "rule of law."

It should be emphasized that *stare decisis* minimizes but does not eliminate the element of judicial discretion or creativity. While legal reasoning presents itself as a deductive process, the reality is a more subtle blend of both inductive and deductive reasoning. Legal reasoning is accurately described as "reasoning by example." The judges are essentially asking, "Whether the present case resembles the plain case 'sufficiently' and in the 'relevant' aspects." In determining what is "sufficient" and what is "relevant," the judge must ultimately make certain choices. Because of this element of choice, a judge is responsible for striking the balance between continuity and innovation. The central thrust of the theory of legal realism has been to emphasize this element of choice and judicial discretion, and the ensuing responsibility of the judge for his choice.

Weiler's analysis of the Supreme Court's responsibility for the development of tort law is based on this legal realist perspective. Weiler argues that judges can no longer claim that precedent "dictates" nonsensical or patently unfair legal conclusions. Judges must be critical in their use of precedent, and go beyond the surface "rule" to discover the animating "principle." The proper function of the common law judge, according to Weiler, is to derive specific rules from more general principles, as the situation demands. Since situations change, rules must change also. While the "cattle trespass" exemption to normal tort law responsibility may have been appropriate to the rural, agricultural society of eighteenth century England, it had become a dangerous anachronism in twentieth century Canada. Similarly in *Boucher v. The King*, the Court was faced with a conflict between the definition of "seditious libel" developed in nineteenth century, homogeneous, protestant Britain, and the norms of freedom of religion and speech in twentieth century, pluralistic Canada. Appeal court judges have a duty, says Weiler, to adapt the common law to the changing needs and circumstances of contemporary society.

Strict adherence to *stare decisis* is yet another aspect of the "adjudication of disputes" function of courts that poses problems for judicial policy-making. Refusal to disavow or change past decisions plays no constructive role in a policy-making institution, as the examples of legislative and executive practice make clear. While certainty and continuity are legal virtues, adaptability and innovation are more important in the policy-making process. The case for abandoning a strict adherence to precedent is especially strong in constitutional law. Not only is policy-impact more probable, but constitutional law lacks the flexibility of common law and statutes. If the courts make a "mistake" in the latter areas, it can be corrected by remedial legislation. But if the Supreme Court makes a constitutional decision with undesirable policy consequences, the only direct way to correct the damage is through formal constitutional amendment, an extremely cumbersome and difficult process. Predictably, the U.S. Supreme Court was the first court of appeal in a common law nation to abandon *stare decisis* as an absolute requirement. The demotion of *stare decisis* from a binding rule to a guiding principle is another index of a court's evolution toward a greater policy-making role.

The recent advent of judicial realism in Canadian jurisprudence has brought with it a decline in the status of the rule of *stare decisis*. Long after the American Supreme Court had abandoned absolute adherence to precedent, the Canadian Supreme Court continued to perceive itself as bound to adhere not only to its own previous decisions but those of the British House of Lords as well. This latter restriction is attributable to the role of the Judicial Committee of the Privy Council as Canada's final court of appeal until 1949. Ten years after the abolition of that role, the Supreme Court declared its independence from British precedents as well. In 1966 the British House of Lords officially declared that, when appropriate, it would no longer follow its own prior decisions. However, the Supreme Court of Canada continued to profess strict adherence to its prior decision until the 1970's. Under the leadership of Bora Laskin, the Canadian Supreme Court began to move in the same direction. In 1972, before his appointment as chief justice, Laskin had written that *stare decisis* was "no longer an article of faith in the Supreme Court of Canada, but it still remains a cogent principle." Speaking as the new Chief Justice at the Centennial Symposium of the Supreme Court in 1975, Laskin repeated that *stare decisis* was no longer "an inexorable rule," but rather,

> simply an important element of the judicial process, a necessary consideration which should give pause to any but the most sober conclusion that a previous decision or line of authority is wrong and ought to be changed.

Practising what he preached, Laskin led the Supreme Court to overturn three precedents during the next three years, including an old Privy Council decision dealing with the federal division of powers. The abandoning of strict adherence to *stare decisis* is yet another indicator of the Supreme Court's institutional evolution toward more of a policy-making court.

The second principal source of law is legislative statutes. Beginning in the nineteenth century, legislatures in Great Britain, Canada, and the United States began to codify large portions of the common law. In large part this was a democratic reaction against the perceived elitism of the "judge-made" character of the common law. By reducing the confusing maze of common law precedent to clearly worded, legislative statutes, it was thought that the law would be made easier for "the people" to understand, and that the democratic authority of "government by consent" would be enhanced.

In 1892 the Canadian Parliament abolished all criminal offenses at common law, and replaced them with a comprehensive statute, the *Criminal Code*. In so doing, Parliament hoped to reap the alleged advantages of codification mentioned above, including restricting judicial discretion in the criminal law. Since crimes were now clearly and authoritatively defined, judges would simply apply the law as Parliament had written it. It would no longer be necessary to refer to a vast and confusing system of precedent to apply the criminal law, or so it was hoped.

In fact, precedent and *stare decisis* quickly found their way back into the criminal law. Perhaps, as Parker has suggested, it was (and still is) impossible for judges and lawyers trained in the common law tradition to properly construe a code of law. More likely the common law "habit" simply compounds a more serious problem — the ultimate ambiguity of statutory terminology itself. Try as they might, legislators will never be able to draft statutes that anticipate and encompass all possible future situations. This is due in part to the inherent tension between the generality of words and the specificity of reality, and in part to human ignorance of the future. As new situations inevitably arise, the applicability of the original wording of statutes becomes increasingly questionable....

The preceding argument notwithstanding, judicial discretion in interpreting statutes, including the *Criminal Code*, is much more circumscribed than in interpreting the common law. As Weiler says, judges can develop new torts, but not new crimes, and there are sound reasons for preferring this arrangement. As issues of tort law are rarely the subject of partisan political controversy, an innovative court cannot be accused of usurping the legislative function. The controversies over capital punishment and abortion show that the same is not true of the criminal law. In the area of tort law, judicial expertise is very high, relative to other policy-making institutions. Finally, judicial initiatives in substantive criminal law would pose the threat of punishing innocent persons. No comparable problem of "due process" arises in tort law.

While codification and statutes clearly circumscribe the limits of judicial law-making, there is still the element of judicial "choice" and its accompanying responsibility. This is especially true of the *Criminal Code*, which authorizes the continued use of common law defenses such as *mens rea*. Once again, Weiler argues that judges should go beyond superficial resemblances of wording of facts and grasp the principles that animate this area of law. The examples used appear to be contradictory decisions concerning the availability of the *mens rea* defense. Weiler suggests that these can be reconciled by reference to the underlying competition between the "crime control" and "due process" principles of criminal law. Different judges could reasonably reach different conclusions in these two cases. The essential point from Weiler's perspective is not so much what a judge decides, but how he decides the case. A final appellate court should explicitly ground its decision in the underlying principles, and explain why the particular circumstances of this case dictated favouring one over the other. Failure to do so is a failure to live up to the standards of judicial craftsmanship that can reasonably be expected from a final appellate court in an age of legal realism.

(ii) Legal Reasoning

John Farrar and A. Dugdale

Legal reasoning and Logic

Lawyers are often thought of as having logical minds. This gives the impression that legal reasoning itself is or should be governed by logic. Certainly logic plays an important role in legal reasoning but as we will see it is only part of the story.

When we refer to logic we are often thinking of the deductive form of argument known as *the syllogism*. It goes like this:

All men are mortal — Major Premise
Socrates is a man — Minor Premise
Therefore Socrates is mortal — Conclusion.

A lawyer advising his client as to the application of a detailed statutory provision will employ this type of reasoning. The statute is a major premise, the lawyer identifies his case as falling within the statute and then deduces as the conclusion the way in which it applies to his client. Deductive logic is only applicable once a clear major premise has been established. If the source is not a statute but case law, no major premise is likely to be clear from just one case decision. Instead the lawyer will have to examine several cases to find a major premise which underlies them all. He will have to reason from particular case decisions to a general proposition. This form of reasoning is often referred to as inductive logic as opposed to deductive logic where the reasoning is from the general proposition to the particular conclusion in the case itself. Thus, a lawyer advising on the application of case law to a particular situation will employ first inductive reasoning to find a general proposition of law and then deductive reasoning to determine how it applies to the facts.

Judges too make use of inductive and deductive logic when deciding cases. Lord Diplock explained very fully how a court uses this form of reasoning in the case of *Dorset Yacht Co.* v. *The Home Office* which concerned the question whether Borstal Officers owed a duty of care to the public to prevent escapes by those in their custody. He said that the court should proceed:

...by seeking first to identify the relevant characteristics that are common to the kinds of conduct and relationship between the parties which are involved in the case for decision and the kinds of conduct and relationships which have been held in previous decisions of the courts to give rise to a duty of care.

The method adopted at this stage of the process is analytical and inductive. It starts with an analysis of the characteristics of the conduct and relationship involved in each of the decided cases. But the analyst must know what he is looking for, and this involves his approaching his analysis with some general conception of conduct and relationships which ought to give rise to duty of care. This analysis leads to a proposition which can be stated in the form;

In all the decisions that have been analysed a duty of care has been held to exist wherever the conduct and the relationship possessed each of the characteristics A, B, C, D, etc., and has not so far been found to exist when any of these characteristics were absent.

For the second stage, which is deductive and analytical, that proposition is converted to: 'In all cases where the conduct and relationship possess each of the characteristics A, B, C, D, etc., a duty of care arises.' The conduct and relationship involved in the case for decision is then analysed to ascertain whether they possess each of these characteristics. If they do the conclusion follows that a duty of care does arise in the case for decision.

In this extract Lord Diplock adds one further element to the model of inductive and deductive reasoning, namely that at the inductive stage the analyst must have some idea of what he is looking for. In other words he must categorise the issue and decide which previous decisions are so closely analogous to the issue in question that this can be used as a basis for inducing the relevant proposition of law. Judges and legal advisers frequently use this form of reasoning, arguing that previous decisions are or are not sufficiently similar to be relevant to the issue in question. Analogical reasoning of this kind is not

From *Introduction to Legal Method*, 2nd ed. (London: Sweet & Maxwell, 1984) at 74–78. Notes omitted. Reproduced by permission of Sweet & Maxwell Limitd, Andover, Hampshire, U.K.

strictly logical. It is a looser form of reasoning which raises broader issues.

Lord Diplock went on to stress one further limitation upon logical reasoning in the following terms:

> But since *ex hypothesi* the kind of case which we are now considering offers a choice whether or not to extend the kinds of conduct or relationships which give rise to a duty of care, the conduct or relationship which involved in it will lack at least one of the characteristics A, B, C or D, etc. And the choice is exercised by making a policy decision as to whether or not a duty of care ought to exist if the characteristic which is lacking were absent or redefined in terms broad enough to include the case under consideration.

Cases which involve a question of what law should be applied come before the court precisely because there is no purely logical answer to the question. Instead there is a choice which according to Lord Diplock, is exercised by making a policy decision. But how does the judge make this decision? Obviously he will be influenced by the rhetoric of the parties' counsel, by the way in which they have framed the issue and the analogies they have suggested. He may have his own personal views, although on legal matters these are likely to have become "institutionalised" over the years of practice before the courts. Perhaps the most important influence on his choice, is the knowledge that he will have to justify his decision in a reasoned judgment. It is to this "justificatory" nature of legal reasoning that we now turn.

Legal Reasoning and Justification

How will a judge justify his decision? Obviously he will appeal to authority, to the sources of law, the past precedents, the statutory wording. Until the last 20 years or so, this might have been the limit of his expressed justification. Judgments were often written in such a way as to suggest that the authorities provided an obvious answer. Nowadays the judges are more willing to recognise that the authorities present a choice and that their decision can be properly justified in other terms.

Professor Neil MacCormick, in his book *Legal Reasoning and Legal Theory*, suggests that two factors in particular may be considered by a judge when justifying his decision. The first is the extent to which a proposed decision will cohere with existing principles and authorities. The greater the inconsistency with the existing legal framework that will result from a proposed decision, the less likely it is to be adopted. The second concerns the broader consequences of the decision for potential litigants, the legal system and indeed the role of law in society. Will these consequences be acceptable in terms of justice or common sense? Other writers have made similar suggestions and if you examine the judgment of Lord Roskill in the *Veitchi* case which we have set out as an appendix to Chapter 8 you will see an example of a judge employing justificatory arguments of this kind. He discussed the existing trend of case law to show how his proposed decision would fit the pattern. He argued that an opposite decision would perpetuate artificial distinctions. He considered the consequences of his proposed decision, the possibility that it would release the "floodgates" of litigation but concluded that although this argument had its place it was overridden by the principle suggesting liability. When you have read this chapter you will understand more of the background to the case and the basis of the principle. Of course, the fact that Lord Roskill justified his decision in terms of coherence and consequence does not prove that he is right. The dissenting Law Lords employed just the same kind of arguments to the opposite effect. What it illustrates is simply the process of reasoned justification.

Other types of argument may be used as justification. Judges may refer to common sense, the supposed view of a reasonable man or they may refer to notions of justice and fairness. In Chapter 10 we describe the way in which the courts have interpreted the statutory phrase "intentionally homeless" and there you will see examples of the appeal to common sense and other factors to justify a particular decision. Professor John Wisdom, a philosopher, has summed up the nature of legal reasoning by saying that it is "not a chain of demonstrative reasoning. It is a presenting and [re-presenting] of those features of the cases which severally co-operate in favour of the conclusion.... The reasons are like the legs of a chair not the links of a chain." In this respect legal reasoning employs the process of practical reasoning we all use in everyday life. We tend to weigh a collection of reasons for or against a particular decision rather than think in terms of deductive logic. However, whilst in our own practical reasoning we can take into account anything within our own knowledge, it is important to realise that a judge can only properly take into account those considerations which can be adequately argued before a court of law ...

(iii) The Doctrine of Precedent

Patrick Atiyah

There are, of course, rules about law-making by courts, rules laid down by the courts themselves. Not everything said by a judge makes law. In the first place, decisions on pure questions of fact clearly do not create precedents. The fact that X shot Y may make him guilty of murder but is of no relevance to another case in which Z is the accused. Even evaluative decisions, such as a decision that a certain piece of conduct constitutes negligence, are not regarded as decisions on points of law which can constitute precedents. To take a simple example, if a judge says that a defendant in a civil action was driving his car at 80 mph in a public street, and that he was therefore guilty of negligence, that is no precedent for holding that it is negligence for another driver in a subsequent case to have driven at the same speed (even on the same road). This is partly because (as is commonly said) evaluative decisions like this must depend on all the circumstances of the case, and so it is impossible to be sure that the relevant facts in the first decision were in all respects the same as in the second. But it also seems pretty clear that one reason why decisions of this kind are not treated as precedents is simply that the courts do not want to make their every decision suffocated under the weight of previous cases. If every case of this kind became a precedent, the volume of case law would become enormous, the argument of simple cases would become inordinately complicated, as each side would support its case with a mountainous pile of precedents, and judges would find it increasingly difficult to explain why and how decision Z was consistent with decisions A, B, C ... in favour of one side, and not inconsistent with decisions M, N, O ... in favour of the other side. So judicial decisions would inevitably appear inconsistent, and this is disliked by judges. Decisions on discretionary matters are also not decisions which can constitute precedents, although the guiding principles on which discretions are to be exercised are treated as questions of law.

The doctrine of precedent, then, is largely concerned with pure questions of law. A decision on a point of law constitutes a precedent which can in principle *bind* other courts to follow it. But before we can say that a decision constitutes a binding precedent two further qualifications need to be made. First, it must indeed be a *decision*, and not merely an *obiter dictum*, that is, a statement made by the way, an aside. In principle the distinction between the binding part of the decision (the *ratio decidendi*) and an *obiter dictum* is clear, but in practice it is not always easy to distinguish between them. Sometimes judges give several reasons for a decision: are they all binding, or is there one binding reason, the others being merely *dicta*? Or again, there may be several different judgements given in an appeal court, and the reasons given by all the judges may not wholly coincide, so what is the *ratio decidendi* then? In any event, the question of *ratio* or *dictum* may be less important than the weight of the remarks in their context, and the tribunal from which they emanate. Fully considered *dicta* in the House of Lords are usually treated as more weighty than the *ratio* of a judge at first instance in the High Court. So the whole distinction is more blurred than it might seem. Further, the distinction often does not matter at all. It does not matter basically when the second court agrees with the decision (or *dicta*) in the previous case, and would arrive at the same conclusion anyhow; it does not matter even when the second court might, if it were to go into the issue in depth, have doubts about the first decision (or *dicta*) but feel disinclined to reopen the issue for any one of a number of possible reasons. Nor does the distinction between *ratio* and *dicta* matter if the second court disagrees so strongly with what was said in the earlier case that it is not prepared to follow it, even if in theory some lawyers might regard the prior case as a binding precedent. Where this happens, the second court may 'distinguish' the first decision by finding some relevant fact to be decisive of the second case which was not present in the first. Every lawyer

---

From *Law and Modern Society* (London, U.K.: Oxford University Press, 1983) at 134–37. © P.S. Atiyah 1983. Reproduced from *Law and Modern Society* by P.S. Atiyah (1983) by permission of Oxford University Press.

(iii) The Doctrine of Precedent

knows that fine distinctions are sometimes seized upon to justify departing from a prior decision without an apparent breach with the rules of binding precedent.

The second qualification that needs to be made to the binding nature of the doctrine of precedent is that the strictly binding feature of the doctrine depends on the relative status of the courts concerned. Decisions of the House of Lords bind all lower courts, and are normally treated as binding by the House itself. Since 1966 the House has claimed the right to overrule previous decisions in exceptional cases, but it has so far been very sparing in its willingness to exercise this power. Decisions of the Court of Appeal bind lower courts, and also in principle bind the Court of Appeal itself. But there is much controversy on this and practice varies. Lord Denning, who as Master of the Rolls presides over the Court of Appeal, has frequently expressed his belief that that court ought to have the same freedom to depart from its own prior decisions as the House of Lords now claims; some of his colleagues appear to agree with him, but a majority do not. Furthermore, while most of those who agree with Lord Denning are generally prepared to accept the majority view that the Court of Appeal should remain bound by its own decisions, Lord Denning himself (and occasionally, it would seem, one or two others) are not. There are, in any event, a number of established exceptions to the rule that that court is bound by its own decisions, but their limits are somewhat ill-defined, so in practice it is really quite rare that the court must seriously face the question whether it is absolutely bound by one of its own decisions.

Decisions of Divisional Courts bind all lower courts, and even decisions of a single High Court judge are treated as binding on magistrates and tribunals, and generally by lawyers in the public service. Decisions of judges below the level of the High Court are not regarded as binding on anyone, and there is no systematic method of reporting such decisions.

The above account of the doctrine of precedent may well give a misleading impression of the importance of single binding decisions. Undoubtedly there are some situations where such decisions settle the law on a clear, simple point. In the interpretation of a statute, for instance, a simple ambiguity may be found which gives two alternative meanings to a section: the choice may be stark and straight-forward, even though the resolution of the ambiguity may be quite difficult. In such a case, a single decision may settle the issue, particularly if it is in the Court of Appeal or the House of Lords. But much more commonly, it is clusters of decisions which are important for the development of the law. Usually it is found that areas of doubt and uncertainty in the law, as well as newly developing areas, give rise to more litigation than other areas: this occurs for the obvious reason that lawyers are unable to advise their clients with the same degree of confidence in these areas, and the prospects of successful appeals may well be higher in such cases. So it quite often happens that a whole series of new cases arises in a relatively short period of time. When this happens, it also often becomes clear that new vistas are opening up, and, perhaps, that new problems, hitherto unsuspected, have been thrown up. Such a cluster of cases may well trigger off academic writing, which in turn may influence counsel in arguing subsequent cases. After a while matters may settle down again, and a new bit of law is, as it were, digested by the law and lawyers. This sort of development does not necessarily raise serious issues about the binding force of particular precedents, though such a development is occasionally triggered off by a loosening-up of the effect of an earlier series of precedents.

One recent illustration of this process, of some general interest, concerns the liability of barristers and solicitors for negligence in handling their clients' affairs. Until the early 1960s the law was taken to be settled that (1) a solicitor was liable for negligence on the same footing as any other professional adviser, but (2) that a barrister was not so liable because a barrister did not have a direct contract with his client—the client being compelled to approach the barrister through the solicitor with whom he contracted. Then in 1964 the House of Lords decided the famous *Hedley Byrne* case [1964] AC 465 which had nothing at all to do with the liability of barristers or solicitors, but which recognized for the first time that liability for negligent professional advice might arise *in tort*, that is, even between parties not in a contractual relationship. Barristers, of course, were quick to appreciate that their own traditional immunities might now be called in question, and in two subsequent decisions the House of Lords has begun to explore this possibility. These two decisions have laid down a new framework of law, much of which remains to be filled in by later decisions. Barristers remain immune from negligence liability in respect of the actual conduct of a case in court and in respect of advisory work which is so closely connected with the conduct of the case that it is in effect preparatory work for the trial, but they are no longer immune in respect of purely advisory work. Further, although none of

61

these cases has so far actually involved the liability of a solicitor, it is pretty clear from *dicta* in them, that a solicitor's liability will now be equated with a barrister's, and he will share the barrister's immunity in respect of the actual conduct of a case in court — and cases in lower courts often are handled by solicitors. What is now likely to happen is that there will be a number of cases defining somewhat more clearly the line between purely advisory work and preparation for actual litigation.

This series of cases (and I have omitted some of the less significant) illustrates the way in which the common law can still develop, step by step, almost as though it were an organic growth. We now have a number of judgments in several cases, each of which offers arguments and opinions in favour of this or that development. Hypothetical examples may also be given, some of the arguments in one judgment may be rebutted in another judgment, and so on. Then for a while, the issues may move into the public domain, particularly where, as in this case, there is a public interest in the legal rules being developed. There may be academic articles and notes, media discussion, perhaps anecdotal evidence of past injustices, and possibly even a parliamentary debate. All this may indirectly feed into the next round of developments, and so the process continues.

(iv) This Case System: Precedent

Karl Llewellyn

We turn first to what I may call the orthodox doctrine of precedent, with which, in its essence, you are already familiar. Every case lays down a rule, the rule of the case. The express ratio decidendi is prima facie the rule of the case, since it is the ground upon which the court chose to rest its decision. But a later court can reexamine the case and can invoke the canon that no judge has power to decide what is not before him, can, through examination of the facts or of the procedural issue, narrow the picture of what was actually before the court and can hold that the ruling made requires to be understood as thus restricted. In the extreme form this results in what is known as expressly "confining the case to its particular facts." This rule holds only of redheaded Walpoles in pale magenta Buick cars. And when you find this said of a past case you know that in effect it has been overruled. Only a convention, a somewhat absurd convention, prevents flat overruling in such instances. It seems to be felt as definitely improper to state that the court in a prior case was wrong, peculiarly so if that case was in the same court which is speaking now. It seems to be felt that this would undermine the dogma of the infallibility of courts. So lip service is done to that dogma, while the rule which the prior court laid down is disembowelled. The execution proceeds with due respect, with mandarin courtesy.

Now this orthodox view of the authority of precedent — which I shall call the *strict* view — is but *one of two views* which seem to me wholly contradictory to each other. It is in practice the dogma which is applied to *unwelcome* precedents. It is the recognized, legitimate, honorable technique for whittling precedents away, for making the lawyer, in his argument, and the court, in its decision, free of them. It is a surgeon's knife.

It is orthodox, I think, because it has been more discussed than is the other. Consider the situation. It is not easy thus to carve a case to pieces. It takes thought, it takes conscious thought, it takes analysis. There is no great art and no great difficulty in merely looking at a case, reading its language, and then applying some sentence which is there expressly stated. But there is difficulty in going underneath what is said, in making a keen reexamination of the case that stood before the court, in showing that the language used was quite beside the point, as the point is revealed under the lens of leisured microscopic refinement. Hence the technique of dis-

---

From *The Bramble Bush: On Our Law and Its Study* by Karl Llewellyn, at 66–69, published by Oceana Publications, Inc., Dobbs Ferry, N.Y., 1960.

(iv) This Case System: Precedent

tinguishing cases has given rise to the closest of scrutiny. The technique of arguing for a distinction has become systematized. And when men start talking of authority, or of the doctrine of precedent, they turn naturally to that part of their minds which has been *consciously* devoted to the problem; they call up the cases, the analyses, the arguments, which have been made under such conditions. They put this together, and call this "*the* doctrine". I suspect there is still another reason for the orthodoxy. That is that only finer minds, minds with sharp mental scalpels, can do this work, and that it is the finer minds — the minds with a sharp cutting edge — which write about it and which thus set up the tradition of the books. To them it must seem that what blunt minds can do as well as they is poor; but that which they alone can do is good. They hit in this on a truth in part: you can pass with ease from this strict doctrine of precedent to the other. If you can handle this, then you can handle both. Not vice versa. The strict doctrine, then, is the technique to be learned. *But not to be mistaken for the whole.*

For when you turn to the actual operations of the courts, or, indeed, to the arguments of lawyers, you will find a totally different view of precedent at work beside this first one. That I shall call, to give it a name, the *loose view* of precedent. That is the view that a court has decided, and decided authoritatively, *any* point or all points on which it chose to rest a case, or on which it chose, after due argument, to pass. No matter how broad the statement, no matter how unnecessary on the facts or the procedural issues, if that was the rule the court laid down, then that the court has held. Indeed, this view carries over often into dicta, and even into dicta which are grandly obiter. In its extreme form this results in thinking and arguing exclusively from *language* that is found in past opinions, and in citing and working with that language wholly without reference to the facts of the case which called the language forth.

Now it is obvious that this is a device not for cutting past opinions away from judges' feet, but for using them as a springboard when they are found convenient. This is a device for *capitalizing welcome precedents*. And both the lawyers and the judges use it so. And judged by the *practice* of the most respected courts, as of the courts of ordinary stature, this doctrine of precedent is like the other, recognized, legitimate, honorable.

What I wish to sink deep into your minds about the doctrine of precedent, therefore, is that it is two-headed. It is Janus-faced. That it is not one doctrine, nor one line of doctrine, but two, and two which, *applied at the same time to the same precedent, are contradictory of each other*. That there is one doctrine for getting rid of precedents deemed troublesome and one doctrine for making use of precedents that seem helpful. That these two doctrines exist side by side. That the same lawyer in the same brief, the same judge in the same opinion, may be using the one doctrine, the technically strict one, to cut down half the older cases that he deals with, and using the other doctrine, the loose one, for building with the other half. Until you realize this you do not see how it is possible for law to change and to develop, and yet to stand on the past. You do not see how it is possible to avoid the past mistakes of courts, and yet to make use of every happy insight for which a judge in writing may have found expression. Indeed it seems to me that here we may have part of the answer to the problem as to whether precedent is not as bad as good — supporting a weak judge with the labors of strong predecessors, but binding a strong judge by the errors of the weak. For look again at this matter of the *difficulty* of the doctrine. The strict view — that view that cuts the past away — is *hard* to use. An ignorant, an unskilful judge will find it hard to use: the past will bind him. But the skilful judge — he whom we would make free — *is* thus made free. He has the knife in hand; and he can free himself.

Nor, until you see this double aspect of the doctrine-in-action, do you appreciate how little, in detail, you can predict *out of the rules alone*; how much you must turn, for purposes of prediction, to the reactions of the judges to the facts and to the life around them. Think again in this connection of an English court, all the judges unanimous upon the conclusion, all the judges in disagreement as to what rule the outcome should be rested on.

Applying this two-faced doctrine of precedent to your work in a case class you get, it seems to me, some such result as this: You read each case from the angle of its *maximum* value as a precedent, at least from the angle of its maximum value as a precedent *of the first water*. You will recall that I recommended taking down the ratio decidendi in substantially the court's own words. You see now what I had in mind. Contrariwise, you will also read each case for its *minimum* value as a precedent, to set against the maximum. In doing this you have your eyes out for the narrow issue in the case, the narrower the better. The first question is, how much can this case fairly be made to stand for by a later court to whom the precedent is welcome? You may well add — though this will be slightly flawed authority — the dicta which appear to have been well considered. The second question is, how much is there in this case that cannot be got around, even by a later court that wishes to avoid it?

You have now the tools for arguing from that case as counsel on *either* side of a new case. You turn them to the problem of prediction. Which view will this same court, on a later case on slightly different facts, take: will it choose the narrow or the loose? Which use will be made of this case by one of the other courts whose opinions are before you? Here you will call to your aid the matter of attitude that I have been discussing. Here you will use all that you know of individual judges, or of the trends in specific courts, or, indeed, of the trend in the line of business, or in the situation, or in the times at large — in anything which you may expect to become apparent and important to the court in later cases. But always and always, you will bear in mind that each precedent has not one value, but two, and that the two are wide apart, and that whichever value a later court assigns to it, such assignment will be respectable, traditionally sound, dogmatically correct.

Above all, as you turn this information to your own training you will, I hope, come to see that in most doubtful cases the precedents *must* speak ambiguously until the court has made up its mind whether each one of them is welcome or unwelcome. And that the job of persuasion which falls upon you will call, therefore, not only for providing a technical ladder to reach on authority the result that you contend for, but even more, if you are to have *your* use of the precedents made as *you* propose it, the job calls for you, on the facts, to persuade the court your case is sound.

People — and they are curiously many — who think that precedent produces or ever did produce a certainty that did not involve matters of judgment and of persuasion, or who think that what I have described involves improper equivocation by the courts or departure from the court — ways of some golden age — such people simply do not know our system of precedent in which they live.

B. Standpoint and "Truth" in Legal Method

(i) The Maleness of Legal Language

Karen Busby

INTRODUCTION

Language is one of the most important determinants of reality. Some would say that it is the primary means by which we construct reality, but others would go further and say that language makes us what we are. Since reality is not experienced in the same way by every person, different societies and groups within a given society have different registers that they use to express their respective concerns, ideas, interests and perspectives. A particular register (that is, a specific stratification within an actually existent language system such as English), will obviously share many features of that system but it will also have its own specialized vocabulary, grammar and style.

Language is not used uniformly by all people nor is it equally accessible to everyone, and not all discourses or language registers are valued in the same way. The most powerful registers such as those used by law, medicine and religion, are controlled by and are fully accessible to a select group of highly trained people. The kind of English spoken by some Black Americans in Harlem could also be described as a specific register: it too is only fully accessible to a select group of individuals, although most people would ascribe to it a very different value than, for example, the register used by lawyers. Rather, use

(1989) 18 Man. L.J. 191 at 191-93, 195-204, 206-208, 210-12. Notes omitted. Reproduced by permission of the author.

within a particular registry is impressed with social ideology: the linguistic structure of a text reflects, affects and helps to maintain the roles, purposes and ideologies of its participants or subjects. As well, these structures assume meanings that impliedly express social and political values.

Since Simone de Beauvoir said that men describe the world "from their own point of view which they confuse with the absolute truth," feminists in all disciplines have begun to show how male voices, perspectives, interests and ideas have prevailed in all thinking. The task of determining how androcentric or "male as norm" thought has come to dominate is difficult because "...it is metaphysically nearly perfect. Its point of view is the standard for universality, its particularity the meaning of universality". Can it be said that language, particularly the language of the legal register, shields a male subjectivity? Is the insidious message of the legal register, therefore, the superiority of the male and its politics, patriarchy? These are two of the important questions that I will address in this article.

I will examine the thesis that grammatical features of the legal register such as pronouns, generics, lexicon, semantics and syntax trivialize, exclude and devalue women and characteristics associated with women. By analyzing the details of language as used in legal texts we can begin to see its preconstructions and preferred meanings and to understand its historical and social genesis. My modest goal in this paper is to collect together and to examine some examples from the legal register in order to begin to see what connections can be made between language, gender and oppression in the context of the legal register.

GENDER

It is necessary for me to touch on the issue of what is gender and the tension between simplistic reductive gender categorizations and the equally unacceptable assumption of no difference at all. In this paper "gender" means the various psychological and social characteristics that are usually attributed to an individual according to biological sex. When a characteristic is described as "female" or "male", I mean that it is one usually attributed to women or to men respectively. Such attribution is not exclusive to one sex or the other as either sex may exhibit the gender characteristics of the other. I do not think that I am expressing preferences in this article for one set of characteristics over another although I think that the present legal system favours the male set over the female. Further, I would deny that there is anything deterministic or immutable about gender. But as long as gender has meaning, an analysis of the effect of gender categorizations will be necessary.

. . . .

PRONOUNS AND OTHER FALSE GENERICS

The first issue to be discussed in any feminist analysis of language is the use of male pronouns when the referent is indefinite or inclusive of both women and men. This issue receives so much attention because of its pervasiveness and, more important, because it is one of the least subtle of sexist forms. According to the [masculinist] theory of marking, male pronouns can be marked or unmarked. The context is supposed to determine whether the referent is a male gender specific noun (marked) or a noun that includes men and women (unmarked).

Marking theory has not always been a "rule of grammar". It was the work of prescriptive grammarians from the 16th century onward to suppress the alternative use of "she" or "they". Ann Bodine has revealed that the authors of grammatical treatises appealed not to the laws of language but to the laws of nature. These authors stated that the generic masculine had the virtue of being first in the natural order and in propriety. These men also said that the male pronoun was more comprehensive.

The connection between language, gender and the suppression of women is clear and present in the use of male pronouns. Use of the generic male pronoun perpetuates and conceals male domination at all levels of conceptualization and language. I cannot assume that I have been included within the ambit of a particular passage; my presence is never a given. The subliminal message that I am not relevant or, even more alienating, that I am the "other" is constantly given and received. Take almost any legal text and count how often a male pronoun is used. You can begin then to realize how often I am told that maybe I am not included.

My personal experience is verified by sociological and psychological studies that reveal that the use of the male pronouns does not bring women into readers' minds. Men use and understand "he" more often in its marked or gender specific sense than its unmarked or generic sense. They are less likely to contemplate women as possible actors. Women are more likely than men to use "he and she" or "they" rather than "he" thereby clarifying whether we have been included. When "he" is used in connection with a neutral noun such as "person" or "clerk", the described individual will be perceived as a man. It seems clear then that the use of male pronouns exerts important subliminal influences on people's perception of women as secondary or marginal.

The problems that arise in connection with generic nouns are even more acute. Throughout the texts studied in the legal philosophy seminar there are of course many references simply to "men" to which I must ask whether it includes women; to "people" to which I ask whether women are truly included; and to "men and women" to which I must ask why there is a specific reference to women. The context rarely provides an answer to these questions. Consider the following examples of seemingly generic or unmarked nouns, most of which are from the materials used in the legal philosophy seminar.

Aristotle's "Just Man"

At first blush, it appears that this usage is generic. However, a passage on "household justice" found near the end of the excerpt suggests that Aristotle does not contemplate women as political actors. Unless readers pick up this clue, they would be unaware of Aristotle's systematic exclusion of women and mistakenly assume that women are included within the concept of "just man".

Hart's "Ordinary Citizen"

In a discussion on the morality of acts performed privately and the indecency of acts performed publicly, H.L.A. Hart discusses recent amendments to English prostitution law and says that

> it has not made prostitution a crime but punished its public manifestations in order to protect the ordinary citizen who is an unwilling witness of it in the street from something offensive.

The offensive act of which he speaks could refer to someone witnessing a prostitute and a customer bargaining over fees in a public place. If this is the case, Hart's ordinary citizen could refer to both women and men as both could witness the event. Alternatively, Hart could be speaking of the offence to a particular man who is solicited by a prostitute and who finds such solicitation unwanted. Since this law was not used to punish men who sought the services of a prostitute, Hart did not have in mind the offence to uninterested women who are solicited by men seeking to pay money to have sex. If this alternative describes what Hart was talking about, and his example is ambiguous, then his ordinary citizen is a man. Hart's perspective on solicitation is not surprising as the legal system has long perceived prostitutes and not their customers as being the cause of prostitution or money for sex.

Hart's ordinary citizen is an example of how language that appears to include the experience of both men and women may be seen on closer examination to exclude the experience of women. Apparently gender neutral language may conceal a possibly male exclusive perspective. Hart, like many men, fails to realize that women are subject to unwanted solicitation by men for sex for money. The failure to perceive problems from alternative perspectives is one of the reasons why men and women, or in this particular case, prostitutes and johns, are not treated in the same way by the legal system.

Rawls' "Rational Man"

In developing his theory of justice, John Rawls is concerned with the choices that rational men would make in a hypothetical situation of equal liberty. To this end, he places his actors in an abstract, decontextualized void that he names the original position. He assumes that parties in the original position are rational and mutually disinterested; they are not concerned with one another's interests. The pursuit of individual liberty therefore is second only to the satisfaction of the most basic of human wants. Social ties are useful only insofar as they further individual interests.

While the assumptions Rawls makes about the primacy of autonomy are accurate in relation to men, recent studies have shown that his assumptions about human nature are not accurate when applied to women. Carol Gilligan and others have shown that women have a more relational and affiliational concept of self. We are less likely than men to be disinterested in the situations of others and social ties are ends in themselves and not the means to individualistic ends. By virtue of his assumptions, it is clear that Rawls' "rational man" is a man. He fails to consider what women in the original position might choose. The very foundation of [Rawls'] legal theory is considerably weakened when it is realized that it has excluded the preferences of half the population.

"Reasonable Man"

The most important concept in law, its standard of the objective, excludes from its ambit women's conduct except in those instances where such conduct in a given situation would be the same as that of men. Dolores Donovan and Stephanie Wildman analyze the idea of the "reasonable man" in the criminal law context of self-defense and provocation.

(i) The Maleness of Legal Language

They concluded that the standard of the "reasonable man" applies only to white middle class male techniques for self-defence and reactions to provocation. The standard fails to account, for example, for any behaviour that may be described as culturally female. Similarly, Leslie Bender reviews the standard of care required in tort negligence law, that of the "reasonable person". She too concludes that this is another example of male naming and acceptance of the implicit male norm.

It should be clear that we cannot resolve the problem of androcentricity implicit in the notion of the reasonable man simply by changing the standard from that of the reasonable man to that of the reasonable person. This nominal change will not, by itself, make the concept more flexible and inclusive. While this is a necessary first step, there must also be a recognition by those using and applying the standard of the built-in bias of the present [masculinist] reasonable man standard and an understanding that the new standard requires that we view situations from different perspectives.

The problems that have been noted in relation to the use of male pronouns and generics amount to much more than an annoying use of language. Such usage leads to serious ambiguities. Because the legal register prides itself on clarity and precision, this reason alone should be sufficient to radically reform the practice. But more insidiously, the use of "he" and "man" and other unmarked generic forms also conceals an inherent bias in favour of the "male as norm" while hiding under the guise of a neutral inquiry. Once this bias is revealed, as for example in the case of Rawls' "rational man", the very foundation of certain ideas becomes questionable. Or, as happens with the example of the "ordinary citizen" and the "reasonable man", the exclusion of women, in situations where it might be different from that of men, may pervert the formation of a legal principle such as the rules on prostitution or provocation.

Solutions to the problems of gender exclusivity and ambiguity arising in relation to pronouns and generics are not easy to find given both the pervasiveness of the problem and the unwillingness of many women and men to recognize that a problem exists. But the starting point must be an identification and understanding of the sexist effects of a linguistic practice. This foundation helps us to recognize when a particular usage has sexist implications.

LEXICON AND SEMANTICS

Mary Daly has said that we have inherited a contaminated language. Dale Spender states that every meaning is man-made and inevitably encodes a male point of view which is at odds with women's experiences. In this part I will simply describe, by way of example, how the lexicon and semantics differentiate between men and women. In particular, I will consider the systematic devaluation of words associated with women, the use and effects of sexual stereotypes, how some metaphorical concepts personify or alienate women, the sexist etymology of some words and the need for new words to describe women's experiences. As will be seen, the observations of Daly and Spender have some truth in the context of the legal register.

Systematic Semantic Derogation

Consider the meanings associated with each word in these word dichotomies: bachelor/spinster; governor/governess; master/mistress; courtier/courtesan; king/queen; baron/dame; and sir/madame. Even the same words have different meanings depending on the sex of the referent: he is a professional/she is a professional; he is a tramp/she is a tramp. The idea of Holmes' "bad man" takes on a different connotation if he becomes, instead, a "bad woman". In *every* case, the female side of the dichotomy has an additional meaning that either has a negative sexual connotation or assumes female subservience. In the absence of the male counterpart, some of the words are best known in the devalued sense, for example, mistress and dame. I cannot think of any dichotomies in which the female word has not been assigned a devalued meaning; the same is not true of the male words.

It has often been said that male qualities include rationality, objectivity, detachment, abstraction, control, principles, aggressiveness, ambition, and autonomy. Notice that many of these words are also used to describe the desirable traits of the law. Women, on the other hand, are emotional, subjective, attached, contextual, spontaneous, personal, passive, supportive and compassionate. Few of these words could be used to describe the law.

If a woman embodies male characteristics, a less valued or devalued word will be substituted for the more positive word used in relation to men: scheming, political, cold, conjectured, manipulative, aggressive, ambitious and selfish. (Note that words like aggressive and ambitious can have very different meanings depending on the sex of the referent.) Finally when female characteristics are attributed to a man the word used will not have a less valued connotation as happens when male characteristics are attributed to women. Rather, these words will often be positive: uninhibited, open minded, loyal, practical, easy going, contemplative, committed and considerate.

Perhaps it could be said that the examples offered so far express sexism through purely emotive meanings and while the prescription would involve a reassessment of usage, there is nothing of particular linguistic interest in the examples. I think such an observation would be incorrect for it would ignore that it is the *female* side which is systematically devalued. If it can be said that there is a "process of systematic semantic derogation of words associated with women," then sexism as reflected in language cuts much deeper than emotive meaning. Spender has observed that *all* words associated with women acquire negative connotations because there is a "fundamental semantic 'rule' in our society that constructs male supremacy."

I think these examples raise several other questions, including: why has the male set of characteristics become personified in the law and the female side regarded as the opposite of what law ought to be? Is Fran Olsen correct in asserting that the law has a sex? What are the implications of gendered character attribution on women in the profession of law? While these are interesting and important questions, they are beyond the scope of this paper.

Stereotypes

Since virtually all the references to human beings in the texts used in legal philosophy seminars are to men, specific references to women attract special attention. Just how am I represented in the casebook? With the sole exception of Kent Greenawalt's reference to a female law teacher and a female villager, all the women in the materials are cultural stereotypes. (However, Greenawalt's women are given the suggestive names of Constance and Faith.) There are sex crime victims, wives (but few husbands) and prostitutes. There is Oliver Holmes' Mrs. Quickly who "would be sure to dwell upon [a client's white hat] along with the parcel gilt goblet and the seacoal fire" rather than the contents of a contract. The implicit message is that women are silly. Next we have Greenawalt's beauty contestants who are judged by men and juxtaposed against the example of "five experienced men". While the reference to the men is necessary because he is discussing Dworkin's reference to the same class, the example of beauty contestants in this context makes the objectivication of women even more apparent. The implicit message is that women are to stand around being pretty while men work.

Ronald Dworkin provides the most examples of women in stereotyped roles. The child who needs to be bussed to school is a girl. Does he use feminine pronouns when speaking of children to reinforce the idea of women as childlike? The archetype for his judge is the Greek hero, Hercules, a curious choice given the more appropriate archetype, Athena, the Greek goddess of justice. Does he doubt the intellectual or rational capacity of women? While men are never afforded courtesy titles, "Mrs. MacPherson" is never described simply as "MacPherson." What could be the possible relevance of her marital status in a legal text?

Finally Dworkin refers to "the timid lady on the streets of Chicago [who] is not entitled to just the degree of quiet that now obtains." Why does he refer to her as "timid" when his style is otherwise free of gratuitous adjectives? Are we to assume that the gender specific reference is relevant and contributes to understanding? By referring to her as a "lady", a word which suggests a certain delicacy, and implying that her concerns are trivial (the noise), is he also commenting on the nature of women? This reference appears in a section on the enforcement of personal rights. Does he use a woman to describe the situations in which personal rights would not prevail because her sex facilitates somehow in understanding his point?

The stereotypes and linguistic structure that Dworkin uses reflects and expresses the roles, purposes and ideologies he ascribes to his subjects just as much as his more apparent content. According to Dworkin, we are childlike, dependent, passive and trite.

Undoubtedly there are stereotypical portraits of men in the seminar materials, but on the whole the range of characteristics attributed to the men represented is broader than the narrow range attributed to women. In a more equal world, the use of stereotypes would not threaten women because the assigned role would be recognized only for its usefulness in a particular context. But as matters now stand, sexual stereotypes reinforce the idea of the limited potential of women by describing them as unintelligent, dependent, passive objects. The systematic use of stereotypes conditions people to believe that women are not capable of doing things.

Metaphors

The use of metaphors, the experience of one thing in terms of another, is pervasive and affects not only how we speak but also how we think and act. The purpose of metaphors is to facilitate

(i) The Maleness of Legal Language

understanding by describing those things that are unknown or difficult to describe in terms of things we know. The assumption is that the person receiving the information knows and understands the original reference in the same sense as the person communicating the information.

Consider for example, the metaphorical concept of WOMEN AS SEXUAL OBJECT as used in legal discourse: "piercing the corporate veil" and "raping the corporation". These notions have to do with control or dominance in the legal sense. The attribution of femaleness to the corporate body facilitates a male conceptualization of the action being described. Rawls may have been using a variation of this metaphorical concept when he speaks of the "veil of ignorance" in developing his notion of the original position. When covered by the veil and therefore on the female side, his subjects are unreal and unknowing; life only truly exists on the other side of the veil. In relying on these metaphorical concepts, the legal register perpetuates the idea of women as passive, submissive and ignorant.

George Lakoff gives a particularly frightening analysis of the relationship between our metaphors for anger and for lust and notes that these metaphors often overlap. For example, ANGER IS HEAT (i.e., I was boiling with anger) and LUST IS HEAT (i.e., you are hot). He states that the connection between these two metaphors has important social consequences as that they enter our reasoning: anger and lust come to be seen as the same thing. Lakoff concludes that these metaphors actually provide a rationale for rape.

Another metaphorical concept well known to the legal register is ARGUMENT AS WAR. Consider the following examples:

i) her defence is weak
ii) he attacked this argument
iii) you can never beat them

The structure of the disagreements as created by the metaphorical concept also dictates the process or how those in the argument will act. Arguments, especially legal arguments, are seen as adversarial and often violent with clear victors and victims. Because women have been socialized to avoid conflict and seek reconciliation and harmony, the pervasive use of ARGUMENT AS WAR alienates women from participation in legal discourse and entrenches a patriarchal or male perspective on legal reasoning and method.

We could of course conceive of argument in a different way. Consider the metaphorical concept of ARGUMENT AS DANCE:

i) his argument does not jive
ii) she never misses a beat
iii) that leads me to

In my view, ARGUMENT AS DANCE creates a structure of agreement and cooperation and embraces the idea of a process that leads to a mutually satisfying conclusion. In one legal philosophy seminar we consciously attempted to use ARGUMENT AS DANCE instead of ARGUMENT AS WAR in our discussion. Most people felt a real change in the dynamics of our interaction. We were less antagonistic and more willing to listen to each other. Tensions that had existed dissolved or at least were dealt with in a positive, constructive way.

Finally, I would like to consider the pervasive use of sport analogies in legal discourse. Llewellyn, Dworkin and Hart liken law to a baseball game. This does not assist those who are unfamiliar with the rules of the game or those who are uncomfortable with participation in sports in understanding the ideas being discussed. The analogy of sport as law excludes many women (and some men) from participation in the discourse and thereby limits its utility. If you have trouble seeing this point, consider how you might feel if a common metaphorical concept in law was CONTRACT AS RECIPE.

We should not view metaphors as a matter of mere language. When we use a metaphor to describe something, the metaphor and the thing become one: woman becomes object, sex becomes anger, argument becomes war and law becomes a game. Each of these metaphors has the effect of oppressing women by objectifying or alienating us, by structuring and legitimating violent actions or by excluding us from the discourse.

Etymology and Word Creation

The study of etymology yields some interesting examples of the connection between language and gender. It was a Jewish custom (and remains an Arabic custom) for men to swear mutual oaths by placing a hand on each other's testicles. Words like testament, testify and testimony find their root in this custom. Women would have been precluded from making such oaths. The word 'rape' once simply meant to steal or to plunder; the victim was not the raped woman but rather it was her father or husband who was thought to have lost something. But while etymology reveals examples of practices that once clearly suppressed women, it may be difficult to prove that the root meanings of words continues to affect the discourse today. Therefore I simply offer these examples and leave it to someone else to discover whether these word histories have a deeper continuing significance.

A more serious problem arises in connection with those experiences for which no descriptive word exists. Without a word to describe an experience, it might be difficult to imagine that the experience has a basis in reality. For example, in her classic feminist work *The Feminine Mystique*, Betty Friedan identifies "the problem that has no name." The problem, briefly, is the lack of utility attached to the work that homemakers do and the resulting frustration they feel. What word describes what homemakers do? When I refer to it as 'work' I am usually misunderstood. Friedan's problem is still unnamed.

The legal register "places great stress upon the legal signifier or legal word as an entity in itself." Therefore, the birth of new words to describe experiences better known to women is important to recognition by the legal system of these experiences when appropriate. "Sexual harassment" and "sexism" are examples of words conceived by feminists that have gradually received wider acceptance. These words have now been accepted into the legal register and have become legal entities with legal consequences. On the other hand, the legal register seems to have adopted the signifier "surrogate mother" to describe a woman who agrees to conceive and bear a child for its biological father. The word "surrogate" detracts from the fact that she is also the biological mother of the child by suggesting that she is external to the process.

Of particular interest are the semantic implications of the expressions "domestic violence" and "wife battering". Why has the expression "domestic violence" prevailed in usage over "wife battering"? The former names neither the wife, nor by implication, the husband; it suggests that the problem is private (and therefore outside the realm of the law) and, as violence is a prevailing problem in our society anyway, there may be the suggestion that this is nothing special. "Wife battering" names the survivor, implicates the criminal and describes the crime that has been committed. The development of the term "domestic violence" itself was an important step in the broader societal recognition of the tragedy of men beating women in the home. Ultimately, however, the term is not strong enough to describe the true dynamics of most situations.

Feminists use the word 'survivor' to describe and empower those adults who have been subject to sexual abuse as children and who continue to bear the emotional and physical scars of that abuse. This word is not, however, widely used outside feminist circles. Perhaps as information on the continuing effects of child sexual abuse is more widely available, the word 'survivor' will also become better known. Should this happen, perhaps this word will join 'sexual harassment' and 'sexism' in the legal register. Survivors might then be eligible for compensation for the abuse suffered. But without a discrete word such as 'survivor' to serve as the legal entity, it would seem less likely that the experience will be seen as one deserving legal redress.

The problems noted in relation to the lexicon and semantics are of a different sort than those that arise in connection with the use of male pronouns and false generics. They are less obvious as their offensiveness is not in isolated usage but rather in their systematic insidiousness. Further, whereas male pronouns and generics conceal an androcentric bias, the semantics of the legal register can be seen as more thoroughly misogynist. The words used to describe women construct an ideal of subservience or sexual usefulness. The roles we are ascribed and the language used to describe legal processes impliedly express accord with patriarchal political values. The consequence is the exclusion of women as actors in the legal system except in very narrowly prescribed roles.

. . . .

TOWARDS A CONCLUSION

Ever since I began studying law, I have had a growing uncomfortableness about what the language of legal discourse seems to say or imply about me as woman. But like most good women law students I avoided raising these issues because they did not seem to be quite on point: language was not a legal problem. When I returned to law school to do a master of law degree and had the opportunity to write a more theoretical paper rather than a paper on doctrine, language seemed an obvious choice. My original plan was to pull together a list of examples from the legal texts — a sort of glossary — and let their obviousness speak for itself.

The paper is well on its way to achieving its original plan, although that has now become its first goal. While the list of examples can be expanded and improved upon, I have said enough to show that the legal discourse systematically excludes, devalues, trivializes and ignores women. Obviously there will be disagreement with what I have and have not included. Hopefully, a dialogue will continue. For now, I will begin to formulate some conclusions.

(i) The Maleness of Legal Language

Deborah Cameron has said that like a wolf whistle, a sexist remark has significance beyond the immediate offence it gives. Not only is it a manifestation of an unacceptable misogyny but it is also the mechanism by which misogyny is constructed and transmitted. One can hope that the worst stereotypes are behind us now. This statement is probably too optimistic, however, as long as expressions like "raping the corporation" are current and if law professors continue to insist in classroom dialogues to refer to women only as wives or sex crime victims. This language so fundamentally alienates women that we cannot participate in the discourse without first denying ourselves.

The original emphasis in writings on women and language focused on "non-sexist" language. Simply stated, writers were to substitute sex-specific terms with generic terms. As was noted earlier, the exclusive use of unmarked masculine pronouns and generics has the effect of excluding women from the readers' mental landscape. Such an exclusion leads to an androcentric view of the world: women are invisible and irrelevant.

By making the important switch to non-sexist language, women come into focus. This is an important first step. There is, however, a problem with thinking that if we use the pronouns "he" and "she" interchangeably and if we refer to policemen as police officers, no further change or analysis is required. Inherent in such a reformist theory is that we ought to reduce some forms of oppression and then, by implication, we legitimate the remaining forms. We must also refuse to accept stultifying stereotypes and alienating metaphors. We need to examine word choices for sexist semantic implications. Non-sexist language also requires that expressions used to describe women have a parallel meaning when used in reference to men. For example, if we speak of a "working mother" we should speak also of a "working father".

The obvious intent of these kinds of changes is to ensure that the content of legal discourse is changed to ensure the inclusion of women. I have stated in this paper that language contributes very significantly to androcentricity in law. We cannot assume that androcentricity is avoided by substituting "reasonable person" for "reasonable man". While the kinds of changes in language that I suggested help change how women are perceived in the legal system, law makers must then be willing to adopt new perspectives that come with that change. Otherwise the end effect will simply make women into honorary men. Analogical reasoning — the meta-metaphor — will bind the law to androcentricity unless lawmakers struggle against it.

There is a problem with stopping at a prescription for non-sexist language. If we use a generic term to describe a sex specific situation, another form of sexism is created. Thus, even if Rawls' "rational man" was styled as a "rational person," this character would still be a man. However, now that fact would be even less apparent. The language that we use must be sensitive to gender when the sex of the referent is a socially significant variable.

In this paper I have tried to show how finely sexist usage is woven into the fabric of legal language. Many of these problems can be redressed by using non-sexist language. However, some problems such as the problems associated with semantics and syntax, require a more heightened sensitivity to their oppressive effect because of the social construction of dominance by men. This sensitivity requires that we probe deeply into meaning. What is not being said? What actors are not named? What are readers being encouraged to imply? Is male dominance encouraged or assumed?

The elimination of sexist language is critical to the elimination of sexism. The first step is to understand how it is expressed in language. To paraphrase Richard Scrutton, each of us inherits in language the sexism of many generations. To rehabilitate this repository of human experience is to alter our most fundamental perceptions. Finally, we must care about what we say and be willing always to challenge, monitor, and change our language.

(ii) Native Culture on Trial

Louise Mandell

Introduction

Several months ago, when I was talking to an Indian elder about the evidence he was to give in a hunting trial, I became concerned that court might be starting momentarily. I asked whether anyone knew the time and the old man replied: "It's almost summer."

The first task in advancing cases involving aboriginal rights through Canadian courts is to make the different world view of the Indian Nations visible.

Judges have a greater responsibility than other professionals to understand Indian world views and property definitions. This is especially so today because since the recent entrenchment of aboriginal and treaty rights in the Constitution Indian Nations are looking to the courts for assistance in righting the wrongs of the past and in shaping their relationship with Canada. Yet in general, judges have no better knowledge than the general public and arguably, as a group, they suffer from a somewhat poorer exposure to the day-to-day life and struggle of the Indian Nations. It can therefore be expected that certain judges will fail to appreciate the history and aspirations of the Indian Nations.

A brief examination of several leading cases illustrates some of the central difficulties facing Indian Nations in their efforts to enforce recognition of their rights through the courts. The cases show the difficulty some judges have experienced in overcoming their learned biases. This paper will demonstrate this point by canvassing judicial reaction and decisions to legal questions of aboriginal title, definitions of aboriginal property rights, recognition of aboriginal religion, and the legal debate involving the extinguishment of aboriginal title.

Judicial Decisions in Relation to Aboriginal Property Rights

The Supreme Court of Canada has placed the onus of proof on the Indian Nations in cases where the Nation asserts an existing title. The onus shifts to the Indians because of an initial assumption that the Crown's "discovery" of this continent (which had been occupied for thousands of years by the Indian Nations) gave it rights to the soil. Alternatively, the assertion is that the Crown conquered the Indian Nations by exercising jurisdiction over the territory. The result of this manifestly arrogant assertion of power is that the courts have said that the extent of Indian title depends upon the degree to which the Nation traditionally possessed their lands. In *Kruger v. R.*, Mr. Justice Dickson said that proof of aboriginal title will be decided when title is directly in issue:

> Interested parties should be afforded an opportunity to adduce evidence in detail bearing upon the resolution of the particular dispute. Claims to aboriginal title are woven with history, legend, politics and moral obligations. If the claim of any Band in respect of any particular land is to be decided as a justiciable issue and not a political issue, it should be so considered on the facts pertinent to that Band and to that land, and not on any global basis.

The Indian elders in British Columbia question why they must subject their relationship to the land to a non-Indian court's strict scrutiny: why they must explain their use of the land to obtain "rights" abstractly defined by others. They believe that the Indians have rights to their land because their people go back with the land for thousands of years. What they do not understand is how the Crown acquired its "rights" to their land.

An example of the Indians' misunderstanding occurred during the course of taking commission evidence in a land claims case presently advancing through the courts in British Columbia. Lawyers for the Crown cross-examined an elder for many days on the extent of his hunting, fishing, trapping and berry-picking practices throughout his territory. The plaintiffs had originally advanced evidence to prove that an aboriginal title was established by these activities. The elder turned to the Crown's lawyers and asked

---

From Sheilah Martin and Kathleen Mahoney, eds., *Equality and Judicial Neutrality* (Toronto: Carswell, 1987), at 358–65. Notes omitted. Reproduced by permission of Carswell, a division of Thomson Canada Limited.

whether the Queen had ever been questioned on whether she had ever shot a deer in his territory and if not, how does she claim her right to his land.

Notwithstanding the inherent problems with where the onus of proof is placed, many Nations, when trying to discharge this burden of proof, find that judges do not recognize their legitimate relationship to the land. In those cases the courts tend to evaluate traditional Indian customs against their own modern non-Indian values. This problem was fatal to the way of life of aborigines in Australia when a court would not give legal weight to Indian concepts of property. In the case of *Milirrpum v. Nabalco Party Ltd. and Commonwealth of Australia* the Indians alleged that they had a legal property right in lands they traditionally used and occupied. The action was brought to stop a mining operation which threatened to harm traditional lands. The plaintiffs introduced complex evidence on their social rules and customs to establish that they had proprietary legal rights in the land. The judge described the Indians' relationships to the land as follows:

> As I understand it, the fundamental truth about the aboriginals' relationship to the land is that whatever else it is, it is a religious relationship ... the physical and spiritual universes are not felt as distinct. There is an unquestioned scheme of things in which the spirit ancestors, the people of the clan, particular land and everything that exists on and in it, are organic parts of one indissoluble whole ... it is not in dispute that each clan regards itself as a spiritual entity having a spiritual relationship to particular places or areas, and having a duty to care for and tend that land by means of ritual observances.

After examining this evidence the judge found it showed:

> A subtle and elaborate system highly adapted to the country in which the people lead their lives which provided a stable order of society and was remarkably free from the vagaries of personal whim or influence. If ever a system could be called a "government of laws, and not of men", it is shown in the evidence before me.

Despite these observations the judge decided that the Indians had no proprietary interest in their lands. He concluded:

> In my view, the proper procedure is to bear in mind the concepts of "property" in our law, and in what I know of how other systems which have the concept, as well as my understanding permits, and look at the aboriginal system to find what there corresponds to or resembles "property".

> In my opinion, therefore, there is so little resemblance between property, as our law, or what I know of any other law, understands that term, and the claims of the plaintiffs for their clans, that I must hold that these claims are not in the nature of proprietary interests.

The judge ruled against the Indian Nations because the Indian view of property was different from that of the colonizers. The result was their traditional lands could be mined, notwithstanding the destruction mining would bring to their way of life.

Judicial Reactions to Aboriginal Religious Values

An example of bias in religious values in a Canadian court is the recent case of *Anderson Jack v. R.*, where the Supreme Court of Canada displayed its incapacity to recognize and give legal force and effect to Indian religious beliefs and practices. The case involved two Indian men who were charged under a provincial Wildlife Act with hunting deer out of season. The hunting took place as part of an ancient traditional ceremony where food is burned for the benefit of deceased relatives. Dr. Barbara Lane, an anthropologist, explained the religious practice to the court:

> Well, this is a very ancient traditional practice among all Coast Salish people and the essence of the ceremony is to provide food for deceased relatives by burning it and the essence of the food, as I understand it, is transmitted through the smoke to the essence of the deceased person.

Many witnesses told the court how this practice of burning expresses the world view of the Coast Salish people. These explanations were summarized by Judge Taggart of the Court of Appeal of British Columbia and repeated in the judgment of Mr. Justice Beetz of the Supreme Court of Canada:

> The religious ceremony was described by witnesses who were members of the Tsartlip Band and by Dr. Barbara Lane. Dr. Lane is an anthropologist who since 1948 has studied the Coast Salish people and especially their religious beliefs and practices. She said that the Coast Salish people were believed to have lived in British Columbia for about 20,000 years. The Coast Salish believe that members of their people who die do not go to another world but that their spirits remain close to where they lived. The belief is that the spirits have the same kinds of needs and desires as living people. Dr. Lane explained the belief in this way:

They become lonely and want to visit their relatives, they become hungry and want to have the kind of foods that they had before, and they have desires for other things that they've left behind here, and they transmit these desires to their close relatives through dreams and other kinds of experiences, and these needs are satisfied and the desires of the deceased relatives are met by the living providing to them the things that they request....

As I was attempting to suggest earlier, the entire world view of Coast Salish Indian people is quite different from that which those of us who are raised in the Judeo-Christian tradition have. Coast Salish Indian people perceive of the world as an intimately inter-related phenomenon in which the living and the dead animals and humans, all things are intimately connected and belong together in this place and do not leave it. And the function of burning food for the dead is to carry on the mutual responsibilities and respect that Indian people here try to accord to all of the other parts of the world as they see it. One of the things that always seems to be incomprehensible to Indian people is how the rest of us can pick ourselves up from one part of the world and move to another and abandon and cut ourselves off from our dead relatives because they perceive of themselves as being in continuous association with and having ongoing responsibilities to the dead.

The hunt took place to assist Elizabeth Jack, the wife of the defendant Anderson Jack and the sister of the defendant George Louie Charlie. Elizabeth Jack had conducted a burning at Christmas in 1977 for her dead great-grandfather. At that burning, she burnt potatoes, hamburger, Indian bread and clams. During the burning, her dead relative communicated through her father, a Shaman, Louie Charlie, that the great-grandfather wanted raw deer meat.

Elizabeth Jack became very sick. She believed her sickness was a reaction to her not having satisfied the wishes of her dead relative for raw deer meat. She went to Louie Charlie for assistance. The power to do the work done by Louie Charlie and perform burnings is handed down from one generation to another. Burnings are considered to be a sacred practice and each burning must be done at set times and by special people who are recognized as able to do the work.

Louie Charlie gave evidence that his instructions must be carried out and exercised precisely, otherwise the family doing the burning would continue to be troubled. Louie Charlie directed Elizabeth and the defendants to hunt deer at Pender Island, an old hunting place of the Saanich People. Elizabeth Jack gave evidence that the deer came forth to be burned for her great-grandfather:

> Then we saw one there, standing, and they wouldn't do anything about it, and I told them, "Well, there it is, it's just standing there, in the grass, like, you can see it clear." So I told them, "That's the one I want, I got to have it, because I want to feed my grandparents." ... Then he looked at us, my brother looked at us, and then he aim, and he was still standing there, so he shot it, and it just dropped there ... then we went back in the camp there, we cleaned it out and all that and I told him, "You have to bury the head", and all that, the guts and things like that. So they did.

Later that morning wildlife officers stopped the hunters, seized the deer, and charged the hunters with offences under the Wildlife Act.

At trial, the Provincial Court judge accepted that the accused were sincere and that the burning practice had its roots in religious practice going back at least 20,000 years. However, he subjected the hunting to the rules of the Wildlife Act, finding that the policy of the Wildlife Act did not impair the defendants' status and capacity as Indians:

> ...if Indians wish to exercise their historic religious practices there are ways within the bounds of the Provincial Statute in which to exercise those religious practices. They can, for example, retain a supply of deer meat in storage for such purposes ... the purpose of the Act is what matters. This Act is being held to be and is, clearly I think, of general application and was certainly not aimed at preventing the Coast Salish from exercising any religious practice. The act of burning food as an offering to the spirit of an ancestor is not prohibited. If it is exercised within the limits of the general law it may be freely carried out by the Sannich people.

On Appeal, the County Court judge found against the accused on another footing. The court distinguished between religious belief and religious practice and said that although freedom of religion protects religious belief, religious practices must be exercised within the limits of law. The British Columbia Court of Appeal divided on the question. The majority judgment agreed with the County Court and held that: "freedom of religion must be exercised within the limits permitted by validly enacted legislation...." The court also said that the Wildlife Act must be directed against Indian religion in its policy in order for the courts to hold that it does not apply to Indians. The court refused to accept the argument that the *effect* of the Wildlife Act was to prevent and prohibit the religious practices of the Indians.

In dissent Mr. Justice Hutcheon held:

> The issue in this case is whether Anderson Jack and George Louie Charlie were guilty of an offense when they hunted and killed a deer out of season. The hunting and killing was part of a religious ritual of the Coast Salish people of 20,000 years duration. The ritual is not harmful to society, is not opposed to the common good and is not in violation of the rights of any other individual. I have concluded that they were not guilty of an offense and that this appeal should be allowed. There is no suggestion that the loss of one deer for the purpose of the ritual would impair the legislative purpose. I think that the freedom of religion of Jack and Charlie ought not to be taken away by the application of an enactment of general application in the absence of evidence of some compelling justification.... In my opinion, the Wildlife Act ought to be read so as to acknowledge the right of Jack and Charlie on these facts to practise their religion where no compelling interest of society exists.

An argument raised for the first time before the Supreme Court of Canada by the province of British Columbia was that the hunting itself was not a religious practice. The Supreme Court of Canada agreed, holding that there was nothing in the evidence to suggest that the hunting and killing of the deer on Pender Island was part of a religious ritual. The court agreed with the trial judge who said that the Wildlife Act did not interfere with the religion of the people because it was possible to use stored or frozen deer meat for the burning. It is significant that although the judges could envision a proper burning with stored deer meat, the Indians could not.

The court also failed to consider that the preparation for the burning was considered by the Indians as a sacred quest directed by the Shaman's strict instructions. It is evident in the following quote analogizing the obtaining of the meat with the obtaining of sacramental wine:

> No clergyman could raise a defence based on religious freedom, to a charge of obtaining wine illegally while liquor stores were closed, simply because it was intended to use the wine for the sacrament of Holy Communion. Similarly a defence based on "freedom of religion" must fail the Appellants in this case, where the charge is killing a deer in the closed season. Since killing the deer is not, in itself, ceremonial, the *actus reus* of the offence cannot be regarded as a religious observance. If it is not such an observance, then logically, its prohibition by the Wildlife Act raises no question of religious freedom.

The reasoning suggests that if the Indian practice more closely paralleled Judeo-Christian religious practices and if some overt act, such as the saying of a prayer, took place when the deer was shot, that kind of evidence would flag to the courts a religious ceremony worthy of judicial protection. By defining religion as a ceremony and ignoring or refusing to give weight to the evidence of the Indian people which described the religious practice as understood and as practised by them, the Supreme Court of Canada set itself as the judge of Indian religious orthodoxy and then failed to understand the evidence which described the essence of the religious practices and beliefs.

. . . .

Conclusion

Since the enactment of the Constitution Act, 1982, which entrenches aboriginal and treaty rights, Indian Nations are increasingly turning to the courts to compel governments to negotiate just land claims. But it is questionable whether the courts can or should settle issues involving aboriginal rights. Relations between Nations is certainly a political matter. However, courts could have a role in building the foundation for meaningful political negotiations between the Indian Nations and the Crown.

Judges hearing cases such as those discussed above must not only be sensitive to their own biases, but they must also hear evidence before them with open minds so that they can understand another world view as it is understood by the Indians. Without such judicial sensitivity, judges will fail to protect the rights Indians say are necessary for their survival. Should the courts fail in this responsibility, future negotiations with governments regarding native rights will be jeopardized.

(iii) *Delgamuukw* v. *B.C.*

(2) Application of General Principles

(a) General Comments

The general principle of appellate non-interference applies with particular force in this appeal. The trial was lengthy and very complex. There were 318 days of testimony. There were a large number of witnesses, lay and expert. The volume of evidence is enormous. To quote the trial judge at pp. 116–17:

> A total of 61 witnesses gave evidence at trial, many using translators from their native Gitksan or Wet'suwet'en language; "word spellers" to assist the official reporters were required for many witnesses; a further 15 witnesses gave their evidence on commission; 53 territorial affidavits were filed; 30 deponents were cross-examined out of court; there are 23,503 pages of transcript evidence at trial; 5898 pages of transcript of argument; 3,039 pages of commission evidence and 2,553 pages of cross-examination on affidavits (all evidence and oral arguments are conveniently preserved in hard copy and on diskettes); about 9,200 exhibits were filed at trial comprising, I estimate, well over 50,000 pages; the plaintiffs' draft outline of argument comprises 3,250 pages, the province's 1,975 pages, and Canada's over 1,000 pages; there are 5,977 pages of transcript of argument in hard copy and on diskettes. All parties filed some excerpts from the exhibits they referred to in argument. The province alone submitted 28 huge binders of such documents. At least 15 binders of reply argument were left with me during that stage of the trial.

The result was a judgment of over 400 pages in length.

It is not open to the appellants to challenge the trial judge's findings of fact merely because they disagree with them. I fear that a significant number of the appellants' objections fall into this category. Those objections are too numerous to list in their entirety. The bulk of these objections, at best, relate to alleged instances of misapprehension or oversight of material evidence by the trial judge. However, the respondents have established that, in most situations, there was *some* contradictory evidence that supported the trial judge's conclusion. The question, ultimately, was one of weight, and the appellants have failed to demonstrate that the trial judge erred in this respect.

One objection that I would like to mention specifically, albeit in passing, is the trial judge's refusal to accept the testimony of two anthropologists who were brought in as expert witnesses by the appellants. This aspect of the trial judge's reasons was hotly contested by the appellants in their written submissions. However, I need only reiterate what I have stated above, that findings of credibility, including the credibility of expert witnesses, are for the trial judge to make, and should warrant considerable deference from appellate courts.

On the other hand, the appellants have alleged that the trial judge made a number of serious errors relating to the treatment of the oral histories of the appellants. Those oral histories were expressed in three different forms: (i) the adaawk of the Gitksan, and the kungax of the Wet'suwet'en; (ii) the personal recollections of members of the appellant nations, and (iii) the territorial affidavits filed by the heads of the individual houses within each nation. The trial judge ruled on both the admissibility of, and the weight to be given to, these various forms of oral history without the benefit of my reasons in *Van der Peet*, as will become evident in the discussion that follows.

(b) Adaawk and Kungax

The adaawk and kungax of the Gitksan and Wet'suwet'en nations, respectively are oral histories of a special kind. They were described by the trial judge, at p. 164, as a "sacred 'official' litany, or history, or recital of the most important laws, history, traditions and traditional territory of a House". The content of these special oral histories includes its physical representation totem poles, crests and blankets. The importance of the adaawk and kungax is underlined by the fact that they are "repeated, performed and authenticated at important feasts" (at p. 164). At those feasts, dissenters have the opportunity to object if they question any detail and, in this way, help ensure the authenticity of the adaawk and kungax. Although they serve largely the same role,

---

[1997] 3 S.C.R. 1010 at 1070–79, per Lamer C.J.

(iii) Delgamuukw v. B.C.

the trial judge found that there are some differences in both the form and content of the adaawk and the kungax. For example, the latter is "in the nature of a song ... which is intended to represent the special authority and responsibilities of a chief...." However, these differences are not legally relevant for the purposes of the issue at hand.

It is apparent that the adaawk and kungax are of integral importance to the distinctive cultures of the appellant nations. At trial, they were relied on for two distinct purposes. First, the adaawk was relied on as a component of and, therefore, as proof of the existence of a system of land tenure law internal to the Gitksan, which covered the whole territory claimed by that appellant. In other words, it was offered as evidence of the Gitksan's historical use and occupation of that territory. For the Wet'suwet'en, the kungax was offered as proof of the central significance of the claimed lands to their distinctive culture. As I shall explain later in these reasons, both use and occupation, and the central significance of the lands occupied, are relevant to proof of aboriginal title.

The admissibility of the adaawk and kungax was the subject of a general decision of the trial judge handed down during the course of the trial regarding the admissibility of all oral histories (incorrectly indexed as *Uukw v. R.*, [1987] 6 W.W.R. 155 (B.C.S.C.)). Although the trial judge recognized that the evidence at issue was a form of hearsay, he ruled it admissible on the basis of the recognized exception that declarations made by deceased persons could be given in evidence by witnesses as proof of public or general rights: see Michael N. Howard, Peter Crane and Daniel A. Hochberg, *Phipson on Evidence* (14th ed. 1990), at p. 736. He affirmed that earlier ruling in his trial judgment, correctly in my view, by stating, at p. 180, that the adaawk and kungax were admissible "out of necessity as exceptions to the hearsay rule" because there was no other way to prove the history of the Gitksan and Wet'suwet'en nations.

The trial judge, however, went on to give these oral histories no independent weight at all. He held, at p. 180, that they were only admissible as "direct evidence of facts in issue ... in a few cases where they could constitute confirmatory proof of early presence in the territory". His central concern [was] that the adaawk and kungax could not serve "as evidence of detailed history, or land ownership, use or occupation". I disagree with some of the reasons he relied on in support of this conclusion.

Although he had earlier recognized, when making his ruling on admissibility, that it was impossible to make an easy distinction between the mythological and "real" aspects of these oral histories, he discounted the adaawk and kungax because they were not "literally true", confounded "what is fact and what is belief", "included some material which might be classified as mythology", and projected a "romantic view" of the history of the appellants. He also cast doubt on the authenticity of these special oral histories (at p. 181) because, *inter alia*, "the verifying group is so small that they cannot safely be regarded as expressing the reputation of even the Indian community, let alone the larger community whose opportunity to dispute territorial claims would be essential to weight". Finally, he questioned (at p. 181) the utility of the adaawk and kungax to demonstrate use and occupation because they were "seriously lacking in detail about the specific lands to which they are said to relate".

Although he framed his ruling on weight in terms of the specific oral histories before him, in my respectful opinion, the trial judge in reality based his decision on some general concerns with the use of oral histories as evidence in aboriginal rights cases. In summary, the trial judge gave no independent weight to these special oral histories because they did not accurately convey historical truth, because knowledge about those oral histories was confined to the communities whose histories they were and because those oral histories were insufficiently detailed. However, as I mentioned earlier, these are features, to a greater or lesser extent, of all oral histories, not just the adaawk and kungax. The implication of the trial judge's reasoning is that oral histories should never be given any independent weight and are only useful as confirmatory evidence in aboriginal rights litigation. I fear that if this reasoning were followed, the oral histories of aboriginal peoples would be consistently and systematically undervalued by the Canadian legal system, in contradiction of the express instruction to the contrary in Van der Peet that trial courts interpret the evidence of aboriginal peoples in light of the difficulties inherent in adjudicating aboriginal claims.

(c) Recollections of Aboriginal Life

The trial judge also erred when he discounted the "recollections of aboriginal life" offered by various members of the appellant nations. I take that term to be a reference to testimony about personal and family history that is not part of an adaawk or a kungax. That evidence consisted of the personal knowledge of the witnesses and declarations of witnesses' ancestors as to land use. This history had been adduced by the appellants in order to establish the requisite degree of use and occupation to make out a claim to ownership and, for the same reason as the adaawk and kungax, is material to the proof of aboriginal title.

The trial judge limited the uses to which the evidence could be put. He reasoned, at p. 177, that this evidence, at most, established "without question, that the plaintiff's immediate ancestors, for the past 100 years or so" had used land in the claimed territory for aboriginal purposes. However, the evidence was insufficiently precise to demonstrate that the more distant ancestors of the witnesses had engaged in specific enough land use "far enough back in time to permit the plaintiffs to succeed on issues such as internal boundaries". In the language of *Van der Peet*, the trial judge effectively held that this evidence did not demonstrate the requisite continuity between present occupation and past occupation in order to ground a claim for aboriginal title.

In my opinion, the trial judge expected too much of the oral history of the appellants, as expressed in the recollections of aboriginal life of members of the appellant nations. He expected that evidence to provide definitive and precise evidence of pre-contact aboriginal activities on the territory in question. However, as I held in *Van der Peer*, this will be almost an impossible burden to meet. Rather, if oral history cannot conclusively establish pre-sovereignty (after this decision) occupation of land, it may still be relevant to demonstrate that current occupation has its origins prior to sovereignty. This is exactly what the appellants sought to do.

(d) Territorial Affidavits

Finally, the trial judge also erred in his treatment of the territorial affidavits filed by the appellant chiefs. Those affidavits were declarations of the territorial holdings of each of the Gitksan and Wet'suwet'en houses and, at trial, were introduced for the purposes of establishing each House's ownership of its specific territory. Before this Court, the appellants tried to amalgamate these individual claims into collective claims on behalf of each nation and the relevance of the affidavits changed accordingly. I have already held that it is not open to the appellants to alter fundamentally the nature of their claim in this way on appeal. Nevertheless, the treatment of the affidavits is important because they will be relevant at a new trial to the existence and nature of the land tenure system within each nation and, therefore, material to the proof of title.

The affidavits rely heavily on the declarations of deceased persons of use or ownership of the lands, which are a form of oral history. But those declarations are a kind of hearsay and the appellants therefore argued that the affidavits should be admitted through the reputation exception to the hearsay rule. Although he recognized, at p. 438, that the territorial affidavits were "the best evidence [the appellants] could adduce on this question of internal boundaries", the trial judge held that this exception did not apply and refused to admit the declarations contained in the affidavits.

I am concerned by the specific reasons the trial judge gave for refusing to apply the reputation exception. He questioned the degree to which the declarations amounted to a reputation because they were largely confined to the appellants' communities. The trial judge asserted that neighbouring aboriginal groups whose territorial claims conflicted with those of the appellants, as well as non-aboriginals who potentially possessed a legal interest in the claimed territory, were unaware of the content of the alleged reputation at all. Furthermore, the trial judge reasoned that since the subject-matter of the affidavits was disputed, its reliability was doubtful. Finally, the trial judge questioned, at p. 441, "the independence and objectivity" of the information contained in the affidavits, because the appellants and their ancestors (at p. 440) "have been actively discussing land claims for many years".

Although he regretted this finding, the trial judge felt bound to apply the rules of evidence because it did not appear to him (at p. 442) "that the Supreme Court of Canada has decided that the ordinary rules of evidence do not apply to this kind of case". The trial judge arrived at this conclusion, however, without the benefit of *Van der Peet*, where I held that the ordinary rules of evidence must be approached and adapted in light of the evidentiary difficulties inherent in adjudicating aboriginal claims.

Many of the reasons relied on by the trial judge for excluding the evidence contained in the territorial affidavits are problematic because they run against this fundamental principle. The requirement that a reputation be known in the general community, for example, ignores the fact that oral histories, as noted by the Royal Commission on Aboriginal Peoples, generally relate to particular locations, and refer to particular families and communities and may, as a result, be unknown outside of that community, even to other aboriginal nations. Excluding the territorial affidavits because the claims to which they relate are disputed does not acknowledge that claims to aboriginal rights, and aboriginal title in particular, are almost always disputed and contested. Indeed, if those claims were uncontroversial, there would be no need to bring them to the courts for resolution.

Casting doubt on the reliability of the territorial affidavits because land claims had been actively discussed for many years also fails to take account of the special context surrounding aboriginal claims, in two ways. First, those claims have been discussed for so long because of British Columbia's persistent refusal to acknowledge the existence of aboriginal title in that province until relatively recently, largely as a direct result of the decision of this Court in *Calder*, supra. It would be perverse, to say the least, to use the refusal of the province to acknowledge the rights of its aboriginal inhabitants as a reason for excluding evidence which may prove the existence of those rights. Second, this rationale for exclusion places aboriginal claimants whose societies record their past through oral history in a grave dilemma. In order for the oral history of a community to amount to a form of reputation, and to be admissible in court, it must remain alive through the discussions of members of that community; those discussions are the very basis of that reputation. But if those histories are discussed too much, and too close to the date of litigation, they may be discounted as being suspect, and may be held to be inadmissible. The net effect may be that a society with such an oral tradition would never be able to establish a historical claim through the use of oral history in court.

(e) Conclusion

The trial judge's treatment of the various kinds of oral histories did not satisfy the principles I laid down in *Van der Peet*. These errors are particularly worrisome because oral histories were of critical importance to the appellants' case. They used those histories in an attempt to establish their occupation and use of the disputed territory, an essential requirement for aboriginal title. The trial judge, after refusing to admit, or giving no independent weight to these oral histories, reached the conclusion that the appellants had not demonstrated the requisite degree of occupation for "ownership". Had the trial judge assessed the oral histories correctly, his conclusions on these issues of fact might have been very different.

In the circumstances, the factual findings cannot stand. However, given the enormous complexity of the factual issues at hand, it would be impossible for the Court to do justice to the parties by sifting through the record itself and making new factual findings. A new trial is warranted, at which the evidence may be considered in light of the principles laid down in *Van der Peet* and elaborated upon here. In applying these principles, the new trial judge might well share some or all of the findings of fact of McEachern C.J.

C. Connecting Law and Society

(i) Legal System and Society

Lawrence Friedman and Stewart Macaulay

Law is assumed to make a difference to the people and groups who are subject to it. Obviously, law as a whole does make a difference, and so, too, do particular laws and particular activities of legal officials. But the effect is not necessarily one which is deducible from a reading of the *words* of statutes and case-law. There are stringent laws in the States against sale and possession of marijuana, but more people seem to smoke marijuana all the time. Prohibition is another example of a classic problem often referred to as the "limits of legal action". The problem is classic, but so far there are no classic answers or even serious attempts at one....

That legal systems, on the other hand, reflect the larger society is undeniable. But this statement by itself is far too general to be very meaningful.

From "Preface to the First Edition" in Lawrence Friedman and Stewart Macaulay, *Law and the Behavioural Sciences*, 2nd ed. (Indianapolis: Bobbs-Merrill, 1977) at xiii, xiv. Reproduced by permission of the authors.

Here too, the problem is classic and the solutions imperfect. What people or groups influence what kinds of legal action and by what means? The reflection of society in the legal system is not easy to trace. Influences travel devious and myriad routes.

There are respects, too, in which it is useful to look at the legal system in isolation — not in the dogmatic, rule-bound isolation of conceptual jurisprudence — but as a little world in itself, a social system which demands responses, role-players, and moving parts. All systems are alike in some general characteristics. Their structures, if comparable, generate comparable internal pressures which drive them to behaviour of this or that kind. People working within a system, for example, will tend to try to make their tasks manageable and personally rewarding. What can one meaningfully say about the legal system as a system?

This does not mean that there are not properties unique to a legal system, compared to other social systems. Legal tasks are different from those undertaken by business corporations, the family or a university. Some of the properties and values of the legal system are of crucial importance to society as a whole. For example, the American legal system is, in part, organized around a set of values for which the phrase "due process" is a shorthand expression. Due process, in turn, has an important impact on American society, both in terms of actual results and as a value that percolates into other parts of the social order. What these consequences are is an important empirical question.

. . . .

...We are convinced for a variety of reasons that an integration of the study of law with social science methods and concepts is both inevitable and desirable. Classical legal research and education thought of itself as "scientific," but it took law to be a deductive science. It did not have much propensity to go out and look at the world. When this idea died (slowly), it was replaced by a new justification: the old materials were preserved, but now they were defended on the grounds that they were just the thing for the inculcation of legal method, that is, skills and habits of thought which a lawyer ought to have.... It ought to be (if one dares use the word) more *relevant* to social problems. It ought to be more empirical. There is now a good deal of emphasis on social science and empirical methods, and the trend is clearly in this direction. But elementary teaching materials for an introductory course in law and social science are badly needed.

Second, we are equally convinced that the social sciences need to study law more closely. It is a social phenomenon of great importance, and it has been unduly neglected, partly because of the insularity of legal scholarship, partly because of the insularity of the social sciences. Here too, the trend is clear: sociology of law, behavioral political science, anthropology of law, psychology and psychiatry and law, and legal economics have all received new infusions of persons and enthusiasm in the last generation. But how does the social science student enter into the legal thickets? It is possible for him to go to law school, or to take particular law school courses, but this is a wasteful method for those who do not intend to practise and who are interested only in certain aspects of the law. Again, the solution is elementary teaching materials and an introductory course in law and social science.

(ii) The New Legal Scholarship: Problems and Prospects

John Hagan

Defining the Field

Legal scholarship has changed dramatically in this century. Early in this century, legal scholarship found form and coherence in a method of study and teaching often referred to as the doctrinal approach. This approach placed its emphasis on the determina-

---

(1986) 1 CJLS/RCDS 35 at 35–37. Notes omitted. Reproduced by permission.

(ii) The New Legal Scholarship: Problems and Prospects

tion of rules, principles and procedures through the detailed analysis of cases — a method that goes back at least as far as Langdell's reforms at the Harvard Law School. There can be little debate as to the professional success of this approach to legal scholarship. It provided a method for teaching and for the writing of legal treatises and law review articles that endures to this day.

Yet if there was a purity to this methodological emphasis on "law in the books", there was also an incompleteness that led others to call for research on the "law in action". Often known as the legal realist movement, and best documented in its emergence at the Yale Law School, this approach to legal scholarship called attention to gaps between doctrine and practice. It is interesting to note that both the traditional doctrinal approach and legal realism were eager to claim the mantle of science. In doing so, the doctrinal approach focused on recorded cases as its units for observation and analysis, while the realists moved beyond these official accounts to examine the way the law actually was applied and affected people's lives. The realist's point was that the law often only affected social life indirectly and that doctrine frequently affected society in uncertain and unanticipated ways.

Today, few scholars conceive of themselves as legal realists *per se*. This is probably because there are now few legal scholars who see the "gap" between the law and the contexts in which it is applied as being as clear cut as the realists seemed once to imply. Rather, legal doctrine and the society out of which it grows are seen as intimately interconnected. That is, we now recognize that the meaning of legal rules resides not only in the internal relations of the principles and value they contain, but also in the ways rules are distributed, achieved and changed — through their career in the real world of claims, counter-claims, negotiations, arbitrations, etc. In these and other ways (made explicit below), we have entered a world of post-doctrinal scholarship that now takes the law and the contexts in which it develops as the combined focus for research.

Two distinguishable streams of work characterize post-doctrinal legal scholarship. The first stream consists of what we will call normative interpretative legal studies, and is most provocatively represented by the critical legal studies movement in prominent American law schools. This work is often historical and sometimes comparative in form, and is most frequently distinguished by the interpretative reanalysis of case law doctrine in the format of contextualized critiques. It is interesting to note that the case law base and library setting of much critical legal study marks a continuation of traditional doctrinal methods. However, the critical and contextualized form of this work makes it radically different from the older doctrinal approach.

The second stream of post-doctrinal legal scholarship has taken on many names but here will be called empirical behavioral legal studies. These studies are not explicitly concerned with either the justification or criticism of case law doctrine, but instead strive to be value neutral. An explicit goal of this approach is to frame legal issues as empirical questions that can be answered without consideration of value preferences. For example, "the gap problem" that so concerned the legal realists is not taken here as inherently good or bad, or as something to be reduced; rather, in empirical behavioral legal studies the gap is taken as something to be explained, as in Stewart Macaulay's classic study of non-contractual relations in business. That is, the purpose is not to find the doctrinal principle that will reestablish legal order, thereby, for example, making all business relations contractual. The purpose instead is to make explicit the discontinuity between law and everyday practice and then to explain this discontinuity, so that what happens on each side of it can be better understood. The emphasis here is on causal and functional explanations, with the explanations made testable by the articulation of propositions that are predictive, and therefore assessable through comparisons of theoretically derived expectations with empirically generated observations. This work can be experimental as well as non-experimental, cross-sectional, longitudinal and comparative as well as historical and critical.

There is increasing reason to believe that the two streams of post-doctrinal scholarship we have described can be joined by a pragmatic tradition of empirical legal scholarship. It is therefore worthwhile taking note of what this new legal scholarship offers, and of what the obstacles to this new tradition might be. We consider the possibilities first, and the obstacles second.

In the most general terms, the new legal scholarship offers a more inclusive look at the interrelationships between law and the surrounding society. It does this first by shifting our attention outward and downward from "law at the top". This means moving our focus from the highly publicized and recognized importance of decisions made, for example, in appellate and trial courts, away from the professionals who "make" these cases, down to the law's users and consumers. Law at the bottom becomes as important and as interesting, and therefore as much in need of explanation, as law at the top. Among other things, we begin to seek explanations of the movement of legal activity up and down this hierarchy.

The downward thrust of the new legal scholarship extends attention simultaneously to less formal manifestations of law. Among the most central of these manifestations is the negotiated outcome. Bargaining is a pervasive feature of law more broadly conceived. Galanter writes that, "[t]he negotiated outcome in the shadow of the law turns out to be the master pattern of disputing ..." What might otherwise be seen as adjudicative processes are now seen as negotiative ones, with authoritative decision makers now cast in the roles of arbitrators and mediators. Legal rules and principles surely still apply, but their role is less determinative, and now understood as less definitive.

The parties to the negotiated outcomes are also more broadly conceived, as are the settings in which they act. The actors in these larger social dramas include legally recognized authorities, users and consumers of law and their authorized and unauthorized agents, other interested parties, and the broader social audience that must be considered in shaping negotiated outcomes. These actors are seen and heard not only in more formal and heavily monitored legal settings, but in a plurality of other places. Private governments, semi-autonomous social and professional fields, indigenous law and other forms of regulation are related to law in ways that depend on one another for mutual effect. Governmental law is intimately interrelated with other kinds of law and social institutions in which regulators and regulatees conduct their everyday business. Law is seen here as plural, not singular.

The influence of law is also understood in symbolic as much as or more than in instrumental terms. Indeed, scarcity of legal resources requires that this must be so, for the cost of direct law enforcement sharply curtails the range over which the law can be applied. However, when law is conceived as symbolic information flows, apart from the direct and instrumental exercise of force, the broad impact of law, albeit indirect and often with unintended effects, is more easily grasped. For example, general deterrence, legal socialization and bargaining in the shadow of the law are all seen as broader manifestations of the law as it symbolically affects people's everyday lives.

In all of these ways, the new legal scholarship has dramatically increased what we know about the way law actually works — about plea bargaining, negotiated settlements, selective prosecution, litigants' strategies, the working routines of courts and judges; about the practice of law, client-lawyer relationships, the structure and politics of the bar; about legal education and the public consumption of law. Journals such as *Law & Society Review*, the *Journal of Legal Studies*, the *Journal of Law & Economics*, the *Journal of Legal Education, Law & Human Behaviour* and the *American Bar Association Research Journal* are alive with the emerging products of this work. An increasing number of monographs and texts are also available. All of this reflects an accumulation of empirical legal study that is impressive compared to the dearth of such material available less than a generation ago.

(iii) The Pedagogic Challenge

Neil C. Sargent

Roger Cotterrell (1986) points out that one of the defining characteristics of any discipline or knowledge-field lies in the fact that its intellectual frame of reference (its object of inquiry, the conceptual and methodological tools relied upon and the manner in which the autonomy of the field of inquiry is established) tends to be autonomous and self-validating. Consequently, one of the problems inherent in any attempt to challenge the intellectual hegemony of any discipline or paradigm lies in estab-

---

From "The Possibilities and Perils of Legal Studies" (1990) 8 *Law in Context* at 4–14.

lishing the intellectual space from which to mount such a challenge.

Cotterrell's insight has particular relevance in relation to the difficulties inherent in developing an interdisciplinary approach to legal studies which is capable of challenging the dominant legal positivist tradition within legal education. This is because the intellectual hegemony of the legal positivist tradition is intimately connected with the professionalization of legal education and the institutional autonomy of the professional law school. This is no accident. The development of legal positivism as a closed form of knowledge-formation, with its own internal canons of enquiry, has played an important role in raising the status of law to that of a 'learned' profession (Arthurs, 1987). Moreover, the focus of legal positivism on the substantive content of legal texts and on internal conventions of reasoning and analysis reflects precisely those areas of knowledge and expertise over which legal professionals have traditionally exercised a monopoly.

The strength of this intellectual tradition lies in the way it colonizes the imagination of legal scholars. As such it imposes a powerful intellectual brake upon their research and teaching agendas, which is all the more insidious for being largely invisible. Legal positivism involves epistemological assumptions about the nature of law as an object of inquiry which reinforce the insularity of legal scholarship from the academic concerns of scholars in other disciplines. At its heart is a conceptualization of law as a normatively closed form of knowledge and system of inquiry which have few, if any, necessary reference points to the social, political or economic environment in which law operates (Cotterrell, 1986). Despite the recent burgeoning of critical perspectives on law which seek to challenge many of the tenets of the dominant positivist tradition, such as the Critical Legal Studies Movement, in one important respect little seems to have changed. The focus of enquiry of most contemporary legal scholarship remains defined by its concern with legal doctrine, notwithstanding the explicitly political agenda of much of the new critical scholarship. Moreover, the modes of inquiry relied upon even by critical legal scholars are still oriented around textual analysis and deconstruction, even if the claimed rationality and objectivity of traditional modes of legal interpretation have become increasingly contested with the new critical scholarship.

Consequently, there is still no obvious mandate for travel outside these conventional boundaries in search of empirical evidence about the impact of law in practice. Nor is there any need to investigate the role of legal institutions or legal actors other than as sources of authoritative texts for analysis or interpretation. In this respect, Supreme Court justices are necessarily more important as authors of legal texts than trial court justices, notwithstanding the claims of the Legal Realists to the contrary. Similarly, the role of the court as a trier of fact and in processing disputes is less significant to most legal scholars than its role as a source of texts for interpretation and analysis.

By contrast, the assumption that legal texts can be read independently from their social, cultural, economic or political environment tends to be viewed by many social scientists with a considerable degree of skepticism, bordering at times on disbelief. Those issues which are of marginal concern to legal scholars in their search for authoritative texts are precisely the issues about the workings of the legal system, the behaviour of legal actors, the effectiveness of legal rules and decision-making processes, that are likely to be of interest to social science researchers. Consequently, the sources of data, the methods of enquiry and the conceptual frameworks utilised by social science researchers in their investigations of law are based on very different foundations than those which inform most conventional legal scholarship (Friedman, 1986; Hagan, 1986).

One of the major problems inherent in attempting to develop an interdisciplinary approach to legal studies which is able to draw from both these disciplinary traditions lies in the fact that they appear to be mutually exclusive of one another. This is borne out by the history of the law-and-society movement in the United States, which despite its promising beginnings and its relatively lengthy history, has largely failed to penetrate the mainstream of American legal scholarship (Friedman, 1986).

As a result, there is sometimes a tendency on the part of social science researchers to regard the disciplinary claims made by legal academics as something of a contradiction in terms. Legal scholarship tends to be dismissed by many social scientists on the grounds that it lacks theoretical or methodological coherence. The question is often asked whether there is anything sufficiently distinctive about law being treated as a separate disciplinary field (Friedman, 1986; Cotterrell, 1986). From this perspective, law is frequently seen as a proper object of inquiry only within the confines of another disciplinary tradition, such as sociology, political science, history, psychology or philosophy.

Why not then simply abandon the legal academics to their search for authoritative texts while the social scientists get on with the work of investigating the way in which law operates as a social phenomenon and impacts upon people's lives? The answer that I would give to this question is two-fold. First, that law is too important a social institution to be left only to lawyers. This implies that the language of law and content of legal doctrine should not be regarded as simply the dry, technical preserve of lawyers. Law plays a crucial ideological role in shaping popular understandings about the nature of power relations and the structure of social ordering within liberal democratic societies. Consequently, the entire terrain of law, which includes the role of legal education, the nature and form of legal reasoning, the hierarchical structure of legal authority, as well as the content of legal rules, needs to be studied as a complex social phenomenon that can only be fully understood through the use of social science concepts and methods of inquiry.

Closely related to this first point is a further observation concerning the limits of empirical enquiry as a means of understanding the social significance of law. Law as a social phenomenon is more than just a set of empirically observable relations or activities that can be examined according to well-established canons of enquiry to produce empirically-testable hypotheses about the behaviour or significance of law or legal institutions in practice. Here I clearly part company with many in the socio-legal studies movement in Britain and Australia and in the law-and-society movement in the United States and Canada. It follows from the point made above that legal discourse and doctrine must also become part of the province of social science enquiry, even if not readily amenable to empirical methods of investigation.

Given the significance of law as a source of contested meanings about the nature of social relations, a crucial question for investigation becomes what are the limits of law as an agency of social or political change? To what extent, for example, is the language of legal rights capable of redressing situations of substantive social, economic or political inequality? Or is the discourse of legal rights so closely wedded to liberal notions of abstract individualism and formal equality that it has the effect of channelling progressive political struggles into narrowly circumscribed legal issues? These are not questions which can be answered solely by reference to internal canons of interpretation and precedent, such as legal academics are used to. Rather, what is at issue are fundamental questions about the relationship between legal concepts and the structure of social, economic and political ordering within Canadian society.

What this translates to in practice is the need to insert questions of theory and method into the design of any legal studies curriculum in a way that is central to the pedagogic enterprise. This implies that conventional legal methods of inquiry are inadequate alone to generate meaningful hypotheses about the nature of law or the connection between legal relations and social relations. It also implies a significant degree of skepticism about the ability of empirical enquiry alone to produce any more meaningful responses to these questions unless explicitly informed by an awareness of wider theoretical issues.

Consequently, the prescription offered is for a legal studies approach which claims law as an appropriate field of inquiry, but which rejects any conception of law as a unitary mode of discourse that can be investigated by reliance on internal canons of inquiry alone. Rather, the focus should be on exploring the multi-faceted character of law as a complex social phenomenon, and the manner in which different theoretical and methodological perspectives give rise to different types of questions about the role and functions of law and the relationship between legal and social change (*cf.* Hunt, 1986; Boyd, 1989). Perhaps it should come as no great surprise that this also reflects the intellectual trajectory followed in the development of the Carleton law program.

4   Citizenship and Human Rights

A. Citizenship

[In the following case the Judicial Committee of the Privy Council, then Canada's final court of appeal, was called upon to decide the question whether women were "persons" within the meaning of section 24 of the British North American Act, and thus eligible to be appointed to the Senate. In an earlier decision the Supreme Court of Canada had unanimously dismissed the petitioners' arguments that women were included in the meaning of "persons" under s. 24.]

(i) *Henrietta Muir Edwards et al. v. Canada (A.G.)*

[LORD SANKEY L.C.:]

By s. 24 of the *British North America Act, 1867*, it is provided that "The Governor General shall from time to time, in the Queen's name, by instrument under the Great Seal of Canada, summon qualified persons to the Senate; and, subject to the provisions of this Act, every person so summoned shall become and be a member of the Senate and a senator."

The question at issue in this appeal is whether the words "qualified persons" in that section include a woman, and consequently whether women are eligible to be summoned to and become members of the Senate of Canada.

Of the appellants, Henrietta Muir Edwards is the Vice-President for the Province of Alberta of the National Council of Women for Canada; Nellie L. McClung and Louise C. McKinney were for several years members of the Legislative Assembly of the said Province; Emily F. Murphy is a police magistrate in and for the said Province; and Irene Parlby is a member of the Legislative Assembly of the said Province and a member of the Executive Council thereof.

On August 29, 1927, the appellants petitioned the Governor General in Council to refer to the Supreme Court certain questions touching the powers of the Governor General to summon female persons to the Senate, and upon October 19, 1927, the Governor General in Council referred to the Supreme Court the aforesaid question. The case was heard before Anglin C.J., Duff, Mignault, Lamont, and Smith JJ., and upon April 24, 1928, the Court answered the question in the negative; the question being understood to be "Are women eligible for appointment to the Senate of Canada."

The Chief Justice, whose judgment was concurred in by Lamont and Smith JJ., and substantially by Mignault J., came to this conclusion upon broad lines mainly because of the common law disability of women to hold public office and from a consideration of various cases which has been decided under

[1930] A.C. 124 (J.C.P.C.).

different statutes as to their right to vote for a member of Parliament.

Duff J., on the other hand, did not agree with this view. He came to the conclusion that women are not eligible for appointment to the Senate upon the narrower ground that upon a close examination of the *British North America Act 1867*, the word "persons" in s. 24 is restricted to members of the male sex. The result therefore of the decision was that the Supreme Court was unanimously of opinion that the word "persons" did not include female persons, and that women are not eligible to be summoned to the Senate.

Their Lordships are of opinion that the word "persons" in s. 24 does include women, and that women are eligible to be summoned to and become members of the Senate of Canada.

The exclusion of women from all public offices is a relic of days more barbarous than ours, but it must be remembered that the necessity of the times often forced on man customs, which in later years were not necessary. Such exclusion is probably due to the fact that the deliberative assemblies of the early tribes were attended by men under arms, and women did not bear arms. "*Nihil autem neque publicae neque privatae rei, nisi armati, agunt*": Tac. Germ., c. 13. Yet the tribes did not despise the advice of women. "*Inessequin etiam sanctum et providum putant, nec aut consilia earum aspernantura ut responsa neglegunt*": Germ., c. 8. The likelihood of attack rendered such a proceeding unavoidable, and after all what is necessary at any period is a question for the times upon which opinion grounded on experience may move one way or another in different circumstances. This exclusion of women found its way into the opinions of the Roman jurists, Ulpian (A.D. 211) laying it down. "*Feminae ab omnibus offiis civilibus vel publicis remotae sunt*": Dig. 1.16.195. The barbarian tribes who settled in the Roman Empire, and were exposed to constant dangers, naturally preserved and continued the tradition.

In England no woman under the degree of a Queen or a Regent, married or unmarried, could take part in the government of the State. A woman was under a legal incapacity to be elected to serve in Parliament and even if a peeress in her own right she was not, nor is, entitled as an incident of peerage to receive a writ of summons to the House of Lords.

Various authorities are cited in the recent case of *Viscountess Rhondda's Claim*, where it was held that a woman was not entitled to sit in the House of Lords. Women were, moreover, subject to a legal incapacity to vote at the election of members of Parliament: Coke, 4 *Inst.*, p. 5; *Chorlton v. Lings*; or of town councillor: *Reg. v. Harrald*; or to be elected members of a County Council: *Beresford-Hope v. Sandhurst*. They were excluded by the common law from taking part in the administration of justice either as judges or as jurors, with the single exception of inquiries by a jury of matrons upon a suggestion of pregnancy: Coke, 2 *Inst.* 119, 3 Bl. Comm. 362. Other instances are referred to in the learned judgment of Willes J. in *Chorlton v. Lings*.

No doubt in the course of centuries there may be found cases of exceptional women and exceptional instances, but as Lord Esher M.R. said in *De Souza v. Cobden*: "By the common law of England women are not in general deemed capable of exercising public functions, though there are certain exceptional cases where a well recognised custom to the contrary has become established." An instance may be referred to in the case of women being entitled to act as churchwardens and as sextons, the latter being put upon the ground that a sexton's duty was in the nature of a private trust: *Olive v. Ingram*. Also of being appointed as overseer of the poor: *Rex v. Stubbs*. The tradition existed till quite modern times: see *Bebb v. Law Society*, where it was held by the Court of Appeal that by inveterate usage women were under a disability by reason of their sex to become attorneys or solicitors.

The passing of *Lord Brougham's Act* in 1850 does not appear to have greatly affected the current of authority. Sect. 4 provided that in all acts words importing the masculine gender shall be deemed and taken to include female unless the contrary as to gender is expressly provided.

The application and purview of that *Act* came up for consideration in *Chorlton v. Lings*, where the Court of Common Pleas was required to construe a statute passed in 1861, which conferred the parliamentary franchise on every man possessing certain qualifications and registered as a voter. The chief question discussed was whether by virtue of *Lord Brougham's Act* the words "every man" included women. Bovill C.J., having regard to the subject-matter of the statute and its general scope and language and to the important and striking nature of the departure from the common law involved in extending the franchise to women, declined to accept the view that Parliament had made that change by using the term "man" and held that the word was intentionally used expressly to designate the male sex. Willes J. said: "It is not easy to conceive that the framer of that Act, when he used the word 'expressly,' meant to suggest that what is necessarily or properly implied by language is not expressed by such language."

(i) Henrietta Muir Edwards et al. v. Canada (A.G.)

Great reliance was placed by the respondents to this appeal upon that decision, but in our view it is clearly distinguishable. The case was decided on the language of the *Representation of the People Act, 1867*, which provided that "every man" with certain qualifications and "not subject to any legal incapacity" should be entitled to be registered as a voter. Legal incapacity was not defined by the Act, and consequently reference was necessary to the common law disabilities of women.

A similar result was reached in the case of *Nairn v. University of St. Andrews*, where it was held under s. 27 of the *Representation of the People (Scotland) Act, 1868*, which provided that every person whose name is for the time being on the register of the general council of such university shall, being of full age and not subject to any legal incapacity, be entitled to vote in the election of a member to serve in any future Parliament for such university, that the word "person" did not include women, but the Lord Chancellor, Lord Loreburn, referred to the position of women at common law, and pointed out that they were subject to a legal incapacity. Both in this case and in the case of the Viscountess Rhondda the various judgments emphasize the fact that the legislature in dealing with the matter cannot be taken to have departed from the usage of centuries, or to have employed loose and ambiguous words to carry out so momentous and fundamental a change.

The judgment of the Chief Justice in the Supreme Court of Canada refers to and relies upon these cases, but their Lordships think that there is great force in the view taken by Duff J. with regard to them, when he says that s. 24 of the *British North America Act, 1867*, must not be treated as an independent enactment. The Senate, he proceeds, is part of a parliamentary system, and in order to test the contention based upon this principle that women are excluded from participating in working the Senate or any other institution set up by the Act one is bound to consider the Act as a whole and its bearings on this subject of the exclusion of women from public office and place.

The communities included within the Britannic system embrace countries and peoples in every stage of social, political and economic development and undergoing a continuous process of evolution. His Majesty the King in Council is the final Court of Appeal from all these communities, and this Board must take great care therefore not to interpret legislation meant to apply to one community by a rigid adherence to the customs and traditions of another. Canada had its difficulties both at home and with the mother country, but soon discovered that union was strength. Delegates from the three maritime Provinces met in Charlottetown on September 1, 1864, to discuss proposals for a maritime union. A delegation from the coalition government of that day proceeded to Charlottetown and placed before the maritime delegates their schemes for a union embracing the Canadian Provinces. As a result the Quebec conference assembled on October 10, continued in session till October 28, and framed a number of resolutions. These resolutions as revised by the delegates from the different Provinces in London in 1866 were based upon a consideration of the rights of others and expressed in a compromise which will remain a lasting monument to the political genius of Canadian statesmen. Upon those resolutions the *British North America Act of 1867* was framed and passed by the Imperial legislature. The Quebec resolutions dealing with the Legislative Council — namely, Nos. 6–24 — even if their Lordships are entitled to look at them, do not shed any light on the subject under discussion. They refer generally to the "members" of the Legislative Council.

The *British North America Act* planted in Canada a living tree capable of growth and expansion within its natural limits. The object of the Act was to grant a Constitution to Canada. "Like all written constitutions it has been subject to development through usage and convention": *Canadian Constitutional Studies*, Sir Robert Borden (1922), p. 55.

Their Lordships do not conceive it to be the duty of this Board — it is certainly not their desire — to cut down the provisions of the Act by a narrow and technical construction, but rather to give it a large and liberal interpretation so that the Dominion to a great extent, but within certain fixed limits, may be mistress in her own house, as the Provinces to a great extent, but within certain fixed limits, are mistresses in theirs. "The Privy Council, indeed, has laid down that Courts of law must treat the provisions of the *British North America Act* by the same methods of construction and exposition which they apply to other statutes. But there are statutes and *statutes*; and the strict construction deemed proper in the case, for example, of a penal or taxing statute or one passed to regulate the affairs of an English parish, would be often subversive of Parliament's real intent if applied to an Act passed to ensure the peace, order and good government of a British Colony": see Clement's *Canadian Constitution*, 3rd ed., p. 347.

The learned author of that treatise quotes from the argument of Mr. Mowat and Mr. Edward Blake before the Privy Council in *St. Catherine's Milling and Lumber Co. v. The Queen*: "That Act should be on all occasions interpreted in a large, liberal and comprehensive spirit, considering the magnitude of the subjects with which it purports to deal in very few words." With that their Lordships agree, but as was said by the Lord Chancellor in *Brophy v. Attorney-General of Manitoba*, the question is not what may be supposed to have been intended, but what has been said.

It must be remembered, too, that their Lordships are not here considering the question of the legislative competence either of the Dominion or its Provinces which arise under ss. 91 and 92 of the Act providing for the distribution of legislative powers and assigning to the Dominion and its Provinces their respective spheres of Government. Their Lordships are concerned with the interpretation of an Imperial Act, but an Imperial Act which creates a constitution for a new country. Nor are their Lordships deciding any question as to the rights of women but only a question as to their eligibility for a particular position. No one, either male or female, has a right to be summoned to the Senate. The real point at issue is whether the Governor General has a right to summon women to the Senate.

The Act consists of a number of separate heads.

The preamble states that the Provinces of Canada, Nova Scotia and New Brunswick have expressed their desire to be federally united into one Dominion under the Crown of the United Kingdom of Great Britain and Ireland with a constitution similar in principle to that of the United Kingdom.

The word "person" as above mentioned, may include members of both sexes, and to those who ask why the word should include females the obvious answer is why should it not? In these circumstances the burden is upon those who deny that the word includes women to make out their case.

Their Lordships do not think it possible to interpret the word "persons" by speculating whether the framer of the *British North America Act* purposely followed the system of Legislative Councils enacted in the *Acts of 1791* and *1840* rather than that which prevailed in the maritime Province for the model on which the Senate was to be formed, neither do they think that either of these sub-sections is sufficient to rebut the presumption that the word "persons" includes women. Looking at the sections which deal with the Senate as a whole (ss. 21–36) their Lordships are unable to say that there is anything in those sections themselves upon which the Court could come to a definite conclusion that women are to be excluded from the Senate.

So far with regard to the sections dealing especially with the Senate — are there any other sections in the Act which shed light upon the meaning of the word "persons"?

Their Lordships think that there are. For example, s. 41 refers to the qualifications and disqualifications of persons to be elected or to sit or vote as members of the House of Assembly or Legislative Assembly, and by a proviso it is said that until the Parliament of Canada otherwise provides at any election for a member of the House of Commons for the district of Algoma in addition to persons qualified by the law of the Province of Canada to vote every male British subject aged twenty-one or upwards being a householder shall have a vote. This section shows a distinction between "persons" and "males." If persons excluded females it would only have been necessary to say every person who is a British subject aged twenty-one years or upwards shall have a vote.

Again in s. 84, referring to Ontario and Quebec, a similar proviso is found stating that every male British subject in contradistinction to "person" shall have a vote.

Again in s. 133 it is provided that either the English or the French language may be used by any person or in any pleadings in or issuing from any court of Canada established under this Act and in or from all of any of the courts of Quebec. The word "person" there must include females, as it can hardly have been supposed that a man might use either the English or the French language but a woman might not.

If Parliament had intended to limit the word "persons" in s. 24 to male persons it would surely have manifested such intention by an express limitation, as it has done in ss. 41 and 84. The fact that certain qualifications are set out in s. 23 is not an argument in favour of further limiting the class, but is an argument to the contrary, because it must be presumed that Parliament has set out in s. 23 all the qualifications deemed necessary for a senator, and it does not state that one of the qualifications is that he must be a member of the male sex.

The history of these sections and their interpretation in Canada is not without interest and significance.

From confederation to date both the Dominion Parliament and the Provincial legislatures have interpreted the word "persons" in ss. 41 and 84 of the *British North America Act* as including female persons, and have legislated either for the inclusion or exclusion of women from the class of persons entitled to vote and to sit in the Parliament and Legislature respectively, and this interpretation has never been questioned.

From confederation up to 1916 women were excluded from the class of persons entitled to vote in both Federal and Provincial elections. From 1916 to 1922 various Dominion and Provincial Acts were passed to admit women to the franchise and to the right to sit as members in both Dominion and Provincial legislative bodies. At the present time women are entitled to vote and to be candidates:

1. At all Dominion elections on the same basis as men.
2. At all Provincial elections save in the Province of Quebec.

From the date of the enactment of the *Interpretation Acts* in the Province of Canada, Nova Scotia and New Brunswick prior to confederation and in the Dominion of Canada since confederation and until the franchise was extended, women have been excluded by express enactment from the right to vote.

Neither is it without interest to record that when upon May 20, 1867, the *Representation of the People Bill* came before a Committee of the House of Commons, John Stuart Mill moved an amendment to secure women's suffrage, and the amendment proposed was to leave out the word "man" in order to insert the word "person" instead thereof: see *Hansard*, 3rd series, vol. clxxxvii., col. 817.

A heavy burden lies on an appellant who seeks to set aside a unanimous judgment of the Supreme Court, and this Board will only set aside such a decision after convincing argument and anxious consideration, but having regard:

1. To the object of the Act — namely, to provide a constitution for Canada, a responsible and developing State;
2. That the word "person" is ambiguous, and may include members of either sex;
3. That there are sections in the Act above referred to which show that in some cases the word "person" must include females;
4. That in some sections the words "male persons" are expressly used when it is desired to confine the matter in issue to males;
5. To the provisions of the *Interpretation Act*; their Lordships have come to the conclusion that the word "persons" in s. 24 includes members both of the male and female sex, and that, therefore, the question propounded by the Governor General should be answered in the affirmative, and that women are eligible to be summoned to and become members of the Senate of Canada, and they will humbly advise His Majesty accordingly.

(ii) Citizenship and Social Class

T.H. Marshall

The sociological hypothesis latent in Alfred Marshall's essay postulates that there is a kind of basic human equality associated with the concept of full membership of a community — or, as I should say, of citizenship — which is not inconsistent with the inequalities which distinguish the various economic levels in the society. In other words, the inequality of the social class system may be acceptable provided the equality of citizenship is recognized. [...]

He recognizes only one definite right, the right of children to be educated, and in this case alone does he approve the use of compulsory powers by the state to achieve his object. He could hardly go further without imperilling his own criterion for distinguishing his system from socialism in any form — the preservation of the freedom of the competitive market. [...] His sociological hypothesis lies as near to the heart of our problem today as it did three-quarters of a century ago — in fact nearer. The basic human equality of membership [...] has been enriched with new substance and invested with a formidable array of rights. It has developed far beyond

---

From David Held et al., eds., *States and Societies* (Oxford: Basil Blackwell in association with The Open University, 1985, © 1983 & originally published by Martin Robertson & Company Ltd., Oxford, 1983) at 248–60. Notes omitted. Reproduced with permission of Cambridge University Press.

what he foresaw, or would have wished. It has been clearly identified with the status of citizenship. [...]

Is it still true that basic equality, when enriched in substance and embodied in the formal rights of citizenship, is consistent with the inequalities of social class? I shall suggest that our society today assumes that the two are still compatible: so much so that citizenship has itself become, in certain respects, the architect of legitimate social inequality. Is it still true that the basic equality can be created and preserved without invading the freedom of the competitive market? Obviously it is not true. Our modern system is frankly a socialist system not one whose authors are, as Marshall was, eager to distinguish it from socialism. But it is equally obvious that the market still functions — within limits. Here is another possible conflict of principles which demands examination. And thirdly, what is the effect of the marked shift of emphasis from duties to rights? Is this an inevitable feature of modern citizenship — inevitable and irreversible? [...]

I shall ask whether there appear to be limits beyond which the modern drive towards social equality cannot, or is unlikely to pass, and I shall be thinking, not of the economic cost (I leave that vital question to the economists), but of the limits inherent in the principles that inspire the drive. But the modern drive towards social equality is, I believe, the latest phase of an evolution of citizenship which has been in continuous progress for some 250 years. [...]

The Development of Citizenship to the End of the Nineteenth Century

[...] I shall be running true to type as a sociologist if I begin by saying that I propose to divide citizenship into three parts. But the analysis is, in this case, dictated by history even more clearly than by logic. I shall call these three parts, or elements, civil, political and social. The civil element is composed of the rights necessary for individual freedom — liberty of the person, freedom of speech, thought and faith, the right to own property and to conclude valid contracts, and the right to justice. The last is of a different order from the others, because it is the right to defend and assert all one's rights on terms of equality with others and by due process of law. This shows us that the institutions most directly associated with civil rights are the courts of justice. By the political element I mean the right to participate in the exercise of political power, as a member of a body invested with political authority or as an elector of the members of such a body. The corresponding institutions are Parliament and councils of local government. By the social element I mean the whole range from the right to a modicum of economic welfare and security to the right to share to the full in the social heritage and to live the life of a civilized being according to the standards prevailing in the society. The institutions most closely connected with it are the educational system and the social services. [...]

By 1832 when political rights made their first infantile attempt to walk, civil rights had come to man's estate and bore, in most essentials, the appearance that they have today. 'The specific work of the earlier Hanoverian epoch', writes Trevelyan, 'was the establishment of the rule of law; and that law, with all its grave faults, was at least a law of freedom. On that solid foundation all our subsequent reforms were built'. This eighteenth-century achievement, interrupted by the French Revolution and completed after it, was in large measure the work of the courts both in their daily practice and also in a series of famous cases in some of which they were fighting against Parliament in defence of individual liberty. The most celebrated actor in this drama was, I suppose, John Wilkes, and, although we may deplore the absence in him of those noble and saintly qualities which we should like to find in our national heroes, we cannot complain if the cause of liberty is sometimes championed by a libertine.

In the economic field the basic civil right is the right to work, that is to say the right to follow the occupation of one's choice in the place of one's choice, subject only to legitimate demands for preliminary technical training. This right had been denied by both statute and custom; on the one hand by the Elizabethan Statute of Artificers, which confined certain occupations to certain social classes, and on the other by local regulations reserving employment in a town to its own members and by the use of apprenticeship as an instrument of exclusion rather than of recruitment. The recognition of the right involved the formal acceptance of a fundamental change of attitude. The old assumption that local and group monopolies were in the public interest, because 'trade and traffic cannot be maintained or increased without order and government', was replaced by the new assumption that such restrictions were an offence against the liberty of the subject and a menace to the prosperity of the nation. [...]

By the beginning of the nineteenth century this principle of individual economic freedom was accepted as axiomatic. You are probably familiar with the passage quoted by the Webbs from the report of the Select Committee of 1811, which states that:

(ii) Citizenship and Social Class

no interference of the legislature with the freedom of trade, or with the perfect liberty of every individual to dispose of his time and of his labour in the way and on the terms which he may judge most conducive to his own interest, can take place without violating general principles of the first importance to the prosperity and happiness of the community. [...]

The story of civil rights in their formative period is one of the gradual addition of new rights to a status that already existed and was held to appertain to all adult members of the community — or perhaps one should say to all male members, since the status of women, or at least of married women, was in some important respects peculiar. This democratic, or universal, character of the status arose naturally from the fact that it was essentially the status of freedom, and in seventeenth-century England all men were free. Servile status, or villeinage by blood, had lingered on as a patent anachronism in the days of Elizabeth, but vanished soon afterwards. This change from servile to free labour has been described by Professor Tawney as 'a high landmark in the development both of economic and political society', and as 'the final triumph of the common law' in regions from which it had been excluded for four centuries. Henceforth the English peasant 'is a member of a society in which there is, nominally at least, one law for all men'. The liberty which his predecessors had won by fleeing into the free towns had become his by right. In the towns the terms 'freedom' and 'citizenship' were interchangeable. When freedom became universal, citizenship grew from a local into a national institution.

The story of political rights is different both in time and in character. The formative period began, as I have said, in the early nineteenth century, where the civil rights attached to the status of freedom had already acquired sufficient substance to justify us in speaking of a general status of citizenship. And, when it began, it consisted, not in the creation of new rights to enrich a status already enjoyed by all, but in the granting of old rights to new sections of the population. [...]

It is clear that, if we maintain that in the nineteenth century citizenship in the form of civil rights was universal, the political franchise was not one of the rights of citizenship. It was the privilege of a limited economic class, whose limits were extended by each successive Reform Act. [...]

It was, as we shall see, appropriate that nineteenth-century capitalist society should treat political rights as a secondary product of civil rights. It was equally appropriate that the twentieth century should abandon this position and attach political rights directly and independently to citizenship as such. This vital change of principle was put into effect when the Act of 1918, by adopting manhood suffrage, shifted the basis of political rights from economic substance to personal status. I say 'manhood' deliberately in order to emphasize the great significance of this reform quite apart from the second, and no less important, reform introduced at the same time — namely the enfranchisement of women. [...]

The original source of social rights was membership of local communities and functional associations. This source was supplemented and progressively replaced by a *Poor Law* and a system of wage regulation which were nationally conceived and locally administered. [...]

As the pattern of the old order dissolved under the blows of a competitive economy, and the plan disintegrated, the Poor Law was left high and dry as an isolated survival from which the idea of social rights was gradually drained away. But at the very end of the eighteenth century there occurred a final struggle between the old and the new, between the planned (or patterned) society and the competitive economy. And in this battle citizenship was divided against itself; social rights sided with the old and civil with the new. [...]

In this brief episode of our history we see the *Poor Law* as the aggressive champion of the social rights of citizenship. In the succeeding phase we find the attacker driven back far behind his original position. By the Act of 1834 the *Poor Law* renounced all claim to trespass on the territory of the wages system, or to interfere with the forces of the free market. It offered relief only to those who, through age or sickness, were incapable of continuing the battle, and to those other weaklings who gave up the struggle, admitted defeat, and cried for mercy. The tentative move towards the concept of social security was reversed. But more than that, the minimal social rights that remained were detached from the status of citizenship. The *Poor Law* treated the claims of the poor, not as an integral part of the rights of the citizen, but as an alternative to them — as claims which could be met only if the claimants ceased to be citizens in any true sense of the word. For paupers forfeited in practice the civil right of personal liberty, by internment in the workhouse, and they forfeited by law any political rights they might possess. This disability of defranchisement remained in being until 1918, and the significance of its final removal has, perhaps, not been fully appreciated. The stigma which clung to poor relief expressed the deep feelings of a people who understood that those who accepted relief must cross the road that separated the community of citizens from the outcast company of the destitute.

The *Poor Law* is not an isolated example of this divorce of social rights from the status of citizenship. The early *Factory Acts* show the same tendency. Although in fact they led to an improvement of working conditions and a reduction of working hours to the benefit of all employed in the industries to which they applied, they meticulously refrained from giving this protection directly to the adult male — the citizen *par excellence*. And they did so out of respect for his status as a citizen, on the grounds that enforced protective measures curtailed the civil right to conclude a free contract of employment. Protection was confined to women and children, and champions of women's rights were quick to detect the implied insult. Women were protected because they were not citizens. If they wished to enjoy full and responsible citizenship, they must forgo protection. By the end of the nineteenth century such arguments had become obsolete, and the factory code had become one of the pillars in the edifice of social rights. [...]

By the end of the nineteenth century, elementary education was not only free, it was compulsory. This signal [*sic*] departure from *laissez faire* could, of course, be justified on the grounds that free choice is a right only for mature minds, that children are naturally subject to discipline, and that parents cannot be trusted to do what is in the best interests of their children. But the principle goes deeper than that. We have here a personal right combined with a public duty to exercise the right. Is the public duty imposed merely for the benefit of the individual — because children cannot fully appreciate their own interests and parents may be unfit to enlighten them? I hardly think that this can be an adequate explanation. It was increasingly recognized, as the nineteenth century wore on, that political democracy needed an educated electorate, and that scientific manufacture needed educated workers and technicians. The duty to improve and civilize oneself is therefore a social duty, and not merely a personal one, because the social health of a society depends upon the civilization of its members. And a community that enforces this duty has begun to realize that its culture is an organic unity and its civilization a national heritage. It follows that the growth of public elementary education during the nineteenth century was the first decisive step on the road to the reestablishment of the social rights of citizenship in the twentieth. [...]

The Impact of Citizenship on Social Class

Citizenship is a status bestowed on those who are full members of a community. All who possess the status are equal with respect to the rights and duties with which the status is endowed. There is no universal principle that determines what those rights and duties shall be, but societies in which citizenship is a developing institution create an image of an ideal citizenship against which achievement can be measured and towards which aspiration can be directed. The urge forward along the path thus plotted is an urge towards a fuller measure of equality, an enrichment of the stuff of which the status is made and an increase in the number of those on whom the status is bestowed. Social class, on the other hand, is a system of inequality. And it too, like citizenship, can be based on a set of ideals, beliefs and values. It is therefore reasonable to expect that the impact of citizenship on social class should take the form of a conflict between opposing principles. If I am right in my contention that citizenship has been a developing institution in England at least since the latter part of the seventeenth century, then it is clear that its growth coincides with the rise of capitalism, which is a system, not of equality, but of inequality. Here is something that needs explaining. How is it that these two opposing principles could grow and flourish side by side in the same soil? What made it possible for them to be reconciled with one another and to become, for a time at least, allies instead of antagonists? The question is a pertinent one, for it is clear that, in the twentieth century, citizenship and the capitalist class system have been at war....

It is true that class still functions. Social inequality is regarded as necessary and purposeful. It provides the incentive to effort and designs the distribution of power. But there is no overall pattern of inequality, in which an appropriate value is attached, *a priori*, to each social level. Inequality, therefore, though necessary, may become excessive. As Patrick Colquhoun said, in a much-quoted passage: 'Without a large proportion of poverty there could be no riches, since riches are the offspring of labour, while labour can result only from a state of poverty.... Poverty therefore is a most necessary and indispensable ingredient in society, without which nations and communities could not exist in a state of civilization. [...]

The more you look on wealth as conclusive proof of merit, the more you incline to regard poverty as evidence of failure — but the penalty for failure may seem to be greater than the offence warrants. In such circumstances it is natural that the more unpleasant features of inequality should be treated, rather irresponsibly, as a nuisance, like the black smoke that used to pour unchecked from our factory chimneys. And so in time, as the social conscience stirs to life, class-abatement, like smoke-abatement, becomes a desirable aim to be pursued as far as is compatible with the continued efficiency of the social machine.

But class-abatement in this form was not an attack on the class system. On the contrary it aimed, often quite consciously, at making the class system less vulnerable to attack by alleviating its less defensible consequences. It raised the floor-level in the basement of the social edifice, and perhaps made it rather more hygienic than it was before. But it remained a basement, and the upper stories of the building were unaffected. [...]

There developed, in the latter part of the nineteenth century, a growing interest in equality as a principle of social justice and an appreciation of the fact that the formal recognition of an equal capacity for rights was not enough. In theory even the complete removal of all the barriers that separated civil rights from their remedies would not have interfered with the principles or the class structure of the capitalist system. It would, in fact, have created a situation which many supporters of the competitive market economy falsely assumed to be already in existence. But in practice the attitude of mind which inspired the efforts to remove these barriers grew out of a conception of equality which overstepped these narrow limits, the conception of equal social worth, not merely of equal natural rights. Thus although citizenship, even by the end of the nineteenth century, had done little to reduce social inequality, it had helped to guide progress into the path which led directly to the egalitarian policies of the twentieth century. [...]

This growing national consciousness, this awakening public opinion, and these first stirrings of a sense of community membership and common heritage did not have any material effect on class structure and social inequality for the simple and obvious reason that, even at the end of the nineteenth century, the mass of the working people did not wield effective political power. By that time the franchise was fairly wide, but those who had recently received the vote had not yet learned how to use it. The political rights of citizenship, unlike the civil rights, were full of potential danger to the capitalist system, although those who were cautiously extending them down the social scale probably did not realize quite how great the danger was. They could hardly be expected to foresee what vast changes could be brought about by the peaceful use of political power, without a violent and bloody revolution. The 'planned society' and the welfare state had not yet risen over the horizon or come within the view of the practical politician. The foundations of the market economy and the contractual system seemed strong enough to stand against any probable assault. In fact, there were some grounds for expecting that the working classes, as they became educated, would accept the basic principles of the system and be content to rely for their protection and progress on the civil rights of citizenship, which contained no obvious menace to competitive capitalism. Such a view was encouraged by the fact that one of the main achievements of political power in the later nineteenth century was the recognition of the right of collective bargaining. This meant that social progress was being sought by strengthening civil rights, not by creating social rights; through the use of contract in the open market, not through a minimum wage and social security.

But this interpretation underrates the significance of this extension of civil rights in the economic sphere. For civil rights were in origin intensely individual, and that is why they harmonized with the individualistic phase of capitalism. By the device of incorporation groups were enabled to act legally as individuals. This important development did not go unchallenged, and limited liability was widely denounced as an infringement of individual responsibility. But the position of trade unions was even more anomalous, because they did not seek or obtain incorporation. They can, therefore, exercise vital civil rights collectively on behalf of their members without formal collective responsibility, while the individual responsibility of the workers in relation to contract is largely unenforceable. These civil rights became, for the workers, an instrument for raising their social and economic status, that is to say, for establishing the claim that they, as citizens, were entitled to certain social rights. But the normal method of establishing social rights is by the exercise of political power, for social rights imply an absolute right to a certain standard of civilization which is conditional only on the discharge of the general duties of citizenship. Their content does not depend on the economic value of the individual claimant. There is therefore a significant difference between a genuine collective bargain through which economic forces in a free market seek to achieve equilibrium and the use of collective civil rights to assert basic claims to the elements of social justice. Thus the acceptance of collective bargaining was not simply a natural extension of civil rights; it represented the transfer of an important process from the political to the civil sphere of citizenship. But 'transfer' is, perhaps, a misleading term, for at the time when this happened the workers either did not possess, or had not yet learned to use, the political right of the franchise. Since then they have obtained and made full use of that right. Trade unionism has, therefore, created a secondary system of industrial citizenship parallel with and supplementary to the system of political citizenship. [...]

A new period opened at the end of the nineteenth century, conveniently marked by Booth's survey of Life and Labour of the People in London and the Royal Commission on the Aged Poor. It saw the first big advance in social rights, and this involved significant changes in the egalitarian principle as expressed in citizenship. But there were other forces at work as well. A rise of money incomes unevenly distributed over the social classes altered the economic distance which separated these classes from one another, diminishing the gap between skilled and unskilled labour and between skilled labour and non-manual workers, while the steady increase in small savings blurred the class distinction between the capitalist and the propertyless proletarian. Secondly, a system of direct taxation, ever more steeply graduated, compressed the whole scale of disposable incomes. Thirdly, mass production for the home market and a growing interest on the part of industry in the needs and tastes of the common people enabled the less well-to-do to enjoy a material civilization which differed less markedly in quality from that of the rich than it had ever done before. All this profoundly altered the setting in which the progress of citizenship took place. Social integration spread from the sphere of sentiment and patriotism into that of material enjoyment. The components of a civilized and cultured life, formerly the monopoly of the few, were brought progressively within reach of the many, who were encouraged thereby to stretch out their hands towards those that still eluded their grasp. The diminution of inequality strengthened the demand for its abolition, at least with regard to the essentials of social welfare.

These aspirations have in part been met by incorporating social rights in the status of citizenship and thus creating a universal right to real income which is not proportionate to the market value of the claimant. Class-abatement is still the aim of social rights, but it has acquired a new meaning. It is no longer merely an attempt to abate the obvious nuisance of destitution in the lowest ranks of society. It has assumed the guise of action modifying the whole pattern of social inequality. It is no longer content to raise the floor-level in the basement of the social edifice, leaving the superstructure as it was. It has begun to remodel the whole building, and it might even end by converting a skyscraper into a bungalow. It is therefore important to consider whether any such ultimate aim is implicit in the nature of this development, or whether, as I put it at the outset, there are natural limits to the contemporary drive towards greater social and economic equality. [...]

The degree of equalization achieved [by the modern system of welfare benefits] depends on four things; whether the benefit is offered to all or to a limited class; whether it takes the form of money payment or service rendered; whether the minimum is high or low; and how the money to pay for the benefit is raised. Cash benefits subject to income limit and means test had a simple and obvious equalizing effect. They achieved class-abatement in the early and limited sense of the term. The aim was to ensure that all citizens should attain at least to the prescribed minimum, either by their own resources or with assistance if they could not do it without. The benefit was given only to those who needed it, and thus inequalities at the bottom of the scale were ironed out. The system operated in its simplest and most unadulterated form in the case of the *Poor Law* and old age pensions. But economic equalization might be accompanied by psychological class discrimination. The stigma which attached to the *Poor Law* made 'pauper' a derogatory term defining a class. 'Old age pensioner' may have had a little of the same flavour, but without the taint of shame. [...]

The extension of the social services is not primarily a means of equalizing incomes. In some cases it may, in others it may not. The question is relatively unimportant; it belongs to a different department of social policy. What matters is that there is a general enrichment of the concrete substance of civilized life, a general reduction of risk and insecurity, an equalization between the more and the less fortunate at all levels — between the healthy and the sick, the employed and the unemployed, the old and the active, the bachelor and the father of a large family. Equalization is not so much between classes as between individuals within a population which is now treated for this purpose as though it were one class. Equality of status is more important than equality of income. [...]

I said earlier that in the twentieth century citizenship and the capitalist class system have been at war. Perhaps the phrase is rather too strong, but it is quite clear that the former has imposed modifications on the latter. But we should not be justified in assuming that, although status is a principle that conflicts with contract, the stratified status system which is creeping into citizenship is an alien element in the economic world outside. Social rights in their modern form imply an invasion of contract by status, the subordination of market price to social justice, the replacement of the free bargain by the declaration of rights. But are these principles quite foreign to the practice of the market today, or are they there already, entrenched within the contract system itself? I think it is clear that they are. [...]

Conclusions

I have tried to show how citizenship, and other forces outside it, have been altering the pattern of social inequality.... We have to look, here, for the combined effects of three factors. First, the compression, at both ends, of the scale of income distribution. Second, the great extension of the area of common culture and common experience. And third, the enrichment of the universal status of citizenship, combined with the recognition and stabilization of certain status differences chiefly through the linked systems of education and occupation. [...]

I asked, at the beginning, whether there was any limit to the present drive towards social equality inherent in the principles governing the movement. My answer is that the preservation of economic inequalities has been made more difficult by the enrichment of the status of citizenship. There is less room for them, and there is more and more likelihood of their being challenged. But we are certainly proceeding at present on the assumption that the hypothesis is valid. And this assumption provides the answer to the second question. We are not aiming at absolute equality. There are limits inherent in the egalitarian movement. But the movement is a double one. It operates partly through citizenship and partly through the economic system. In both cases the aim is to remove inequalities which cannot be regarded as legitimate, but the standard of legitimacy is different. In the former it is the standard of social justice, in the latter it is social justice combined with economic necessity. It is possible, therefore, that the inequalities permitted by the two halves of the movement will not coincide. Class distinctions may survive which have no appropriate economic function, and economic differences which do not correspond with accepted class distinctions. [...]

(iii) Return of the Citizen: A Survey of Recent Work on Citizenship Theory

Will Kymlicka and Wayne Norman

INTRODUCTION

There has been an explosion of interest in the concept of citizenship among political theorists....

There are a number of reasons for this renewed interest in citizenship in the 1990s. At the level of theory it is a natural evolution in political discourse because the concept of citizenship seems to integrate the demands of justice and community membership — the central concepts of the political philosophy in the 1970s and 1980s, respectively. Citizenship is intimately linked to ideas of individual entitlement on the one hand and of attachment to a particular community on the other. Thus, it may help clarify what is really at stake in the debate between liberals and communitarians.

Interest in citizenship has also been sparked by a number of recent political events and trends throughout the world — increasing voter apathy and long-term welfare dependency in the United States,

---

From Ronald Beiner, ed. *Theorizing Citizenship* (Albany: State University of New York Press, 1995) AT 283–91, 301–309. Notes omitted. This article is originally published in the journal *Ethics*, vol. 104, #2 (1994): 351–81. Reproduced with permission of University of Chicago Press.

the resurgence of nationalist movements in Eastern Europe, the stresses created by an increasingly multicultural and multiracial population in Western Europe, the backlash against the welfare state in Thatcher's England, the failure of environmental policies that rely on voluntary citizen cooperation, and so forth.

These events have made clear that the health and stability of a modern democracy depends, not only on the justice of its "basic structure" but also on the qualities and attitudes of its citizens, for example, their sense of identity and how they view potentially competing forms of national, regional, ethnic, or religious identities; their ability to tolerate and work together with others who are different from themselves; their desire to participate in the political process in order to promote the public good and hold political authorities accountable; their willingness to show self-restraint and exercise personal responsibility in their economic demands and in personal choices which affect their health and the environment. Without citizens who possess these qualities, democracies become difficult to govern, even unstable.

. . . .

THE POSTWAR ORTHODOXY

Before describing the new work on citizenship, it is necessary to outline quickly the view of citizenship that is implicit in much postwar political theory and that is defined almost entirely in terms of the possession of rights.

The most influential exposition of this postwar conception of citizenship-as-rights is T.H. Marshall's "Citizenship and Social Class," written in 1949. According to Marshall, citizenship is essentially a matter of ensuring that everyone is treated as a full and equal member of society. And the way to ensure this sense of membership is through according people an increasing number of citizenship rights.

. . . .

For Marshall, the fullest expression of citizenship requires a liberal-democratic welfare state. By guaranteeing civil, political, and social rights to all, the welfare state ensures that every member of society feels like a full member of society, able to participate in and enjoy the common life of society. Where any of these rights are withheld or violated, people will be marginalized and unable to participate.

This is often called "passive" or "private" citizenship, because of its emphasis on passive entitlements and the absence of any obligation to participate in public life. It is still widely supported, and with good reason: "the benefits of private citizenship are not to be sneezed at: they place certain basic human goods (security, prosperity, and freedom) within the grasp of nearly all, and that is nothing less than a fantastic human achievement" (Macedo 1990, p. 39).

Nevertheless, this orthodox postwar conception of citizenship has come increasingly under attack in the past decade. For the purposes of this article, we can identify two sets of criticisms. The first set focuses on the need to supplement (or replace) the passive acceptance of citizenship responsibilities and virtues, including economic self-reliance, political participation, and even civility. These issues are discussed in section III.

The second set focuses on the need to revise the current definition of citizenship to accommodate the increasing social and cultural pluralism of modern societies. Can citizenship provide a common experience, identity and allegiance for the members of society? Is it enough simply to include historically excluded groups on an equal basis, or are special measures sometimes required? This issue is discussed in section IV.

THE RESPONSIBILITIES AND VIRTUES OF CITIZENSHIP

A. The New Right Critique of Social Citizenship and the Welfare State

The first, and most politically powerful, critique of the postwar orthodoxy came from the New Right's attack on the idea of "social right." These rights had always been resisted by the right, on the grounds that they were *(a)* inconsistent with the demands of (negative) freedom or (desert-based) justice, *(b)* economically inefficient, and *(c)* steps down "the road to serfdom." But in the public's eye, these arguments were seen as either implausible or, at any rate, as justifiably outweighed by considerations of social justice or by a citizenship-based welfare state such as Marshall's.

One of the revolutions in conservative thinking during the Thatcher/Reagan years was the willingness to engage the left in battle over the domain of social citizenship itself. Whereas Marshall had argued that social rights enable the disadvantaged to enter the mainstream of society and effectively exercise their civil and political rights, the New Right argues that the welfare state has promoted passivity among the poor, without actually improving their life chances, and created a culture of dependency. Far from being the solution, the welfare state has itself perpetuated the problem by reducing citizens to passive dependents who are under bureaucratic tutelage. According to Norman Barry, there is no evidence that welfare programs have in fact promoted more active citizenship (Barry 1990, pp. 43–53).

The New Right believes that the model of passive citizenship underestimated the extent to which fulfilling certain obligations is a precondition for being accepted as a full member of society. In particular, by failing to meet the obligation to support themselves, the long-term unemployed are a source of shame for society as well as themselves (Mead 1986, p. 240). Failure to fulfill common obligations is as much of an obstacle to full membership as the lack of equal rights. In these circumstances, "to obligate the dependent as others are obligated is essential to equality, not opposed to it. An effective welfare [policy] must include recipients in the common obligations of citizens rather than exclude them" (Mead 1986, pp. 12–13).

According to the New Right, to ensure the social and cultural integration of the poor we must go "beyond entitlement," and focus instead on their responsibility to earn a living. Since the welfare state discourages people from becoming self-reliant, the safety net should be cut back and any remaining welfare benefits should have obligations tied to them. This is the idea behind one of the principal reforms of the welfare system in the 1980s: "workfare" programs, which require welfare recipients to work for their benefits, to reinforce the idea that citizens should be self-supporting.

This New Right vision of citizenship has not gone unchallenged. For example, the claim that the rise of an unemployed welfare-underclass is due to the availability of welfare ignores the impact of global economic restructuring, and sits uncomfortably with the fact that many of the most extensive welfare states (in Scandinavia, e.g.) have traditionally enjoyed among the lowest unemployment rates.

Moreover, critics charge, it is difficult to find any evidence that the New Right reforms of the 1980s have promoted responsible citizenship. These reforms aimed to extend the scope of markets in people's lives — through freer trade, deregulation, tax cuts, the weakening of trade unions, and the tightening of unemployment benefits — in part in order to teach people the virtues of initiative, self-reliance, and self-sufficiency (Mulgan 1991, p. 43).

Instead, however, many market deregulations arguably made possible an era of unprecedented greed and economic irresponsibility, as evidenced by the savings and loan and junk bond scandals in America (Mulgan 1991, p. 39). Also, cutting welfare benefits, far from getting the disadvantaged back on their feet, has expanded the underclass. Class inequalities have been exacerbated, and the working poor and unemployed have been effectively "disenfranchised," unable to participate in the new economy of the New Right (Fierlbeck 1991, p. 579; Hoover and Plant 1988, chap. 12).

For many, therefore, the New Right program is most plausibly seen not as an alternative account of citizenship but as an assault on the very principle of citizenship. As Plant puts it, "Instead of accepting citizenship as a political and social status, modern Conservatives have sought to reassert the role of the market and have rejected the idea that citizenship confers a status independent of economic standing" (Plant 1991, p. 52; cf. Heater 1990, p. 303; King 1987, pp. 196–98).

B. Rethinking Social Citizenship

Given these difficulties with the New Right critique of welfare entitlements, most people on the left continue to defend the principle that full citizenship requires social rights. For the left, Marshall's argument that people can be full members and participants in the common life of society only if their basic needs are met "is as strong now ... as it ever was" (Ignatieff 1989, p. 72). However, many on the left accept that the existing institutions of the welfare state are unpopular, in part because they seem to promote passivity and dependence, and to "facilitate a privatist retreat from citizenship and a particular 'clientalization' of the citizen's role" (Habermas 1992, pp. 10–11; cf. King 1987, pp. 45–46).

How then should the state foster self-reliance and personal responsibility? The left has responded ambivalently to issues such as "workfare." On the one hand, the principle of personal responsibility and social obligation has always been at the heart of socialism (Mulgan 1991, p. 39). A duty to work is, after all, implicit in Marx's famous slogan, "From each according to his talents, to each according to his needs." Some people on the left, therefore, express qualified acceptance of workfare, if it "gives both responsibility and the power to use it" (Mulgan 1991, p. 46).

On the other hand, most people on the left remain uncomfortable with imposing obligations as a matter of public policy. They believe that the dependent are kept out of the mainstream of society because of a lack of opportunities, such as jobs, education, and training, not because of any desire to avoid work. Imposing obligations, therefore, is futile if genuine opportunities are absent, and unnecessary if those opportunities are present, since the vast majority of people on welfare would prefer not to be (King 1987, pp. 186–91; Fullinwider 1988, pp. 270–78). Rather than impose an obligation to work, the left would try to achieve full employment through, for example, worker-training programs. So while the left accepts the general principle that citizenship involves both rights and responsibilities, it feels that rights to participate must, in a sense, precede the responsibilities — that is, it is only appropriate to demand fulfillment of the responsibilities after the rights to participate are secured.

A similar rejection of the New Right's view of citizenship can be found in recent feminist discussions of citizenship. Many feminists accept the importance of balancing rights and responsibilities — indeed, Carol Gilligan's findings suggest that women, in their everyday moral reasoning, prefer the language of responsibility to the language of rights (Gilligan 1982, p. 19). But feminists have grave doubts about the New Right rhetoric of economic self-sufficiency. Gender-neutral talk about "self-reliance" is often a code for the view that men should financially support the family, while women should look after the household and care for the elderly, the sick, and the young. This reinforces, rather than eliminates, the barriers to women's full participation in society.

When the New Right talks about self-reliance, the boundaries of the "self" include the family — it is families that should be self-reliant. Hence, greater "self-reliance" is consistent with, and may even require, greater dependency within the family. Yet women's dependence on men within the family can be every bit as harmful as welfare dependency, since it allows men to exercise unequal power over decisions regarding sex, reproduction, consumption, leisure, and so on (King 1987, p. 47; Okin 1989, pp. 128–29).

Since perceptions of responsibility tend to fall unequally on women, many feminists share the left's view that rights to participate must, in a sense, precede responsibilities. Indeed, feminists wish to expand the list of social rights, in order to tackle structural barriers to women's full participation as citizens that the welfare state currently ignores, or even exacerbates, such as the unequal distribution of domestic responsibilities (Phillips 1991a, 1991b; Okin 1992). Given the difficulty of combining family and public responsibilities, equal citizenship for women is impossible until workplaces and career expectations are rearranged to allow more room for family responsibilities and until men accept their share of domestic responsibilities (Okin 1989, pp. 175–77).

However, if rights must precede responsibilities, it seems we are back to the old view of passive citizenship. Yet the left, as much as the right, accepts the need for change. The most popular proposal is to decentralize and democratize the welfare state, for example, by giving local welfare agencies more power and making them accountable to their clients (Pierson 1991, pp. 200–207). Hence, the now-familiar talk of "empowering" welfare recipients by supplementing welfare rights with democratic participatory rights in the administration of welfare programs.

This is the central theme of the contemporary left view of social citizenship. Whether it will work to overcome welfare dependency is difficult to say. Service providers have often resisted attempts to increase their accountability (Rustin 1991, p. 231; Pierson 1991, pp. 206–207). Moreover there may be some tension between the goal of increasing democratic accountability to the local community and increasing accountability to clients (Plant 1990, p. 30)....

. . . .

CITIZENSHIP, IDENTITY, AND DIFFERENCE

Citizenship is not just a certain status, defined by a set of rights and responsibilities. It is also an identity, an expression of one's membership in a political community. Marshall saw citizenship as a shared identity that would integrate previously excluded groups within British society and provide a source of national unity. He was particularly concerned to integrate the working classes, whose lack of education and economic resources excluded them from the "common culture" which should have been a "common possession and heritage" (Marshall 1965, pp. 101–102).

It has become clear, however, that many groups — blacks, women, Aboriginal peoples, ethnic and religious minorities, gays and lesbians — still feel excluded from the "common culture," despite possessing the common rights of citizenship. Members of these groups feel excluded not only because of

(iii) Return of the Citizen: A Survey of Recent Work on Citizenship Theory

their socioeconomic status but also because of their sociocultural identity — their "difference."

An increasing number of theorists, whom we will call "cultural pluralists," argue that citizenship must take account of these differences. Cultural pluralists believe that the common rights of citizenship, originally defined by and for white men, cannot accommodate the special needs of minority groups. These groups can only be integrated into the common culture if we adopt what Iris Marion Young calls a conception of "differentiated citizenship" (Young 1989, p. 258).

On this view, members of certain groups would be incorporated into the political community not only as individuals but also through the group, and their rights would depend, in part, on their group membership. For example, some immigrant groups are demanding special rights or exemptions to accommodate their religious practices; historically disadvantaged groups, such as women or blacks, are demanding special representation in the political process; and many national minorities (Québécois, Kurds, Catalans) are seeking greater powers of self-government within the larger country, if not outright secession.

These demands for "differentiated citizenship" pose a serious challenge to the prevailing conception of citizenship. Many people regard the idea of group-differentiated citizenship as a contradiction in terms. On the orthodox view, citizenship is, by definition, a matter of treating people as individuals with equal rights under the law. This is what distinguishes democratic citizenship from feudal and other premodern views that determined people's political status by their religious, ethnic, or class membership. Hence "the organization of society on the basis of rights or claims that derive from group membership is sharply opposed to the concept of society based on citizenship" (Porter 1987, p. 128). The idea of differentiated citizenship, therefore, is a radical development in citizenship theory.

One of the most influential theorists of cultural pluralism is Iris Marion Young. According to Young, the attempt to create a universal conception of citizenship which transcends group differences is fundamentally unjust because it oppresses historically excluded groups: "In a society where some groups are privileged while others are oppressed, insisting that as citizens persons should leave behind their particular affiliations and experiences to adopt a general point of view serves only to reinforce the privilege; for the perspective and interests of the privileged will tend to dominate this unified public, marginalizing or silencing those of other groups" (Young 1989, p. 257). Young gives two reasons why genuine equality requires affirming rather than ignoring group differences. First, culturally excluded groups are at a disadvantage in the political process, and "the solution lies at least in part in providing institutionalized means for the explicit recognition and representation of oppressed groups" (Young 1989, p.259). These procedural measures would include public funds for advocacy groups, guaranteed representation in political bodies, and veto rights over specific policies that affect a group directly (Young 1989, pp. 261–62; 1990, pp.183–91).

Second, culturally excluded groups often have distinctive needs which can only be met through group-differentiated policies. These include language rights for Hispanics, land rights for Aboriginal groups, and reproductive rights for women (Young 1990, pp. 175–83). Other policies which have been advocated by cultural pluralists include group libel laws for women or Muslims, publicly funded schools for certain religious minorities, and exemptions from laws that interfere with religious worship, such as Sunday closing, animal-slaughtering legislation for Jews and Muslims, or motorcycle helmet laws for Sikhs (Parekh 1990, p. 705; 1991, pp. 197–204; Modood 1992).

Much has been written regarding the justification for these rights and how they relate to broader theories of justice and democracy. Young herself defends them as a response to "oppression," of which she outlines five forms: exploitation, marginalization, powerlessness, cultural imperialism, and "random violence and harassment motivated by group hatred or fear" (Young 1989, p. 261). It would take us too far afield to consider these justifications or the various objections to them. Instead, we will focus on the impact of these rights on citizenship identity.

Critics of differentiated citizenship worry that if groups are encouraged by the very terms of citizenship to turn inward and focus on their "difference" (whether racial, ethnic, religious, sexual, and so on), then "the hope of a larger fraternity of all Americans will have to be abandoned" (Glazer 1983, p. 227). Citizenship will cease to be "a device to cultivate a sense of community and a common sense of purpose" (Heater 1990, p. 295; Kristeva 1993, p. 7; Cairns 1993). Nothing will bind the various groups in society together and prevent the spread of mutual mistrust of conflict (Kukathas 1993, p. 156).

Critics also worry that differentiated citizenship would create a "politics of grievance." If, as Young implies, only oppressed groups are entitled to differentiated citizenship, this may encourage group leaders to devote their political energy to establishing a perception of disadvantage — rather than working to overcome it — in order to secure their claim to group rights.

These are serious concerns. In evaluating them, however, we need to distinguish three different kinds of groups and three different kinds of group rights, which both Young and her critics tend to run together: *(a)* special representation rights (for disadvantaged groups); *(b)* multicultural rights (for immigrant and religious groups); and *(c)* self-government rights (for national minorities). Each of these has very different implications for citizenship identity.

Special representation rights. — For many of the groups on Young's list, such as the poor, elderly, African-Americans, and gays, the demand for group rights takes the form of special representation within the political process of the larger society. Since Young views these rights as a response to conditions of oppression, they are most plausibly seen as a temporary measure on the way to a society where the need for special representation no longer exists. Society should seek to remove the oppression, thereby eliminating the need for these rights.

Self-government rights. — In some of Young's examples, such as the reservation system of the American Indians, the demand for group rights is not seen as a temporary measure, and it is misleading to say that group rights are a response to a form of oppression that we hope someday to eliminate. Aboriginal peoples and other national minorities like the Québécois or Scots claim permanent and inherent rights, grounded in a principle of self-determination. These groups are "cultures," "peoples," or "nations," in the sense of being historical communities, more or less institutionally complete, occupying a given homeland or territory, sharing a distinct language and history. These nations find themselves within the boundaries of a larger political community, but claim the right to govern themselves in certain key matters, in order to ensure the full and free development of their culture and the best interests of their people. What these national minorities want is not primarily better representation in the central government but, rather, the transfer of power and legislative jurisdictions from the central government to their own communities.

Multicultural rights. — The case of Hispanics and other immigrant groups in the United States is different again. Their demands include public support of bilingual education and ethnic studies in schools and exemptions from laws that disadvantage them, given their religious practices. These measures are intended to help immigrants express their cultural particularity and pride without its hampering their success in the economic and political institutions of the dominant society. Like self-government rights, these rights need not be temporary, because the cultural differences they promote are not something we hope to eliminate. But unlike self-government rights, multicultural rights are intended to promote integration into the larger society, not self-government.

. . . .

Would adopting one or more of these group rights undermine the integrative function of citizenship? A closer look at the distinction between the three kinds of rights suggests that such fears are often misplaced. The fact is that, generally speaking, the demand for both representation rights and multicultural rights is a demand for inclusion. Groups that feel excluded want to be included in the larger society, and the recognition and accommodation of their "difference" is intended to facilitate this.

. . . .

Self-government rights, however, do raise deep problems for traditional notions of citizenship identity. While both representation and multicultural rights take the larger political community for granted and seek greater inclusion in it, demands for self-government reflect a desire to weaken the bonds with the larger community and, indeed, question its very nature, authority, and permanence. If democracy is the rule of the people, group self-determination raises the question of who "the people" really are. National minorities claim that they are distinct peoples, with inherent rights of self-determination which were not relinquished by their (sometimes involuntary) federation with other nations within a larger country. Indeed, the retaining of certain powers is often explicitly spelled out in the treaties or constitutional agreements which specified the terms of federation.

Self-government rights, therefore, are the most complete case of differentiated citizenship, since they divide the people into separate "peoples," each with its own historic rights, territories, and powers of self-government, and each, therefore, with its own political community.

It seems unlikely that differentiated citizenship can serve an integrative function in this context. If citizenship is membership in a political community, then in creating overlapping political communities, self-government rights necessarily give rise to a sort of dual citizenship and to potential conflicts about which community citizens identify with most deeply (Vernon 1988). Moreover, there seems to be no natural stopping point to the demands for increasing self-government. If limited autonomy is granted, this may simply fuel the ambitions of nationalist leaders who will be satisfied with nothing short of their own undifferentiated nation-state. Democratic multination states are, it would seem, inherently unstable for this reason.

. . . .

What, then, is the source of unity in a multination country? Rawls claims that the source of union in modern societies is a shared conception of justice: "Although a well-ordered society is divided and pluralistic ... public agreement on questions of political and social justice supports ties of civic friendship and secures the bonds of association" (Rawls 1980, p. 540). But the fact that two national groups share the same principles of justice does not necessarily give them any strong reason to join (or remain) together, rather than remaining (or splitting into) two separate countries. The fact that people in Norway and Sweden share the same principles of justice is no reason for them to regret the secession of Norway in 1905. Similarly, the fact that the anglophones and francophones in Canada share the same principles of justice is not a strong reason to remain together, since the Québécois rightly assume that their own national state could respect the same principles. A shared conception of justice throughout a political community does not necessarily generate a shared identity, let alone a shared citizenship identity that will supersede rival identities based on ethnicity (Nickel 1990; Norman 1993a).

It seems clear, then, that this is one place where we really do need a theory of citizenship, not just a theory of democracy or justice. How can we construct a common identity in a country where people not only belong to separate political communities but also belong in different ways — that is, some are incorporated as individuals and others through membership in a group? Taylor calls this "deep diversity" and insists that it is "the only formula" on which a multination state can remain united (Taylor 1991). However, he admits that it is an open question what holds such a country together.

Indeed, the great variance in historical, cultural, and political situations in multination states suggests that any generalized answer to this question will likely be overstated. It might be a mistake to suppose that one could develop a general theory about the role of either a common citizenship identity or a differentiated citizenship identity in promoting or hindering national unity (Taylor 1992b, pp. 65–66). Here, as with the other issues we have examined in this survey, it remains unclear what we can expect from a "theory of citizenship."

(iv) Left and Rights

Stuart Hall and David Held

'Citizenship' has been largely absent from political discussion and debate for more than two decades. Only in relation to questions of race and immigration did it carry a deep political charge. Were the boundaries of citizenship to be redrawn with the end of empire? Could there be more than one class of citizenship for people of different ethnic backgrounds? The debate, crowned by the intervention of Enoch Powell in the late 1960s, marked a high point in the political currency of this dimension of citizenship. Elsewhere, the concept seemed rather out-of-date. Suddenly, however, citizenship is once more on the lips of politicians, academics and commentators of all political complexions. Why this renewed concern? What is at stake in this debate about citizenship between Right and Left?

This article first appeared in June 1989, *Marxism Today* 33(b) at 16–23. Reproduced with permission.

A number of different factors seem to be responsible for the return of citizenship to the political agenda. Some derive from the experience of Thatcherism itself: the dismantling of the welfare state, the growing centralisation of power, the erosion of local democracy, of free speech, trade-union and other civil rights.

Some have a wider, more 'global', context: the growth of regional nationalism in Scotland and elsewhere; the prospects for greater European integration; the weakening of the old East-West frontiers under the Gorbachev offensive; the growing pace of international interdependence and globalisation — all, in one way or another, exposing and eroding the sovereignty of the nation-state, the entity to which, until now, the modern language of citizenship primarily referred.

These changes have been accompanied by shifts in attitude towards the idea of citizenship on both the Right and the Left. It used to be fashionable in some sections of the Left to dismiss the question of 'rights' as, largely, a bourgeois fraud. But the experience of Thatcherism in the West and of stalinism in the East has gradually shifted the Left's thinking on this question. The shift on the Right is more complex and uncertain. Thatcherism's drive towards unrestricted private accumulation, its attack on public expenditure, collectivism and the 'dependency culture' made it the natural enemy of citizenship in its modern, welfare-state form. As the prime minister put it: 'There is no such thing as society, only individual men and women and their families.'

However, this unswerving commitment to individualism and the competitive ethic has awakened, in its turn, the spectre of Hobbes' 'war of all against all': the breakdown of a sense of community and interdependence, the weakening of the social fabric and the loosening of the bounds of social violence — so often features of a society dedicated exclusively to competitive self-interest. Thatcherism has therefore rediscovered the need for some concept to help integrate and 'bind' society and has come up with the idea of the 'active citizen', who engages in 'doing good' but in a purely private capacity. In this discourse, citizenship is detached from its modern roots in institutional reform, in the welfare state and community struggles, and rearticulated with the more Victorian concepts of charity, philanthropy and self-help. In more recent versions, the 'active citizen' is decked out in the pious homilies of Thatcherism's version of the New Testament.

Clearly, we need a framework for thinking about citizenship and its place in the agenda of the Left which sets it in the context of recent developments. Far from simply returning us to the old language of citizenship, such an exercise requires us to confront new questions and to rethink the concept itself in the light of a new historical situation.

Does 'citizenship' belong, naturally and exclusively, to the Left? It has been part of what can broadly be identified as a variety of progressive historical movements — from older ideas of a just moral order to Paine's *Rights of Man* and Chartism. Nevertheless, it seems to be the case that citizenship belongs *exclusively* to neither Right nor Left, nor indeed to centre-ground. Like all the key contested political concepts of our time, it can be appropriated within very different political discourses and articulated to very different political positions — as its recuperation by the new Right clearly shows. The concept can only mean something decisive for the Left if we are prepared to do some theoretical and political work around it, actively integrating it within a whole set of related political ideas.

While there is no 'essence' to citizenship, it does have a long and rich history with which any new conception must come to terms. From the ancient world to the present day, citizenship has entailed a discussion of, and a struggle over, the meaning and scope of membership of the community in which one lives. Who belongs and what does 'belonging' mean in practice? Membership, here, is not conditional: it is a matter of right and entitlement. But it is two-sided, reciprocal: rights in, but also responsibilities towards, the community. These rights have to be defined and specified, because otherwise their loss cannot be challenged, and may even go undetected. But formal definition alone will not suffice. Rights can be mere paper claims unless they can be practically enacted and realised, through actual participation in the community. These then are citizenship's three leading notions: membership; rights and duties in reciprocity; real participation in practice.

The issues around membership — who does and who does not belong — is where the *politics* of citizenship begins. It is impossible to chart the history of the concept very far without coming sharply up against successive attempts to restrict citizenship to certain groups and to exclude others. In different historical periods, different groups have led, and profited from this 'politics of closure': property-owners, men, white people, the educated, those in particular occupations or with particular skills, adults. However, as the struggles against exclusion have developed and broadened across history, so those stemming from the exclusive enjoyment of the advantages of property, ownership, wealth and privilege — in short, questions of *class* — have come to dominate

(iv) Left and Rights

the 'politics of citizenship', absorbing a wide variety of different struggles against different forms of exclusion under their rubric.

Certainly, class has constituted, historically, one of the most powerful and ramified of barriers to membership and participation by the majority. But this has also set up a tension within the idea of citizenship itself. For, as the politics of citizenship has been absorbed into class politics, so the citizenship idea has lost something of its specific force.

However, this exclusive reference to class is one of the things which is changing with the renewed interest in citizenship. In reality, attempts to restrict membership and participation take many different forms, involving different practices of exclusion and affecting different groups. This should be enough to convince us that questions of citizenship, though bound to place the issues of class at their centre, cannot simply be absorbed into class politics, or thought of exclusively in class terms, and in relation to capitalist relations of production.

A contemporary 'politics of citizenship' must take into account the role which the social movements have played in *expanding* the claims to rights and entitlements to new areas. It must address not only issues of class and inequality, but also questions of membership posed by feminism, the black and ethnic movements, ecology (including the moral claims of the animal species and of Nature itself) and vulnerable minorities, like children. But it must also come to terms with the problems posed by 'difference' in a deeper sense: for example, the diverse communities to which we belong, the complex interplay of identity and identification in modern society, and the differentiated ways in which people now participate in social life. The diversity of arenas in which citizenship is being claimed and contested today is essential to any modern conception of it because it is inscribed in the very logic of modern society itself.

However, this expansion of the idea of citizenship may run counter to the logic of citizenship, which has tended to absorb 'differences' into one common universal status — the citizen. In the year of the anniversary of the French Revolution, it is worth recalling that its three cardinal principles — liberty, equality and fraternity — formed a matrix within which the citizens of the new Republic claimed *universal* recognition on the basis of a common *equality*. This language of theoretical universality and equality is what distinguished this moment — the moment of the 'Rights of Man' — from earlier phases in the long march of citizenship. But in the light of the expansion and diversity of claims discussed above, the question must be posed as to whether the variety and range of entitlements can be adequately expressed through or represented by a single, universal status like 'citizenship'. Is there now an irreconcilable tension between the thrust to equality and universality entailed in the very idea of the 'citizen', and the variety of particular and specific needs, of diverse sites and practices which constitute the modern political subject?

We will come back to this question of 'difference' later — it is, in some ways, the joker in the citizenship pack. However, what the previous discussion makes clear is that contemporary claims to citizenship are interrelated with a range of other political questions. What we think about this range of political questions will inevitably affect what we think about citizenship itself.

What does the language of citizenship rights really mean in contemporary society? And who are the subjects of such rights? Citizenship rights are *entitlements*. Such entitlements are public and social (hence Mrs. Thatcher's difficulties with them). They are 'of right' and can only be abrogated by the state under clearly delimited circumstances (e.g., in the case of imprisonment, which curtails liberties which all citizens should otherwise enjoy). However, though citizenship is a social status, its rights are entitlements to individuals. Individual citizens enjoy such entitlements on the basis of a fundamental equality of condition — i.e., their membership of the community.

Citizenship rights establish a legitimate sphere for *all* individuals to pursue their actions and activities without risk of arbitrary or unjust political interference. Early attempts to achieve citizenship involved a struggle for the autonomy or independence of individuals from the locale in which they were born and from prescribed occupations. Later struggles have involved such things as individual entitlement to freedom of speech, expression, belief, information, as well as the freedom of association on which trade-union rights depend, and freedom of women in relation to marriage and property. Citizenship rights can therefore be thought of as a measure of the autonomy an individual citizen enjoys as a result of his or her status as 'free and equal' members of a society. The other important feature is that, though they are guaranteed to citizens by the state, they are also, in an important sense, guaranteed *against* the arbitrary exercise of state power. Citizenship in its full sense therefore combines, in rather unusual ways, the public and the social with the individual aspects of political life.

The left critique of this position is by now quite familiar, and carries considerable weight. It centres on the emphasis, in the language of rights, on *individual* entitlement. There are really three strands to this critique. First, the degree to which individuals really are 'free' in capitalist democracies is open to question. Second, everything depends on how freedom is defined. The rights and freedoms which interest the new Right refer to a very narrow arena of social action, and are constructed around a very limited conception of individual needs and desires. Largely, these are restricted to individuals as isolated atoms, acting in their own interests, maximised through exchange in the marketplace. Rights are not considered to have a social dimension or an interdependent character. Third, citizenship rights, particularly in Britain, are largely defined negatively. There are no laws preventing you entering the Ritz or buying property in Docklands or applying for most jobs. Whether in fact you have the means or the capacity to do or achieve any of those things, positively, is a quite different matter. In the famous words of Anatole France: 'The law in its majestic equality gives every man (prince and pauper alike) an equal right to sleep under a bridge or eat at the Ritz.'

This is really another way of restating the Left's critique of classic liberalism in terms of the tension between 'formal' and 'substantive' rights. The citizen may formally enjoy 'equality before the law'. But, important though this unquestionably is, does he or she *also* have the material and cultural resources to choose between different courses of action in practice? The 'free and equal individual', as one commentator suggests, is a person found more rarely in practice, than liberal theory suggests. What liberal theory, in both its classic and contemporary forms, takes for granted has, in fact, to be seriously questioned. Namely, whether the existing relations between men and women, between employers and employees, between the social classes, or blacks, whites and other ethnic groups, allow citizenship to become a reality in practice.

This question lies at the centre of the 'politics of citizenship' today. Any current assessment of citizenship must be made on the basis of liberties and rights which are tangible, capable of being enjoyed, in both the state and civil society. If it is not given concrete and practical content, liberty as an abstract principle can scarcely be said to have any very profound consequences for everyday life. It is difficult to hymn the praises of liberty, when massive numbers of actual individuals are systematically restricted — for want of a complex mix of resources and opportunities — from participating actively in political and civil life. Gross inequality of class, sex and race substantively hinder the extent to which it can legitimately be claimed that individuals are really 'free and equal' in contemporary society.

There is therefore, much of substance to the Left's critique of the liberal conception of citizenship. On the other hand, this may have led us to go too far in the opposite direction. We must test every 'formal' right we are supposed to enjoy against its substance in practice. But this does not mean that the formal definition of rights — for example, in a constitution or bill of rights — is unimportant, or a matter of 'mere form'. Until rights have been specified, there is no way of monitoring their infringement or of calling to account their practical implementation.

In general, what this discussion suggests is that the 'politics of citizenship' today must come to terms with, and attempt to strike a new balance between, the individual and the social dimensions of citizenship rights. These two aspects are interdependent and cannot be separated. Neither, on its own, will suffice. On the other hand, there is no *necessary* contradiction between them.

The new Right would argue exactly the opposite, and this is one reason why the relationship between the individual and the social dimensions of rights becomes one of the key issues at stake in exchanges between the new Right and its left critics. The new Right has a very clear and consistent position on the question and the related issues of freedom and equality.

The new Right is committed to the classic liberal doctrine that the collective good can be properly realised in most cases *only* by private individuals acting in competitive isolation, pursuing their interests with minimal state interference. At root, the new Right is concerned with how to advance the cause of 'liberalism' against 'democracy' (or, as they put it, 'freedom' against 'equality') by limiting the possible uses of state power. On this view, the government can only legitimately intervene in society to enforce *general rules* — formal rules which broadly protect, in John Locke's works, the 'life, liberty and estate' of the citizen. Hayek, a leading advocate of these ideas, argues that a free liberal order is incompatible with rules which specify how people should use the means at their disposal. Governments become coercive if they interfere with people's capacity to determine their own objectives. Hence the reliance in Hayek's work on 'law', his critique of the so-called 'totalitarianism' involved in social planning and rejection of

(iv) Left and Rights

the idea that the state can represent the 'public interest'.

Hayek's prime example of coercive government is legislation which attempts to alter the 'material position of particular people or enforce distributive or "social" justice'. Distributive justice, he argues, always imposes on some person or group someone else's conception of merit or desert. It requires the allocation of resources by a central authority acting as *if* it knew what people should receive for their efforts or how to behave. In this view, there is only one mechanism sufficiently sensitive to determine collective choice on an individual basis without such imposition — the free market. When protected by a constitutional state and a framework of law, it is argued, no system provides a mechanism of collective choice as dynamic, innovative and responsive. The free market is, for the new Right, the key condition of the liberty of citizens. When operating within the framework of a minimal state, it thus becomes constitutive of the nature of citizenship itself.

The Left has always taken issue with this line of argument. The free market, it has argued, produces and reinforces those very forms of exclusion and 'closure' associated with private property and wealth, against which the idea of citizenship was directed. Hence, through the redistributive welfare state, the prerogatives of property and wealth had to be cross-cut, modified or, in T.H. Marshall's famous phrase, 'abated', by the countervailing rights of citizenship. In practice, the only force of sufficiently compelling weight to bring to bear against the powers of property and capital was that of the state. Hence, for the Left, the state was not inimical but essential to the very idea of citizenship.

It is indeed difficult to see how a proper conception of citizenship could be established or effectively secured without the intervention of the state. On the other hand, it is not necessary to accept Hayek's line of reasoning to see that citizenship also entails the protection of the citizen *against* the arbitrary overweening exercise of state power. The weaknesses and limitations of a purely 'statist' conception of citizenship have become much more obvious in the light of recent history.

There is, then, an inevitable tension in the Left's position on citizenship, since it both requires and can be threatened by the state. One tendency of the Left has been to resolve or bypass this difficulty by, so to speak, dissolving the whole question into that of democracy itself. The extension of popular democracy, it is thought, will resolve all these knotty problems. Hence the Left's advocacy of collective participation as a resolution to all the problems of citizenship. Why bother to define and entrench specific rights if, in an expanded democracy, every individual is destined to become 'fully sovereign'? Thus, by focusing squarely on the extension of democracy, the Left has tended to leave any further specification of particular citizenship rights, and the complex relations between liberty, social justice and democratic processes, to the ebb and flow of democratic negotiation. From Karl Marx to Lenin to Roy Hattersley (in his recent defence of Labour Party policy against Charter 88) this is a constant and recurring theme. 'The people' are to become sovereign (via, respectively, the Commune, Soviets, Parliament). 'The people' are to become governors of their own affairs — without limit; so the argument runs. Within this broad democratic advance, the specific questions of citizenship and the difficulty of defining particular rights will take care of themselves.

This 'democratic' solution is in many ways an attractive argument. But it presents certain real difficulties. It is vulnerable to the charge of having failed to address the highly complex relations in modern societies between individual liberty, distributional questions of social justice, and democratic processes. It does not really resolve the question of who 'the people' are whose democratic sovereignty and enfranchisement is supposed to settle at a single stroke so many questions about particular rights. And it poses the extremely awkward issue of whether there are to be any specifiable limits to democracy. In short, is 'democracy' alone, unsupplemented and unmodified by any concept of citizenship any longer enough?

Should there be any limits on the power of 'the people' to change or alter political circumstances? The experience of 10 years of 'elective dictatorship' under Mrs. Thatcher may have changed the Left's thinking on this question. For example, should the winning of a majority vote at an election constitute a mandate to destroy parts of the system of local government which has been so important a counterweight to the encroaching powers of a centralising state — especially if achieved under our highly lopsided, first-past-the-post electoral system? Should the nature and scope of the liberty of individuals be left entirely to the 'play' of democratic decision? Don't individuals need to have their rights to freedom of speech, thought and expression protected? Must minorities conform, simply because they are minorities?

By answering questions about the necessary limits to democracy in the affirmative, the new Right at least recognises the possibility of real tensions between individual liberty, collective decision-making and the institutions and processes of democracy. By not systematically addressing these issues, the Left, in contrast, has perhaps too hastily put aside the problems. In making democracy, at all levels, the primary social objective to be achieved, the Left has relied on 'democratic reason' — a wise and good democratic will — for the determination of all just and positive social outcomes. But can 'the people' always be relied upon to be just to minorities or to marginal and so-called 'unpopular' interests? Can one assume that the democratic will will always be wise and good?

This is not a matter of abstract theoretical debate. It is around some of these tensions that the new Right generated so much political capital against the Left. It forced the Left to acknowledge the uncertain outcomes of democratic life: the ambiguous results of the welfare state, for example. It highlighted the fact that distributive justice can also lead to bureaucracy, surveillance and the excessive infringement of individual options (and not only in Eastern Europe). It represented the reallocation of resources by the local state (for example, in the form of 'equal opportunities' and 'anti-racist programmes') as an imposition of minority interests on the majority! These experiences have not necessarily made people more optimistic about collective democratic decision-making or more ready to fight to defend it.

Take the question of 'popular sovereignty'. Will the fact that we are all members of the great, collective democratic subject — 'the people' — provide a guarantee of the rights and the liberties of the individual citizen? Not necessarily. 'The people' is, after all, also a discursive figure, a rhetorical device, a mode of address. It is open to constant negotiation, contestation and redefinition. It represents, as a 'unity', what are in fact a diversity of different positions and interests. In its populist form — 'giving the people what they want' — it has been exploited by Thatcherism as a form of populist mobilisation against a range of different minorities who are 'not one of us'.

'The people' has also functioned so as to silence or marginalise the conflicts of interest which it claims to represent. Thatcherism has operated within a narrow and exclusive definition of 'the people'. It defines 'the people' as those who identify with or have done well out of the enterprise culture. But since, in reality, only a small number of prosperous people, mainly living in parts of the south east, can be represented in this figure, it is in effect a way of suppressing the rights, marginalising the needs and denying the identities of large numbers of other 'people' — including the Scots, the poor, the unemployed, the homeless, the underclasses, black people, many women, single-parent mothers, gay and lesbian people, and so on. Far from resolving anything, it is a highly-contested and contestable idea, around which a great deal of 'ideological work' is constantly going on.

Then there is the problem of what political entity the citizen is a citizen *of*. Everywhere, the nation-state itself — the entity to which the language of political citizenship refers — is eroded and challenged. The processes of economic, political, military and ecological interdependence are beginning to undermine it as a sovereign, self-contained entity from above. The rise of regional and local 'nationalisms' are beginning to erode it from below. In certain respects, this may have negative consequences for citizenship: how to give effect to the 'rights' of the citizens of Bhopal against chemical pollution caused by a multinational company registered in New York and operating worldwide? In other respects, its consequences for citizenship may be positive. The European Court has certainly provided a critical bulwark for the citizen of the UK against the steady erosion of civil liberties under Thatcherism. But whether these processes work to the advantage or disadvantage of citizenship, the question remains: is this the right moment, historically, to be trying to define claims and entitlements made in terms of membership of the nation-state?

There are then all kinds of problems which undermine any certainty that greater democracy will, in and of itself, resolve the dilemmas of citizenship. Is there any way through this impasse?

One point which does follow directly from the foregoing discussion can be stated clearly, and provides us with a fresh start. There is a need to think through, and give institutional expression to the demands of citizenship and democracy as closely-related issues: but it is important to keep these questions distinct. Democracy can only really exist on the basis of 'free and equal citizens'. But citizenship requires some specification, and some institutional and political protection, separate from and beyond the extension of democracy. In short, in the relationship between citizenship and democracy is entailed a new balance — a new settlement — between liberty and equality.

Can the parameters of such a 'new settlement' be further specified? It appears that a plausible resolution of some of the dilemmas of contemporary politics can only be provided if enhanced political participation is embedded in a legal and constitu-

(iv) Left and Rights

tional framework that protects and nurtures individuals and other social categories as 'free and equal citizens'. However, to go down that road has some real political consequences. It requires us, for example, to recognise the importance of a number of fundamental tenets, often dismissed because of their association with liberalism; for example, the centrality, in principle of an 'impersonal' structure of public power; to guarantee and protect rights; a diversity of power centres, both within the state and outside it, in civil society; mechanisms to promote open debate between alternative political platforms; an institutional framework of enforceable and challengeable rights.

In many countries, West and East, the limits of 'government' are explicitly defined in constitutions and bills of rights which are subject to public scrutiny, parliamentary review and judicial process. The Left has sometimes been impatient with this procedural approach — and it is certainly true that no written constitution or judicial review, alone, has been able to guarantee the rights of the citizen against a state which is determined to abolish or reduce them. Nevertheless, the experience of recent history suggests that this idea is fundamental to democracy, conceived as a process which bites deep into the structure of state and society. Constitutional entrenchment, however, is not enough. Any conception of democracy which seeks to elaborate it as a form of 'socialist pluralism' requires the limits on the 'public power' to be reassessed in relation to a far broader range of issues than had been hitherto commonly presupposed.

What would be included in such an expanded system of rights? A constitution or bill of rights which enshrined the idea of the 'double focus' of citizenship — equal rights and equal practices — would have to specify rights with respect to the *processes* that determine outcomes. Thus, not only equal rights to cast a vote, but also to enjoy the conditions of political understanding, involvement in collective decision-making and setting of the political agenda which make the vote meaningful. These conditions for real political participation include, rights with respect to information, education, the 'right to know', including the defence of the right to make public things which governments prefer to keep under official restriction. There would have to be a bundle of social rights linked to reproduction, childcare and health; and economic rights to ensure adequate economic and financial resources for a citizen's autonomy. Without tough social and economic rights, rights with respect to the state could not be enjoyed in practice; and without rights in respect of the state, new forms of inequality of power, wealth and status could systematically disrupt the implementation of social and economic liberties.

For example, a right to reproductive freedom for women entails making public authorities responsible not only for medical and social facilities to prevent or assist pregnancy, but also for providing the material conditions which help to make the choice to have a child a genuinely free one. A right to the capacity really to choose between courses of action obliges the state to implement ways of distributing wealth and income much more equitably. One way of making such resources available may be a guaranteed minimum income for all adults, irrespective of whether they are engaged in wage or household-labour. Strategies of this type have to be treated with caution since their implications for collective or societal wealth-creation are complex and not fully clear. However, without a minimum guaranteed resource-base, many people will remain highly vulnerable and dependent on the charity or goodwill of others — a condition which, despite Mrs. Thatcher's passion for replacing welfare rights with private philanthropy, is in contradiction with the very idea of citizenship.

Such a system of rights must specify certain responsibilities of the state to groups of citizens which particular governments could not (unless permitted by an explicit process of constitutional amendment) override. The authority of the state — even of a much more democratic one than we enjoy at the moment — would thus, in principle, be clearly circumscribed; its capacity for freedom of action to a certain degree bounded. This challenges some fundamental assumptions still widely held on the Left.

We would go further. The important point about such a constitution or bill of rights would be that it radically enhances the ability of citizens to take action *against* the state (including a socialist state) to redress unreasonable encroachments on liberties. This would help tip the balance from state to parliament and from parliament to citizens. It would be an 'empowering' system, breaking with any assumption that the state can successfully define citizens' wants and needs for them, and become the 'caretaker of existence'. It would redefine the balance between state and civil society, which is at the heart of so much rethinking, from Left and Right alike.

Of course, empowerment would not thereby be guaranteed. But rights could be fought for by individuals, groups and movements and could be tested in, among other places, open court. The American system makes it clear that this can lead to interminable wrangles, social change getting delayed and bogged down in 'due process' within the system. On the other hand, the *European Convention on Human Rights* has been a better defence of civil liberties than Britain's more venerable, customary arrangements. On balance, the gains from going in this direction are preferable to the present situation where it is extremely difficult to bring our archaic state system, operating so much of the time on the basis of undefined 'club' rules, to any open accountability.

Enter Charter 88. Charter 88 is rightly concerned with enshrining the rights and liberties of British subjects in a bill of rights and a constitution — and thereby making them 'citizens' for the first time in their history. The Charter is an immediate and practical intervention in current political discussion of the first importance and, as such, is to be welcomed and endorsed. But, if the argument above is correct, then it is a necessary but not a sufficient means for people to establish themselves in their capacity as citizens. In the contexts of the long-term struggle for socialism, it can be seen as one, but only one, essential moment in the elaboration of a diverse range of new rights and their conditions of existence.

The question of difference, however, which we discussed earlier, raises much deeper, more troubling issues, which are not easily resolved in the short term. Older European ideas of citizenship assumed a more culturally-homogeneous population, within the framework of a strong and unitary national state. It seemed appropriate, therefore, to believe that widening the democratic franchise and participation of all citizens would naturally enlarge the freedoms, rights and liberties of everyone.

But social and cultural identities have become more diversified and 'pluralised' in modern society. The modern nation-state is increasingly composed of groups with very different ethnic and cultural identities. Many of these groups belong to other histories, cultures and traditions very different from those of the indigenous people. These cultural differences are crucial to their sense of identity, identification and 'belongingness'. Similar differences are also beginning to show through in the communities and regions which originally constituted the United Kingdom. These differences present new challenges to, and produce new tensions within, what we called earlier the 'universalising' thrust in the idea of citizenship.

Of course, permanent residents in the society, whatever their differences of origin, history and culture, must be able to claim common rights and entitlements, as full members of the political community, without giving up their cultural identities. This is a key entitlement in any modern conception of citizenship — especially in societies whose populations are increasingly culturally and ethnically diverse. But this may not resolve all the problems. Differences of all kinds will continue to create *special and particular* needs, over and above those which can be addressed within a universalistic conception of citizenship. As the Rushdie affair demonstrates, it is not always possible to keep universal political claims and particularly cultural ones in separate compartments. They keep overlapping and invading each other's territory.

The politics of citizenship, in sum, throws us into the deep end of some very profound, general, theoretical concerns about politics as well as posing a set of complex organisational issues. To think it through — a project only just beginning — we need to attend to both dimensions. The elements of equality and universality associated with the idea of 'the citizen', and the diverse and particular requirements of different groups which have to be met if they are to enjoy 'free and equal' status, demand that the Left clarify, more profoundly than it has so far, both the principles of the politics of citizenship and their institutional requirements. What is at stake is nothing less than reformulating socialism to take better account of 'citizenship' and the conditions and limits this imposes on state action and political strategy.

B. The Charter of Rights

(i) The Legalisation of Politics in Advanced Capitalism: The Canadian Charter of Rights and Freedoms

Harry J. Glasbeek and Michael Mandel

THE ENTRENCHMENT OF THE CHARTER AND THE EMERGENCE OF THE COURT

As recently as 1977, the leading Canadian constitutional law treatise stated that, despite the lack of entrenched guarantees,

> ...[i]t is a fact, however, that in Canada — as in the United Kingdom, Australia and New Zealand — civil liberties are better respected than in most other countries.

This opinion was echoed by constitutional lawyers and civil libertarians up to and before that time. While this does not prove that Canadians did have all the rights and freedoms they might have wanted, it does demonstrate that conventional wisdom sensed no serious lack of protection for individuals in Canada. Yet, a mere five years later, a *Charter of Rights and Freedoms* was entrenched in the Canadian *Constitution* to the applause of most of the same conventional wisdomeers.

The entrenchment is supposed to ensure that certain rights and freedoms will not be taken from individuals by acts of government. This is to be provided by giving the judiciary the power to disallow government action which infringes the rights and freedoms entrenched. Thus, the judiciary has been given a central role to play in Canadian sociopolitical affairs, beyond the role of umpire between the two levels of government. It has become a recognised participant. There had been no public demand for this change. Indeed, the process of constitutional rearrangement was remarkable for the lack of popular participation. Given that the entrenchment of rights and freedoms was not a response to either a series of triggering events or to a palpable public demand, we may search for its origins in political economy.

. . . .

This is of interest because the judiciary has always had implicit opportunities and, with the *Bill of Rights*, was given some encouragement to enforce human rights and freedoms in Canada well before the entrenchment of the *Charter*. The inhibition demonstrated by the courts raises two issues. First, why would it ever be thought useful to make that very judiciary, whose record on human rights and freedoms was anything but progressive, the dominant means of safe-guarding civil liberties? Second, why would an historically reluctant judiciary play a major role in the creation of this very situation, one in which it would be asked to play a role it had up to then abjured? ...

. . . .

THE LEGALISATION OF POLITICS

The *Charter of Rights and Freedoms* grants to the judiciary a supervisory role over legislation and government activity in general. It constitutes a substantial step in a modern trend towards giving the judiciary a central role in Canadian politics. What view should socialists take of this development? Two possible criteria for appraisal suggest themselves, analogous to Wright's distinction between immediate and fundamental interests of the working class. While it is notorious that these interests may conflict, in that reform in the immediate interests of working people may indeed prolong the existence of capitalism, this is not always the case. Marx argued convincingly that legislative limitations on the hours

---

(1984) 2 *Socialist Studies* 84 at 84, 88, 95–101, 103–104, 106–109, 115. Notes omitted. Reproduced by permission of Society for Socialist Studies.

of work were both in workers' immediate and fundamental interests. Is the *Charter* such a "reform"? What, if anything, does it do for workers, either in the long or the short run? We want briefly to review a number of traditional approaches to *Bills of Rights* which can be adapted to this perspective, before coming to what we believe to be the main point.

The "Content" of Judicial Review

One approach is to analyse judicial review in terms of the "content" of court decisions. Are the courts likely to make more or less progressive decisions than legislatures? Are they likely to cause legislatures to make more or less progressive laws? One way of answering these questions is to look at the historical record. As we have seen, the Canadian Supreme Court's record under the *Canadian Bill of Rights* is one of deference to the federal Parliament. On the other hand, it might be argued that decisions concerning the *Bill of Rights* are not a good test because of the *Bill*'s "non-constitutional" nature. To this it could be said that the courts had power to give it much more reach than they did. Such arguments are inconclusive.

The long experience in the United States with an entrenched *Bill of Rights* provides a richer testing ground. But the record there is, at the very best, equivocal. Proponents of the *Charter* as a potentially progressive tool might cite the desegregation decisions, starting with *Brown* v. *Board of Education of Topeka* in 1954, and the pro-abortion decision of *Roe* v. *Wade* in 1973. On the other hand, the period of time which elapsed between these two cases seems to be the only really progressive one in the Supreme Court's entire 200 year history. Its most active period other than that one (that is to say, active in the enforcement of the *Bill of Rights* against legislation, as opposed to activism in respect of issues of federalism) was one in which it fought a vigorous rearguard action on behalf of laissez-faire capitalism against the regulation of business between 1900 and 1937. The Court struck down hard-fought-for maximum hours, minimum wage, child labour and anti-trust legislation, and so on, until the confrontation with Roosevelt in 1937, after it had "cut the heart from the New Deal Program":

> There is no way of estimating reliably the restraining effect of this cloud of negativisms on state legislators and congressmen who might otherwise have made haste more speedily along the road to the welfare state. No doubt the pace of social change was moderated; a respectable number of "excesses" were prevented; a respectable amount of money was saved for the businessmen; a good many labourers were left a little hungrier than they might have been if the Court had not been there to defend economic liberty.

More recently, the Supreme Court of the United States has invalidated legislation limiting corporate spending in political campaigns as an infringement on "freedom of speech" and local affirmative action programmes intended to benefit historically deprived racial minorities as an infringement of "equal protection of the law". Then, there have been numerous instances throughout its history when the Supreme Court has merely sanctioned reactionary legislation. Famous examples include *Plessy* v. *Ferguson*, which upheld legislation requiring blacks to ride in separate railway cars, the genesis of the "separate but equal doctrine" that stood for sixty years until Brown; the *Korematsu* case in 1945, sustaining removal of Japanese-Americans from their homes to internment camps without proof of anti-government activity by them; and, more recently, decisions sustaining legislation withholding medicare for abortions even where medically necessary. These are all examples of how weak a protector of even "bourgeois" liberty a judicially enforced *Bill of Rights* is. To suppose, on the basis of this record, that a court administering the *Charter* would be likely to launch an attack on the dominant relations of production, even without "property" enshrined therein (for now), would be naive. Moreover, there is nothing in the historical record to indicate that courts will protect those crucial political rights of criticism and dissent to which we are theoretically entitled, even under capitalism. During the prelude to the McCarthy period the *Bill of Rights* did not prevent the Supreme Court of the United States from upholding criminal convictions against Communists because they were Communists. And when, during the same period, an otherwise qualified Canadian candidate was refused admission to the Bar on the sole ground that he was a Communist, none other than Judge C.H. O'Halloran, the Canadian advocate of an entrenched *Bill of Rights* mentioned earlier, approved of the action, notwithstanding the value he put on the principle (entrenched or not) of freedom of speech, thought or opinion:

> Freedom of expression cannot be given to Communists to permit them to use it to destroy our constitutional liberties, by first poisoning the minds of the young, the impressionable, and the irresponsible.
>
> ...
>
> [I]n Canada the accepted and non-technical use of the term "political opinions" is not

(i) The Legalisation of Politics in Advanced Capitalism: The Canadian Charter of Rights and Freedoms

related to the philosophies underlying different systems of Government, but is directed to adherence to or acceptance of the policies of a political party that upholds the constitution and is not subversive in its programme and tendencies.

Nor did the freedom of speech clause in the American *Constitution* prevent the United States from denying the Marxist Ernest Mandel admission to the country for a speaking engagement, long after the McCarthy period had ended.

Horrible though these decisions may seem, they are in no sense aberrations, though there are counter-examples in very different circumstances (besides cases like *Buckley*) where the courts have defended species of political freedom.

The Enforceability of Judicial Decisions

There is also the problem of what one wins when one wins progressive court decisions, since they do not, after all, enforce themselves:

> In 1955, the U.S. Supreme Court, in "Brown II", ordered that Topeka's schools racially desegregate "with all deliberate speed". Presently a federal district court judge is examining Topeka's schools to determine if they are in compliance with that original 1955 decision. Yet this remarkable fact should not surprise us, for in substantive areas as diverse as desegregation, school prayer, and criminal procedure, voluminous impact studies consistently informed us throughout this twenty-five year period of the difficulties encountered in implementing judicial decisions that mandate policy reform and social change.

Enforcement depends on the alignment of real flesh-and-blood social forces, which are much more likely to be in favour of the overruled legislation than vice-versa. Indeed, more than one commentator has noticed that the abortion victories in the American courts in the seventies did more for the "pro-life" movement than for the pro-choice movement. While the legal victories "did not significantly move public opinion toward greater acceptance of abortion", they "triggered almost immediately a strong counterreaction, and the generation of a broad-based, well-organized right-to-life movement" which "gained political momentum throughout the 1970s and now threatens to recriminalize abortion at the level of a constitutional amendment or a human life statute". This may be too sanguine a view of the pro-life movement's chances of success. It may be as hard to *reverse* progressive decisions such as *Roe* v. *Wade* (not to mention reactionary decisions) as it is to *enforce* progressive decisions such as *Brown*. But the argument, that a preferable strategy would have consisted of ordinary political efforts to repeal abortion laws on a state by state basis, seems sound. At least this would have avoided confusing the abortion issue with the different one of democracy versus "government by judiciary" (of which more later).

The Forum of Judicial Review

Disappointment with the "content" of judicial review of legislation, and with the enforceability and impact of even successful litigation, has led some of its supporters to take a different tack altogether, one which emphasizes the political value of the litigation process itself, win or lose....

In other words, litigation provides a forum with special, mostly attention-getting, features for causes that are politically weak or unpopular, as progressive causes frequently are. Why should these features inhere in the judicial process and not in the legislative one? Why should the media pay more attention when interests or positions with minority support are advanced in court than when they are advanced out of court? Assuming that this is the case, we think that the answer has to do with the special nature of legal argument which seems to many to be capable of leading to a special sort of result. In legal argument, the ordinary indicia of political power (for example degree of mass support, wealth) are not supposed to count, and "reason" is supposed to prevail. So, win or lose, the judicial forum provides an opportunity to advance the superior reasoning supporting progressive causes, to challenge laws, to raise consciousness, etc., in a setting where one is likely to be listened to no matter how weak one's political support is. We think that this is an important point — for different reasons — and we return to it shortly. For now, we want to reiterate what we suggested in Part I in connection with the constitutional reference cases, namely that it is a specific kind of "reason" that prevails in court, specifically the kind in which numbers or, to be more precise, *classes* do not count. In other words, you cannot say anything you want in court. Argument must take a particular form. Furthermore, not anyone can speak in court. In most courts, particularly the ones in which these kinds of issues are decided, only lawyers do the actual debating. This may be why lawyers find this forum so appealing. But the problem is not that it is lawyers who do the speaking; it is the language they speak.

Democracy and Judicial Review

. . . .

For all their faults, modern bourgeois legal systems, such as Canada's, do contain substantive and procedural legal rights in many realms of life which are not only of great value to workers, but which are the product of many years of working class struggle. Thus, many Marxists have greeted with approval E.P. Thompson's celebration of "the rule of law" as an "unqualified human good". But the *rule of law* must be sharply distinguished from the *legalisation of politics*. The rule of law is a democratic ideal under which the judicial function is impartially to apply the law to the facts of each case. The ideal of the rule of law is most closely approached when laws are specific and leave little room for personal discretion. It is most democratic when there is popular participation in law making. But the rights in the *Charter* differ from the ordinary legal rights evoked by the notion of the rule of law in both of these respects. In the first place, most of them are entirely *abstract*. The *Charter* does not spell out with precision the nature of these rights. For example, instead of the right to strike in specified circumstances, the *Charter* enshrines "freedom of association" and the "right to liberty". Do these include the right to strike? If so, when? As the American legal philosopher, Ronald Dworkin, has pointed out, rights such as those in the *Charter*, are "appeals to moral *concepts*", not "attempts to lay down particular *conceptions*". They remain to be worked out. Worked out by whom, though? By the courts, of course. The government, on the other hand, has tried to give the impression that the rights in the *Charter* are as precise as can be, that indeed the *Charter* is meant to "clarify" as well as to "strengthen" them, and that the judges have merely to apply them:

> Now, these rights *are* written into the *Constitution* so that you will know exactly where you stand.... The courts are there as an impartial referee to correct injustices in the event that you find that your constitutional rights are being denied.

This is an attempt to conceal the basic democratic dilemma. Whereas without the *Charter*, the nature of rights can be, and is, largely worked out and made concrete by legislatures, with the *Charter*, a more or less substantial chunk of this job is handed over to the courts. The task is taken from people who must be elected on the basis of universal adult suffrage in constituencies all over the country, and who must face re-election on the basis of decisions they or their party have made, and handed over to a handful of lawyers appointed once and for all. Though these lawyers are appointed by the government of the day, their tenure typically outlasts that of their appointers and a relatively rigid hierarchy of judicial authority reposes the ultimate say in nine persons (to paraphrase Marx, nine "kings in the shape of irremovable inquisitors of legality"), all appointed by the federal government. Not only are these people not responsible to any constituency, it is an offence even to criticise their decisions (disrespectfully at least), unless *they* should decide the contempt power is an infringement on "freedom of expression"!

. . . .

What is presented by the government as a strengthening of popular power, turns out to be a restriction on the universal suffrage for which so many bloody struggles were fought over so many bitter years. (Viewed in this light, the absence of the holding of a referendum or the creation of a deliberative constituent assembly in the patriation process seems almost to have been a matter of principle!)

. . . .

Then there is the mystique surrounding the *Charter* itself, deliberately cultivated by such schemes as Ed Broadbent's to hang it "on the wall of every classroom in every school in every region of Canada", which makes *Charter* interpretation a rather awesome process. So, a court administering the *Charter* is a force to be reckoned with by elected representatives. This means, in addition, that political activists must devote enormous resources to litigation which, besides promoting the direct extraction of surplus value in favour of the legal profession, is a drain on the reservoir of energy and material available for direct participation in the political process. The last several years have seen the energies of the Native peoples and the women's movement consumed in the process of constitution-making, the end-result of which is to entrench a series of concepts to be worked out by judges (mostly male and all non-native). Constitutionalism has reached such proportions that, in the case of aboriginal rights, the right to discuss the issues is being entrenched!

. . . .

(i) The Legalisation of Politics in Advanced Capitalism: The Canadian Charter of Rights and Freedoms

The Legalisation of Political Discourse

We are concerned here with a change in discourse, not in the linguistic sense, but in the sense of the structure of discussion, the way in which political issues are categorised and dealt with and, most important, the way in which political decisions are justified. It is the *form of legitimation* which concerns us here. Naturally, a legalisation of political discourse involves a concomitant increment in the peculiar legalese spoken by lawyers, the acquisition of which comprises almost all of their training and which is largely incomprehensible to ordinary human beings. We are concerned that political debate will henceforth have to take this form and be that much more removed from ordinary language. But this is an effect, not the essence, of the phenomenon we seek to identify. Nor are we suggesting that the discourse peculiar to courts imposes significant restraints on them, which force them to come to results very different from those reached by politicians who use a different form of discourse. We accept what the so-called "legal realists" established long ago and what is demonstrated in every courtroom every day, namely that enormous "leeway" exists within judicial reasoning which enables judges to reach conclusions consistent with prevailing interests and values.

Any alternative hypothesis requires (for example) that we believe that differences of judicial opinion such as those in *Re Resolution to Amend the Constitution* are based on profound stupidity on somebody's part (because neither majority nor dissent express any doubt about their positions) and that these differences are uninfluenced by consideration of the social impact of the decision. In other words, judges seem to be no more restrained by their rhetoric than politicians are by theirs. They too can, and do, choose between competing policies and interests, and they too legitimate such choices by reference to reasons which may not reflect their real thinking and motivation. In this they are like legislative politicians. Judges may occasionally support different interests or values than do legislators, reflecting their particular personal biases and the judiciary's separate institutional needs. That they do so is shown by those instances, mentioned earlier, when courts administering Bills of Rights have invalidated legislation. But the evidence also indicates that courts and legislatures generally agree. In other words, legal discourse legitimates decisions necessitated on other grounds, as do other forms of political discourse. Thus, the legalisation of political discourse is a change in the nature of legitimation, not in what is legitimated (though it may *signify* a change in what is legitimated, a point we will pursue later). We should now indicate what we mean by a legal form of discourse.

. . . .

The work of the Soviet legal scholar E.B. Pashukanis is of assistance here. In the 1920s Pashukanis attempted to develop a Marxist theory of law on the basis of the commodity form. His point of departure was the fully developed legal subject of jurisprudence which differed greatly from the zoological human being, in that the legal subject was private, isolated, autonomous, egoistic and possessed of a free will. "Idealist" and "dogmatic" jurisprudence "explained" these strange attributes as innate eternal qualities of human personality: "from this point of view, being a legal subject is a quality inherent in man as an animate being graced with a rational will". And the legal powers of legal subjects were "explained" as emanations from these capacities. This, argued Pashukanis, was completely upsidedown:

> In the logical system of judicial concepts, the contract is merely a form of legal transaction in the abstract, that is, merely one of the will's concrete means of expression which enable the subject to affect the legal sphere surrounding him. Historically speaking, and in real terms, the concept of the legal transaction arose in quite the opposite way, namely from the contract. Outside of the contract, the concepts of the subject and of will only exist, in the legal sense, as lifeless abstractions. These concepts first come to life in the contract. At the same time, the legal form too, in its purest and simplest form, acquires a material basis in the act of exchange.

So, according to Pashukanis, it was the social practice of the contract that gave birth to all these innate qualities, which had no existence in the feudal world of serfdom and Guilds which lacked "any notion of a formal legal status common to all citizens", especially one which included the freedom to contract. In fact, it was the requirements of capitalist exchange relations, especially in labour, first developed in practice and then in theory, that gave birth to the legal subject:

> After he has become slavishly dependent on economic relations, which arise behind his back in the shape of the law of value, the economically active subject — now as a legal subject — acquires, in compensation as it were, a rare gift: a will, juridically constituted, which makes him

absolutely free and equal to other owners of commodities like himself.

Anyone who doubts this should ask why the notion of free will demands that there be a total absence of all forms of coercion, *except those of history and class*. In other words, why is the concept of freedom so limited that a bargain entered into under *normal* economic pressure is nevertheless considered to be "free"? The answer is because it is precisely the real compulsions of class which are the essential preconditions for the unequal bargains between capitalist and worker being entered into [at] all. The notion of freedom is limited, that is determined, by its concrete role of legitimating the acute unfreedom of the status quo. According to Pashukanis, then, the juridical approach requires that class and history be denied and rendered irrelevant:

> The free and equal owners of commodities who meet in the market are free and equal only in the abstract relation of appropriation and alienation. In real life, they are bound by various ties of mutual dependence. Examples of this are the retailer and the wholesaler, the peasant and the landowner, the ruined debtor and his creditor, the proletarian and the capitalist. All these innumerable relationships of actual dependence form the real basis of state structure, whereas for the [juridical] theory of the state it is as if they did not exist.

A good example of the juridical approach is the treatment of abortion by the Supreme Court of the United States. The decriminalisation of abortion in the United States was achieved, almost single-handedly, by the six judges of the majority in the 1973 decision of *Roe* v. *Wade*. In that case it was held that the Due Process clause of the *Bill of Rights* implicitly included "a freedom of personal choice in certain matters", including "the freedom of a woman to decide whether to terminate a pregnancy". Consequently, a Texas statute making abortion a crime (except where there was medical evidence that it was necessary to save the potential mother's life) was unconstitutional, as would be any statute preventing any abortion during the first trimester of pregnancy or preventing one during the second trimester, unless it could be shown that the mother's health would be adversely affected. We have already mentioned the reaction that this decision engendered. Whether or not this reaction influenced the subsequent decisions on the availability of financial assistance to indigents wanting abortions is neither here nor there. Nevertheless, various statutes were subsequently enacted by federal and state legislatures severely limiting the availability of "medicaid" funds for the abortions which had been legalised by the *Roe* v. *Wade* decision. In 1976, the Supreme Court upheld a Connecticut regulation restricting such funds to abortions that were "medically necessary". In 1980, it upheld the federal "Hyde Amendment" which restricted funding to abortions "where the life of the mother would be endangered if the fetus were carried to term" or "for the victims of rape or incest when such rape or incest has been reported promptly to a law enforcement agency or public health service". The reasoning in *Harris* v. *McRae* is a classic illustration of the judicial approach which holds class entirely irrelevant and no obstacle to "freedom by choice". Here we find the fundamental and rigid distinction made by judicial reasoning between the public sphere of "Freedom, Equality, Property and Bentham" and the private sphere of despotism and dependence:

> But, regardless of whether the freedom of a woman to choose to terminate her pregnancy for health reasons lies at the core or the periphery of the due process liberty recognized in *Wade*, it simply does not follow that a woman's freedom of choice carries with it a constitutional entitlement to the financial resources to avail herself of the full range of protected choices. The reason why was explained in *Maher*; although government may not place obstacles in the path of a woman's exercise of her freedom of choice, it need not remove those not of its own creation. Indigency falls in the latter category. The financial constraints that restrict an indigent woman's ability to enjoy the full range of constitutionally protected freedom of choice are the product not of government restrictions on access to abortions, but rather of her indigency. Although Congress has opted to subsidize medically necessary services generally, but not certain medically necessary abortions, the fact remains that the Hyde Amendment leaves an indigent woman with at least the same range of choice in deciding whether to obtain a medically necessary abortion as she would have had if Congress had chosen to subsidize no health care costs at all. We are thus not persuaded that the Hyde Amendment impinges on the constitutionally protected freedom of choice recognized in *Wade*[ ].

Another example of the quintessential judicial approach can be found in *Buckley* v. *Valeo* where the Supreme court of the United States struck down a federal law imposing serious limitations on private campaign expenditures in the wake of the Watergate controversy. The court held that this was an infringement on freedom of speech, thereby denying the relevance of class to political influence or, in other words, denying that limitations of class (*viz.* lack of wealth) could adversely affect people's right to participate in politics.

Yet another example of the "principled" approach characteristic of judicial reasoning is the famous decision of the Supreme Court of the United States in *Regents of the University of California* v. *Bakke*. In this case, a California medical school's affirmative action programme, which gave preferential admission to members of historically disadvantaged minority groups (blacks, Chicanos, Asians, American Natives) who were also "economically and/or educationally disadvantaged", was ruled unconstitutional on the basis that it offended the Equal Protection clause. The decision embraces several classic elements including the preference of individual rights over collective interests and the requirement of individual blame as a justification for a deprivation ("a classification that imposes disadvantages upon persons like the respondent, who bear no responsibility for whatever harm the beneficiaries of the special admissions programme are thought to have suffered"). But the most significant aspect of the decision is its denial of the relevance of history. When the majority held that "[t]here is no principled basis for deciding which groups would merit 'heightened judicial solicitude' and which would not", it was ignoring the historical and concrete fact of racism in the United States, as well as the fact that the specific clause under which it struck down the programme was supposed to have been enacted for the benefit of blacks. As the dissent pointed out, "during most of the past 200 years, the *Constitution* as interpreted by this Court did not prohibit the most ingenious and pervasive forms of discrimination against the Negro. Now, when a state acts to remedy the effects of that legacy of discrimination ... this same *Constitution* stands as a barrier".

. . . .

No doubt, some of the concrete rights that might be comprehended by the abstract formulations in the *Charter of Rights and Freedoms* are rights that socialists should fight for. Others, however, are rights that we should fight against. As we noted earlier, given that the interest, points of view and strategic judgments of courts sometimes diverge from those of the legislators, and even from those of the bourgeoisie, victory in the courts is sometimes possible. But history tells us that there will be many more losses than victories. And, for judicial victories to become concrete gains, legitimacy must be accorded to the judicial process *in general*. Thus, each isolated victory legitimates the inevitably greater number of losses which will be suffered by the working class. We should not be seduced or forced to do our fighting in courts according to rules devised for capitalism's maintenance and survival. We should not do our fighting by *pleading*. We should not do our fighting in a form that presupposes that what rights we have [depend] on something other than what we have won by our struggles; that they fell from the sky to be interpreted by wise, rich men. But, most important, we should not do our fighting by denying the existence of class. To the contrary: it is at this moment that we should be doing our fighting on the basis of class. Collaboration in the legalisation of politics will prevent us from doing this.

(ii) The Concept of Human Dignity

Trudeau, Pierre Elliott

The very adoption of a constitutional charter is in keeping with the purest liberalism, according to which all members of a civil society enjoy certain fundamental, inalienable rights and cannot be deprived of them by any collectivity (state or government) or on behalf of any collectivity (nation, ethnic group, religious group, or other). To use Maritain's phrase, they are "human personalities," they are

---

From *The Essential Trudeau* edited by Ron Graham (Toronto: McClelland and Stewart, 1998) at 80. Used by permission, McClelland & Stewart, Ltd. The Canadian Publishers.

beings of a moral order—that is, free and equal among themselves, each having absolute dignity and infinite value. As such, they transcend the accidents of place and time, and partake in the essence of universal Humanity. They are therefore not coercible by any ancestral tradition, being vassals neither of their race, nor to their religion, nor to their condition of birth, nor to their collective history.

(iii) Judging and Equality: For Whom Does the Charter Toll?

A. Wayne Mackay

The Promise of Judges and the Charter

Unless this Court is willing to say that the condition of Duncan's (the accused) purse is no ground upon which to qualify or limit his rights as a citizen of the United States ... then our heritage of constitutional privileges and immunities is only a promise to the ear to be broken to the hope, a teasing illusion like a munificent bequest in a pauper's will.

Canada's *Charter* has real potential in its broad and open-ended language and invites lawyers and judges to engage in a debate about basic values in Canadian society. The critical question raised by the opening quotation is whether the promise of the *Charter* is only a "promise to the ear to be broken to the hope." If the *Charter* creates an illusion of rights that cannot in fact be enforced, it is a bad thing for Canadians. Not only will raised expectations be dashed, but the limited energy for reform will have been diverted from more useful channels. After four years it is far from clear whether the *Charter* is a good or bad thing for the real protection of rights in Canada.

Legal academics are divided on the potential of the *Charter*. There are the *Charter* optimists, who, either as a matter of prediction or advocacy, make broad claims about the *Charter* as a vehicle for change. Another group of academics might be labelled as the *Charter* skeptics. A third group is the *Charter* pessimists. This latter group views the *Charter* as an obstacle to real change in society. If the *Charter* can be analogized to a religion, as Professor McBride does in his article, the optimists are the true believers, the skeptics are the agnostics and the pessimists are the atheists or heretics. Heretics may be the better term for the last group as they reject the *Charter* but embrace other religions. Practising lawyers and judges would also divide along similar lines.

Assessment of the *Charter* and its implications for change may, for sake of clarity, be considered at three separate levels:

1. the choice of the rights paradigm as the central means of addressing the relationships amongst individuals and between individuals and the state;
2. the judicial treatment of the *Charter*;
3. the content of the *Charter* itself.

Most of what follows this part of the article will be concerned with the first two levels of analysis. This part of the article examines the *Charter* as a document. Since the words of the *Charter* only gain life from judicial interpretation, it is impossible to totally ignore the second level analysis but it will be kept to a minimum. I shall begin by considering the positive side of the *Charter*—its potential.

Broad Potential

The *Charter* contains broad and ringing phrases that invite creative arguments from lawyers and innovative responses from judges. While the catalogue of rights and their expression is not ideal, the wording

---

(1986) 10:2 Dalhousie L.J. at pp. 39–51. Notes omitted. Reproduced by permission of A. Wayne Mackay, Professor of Law, Dalhousie University, Halifax, N.S.

(iii) Judging and Equality: For Whom Does the Charter Toll?

is broad enough to encompass most of the important value disputes in Canadian society. Sections 7 and 15 are prime examples. The former has already been used on both sides of the abortion debate and in respect to the testing of cruise missiles in Canada. Out of section 7 there have also been claims of a right to die, a right to an education and a right to basic social security, to name but a few. The equality guarantees in section 15 offer an even broader scope and the kind of issues that will arise under it will be discussed in Part 2 of this article.

Implicit in the *Charter* is a balancing of interests that moves judges to a more overt policy-making role. This balancing will involve not only a weighing of individual rights against societal claims to reasonable limits in section 1 but also the weighing of one individual right against another. Often an equality right will be on one side of the scale and one of the liberty rights on the other. Thus the structure of the *Charter* may force judges to be more overtly political than they have been in the past. Patrick Monahan views this interest balancing role with some alarm:

> Even a cursory analysis of the language and structure of the *Charter* indicates that most *Charter* litigation may well turn on the issue of the "wisdom" of legislative choices. In part, this is a product of the abstract and generalized nature of the rights protected by the *Charter*. The very process of defining the content of the rights protected by the *Charter* seems inherently political. Many of these rights — most notably the right to "equality" and "liberty" — contain little or no substantive criteria; they resemble blank slates on which the judiciary can scrawl the imagery of their choice. But there is a second problem. Having given content to these open-ended rights, the judiciary must then "balance" these rights against considerations of the general welfare under section one. This process of "interest balancing" seems just another way of asking the fundamental legislative questions; "is this worth what it costs?" The process of balancing individual against collective interests is a calculation which would have already been made by the legislature when it passed the statute under review. Since the government passed the statute, it must have calculated that the interests to be served outweigh those to be sacrificed. Section one of the *Charter* appears to invite the Court to assess and second-guess the "wisdom" of the balance struck by the legislature.

In response to his concern about courts that may become too actively involved in assessing the wisdom of government action, Professor Monahan articulates a theory of judicial review based upon the promotion of democratic values; these include the rights to participate in decision-making, equality of access and fair distribution of benefits. He goes beyond a strict process standard of review but stops short of having the judges evaluate outcomes. Monahan's touchstone is the democratic values implicit in Canadian society, which are distinct from those in the United States. This evolution of a distinct Canadian jurisprudence is one of the promising features of the *Charter*.

W.R. Lederman has also fixed his attention on the phrase "free and democratic society" in section 1 of the *Charter*, but to a rather different purpose than that of Monahan. Professor Lederman predicts that independent courts and democratic legislatures will both pursue the goals of the *Charter* in a spirit of partnership. The re-thinking of the comparative roles of legislators, administrators and courts is another promising feature of the *Charter* that is likely to be realized.

Part of the above reconsideration of institutional roles is a concern about the best way to protect minorities, defined as those who have been excluded from power; this includes all the groups specified in section 15 of the *Charter* and many more as well. Courts may offer minorities a shield against the majority, and this may be particularly important in times of political conservatism and economic restraint. Even those who are *Charter* skeptics see a useful role for the courts in relation to minorities.

> Nevertheless, we should also see the *Charter* as a brave and necessary step in enhancing the civility of the Canadian state. The diversity of Canada has made it a polity with many minorities, which are everywhere vulnerable to the passing whims of majorities. Our history is full of instances where a national majority has imposed its will on local minorities, as in the imposition of the tariff or conscription in a way that created deeply-rooted resentments which lasted for generations, or where local majorities in particular provinces or regions abused the rights of their own minorities, such as Japanese-Canadians in British Columbia, Jehovah's Witnesses in Quebec and francophones in Manitoba. The *Charter* as it stands might not have been strong enough to protect or help them, but its ultimate object was to nourish an atmosphere of civility which will act as a restraint on the old Adam in us all. A truly civil polity is a very fragile thing, as it is, as Frank Scott said, a work of art that is never finished. It is very easy to destroy or damage it. It requires restraint and discipline to preserve it.

Another promising aspect of the *Charter* is the opening up of legal discourse to a wider range of sources and influences. Courts will have to reconsider what sources to use in resolving a *Charter* question and how they can become informed on matters beyond the law. Mr. Justice Gerald La Forest made the following encouraging statement about *Charter* sources before being appointed to the Supreme Court of Canada and it appears to be a view shared by many of his present colleagues on the Court:

> the *Charter* forces us to look at questions differently than before. However clear a statute or its purposes may be, courts will be asked to make a value judgment about it, a duty that is very different from the traditional role of the court. This should profoundly affect the sources on which courts must rely for guidance.... Our courts must be guided by the felt needs and traditions of our own society. But they will be invaluable in raising the issues that must be considered. So often we fail to see that a course of action may unnecessarily infringe on the rights of the individual because we have simply become accustomed to that way of doing things.
>
> I hope, too, that our search will also lead us to seek light from disciplines other than the law, for many of the questions we will have to consider transcend the legal system. Rights continue to emerge from the human experience.

Perhaps the greatest potential for the *Charter* lies in its use outside the courtrooms, but it has important uses within too. While the judges play a crucial role in interpreting the *Charter*, it is the front-line lawyers who must take the lead in this new constitutional dance. Lawyers must be open to representing a wider range of clients and be prepared to raise innovative arguments, supporting alternative versions of reality. Judges, particularly those at the lower levels, are likely to resist such creative advocacy but there will be judges willing to break new ground. Furthermore, the polycentric nature of issues that arise under the *Charter* beg a larger role for intervenors and Brandeis style briefs in the litigation process. This opening up of the adjudicative process will have a positive effect even beyond *Charter* cases.

The growing media interest in *Charter* litigation also invites the use of the *Charter* as a political tool. This was high on the agenda of Operation Dismantle when they challenged the testing of cruise missiles in Canada on the basis of the *Charter*. Such litigation is expensive but for the amount of media exposure it may be a bargain. Some groups, however, cannot afford to litigate even if it offers an opportunity for political education. For such groups, the *Charter* may be used as part of the public debate about the issue, which may result in concessions in order to avoid bad press or possible litigation.

Whether Canadians like it or not, courts will become a more overt political forum under the *Charter*. As J.R. Mallory observes, this has been the situation in the United States for many decades:

> The *Charter* opens up a new avenue — one which has for a long time been available to interest groups in the United States. Attempts to extend civil rights to blacks could never succeed as long as there were powerful veto groups in the Congress which could stop any law on the subject. Accordingly, the strategy of shifting the action to the courts not only prodded the courts into interpreting the law and the constitution in a more liberal way, but also created a great deal of publicity which helped to mobilize public opinion and thus encourage legislative and executive compliance. In the past there were slight prospects for this strategy to succeed in Canada. Now that the *Charter* is part of the constitution we may expect a substantial number of issue-groups, from environmentalists to pro- and anti-abortion groups, to fight their battles in the courts, which will greatly enhance their capacity to mobilize public opinion.

The new political use of courts is not as novel as many people suggest. What may be new is the extent to which courts can now provide a forum for a wider range of political views. If minority interests will have as much chance to state their case in court as large corporate interests, that would be a promising step towards equality. I shall explore in the next part of the paper whose voices have been heard in the courts during the first four years of the *Charter*.

Some writers would dispute the distinction between the legal and political uses of the courts. As Professor McBride suggests in the preceding article in this volume, there is politics at some level in all adjudication. It is really a question of kind and degree. Mark Gold has argued that judges are advocates in rendering a decision and aware of the value of rhetorical devices. In some senses, judges are political actors in the adjudicative process, but they are restrained by training and institutional structures in ways that distinguish them from naked legislators. I shall return to this theme in the concluding part of this article.

A final promising feature of the *Charter* is its value as an educational tool. The role of the judge as teacher and expositor of the law was recognized before the *Charter*. As McBride indicates in the preceding article, this role is extended to broader audiences by the *Charter*. To a significant extent, the Supreme Court of Canada has become the leader of a national symposium on fundamental rights and values. While education in itself offers no panacea, the value of raising a "rights consciousness" should not be discounted. There is a potential in the *Charter* that suggests that it may be more than "a promise to the ear," but there are also limitations.

Charter Limitations

Section 52 of the *Constitution Act, 1982* declares that the *Charter*, as part of the Canadian Constitution, is the supreme law of the land and any conflicting policy is void. In spite of this declaration of judicial supremacy, there are limitations in the *Charter* as a document that make the label "judicial primacy" more applicable to the Canadian scene. While some lament the dilution of judicial power, others argue that the "joint primacy" of judicial and legislative institutions is both desirable and appropriate in the Canadian context. Supremacy of parliament as inherited from the United Kingdom has been qualified but not discarded. Whether this is a strength or limitation is a matter of opinion, but in terms of what judges can do with the *Charter* it is a limitation.

The clearest indication that supremacy of parliament is still alive is section 33 of the *Charter*. This section allows legislators to over-ride sections 2 and 7–15 of the *Charter* for a five-year period, which can then be renewed. It is significant that both sections 7 and 15, which are the broadest ones in the *Charter* with respect to equality, are included. Interestingly, section 28, dealing with sex discrimination, is outside the scope of the over-ride clause. On most important issues the legislators can still have the final say.

During the patriation process, the *Charter* sales people (mostly at the federal level) argued that it would be politically unpopular to use section 33 and it would thus have little impact. That has not been the case. In Quebec, under René Levesque's Parti Quebecois, every Quebec statute contained a section 33 over-ride clause. In early 1986, the province of Saskatchewan became the first province outside of Quebec to use section 33. It was used in the context of back-to-work legislation to end rotating strikes by the Saskatchewan Government Employees Union. These uses were not overwhelmingly unpopular and other such uses will emerge in the future.

Section 33 represents a political limit on the use of the *Charter* and is a reaffirmation of majority rule. Whatever the courts say about what rights should be protected in Canadian society, these same rights can be over-ridden if there is the political will to do so. This has led some critics of the *Charter* to question the value of a document that only protects politically acceptable rights. Dean Rod MacDonald of McGill Law School is one such critic, and he argues that a proper analysis of the *Charter* requires an examination and justification of the basic tenets of liberal political theory. An attempt will be made in Part 4 of this article to assess the *Charter* in its legal and political context. Only when painting on this broader canvas will the strengths and limitations of the *Charter* appear.

MacDonald asserts that history teaches that charters of rights are ineffective in intolerant societies and unnecessary in tolerant ones. I would question the historical accuracy of this generalization, but even if it is true in most cases, does this undercut the value of the *Charter*? Surely there will be a few victories under the *Charter* that would not otherwise have occurred, and these will have some effect on unlitigated claims and administrative practices. Furthermore, the *Charter* itself and the litigation and debate that emerges from it has an educational component that can change social attitudes about rights.

There will be cases where political actors are more progressive than their judicial counterparts. In such cases, judges may use the *Charter* to impede rather than promote change. This is a limitation on the *Charter* but not a case for discarding it. When there is no political will to uphold civil liberties a judicial entrenchment of rights can buffer the effect of this absence. When there is such a political will the existence of the *Charter* may expedite the judicial acceptance of a similar view. The approach to the *Canadian Bill of Rights* offers some evidence of the value of a *Charter* as an education for judges. In an increasingly conservative political climate there is also some solace in the fact that even a conservative judiciary can hold the fort against an extreme shift away from human rights.

Many of MacDonald's complaints, and he is typical of many of the *Charter* skeptics, are against what judges will do with the *Charter* rather than the *Charter* itself. It is difficult to distinguish judicial interpretation from the words of the *Charter* as they converge to give meaning to the guaranteed rights. Whether the *Charter* should be read expansively or narrowly depends on assumptions about whether judges are promoters or inhibitors of rights. I shall return to the role of judges as protectors of equality in the latter parts of this article.

Section 1 of the *Charter* is the vehicle by which judges can limit the rights guaranteed in the document:

> *The Canadian Charter of Rights and Freedoms* guarantees the rights and freedoms set out in it subject only to such reasonable limits prescribed

by law as can be demonstrably justified in a free and democratic society.

What are the reasonable limits on broad rights such as equality, that judges will find acceptable? The burden of demonstrable justification rests with the state but judges will be the final arbiters of what limitations are reasonable in "a free and democratic society." To put the question in the present context, what reasonable limitations on equality will be tolerated in Canada, as a free and democratic society? Judges will claim to reflect broader social values in making such judgment but they will inevitably impose their own values as well. Thus, the extent to which section 1 limits the impact of the *Charter* depends on the value structure implicit in both the judicial and the larger political process. These values will be examined later.

A significant limitation on the reach of the *Charter* is the application of section 32. The majority view on this section is that the *Charter* will encompass legislative and government action, broadly defined, but will not be extended to the private sector. There is a minority view that section 32 can be read to include the private sector and thus extend the *Charter* to all activity. Many violations of equality do occur in the private sector, and if it is immune from the *Charter*, the *Charter* will be blunted as an instrument of equality. Hester Lessard's article in this volume emphasizes the negative impact that a state action interpretation of the *Charter* would have on combating discrimination against women. The division of the world into public and private spheres has been identified by others as a limitation on legal reform generally.

Perhaps the most important limitation on the *Charter* is in the form of things that were omitted from the document. One such omission is a guarantee of the funding necessary to pursue a *Charter* challenge. This limits the real access to the *Charter*, as is discussed in the next part of this article. Limitations are also inherent in the choice of rights for inclusion in the *Charter* and the inferential exclusion of others.

One of the best critiques of the *Charter* on a philosophical basis is that presented by Robert Samek. He argues that the rights protected in the *Charter* are the predictable legal and political rights that characterize the liberal state. They are aimed at removing the negative constraint of the state on individual freedom of choice. There is a notable absence of social and economic rights that would require a more positive intervention on the part of the courts.

As the title of his article suggests, Professor Samek is concerned about "untrenching" fundamental rights. In his view, real fundamental rights have a dynamism that denies a specific ideological content and precludes a static articulation and interpretation by the courts. Furthermore, he argues that most of the rights protected by the *Charter* are not fundamental. Samek takes the word "fundamental" in the term "fundamental rights" very seriously. He states that fundamental rights are rights that inhere in us *qua* human beings and not as participants in a particular political and social mix. Thus, the equality provision comes closest to capturing what Samek feels is a fundamental right. Language rights and mobility rights may be rights, but they are not fundamental rights, in Samek's view. Rights that are fundamental do not arise from conferral by the state. Neither can they be removed by the state. This is clearly a philosopher's objection to the *Charter*.

While I am in general agreement with the Samek critique and particularly like his link between rights and needs, there are also some problems with his analysis. Even if rights do inhere in people, the regulation of their exercise must involve the state. Another philosopher, Jacques Maritain, has argued that while fundamental rights are possessed by people and not conferred by the state, their exercise is a function of being recognized or limited by the state. Petter makes the perceptive comment that the *Charter* is not a distributive document but represents a "zero sum" game in which rights are given to citizens at the expense of governments.

The argument about what rights should be included in the *Charter* presupposes an assumption about the value of courts as protectors of fundamental rights. Since Samek is opposed to the entrenchment of fundamental rights, it appears that he is skeptical about the role of courts as a protector. Thus, one would expect him to be happy with the fact that social and economic rights, which he regards as real fundamental rights, are outside the *Charter*. This is not the case. Indeed section 7 and 15 could be broadly interpreted to encompass social and economic rights. A more difficult question is whether this would be a good thing.

When dealing with the issue of entrenchment of economic rights, *Charter* critics are as blind and legalistic as the objects of their scorn. More would be required than the simple entrenchment of an economic or social right. Such a move would give the *Charter* more clout, but entrenchment is only the legal act. What would this entail in terms of an egalitarian redistribution of wealth in our society? Would those from whom this wealth would be taken remain in Canada? Would the capital flight from a country contemplating such a move result in an economy that could not maintain its present standards of welfare or jobs, let alone give effect to the legal right to a job or a guaranteed minimum income? Failure by legal commentators to recognize and address such concerns gives real meaning to the term disciplinary blindness. MacDonald appears blind to this, while Samek says only that we must be willing to pay the price for economic rights; on what that price is, he is conspicuously silent.

Is the *Charter* negative, positive or neutral as a means of promoting equality? The answer to this question has less to do with the document itself than how it is used. If the *Charter* will be used negatively, then the limitations on it are positive for equality. If the *Charter* will be used positively, then the opposite is true. The *Charter* has the potential for positive use, although such use is limited. Whether this potential will be realized depends on the political and judicial context. The rest of this article turns to these matters.

I have identified myself as a *Charter* skeptic or agnostic, rather than a true believer. The basis for my skepticism is not the *Charter* document itself but rather the limits that are inherent in the ideology of the liberal state and the process of judging. While the *Charter* is not self-enforcing, it offers the potential for significant change. There will be no revolution in Canadian society and none was intended by its drafters. The *Charter* will, however, change the lot of some Canadians. Whether the protection of fundamental rights will be extended to those with fundamental needs will be the true test of the *Charter*.

(iv) Popular Rights In (and Out of) the Constitution

Gail Starr

INTRODUCTION

So many fears are calmed. For those who thought the Trudeau *Charter* was opening a future of godless communism, it is declared that we recognise "the supremacy of God and the rule of law". Those who worry about the erosion of their property rights are re-assured by the continuance of the *Canadian Bill of Rights* and such provincial equivalents as there are. And monarchists and others who dread republicanism find, under the heading "Democratic Rights", nothing more threatening than a right to vote and the ancient constitutional provisions respecting the frequency of elections and the sittings of legislative bodies; what had been merely statutory in the *War Measures Act* is made constitutional through provision for abrogation in time of "real or apprehended war, invasion or insurrection". The searcher for evidence of the rights of the people to participate in the political life of Canada will find virtually "no new thing under the sun". The cynic within will easily conclude that the *Charter* is a creature of smoke and mirrors.

This paper proposes, however, that, while there is only one provision in the *Constitution Act, 1982*, which actually enhances the power of the people, there is a possibility of using the *Charter* to broaden the base of popular power. Although the expansion of judicial power by the *Charter* has received considerable attention in the last two years, there are actually important limitations on the judicial power (and on the legislative power) introduced by the *Constitution Act, 1982*. Some of these limitations can be used to broaden and deepen popular power, to add to the weight of public opinion and to sharpen the impact of the popular will. At least in theory.

Sections 2 to 5, although divided under the two headings, "Fundamental Freedoms" and "Democratic Rights", include the *Charter* provisions which deal directly with what I characterise as "popular rights". In these four sections are embodied all the guarantees we have of the right of people to participate in the "free and democratic society" contemplated by section 1.

What the *Charter* denominates "fundamental freedoms" have been called either "political rights"

(1984) 2 *Socialist Studies* 8. Notes omitted. Reproduced by permission of the Society for Socialist Studies.

(as by then Minister of Justice Trudeau in his 1968 document *A Canadian Charter of Human Rights*) or "civil liberties" (as by many whose views on the subject are strongly influenced by American individual rights theories). Implicit in both "fundamental freedoms" and "civil liberties" as labels is the individualistic notion, a progeny of the Enlightenment, of creating a sphere of individual autonomy on which the sovereign power might not intrude. Historically, and continuing well beyond the zenith of natural law, private property was at the conceptual core of this notion. Viewed through these lenses, the "freedoms" protected by section 2 might be summed up (more emphatically if property were in their midst) by the revealing Anglo-American phrase "the right to be left alone".

Although they will be invoked (and upheld) in support of individualistic and selfish causes, I will consider these "freedoms" here for their importance to collective action. Indeed, with possible factual exceptions in the areas of conscience, religion, thought, belief and opinion, the freedoms protected by section 2 presuppose co-operation and community of purpose. Were it otherwise, freedom of the press (even as a concept) would indeed be limited to those who own one. To state the obvious, "assembly" requires three or more people and "association" two as a notional minimum.

While I will not shun the expression "fundamental freedoms", I will regard the areas of activity protected by section 2 as "political rights". With the right to stand for election and the right to vote classed by *Charter* headings as "democratic rights", the total of "political rights" and "democratic rights" may be regarded as "popular rights" — rights of "everyone" or "every citizen" to participate, if only in the extra-parliamentary opposition, in the political determination of the path of the state.

POLITICAL RIGHTS

The first observation about section 2 is that it is subject to section 1. By having the standards of permissible limitations enunciated in s. 1 of the *Charter*, we avoid the untenable proposition, as espoused in the American *Bill of Rights*, that the legislature "shall make no law abridging". A function of this express limitation in s. 1 is that we also preclude judges and administrators from making up limitations *ex post facto*. Limitations, to be recognised at all, must be "prescribed by law". Commentators (and most judges who have expressed themselves on the matter) agree that "demonstrably justified" places the onus on the party seeking to uphold the challenged law. While awaiting a stable articulation of judge-made law on this issue, the defence of political rights will require advocacy that prevents judges adopting easy conclusions that "limits prescribed by law" are *prima facie* "reasonable", thereby begging the question as to whether they are "demonstrably justified". As our judges, both home-grown and imperial, have displayed a propensity for skipping over an inquiry into "matters coming within classes of subjects" to get to heads of legislative competence, we should, by now, know how to expose such practices.

The second internal *Charter* limitation on section 2 is the legislative override provided by section 33. Parliament or a provincial legislature may by legislative declaration override any provision of section 2 (and of section 7 through 15). Section 33, which Professor David Cruickshank appropriately suggests we should call "the rights-denial clause", seems to provide only for the *negation* of rights granted or affirmed by section 2 and 7 to 15 of the *Charter*. However, ironically in view of the way it is formulated, it may also have important uses in the *protection* of popular rights. Most relevant are those rights declared in section 2.

The legislative override is available only within the sphere of legislative competence possessed by the legislature seeking to override the *Charter*. This refers to the division of powers represented principally by sections 91 and 92 of the *Constitution Act, 1867*. And section 31 of the *Charter* provides, unambiguously, that "(n)othing in this *Charter* extends the legislative powers of any body or authority." To the extent, therefore, that legislative denial of section 2 rights would be aimed at making criminal certain exercises of those rights, only Parliament would be competent to do so. Accordingly, with a clear sense of *deja vu*, provincial legislative attempts to override section 2 protection may be challenged as invasions of the exclusive federal criminal law power. Suggestions for employing this argument will be offered in the context of specific section 2 rights, especially freedom of peaceful assembly.

This argument will in some cases have to draw on the "implied Bill of Rights", a Canadian judicial approach to the relationship between citizen and state which is, with respect to our pre-*Charter* jurisprudence, of doubted vitality. However, to the extent that the implied Bill of Rights survives, it could be a weapon for challenging provincial legislation restricting political rights. Strong *dicta* exist suggesting that the fundamental freedoms implicit in having a constitution "similar in principle to that of the United Kingdom" can never be "local matters". Some *dicta* are available, in the implied Bill of Rights cases, to suggest that neither level of government can limit certain of these rights.

Freedom of Conscience and Religion

Some have suggested that the addition of "conscience" to the freedom as it was expressed in the *Canadian Bill of Rights* will extend the protection to quasi-religious groups and to "non-religious aspects" of religious systems. This remains to be seen; bigamy will not be excused by the courts merely because it is allowed by the religion of the accused. The balancing required by section 1 will test the boundaries of whatever may be newly permitted by the change in phrasing.

What the change in wording does make possible is the development of a concept of freedom *from* religion. Freedom from religion would include freedom from having elements of one's life dictated by prevailing patterns of religious belief. Prayers and religious study in public schools and Sunday observance legislation come to mind. The Provincial Court of Alberta, in Calgary, has declared section 4 of the *Lord's Day Act* contrary to the provisions of the *Charter* and, therefore, of no force or effect. Sunday observance legislation was recharacterised as having nothing to do with the criminal law power. Further, although not mentioned specifically in the reasons for judgment, the provision of section 27 of the *Charter*, that it should be interpreted "in a manner consistent with the preservation and enhancement of the multi-cultural heritage of Canadians", provides an additional buttress to the reasoning of Judge Stevenson.

While the general prospect held out by section 2(a), especially when read with section 27, is of a secular society, section 29 makes clear that existing Constitutional guarantees relating to separate schools remain undisturbed. Whether the preamble to the *Charter* can be invoked for any particular purpose is an open question.

Freedom of Expression

Subsection (b) of section 2 identifies a number of elements of the freedom of expression. The *Canadian Bill of Rights* protected only speech. Gestures and other forms of symbolic speech will now come under the protection. In a technologically forward-looking expansion, freedom of the press is extended to "other media of communication". This larger collocation of phrases elaborating the identified freedoms suggests that the whole may be greater than the sum of its parts. There are concepts here to work with in building arguments for the right to effective speech, for the right to be heard, for the right to respond to image advertising, for the right of access to outlets of information, etc. More will be said about the protection of thought, belief, and opinion.

Freedom of Peaceful Assembly

The *Canadian Bill of Rights* protected "freedom of assembly and association". The *Charter* divides the two and qualifies assembly by the requirement that it be peaceful. I hope that this change, read with the expansion of "expression" described above, will render the reasoning of Mr. Justice Beetz in *Dupond* obsolete.

Under the *Canadian Bill of Rights*, the protection offered to assembly and association rights was never successfully invoked. We grew used to there being no effective protection of the right to assemble. In Vancouver the city's interest in having its noise by-law enforced was held to be sufficient to prohibit Hare Krishna groups from chanting along the sidewalks. In Calgary the whimsical issuance, or non-issuance, of parade permits was upheld against Chilean exiles seeking to mount a modest demonstration against the excesses of the Pinochet regime. And in Montreal, in the only case of its type to reach the Supreme Court of Canada, the dual fear that either assembly might become effective to mobilise public opinion or that the police budget would be exhausted in preventing it, was sufficient to justify city by-laws prohibiting *any* demonstration for a period of 60 days. Thus, even during the period of our history when the *Canadian Bill of Rights* expressly protected assembly and association, we saw our highest court approve a local measure as repressive as the 1920's Toronto by-laws which forbade meetings at which anyone was to speak in a language other than English.

With the constitutional recognition of the right of assembly now qualified, in terms, only by the requirement that it be "peaceful", it may be argued that the only justification for restricting the exercise of the right would be to prevent riot, and that that is covered by the *Criminal Code*. As, historically, almost all limitations on the right of assembly have been placed there by local and provincial authorities, this may be a potent argument. Again, the "implied Bill of Rights" argument, to the effect that this right is so fundamental to Canadian society as to be beyond the reach of either level of government, must be pressed.

Freedom of Association

The most continuous struggle for recognition of the freedom of association has been waged by trade unions. Major episodes have also included the occasional banning of the Communist Party of Canada, through the *Criminal Code*, and of the F.L.Q., first under the *War Measures Act* and then under the "Turner law". It is not known whether this characteristic of the freedom's history played any part in the drafter's decision to separate assembly from association, but the decision to recognise association as a separate right may help us argue that it be broadened. Because of this history of the concept and its realisation, it may now be easier to argue that it includes the right to form a union, the right to bargain collectively, and the right to strike. In any event, its separate recognition may contribute to pushing back the lines drawn by prohibitions on conspiracy and sedition.

The history of the struggle for recognition of the right will also need to be employed to argue that the constitutional recognition of the positive right does not include recognition of its converse. (It is suggested that the differences in historical development of recognition of the two rights mandate the contrary argument, as set out above, with respect to the freedom of religion.) Thus, the freedom of *dis*association, contrary to the results obtained under the *European Convention* with respect to the closed shop, must be seen as a right *not* protected by the *Charter*.

Section 2 as an Entity

Subsection (b) expressly contemplates a freedom of "thought, belief and opinion". The presence of these words might be dismissed as conferring nothing, recognising nothing. Many would dismiss them as hollow; a few contend that they cannot be invaded anyway. But they can be and are invaded daily. This recognition in the *Charter* may presage a broadening of popular rights.

The experience of the left in Canada demonstrates, even if Orwell had not already shown it to be possible, that the state can know every preference, every value, every deeply held opinion by simply taking note of what an individual does. Through surveillance, through intimidation and through harassment, both subtle and unsubtle pressure is exerted to conform, to be quiet, to cease challenging, to be inactive except in harmless individualistic pursuits.

The seemingly innocuous words of subsection 2(b), taken together with the other rights protected by section 2, constitute a whole larger than the sum of its parts. This may be a kind of right to privacy, but one founded on the dignity and worth of persons as social and political beings, rather than on the licence of the individual in relation to his own property. We will make more headway in using section 2 to broaden collective interests if we regard it as a right *to be with* and consistently oppose its interpretation to vindicate the dubious right to be left alone. In this way it becomes the basis upon which we can, together, demand the recognition of additional political rights.

DEMOCRATIC RIGHTS

"Democratic rights" in sections 3 through 5 of the *Charter* provide for the merely elementary components of electoral democracy. Only s. 3 contains anything new. Section 4 and 5 enshrine British norms developed well before Confederation and already a part of our constitutional law.

Any Canadian who paid much attention to the ten year build-up which culminated in patriation will have noticed that, whether the bargaining table was situated in Victoria, Ottawa or Quebec, the only people at it were politicians. To be sure, Liberal roadshow after Liberal roadshow toured the country, listening conspicuously to what real people might like to have in their constitution. The only groups to have any effect on the final text were women and native people, the two groups politically astute enough to act on the knowledge that politicians seizing a once-in-a-lifetime opportunity to divide up the pie would be influenced only by those who stayed within a figurative shouting distance of the bargaining table. The historic gains won by these two groups are outside the scope of this paper. But these victories represent the only concessions wrested by the people from the politicians.

The guarantee, provided by s. 3, that "every citizen of Canada" can vote in an election to the House of Commons or to the Legislative Assembly of a province represents an expansion of the right, at least insofar as it has received statutory recognition. Judges, convicted prisoners and mentally incompetent persons are today generally denied the right to vote. Since patriation, challenges to denials of the right to vote have been brought by remand prisoners, convicted prisoners, judges, and probationers. Such statutory restrictions will be subject to judicial "bal-

(iv) Popular Rights In (and Out of) the Constitution

ancing" of the restriction as against the provisions of s. 1.

Section 3 also provides that "every citizen of Canada has the right ... to be qualified for membership" in the House of Commons or a Legislative Assembly. Again, age and residency requirements might be challenged through a combination of s. 3 provisions and equality (s. 15) or mobility (s. 6) arguments. But these provisions will not be of crucial significance to many people. As s. 3 is limited, by its own terms, to House of Commons and provincial legislature members, there is no threat to the prohibition against a bankrupt being a Senator. Accordingly, we can expect a continuation of the tradition that Senators will be appointed only from the ranks of the suitably privileged.

Sections 4 and 5, as we suggested above, continue the requirements that, "real or apprehended war, invasion or insurrection" not intervening, there shall be elections at least every five years, and that parliament and provincial legislatures shall sit at least once every twelve months. Little is new, and no significant additional power is conferred upon the people.

LEGISLATIVE OVERRIDE

It was suggested in the introduction that there were important limitations on both legislative and judicial power, provided for in the *Charter*, which might operate to add to the power of people. These possibilities lie within the provisions of s. 33 of the *Charter*, the "legislative override" of the "rights denial" section. Underlying this section is a schizophrenic theory which will be argued and applied in a schizophrenic fashion. A major theme of the *Constitution Act, 1982*, as chiefly expressed in sections 52 and 24, is that the *Constitution* is "the supreme law of Canada" and that courts are the final arbiters as to when it has been violated and what remedy should be provided. Citizens can claim from the judiciary a remedy for wrongs committed by the state through its executive and legislative organs. Yet, over against this lies a (sometimes grudging) recognition that judicial review, even when undertaken by an independent judiciary, is fundamentally anti-democratic. The conflicting impulses — now to trust an independent judiciary, now to trust elected representatives — produce a "clear" mandate which, with respect to s. 2 or sections 7 to 15, can always be drawn back.

It is the quintessential Canadian solution. What can be said in its favour is this: when, and to the extent that, Canadian electoral democracy can be made to function in objectively democratic ways, the Canadian people (or, as appropriate, the people of a province) *may* have the last word about what the *Charter* should provide. That statement is supportable only by calling attention to the fact that if a government, through the legislature it controls, deliberately and in terms enacts legislation which is to operate notwithstanding *Charter* protections, such an enactment can be an election issue and, if opposition to that enactment is sufficiently popular and effective, the people can "throw the rascals out".

The provinces, from whom most legislative derogations from the *Charter* may be expected in the short run, have not had their legislative powers broadened in any respect by the *Charter*; s. 31 makes that clear. "Distribution of powers" arguments will still be pertinent. With respect to s. 2, therefore, when a provincial legislature seeks to deny one of the protected rights, it will be possible to argue that such legislation cannot be "demonstrably justified" except as an exercise of the criminal law power, which is exclusively federal. And here again, the "implied Bill of Rights" argument may be marshalled. Similar arguments will be telling where provincial legislation seeks to override the protections offered by section 7 through 15. The provincial interest in quasi-criminal offences and penalties is not momentous enough to demonstrably justify overriding these fundamental legal rights.

Insofar as equality rights are concerned, s. 15 can be overridden by either Parliament or a provincial legislature; however, section 28 (with respect to which there is no override) prohibits, to both levels of government, discrimination based on gender. Section 28 also suggests that gender-based discrimination that does not meet the s. 1 requirement can be challenged immediately, notwithstanding the three year suspension of other equality rights provided by s. 32(2).

"DISAPPEARED" RIGHTS

There was, in most drafts of the *Constitution Act, 1982*, save for the one that was enacted, an important provision of a popular right. In the early drafts, part or all of the patriation package would have been the subject of a referendum. When the politicians reached the final bargaining table the referendum provision was quietly abandoned. The first of the Liberal roadshows to begin to focus public attention on constitutional issues aimed at amendment and patriation was the MacGuigan-Molgat Committee, the Special Joint Committee of the Senate and the House of Commons on the Constitution of Canada, which submitted its report in 1972. A number of the individuals appearing before the MacGuigan-Molgat Committee suggested that a referendum mechanism be incorporated into the constitutional amendment process. The report of the committee did not mention the issue.

A few years later another road show was mounted, this one carrying out its consultations with the public at the same time as federal and provincial politicians were working away at the real bargaining tables. A similar pattern of representations was made to the Pepin-Robarts Commission. It did recommend the referendum mechanism.

Meanwhile, at the bargaining table, referendum provisions found their way into some of the tentative agreements reached among politicians, most notably the *Victoria Charter*. Accounts of discussions leading to these various (and ultimately abortive) proposals suggest that only the federal delegation held any brief for the referendum. Only a few of Mr. Trudeau's closest advisors, notably Michael Kirby, actually favoured such a provision.

In the end, or at least as close to the end as 5 November is to 2 December 1981, this provision (as it appeared in the penultimate version) disappeared. There was never an explanation. So far as can be ascertained, politicians actually at the various bargaining tables never made strong public statements against the notion of the referendum. But there was no commitment to it.

What is at least as important as the disappearance of referendum provisions in 1982 is that the politicians assured themselves the same closed forum for the next mandatory review of the *Constitution*. Section 49 of the *Constitution Act, 1982* provides:

> A constitutional conference composed of the Prime Minister of Canada and the first ministers of the provinces shall be convened by the Prime Minister of Canada within 15 years after this Part comes into force to review the provisions of this Part.

The "Part" being referred to is Part V of the *Constitution Act, 1982*, headed *Procedure for amending Constitution of Canada*.

If the political aspirations and values of people other than elected politicians are to be given expression in the development of the Canadian constitution, less than 13 years remain in which to create a climate in which politicians would find it unthinkable to sit down alone for the further amendment of the constitution. We will need every "popular right" we can argue for.

(v) Aboriginal Peoples and the Canadian Charter of Rights and Freedoms: Contradictions and Challenges

Aki-Kwe/Mary Ellen Turpel

> Whereas Canada is founded upon principles that recognize the supremacy of God and the rule of law ...
> Preamble to Part I, *Canadian Charter of Rights and Freedoms*).

> Your religion was written upon tables of stone by the iron finger of your God so that you could not forget. The Red Aboriginal people could never comprehend nor remember it. Our religion is the traditions of our ancestors — the dreams of our old men, given them in solemn hours of night by the Great Spirit; and the visitations of our sachems: and it is written in the hearts of our people
> (Chief Seattle to the Governor of Washington Territory, 1854).

> When anthropologists, government officials, and churchmen have argued that our ways have been lost to us, they are fulfilling one of their own tribal rituals — wish fulfilment.
> (Chief George Manuel, *The Fourth World*).

From Elizabeth Comack and Stephen Brickey, eds., *The Social Basis of Law*, 2d ed. (Halifax: Garamond Press, 1991) 223. Notes omitted. This article was originally published in (1989) 10:2 and 10:3 *Canadian Women Studies*. Reproduced by permission of the author.

(v) Aboriginal Peoples and the Canadian Charter of Rights and Freedoms: Contradictions and Challenges

The contemporary world of aboriginal politics is inhabited by discussions about rights — the right to self-government, the right to title of land, the right to equality, the right to social services, and the right to practice spiritual beliefs. None of this is very new, nor is it surprising, given that non-aboriginal people have been writing on behalf of the "rights" of aboriginal people since the 16th century.

The earliest of these works were concerned primarily with how the colonial powers (Spain) should treat the "uncivilized" and savage peoples discovered in America (see, for instance de Las Casa, 1656 and de Victorio, 1917). Many would argue that there have been no real advances in "rights" for aboriginal people in America since the 16th century, but to seek advances in "rights" presupposes the acceptance of terminology. It strikes me that when aboriginal people discuss rights and borrow the rhetoric of human rights in contemporary struggle, we are using the paradigm of human rights, both nationally and internationally, as an instrument for the recognition of historic claims — and in many cases as the "only" resort. Is that really buying into the distinctly western and liberal vision of human rights concepts?

Underlying the use of human rights terminology is a plea for recognition of a different way of life, a different idea of community, of politics, of spirituality — ideas which have existed since time immemorial, but which have been cast as differences to be repressed and discouraged since colonization. In asking for recognition by another culture of the existence of your own, and for toleration of, and respect for, the practical difference that it brings with it, there seems to be something at stake which is larger than human rights, and certainly larger than the texts of particular documents which guarantee human rights, such as the *Canadian Charter of Rights and Freedoms*: a more basic request — the request to be recognized as peoples. I believe that from early colonization up to the present, no government or monarch has ever recognized aboriginal peoples as distinct peoples with cultures different from their own, in other words, as peoples whose ways of life should be tolerated and respected, even though certain customs may challenge the cultural assumptions of the newcomers.

I also believe that one reason for this, aside from the obvious one of the assertion of government power and the quest for economic dominance, is that aboriginal ways have been and still are presumed to be primitive, in the sense of "lesser" states of development. This presumption denies genuine differences by presuming that another culture is the same, just not quite as "civilized" yet. Hence, it is important for the colonial governments to take jurisdiction over aboriginal peoples in order to guide them to a more reasoned state where they can become just like them (it is not surprising that the church was usually the state's best ally).

No government has ever dealt with aboriginal peoples on an equal basis — without seeing us as means to an economic goal (settlement and development), as noble savages, the pagans without civilization, or as specimens for anthropological investigation and scientific collection. Genuinely recognizing another people as another culture is more than recognizing rights of certain persons. It is not simply recognizing peoples of another colour, translated in European terms as "race", nor is it recognizing the presence of a minority because the minority is always defined by and in subordination to the majority. Placing the emphasis on race or minority (and consequently on rights) has the effect of covering over the differences at work to the majority's advantage. Aboriginal cultures are not simply different "races" — a difference explained in terms of biology (or colour): aboriginal cultures are the manifestations of a different human (collective) imagination.

To borrow the words of a non-aboriginal writer, [aboriginal] cultures "are oriented as wholes in different directions. They are travelling along different roads in pursuit of different ends, and these ends and these means in one society cannot be judged in terms of those of another society because essentially they are incommensurable ..." (Benedict, 1935). While it seems that, in the Canadian context, aboriginal peoples and non-aboriginal persons have some understanding and recognition of each other, it also seems that aboriginal peoples have been the ones who have had to suffer for tolerance (even by force and imprisonment).

It is true that there have been treaties between aboriginal peoples and the British Crown. However, these do not amount, in my view, to a genuine recognition of diverse indigenous cultures; they were really Western-style (written in a highly legalistic form in most cases) methods to make way for progress, with "progress" defined according to the standards of the newcomers. After all, signing treaties was the British practice in almost all of the colonies, irrespective of cultural differences among those they "discovered" or "conquered". It is no wonder, then, that in studying the law of treaties, we quickly learn that, according to Anglo-Canadian legal standards, treaties (even before Confederation) are not seen as agreements between sovereign peoples or nations. When we inquire as to why treaties are not viewed as agreements between two (or more) sovereign peoples, we are generally led to the theory that aboriginal people (either at the time of treaty-making or now) were not sufficiently "civilized" and organized to qualify as "sovereign" peoples, or that they had already "lost" their sovereignty through some predestined and mysterious process for example, by virtue of being "discovered").

Of course, there is no compelling reason, according to the doctrines and principles of international law, to view treaties between aboriginal peoples and the Crown as anything other than treaties between sovereigns, or *international* treaties. Nor does there seem to be any compelling reason for continuing to pretend that aboriginal peoples do not have distinct cultures, cultures which are deserving of recognition by the dominant (European) one which has been imposed in Canada. Why is it, then, that aboriginal peoples, and aboriginal claims, must be "fit-in" to the categories and concepts of a dominant culture, in some form of equivalence, in order to be acknowledged? There appears to be a contradiction at work in areas like human rights, that is, a contradiction between pretending, on the one hand to accept aboriginal peoples as distinct peoples and, on the other, of accepting something called aboriginal peoples' rights. This contradiction, which I explore briefly in the following pages, has led to a great deal of misunderstanding and has given the dominant culture (as represented by the government of Canada) plenty of scope in which to maneuvre, while avoiding a difference-based approach to aboriginal peoples as equals or as sovereigns.

"Aboriginal rights" is a category, primarily a category of law, in which most discussions about our historic claims and cultural differences are carried out in Canadian society. It is a category with severe limitations politically and legally — limitations which have been set, whether or not intentionally, by those who thought up the category — mostly non-aboriginal people. It is a realm in which discussions focusing on strange expressions like "title", "usufructory rights", "mere premises", "status", "referential incorporation", "extinguishment", and "existing" take on enormous significance, even though they do not seem to have anything to do with the everyday lives of aboriginal people. A frightening and frustrating thing about the centrality of these expressions is that they were thought up by the same non-aboriginal people that brought us the "rights" category; they seem incompatible with aboriginal ideas about land, family, social life, and spirituality. Yet, somehow, they are supposed to be helping us out, assisting in our struggle to continue to practice our cultures. Could it be that they just serve to limit the possibilities for genuine acknowledgement of the existence of aboriginal peoples as distinct cultures and political communities possessing the ability to live without external regulation and control?

I chose the first two quotations prefacing this article to illustrate the contradiction here. A *Charter* based on the supremacy of a foreign God and the (Anglo-American) rule of law just doesn't seem to be the kind of constitution that aboriginal peoples can get too excited about. Rather, it is the kind of constitution which we can get rather angry about because it has the effect of excluding aboriginal vision(s) and (diverse) views about the land and the society now called Canada. Clearly, as an historical document, it represents only one story of Canada — that is, the story of the colonialists. As a document held out to be the "supreme law of Canada" (according to Section 52 of the *Constitution Act*, 1982), it represents an act of ethnocentrism and domination, acknowledging at no point The Great Law of customary laws of the First Peoples of this territory (except unless through wish-fulfilment Section 35 is read in this way).

Could aboriginal spirituality ever be represented by the likes of the preamble to the *Canadian Charter of Rights and Freedoms*? Do Chief Seattle's words render this impossible? Are we travelling along a different road, one which does not need formal written declarations to convince ourselves of what kinds of societies we are? Should we even try to do things this way? Who are we trying to please in doing so? Is it inevitable that aboriginal traditions and customs have to take the form of "rights" which are brought to courts, proven to exist, and then enforced? Is not the fundamental problem here the fact that everything has to be adjusted to fit the terms of the dominant system?

I view the problems of the aboriginal peoples[-] human rights area as further evidence of the fact that the dominant culture has never recognized aboriginal peoples as distinct peoples and cultures. I suppose that the exclusion or repression of the "aboriginal fact" of Canada in the present *Constitution Act* in a strange way bolsters the idea that aboriginal peoples are sovereign and distinct (yet entrapped) nations. Unless there was a conscious strategy of "ignore them and they'll go away", one would presume more ink would have been spilt on setting out the nature of the relationship between the Crown and the First Peoples of Canada; or at least on mentioning it more directly than in two perfunctory sections in the *Constitution Act*.

(v) Aboriginal Peoples and the Canadian Charter of Rights and Freedoms: Contradictions and Challenges

Larger questions loom over all of these problems. What does it mean for aboriginal peoples to advance claims enveloped in the rhetoric of human rights? While there is no question that there are serious human problems in aboriginal communities which seem to warrant redress as "human rights" violations, are such claims too piecemeal? Is there a difference between having discrete "rights" incrementally recognized, and being recognized as a people? What alternatives to rights-based claims are available? In the very pragmatic-oriented work of human rights lawyers and activists in Canada — a discourse about litigation strategies and legal doctrines — there hardly seems to be an opportunity to stop and consider these kinds of questions about aboriginal rights and the *Canadian Charter of Rights and Freedoms*. I wonder to what extent those who support struggles for the recognition of aboriginal rights have really considered these issues?

Generally, we have never really had to address these problems during the first five years of the *Charter* because we were too preoccupied with negotiations to recognize (both within the *Charter* and within another specific section of the *Constitution Act*) the "right to self-government". When these negotiations failed miserably at the final meeting of the First Ministers in 1987 — a failure which was something of a foregone conclusion given that the aboriginal peoples were never seen as equal parties in the negotiation process from the beginning (instead we were given special "observer" status) — people returned to the *Charter* and the vague provision on the aboriginal rights in section 35 of *Constitution Act, 1982* to consider legal challenges and claims based upon these provisions. It is my belief that questions regarding *which* forums and laws are especially urgent now. Such questions can hardly be avoided any longer, especially in light of the fact that aboriginal peoples are turning more to the *Charter* for recognition of their rights vis-à-vis the Canadian Crown, and perhaps more disturbingly, turning to the *Charter* to fight out internal battles in communities.

I would like to explore some of the layers of contradiction or conflict which are raised in the context of aboriginal peoples' claims and the *Charter*, and describe briefly an effort to meet one aspect of these contradictions which has been made by aboriginal women through the Native Women's Association of Canada. The views put forward here are my own, many of which have been developed in the course of advising the Native Women's Association of Canada on human rights matters in recent years. I have been greatly influenced in these questions by situations facing the Association and its constituents, and by both my mixed education and ancestry. I do not propose to consider in any detail traditional and customary practices of specific aboriginal peoples, both for reasons of the limits of space here and because I have reservations about the extent to which knowledge about these matters can be transmitted in such a medium.

The Origins of Human Rights

While it might seem obvious that human rights and the *Canadian Charter of Rights and Freedoms* are incompatible with aboriginal culture and traditions, it is helpful to trace the origin of the idea of human rights in the modern era in order to locate the differences here. The Anglo-American concept of rights was set out, for the most part, by two 17th century English political theorists, Thomas Hobbes (1651) and John Locke (1690). Locke is the more famous of the two on these matters. He developed a theory of "natural rights" — later "human" came to be substituted for "natural," after the recognition (post-Holocaust) that peoples are capable of barbaric actions in the name of what is "natural." Locke's theory of natural rights was based around his idea that every *man* (and emphasis should be on *man* because Locke is famous for his theory that society was naturally patriarchal) possesses a right to private property, or the right to own property. This right, he suggested, flowed from the fact that human beings are God's property ("God" as in the preamble to the *Canadian Charter*). He argued that people enter into "civil society" for the central, and negatively conceived, purpose of protecting their right to private property against random attack.

The idea of the absolute right to property, as an exclusive zone of ownership capable of being transmitted through the family (through males according to a doctrine called "primogenitor"), is the cornerstone of the idea of rights — the idea that there is a zone of absolute human right where the individual can do what he chooses: "The right is a loaded gun that the right holder may shoot at will in his corner of town" (Unger, 1986). It does not take much of a stretch of the imagination to see where slavery and the subordination of women found legitimacy in the Anglo-American tradition — with the absolute ownership of property, and autonomous domains, "naturally" rights will extend "even to another person's body" (Hobbes, 1651).

Although there is no pan-aboriginal culture of iron-clad system of beliefs, this notion of rights based on individual ownership is antithetical to the widely-shared understanding of creation and stewardship responsibilities of First Nations peoples for the land, or for Mother Earth. Moreover, to my knowledge, there are no notions among aboriginal Nations of living together for the purposes of protecting an individual interest in property. Aboriginal life has been set out in stories handed down through generations and in customary laws sometimes represented by wampum belts, sacred pipes, medicine bundles, and rock paintings. For example, the teachings of the Four Directions is that life is based on four principles: trust, kindness, sharing and strength. While these are responsibilities which each person owes to others, they represent the larger function of social life, that is, to honour and respect Mother Earth. There is no equivalent of "rights" here because there is no equivalent to the ownership of private property. The collective or communal bases of aboriginal life [do] not really have a parallel to individual rights; they are incommensurable. To try to explain to an Elder that, under Canadian law, there are carefully worked-over doctrines pertaining to who owns every inch of the country, the sky, the ocean, and even the moon, would provide disbelief and profound sadness.

The Structure of the *Canadian Charter*

Nevertheless, the Canadian human rights system, having been distanced in time and space somewhat from its origin and conceptual basis in the theories about the right to individual ownership to property, seems little less foreign, especially since so much is said of aboriginal matters in the context of human rights. Some writers even argue that, in Canada, the *Charter* recognized certain collective rights, such as aboriginal rights, and not merely individual rights. However, my reading of the law leads me to believe that the individual property basis of human rights is revealed clearly in the text of the *Canadian Charter*, as well as in recent cases which have been decided under the *Charter*. The language of the *Charter* refers to human rights enjoyed by "every citizen of Canada", "every individual", "any person", etc. The section of the *Charter* on enforcement applies to "[a]ny *one* whose rights or freedoms ... have been infringed", permitting them to apply to court for the order the court considers appropriate in the circumstances — almost always the singular subject.

The extent to which a human rights law set out in such individualist terms could ever either (i) be interpreted as including a collective understanding of rights, or (ii) lead to judges acknowledging that other peoples might not base their social relations on these individual "rights" notions, is highly questionable. There is nothing strong enough in the *Charter* to allow for either a collectivist idea of rights (or responsibilities), if such a theory is conceivable, or toleration of a community organized around collective values. When cases involving aboriginal peoples come before the courts, it is doubtful that different standards of legal analysis will be applied. Already the case law has taken a disturbing course from the viewpoint of aboriginal peoples.

With shades of private property notions in mind, the Supreme Court of Canada in the recent *Morgentaler* case on abortion suggested that "the rights guaranteed in the *Charter* erect around each individual, metaphorically speaking, an invisible fence over which the state will not be allowed to trespass. The role of the courts is to map out, piece by piece, the parameters of the fence". In an earlier decision, one involving aboriginal persons, the Federal Court of Canada took the view that "in the absence of legal provisions to the contrary, the interests of individual persons will be deemed to have precedence over collective rights. In the absence of law to the contrary, this must be as true of Indian Canadians as of others".

Even in the area of language rights — an area said to be a cornerstone of collective rights in the *Charter* — the Supreme Court of Canada in the recent case involving Québec's former *Bill 101* has indicated that this right is somehow both an individual and a collective one: "Language itself indicates a means by which a people may express its cultural identity. It is also the means by which the individual expresses his or her personal identity and sense of individuality". How to go about reconciling these two aspects when they conflict is no easy task, and the Court gives little guidance here on its view of collective rights, except to say that the right to speak their language must be protected at law against the community's prohibition of it.

Even in the area of equality rights, as recognized in section 15 of the *Charter*, the text applies to "every individual". This provision has been interpreted by the courts not as a general recognition of the idea of equality (which, if read as "sameness", would be deeply disturbing to aboriginal people), but simply as a principle in relating to the application of given laws. In a recent equality case, the Supreme Court of Canada stated that section 15 "is not a general guarantee of equality, it does not provide for equality between individuals or groups within society in a general or abstract sense, nor does it impose on

(v) Aboriginal Peoples and the Canadian Charter of Rights and Freedoms: Contradictions and Challenges

individuals or groups an obligation to accord equality treatment to others. *It is concerned with the application of the law.*" The scope for aboriginal rights claims under section 15 is limited, even if such a course was seen as desirable by aboriginal leaders.

Moreover, we can begin to see the broader implications of these cases for aboriginal peoples or aboriginal claims. It is difficult to move in a certain direction as a people if individuals can challenge collective decisions based on infringement of their individual rights and if collective goals will not be understood or prioritized. Some people may view this as the triumph of democracy, but it makes the preservation of a different culture and the pursuit of collective political goals almost impossible.

In aboriginal communities where customary political and spiritual institutions are the guiding force (even alongside the imposed *Indian Act* system of Band Councils), such as the Haudenosaunee of the Iroquois Confederates, recourse to an individual-rights based law like the *Charter* could result in further weakening of the cultural identity of the community. This could take one of two forms: either a member of the community would challenge aboriginal laws based on individual rights protections in the *Charter* arguing that they have not been respected by their government (an internal challenge); or a non-aboriginal person could challenge the laws of an aboriginal government on the basis that they do not conform with *Charter* standards (an external challenge).

In the case of an external challenge, for example, on the basis of voting or candidacy rights where a non-aboriginal complainant argued that they could not vote or stand for elections in an aboriginal community because of cultural restrictions, the court would be given the authority to decide on an important part of the future of an aboriginal community. It would have to consider the protections of aboriginal rights in the *Charter* and weigh these against the individual right to vote recognized in section 3. Should Canadian courts (and non-aboriginal judges) have authority in these cases? Given the highly individualistic basis of the *Charter*, and of the history of human rights, would the collective aboriginal right stand a chance? I doubt it. As the Assembly of First Nations argued before the Parliamentary Committee on Aboriginal Affairs in 1982:

> [as] Indian people we cannot afford to have individual rights override collective rights. Our societies have never been structured that way, unlike yours, and that is where the clash comes ... If you isolate the individual rights from the collective rights, then you are heading down another path that is even more discriminatory ... The *Canadian Charter of Rights* is in conflict with our philosophy and culture ...

The other possible challenge, the internal challenge, where a member of an aboriginal community felt dissatisfied with a particular course of action the aboriginal government was taking and turned to the *Charter* for the recognition of a right, is equally if not more worrisome. This kind of challenge would be a dangerous opening for a Canadian court to rule on individual versus collective rights *vis-a-vis* aboriginal peoples; it would also break down community methods of dispute-resolution and restoration. Here, the example of the *Indian Civil Rights Act* in the United States is instructive. This act, based on the idea that protections for the *American Bill of Rights* should be extended to aboriginal communities, along with the establishment of tribal courts which would have the same function as American courts generally, has been greatly criticized by aboriginal people as imposing alien ways of life. As two noted scholars suggest:

> In philosophical terms, it is much easier to describe the impact of the ... Act. Traditional Indian society understood itself as a complex of responsibilities and duties. The [Act] merely transposed this belief into a society based on rights against government and eliminated any sense of responsibility that people might have felt for one another. Granted that many of the customs that made duties and responsibilities a serious matter of individual action had eroded badly in the decades since the tribes had agreed to move to the reservations, the impact of the [Act] was to make these responsibilities impossible to perform because the Act inserted the trial court as an institution between the people and their responsibilities. People did not have to confront one another before their community and resolve their problems; they had only to file suit in tribal court (Deloria and Lytle, 1984).

The lessons of the *American Indian Civil Rights Act* and of the establishment of tribal courts are important ones in light of the *Charter*. If internal disputes are brought before Canadian courts, it will seriously undermine the aboriginal system of government based on responsibility (like the Four Directions) and interpose a system of individual-based rights. It also has the effect of encouraging people to go outside the community, and outside of custom, to settle disputes in formal courts — instead of having to deal with a problem within a community.

This might sound like a hard line to take, especially when one considers the extent to which customs and traditional methods of governance and dispute-resolution have been dislodged in aboriginal communities after more than a century of life under the *Indian Act*. The experience of gender-based discrimination was employed as a technique of assimilation up until the 1985 amendments to the *Indian Act* (many see the gender-based discriminatory provisions as having continuing effect despite the amendments), and scarred many aboriginal communities as male-dominated Band councils frequently sided against women and with the Canadian government in the belief that to do otherwise would undermine the Crown's responsibility for aboriginal peoples.

As a consequence, women were forced to go outside the community to resolve the injustices of gender discrimination, so cases were brought under the *Canadian Bill of Rights* and eventually under the *United Nations Covenant on Civil and Political Rights*. Changes were made to the *Indian Act*, but many of the after-effects of gender discrimination still plague aboriginal communities, including problems associated with women returning to communities and being able to take up residence, educate their children, share in social services, and receive per capita payments from resource exploitation on aboriginal lands.

Communities have been slow to address questions related to the aftermath of gender discrimination in the *Indian Act*, and the mechanisms available to resolve disputes according to customary practices are not necessarily available. This places a great deal of pressure on aboriginal communities, which could lead to cases being taken to Canadian courts pursuant to the *Charter* for recognition of rights against aboriginal governments. As a result of concern over what this could lead to, in light of the individual-based notions of rights under Canadian law, and in light of lessons derived from the United States experience with the *Indian Civil Rights Act*, aboriginal women have been working on projects to encourage the development of First Nations laws in areas like "citizenship" and human rights and responsibilities — laws based, as far as possible, on inherent First Nation jurisdiction and customary practices.

An Alternative Approach: First Nations Human Rights and Responsibilities Laws

The Native Women's Association of Canada has addressed questions relating to gender discrimination in the *Indian Act* and related problems in aboriginal communities since the late 1970s. In 1985, when amendments to the *Indian Act* aimed at eliminating gender discrimination were finally passed, the Native Women's Association took the position that, while aboriginal women could support the end of unfair bias against women, they could not simply support the Federal government's efforts to "improve" the *Indian Act* and the extension of legislative control over the lives of aboriginal peoples through its paternalistic provisions. Consequently, the Association turned its attention to the development of a "First Nation Citizenship Code", or a model law which would address the issues of membership or citizenship in a First Nation, but would base its principles and jurisdiction not on Canadian law, but on the inherent jurisdiction of First Nations to regulate citizenship as practices since time immemorial.

The model code was distributed to every aboriginal community in Canada with a letter encouraging communities to take a First Nations approach to citizenship (and not an *Indian Act* approach) and to set up local mechanisms based, as much as possible, on customary principles for settling disputes, so that problems regarding citizenship could be addressed in the community itself and not in the Canadian courts. As it became clear that citizenship was not the only area of concern in communities (although the issue of Indian status was by far the most divisive), it was evident that some other efforts would need to be expended to discourage internal challenges of aboriginal government actions getting into Canadian courts under the *Charter*. In 1986, the Native Women's Association of Canada began to consider the development of another model law, parallel to the Citizenship Code, which would be a First Nations human rights and responsibilities law.

It appears that this Code (which at the time of writing is still in the draft stages) will be based on the inherent jurisdiction of First Nations to make laws for their peoples. It will include a very loosely and generously worded part on human rights and responsibilities, corresponding to the four groups of rights and responsibilities which come from the teachings of the Four Directions. Hence, there are the following responsibilities and rights:

(i) *kindness* — social rights
(ii) *honesty* — political and civil rights
(iii) *sharing* — economic rights, and
(iv) *strength* — cultural rights.

For example, the responsibility and rights category of strength / cultural rights would include provisions on the right to pursue traditional occupations, the right to education in aboriginal languages, the right to customary marriage and adoptions, the right

(v) Aboriginal Peoples and the Canadian Charter of Rights and Freedoms: Contradictions and Challenges

to participate in ceremonies according to laws and traditions of the Nation, and, most importantly, the recognition of the fundamental importance of Elders and spiritual leaders in the preservation of ancestral and customary law and in the health and well-being of the community as a whole.

The provisions on the model law developed by the Native Women's Association on dispute-resolution provide options for a particular community to consider creating a law which fits within its customs and aspirations. These include mediation, the establishment of a Human Rights Committee, and a Council of Elders. Also included are options for setting up methods to deal with conflicts on a regional basis (for example, an Iroquois or Ojibway council of Elders). It is hoped that the work of the Association will contribute to the development of community laws and less formal community solutions to reduce the possibilities that individual members of the First Nations communities will have to go outside their communities (to foreign courts) for redress of grievances. It appears that the development of community codes is the best available solution to the problems in communities and to the threat of the (further) imposition of a Western individualistic human rights system on aboriginal communities.

Future Challenges

The work of the Native Women's Association of Canada really only addresses the problem of internal challenges based on the *Charter* by members of First Nations communities. It does not attempt to deal with other areas of concern, such as external challenges or claims brought by non-aboriginal peoples pursuant to the *Charter*, calling into question the collective basis of aboriginal communities. Even claims brought by aboriginal communities against the Federal Government based on provisions of the *Charter* seem to present a dangerous opportunity for the court to take a restrictive view of collective-based community goals. Any case which presents a Canadian court with the opportunity to balance or weigh an individual right against a collective understanding of community will be an opportunity to delimit the recognition of aboriginal peoples as distinct cultures.

This is something quite different from dealing on an equal footing with aboriginal peoples about historic claims and cultural differences which have to be addressed and settled. These cases permit the court to say, "Yes, we do have jurisdiction over you, and we will decide what is best for you under Canadian law". It is not that different from the imposed system of rule under the *Indian Act*, except in the *Charter* cases, the court can cloak its decision in the rhetoric of democratic freedom, emancipation, multiculturalism and human rights for "all Canadians". The only way to really consider the political and cultural differences between aboriginal peoples and the Canadian state is through discussions which are quasi-international, so that the respective "sovereignty" of the parties will be respected.

Aboriginal peoples have been trying to pursue this (international) course during the past decade. The United Nations has established a special Working Group on Indigenous Populations to consider the human rights violations (really historic claims under international law) of indigenous peoples from around the globe. During the past seven years, there have been six meetings of the Working Group, and recently efforts have been directed at the development of a United Nations [Declaration] on Indigenous Rights. Although aboriginal peoples have been participating quite actively in this process of development of a United Nations Declaration, once again, we are really on the outside of the United Nations system. Nevertheless, certain States which are part of the United Nations structure have been willing to advocate for the recognition of indigenous rights in a declaration.

The matters dealt with in the proceedings of the Working Group and in the Draft Declaration can hardly be ignored, especially when one considers the extent to which they are present in all areas of the globe. As one noted international scholar has suggested, "[t]he peoples of entrapped nations are a sleeping giant in the workings of power politics" (Falk, 1987). A cornerstone of an eventual declaration would have to be, from the aboriginal perspective, a recognition and explicit extension of self-determination to indigenous peoples under international law. There are persuasive arguments that, even without a specific declaration, international law already recognizes the right of all peoples (including aboriginal peoples) to self-determination.

Self-determination is something different than self-government, although it could include the latter. Self-government (which has been the pinnacle of all human rights discussions in the Canadian context) implies that aboriginal peoples were not previously able to govern themselves because they were not at an advanced enough stage of civilization, but can now take on some responsibility for their own affairs. Very few people make a distinction between self-government and self-determination. In a recent (1988) report by the Canadian Bar Association Special Committee on Native Justice, the idea of self-government is used throughout without any distinction as to its historical context or political implications. On this point, aboriginal women in Canada, through the voice of the Native Women's Association, have again made their position in support of self-determination over self-government quite clear.

In the international context, the draft declaration on indigenous rights is silent on the issue of self-determination. It contains many disturbing provisions on lesser notions like "autonomy ... in local affairs" and the "right to exist". While these might seem progressive in some situations where the very life of aboriginal people is systematically threatened on a daily basis, the provisions do not go far enough in recognizing aboriginal people as distinct cultures and political entities, equally as capable of governing and making decisions as European sovereigns, except with different political and cultural goals.

A great deal more work will have to be done in the next few years to ensure that the text of the draft declaration is one which will recognize indigenous people as legitimate, though different, governments and cultures. The only way to do this, in international law, is through a recognition of self-determination. Realizing this goal will require broad-based support from international society, manifested in the work of non-government organizations, women's movements, and sympathetic States. The Canadian government and Canadian people could do much to assist the international process if the government would simply recognize aboriginal peoples as distinct peoples with different but equally legitimate cultures and ways of life. This cannot be done through Canadian courts and in the rhetoric of Canadian human rights — it has to be done through a joint aboriginal-Canadian discussion process where, unlike the series of discussions held on Canadian constitutional amendments, aboriginal peoples are equal participants in the process, along with the Prime Minister and perhaps Provincial Premiers.

In the meantime, aboriginal women will continue to do what can be done to ensure that aboriginal communities are governed by customary laws and practices, through the development of First Nations laws, and through the political and spiritual voice of the Native Women's Association of Canada as guided by its Elders and affiliated women's organizations.

5 Law, Crime and Social Order

(i) The Treason Trial of David Maclane

R. DeSalaberry

The Court opened at 7 o'clock a.m. precisely. David Maclane was placed at the bar. The jurors empanelled by the sheriff were called over — eleven were challenged on the part of the Crown, and twenty-four by the prisoner. The following gentlemen were sworn: John Blackwood, John Crawford, John Mure, John Jones, James M. Goddard, Henry Cull, John Painter, David Munro, James Irvine, James Orkney, Robert Morragh, Georges Symes. Then Mr. Lind, Clerk of the Arraigns said: "David Maclane, hold up your hand. Gentlemen of the Jury, the prisoner David Maclane stands indicted (here he read the indictment of which I have presented already the substance). Upon this indictment he hath been arraigned and upon his arraignment hath pleaded not guilty, and for his trial hath put himself upon God and the country, which country you are. Your charge is to enquire whether he be guilty of the felony and high treason whereof he stands indicted or not guilty. If you find him guilty, you are to enquire what goods or chattels, lands or tenements he had at the time of the felony and high treason committed, or at any other time since. If you find him not guilty, you are to enquire whether he fled for it. If you find that he did fly for it, you shall enquire of his goods and chattels as if you had found him guilty. If you find him not guilty and that he did not fly for it, say so, and no more. Hear you evidence."

Then Mr. Caron addressed the jury on behalf of the Crown and was followed by the Attorney-General who gave them the law and the facts on which the charge was based and which were to be brought forth by the witnesses William Barnard, Elmer Cushing, Francis Chandonet, Thomas Butterfield, Charles Frichette, John Black and Herman W. Ryland. Barnard had met the accused for the first time in Vermont at dark in a house near the border line. Maclane confidentially told him under a solemn promise of secrecy that his business was to bring about a revolution in Canada, and that the Canadians would have everything done for them for that purpose. He offered him to take the lead, adding that if Barnard undertook the task his fortune would be made.

A second interview took place at Montreal a few days later and again the matter was pressed upon Barnard, who this time informed Mr. McCord, one of the magistrates at Montreal. Barnard met the accused a third time at Laprairie, a village on the south shore of the St. Lawrence, about 9 miles above Montreal, on the second of November, when the same proposals were renewed and the promise made that an army would invade the province in the spring. He wanted to know where the seminary of Montreal kept their money and wished to be informed who the principal merchants were and in what part of their houses they kept their cash.

Elmer Cushing the second witness kept a tavern called the "American Coffee House" at Montreal, and the accused stopped at his place on the 5th of November. Cushing observed that his clothes were covered with small burrs, and asked him where he

---

Originally appeared as "The First State Trial in Lower Canada" (Sept. 1927) VII *Canadian Bar Review* 469 at 472–77. Note omitted. Reproduced by permission of Canadian Bar Association.

had been. He answered that he had been on every part of the mountain, which might be made a place of great command over Montreal in case of war. Maclane then exacting a promise of secrecy, which was given, told the witness that there would be a severe attack upon the province early in the spring; that he was employed by the French Minister at Philadelphia in forwarding the plan; that the attack would be made by a fleet from France, which would bring from ten to fifteen thousand land forces. He went to his saddlebags, took out a pair of shoes, one of which had a hole near the toe, and pulled out a paper signed Adet. He assured Cushing he would have any reward he might ask for if he took an active part and that if he ever revealed what he had heard it should fare hard with him; that his life would be taken immediately.

Francis Chandonet, the third witness, was an American subject. He had met the prisoner at Watson's Tavern in the course of the previous summer, a little below "Ile aux Noix" and sometime also in the beginning of the winter. Maclane had come across Lake Champlain, and told the witness that he had come on most important business which he would reveal under promise of secrecy. He then told him he was employed by the French to sound the minds of the people, and that the plan was to secrete a quantity of arms and ammunition on rafts in the spring to be brought into the province by Lake Champlain, and the St. Lawrence, that he thought a quantity might likewise be concealed in the rafts of firewood made in the Chateauguay River, and he pressed very hard upon the witness to take part with him, which the latter refused to do.

Thomas Butterfield, from Swaton, U.S., the next witness, was an accomplice. He had promised to assist Maclane in all his enterprises against Canada and also was under his pay. The prisoner had told him he and a man named Frichette were going to Quebec to lay some plan to take the garrison.

Frichette was then heard. He met the prisoner at St. John's, who asked him if he had horses to sell. Both went into the field where Frichette, being bound by an oath to secrecy, was asked by the accused if the Canadians were disposed to revolt, to which Frichette answered they were not desirous of war, and the prisoner then stated that he had come to take Quebec — that five hundred men with pikes could do it. He asked him to conduct him to Quebec through the land, to which the witness agreed. They passed behind the Fort of St. John's before daylight, and proceeded on the south shore road to St. Nicholas. They left St. Nicholas, and crossed the St. Lawrence to Wolfe's Cove. The prisoner sent Frichette from there to Quebec to bring one Mr. Black to him. When Mr. Black arrived he told the prisoner that Frichette had informed him of the intentions of his journey. He advised him to go back without making the attempt, as he thought it could not succeed as the Canadians were not disposed to rise and could not therefore be depended upon.

The prisoner afterwards informed Mr. Black he had a letter for him, and another person. Mr. Black opened and read the letters and advised the prisoner to tear them to pieces, and bury them, which was done. At Mr. Black's request he explained his plan of the taking of Quebec. The troops he said would be so surprised that they would not know which way to turn. Mr. Black told Maclane not to be afraid and to come to Quebec to his house, dressed like a gentleman, and take a walk about the town. The prisoner expressed his dislike to come into town, but Mr. Black insisted and finally Maclane consented to go. Mr. Black did not approve of his coming in company with him, to avoid suspicion. He wanted Frichette to bring Maclane to his house in the evening which accordingly was done. The prisoner desired to be called by the name of Felt, from St. John's, till he went to Mr. Black's.

Mr. Black then gave evidence. He corroborated Frichette and related to the Jury that the prisoner had explained his plan, which was that of humanity. That he was sorry to see a great people labouring under the tyranny of England; that he proposed to push the British from the continent of America. He said he left Mr. Adet on the 7th of April, who was going to France on the 10th, and that both he and the Spanish minister were concerned in the measures. That besides these measures there were fifteen thousand men at the line ready at a nod. He inquired much concerning the property, public and private, that there was at Quebec, and he said the property was intended to be given to those who should take the city. Black advised him to come to town after dark. The prisoner finally consented and was conducted to his house by Frichette. As soon as Black came back to town he gave information to a magistrate, Mr. Young, and the prisoner was apprehended the same evening, about eleven o'clock at his house.

The last witness was Herman Witsius Ryland, Secretary to His Excellency the Governor-General, who made the arrest. This concluded the evidence of the Crown. The defence produced no witnesses. David Maclane made a long speech to the Jury in which he denied the charge, but unfortunately it was not conclusive. His two counsel made a strong appeal to the feelings of the Jury. The Attorney-

(i) The Treason Trial of David Maclane

General replied. Chief Justice Osgood then made a forcible address to the Jury, but very fair and moderate, summing up the evidence in a clear, precise and impartial manner.

Then the Jury withdrew for twenty minutes and returned. The Clerk of Arraigns then said: "Gentlemen answer to your names."

"Gentlemen, are you all agreed upon your verdict?" — "Yes."

"Who shall speak for you?" — "Our foreman."

"David Maclane hold up your hand. Jurors, look upon the prisoner; how say you — is he guilty of the felony and high treason whereof he stands indicted, or not guilty?"

Foreman: "Guilty."

"What goods or chattels, lands or tenements had he at the time of the felony and high treason by him committed?"

Foreman: "None to our knowledge."

"Gentlemen of the Jury, the Court discharges you and thanks you for your services."

The Attorney-General: "Upon the verdict as recorded, I humbly move for judgment of death against the prisoner."

Clerk of Arraigns: "David Maclane, hold up your hand. You have been indicted of felony and treason, have been arraigned and pleaded not guilty thereto, and for your trial have put yourself on God and country, which country has found you guilty — what have you to say for yourself why the court should not give judgment of death upon you according to law."

Prisoner: "I have nothing more to say."

Proclamation being made, the Chief Justice Pronounced the sentence of death as follows: —

> It remains that I should discharge the painful duty of pronouncing the sentence of the law which is: That you, David Maclane, be taken to the place from whence you came, and from thence you are to be drawn to the place of execution, where you must be hanged by the neck, but not until you are dead; for you must be cut down alive and your bowels taken out and burnt before your face; then your head must be severed from your body, which must be divided into four parts, and your head and quarters be at the King's disposal — and may the Lord have mercy on your soul.

The Attorney-General moved that a day should be fixed for the execution, and the Court appointed Friday, the 21st of July.

The trial had commenced at 7 a.m. and was concluded at 9 p.m. the same day.

On Friday, the 21st, the prisoner was taken from the gaol and placed upon a hurdle which moved in slow solemnity towards the place of execution. At about a quarter after ten, the hurdle drew up close to the gallows. As soon as it stopped, Maclane rose up dressed in white linen and wearing a white cap on his head. The Rev. Mr. Mountain and the Rev. Mr. Sparks attended him, and with them he continued in fervent prayer for some minutes. He then informed the executioner that he was ready and was by him directed to ascend the ladder, which he immediately did. But the executioner observing that he was too high, he descended a step or two and then addressed the spectators in the following words:

> This place gives me pleasure; I am now going where I have long wished to be and you, who now see me, must all follow me in a short time, some of you perhaps in a few days; let this be a warning to prepare for your own deaths.

Then addressing himself to the military who were drawn up in a hollow square, he added: "You with arms in your hands, you are not secure here even with your arms. I am going where I shall be secure without them." He immediately drew the cap over his face, exclaiming: "Oh! God, receive my soul. I long to be with my Jesus," and dropped his handkerchief as a signal to the executioner, who instantly turned him off. He struggled with death but a short time. The body hung for about twenty-five minutes, and was then cut down. A platform, with a raised block upon it, was brought near the gallows, and a fire was kindled for executing the remainder of the sentence. The head was cut off, and the executioner holding it up to public view proclaimed it "the head of a traitor." An incision was made below the breast and a part of the bowels taken out and burnt. The four quarters were marked with a knife but not divided from the body.

The whole of the execution took about two hours.

(ii) Law, State, and Class Struggle

Alan Hunt

Introduction

This chapter sets out to examine the way in which law operates to maintain class domination. The argument that is developed shows that law should not simply be regarded as part of the coercive armoury of the state; but also must be understood as making a major contribution to what will be called "ideological domination." Ideological domination consists of those processes that produce and reaffirm the existing social order and thereby legitimize class domination. The processes involved in creating and reproducing ideological domination play a major part in ensuring the continuation of capitalist social relations.

There has been relatively little attention paid by Marxists to law. This absence of discussion has resulted in a tendency for the more obvious repressive characteristics to be stressed; and as a consequence the more pervasive contribution of law to the maintenance of capitalist society has not been sufficiently explored. The analysis of law in this wider context is of considerable political importance. Marxists are increasingly being forced to come to grips with the fact that modern capitalism has exhibited very considerable "staying power." In the period since the Second World War capitalism in Western Europe has shown what may be best described as relative stability; that is to suggest that despite the occurrence of very deep economic, social and political crises the capitalist social order in the major Western European states has survived substantially intact. This chapter examines the extent and the manner in which legal systems contribute to the perpetuation of capitalist systems.

State and Law

In class societies the economic and social dominance of an exploiting class does not sustain itself automatically. The exploiting class always strives to turn itself into a ruling class by means of an institutional structure, the state, which operates to sustain and to reproduce that position. While the state is a product of class antagonism it takes on the appearance of being an entity which stands above society and which embodies the interests of the community as a whole. This apparently *universal* quality is especially significant with reference of legal systems:

> Right, law, etc. are merely the symptom, the expression of *other* relations upon which State power rests.... These actual relations are in no way created by the State power; on the contrary they are the power creating it. The individuals who rule in these conditions, besides having to constitute their power in the form of the *State*, have to give their will, which is determined by these definite conditions, a universal expression as the will of the state, as law. (Marx/Engels 1968: 366)

The distinctive feature then of legal systems of class societies is the fact that they embody the material interests of the ruling class in a universal form, and thus present law as the embodiment of the interests of the community as a whole:

> In a modern state, law must not only correspond to the general economic condition and be its expression, but must also be an *internally coherent* expression which does not owing to inner contradictions, reduce itself to nought. And in order to achieve this, the faithful reflection of economic conditions suffers increasingly. All the more so the more rarely it happens that a code of law is the blunt, unmitigated, unadulterated expression of domination of a class — this in itself would offend the "conception of right". (Engels 1890: 504)

This striving of "internal coherence," in which law comes to be seen as the embodiment of universal notions of "justice" and "right," needs to be explored. At the hands of bourgeois legal and political theorists it has been used to provide an ideological dogma, important in bourgeois political and legal theory, of the doctrine of the "separation of powers." The essence of this view is that the character of the democratic state is defined as one in which

---

From *Explorations in Law and Society: Towards a Constitutive Theory of Law* (London: Routledge, 1993) at 17–35. Notes omitted. Originally from (1976) 20 *Marxism Today* at 178–87. © New Statesman, 2000. Reproduced by permission.

there exists a separation between the major components of the state. Specifically it is argued that not only is there, but also that there ought to be, a separation between the legislature, which makes the laws, and the judiciary, which apply those laws.

The doctrine of the separation of powers has played, and continues to play a central part in bourgeois theory of the law and the state. There has been a tendency of Marxists in seeking to expose the ideological character of this doctrine to react against it by asserting the identity of the state and law. Thus the legal system has been presented simply as the direct and totally subservient agent of the state. Such a position is too simple, but more importantly it obscures the real class character of the legal system as a mechanism whereby the existing form of class domination is perpetuated and reproduced.

We need to start by asking, how does it come about that a separation appears to exist between law and state? Engels provides a useful starting point:

> But once the state has become an independent power *vis-à-vis* society, it produces forthwith a further ideology. It is indeed among professional politicians, theorists of public law and jurists of private law that the connection with economic facts gets lost for fair [*sic*]. Since in each particular case the economic facts must assume the form of juristic motives in order to receive legal sanction; and since, in so doing, consideration of course has to be given to the whole legal system already in operation, the juristic form is, in consequence, made everything and the economic content nothing. (Engels 1958: 396–97)

If these ideological functions are to be fulfilled they cannot operate exclusively as ideological forces, they must find some expression in the actual practice embodied within the legal system. As a consequence the legal system operates in a manner which cannot be explained exclusively by reference to the dictates of the state as a whole.

The doctrine of the separation of powers appeals to the independence of the judiciary. Yet this independence is clearly very restricted. Judicial appointments are made by the highest representatives of the political apparatus of the state.

But what does need to be stressed is that even the relative degree of autonomy sets up stresses and contradictions within the state as a whole. Decisions by courts do not always please the holders of state power. The protracted struggle between the courts and Nixon throughout the "Watergate affair" is perhaps the most important recent example of such a tension in operation, in which the conflict between court and state contributed in no small measure to the downfall of Nixon.

But the tension between courts and state may also have advantages for the holders of state power. The institutional complexity of the English legal system allowed the government to brush the cobwebs off the Official solicitor whose intervention facilitated the release of the "Pentonville 5" in 1972 when faced with the prospect of a General Strike. Frequently it serves as a convenient smoke-screen behind which to hide; Roy Jenkins, as Home Secretary, consistently used the excuse of separation between government and courts to refuse to intervene and secure the release of the Shrewsbury pickets.

This discussion points toward the general conclusion that the relationship between the state and the legal system must always be a matter for concrete examination. While the general dependence of the law on the state as a whole is an important proposition within Marxist theory, this must not be treated as if it suggested a complete identity between law and state.

Domination and Hegemony

Domination is a universal feature of class society. It consists in the subjection of one or more classes to another class (or grouping of classes) in such a way that exploitative relations are perpetuated. But the form that domination takes varies with the form of the exploitative class relations; thus the domination of slave by slaveholder differs from the employer's domination of the factory worker. Domination must be viewed not as a single act but as a process that reproduces the conditions for exploitative social relations.

Domination can only be based for very short periods of time on direct physical coercion. Even the most barbarous and coercive systems do not rely exclusively upon coercive violence. Direct coercion will often play a major part in the establishment of a new system of class power, but, however much it continues to depend on physical repression, it will strive to promote other means of consolidating its domination.

An extremely fruitful approach to the discussion of domination is provided by the early leader of the Italian Communist Party, Antonio Gramsci, who made use of the concept of "hegemony." He used it to identify the processes that create

> the "spontaneous" consent given by the great mass of the population to the general direction imposed on social life by the dominant funda-

mental group (i.e., the ruling class). (Gramsci 1971: 12)

The vital characteristic of "hegemony" is that it is an active process; it is concerned not only with the *fact* of consent, but focuses on the creation and the mobilization of that consent. One major facet of the class struggle that takes place within capitalist societies is the continual struggle for influence over the ideas, perceptions, and values of members of the different classes. The maintenance of capitalism would be impossible unless the capitalist class was able to decisively influence the ideas, attitudes and consciousness of the working class.

It is important to stress that the ideological struggle is not simply concerned with the conflict between general theories of society. It is concerned with every aspect of the way in which people think about, react to, and interpret their position in class society.

Coercive and Ideological Domination

In examining the part that is played by law in the class struggle it is useful to distinguish between two different aspects. Law plays an important role in sustaining the domination of the ruling class because it operates both as a form of *coercive domination* and of *ideological domination*. It will also be necessary to stress that they are not simple alternatives. I hope to show the way in which these two elements are closely bound together and as such contribute to the special effectiveness of law as a mechanism of social order.

Let us first consider the coercive character of law. The legal system is able to call upon the organized power of the state. This repression operates both through specific institutions, which range from the courts themselves to the prison system, probation service, etc. In addition it also operates more generally through the police system that operates with wide-ranging powers, sanctioned by law, but able to act with a very considerable degree of autonomy.

Legal coercion operates at a number of different levels. Of greatest importance is the application of coercion to protect the *general conditions* of the capitalist order. First and foremost coercion is applied to protect and reinforce the property relations of capitalist society. There exists an increasingly complex body of "offences against property" that are concerned with the defense of private property. First they are important in demarcating the "lawful" from the "unlawful"; they differentiate between the unlawful appropriation of property, the acts of the "criminals," and the lawful forms of appropriation that are the hallmark of the capitalist system. Just how close is the dividing line between lawful and unlawful appropriation has been clearly revealed by recent bribery and corruption cases. But second, it is not only the offender that is coerced, but all members of society because the coercion of the offender reinforces the values, attitudes, and behavior associated with the existence of private property. It is for this reason that it was stressed above that the coercive and ideological functions of law are closely related.

While the criminal law protects the property interests of the capitalist class it operates more generally to protect the "private property" of all members of society. Indeed it is important to recognise that the vast majority of "property offences" are committed, not against the property of the capitalist class, but rather against the property of noncapitalists. Property offences are usually directed against the privately owned consumption goods of working people.

Another way in which legal coercion is applied to defend the *general* conditions of capitalist society is with respect to "offences against the person." Again this area of the criminal law does not merely act against offences against members of the capitalist class. The significance of this type of legal coercion is that some level of general social order is a necessary precondition for the maintenance of its specifically capitalist content.

One of the most important manifestations of legal coercion is the application of law for the direct protection of the state itself. The state has at its disposal a veritable armory of measures that are ready to be invoked to defend the existing political order. These range from a number of traditional offences such as treason, treachery, and sedition (which have been invoked fairly infrequently in the recent past), through such legislation as the *Official Secrets Act* of 1911 and 1920 and the *Incitement to Disaffection Act* 1934, to the wide ranging emergency powers that the ruling class has gradually accumulated. *The Emergency Powers Acts* of 1920 and 1964 give very extensive powers to the civil and military authorities to intervene in the class struggle. These powers have been used on no less than eight occasions since the War; on four of these occasions by the Heath government against dockers, power supply workers, and the miners; Labour Governments have not shrunk from invoking them.

In the recent past Northern Ireland has been a fertile source of emergency regulations. *The Northern Ireland (Emergency Provisions) Act* 1973 and the *Prevention of Terrorism (Emergency Powers) Act* 1974 have aided the British government's struggle against the Irish people and their scope has been extended to the mainland.

The ruling class also has at its disposal a wide range of legal devices that can be used against offences against public order. These range through riot, affray, unlawful assembly and breach of the peace. Of particular importance is the *Public Order Act* 1936, supposedly introduced to curb the Fascists, but used systematically against the Left. It is interesting to observe the skill of the police and courts in making use of "appropriate" legal mechanisms. A good example has been the recent resuscitation of the *Conspiracy and Protection of Property Act* 1875.

In protecting the existing political order the law does not only have at its disposal the wide ranging powers contained in the legislation discussed above. The general principles of criminal law offer not only ample scope, but also special advantage. It is often in the interest of the ruling class to seek to depoliticize the class struggle. One of the means that is frequently invoked is to charge the "political offender" with ordinary crimes. This can be achieved by using a charge that is incidental to the main social or political issue involved; the most favored police strategy being to invoke charges involving or implying violence. A very good example of this technique is to be seen in the trial of the Shrewsbury pickets. The use of such charges allows the political issues to be ignored while branding the defendants as "common criminals," a tactic favored by Roy Jenkins and Frank Chapple in their attacks on the Shrewsbury pickets.

A related prosecution strategy is to use blanket charges; much in favor in the recent past has been the use of conspiracy charges. These are not only significant in that they allow the prosecution to evade some of the restrictions with regard to the evidence and procedure that normally apply. But in addition, through the orchestration by the mass media, to create impressions of the existence of an unspecified "threat to law and order."

The legal order has at its disposal this powerful armoury of techniques of legal coercion that enable it to directly intervene in the class struggle to defend the interest of the existing order. This direct intervention in the class struggle stands out most sharply in the case of industrial and trade union laws. The history of trade union law, from the *Combination Act* 1800 to the *Industrial Relations Act* 1971, is testimony to the attempt to provide a legal framework favorable to the interests of capital as opposed to those of labor. Yet it is also testimony to the extent of the resistance that over the period as a whole has not only forced tactical retreats, but has also witnessed significant advances in the legal positions of trade unions. I will return later to take up this question of law as an arena of class struggle.

What stands out in sharp relief is the extent to which the ruling class utilizes a legal framework for sustaining and buttressing their class interests. But a certain degree of care is needed in drawing conclusions from this common ground. The argument is frequently advanced that in periods of crisis the capitalist class resort to an increasingly repressive strategy and embark on major attacks on civil liberties. This type of analysis is very clearly presented in John Hostettler's article "Trends to Authoritarian Rule in Britain" (*Marxism Today*, Dec. 1973). This line of argument is sometimes presented in such a way that it obscures important contradictory dimensions, which if correctly considered throw much light on the specific role of law within capitalist society.

The lurch of legal authoritarianism is checked by an equally strong need on the part of the ruling class to maintain the legitimacy of their class rule. This contradiction is not an interaction between two equal forces that smoothly balance each other out; hence there are periods in which there are major shifts toward authoritarianism, but equally there are periods of movement toward more liberal and less coercive forms. The particular result at any point in time is a complex result of the level of class struggle itself.

There is a more general, and possibly more fundamental, political point that underlies this discussion that needs to be more fully discussed. Lenin was correct when he argued that

> bourgeois states are most varied in form, but their essence is the same; all these states, whatever their form in the final analysis are inevitably the dictatorship of the bourgeoisie. (CW 25: 413).

Yet there has been a tendency (which is present in Lenin as well as in others) to regard bourgeois democracy as simply a sham or fraud designed to conceal the class character of the rule of the bourgeoisie. Capitalism has been in existence long enough to demonstrate that its most persistent, stable and "successful" form has proved to be the *bourgeois democratic* political form. Thus for the bourgeoisie whatever pressures manifest themselves toward the "authoritarian solution" there is at the same time a profound concern to sustain the legitimacy of the capitalist order.

This analysis does not lead to the conclusion that the resort by the ruling class to fascism or to military coup is impossible. The tragic example of

Chile is too urgent to allow such a naive conclusion. But this analysis does insist that the resort to fascism is not the automatic response of a capitalist class in crisis. We should have no illusions about the fact that the capitalist class has been prepared, in the final analysis, to abandon bourgeois democracy. But we should be equally insistent that the interests of the bourgeoisie have been best served where they have been able to sustain their class rule within the bourgeois democratic form and that the ruling class itself has an interest in the preservation of bourgeois democracy.

The legal order plays a central role within bourgeois democracy. Thus while the coercive role of the legal order has been emphasized in the first half of this article it is now necessary to draw attention to and to examine the contribution made by the legal system to sustaining the legitimacy of the bourgeois democratic order. In other words it is necessary to discuss law as a method of ideological domination.

Law as Ideological Domination

Repressive and ideological domination are in no sense alternatives. On the contrary they are interdependent; they interact and reinforce each other. While the coercion of the criminal law is directed against those it punishes, its ideological effects are directed much wider. For example, the jailing of the Shrewsbury pickets was legal violence against the accused which was concerned with more than "deterring" others; it was an ideological offence against the strategy of the "flying picket" developed by the miners and applied so effectively by building workers.

Ideological domination describes those activities and processes whereby the assent to the existing social order is produced and mobilized. The notion of assent embraces both the idea of legitimacy as active assent and also acceptance as the passive form. The means by which assent is produced are ideological in that it involves the production and dissemination of ideas that affect social practice through the determination of the social consciousness of individuals, groups, and classes. This process is one of domination in that it involves two elements; first, a differential ability of groups and classes in society to produce, communicate, and disseminate ideas, and second, these ideas, directly or indirectly, have consequences for the maintenance of the existing social order.

Law is ideological in that it conveys or transmits a complex set of attitudes, values, and theories about aspects of society. Its ideological content forms part of the dominant ideology because these attitudes, values, etc. are ones that reinforce and legitimize the existing social order.

The most pervasive ideological effect of law is to be found in the fact that legal rules and their application give effect to existing social relations. The rules of law affirm the social and economic relations that exist within capitalist society. Thus the law of property is not only based on the inequality of property ownership but it reinforces it by allowing and facilitating the owners of property to make use of that property as capital. The complex of legal rules relating to mortgages, trusts, leases, etc. not only allows but also enables property to be used as capital. The law relating to contracts and commercial activity gives effect to the mechanisms of the market.

Similarly labor law facilitates the capitalist form of the relationship between labor and capital; it gives effect to the economic fact of the dependence of the majority on the sale of their labor power. It embodies the economic power of capital over labor by granting to the employer rights regarding not only the control of labor but also over hiring and firing of labor.

Rules of law impinge on almost every form of social relations. For example, family law, despite the reforms of the past decades, incorporates the fact of the dominant role of the husband over the wife, of the parents over the children. Likewise the law of landlord and tenant underlines the power of landlords over tenants in regard to the supply of housing. It is important to stress that the legal rules do not *create* the social relations that make up capitalist society. But by stating them as principles and by enforcing them the law operates not only to reinforce these relations but also to legitimize them in their existing form. This function is further advanced by the role of law in conferring authority upon officials such as the police, magistrates, etc.

The rules of law not only define social relations but confer rights and powers on certain categories of individuals. Thus, for example, landlord and tenant law not only incorporates the economic fact of the monopolization of housing by private interests, but it also legitimizes that economic power by granting rights to landlords to extract rent, to impose conditions, and to evict tenants. The legal system not only reinforces existing social and economic relations, but in addition it confers authority on dominant social interests.

One important aspect that should not be overlooked is the extent to which law operates to regulate the mutual interests of the bourgeoisie. It provides a mechanism for the resolution of disputes and conflicts that arise *between* capitalist interests:

(ii) Law, State, and Class Struggle

> The administration of ... civil justice is concerned almost exclusively with conflicts over property and hence affects almost exclusively the possessing classes. (Marx 1958: II, 34)

Company law, for example, is concerned in the main with the respective interests of shareholders and directors. Much commercial law is likewise concerned with the interests of merchants, middlemen, and dealers.

The law regulating the interests of the propertied classes is detailed and complex, but it has a significant common core. The operation of capitalistic functions is facilitated where the law provides a degree of certainty and predictability. What bourgeois legal theory fails to recognize is that it is only that element of law that regulates the mutual interests of the bourgeoisie, and not the whole of law in a capitalist society that exhibits this quest for certainty.

It is necessary to consider more closely the nature of the correspondence between legal rules and the social relations to which they relate. Legal rules do not simply "reflect" social relations. The rules of law have an added ideological dimension. To explain this it is important to recall that a central feature of capitalist society is that its essential features are obscured or concealed by the very nature of the operation of the capitalist economy. Marx insisted on the need to distinguish between how things appear (the "appearance" or "phenomenal form") and how they really are ("real substratum" or "essence").

The "real" relations that exist find themselves expressed in legal rules in a distorted or truncated form because the law gives effect to only the appearance ("phenomenal form") of social relations. This theoretical point could be taken further by applying the argument developed by Marx in the famous section on "the fetishism of commodities" in *Capital* Vol. I in which he shows how our comprehension of commodities embodies not the real social relations of production which create them, but simply as things; and as a result what are relations between people come to be seen as relations between things.

So legal rules appear abstracted from social relations, and are therefore a "fetishistic" expression of social relations. Legal rules are further divorced from the social relations to which they refer because they (like the state itself) appear separated, independent of society; they seem to have an independent origin and life of their own. Thus as ideological forms of social relations legal rules are doubly removed from the real world.

Legal rules express the appearance of social relations:

> This phenomenal form, which makes the actual relations invisible ... forms the basis of all the juridical notions of both labourer and capitalist, of all the mystifications of the capitalist mode of production, of all its illusions as to liberty. (Marx 1961: I, 540)

Marx showed how our initial perception of the capitalist economy focuses on the process of circulation and exchange, and thus ignores the production process itself. It is significant to note that legal rules follow this pattern and reduce social relations to a system of exchanges. The key legal concept of bourgeois law is that of *contract*. All the most important relations within capitalist society are moulded into the form of contractual relations.

By treating social relations as "contracts" bourgeois law strips them of their most important characteristics. Perhaps the most important example is in the labor relationship between employers and workers. At law the labor relation is a contract between individual employer and individual employee; they are therefore presumed to bargain over the terms of the contract. This individualizing of the contract of employment by focusing on it as an individual exchange excludes the social character of the relation between capital and labor. It is incapable of embracing the increasingly collective determination of labor relations through negotiations between trade unions and employers' federations. English law has reduced itself to great confusion in attempting to preserve the "individual contract" while taking some note of the real "collective contract."

It is not only economic relations that are reduced to contractual form. A wide range of other social relations is similarly treated. Thus, for example, the social institution of marriage is enshrined in law as a contract within which the "parties" have obligations that derive from the contract, and the "breach" of which can result in the contract being terminated, i.e., in divorce. Yet by expressing the marriage relationship in contractual form the law inadvertently exposes something of the real economic basis on which the bourgeois marriage is based, founded on the economic dependence of women.

The principles of contract have been so pervasive that they have been developed into a contractual ideology which continues to have wider ranging influences. Contractual ideology leans heavily on the notions of freedom and equality. But the "freedom" and "equality" to which it refers is purely *formal*; that is individuals are regarded as free if there is no legal bar to them entering into a contract, and are therefore deemed to be equal. It is a notion of equality brilliantly captured by Anatole France:

> The law in its majestic impartiality forbids rich and poor alike to sleep under bridges, to beg in the streets and steal bread (1927: 91)

These formal notions of freedom and equality are characteristic of bourgeois legal and political theory. They do violence to social reality because they are incapable of grasping the real inequality and lack of freedom that results from the dependence of all workers on the sale of their labor.

This discussion has focused on the way in which the rules of law, far from being pure or independent creations, are but a distorted expression of the existing social relations which are thereby reinforced and legitimised. This ideological character of legal rules is extended by two further considerations.

One of the difficulties in penetrating the ideological form of bourgeois law stems from the fact that it operates by abstracting the cases that come before the courts from their social and class context. They are thereby reduced to the status of being pure *technical* issues, apparently divorced from any political or ideological overtones. If, for example, a householder inquires why it is that tax relief is granted on mortgage payments but not on rent, the law replies that it is not a question of relief on mortgage or rent, but on interest repayments. By focusing on a technical distinction the law thereby obscures the social and economic reality.

Second, the law further depoliticizes social issues through the universal form of many legal rules. The fact that rules of criminal law protect the person and property of all members of society not only hides the fundamental class differences, but it also treats the capital of the employer and the personal belongings of the worker as if they were the same. The ideological significance is that it induces the view that all classes in society have a common interest in the protection of private property. Thereby the legal system is aided in fulfilling the ideological function of asserting the unity of interests of all classes. The ideology of the "rule of law" operates to assert and reinforce, and even seeks to celebrate, a social unity and cohesion in the face of the manifest class differentiation of capitalist society.

There is one further facet of the ideological character of law. It is directly ideological in the sense that the legal system propagates a range of views about the nature of the social and political system. This general ideological character of law is contained in what I will call "bourgeois legal ideology."

Bourgeois legal ideology is the fundamental component of the justification of the bourgeois democratic state; many of its elements directly enter into the consciousness of wide sections of the population. The central element of this ideology is the doctrine of "the rule of law." Its classic expression is to be found in Dicey:

> When we speak of the "rule of law" as a characteristic of our country we mean, not only that with us no man is above the law, but (what is a different thing) that every man, whatever be his rank or condition, is subject to the ordinary law of the realm.... With us every official, from the Prime Minister down to a constable ... is under the same responsibility for every act done without legal justification as any other citizen. (1967: 193)

The fundamental tenet is that both the ruled and the rulers are equally subject to a common system of the law. The "law" itself is thus viewed as something separate from the interests of classes. As such it plays a central role in the legitimation of the bourgeois democratic political order.

One particularly interesting feature of bourgeois legal ideology in the context of English law is the way in which it holds itself out as the protector of the individual against the incursions of the state. This antithesis between individual and state has a lengthy history in bourgeois legal thought. Its roots were in the historical alliance between the common law judges and the bourgeois interests against the absolutism of the Stuarts. It became more fully elaborated during the nineteenth century as the legal reflex of laissez-faire ideology. And in the twentieth century it has been used as the basis of antistate attitudes that characterize one element of the conservative reaction to the growth of the Welfare State.

In addition to explicit constitutional principles bourgeois legal ideology consists of a range of important background or implicit assumptions. The intention is only to roughly sketch some of these assumptions, but at the same time to argue that the more the "law and order" debate moves into the center of the political stage the more important it becomes to develop a systematic critique of bourgeois legal ideology.

Almost all discussion about law is based on the assumption that the existence of law is an inevitable or natural feature of social life. Hence law becomes identified with "civilization"; the absence of law is seen as synonymous with the absence of civilization. The classic expression of this assumption is the equation of the absence of law with anarchy; in its classical form in the political philosophy of Hobbes the absence of law implies a condition of "the war of all against all." The whole of society is presumed to have an interest in the existence of law, and is therefore closely connected with the "universalism" of law discussed above.

A closely associated assumption insists on the inherent rationality of law. The existence of rules of social life brought together or codified as law is presented as socially desirable in that it makes social life more certain and predictable. Social life is viewed as if it were a game or a sport in which it is essential that all the "players" adhere to the same rules; without this common set of rules social life would revert to anarchy. Such an attitude places stress on the desirability of rules *as such*, and hence leaves unquestioned the content of those rules and any questions concerning the social and economic interests that are embodied in the rules.

Flowing directly from the insistence on the naturalness and rationality of law is the insistence that adherence to law is natural, and as a corollary, that nonadherence to law is unnatural or deviant. The very existence of a state is treated as a sufficient condition to make obedience to law obligatory for all citizens. The assumption is made that the offender who violates the law is a deviant whose deviation stems from some pathological condition. While the nature of the pathology appealed to has varied, from the genetic inferiority of the "lower orders" to deficiencies in "socialization," the same assumption of the naturalness of obedience to law persists. It is interesting to note that in the recent past this essentially conservative tradition has come under increasing attack from criminologists, and that radical theories of crime are being developed which draw upon Marxism (Taylor, Walton, and Young 1972).

These interrelated attitudes and assumptions about law are not usually expressed in a coherent form: they are a cluster of ideas, but they add up to an assertion of the "sanctity of law" that forms the heart of the pervasive and powerful "law and order" ideology. This ideology finds expression not only in the moralizing editorials of the *Times*, but also forms an important part of widespread and diffuse social attitudes. The essential substance of these views is that they appeal to the sanctity of law, elevated above social life itself, and thereby ignore the class content of law and its role in legitimising the existing forms of class domination.

There is one final aspect of the ideological character of law that needs to be mentioned. The most formal and systematic expression of legal ideology is provided by jurisprudence or legal theory. The history of jurisprudence consists in successive attempts to provide a justification for obedience to law. The central concern has been to provide a socially persuasive account of the legitimacy of the existing legal order, and through that of the social order itself. However, a very interesting development has occurred within jurisprudence which is worth noting. Increasingly a number of liberal academics have been afflicted with growing self-doubt and disillusionment with the whole edifice of law, and are increasingly aware of a very real decline in the legitimacy of the existing legal order (Rostow 1970; Wolff 1971).

The operation of law is, therefore, not confined to simply giving effect to the direct and immediate interests of the ruling class. It must be understood as having an ideological function of an extensive character. Within capitalist society the legal system not only provides substantial ideological underpinnings to the existing capitalist organization of society. It also provides a consistent and coherent legitimation of a multitude of key institutions and principles that are central to the smooth operation of a system of capitalist social relations.

It is this ability to integrate two critical functions, on the one hand to give practical effect to the interests of the dominant class, and, at the same time, to provide a justification or legitimation for these interests in terms of some higher and apparently universal interest of all classes that demonstrates the real power and influence of law in capitalist society.

Law and Class Struggle

Our attention has been focused on the part that law plays in the process of reproducing capitalist social order. Yet law is not simply an instrument which can be wielded at will by an omnipotent ruling class. Precisely because it is an active element in the class struggle, it is at the same time affected by and involved in the class struggle. The law and the legal system form part of the context within which the class struggle takes place, and it is itself an arena in which that struggle occurs. To recognize that class struggle occurs *within* the legal system is not to suggest that the legal system is some neutral territory over which the class struggle wrestles for control. As a major component of the state law is necessarily part of the process through which the ruling class seeks to preserve its domination.

To argue that class struggle occurs within law is only the first step in examining the way in which class struggle makes itself evident within law. It has been argued above that law plays a central part in bourgeois democratic society, not only in theory but also in practice. The form taken by the class struggle has its boundaries broadly defined by the existing law. Thus, for example, trade union activity in Britain is pursued by forms of struggle that are recognized as being lawful. Some of the most important stages in the history of British trade unionism have been periods when struggle has occurred around attempts by the ruling class to narrow or restrict this lawful sphere of operations. The struggle against the *Industrial Relations Act* was a classic example of this type of struggle.

While law plays this important part of defining the parameters of class struggle, it also needs to be recognized that it does not necessarily stay confined within this framework. Indeed a change in this boundary or its breach will normally mark a critical phase in the class struggle. For example, a very important stage of the struggle against the *Industrial Relations Act* occurred in the months after it had been put on the statute book. The right-wing inside the Labour Movement argued that despite the objection they had to the Act it was now "law" and had to be accepted. The critical phase was the decisions made in the individual unions and within the TUC (Croydon and Blackpool Congresses 1971) as to whether they would "register" under the Act, and thus come within "the law," or whether to remain unregistered and to conduct trade union activity without the forms of protection that had been established since the beginning of the century.

Not only does law play an important part in defining the parameters of the class struggle, but many important stages in the class struggle take place around demands for legislative reforms. Marx himself gave considerable attention to one very important example of such struggles, the early *Factory Acts* (in particular the *Factories Regulation Act* of 1833). His chapter in *Capital* Volume I, on "The Working-Day" is a classic study of the interrelation and interaction of class forces in a struggle for legislative control of working hours.

> The creation of a normal working-day is, therefore, the product of a protracted civil war, more or less dissembled, between the capitalist class and the working-class. (1961: I, 231–302)

Elsewhere he summarized the significance of the victory underlying the Act in the following terms:

> it was the first time that in broad daylight the political economy of the middle class succumbed to the political economy of the working class. (1958: I, 383)

His analysis makes clear that the Factory Acts were not simply the direct result of class struggle between the capitalist and working classes. Two particular features of the analysis are worth drawing attention to. The first concerns the relationship between the state and the capitalist class. The advent of machinery and industrial production in the textile industry gives rise to a veritable orgy of exploitation in which the working-day is extended to such lengths that a real threat is posed to the survival of the work force. At this stage the state represents the collective interests of capital, as distinct from the interests of individual capitalists.

Second, he stresses the divisions between the various sections of the capitalist class. Not only is there the division between the landed and industrial capitalists, which led the Tories as representatives of landed capital, to support factory legislation. But more important are the divisions between the more advanced sections of industrial capital and the smaller, more traditional employers. The passage of the factory acts represented a victory not only for the working class, but also for the more advanced sections of capital, who triumphed over their less efficient rivals. The overall analysis therefore brings out with great sharpness the way in which the development of the productive forces, in association with the more or less conscious struggle of various classes, finds its expression in legislation.

In his discussion of factory legislation Marx showed clearly how each legislative victory was only partial; while each was a major practical and ideological victory, the employers, with the direct complicity of the magistrates and judges, impeded the effective enforcement of the provisions of the statutes.

Conclusion

In this chapter I have stressed the importance of law in capitalist society, and as a consequence argued that it is a question that requires a more thorough analysis by Marxists. While this chapter does not complete that task, it has sought to raise a number of questions, and to stress a number of areas for discussion. Some of these have been of a general nature that revolve around an assertion of law as an important agency in the maintenance of capitalist social relations. In particular I have argued the need to understand the significance of law as a system of ideological-coercive domination. It is through this emphasis on this combined process, rather than as two distinct or separate processes, that we can achieve a better understanding of the specific functioning of law within capitalist society, and is also of assistance in achieving a fuller theoretical treatment of the capitalist state.

The legal system within the bourgeois democratic state operates in such a way as to legitimize the class rule of the bourgeoisie. This legitimation involves not only the recognition and reinforcement of the social and economic relations of capitalism. It also encompasses the reification of law (through which law appears to be a power above and outside society) in which the social and political relations of capitalist society are presented as natural and universal. Law then operates to provide ideological reinforcement to those processes that make the reality of class and class power less visible.

The really difficult question is posed by the fact that bourgeois democratic society is not entirely a facade and a fraud. If it were its veils and deceits would have been stripped away long ago. Its strength and persistence result from the fact that in varying degrees it has successfully combined the continued social, political and economic dominance of the capitalist class with, at the same time, a significant level of involvement of the exploited classes sufficient to ensure a relatively high level of acceptance of, and even commitment to, the existing order.

Within the bourgeois democratic state law provides, alongside those aspects that reinforce the domination of the ruling class, an important set of rights, protections, and powers that in varying degrees incorporate certain class interests of the nonruling classes. The most obvious examples of these are such things as the right to vote, to form trade unions, to take strike action, etc.

It is important to recognize that most of these have been secured as the result of class struggle. But these facts should not lead us to view them simply as concessions wrung from the capitalist. Once granted they become woven into the fabric of bourgeois democracy. It should also be noted that we need to recognize that the range of legal rights that may be used to the advantage of the working class extends beyond the range of the more obvious "political" rights mentioned. The law confers rights and protections on all classes as "citizens" in bourgeois democracy. It is of course important to stress the inequality of their application and the inequality of access to legal redress. Yet this does not negate their political and ideological importance. Their very existence plays a significant part in securing the acceptance of, and allegiance to, the existing capitalist social order.

(iii) Police Under Fire

Chris Wood et al.

At 7:45 p.m. on Dec. 8, a .38–calibre bullet smashed through the rear window of a stolen black Nissan Maxima sedan and into the brain of its 17-year-old driver. Fifteen hours later, Michael Wade Lawson died when doctors disconnected his body from a life-support system at Mississauga Hospital, just west of Toronto. The moments of shattering gunfire left a legacy of anger and distrust. The youth happened to be black. The bullet that killed him was one of several fired by two plainclothes policemen. The next day, the Peel Regional Police Force declared that the officers had fired at the high-powered Maxima in self-defence after its driver, ignoring an order to stop, drove directly at them. But Lawson's grieving family and friends accused the police of racist violence. Lawson, said mourner Milton Blake at the youth's funeral, had been "cut down by the hunter's gun, sealed by the badge of law." Added Dari Meade, a member of Toronto's Black Action Defence Committee: "We want murder charges."

Tragedies

Lawson's death was a sad addendum to a growing list of tragedies that has forced a painful reassessment of relations between Canadian police and the communities they are sworn to serve. Among some Canadians — especially the expanding communities of visible minorities — there is vocal suspicion

---

From *Maclean's* (9 January 1989) 30. Reproduced by permission of Maclean's Magazine.

that police forces are, at best, out of touch with a changing society and, at worst, racist. In squad cars and station houses across the country, meanwhile, policemen and a growing number of policewomen say that it has become more difficult and dangerous to keep the peace and enforce the law. As grievances mount on both sides, so do the number of victims. Spokesmen for police point to the toll of suicide and divorce among serving officers, while the mourning relatives of police shootings point to the dead.

Controversial

Lawson was the second black Toronto-area resident in four months to die after being shot by police, and the most recent in a series of controversial killings. Last Aug. 9, a policeman shot and killed Lester Donaldson, a 44-year-old black man, in a Toronto rooming house. A police spokesman quoted Const. David Deviney as saying that he fired at Donaldson to defend his partner when Donaldson lunged at him with a knife. In Montreal last February, black leaders alleged racism when a jury acquitted Const. Allen Gosset of a manslaughter charge after he had shot and killed an unarmed black 19-year-old, Anthony Griffin, the previous November. Griffin — wanted for breaking and entering — had heeded an order to surrender after briefly bolting from police custody.

During the month following Gosset's acquittal — which the Crown is now appealing — Manitoba Indian leader John Joseph Harper died from a police bullet fired during a scuffle with Winnipeg constable Robert Cross on a city street. Then, in June, Vancouver police shot and killed a distraught, knife-wielding psychiatric patient, Gregory Coghlan, in what a coroner's jury later determined to be "victim-precipitated homicide ... a species of suicide."

After each eruption of fatal police gunfire, investigators groped for explanations. In Quebec and Manitoba, commissions have begun inquiries into police treatment of racial minorities. And one week after Lawson's death, Ontario Solicitor General Joan Smith named a five-member civilian panel to examine relations between the police and minority groups.

Spokesmen for ethnic minorities are the most vocal critics of police conduct across the country. Among the general public, surveys conducted by Gallup Canada Inc. show that 50 per cent of Canadians consider the country's 52,500 police officers to be highly or very highly trustworthy — as many as had expressed the same opinion in 1976. But even among those who express general satisfaction with the police, say observers of community attitudes, personal contacts with police officers are seldom either welcome or relaxed. "We have a love/hate relationship with police," observed John Sewell, a former mayor of Toronto and author of the 1985 study *Police*. "We need them to save us from dangerous situations yet we feel they impinge on our lives."

For their part, police officers across Canada told *Maclean's* that they view their fellow citizens with growing distrust, frustration and a sense of deepening isolation. "A police officer coming on a case is resented by everyone," said Robert Menard, 54, a burly 30-year veteran of the Montreal Urban Community police force, for one. "But how the hell can a civilian understand what we deal with every day? You are God damned right we are frustrated."

Pressures

There are 13,483 Royal Canadian Mounted Police who enforce federal law and provide rural service in eight provinces and the North. Provincial police forces operate in Ontario and Quebec, while most cities and towns have their own municipal police. Many of them who spoke to *Maclean's* correspondents said that the mounting pressures of their work — and the strident pitch of public criticism — have resulted in low morale and a growing number of stress-related personal problems. According to one survey, as many as 75 per cent of police marriages end in divorce (page 36). In Halifax, Montreal and Calgary, among other cities, the rising number of stress-linked complaints — including alcohol abuse, domestic violence and depression — has prompted the establishment of counselling services for emotionally troubled officers. Social scientists and other observers say that a number of factors have converged to raise the level of stress on Canadian police. In an increasingly urbanized society, economic pressures, the growing use of drugs and an influx of immigrants from cultures with different traditions and attitudes toward the law have contributed to a rising level of violent crime that police must routinely deal with (page 34). At the same time, the 1982 *Charter of Rights and Freedoms*, with its clear definitions of individual rights, and the 1984 *Young Offenders Act* — which some officers say limits their ability to deal with criminals under 18 — have intensified the scrutiny when police fall short of demanding standards of conduct.

Discipline

There is impassioned debate, however, over what must be corrected in order to restore the tarnished honour of the policeman's badge. Sewell blames the military-style discipline that still pervades most police forces. "Look at the conditions of the normal cop on the beat," he said in an interview. "They are treated badly in a 19th-century management structure. And they lash out." On the other hand, the director of the University of Regina's Prairie Justice Research School, James Harding, criticizes the recruitment into uniform of "kids who see police work as a mandate to play rough." In Montreal, newspaper columnist George Springate, a former city policeman who also served for 11 years in the Quebec legislature, says that the public demands too much of police. "We have to stop picking on the police, expecting them to be saviours for everything that goes wrong in society," said Springate. "They aren't miracle workers."

The debate has acquired new urgency with the recent rash of controversial shootings involving police officers. On the Mississauga street of new brick homes where Wade Lawson's life ended, the red spray paint that investigators had used to mark the spot where the stolen Maxima came to rest quickly disappeared under a mid-December dusting of snow. Other details have emerged slowly in brief statements by police and in news reports.

Tip

The events that led to Lawson's death began shortly after midnight on Dec. 8, when the Grade 11 high-school student stepped from a car driven by his cousin, Dale Ewers, and crossed a Mississauga street to the parking lot of a Nissan dealership at about the time that someone stole a black Maxima. Within hours, a tip from a security guard at a nearby motel led constables Darren Longpre and Anthony Melaragni to set up a daylong surveillance near Ewer's home. Shortly after 7:30 p.m., a Maxima, bearing stolen New York state licence plates, pulled into a driveway facing the house and a passenger got out. As the car backed onto the street and began to drive away, Longpre and Melaragni got out of their own car to intercept it.

According to the statement issued by the Peel regional police, Longpre and Melaragni approached the stolen Maxima and identified themselves to two occupants with the intention of placing them under arrest. But when the car "accelerated directly at" the two officers, the statement continued, they opened fire "in defence of their lives," unleashing at least half a dozen bullets. Indeed, the Toronto *Globe and Mail* later reported that officers close to the investigation had said that the Maxima knocked one of the policemen to the ground as it sped away, prompting both officers to fire at the fleeing automobile. That report added that one of the bullets fired had penetrated the car's rear window, ricocheted inside the vehicle and struck Lawson in the back of the head.

'Nigger'

However, another youth who was in the car at the time of the shooting, but who escaped uninjured, told a Lawson family lawyer that he had heard nothing before the police opened fire. And the 17-year-old youth, who has been charged with possession of stolen property and cannot be named under the *Young Offenders Act*, added that after the officers pulled him from the Maxima, one policeman kicked him and called him a "nigger."

The day after the shooting, Peel Police Chief William Teggart requested an Ontario Provincial Police investigation of the affair. The OPP report, which could recommend criminal charges against the Peel police officers, is expected to be completed late this month. Still, even while the investigation continued, one local black activist, Al Peabody, predicted that its findings would be "a whitewash." Added the youth's father, Winston Lawson, who owns a gravel business: "They are police investigating other police. Naturally, they have sympathy for each other." The charge was dismissed by OPP spokesman Insp. Robert Guay. Declared Guay: "The OPP is a credible force. The family can be assured of a thorough, unbiased investigation." By late last week, however, the OPP had not laid charges against either Longore or Melaragni.

Risk

Many police officers express a growing sense of injury. Complaints of police brutality are far outnumbered by police accounts of violence suffered at the hands of the public. A badge and uniform are no protection against daily dangers that range from a drunk's wildly thrown punch to the fear of AIDS infection through contact with an accident victim's blood. In addition, there is the ever-present risk of death from criminal gunfire. Between 1978 and 1987, 35 on-duty police officers have been killed in Canada.

Beyond the fear for their own safety, police officers interviewed by *Maclean's* expressed a deepening sense of grievance. They complained about high demands and low salaries. First-class constables typically earn between $42,000 and $47,000 a year across the country. As well, work loads have become heavier, as Canada's crime rate recorded a 27 per cent increase between 1978 and 1986 — with violent crimes jumping by 45 per cent — while police forces grew by only six per cent over the same period. At the same time, the very nature of police work forces officers into close daily contact with society's least successful members. "We deal with the dregs of society," said Montreal's Menard, who was shot in the left lung and right leg while trying to prevent a bank robbery in 1985. "We deal with violence, with abuse. We deal with what you as a civilian don't want to have anything to do with."

Often there is little time to weigh choices before reacting. Noted Menard: "We make a judgment call in very tense and explosive situations in an instant, and we must be right the first and only time." In such conditions, said John Sawatsky, a Toronto-based psychologist who counsels OPP members, it is not surprising that an officer sometimes makes a wrong decision. "People who are stressed as much as police officers," said Sawatsky, "sometimes lose their judgment." The consequences for a reaction that appears in retrospect to have been wrong can be a fine, dismissal from the force or criminal charges. "At the back of a policeman's mind," said Jacques Duchesneau, the head of Montreal's organized crime squad, "is always the thought that one quick reaction could live with you for a long time."

Duchesneau, like many police officers, says that the decisions have become more complex in the 1980s. Growing Caribbean, Chinese and Vietnamese communities have become targets for ethnic criminal organizations that are difficult for Canadian police — still overwhelmingly white — to penetrate. Calgary Police Chief Ernest Reimer, who will retire this month at 55, says that "there is a heavy degree of mistrust [of the police] in these new ethnic communities." In many cities, the mistrust is reinforced by an imbalance between the ethnic makeup of police and that of the city they serve. In Toronto, although visible minorities account for 20 per cent of the city's 2.2 million people, according to Sher Singh, chairman of the Toronto Council on Race Relations and Policing, they number only five per cent of its 5,400 police — and hold no ranks above staff inspector.

Work Load

Beyond the charged emotions that radiate from each controversial shooting, however, statistics suggest that Canadian policemen fare well when breakdowns in discipline are weighed against their work load. Among the few forces that release such figures, the RCMP recorded 2,500 complaints about its officers in 1987 — fewer than 0.09 per cent of its three million contacts with the public. The figure for Toronto's force was even lower: fewer than 0.08 per cent of the 1,045,000 calls Toronto police answered last year led to complaints against the force. Fatal shootings by Canadian police — an average of eight each year between 1961 and 1981 — are few by comparison with those in the United States, where police kill at least one person every day.

Still, many Canadian police officers acknowledge that they must do more to regain public confidence. Some steps have already been taken. Educational standards for police recruits have risen. As well, police training programs have been redesigned to emphasize psychology and communication skills and to discourage cadets from viewing themselves as gun-toting enforcers. In answer to allegations that they fail to reflect their community's ethnic mix, urban forces in Toronto and Vancouver have launched active recruiting drives in the two cities' burgeoning immigrant communities.

At the same time, governments increasingly are moving toward the establishment of civilian review boards to investigate complaints against the police. Complaints against RCMP members have been handled by a civilian review panel since last September. And legislation introduced in the Quebec national assembly in November will give civilian panels the right to hold public inquiries into allegations of police misconduct in that province. Similar boards already exist in Nova Scotia and in the cities of Calgary and Toronto. But the spread of civilian panels has been slowed by police resistance.

Tension

Meanwhile, the commissions appointed after the Lawson, Griffin and Harper shootings continue to search for new measures to restore the corroded relationship between police and the public. Their tasks are complicated by deep emotions on both sides of a complex issue. "Police feel abandoned," said Springate. "And as they come under public criticism, they tend to withdraw more into themselves." In Mississauga, meanwhile, Milton Blake told Wade Lawson's mourners last month that "we must rise up to become the protectors of our own interests." But such sentiments seemed unlikely to help reduce the tension in any future confrontation between armed police and the citizens they are sworn to protect.

(iv) The [Nova Scotia] Royal Commission on the Donald Marshall Jr., Prosecution

FACTUAL FINDINGS

Introduction

We find:

- That the criminal justice system failed Donald Marshall, Jr. at virtually every turn from his arrest and conviction in 1971 up to — and even beyond — his acquittal by the Supreme Court of Nova Scotia (Appeal Division) in 1983.
- That this miscarriage of justice could have and should have been prevented if persons involved in the criminal justice system had carried out their duties in a professional and/or competent manner.
- That Marshall was not the author of his own misfortune.
- That the miscarriage of justice was real and not simply apparent.
- That the fact that Marshall was a Native was a factor in his wrongful conviction and imprisonment.

On May 28, 1971, four people came together in a brief, unplanned nighttime encounter in Wentworth Park in Sydney, Nova Scotia. One of them, a 17-year-old black youth named Sandford (Sandy) William Seale, was killed. Another, a 17-year-old Micmac Indian named Donald Marshal, Jr., was wrongfully convicted of his murder, and was sentenced to life imprisonment in November 1971. Eleven years later, after Marshall's lawyer, Stephen Aronson, brought forward information suggesting Marshall did not commit the murder, the RCMP reinvestigated the case for a second time. After that investigation confirmed that Marshall did not kill Seale, he was released on parole and subsequently acquitted by the Supreme Court of Nova Scotia (Appeal Division) in May 1983. A third man, Roy Newman Ebsary, who was one of the four people who had come together in Wentworth Park that night, was charged with killing Seale and was convicted of manslaughter following three trials. He was sentenced to three years in prison. In 1986, the Court of Appeal reduced his sentence to one year. He died in 1988.

The events that took place in Wentworth Park in those few moments on that spring night in 1971 have spawned numerous official inquiries and proceedings, including three formal police investigations, two preliminary inquiries, four trials, three appeals to the Supreme Court of Nova Scotia (Appeal Division), a Reference to the Court of Appeal and two Royal Commissions, including this one. The cost in dollars has been tremendous. The toll in human anguish has been incalculable.

The principal task of this Royal Commission has been to determine why Donald Marshall, Jr. was wrongfully convicted and to make recommendations to ensure that such a miscarriage of justice does not happen again.

First, what did go wrong? Although we will examine in detail each of the relevant events of the Marshall case from its beginning on May 28, 1971, to our appointment on October 28, 1986, we can begin with the following general conclusions that flow from our consideration of all of the evidence.

The criminal justice system failed Donald Marshall, Jr. at virtually every turn, from his arrest and wrongful conviction in 1971 up to — and even beyond — his acquittal by the Court of Appeal in 1983. The tragedy of this failure is compounded by the evidence that this miscarriage of justice could have — and should have — been prevented, or at least corrected quickly, if those involved in the system had carried out their duties in a professional and/or competent manner.

If, for example, the Sergeant of Detectives of the Sydney City Police Department had not prematurely concluded — on the basis of no supporting evidence and in the face of compelling contradictory evidence — that Donald Marshall, Jr. was responsible for the death of Sandy Seale, Marshall would almost certainly never have been charged with the crime. If the Crown prosecutor had provided full disclosure to

---

Nova Scotia, *Report of the Royal Commission on the Donald Marshall, Jr., Prosecution*: Findings and Recommendations, Vol. 1 (Halifax, N.S.: The Commission, 1989) at 15–18 (Chair: T. Alexander Hickman). Copyrighted by the Province of Nova Scotia.

Marshall's lawyers of the conflicting statements provided by alleged eyewitnesses; if Marshall's lawyers had conducted a more thorough defence, including pressing for such disclosure and conducting their own investigations into the killing; if the judge in the case had not made critical errors in law; Marshall would almost certainly not have been convicted.

Even after he was convicted and sent to prison, however, there were numerous other occasions when this miscarriage of justice should have been discovered and rectified, but was not.

For example, when the Crown received evidence shortly after Marshall's conviction suggesting Roy Ebsary might have been involved in the killing, it did not disclose this information to Marshall's counsel. When the RCMP reinvestigated the murder as a result of that new evidence, it did so in such an entirely inadequate and unprofessional manner that it prevented his wrongful conviction from being discovered. During Marshall's appeal of his conviction, his lawyers failed to identify and argue critical errors of law which occurred during the trial. Similarly, the Court of Appeal failed to identify these errors.

When Marshall's wrongful conviction was finally discovered in the early 1980s, the Court of Appeal compounded the miscarriage of justice by describing Marshall as having contributed in large measure to his own conviction and by stating that any miscarriage of justice in the case was more apparent than real.

This Commission has concluded that Donald Marshall, Jr. was not to blame for his own conviction and that the miscarriage of justice against him was real.

That is the inescapable, and inescapably distressing, conclusion we have reached after listening to 113 witnesses during 93 days of public hearings in Halifax and Sydney in 1987 and 1988 and after sifting through 176 exhibits submitted in evidence during those hearings.

But concluding that Donald Marshall, Jr. was the victim of a miscarriage of justice does not answer the complex question of why Marshall came to be wrongfully convicted and imprisoned in the first place. Was it because he was a Native? Was it because he was poor?

To answer those admittedly difficult questions, this Commission has looked not only at how the criminal justice system in Nova Scotia operated in the Marshall case, but it has also compared the handling of the Marshall case with the way in which the system dealt with cases involving powerful and prominent public officials. At the same time, we commissioned independent research studies to find out how Natives and Blacks are treated in the criminal justice system.

From all of that, the evidence is once again persuasive and the conclusion inescapable that Donald Marshall, Jr. was convicted and sent to prison, in part at least, because he was a Native person. We will look at these issues in more detail in our section on visible minorities in the justice system later in this volume.

Having reached these conclusions, we take the next logical step in fulfilling our mandate and ask what can and should be done to make sure that the criminal justice system lives up to this promise of equal justice for all? That too is a question we will deal with later in this volume of our Report.

There are certain issues, however, that we will not be addressing in our Report. For example, this Royal Commission is not recommending that criminal charges be laid against any specific individuals arising out of the findings of fact we will make. Although some counsel urged us to do so during their final arguments to the Royal Commission, it is our opinion that a decision on whether or not any charges should be laid is one that should be taken by the appropriate authorities after due consideration of all relevant factors. We agree with the sentiments expressed by the Attorney General of Ontario when establishing the Grange Commission, sentiments which were concurred in by the Ontario Court of Appeal in *Re Nelles et al. and Grange et al.* (1984), 9 D.L.R. (4th) 79 at p. 84:

> The purpose of a public inquiry is not to attach criminal culpability. It is not a forum to put individuals on trial. The just and proper place to make and defend allegations of crime or civil liability is in a court of law.
>
> In this context, I am reminded of the remarks of an eminent Ontario jurist, Mr. Justice Riddell of the Ontario Court of Appeal, whose observations almost 50 years ago are equally applicable today.
>
> A Royal Commission is not for the purpose of trying a case or a charge against anyone, any person or any institution — but for the purpose of informing the people concerning the facts of the matter to be enquired into. The object of a Royal Commission is to determine facts, not try individuals or institutions, and this consideration is sufficient to guide the Commissioner in the performance of his duty.

The Court went on to say:

> A public inquiry is not the means by which investigations are carried out with respect to the commission of particular crimes.... Such an inquiry is a coercive procedure and is quite in-

compatible with our notion of justice in the investigation of a particular crime and the determination of actual or probable criminal or civil responsibility.

We share this view.

Further, we are not — as some have also urged us to do — specifically recommending that Donald Marshall, Jr. receive additional compensation. The Commission accepted that a settlement had been negotiated, and accordingly, heard no evidence on the amount of compensation that may have otherwise been appropriate. However, the Commission did examine the process by which compensation was ultimately negotiated and paid. We have concluded that the negotiations were strongly influenced by factors which, in our view, were either wrong or inappropriate, and that as a result the compensation process was so seriously flawed that the amount paid should be re-evaluated.

(v) Understanding Over-representation

Why are black people over-represented among prison admissions? What explains the dramatic increase in the imprisonment of black women and men since 1986/87? Why is there such a large difference in imprisonment rates of black and white people for some offences and much smaller differences, or even under-representation of black people, for other offences?

A superficial answer might be that the data "prove" that black people are inherently criminal. This explanation does not fit the facts. Equally superficial — and equally unconvincing — is the conclusion that all white police officers, lawyers and judges are blatantly racist and deliberately criminalize black people.

Consider the superficial view that race determines criminal behaviour, and that racial inequality in prison admissions merely reflects black people's inherent criminality.

How could race cause people to commit criminal offences? Is the answer in biology — could a gene related to dark skin, curly hair and broad noses cause people to commit crimes? Would this gene lead black people to specialize in drug trafficking? Does a gene cause white people to drive after drinking alcohol? Does pale skin and straight hair, or a gene related to these characteristics, prevent people from obstructing justice?

Consider also the dramatic increase in prison admissions of black people. How could a biological link between race and crime explain this? Surely the genetic make-up of black Ontarians did not suddenly change during the late 1980s and early 1990s.

Most important, if biology causes criminality, why are only a small percentage of black Ontarians in conflict with the law? Even if each prison admission represented one individual (which is not the case), 96 percent of black people were not admitted to prison in 1992/93. If a "race gene" caused black people to commit crimes, then most of Ontario's black residents, and few or no white Ontarians, would be in jail.

Such questions are absurd, as is the belief that biology explains criminal behaviour. There is no such thing as a criminality gene, nor, more fundamentally, is there any scientific evidence of a race gene. As Stephen Jay Gould states:

> Intense studies ... have detected not a single "race gene" — that is a gene present in all members of one group and none of another. Frequencies vary, often considerably, among groups, but all human races are much of a muchness.... [T]he great preponderance of human variation occurs within groups, not in the differences between them....
>
> Human groups do vary strikingly in a few highly visible characteristics (skin colour, hair form) — and these external differences may fool

---

From the *Report of the Commission on Systemic Racism in the Ontario Criminal Justice System* (Toronto: Queen's Printer, 1995) at 95–105. Notes omitted. © Queen's Printer for Ontario, 1995. Reproduced with permission.

us into thinking that overall divergence must be great. But we know now that our usual metaphor of superficiality — skin deep — is literally accurate.

Clearly then, the dark skins and curly hair of black people do not cause criminal behaviour. Nor does some other genetic difference lead black people to commit crimes. Since biology is not destiny, the explanation of racial inequalities in prison admissions must lie elsewhere.

Some people who rightly reject biological explanations of criminal activity find cultural ones persuasive. Recognizing that racial appearance cannot determine behaviour, they may think, nonetheless, that culture does. Are cultural propensities to criminality, violence or lack of respect for law and authority the reasons for racial differentials in admissions to Ontario's prisons?

If all or some black cultures are inherently criminal, but white cultures are not, why are the vast majority of prison admissions people from white cultures? Why are most black people (like most white people) not in conflict with the law? If black culture causes criminality, what explains the relatively low proportions of black admissions in 1986/87 and the massive increase since then?

Finally, how do cultural explanations of criminality account for what John Pitts calls "one of the few things we know with any certainty about the relationship between race and crime" — the evidence, documented in many countries, that crime rates among immigrants are lower than among persons born in the country? Crime rates among descendants of immigrants, however, tend to be the same as or higher than crime rates of the dominant culture. If culture explains crime, why are members of the immigrant generation, who presumably have the allegedly criminal tendencies of an "alien" culture in its strongest form, less likely to commit offences than their children and grandchildren raised in the culture of the new society?

The answer, of course, is that cultural characteristics do not explain the evidence. As Pitts states,

> Crime rates are neither a simple product of the proclivities of individuals nor of the cultural penchant of particular ethnic groups but, rather, a product of the chances, choices and solutions available within the milieu they enter. The rise in crime rate among the second and subsequent generations of an immigrant group is a product of ... [the] process whereby people make an accommodation with, and establish ways of being within, a new social environment. In the process some "incoming" young people will adopt the strategies and behaviours of the established social group [where they live].

Cultures may be real and enriching forces in people's lives, but they are not "timeless and inexorable determinants of behaviour." They do not, in other words, dictate what people do. Culture cannot cause people to commit crimes or account for racial inequalities in prison admissions. Far from explaining anything, beliefs that some cultures are inherently violent, criminal, anti-social or disrespectful of law are stereotypes that racialize others. They promote constructions of races as real, different and unequal, and allow people to act as if such constructions were true.

Cultural characteristics of specific racialized groups or minority groups in general clearly cannot explain racial differentials in prison admissions. So how do we explain these differentials in Ontario prisons? In jurisdictions where disproportionate imprisonment of black people has been openly recognized for years, research suggests two general explanations, which may overlap. One explanation emphasizes the influence of social and economic inequality on behaviour; the other points to differential enforcement of the criminal law, including racial discrimination in the administration of justice.

SOCIAL AND ECONOMIC INEQUALITY

Some studies of differential imprisonment emphasize failures to integrate black and other racialized people into the wider society. They draw on evidence of disproportionately high rates of unemployment and dead-end jobs among racialized people, particularly young adults. They also cite poor housing conditions and lack of educational opportunities. These studies make the important point that social and economic opportunities are racialized. That is, members of racialized groups are much more likely than members of non-racialized groups to have limited opportunities. Since people with limited social and economic opportunities are most likely to be policed, prosecuted and punished as criminals, racialized people are more likely than white people to be in conflict with the law. Thus they are over-represented at all stages of the criminal justice process, including prisons.

Three important elements of this explanation are worth emphasizing. First, those who adopt it may generally accept that racialized people are over-represented in prison populations, at least in part, because of greater participation in some criminal activities. They do not accept, however, that biology or culture is the reason for higher rates of participation. Nor do they always see racism in the wider society as the only contributing factor.

According to this view, the social and economic conditions of people's lives are crucial to their participation in criminal activity. The criminality rate should be the same for racialized and non-racialized people where these conditions are the same. If, on the other hand, opportunities are unequally distributed, members of the socially disadvantaged groups are likely to commit a higher proportion of crimes than others. If a higher proportion of a particular racialized group has limited opportunities, compared with other groups, then the average crime rate for this group is likely to be higher.

Second, according to this approach sub-groups with similar life opportunities — in racialized and non-racialized communities alike — are likely to display similar levels of criminality. Young, unemployed white men living in areas of social stress and economic deprivation, for example, would be [as] likely to commit crimes as their young, male, unemployed black neighbours. Conversely, as Pitts noted of the British context, "...the amount of street crime perpetrated by 28-year-old, male, British Afro-Caribbean chartered accountants is the same as that perpetrated by 28-year-old, male, British Caucasian chartered accountants, namely 0.0 per cent." The point is that any difference in street crime rates of British Afro-Caribbean men and British Caucasian men arises because fewer of the former have opportunities for economic advancement.

Finally, this viewpoint does not imply that lack of opportunities or social inequality causes individuals — whether white or racialized — to commit crimes. It does say, rather, that people with limited life-chances may be more likely to view some forms of criminal activity as more attractive or exciting than their other choices. They may see crime as a means to acquire material goods otherwise unobtainable. They may fail to respect the rules of a society that excludes them from its benefits. They may feel they have much to gain and little to lose from criminal activity. Crime may make them feel powerful. It may add excitement to, or provide a means of escape from otherwise dreary lives. Crime, in short, may be a rational choice.

Experts who make these observations do not, of course, excuse or condone the actions of any individual who harms others. They recognize that crime is a serious social problem, hurting immediate victims and the families and friends of victims and perpetrators. They know that fear of crime may severely restrict people's lives. But since imprisonment does not appear to deter or in any other way significantly to reduce crime, it is important to develop strategies likely to work rather than to continue with those known to fail. More emphasis on or investment in crime prevention, as opposed to punishment, is their answer.

DIFFERENTIAL ENFORCEMENT

Other explanations of racialized patterns in prison admissions also stress social and economic conditions, but from a different perspective. These conditions are seen as explanations of who is caught, not who commits crimes. Enforcement practices, rather than offending behaviours, are key.

People who hold this view argue that involvement in criminal activity is not limited to an identifiable group of anti-social and marginal individuals. Criminality is instead a widespread social phenomenon in which many ordinary and apparently respectable people participate. Drawing on studies of employers, employees, taxpayers, retailers and service suppliers, police officers, university students, youths and drug users, and women and children abused by men, these experts conclude that with regard to crime "everybody does it" at least occasionally.

If criminal activity is indeed widespread among the population, the explanation for racial inequality in prison admissions cannot be attributed mainly to disproportionate involvement in crime. Studies in Canada and elsewhere consistently show, for example, that more than 90 percent of young men say they have committed criminal offences. This indicates that variations in offending rates by race or economic class may be small. Variations in enforcement practices likely make the difference.

Law enforcement is not the only possible response to crime, nor is it always desirable. Many studies suggest that law enforcement is costly, blunt and not very effective in reducing crime. Since law enforcement resources are finite, priorities must be established and variations in enforcement practices are inevitable. The critical question is what criteria are used to decide which offenders and which offences the criminal justice system should select.

Formal and informal selection criteria are used in law enforcement. Experts suggest that these criteria make black and other racialized people particularly vulnerable. They point, first, to poverty. Study after study shows that offences by those at the bottom of social and economic hierarchies are more likely to be policed, prosecuted and punished severely than offences committed by wealthier people. The implication is clear: a society that allows racialization to influence people's economic opportunities is likely to produce racial inequality in its prison populations.

Even if criminal activity is widespread, patterns of offending behaviour differ according to the opportunities available. Those with access to other people's money through their employment or profession, for example, are much more likely to embezzle funds than to sell drugs on a street corner. They are also less likely to be caught. Crimes committed in the privacy of corporate offices tend to be more difficult to detect and prosecute than street crimes because of their low visibility, and because the law generally shelters these private spaces from state officials.

Enforcement practices clearly vary with the seriousness of offences committed, and also with factors such as whether and how offences are reported, ease of identification and apprehension, and likelihood of conviction. Racialization in the wider society may also influence law enforcement practices. The criminal justice system requires police officers, lawyers, justices of the peace and judges to make judgments about individuals and their behaviour. Though the law provides a general framework for these judgments, it seldom specifies fixed rules that dictate outcomes. Instead, the law sets out broad standards that allow considerable scope for interpretation of the standards, the individual and the (alleged) offence.

For example, when deciding if someone should be imprisoned before trial, judges or justices of the peace are expected to predict whether the accused, if released, will fail to appear for trial or is substantially likely to commit a criminal offence before the trial. Rarely does a judge or justice of the peace have much information about the accused relevant to such a prediction.* Consequently their decisions must draw more heavily on intuition and what lawyers responding to our survey describe as "empathy." This in turn increases subjectivity in decision-making. It creates conditions under which lack of familiarity with racialized communities may lead a decision-maker to rely subconsciously on stereotypes.

Because the processes leading to discretionary choices in the criminal justice system are subtle and complex, studies of racial discrimination in this system use an approach that is now well established in human rights law. They begin with evidence of adverse impact — such as our findings of racial disproportion in prison admissions — and investigate how far legitimate non-discriminatory factors explain the adverse impact. Racial inequalities that remain after these factors have been taken into account are then treated as evidence of racial discrimination that is tolerated by the criminal justice system.

Using this approach, studies in many jurisdictions have documented direct and indirect discrimination that results in over-representation of black or other racialized people in prisons. Later in this Report we document the Commission's findings that racial discrimination in policing, bail hearings and sentencing decisions affects Ontario prison admissions. The remainder of this chapter presents a brief overview of the various stages where the exercise of discretionary authority may be susceptible to the introduction of racialization.

DECISIONS THAT PRODUCE IMPRISONMENT: AN OVERVIEW

The criminal justice process involves a great deal of interaction among different people with different roles. Decisions made at one stage affect those made later. It is essential to view the system as a whole. Imprisonment is always ordered by a particular judge or justice of the peace, but that decision results from the cumulative choices made by police officers, crown attorneys, defence counsel and probation officers.

Entry into the Criminal Justice Process

In general, accused persons are drawn into the criminal justice system in two ways. Reports of crime may come from victims or observers. In addition, accused persons may be identified by proactive policing.

Victims are an important source of information about violent offences and property crimes, Their decision about whether to report a crime is crucial. Surveys in Canada and elsewhere show that large proportions of individuals harmed by criminal offences do not report them to the police.

These surveys raised the question of whether racialization influences people in selectively reporting offences. As yet, no Canadian data deal with this question, and evidence from other jurisdictions is mixed. Some studies indicate racial inequalities result from victim reporting; other do not show such patterns.

Offences may also be identified through planned and systematic police work. Police may seek evidence of specific offences or focus their attention on specific geographic areas or particular communities. Police may also initiate encounters, such as stopping vehicles and people on the street during routine

156

patrols. Whether or not it is planned, such proactive policing is highly discretionary.

Much evidence from other jurisdictions indicates that this type of policing disproportionately pulls black people into the criminal justice system. Officers working on "gut feelings" or popular stereotypes may stop black people more than others, and may question them more aggressively. Hostile encounters may not only uncover offences but also produce them.

Police Discretion to Charge

Once the police have information identifying a person with an alleged criminal offence, they must decide whether to charge the suspect. Police officers are not legally or professionally obligated to lay charges, even if they believe they have enough grounds (evidence) to meet the test. They may instead do nothing, simply caution suspects, or advise victims how to lay charges themselves.

The scope of police officers' discretion in laying charges is extremely broad. For example, an 18-year-old who shoves another and runs off with the other's baseball cap could be charged with robbery (punishable by up to life imprisonment), theft (two years), assault (five years) or possession of stolen property (two years). As an alternative to laying charges, the police could instead talk with the teenager, perhaps in the presence of family members. This range of choices provides considerable scope for police officers' personal attitudes, perceptions and stereotypes to influence their decision. Even when an officer is acting with conscious fairness and objectivity, subtle influences may arise such as, in this example, whether the teenager comes from what the officer perceives to be a "good" or "stable" family. This assessment might lead to the conclusion that a black youth should be subjected to the criminal justice process, whereas a white youth could be dealt with adequately in the home.

Studies of the extent to which racialization influences police discretion over charging tend to concentrate on outcomes because police interpretations of alleged criminal incidents and their classification are not open to scrutiny. Formal records of officers' conclusions on whether and what to charge are available and may be studied, but the process by which officers arrive at these conclusions is not always obvious. Evidence from some jurisdictions, such as Britain, clearly shows that police discretion not to charge has racialized outcomes, at least with regard to youths. Canadian studies document class and other biases in police practices, particularly in their processing of Aboriginal people.

Imprisonment before Trial

Once a charge is laid, the next critical set of decisions concern whether to hold accused persons in prison or to seek other controls on them during the period before trial. *Criminal Code* provisions suggest that once the accused have been processed by police and told of their duty to appear in court to answer the charges against them, the vast majority of accused persons should be set free.

However, a judge or justice of the peace may order imprisonment before trial if it is necessary to ensure that the accused person will attend court for trial. The accused may also be detained if it is necessary to protect the public. The decision to detain or free the accused takes into account the seriousness of the charges and accused's criminal record as well as criteria such as "ties to the community," employment status and mental health.

Racialization may influence police decisions about whether to release accused persons, and may affect the bail process through information the police supply to crown attorneys. Racialization may also be introduced through the criteria used to predict whether the accused will fail to appear at trial or is "substantially likely" to commit a criminal offence before trial. There is little Canadian research on imprisonment before trial. Some studies conducted in other jurisdictions have found evidence that racialization influences pre-trial release decisions; others are inconclusive. Chapter 5 reports our findings that racial inequalities do appear in the outcomes of bail decisions.

Processing Charges

Once charges have been laid, crown attorneys assume responsibility for how they are processed. Crown attorneys have a professional duty to scrutinize charges and decide whether some or all should be withdrawn because of lack of evidence or because prosecution would not be in the public interest. They may also engage in resolution discussions with defence counsel to see if charges can be disposed of without a contested trial. This may also be an important step for the exercise of crown discretion.

Since crown attorneys make these decisions mostly on the basis of written material rather than interaction with accused persons, there seems to be little scope for racialization to influence their choices. Nonetheless, research in other jurisdictions suggests that the possibility cannot be dismissed. Much of the information available to crown attorneys is supplied by police officers who have met the accused and may have formed racialized judgments. For example, clues to accused persons' racial origin may be recorded on paper. Their names, countries of birth and physical descriptions are all normally included in the information available to crown attorneys. Moreover, some residential areas are identified with racialized communities, so that even an address may be taken to indicate the race of an accused. The exercise of crown discretion is discussed later in this Report (see chapters 5, 6 and 7).

Court Resolutions

Even if charges have been resolved through plea discussions, the accused person still appears in court. This appearance is a public announcement of the conviction and sentence. If the crown attorney and defence counsel have agreed on sentence before the court appearance, they present their agreement to the judge. Judges always have discretion to decide on an appropriate sentence, but they generally accept joint proposals. Consequently, in cases with a guilty plea, potential for facial inequality in sentencing may arise from the resolution discussions that led to the plea and from judges' responses to sentencing proposals.

An accused who contests the charge(s) appears in court for a trial at which verdicts and any punishment are determined. These are adversarial processes in which crown attorneys and defence lawyers compete to influence decision-makers (judges and juries). If there is any possibility that decision-makers may be swayed by racialization, one side or the other may use it (see Chapter 7).

This risk has been raised concerning jury trials of white police officers charged with shooting black persons. It has also been addressed concerning jury trials of black and other racialized accused. In *R. v. Parks*, the Ontario Court of Appeal specifically acknowledged that anti-black racism may influence potential jurors in criminal trials. Sentencing is highly discretionary. The *Criminal Code* sets out maximum sentences for each offence, but offers judges little further guidance about the appropriate penalty for a typical offender who commits a routine offence. Although appellate decisions provide a framework for sentencing, the trial judge retains a broad discretion to determine sentence.

Concerns about inconsistency in sentencing decisions in Canada and other jurisdictions are long-standing. Research has identified "extraordinary discrepancies in almost all aspects of sentencing" and noted that "disparity between courts in sentencing practices ... is an established fact." In this connection the prison admissions data presented earlier in this chapter raises the question of how far the disparity reflects racialization in the criminal justice system.

There are clearly strong and widespread perceptions that judges discriminate against accused people from racialized groups.* Evidence concerning sentencing practices in Canada and other jurisdictions is mixed. Many studies show racial inequalities in sentencing practices; others do not or are inconclusive. In Chapter 8 we report the Commission's findings that racial inequalities do appear in sentencing decisions.

CONCLUSION

There can be few more significant interventions by the public into the private than imprisoning someone ... the decision to imprison a person, to take away their capacity to act in private society and to subject them constantly and totally to the supervision of the state, stands therefore in need of particularly clear justification by law.

Imprisonment is society's most vivid and extreme form of exclusion. The dramatic findings presented in this chapter show that black women, men and youth in Ontario disproportionately experience imprisonment, and that this massive inequality in Ontario prison admissions is a relatively recent occurrence. Ontario simply must not continue to admit black people to prisons at the current rates.†

These findings simply cannot be rationalized by suggesting that black people are inherently more criminal than others. Nor can they be rationalized as reflecting a criminal justice system consisting of officials who are driven by racial hatred.

However, racialization in Canadian society is a recognized fact both inside and outside the criminal justice system. Wherever broad discretion exists, racialization can influence decisions and produce racial inequality.

The criminal justice system operates through a series of highly discretionary decision-making stages. Discretion is exercised in subtle, complex and interactive ways, which leave considerable scope for racialization to influence practices and decisions, and for bias to be transmitted from one stage of the process to others.

In the remainder of this Report we document evidence of the influence of racialization on criminal justice practices, and evidence that this influence is tolerated — evidence of systemic racism. We also make recommendations for securing racial equality in the criminal justice system.

(vi) Is There a Place for the Victim in the Prosecution Process?

Patricia Clarke

Victims of crime once were the central actors in bringing offenders to justice. Today they are neglected outsiders in a system which could not function without them, yet is not accountable to them, provides no role for them and does not necessarily serve them, for ours is "an adversary system in which the victim is not one of the adversaries" (Federal-Provincial Task Force, 1983:5).

Victims are organizing, in one of the significant developments in the justice system, to complain of their expulsion and to demand more participation. Sometimes they bypass the system entirely, either by systems of private justice or in extreme cases by becoming their own prosecutor, judge and executioner.

A number of jurisdictions have tried a number of ways over the past twenty years to answer the demands of victims, and in Canada a Federal-Provincial Task Force on Justice for Victims has made recommendations some of which have been embodied in proposed legislation. The question is no longer, the Task Force says, "whether the victim should participate in the (criminal justice) process or not. The question is rather the extent of that participation" (1983:7).

This paper will look at the current status of the victim in the prosecution process, the reasons for that status in the historic development of the process, and some reasons for the growth of the victims' rights movement. It will review proposals to change the victim's status but will argue that, as far as genuine participation is concerned, the proposed changes will be more cosmetic than real. That is because of the nature of the process, the nature of bureaucratic systems to resist change, and the aims and purposes of the criminal justice system. The exclusion of victims is not an accident or oversight which can be remedied by minor tinkering with a process whose purpose is to provide justice for victims. It is a necessary and inevitable fact of a process with a totally different purpose. If victims dare to find remedies for their victimization, they must find them outside the prosecution process.

Evolution of the Prosecution Process

Before there was a formal legal system, all wrongs were private wrongs. Victims and their families exacted the penalties. To temper and regulate such private justice, in Anglo-Saxon law there gradually grew a system of restitution with fixed payments for various wrongs. At the same time there grew the notion that while some incidents were private disputes, which in the development of law became torts to be dealt with in civil courts, other acts threatened the fabric of society and destroyed "the King's peace". For such acts the offender made payment not only to the victim but also to the lord or the king. Holdsworth (1909:38) claims this was "the germ of the idea that wrong is not simply the affair of the injured individual — an idea which is the condition precedent to the growth of a criminal law".

Gradually as this idea developed, the victim lost control of the conflict and it became the property of the state. The focus shifted from a dispute between the offender and the victim, in which the offender was bound to make reparation to the person he had injured, to the relationship between the offender and society, in which the offender had injured society and must be punished by society. Common law developed to prevent victims from receiving reparations until they did all they could to bring the offender to justice and forbid victims to agree not to prosecute in order to get back their property. Individuals could not condone a crime against the state (Hudson and Galway, 1975:24).

The key to a criminal proceeding thus became, in essence, the exclusion of the victim as one of the parties. Full participation by the victim, Christie says (1977:3), presupposes elements of civil law.

Just as the state came to replace the victim as the injured party, so it gradually replaced the victim as the prosecuting party. Until the late 18th century, trials normally were conducted by the victim-prosecutor and the defendant (Beattie, 1986:13). By the 19th century Blackstone was able to state

---

(1987) 8 *Canadian Criminology Forum* at 31–42. Notes omitted. Reproduced by permission.

categorically that the sovereign "is therefore the proper person to prosecute for all public offences and breaches of the peace, being the person injured in the eye of the law" (Hagan, 1983:268).

In the evolution of the prosecution process, then, two important things have happened, according to Christie (1977:3), one, that both parties are being represented; and second, that the one represented by the state, the victim, "is so thoroughly represented that for the most part he has been pushed completely out of the arena". The victim is a double loser: his property may have been stolen by the offender, but "his conflict has been stolen by the state" (Christie, 1982:93). When the private conflicts become state property, they are made to serve "the ideological interests of state-subject authority relations and the organizational interests of the individual citizens" (Ericson and Baranek, 1982:4).

Role of the Victim in the Prosecution Process

This transfer of the dispute between two persons into a dispute between one of them and the Crown means, according to Shearing and Stenning (1983:9), that victim neglect is not a "minor deficiency" in the justice system but arises from a "fundamental feature". The state owns the conflict and the roles left to victims are; (1) to supply the system with raw material; (2) to give the evidence the system requires; and (3) to serve as a "ceremonial" or "symbolic" presence (Hagan, 1983:7) which legitimizes the mobilization of the law against the accused.

The fundamental policy objectives of the criminal justice system are based on a classical concept of society as a contract between a neutral arbitrating state and rational individuals. The state provides society and its members with a reasonable degree of security, and ensures just treatment for the accused (Griffiths et al., 1980:6). Punishments must be established if the sovereign is to "defend the public liberty, entrusted to his care, from the usurpation of individuals" (VOLD, 1979:24), and they must be fixed, known and in relation to the crime. These policy objectives ignore the victim as such, other than as a member of society. The second objective implies, far from participation by the victim, a moderation and rationality in the punishment the accused might otherwise receive from those who believe themselves wronged. The resulting court process may be seen as a sort of morality play where certain values are publicly affirmed, certain conduct publicly denounced, and certain persons identified, blamed and rejected as "criminals". "The process uses accused persons to help define the relationship between the individual and the state" (Ericson and Baranek, 1982:215). Victims and their needs simply are not part of the script.

As the process has evolved, the chief power left to victims is the power not to surrender their conflict to the state — not to report the victimization. More than half of victims appear to exercise this right (Task Force, 1983:14). Once the state takes over, they lose virtually all other power. They have no right to testify, although they may do so if they are called by the Crown and if theirs is the uncommon case which goes to trial. Approximately up to 70% of cases are settled by a guilty plea. They have no right to express their views on bail or sentencing, though a judge or prosecutor is free to ask for them. They have no right to receive restitution, although they may in certain circumstances have a right to apply for it.

In the prosecution, the Crown represents the interests of the community, which may or may not coincide with the interests of the victims. The Crown must consider, for example, priorities on police time and court time for investigating and prosecuting, availability of evidence, chances of a conviction, public attitudes toward the offence, desirability of plea negotiations, the protection of the community and the rehabilitation of the offender. The victim has no way to challenge these Crown decisions.

Not only does the Crown have to consider wider concerns than those of the victim, but it can be argued that to seem to represent the victim, or to press the victim's claim, might prejudice the Crown's function as an impartial presenter of all the evidence. Indeed, for the Crown to give any assistance or status to the alleged victim, which would not be given to any witness, might compromise the rights of the accused. Even to equate the complainant with a victim could prejudge facts to be proved, for instance in a sexual assault case where consent is an issue.

The Victim Movement

Having been detached over the centuries from the prosecution process, some victims have organized to attempt to get back in. In the last few years such groups have mushroomed across North America. In Canada 28 groups claim 150 chapters in every province and 250,000 to 400,000 members (Toronto Star, 1984:1). Their numbers comprise an effective lobby, but are only a fraction of those eligible. Individual victims in Canada number at least 1.6 million a year. Organizational victims may be even more numerous:

(vi) Is There a Place for the Victim in the Prosecution Process?

in a study by Hagan (1983:35) they made up two-thirds of a random sample.

A number of factors appear to be involved in the birth and growth of victim groups. First, is "a widespread and apparently increasing fear of crime" of which Taylor (1983:93) says "countless research studies" have provided evidence. The fear, partly justified and partly promoted by the media, is expressed in purchases of burglar alarms and double-locks, in self-defence classes, in private security patrols and programmes such as Neighbourhood Watch, and in victim groups.

Second, is the law and order movement, which argues that the criminal justice system is "soft on criminals", thereby turning them loose to create more victims. It supports more "rights" for victims to balance what it claims are too many rights for "criminals".

Third, is the women's movement, which began with advocacy and assistance for rape victims and in some jurisdictions achieved changes in statutes and rules of evidence which provided more rights for victim-witnesses.

Fourth, is the self-help movement, growing out of the protest movements of the 1960's, which leads people who don't trust big government or bureaucracy to form their own groups to represent themselves.

Fifth, is the general humanitarian impulse to help people in trouble (and earn political points) which in other fields has led to worker compensation programmes or the motorists' unsatisfied judgement fund.

Victim advocacy groups differ in their concerns and their goals. Some complain most about neglect, carelessness and insensitivity from police and the courts. They can't find out what is happening in their case, they can't understand what goes on in court and they are not notified when their case is coming up or when it is settled. These groups want more information, more support services, more "sensitivity".

Others complain that victims cannot get restitution for their losses, or even get back their stolen property promptly. According to a 1976 survey in Alameda County, California (Karmen, 1984:148), 30% of victims never got back the stolen property used as evidence, 42% never learned the outcome of their case, and 61% of those eligible for the state's crime compensation fund were not informed of its existence. These victims want more effective compensation schemes and help in applying to them.

Still others such as Mothers Against Drunk Driving want stiffer laws for specific offences. And some want an active role in the prosecution process. They ask to be acknowledged as a party to the proceedings, to be given access to the Crown case, to be supplied with reasons for every decision, even given a veto on plea negotiations and sentence submissions. Donald Sullivan, spokesman for a Canadian conference of victims' groups, says they want laws to give victims "a place in the courtroom" and rights in court "equal to those of the offender" (Toronto Star, 1985:2).

Source of Rights for Victims

A right has three key features (Task Force 1983:130). It is a legal recognition of interest, in this case the victim's interest in this court proceeding. A right for one party implies a responsibility or duty on another party. And it must be legally enforceable, so that one can secure either the right or damages.

At present the justice system is a balance (equal or not) of rights between prosecution and accused. If victims are to have more rights in the prosecution process, are they to come at the expense of the rights of police or the Crown or court officials? These have the greatest interest in encouraging the co-operation of victims, for as much as 87% of police workload — and consequently much of the court workload — comes from incidents reported by citizens (Griffiths et al., 1980:33). Clearly it is in the bureaucratic interests of the system to encourage a steady and increasing clientele. The more incidents that are reported, the higher the crime rate; and high crime rates are an effective argument for bigger budgets. Yet as we have seen, more than half of victimizations are not reported, and many victims "appear to feel that the system would only fail them or ignore them if they involved it" (Task Force, 1983:3).

Victims are essential not only to bringing in the cases but, as witnesses, to prosecuting them successfully. Treating victims in a "sensitive manner" will encourage their "constructive assistance", says a paper prepared for the Federal Department of Justice (Weiler and Desgagne, 1984:27). Or as Weigend (1983:93) puts it, "Happy victims make better witnesses" — a claim he says is unsubstantiated by any evidence except the "feelings" of the staff of victim/witness assistance programmes.

Sensitivity however does not confer power. It is not a right enforceable by law (Task Force 1983:131). It does not conflict with any of the prerogatives of the prosecution. None of the proposals of the Task Force on Justice for Victims involves any mandatory transfer of power from police or court to victims. They contain phrases such as "to be considered" or "where appropriate". Indeed, the Task Force says the key words in its proposals for victims are "concern, consideration and communication" and that these words sum up how the system can respond to the concerns of victims "without compromising its basic aims". (1983:152)

But the "basic aims", as we have seen, have no necessary connection with justice for victims. There is no transfer of power to victims in proposals which allow them to participate in their cases only at the discretion of judge or Crown. There is no transfer of power, either in the guidelines for fair treatment of victims set out by the Victim Committee of the American Bar Association and quoted with approval by the Task Force. (1983:152) They deal mainly with ways to improve communication between victims and decision-makers in the criminal justice system. Similarly, a case management programme in British Columbia "improved convenience" for victims with no change in the "aims and purposes" of the system (Task Force, 1983:96).

If rights for victims are not to come from the prosecution, then they must come from the accused. If the victim of sexual assault, for instance, wins the right not to have evidence of sexual reputation considered, the accused loses the right to present that evidence. The transfer of rights is particularly evident in the California *Victims' Bill of Rights* of 1982 (Karmen, 1984:232–3), which limits the accused's opportunities for bail, restricts plea bargaining, restricts insanity defence, broadens standards for admissibility of evidence, and permits victims to press for greater penalties in sentencing, to appeal sentences they view as lenient and to argue against parole.

That is further than Canadians appear willing to go. The rhetoric is that the rights of the accused are inviolate, and the Task Force cautions that in focussing on the plight of the victim "we must not lose sight of the need to safeguard the accused" (1983:5). Perhaps it would be more realistic to say, with Ericson and Baranek (1982:233), that both accused and victim are dependents in the prosecution process and that neither has more "rights" than is expedient to allow and not "upset the operation of criminal control in the interests of the state".

Proposals for Change

It appears then that victims have almost no enforceable rights in the prosecution process. It also appears that they are excluded from any real rights in the process by its very nature as a conflict between the state and the accused. Within those limits, several ways have been suggested to recognize and recompense the victim.

One is financial reparation. Three of the 79 recommendations of the Task Force deal with this. A second is a "victim impact" statement, to be requested before sentencing, the subject of another Task Force recommendation. A third is a "victims' advocate" who attempts to influence the prosecution process. Two such experiments have been tried in the United States (McDonald, 1976:153). In one a lawyer was employed as a "victim advocate" to attempt to influence the process through out-of-court negotiations. In the other, a volunteer group of victim advocates attended court hearings en masse for a time, until they tired of it, and claimed fewer charges were dismissed or remanded when they were present. The second programme raises questions about fairness to the accused. As Griffiths says (1980:32), "The prototype of community involvement ... is the lynch mob." The first raises questions about who pays the advocate. If the victims pay, they may feel twice victimized. If the state pays, that may compromise its stance that the community, not the victim, is the injured party. In any case, such advocates have no standing in court since the victim is not one of the adversaries.

Restitution and Compensation

The Task Force proposals on reparation would; (1) amend s. 653 of the *Criminal Code* to require judges to consider restitution "in all appropriate cases" and to provide an opportunity for victims to make representations about their ascertainable losses; (2) empower the court to impose a jail term for wilful default on a restitution order; (3) amend s. 388 to raise its present limit on restitution for property damage from $50 to $500. Restitution as part of a probation order under s. 663 would continue unchanged.

"Whenever possible," the Task Force explains, "victims should be restored to the position they enjoyed prior to the victimization" (Task Force, 1983:35). The Law Reform Commission of Canada in its paper on Restitution and Compensation describes restitution as a "natural and just response" to the victim's plight which should be a "central consideration" in sentencing (Working Paper 5, 1974:6,8).

Yet such remedies for the victim already exist. Several sections of the *Criminal Code* make it possible for the court to order restitution. These remedies appear to be seldom used. While Canadian data are lacking (Burns, 1980:29), the Task Force thinks judges are "reluctant" to use them (Task Force, 1983:54). It does not explain why judges would be less reluctant to use its new proposals.

Outside the criminal process, victims may apply to provincial crime injury compensation boards in all provinces except Prince Edward Island, or collect for property losses from private insurance, or file a civil suit both for property loss and for suffering and get judgement not only against the offender but, where negligence can be proved, against third parties.

Restitution provisions in other jurisdictions appear to be an ineffective remedy for victims. In Britain, after passage of new restitution legislation in 1972, of those sent to custody and also given restitution orders only 12% paid the whole sum (Burns, 1980:15). In practice, said the British Advisory Council on the Penal System, a victim's prospects for restitution through a criminal court order "are remote" (Burns, 1980:15). After a study of United States restitution schemes, Burns found them of relatively little use to victims and concluded that their popularity reflected a conception of them as "potentially useful tools for rehabilitating the offender rather than as devices for restoring the victim" (Burns, 1980:12).

The compensation schemes outside the criminal process are not well used either. They are usually limited to victims of violent crime but are available regardless of whether an offender has been identified or convicted. In Ontario, one in 55 eligible victims actually seeks compensation (*Globe & Mail*, 1984:2). A study of the New York and New Jersey schemes showed that fewer than 1% of all victims of violent crime even applied to the boards, and only 35% of those who applied were compensated (Elias, 1983:219).

As for the possibility of civil suit, Allen Linden reported that 1.5% of victims surveyed collected anything by suit, although 74.2% of those studied suffered some economic loss (Linden, 1968:29).

Whether or not restitution is a "natural response", there appear to be a number of reasons why judges are reluctant to use the existing provisions and legislators are reluctant to impose more effective ones — reasons involving the nature of the criminal process, the objectives of sentencing, constitutional division of powers, and sometimes no doubt a combination of ignorance and inertia. Judge Cartwright of York County, in *Regina v. Kalloo* (Unreported; quoted in Moskoff, 1983:11), commented:

> those few Crown counsel who are even aware of the existence of this section (653) which allows the victim of an indictable offence to apply for an order to satisfy loss or damage to property caused in the commission of a crime are equally indifferent to its application.

He went on to suggest that if the Attorney General were paid by commission on completed restitution orders, "blood would be flowing from stones" all over Ontario (Moskoff, 1983:11).

The difficulty of getting blood from stones, however, is one reason restitution orders are seldom made, and civil suit is often useless as well. In making restitution a condition of probation under s. 663(2)(e), a judge is bound to consider an offender's ability to pay. (He is not so bound under s. 653.) Observation of the courts indicates that many offenders, particularly against property, have neither jobs nor assets.

A further reason for caution is the Supreme Court of Canada ruling in *R. v. Zelensky* ((1978), 2 C.R. (3d) 107 (S.C.C.)) that proceedings for restitution under s. 653 must not take on any character of a civil suit, and therefore the criminal court must not determine issues regarding the amount to be awarded. Restitution can be imposed, then, only when the amount is not in dispute, which Moskoff comments makes the section a "toothless tiger" (Moskoff, 1983:11). Burns comments that judges hesitate to order restitution under s. 663 as well, first because they fear using criminal law to enforce civil obligations, and second because they see it as suitable only for simple cases in which there is no dispute either over the amount involved or over the offender's ability to pay (Burns, 1980:25).

In addition, a restitution order once made is hard to enforce. Those made under s. 653 must be enforced by the victim as a civil judgement, if the offender has assets and can be located. Those made under s. 663(2)(e) are intended to be monitored by probation officers. If the probation officers notice that payments have not been made, and if they decide to charge the offender with failure to comply with probation, and if the offender can be located, they must prove the offender "wilfully" defaulted. If they succeed, the maximum penalty is a $500 fine and/or six months in jail. Note that the victim is not the complainant in the enforcement procedure.

The most serious problem with restitution involves the nature of the criminal process. Civil wrongs have grown in law to be those for which injured persons seek their own monetary compensation. Criminal wrongs have become a public relationship between offenders and the state with a public response applied through penal sanctions. The historical tie between the two remains in the *Criminal Code* provisions for restitution (s. 653 and s. 663) which the Law Reform Commission describes as carry-overs "grudgingly grafted onto penal law to save the victim the expense of a civil suit" (Working Paper 5, 1974:9). They enable the victim to circumvent civil procedure by obtaining a criminal judgement, enforceable as if it were civil, by a more expeditious and less expensive process. An example of the civil nature of s. 653 is that it comes into operation "on application" of the victim, not on the initiative of the court.

The *British North America Act* gives jurisdiction over criminal law and procedure to the federal parliament (1867: sect. 91(27)) but authority over property and civil rights to the provinces. This division, says Burns, means "an almost insurmountable obstacle to the establishment of efficient restitution systems in Canada" (1980:29).

Further, criminal courts are constituted to determine a person's criminal responsibility, not his/her civil liability. The two have different standards of proof and different rules of evidence. For example, examination for discovery is a civil procedure not available in the criminal court. An accused person would not have the same safeguards around challenging a victim's claim for damages in criminal court than would be available in civil court. For the criminal court to try to make such a determination raises the danger of infringing on the powers reserved to the civil court. Widespread use of restitution orders might encourage use of the criminal courts as a collection agency, and lead to threatening prosecution to collect a debt.

A further set of problems arises because the focus in sentencing is not on what is pleasing to the victim but on what is good for the offender and for society. Though the Law Reform Commission saw restitution as a "rational sanction" and the Zelensky decision accepted its "valid character" as part of the sentencing process, restitution cannot be argued in the criminal court on the basis that it would return the victim to wholeness or compensate for suffering. The only constitutional way to make the civil liability to the victim a valid part of the criminal sentence is to actively locate it within criminal law. The purpose which has been alleged is that it will deprive the offender of the fruits of crime, deter those who might hope to profit illegally, and facilitate the rehabilitation of the accused.

The Law Reform Commission argues that restitution, "involves acceptance of the offender as a responsible person with the capacity to undertake constructive and socially approved acts.... To the extent that restitution works toward self-correction and prevents or at least discourages the offender's commitment to a life of crime, the community enjoys a measure of protection.... The offender too benefits.... He is treated as a responsible human being" (1974:7–8).

These desirable effects, Burns comments, are "entirely speculative" (1980:8). The momentum toward restitution as a sentence seems to him to depend on little more than "an intuitive sense of its rationality" (1980:7).

The Task Force, although it supports expanded restitution proposals, admits "there is little of the kind of 'hard' evidence which might allow us to decide conclusively whether the benefits of restitution outweigh its costs" (1983:92). To be fair, there is little hard evidence on whether any other sentencing dispositions work any better (Griffiths et al., 1980:233–34). The "safest conclusion", says Klein, is that restitution "as a correctional measure simply will not make any difference" (1978:400).

And finally, there are difficulties in implementing effective and just restitution schemes.

Crown attorneys will have discretion whether to recommend restitution, and judges will have discretion whether to order it. Can justice then be equal for offenders, or victims? The victims cannot "shop" for a judge who is known to make restitution orders.

Would the law fall unevenly on the person who steals $10 million and cannot possibly make restitution, and the person who steals $100 and can? If restitution is a correctional measure, imposed for the good of the offender, should it not then be imposed regardless of whether the victim has been paid for the loss by insurance?

Defence counsel often tell the court, in a bid for a more lenient sentence, that full or partial restitution has been made. If this does in fact result in leniency, does that mean that if a rich man and a poor man both break a window, and the rich man can afford to replace it, then he receives a less severe sentence than the poor man for the same offence?

What happens if there are several offenders? If one has no ability to pay, or reneges on payment, do the others pay more to make up the victim's total loss? Suppose there are multiple victims, and as part of plea negotiations some charges are dropped. Which victims are then to receive restitution?

Finally, if victims of crime are entitled to be restored to their original status, why not every victim? Why limit the recompense to those cases of property loss in which an offender can not only be identified, charged, convicted, and sentenced to make restitution but can actually pay damages?

Yet with all their flaws, restitution programmes (inside the criminal process) and compensation

(vi) Is There a Place for the Victim in the Prosecution Process?

schemes (outside of it) have been legislated in many jurisdictions in the last 20 years. Though often underfunded, unadvertised and underused, obviously they have merits for lawmakers. For one, they enable governments faced with rising crime rates and rising public concern over crime to say, "Look what we're doing for the victims." Roger Meiners points out that large numbers of compensation programmes were established at least in part as a palliative for increasing crime and relatively inefficient restitution (Meiners, 1978:9–44). Voters are told that something will be done for them when and if they are victimized and few will find out otherwise. Elias claims compensation has:

> justified strengthened police forces, provided political advantages to its supporters, facilitated social control of the population and yet substantially failed in providing most victims with assistance (1983:213).

A second purpose is to keep the victim from demanding a real role in the prosecution process. As Hagan says, such programmes open the possibility of bringing the victim back into the system without actually doing it, symbolically conveying a sense of concern while doing little to alter the actual origin of the concern (1983:60).

Victim Impact Statements

The other proposal of the Task Force, aside from restitution, to bring the victim back into the prosecution process was to amend the *Criminal Code* to "permit" the introduction of a victim impact statement "to be considered" at the time of sentencing (Task Force, 1983:157). Such a statement would presumably enable victims to tell the judge of their suffering and of any monetary loss as a result of the crime. Presumably they would then feel that somebody was paying attention to what happened to them.

At present nothing, except pressure of time, prevents a judge from asking to hear from a victim, or when ordering a pre-sentence report from asking that the victim be consulted. The intent of the Task Force proposal is to require the judge to request such a statement.

That proposal raises serious questions. To the degree that the statement dealt with monetary loss, it could be considered in assessing restitution as part of a sentence, subject to concerns already discussed about the purposes of sentencing and conflict with civil courts, particularly if the amount of the loss were in dispute. Questions arise whether the determination of loss would have to be based on receipts of appraisals, which might be difficult for some victims to produce; whether the statement would have to be sworn; whether it would be subject to contest by the accused, and if contested, whether the whole question would not then have to be referred to a civil court for adjudication.

To the degree that the statement dealt with pain or suffering, its usefulness would be questionable as long as the focus in sentencing is on the protection of society and the rehabilitation of the accused. A shut-in widow whose television set is stolen may suffer more from its loss than the wealthy bachelor who is seldom home, but that should weigh less with the judge than the characteristics of the offence, the previous record of the offender and the perceived need to deter such behaviour in the community. If the purpose of the sentence is to rehabilitate the offender, then its nature should be determined by presumed experts. If its purpose is deterrence, then it should be certain and predictable, not subject to modification by the victim. If the purpose is retribution, then the punishment must fit the crime rather than the victim (Karmen, 1984:155).

Then there is the problem of how the statement will be submitted. Ninety-eight percent of cases are concluded in the provincial courts (Griffiths et al., 1980:146) and about 70% of these without a trial (Griffiths et al., 1980:147). Dockets are crowded, hearings are rushed and pre-sentence reports are rare. If the victim is not present when the accused pleads guilty, how often will judges be willing to delay sentence to hear from the victim?

Perhaps too, it is only an assumption that many victims really want this input, or any input, into their cases. A Philadelphia judge, Lois Porer, who routinely offers victims a chance to speak on sentence, says they seldom do (Karmen, 1984:230). Since victim impact statements were legislated in Connecticut in 1981, only 3% of victims appear at sentence hearings (Karmen, 1984:231). When as an experiment victims were invited to take part in plea-bargaining sessions on their cases in Dade County, Florida, only a third attended. Those who were present generally spoke only in answer to questions, approved what the professionals suggested and were "passive and docile" (Heinz and Kerstetter, 1980:172).

Resistance to Change

Having looked at the "rights" of the victim in the prosecution process and at proposals to give victims a larger role, it remains to ask: would these proposals, or any proposals, make any real difference in the conduct of the courts?

As we have seen, restitution is seldom ordered. Compensation schemes are seldom used. The majority of victims do not accept the limited opportunities to participate which are offered to them. It is not clear whether the last is because they don't care, or because they don't think it will make any difference, or because as the Dade County study suggests the system is not diligent in notifying them of opportunities (Heinz and Kerstetter, 1980:173).

One of the reasons advanced for helping victims is to encourage them to cooperate with the system in reporting more victimizations. In the United States, the percentage of incidents of violence which were reported to police went from 46% in 1973 to 47% in 1981, and of household burglaries from 47% in 1973 to 51% in 1981, despite the launching of numerous victim-assistance programmes during that period (Karmen, 1984:168).

After reviewing a decade of action and advocacy on behalf of victims in the United States, Weigend concluded it had generated "much rhetoric, more knowledge ... but little change" (1983:91).

Criminal justice systems are like any bureaucracy. They operate in their own interests. They are subject to what Karmen calls "goal displacement" (1984:169), which means that they substitute for the official goals of doing justice and serving the public, the unofficial goals of getting through the workload expeditiously, covering up mistakes and making themselves look as essential as possible so funding won't be cut. As King points out:

> Imagine for example the approach of the victim of a serious crime. He wishes to see the offender punished and deterred from further offences. Now compare that approach with that of a court administrator, whose major concern is the efficient running of the system, clearing the workload for the day and avoiding any unnecessary delays.... The one looks to the magistrate to revenge his loss ... and to compensate him, the victim, while another looks at his watch and wonders how long the case is going to last and whether the morning list will be completed by one o'clock (1981:13–14).

A place for victims in the prosecution process is limited to one that does not interfere with the smooth working of the system or the privileges and convenience of its principles.

Most reforms, as we have seen, seem to be intended to inform or assist or conciliate the victim, and these are worthy goals, but they involve no real rights or participation. Where the victim has been granted a role in the process, it appears to be subject to foot-dragging (the Dade County experiment), discretion (to be "considered" or to be applied "where appropriate") or co-opting.

The fate of reforms in the role of the victim is not surprising. Ericson and Baranek state:

> It is a common feature of bureaucratic organizations that rules intended to influence the action of agents are routinely absorbed by the agents to conform with their existing practices (1982:224).

Exciting reforms are "translated into mechanisms of convenience by control agents and relegated to their pragmatically appropriate place" (Ericson and Baranek, 1982:231).

Conclusion

If the public criminal justice process is impervious to change which would allow the victim any real participation, what then?

Organizational victims already bypass the public prosecution and set up their own system to deal with incidents which are classified not as "crime" (which by definition involves the public interest) but as "loss" (Shearing and Stenning, 1983:7). In these victim-oriented systems, run by and for victims, the priority is on restitution or compensation for the loss and prevention of future losses.

Then there are proposals, for example Christie's (1977, 1982), for similar decriminalization of offences against individuals. Christie argues that we "create crime by creating systems that ask for the word" (1982:74). He proposes to remove conflicts from the professionals and return them to the accused and the victims, and to set up quasi-civil procedures to assess compensation and penalties. Pointing out that "several less-industrialized countries" apply civil law where Europe applies criminal law (1982:92), he asks, "Could we imagine social systems where the parties by and large relied on civil solutions?" (1982:96).

Ericson and Baranek, discussing such proposals, are skeptical. Decriminalization may simply imply some other form of social control. Diversion programmes may lead to more cumbersome procedures and increase the number of persons subject to control (1982:228). They add, "All reform alternatives include an added role for some group of professionals" (1982:233).

It is also important to note that there is the vigilante, who tries his own case and administers his own justice, celebrated in the movies *Death Wish* and *Deadly Force* ("When the cops won't and the courts can't ... he will give you justice!" (Karmen, 1984:247)) and emulated by Bernhard Goetz of New York.

In Canada, at least, rates of reported crime are not escalating in a way that justifies the vigilante. But one of the arguments for compensating victims of crime rests on the assumption that they do not carry out their own justice. In Taylor's analysis (1983), a crucial function of the capitalist state is to maintain conditions under which production can flourish. One of these conditions is a "justice" system. There must be an overall sense in society of a free contract whereby the state protects the person and the property of its citizens, in exchange for those citizens subjugating themselves to the state. The loss of liberty thereby involved is offset and made legitimate by the overall protection of the freedom of the citizen which is provided by a police force and a legal and penal system (1983:135). In other words, citizens give up the right to protect themselves and to pursue their own vengeance, and the state contracts to protect them and collects taxes from them to do so. Therefore, it can be argued that if the state fails in its side of the contract, it should compensate the victims.

Similar arguments for compensating crime victims can be raised on the basis of sociologist Emile Durkheim's theories that crime is normal, even necessary to a healthy society (Vold, 1979:204–208). Durkheim argued that society makes certain demands on its members, and fulfilling these demands is an important source of social solidarity. But the demands are constructed so that inevitably a certain identifiable group will not be able to fulfill them. This enables the rest to feel a sense of moral superiority which he says is the primary source of the social solidarity.

Durkheim informed us that it is not only inevitable that some will oppose the collective conscience, it is also healthy. Progressive social change comes about because some people dare to differ. Thus crime is the price society pays for the possibility of progress — all the more reason why society should compensate those few who are martyrs to its health.

What would we do if we were really serious about helping victims of crime? We would fund adequately and advertise widely a government-supported compensation fund. It would not be funded, as is often suggested, by convicted offenders, for that would imply that offenders are a distinct group and would hold all in that group, who happened to be caught, liable for the damage inflicted by some. Rather it might be funded like medical insurance (one might contribute to OHIP and to VICE — Victims Insurance (against) Criminal Enterprises), recognizing first, that there are more offenders than ever that are caught; second, that the definition of which acts are crimes and therefore which persons are offenders is made by society and changes from time to time; and third, that society has an obligation to those who suffer from one of its inevitable features. We would allow compensation both for material loss and for pain and suffering, and whether or not an offender has been identified. Yes, there would be cheating, just as people cheat now on claims for private insurance. But if private insurers live with that risk, surely a public scheme can.

[NOTE: See also the excerpt from Nils Christie, "Conflicts as Poverty," in Chapter 1A, above at pages 6–9.]

(vii) Restorative Justice and Mediation: Is the Public Interested?

Mark S. Umbreit

Linda and Bob Jackson had their house broken into while they were away visiting friends in another city. The frustration, anger, and growing sense of vulnerability they felt far exceeded the loss of their television set and stereo. The young person,

---

Reproduced with permission from Mark S. Umbreit, *Victim Meets Offender: The Impact of Restorative Justice and Mediation* (Monsey, N.Y.: Criminal Justice Press, 1994) at 1–13.

Allan, who committed this crime was caught and entered a plea of guilty. When the Jacksons were invited to participate in a program that allowed them to meet their offender, they were eager to get answers to questions such as "why us?" and "were you watching our movements?" The mediation session allowed them to get answers to these and other questions, let Allan know how personally violated they felt and negotiate a plan for him to pay them back. While nervous at first, Allan felt better after the mediation. Everyone treated him with respect even though he had committed a crime, and he was able to make amends to the Jacksons. Linda and Bob felt less vulnerable, were able to sleep better and received payment for their losses. All parties were able to put this event behind them.

The Jacksons are among many thousands of people who have been victimized and have been given the opportunity to experience a radically different way of "doing justice." Through their participation in a victim-offender mediation program, they were able to experience firsthand what the emerging theory of restorative justice is about.

Our contemporary understanding of social theory related to crime and victimization can be traced back to a major paradigm shift that occurred during the Norman invasion of Britain in the twelfth century. This marked a turning away from viewing crime as a victim-offender conflict within the context of community. Crime became a violation of the king's peace, and upholding the authority of the state replaced the practice of making the victim whole.

One of the most significant current developments in our thinking about crime is the growing interest in restorative justice theory (Mackey, 1990; Umbreit, 1993a, 1991b; Umbreit and Coates, 1993; Van Ness, 1986; Van Ness et al., 1989; Wright, 1991; Wright and Galaway, 1989; Zehr, 1990, 1985; Marshall and Merry, 1990; Galaway and Hudson, 1990; Messmer and Otto, 1992), which is based upon principles that were widely practiced prior to the Norman invasion of Britain. At a time in modern society when the current paradigm of justice has demonstrated very little positive impact on offenders, crime victims or the larger community, it is understandable that a promising theory of criminal justice is increasingly being embraced in a growing number of communities throughout the world.

Restorative justice theory provides an entirely different theoretical framework for responding to crime. Rather than defining "the state" as the victim, restorative justice theory postulates that criminal behavior is first a conflict between individuals. The person who was violated is the primary victim, and the state is a secondary victim. The current retributive paradigm of justice focuses on the actions of the offender, denies victim participation and requires only passive participation by the offender. The very definition of "holding offenders accountable" changes when viewed through the lens of restorative justice. As Zehr (1990) notes: "Instead of 'paying a debt to society' by experiencing punishment, accountability would mean understanding and taking responsibility for what has been done and taking action to make things right. Instead of owing an abstract debt to society, paid in an abstract way by experiencing punishment, the offender would owe a debt to the victim, to be repaid in a concrete way."

Restorative justice places both victim and offender in active problem-solving roles that focus upon the restoration of material and psychological losses to individuals and the community following the damage that results from criminal behavior. Whenever possible, dialogue and negotiation serve as central elements of restorative justice. This is true primarily of property crimes, although also of a growing number of more violent offenses. Problem solving for the future is seen as more important than establishing blame for past behavior. Public safety is a primary concern, yet severe punishment of the offender is less important than providing opportunities to: empower victims in their search for closure and healing; impress upon the offender the human impact of their behavior; and promote restitution to the victim.

By far the clearest distinction between the old paradigm of retributive justice and the new paradigm of restorative justice has been developed by Zehr (1990), as outlined in Table 1.

While clearly more difficult to apply in violent crimes, the principles of restorative justice theory are having an increasing impact on social policy. Many of these principles can also be seen in the pioneering work of an Australian scholar who addresses the issues of crime, shame and reintegration. Braithwaite (1989) argues for "reintegrative shaming," a type of social control based upon informal community condemnation of wrong-doing, but with opportunities for the reintegration of the wrongdoer back into the community. He states that the most effective crime control requires active community participation "in shaming offenders, and, having shamed them, through concerted participation in ... integrating the offender back into the community" (Braithwaite,

TABLE 1
PARADIGMS OF JUSTICE — OLD AND NEW

Old Paradigm	New Paradigm
1. Crime defined as violation of state.	1. Crime defined as violation of one person by another.
2. Focus on establishing blame based on guilt, on past (did he/she do it?).	2. Focus on problem solving, on liabilities/obligations, on future (what should be done?).
3. Adversarial relationship and process are normative.	3. Dialogue and negotiation are normative.
4. Imposition of pain to punish and deter/prevent future crime.	4. Restitution as means of restoring both parties; goal of reconciliation/restoration.
5. Justice defined by intent and process: right rules.	5. Justice defined as right relationships; judged by outcome.
6. Interpersonal, conflictual nature of crime obscured, repressed; conflict seen as individual versus the state.	6. Crime recognized as interpersonal conflict; value of conflict is recognized.
7. One social injury replaced by another.	7. Focus on repair of social injury.
8. Community on sidelines, represented abstractly by state.	8. Community as facilitator in restorative process.
9. Encouragement of competitive, individualistic values.	9. Encouragement of mutuality.
10. Action directed from state to offender • victim ignored, • offender passive.	10. Victim and offender's roles recognized in problem/solution: • victim rights/needs recognized, • offender encouraged to take responsibility.
11. Offender accountability defined as taking punishment.	11. Offender accountability defined as understanding impact of action, and helping to decide how to make things right.
12. Offense defined in purely legal terms, devoid of moral, social, economic, political dimensions.	12. Offense understood in whole context — moral, social, economic, political.
13. "Debt" owed to state and society in the abstract.	13. Debt/liability to victim recognized.
14. Response focused on offender's past behavior.	14. Response focused on harmful consequences of offender's behavior.
15. Stigma of crime unremovable.	15. Stigma of crime removable through restorative action.
16. No encouragement for repentance and forgiveness.	16. Possibilities for repentance and forgiveness.
17. Dependence upon proxy by professionals.	17. Direct involvement by participants.

1989). Braithwaite notes that societies with low crime rates consist of people who do not mind their own business, where there exist clear limits to tolerance of deviance and where communities have a preference for handling their own problems.

While Braithwaite does not specifically address restorative justice or victim-offender mediation, he argues for principles of justice which emphasize personal accountability of offenders, active community involvement, and a process of reconciliation and reaffirmation of the offender that directly relates to the restorative justice paradigm.

Victim-Offender Mediation

The clearest expression of restorative justice theory is seen in the emerging field of victim-offender mediation (Fagan and Gehm, 1993; Galaway, 1989, 1988; Galaway and Hudson, 1990; Umbreit, 1993a, 1986a; Zehr, 1990, 1980). Developed extensively in recent years, it represents one of the most creative efforts to: hold offenders personally accountable for their behavior; emphasize the human impact of crime; provide opportunities for offenders to take responsibility for their actions by facing their victim and making amends; promote active victim and

**FIGURE 1
INTERNATIONAL DEVELOPMENT OF VICTIM-OFFENDER MEDIATION**

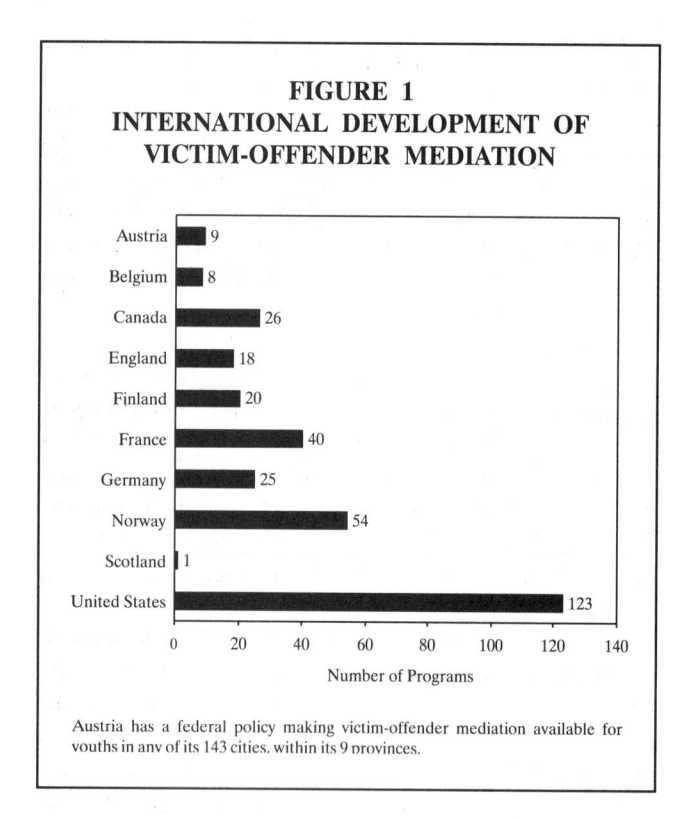

Country	Number of Programs
Austria	9
Belgium	8
Canada	26
England	18
Finland	20
France	40
Germany	25
Norway	54
Scotland	1
United States	123

Austria has a federal policy making victim-offender mediation available for youths in any of its 143 cities, within its 9 provinces.

community involvement in the justice process; and enhance the quality of justice experienced by both victims and offenders. There are more than 120 victim-offender mediation programs in the U.S., 26 in Canada and an even larger number in Europe (Umbreit, 1991b), as noted in Figure 1.

A widespread network of victim-offender mediation programs is now developing throughout the U.S., Canada, England, Germany, France, Austria, Norway and Finland. While interest in restorative justice theory has grown extensively throughout North America and Europe, there exists a significant lack of empirical research to assess the impact of the theory.

The ultimate strength of any social theory is to be found in how accurately it captures the reality of people who are subject to it. Restorative justice theory makes bold claims about the needs of people affected by crime within community structures. Its validity as a new social theory must be grounded in empirical evidence offered by those most affected by crime — victims and offenders. Should restorative justice fail to become a "grounded theory" (Glazer and Strauss, 1967) from the bottom up, it risks the likelihood of becoming an abstraction — a philosophical exercise in criminal justice policy reform with little relevance to the reality of how justice is actually done in a free and democratic society. On the other hand, a grounded theory of restorative justice contains the powerful and prophetic potential for a fundamental change in how society understands and responds to crime in the community.

This book will offer such empirical grounding for the theory of restorative justice. It will report on the largest and most extensive multi-site analysis of victim-offender mediation to occur in North America (Umbreit, 1991a, 1993b; Umbreit and Coates, 1992, 1993). Over a two-and-one-half-year period, victim-offender mediation programs working with the juvenile courts in Albuquerque (NM), Austin (TX), Minneapolis (MN) and Oakland (CA) were examined. A total of 1,153 pre- and post-mediation interviews with victims and offenders were conducted. Two different comparison groups were used to examine the impact of mediation, along with numerous interviews with court officials and program staff, a review of court and program records, and 28 observations of actual mediation sessions.

The conclusions that emerged from this multi-site study, as will be noted in the final chapter, are consistent with a growing body of literature, particularly two recent studies conducted in England (Dignan, 1990; Marshall and Merry, 1990). Together, these studies provide important empirical evidence to support the basic propositions put forth by the restorative justice paradigm.

The Mediation Process

Victim-offender mediation and reconciliation programs differ in a variety of ways related to referral source, diversion versus post-adjudication referral, case management procedures, use of volunteer mediators, etc. A basic case management process, however, tends to be present in most of the programs in the U.S. and Canada, particularly those that have been influenced by the VORP (Victim Offender Reconciliation Program) model (Umbreit, 1988).

Nearly all victim-offender mediation and reconciliation programs focus upon providing a conflict resolution process that is perceived as fair to both parties. It is the mediator's responsibility to facilitate this process. First, the parties are given time to address informational and emotional needs. Once questions have been answered and feelings expressed, the mediation session then turns to a discussion of losses and the possibility of developing a mutually agreeable restitution plan (i.e., money, work for victim, work for victim's choice of a charity, etc.).

The process typically begins when judges, probation staff, prosecutors or victim assistance staff refer juvenile or adult offenders (most often those con-

(vii) Restorative Justice and Mediation: Is the Public Interested?

victed of such crimes as theft and burglary) to the victim-offender mediation program. Many programs accept referrals after a formal admission of guilt has been entered with the court. Some programs accept cases that are referred prior to formal admission of guilt, as part of a deferred prosecution or diversion effort. Each case is then assigned to either a staff or volunteer mediator. Prior to scheduling the mediation session, the mediator meets with both the offender and victim separately. These individual meetings with each party play a very important role in the mediation process. The mediator listens to the story of each party, explains the program and encourages their participation.

Usually mediators meet first with the offender. If he or she is willing to proceed with mediation, they meet later with the victim. In addition to collecting information about the criminal event and explaining the program, these individual meetings provide an opportunity for the mediator to build rapport and trust with the individuals involved. Particularly since both parties are likely to have already been dealt with in an impersonal fashion by a variety of criminal justice officials, having the mediator meet with both individually before even scheduling the mediation is extremely important. It tends to humanize the justice process and result in a higher "getting-to-the-table" rate of actual mediation participation. These preliminary meetings, held separately with victims and offenders, require effective listening and communication skills. They are critical to building rapport and trust with both parties.

While crime victims are encouraged to consider the possible benefits of mediation, they must not be coerced into participating. To do so, even with the best of intentions, would be to revictimize them. Voluntary participation by crime victims and offenders — although for offenders it is a choice within a highly coercive context — is a strong ethical principle of the victim-offender mediation process. Presenting the mediation process as an option helps victims and offenders to feel empowered.

Program literature in the field implies that offender participation in the mediation process is also totally voluntary. Actual practice suggests something quite different. A rather significant amount of state coercion is exercised when offenders are ordered to participate in mediation by the court, via probation, or are diverted from prosecution if they complete the program. One early study (Coates and Gehm, 1985) found that offenders certainly did not perceive the process as voluntary. A more recent and much larger study (Umbreit and Coates, 1992, 1993), as will be reported in this book, found the vast majority of offenders believed they had a choice as to whether to participate in mediation.

A more honest approach is used by programs that attempt to secure offender participation in the least coercive manner possible. Offenders who are strongly opposed to participating are allowed to bow out of the program, while those who are determined by the program staff to be inappropriate for mediation are referred back to the referral source.

Once the victim and offender have indicated their willingness to participate, the mediator then schedules a face-to-face meeting. The mediation session begins with the mediator explaining his or her role, stating any communication ground rules that may be necessary, and stating the agenda for the meeting (first to talk about what happened and how they felt about it, and then to discuss losses and negotiate restitution).

During the first part of the mediation session, the focus is on the facts and feelings related to the crime. Crime victims are given the unusual opportunity to express their feelings directly to the person who violated them. They can get answers to questions such as "why me?", "how did you get into our house?", and "were you stalking us and planning on coming back?" Upon seeing their offender, victims are often relieved. This "criminal" usually bears little resemblance to the frightening character they may have conjured up in their minds.

Facing the person they violated is not easy for most offenders. While it is often an uncomfortable position for offenders, they are given the equally unusual opportunity to display a more human dimension to their character. For many, the opportunity to express remorse in a very direct and personal fashion is important. The mediation process allows victims and offenders to deal with each other as people, often times from the same neighborhood, rather than as stereotypes and objects.

When both parties have concluded discussing the crime and how they felt about it, the second part of the meeting is then initiated. The losses incurred by the victim are reviewed, and a plan for making things right is discussed. The principles of fairness and realism are emphasized during the final negotiation of the restitution agreement. When courts refer cases to mediation, they do not usually order a specific restitution amount. Cases in which the parties are unable to agree upon the amount or form of restitution are referred back to the referral source, with a good likelihood that the offender will be placed in a different program. Mediators do not impose a restitution settlement.

Most programs report that in more than 95% of all mediation sessions a written restitution agreement has been successfully negotiated and signed by the victim, offender and mediator. Joint victim-offender meetings usually last about one hour, with some meetings in the two-hour range.

It is important to note that there exist a number of significant exceptions to the "typical" process described, particularly among community dispute resolution centers that have mediated quite a few disputes among crime victims and offenders, but that did not frame the mediation as a "victim-offender mediation." For example, many of these community dispute resolution centers would have staff be responsible for all of the case development work, including any separate meetings or conversations with the parties prior to mediation. The mediator would first meet the victim and offender at the time of the mediation session.

Is the Public Interested?

Even in view of the empirical evidence in support of restorative justice theory and mediation to be offered in this book, the question remains "Is the larger public really interested?" Certainly the data that have emerged from examination of a number of individual programs are rather persuasive. Yet is there evidence of public support for the principles of restorative justice? The strong "law-and-order" and "get-tough" rhetoric that dominates most political campaigns would suggest not. After all, how often have we heard ambitious politicians or criminal justice officials state that "the public demands that we get tougher with criminals"? This perception — or some would argue, misperception — fuels the engine that drives our nation toward ever-increasing and costly criminal punishments, as seen in lengthy sentences and the highest per capita incarceration in the world (Mauer, 1991).

There is, however, a growing body of evidence to suggest that the general public is far less vindictive than often portrayed and far more supportive of the basic principles of restorative justice than many might think. A recent statewide public opinion survey, conducted by the University of Minnesota (Pranis and Umbreit, 1992) using a large probability sample, challenges conventional wisdom about public feelings related to crime and punishment.

A sample of 825 Minnesota adults, demographically and geographically balanced to reflect the state's total population, were asked three questions with implications for restorative justice as part of a larger omnibus survey. A sample of this size has a sampling error of plus or minus 3.5 percentage points. The first question was: "Suppose that while you are away, your home is burglarized and $1,200 worth of property is stolen.

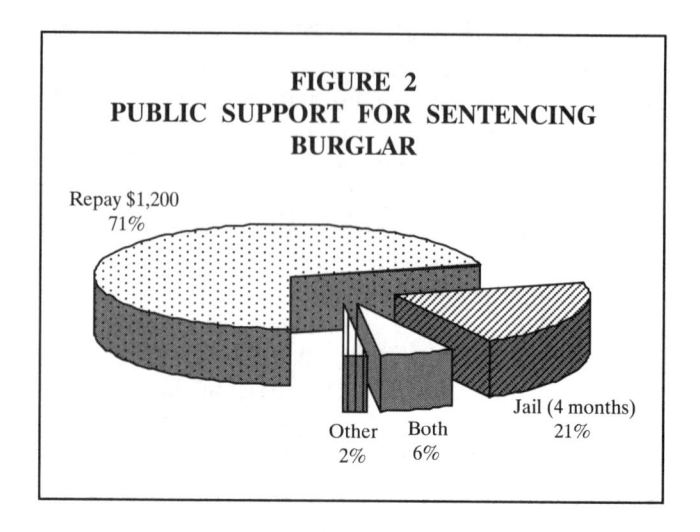

"The burglar has one previous conviction for a similar offense. In addition to 4 years on probation, would you prefer the sentence include repayment of $1,200 to you or 4 months in jail?" Nearly three of four Minnesotans indicated that having the offender pay restitution was more important than a jail sentence, as indicated in Figure 2.

To examine public support for policies that address some of the underlying social problems that often cause crime, a concern that is closely related to restorative justice, the following question was asked: "For the greatest impact on reducing crime, should additional money be spent on more prisons, or spent on education, job training and community programs?" Spending on education, job training and community programs rather than on prisons to reduce crime was favored by four of five Minnesotans, as seen in Figure 3.

The third and final question related to restorative justice addressed the issue of interest in victim-offender mediation. This question was presented in the following manner: "Minnesota has several programs which allow crime victims to meet with the person who committed the crime, in the presence of a trained mediator, to let this person know how the crime affected them, and to work out a plan for repayment of losses. Suppose you were the victim of a non-violent property crime committed by a juvenile or young adult. How likely would you be to participate in a program like this?"

More than four of five Minnesotans expressed an interest in participating in a face-to-face media-

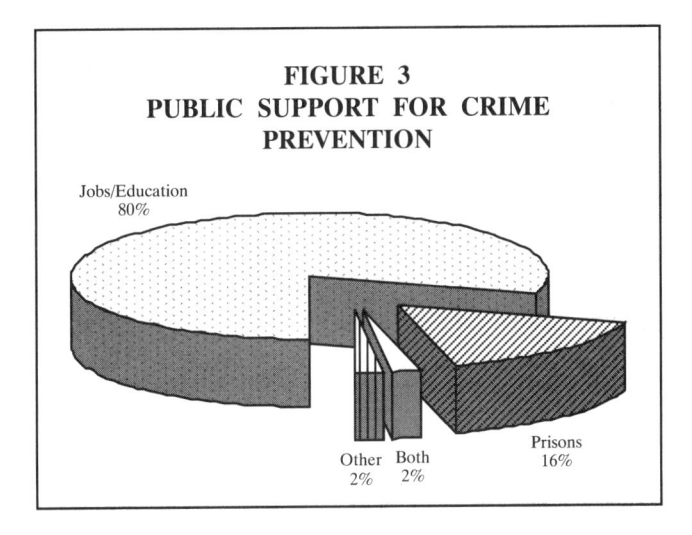

(vii) Restorative Justice and Mediation: Is the Public Interested?

**FIGURE 3
PUBLIC SUPPORT FOR CRIME PREVENTION**

- Jobs/Education 80%
- Other 2%
- Both 2%
- Prisons 16%

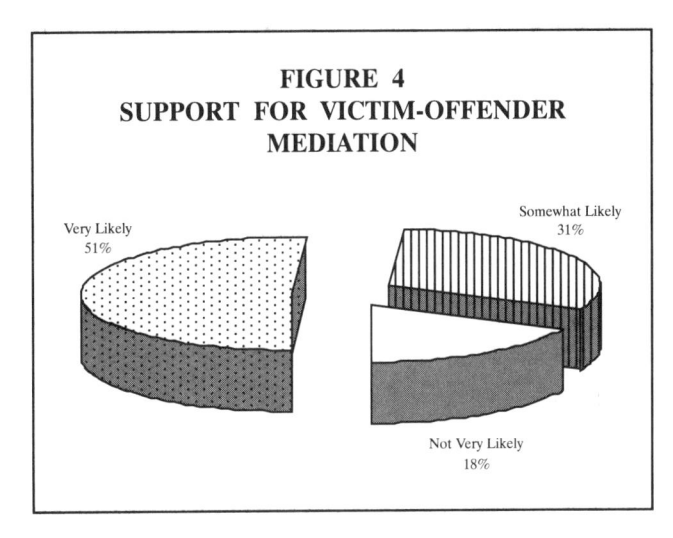

**FIGURE 4
SUPPORT FOR VICTIM-OFFENDER MEDIATION**

- Very Likely 51%
- Somewhat Likely 31%
- Not Very Likely 18%

tion session with the offender. This finding is particularly significant in that criminal justice officials and program staff who are unfamiliar with mediation often make such comments as "there is no way in the world that victims in my community would ever want to confront the offender," or "only a small portion of victims would ever be interested." The finding is particularly important since the vast majority of crime is committed by either juveniles or young adults. Some would suggest that the victim-offender mediation process is likely to be supported only for crimes involving juvenile offenders. This is certainly not the case in Minnesota. As noted in Figure 4, 82% of respondents indicated they would be likely to participate in a program that would allow them to meet the juvenile or young adult who victimized them.

A picture of a far less vindictive public than often portrayed emerges from this statewide survey. Respondents indicated greater concern for restitution and prevention strategies that address underlying issues of social injustice than for costly retribution. Holding offenders personally accountable to their victim is more important than incarceration in a jail. Public safety is understood to be more directly related to investing in job training, education and other community programs than incarceration.

While it might be tempting to suggest that this public opinion survey simply reflects the rather unique liberal social policy tradition of Minnesota, its findings are consistent with a growing body of public opinion research across the U.S. (Bae, 1991; Gottfredson, Warner and Taylor, 1988; Clark, 1985; Public Agenda Foundation, 1987, 1989, 1991; Public Opinion Research, 1986). These previous studies have found broad public support for payment of restitution by the offender to their victim instead of incarceration for property crimes, and support for crime prevention strategies instead of prison strategies to control crime. The studies did not explicitly ask respondents if they supported "restorative justice." The questions asked, however, addressed important underlying principles that are fundamental to the theory of restorative justice, which places far more value on crime prevention and restoration of physical and emotional losses than on retribution and blame for past behavior.

6 Law, Economy and Society

A. Formal Legal Regulation

(i) Max Weber on Law and the Rise of Capitalism

David M. Trubek

III. LEGALISM AND CAPITALISM: A RECONSTRUCTION OF WEBER'S THEORY OF LAW IN ECONOMIC LIFE

We now have most of the elements needed to understand Weber's theory of the relationship between the rise of modern law and capitalism. We have examined his legal sociology, which identifies distinctive types of legal systems, and his political sociology, which shows that the structure of power determines to some degree the type of legal order that can exist. We have seen why Weber thought legalism developed in Europe. Now we must turn to his economic sociology, in which the dynamics of the market are developed. This analysis will show why capitalism and legalism are intimately related.

In his economic sociology, Weber stressed the importance for capitalist development of two aspects of law: (1) its relative degree of *calculability*, and (2) its capacity to develop *substantive* provisions — principally those relating to freedom of contract — necessary to the functioning of the market system.

The former reason was the more important of the two. Weber asserted that capitalism required a highly calculable normative order. His survey of types of law indicated that only modern, rational law, or logically formal rationality, could provide the necessary calculability. Legalism supported the development of capitalism by providing a stable and predictable atmosphere; capitalism encouraged legalism because the bourgeoisie were aware of their own need for this type of governmental structure.

Legalism is the only way to provide the degree of certainty necessary for the operation of the capitalist system. Weber stated that capitalism "could not continue if its control of resources were not upheld by the legal compulsion of the state; if its formally 'legal' rights were not upheld by the threat of force." He further specified that: "[T]he rationalization and systematization of the law in general and ... the increasing calculability of the functioning of the legal process in particular, constituted one of the most important conditions for the existence of ... capitalistic enterprise, which cannot do without legal security."

Weber never worked out in detail a model of capitalist production which might explain why legal calculability was so important to capitalist development. I have developed such a model, and I believe that underlying Weber's repeated emphasis on legal calculability is a vision similar to this latter-day ideal type.

The essence of the model is the conflict of egoistic wills, which is an inherent part of competitive capitalism. In pure market capitalism of the type

---

(1972) Wisconsin L. Rev. 720 at 739–45, 748–50. Notes Omitted. Copyright 1972 by The Board of Regents of the University of Wisconsin System. Notes omitted. Reproduced by permission of the author and the Wisconsin Law Review.

idealized in micro-economics texts, each participant is driven to further his own interests at the expense of all other participants in the market. Theoretically, the profit motive is insatiable, and is unconstrained by any ethical or moral force. Thus, each actor is unconcerned with the ramifications of his actions on the economic well-being of others.

At the same time, however, economic actors in this system are necessarily interdependent. No market participant can achieve his goals unless he secures power over the actions of others. It does little good, for example, for the owner of a textile plant to act egocentrically to further his interests if at the same time he cannot be sure that other actors will supply him with the necessary inputs for production and consume his product. If suppliers do not provide promised raw materials, if workers refuse to work, if customers fail to pay for goods delivered, all the ruthless, rational self-interest in the world will be of little value to the textile producer in his striving for profits.

Now if all the other actors were nice, cooperative fellows, our textile manufacturer might not have to worry. Others would play their roles in the scheme and he would come out all right. But this may not always happen because they are, by hypothesis, as selfish as he is. Thus, they, too, will do whatever leads to the highest profit; if this means failing to perform some agreement, so be it. And since one can assume that there will frequently be opportunities for other actors to better themselves at the expense of providing him with some service or product necessary to the success of his enterprise, our hypothetical businessman lives in a world of radical uncertainty.

Yet, as Weber constantly stressed, uncertainty of this type is seriously prejudicial to the smooth functioning of the modern economy. How can the capitalist economic actor in a world of similarly selfish profitseekers reduce the uncertainty that threatens to rob the capitalist system of its otherwise great productive power? What will permit the economic actor to predict with relative certainty how other actors will behave over time? What controls the tendency toward instability?

In order to answer these questions, Weber moved to the level of sociological analysis. The problem of the conflict between the self-interest of individuals and social stability—what Parsons calls "the Hobbesian problem of order"—is one of the fundamental problems of sociology, and, to deal with it, Weber constructed his basic schemes of social action. Weber recognized that predictable uniformities of social action can be "guaranteed" in various ways and that all of these methods of social control may influence economic activities. Actors may internalize normative standards, thus fulfilling social expectations "voluntarily." Or they may be subjected to some form of "external effect" if they deviate from expectations. These external guarantees may derive from some informal sanctioning system or may involve organized coercion. Law is one form of organized coercion. All types of control may be involved in guaranteeing stable power over economic resources; factual control of this type, Weber observed, may be due to custom, to the play of interests, to convention, or to law.

As I have indicated, however, Weber believed that the organized coercion of *law* was necessary in modern, capitalist economies. While internalization and conventional sanctions may be able to eliminate or resolve most conflict in simpler societies, it is incapable of serving this function in a way that satisfies the needs of the modern exchange economy. For this function, law, in the sense of organized coercion, was necessary. Weber stated:

> [T]hough it is not necessarily true of every economic system, certainly the modern economic order under modern conditions could not continue if its control of resources were not upheld by the legal compulsion of the state; that is, if its formally "legal" rights were not upheld by the threat of force.

Why is coercion necessary in a market system? And why must this coercion take legal form? Finally, when we speak of *legal* coercion, do we mean state power, regardless of how it is exercised, or do we mean power governed by rules, or legalism? Weber gives no clear-cut answer to these questions. The discussion suggests answers but the issues are not fully developed. And the most crucial question, the interrelationship between the need for coercion and the model of legalism, is barely discussed at all. However, I think answers to the questions can be given which fit coherently with other aspects of his analysis.

Coercion is necessary because of the egoistic conflict I have identified above. While Weber never clearly identified this conflict, he himself was aware of it. Some principle of behavior other than short term self-interest is necessary for a market system. Tradition cannot function to constrain egoistic behavior because the market destroys the social and cultural bases of tradition. Similarly, the emerging market economy erodes the social groupings which could serve as the foci for enforcement of conventional standards. Indeed, the fact that the type of conflict I have described comes into existence is evidence of the decline of tradition and custom. Only law is left to fill the normative vacuum; legal coercion is essential because no other form is available.

A second reason why the necessary coercion must be legal is tied to the pace of economic activity and the type of rationalistic calculation characteristic of the market economy. It is not enough for the capitalist to have a general idea that someone else will more likely than not deliver more or less the performance agreed upon on or about the time stipulated. He must know exactly what and when, and he must be highly certain that the precise performance will be forthcoming. He wants to be able to predict with certainty that the other units will perform. But given the potential conflict between their self-interests and their obligations, he also wants to predict with certainty that coercion will be applied to the recalcitrant. The predictability of performance is intimately linked to the certainty that coercive instruments can be invoked in the event of nonperformance.

In this context, it becomes clear why a calculable legal system offers the most reliable way to combine coercion and predictability. Here the model of legalism and the model of capitalist dynamics merge. A system of government through rules seems inherently more predictable than any other method for structuring coercion. Convention is inherently too diffuse, and, like custom, was historically unavailable given the market-driven erosion of the groups and structures necessary for effective constraint of egoism. Like Balzac, Weber saw how the decline of family, guild, and Church unleashed unbridled egoism. Pure *power*, on the other hand, is available in the sense that the state is increasingly armed with coercive instruments. But untrammeled power is unpredictable; wielders of power, unconstrained by rules, will tend not to act in stable and predictable ways. Legalism offers the optimum combination of coercion and predictability.

It is here that the significance of legal autonomy can be seen. Autonomy is intimately linked to the problem of predictability. The autonomous legal system in a legalistic society is an institutional complex organized to apply coercion only in accordance with general rules through logical or purely cognitive processes. To the extent that it truly functions in the purely logical and, consequently, mechanical manner Weber presented, its results will be highly predictable. If it is constantly subject to interference by forces which seek to apply coercion for purposes inconsistent with the rules, it loses its predictable quality. Thus Weber observed that authoritarian rulers (and democratic despots) may refuse to be bound by formal rules since:

> They are all confronted by the inevitable conflict between an abstract formalism of legal certainty and their desire to realize substantive goals. Juridical formalism enables the legal system to operate like a technically rational machine. Thus it guarantees to individuals and groups within the system a relative maximum of freedom, and greatly increases for them the possibility of predicting the legal consequences of their actions.

Of course, the idea of legal autonomy is a much more complex one than this simplified model suggests. In Weber's work, the emergence of the autonomous legal order is correlated with other important phenomena. An autonomous legal order was essential if certain norms of a certain type were to emerge. Neither theocratic nor patrimonial rulers would allow the development of the substantive norms of economic autonomy contained in the idea of freedom of contract. Only an independent structure of normative order could guarantee these, and only a universal and supreme structure could guarantee that these norms would be adhered to. Thus the legal system had to be autonomous of other sources of normative order on the one hand, and of pure power on the other, and simultaneously control the adverse effects of both for capitalism. At least some areas of social life had to be freed of the bonds of kinship, religion, and other foci of traditional authority, and, at the same time, insulated from the arbitrary action of the state. This required that the state, as legal order, be strengthened, so that it superseded other sources of social control, and at the same time be limited, so that it did not encroach upon areas of economic action. The state was to provide a formal order, or facilitative framework within which free economic actors could operate. Contained in the idea of an autonomous legal order are fundamental paradoxes of the 19th-century idea of the liberal state.

. . . .

V. LEGALISM AND THE LEGITIMIZATION OF CLASS DOMINATION

Up to this point, "capitalism" has been presented as a vague abstraction. While Weber thought that capitalism was in some ways the most rational possible economic system, he was no apologist for it. He could be scathingly critical of the moral effects of this system. These criticisms can be seen in several points; they emerge clearly in another part of the sociology of law where Weber takes up an issue raised by Marx: the role of legalism in legitimizing capitalist domination.

Legalism served more than purely economic functions under capitalism. Weber showed how the idea of an autonomous legal system dispensing formal justice legitimizes the political structure of capitalist society.

Legalism legitimizes the domination of workers by capitalists. The relationships between law, the state, and the market are complex. Legalism, while seeming to constrain the state, really strengthens it, and while the system guaranteed formal equality, it also legitimized class domination. Legalism strengthens the state by apparently constraining it, for the commitment to a system of rules increases the legitimacy of the modern state and thus its authority or effective power. And as the liberal state grows stronger, it reduces the hold of other forces on the development of the market. This strengthens the position of those who control property, since market organization increases the effective power of those individuals and organizations that control economic resources. "[B]y virtue of the principle of formal legal equality ... the propertied classes ... obtain a sort of factual 'autonomy'...," Weber observed.

He believed that these effects of legalism stem from the fundamental antinomy between formal and material criteria of justice, and the negative aspects of purely formal administration of justice under modern conditions. Formal justice is advantageous to those with economic power; not only is it calculable but, by stressing formal as opposed to substantive criteria for decisionmaking, it discourages the use of the law as an instrument of social justice. In a passage reminiscent of Anatole France's famous quip that the law forbids both rich and poor to sleep under the bridges of Paris, Weber observed:

> Formal justice guarantees the maximum freedom for the interested parties to represent their formal legal interests. But because of the unequal distribution of economic power, *which the system of formal justice legalizes*, this very freedom must time and again produce consequences which are contrary to ... religious ethics or ... political expediency.

Formal justice not only is repugnant to authoritarian powers and arbitrary rulers; it also is opposed to democratic interests. Formal justice, necessarily abstract, cannot consider the ethical issues raised by such interests; such abstention, however, reduces the possibility of realizing substantive policies advocated by popular groups. Thus, certain democratic values and types of social justice could only be achieved at the cost of sacrificing strict legalism. Weber also pointed out that formal legalism could stultify legal creativity, and that legal autonomy could lead to results opposed to both popular and capitalist values.

[Note: For a similar analysis of the legitimating role of law in capitalist society, see the article by Alan Hunt, "Law, State and Class Struggle," in Chapter 5, above.]

(ii) *Donoghue* v. *Stevenson*

The defendant was the manufacturer of a well-known brand of ginger-beer which was sold in opaque bottles. The plaintiff consumed part of a bottle of the defendant's ginger-beer in which she found the remains of a decomposed snail. The bottle had been purchased by the plaintiff's friend at a railway café.

The defendants denied liability on the basis that as a manufacturer it owed no duty of care to the plaintiff consumer.

[LORD ATKIN:]

The sole question for determination in this case is legal: Do the averments made by the pursuer in her pleading, if true, disclose a cause of action? I need not re-state the particular facts. The question is whether the manufacturer of an article of drink sold by him to a distributor in circumstances which prevent the distributor or the ultimate purchaser or consumer from discovering by inspection any defect

[1932] All E.R. 1 at 10–13, 20. (H.L.)

is under any legal duty to the ultimate purchaser or consumer to take reasonable care that the article is free from defect likely to cause injury to health. I do not think a more important problem has occupied your Lordships in your judicial capacity, important both because of its bearing on public health and because of the practical test which it applies to the system of law under which it arises. The case has to be determined in accordance with Scots law, but it has been a matter of agreement between the experienced counsel who argued this case, and it appears to be the basis of the judgments of the learned judges of the Court of Session, that for the purposes of determining this problem the laws of Scotland and the law of England are the same. I speak with little authority on this point, but my own research, such as it is, satisfies me that the principles of the law of Scotland on such a question as the present are identical with those of English law, and I discuss the issue on that footing. The law of both countries appears to be that in order to support an action for damages for negligence the complainant has to show that he has been injured by the breach of a duty owed to him in the circumstances by the defendant to take reasonable care to avoid such injury. In the present case we are not concerned with the breach of the duty; if a duty exists, that would be a question of fact which is sufficiently averred and for the present purposes must be assumed. We are solely concerned with the question whether as a matter of law in the circumstances alleged the defender owed any duty to the pursuer to take care.

It is remarkable how difficult it is to find in the English authorities statements of general application defining the relations between parties that give rise to the duty. The courts are concerned with the particular relations which come before them in actual litigation, and it is sufficient to say whether the duty exists in those circumstances. The result is that the courts have been engaged upon an elaborate classification of duties as they exist in respect of property, whether real or personal, with further divisions as to ownership, occupation or control, and distinctions based on the particular relations of the one side or the other, whether manufacturer, salesman or landlord, customer, tenant, stranger, and so on. In this way it can be ascertained at any time whether the law recognises a duty, but only where the case can be referred to some particular species which has been examined and classified. And yet the duty which is common to all the cases where liability is established must logically be based upon some element common to the cases where it is found to exist. To exist a complete logical definition of the general principle is probably to go beyond the function of the judge, for, the more general the definition, the more likely it is to omit essentials or introduce non-essentials. The attempt was made by Lord Esher in *Heaven v. Pender* in a definition to which I will later refer. As framed it was demonstrably too wide, though it appears to me, if properly limited, to be capable of affording valuable practical guide.

At present I content myself with pointing out that in English law there must be and is some general conception of relations giving rise to a duty of care, of which the particular cases found in the books are but instances. The liability for negligence, whether you style it such or treat it as in other systems as a species of "culpa," is no doubt based upon a general public sentiment of moral wrong-doing for which the offender must pay. But acts or omissions which any moral code would censure cannot in a practical world be treated so as to give a right to every person injured by them to demand relief. In this way rules of law arise which limit the range of complainants and the extent of their remedy. The rule that you are to love your neighbour becomes in law: You must not injure your neighbour, and the lawyers' question: Who is my neighbour? receives a restricted reply. You must take reasonable care to avoid acts or omissions which you can reasonably foresee would be likely to injure your neighbour. Who then, in law, is my neighbour? The answer seems to be persons who are so closely and directly affected by my act that I ought reasonably to have them in contemplation as being so affected when I am directing my mind to the acts or omissions which are called in question. This appears to me to be the doctrine of *Heaven v. Pender* as laid down by Lord Esher when it is limited by the notion of proximity introduced by Lord Esher himself and A.L. Smith, L.J., in *Le Lievre and another v. Gould*. Lord Esher, M.R., says ([1893] 1 Q.B. at p. 497):

> That case established that, under certain circumstances, one man may owe a duty to another, even though there is no contract between them. If one man is near to another, or is near to the property of another, a duty lies upon him not to do that which may cause a personal injury to that other, or may injure his property.

So A.L. Smith, L.J., says ([1893] 1 Q.B. at p. 504):

> The decision of *Heaven v. Pender* was founded upon the principle that a duty to take due care did arise when the person or property of one was in such proximity to the person or property

of another that, if due care was not taken damage might be done by the one to the other.

I think that this sufficiently states the truth if proximity be not confined to mere physical proximity, but be used, as I think it was intended, to extend to such close and direct relations that the act complained of directly affects a person whom the person alleged to be bound to take care would know would be directly affected by his careless act. That this is the sense in which nearness or "proximity" was intended by Lord Esher is obvious from his own illustration in *Heaven* v. *Pender* (11 Q.B.D. at p. 510) of the application of his doctrine to the sale of goods.

> This [*i.e.*, the rule he has just formulated] includes the case of goods, [etc.], supplied to be used immediately by a particular person or persons, or one of a class of persons, where it would be obvious to the person supplying, if he thought, that the goods would in all probability be used at once by such persons before a reasonable opportunity for discovering any defect which might exist, and where the thing supplied would be of such a nature that a neglect of ordinary care or skill as to its condition or the manner of supplying it would probably cause danger to the person or property of the person for whose use it was supplied, and who was about to use it. It would exclude a case in which the goods are supplied under circumstances in which it would be a chance by whom they would be used, or whether they would be used or not, or whether they would be used before there would probably be means of observing any defect, or where the goods would be of such a nature that a want of care or skill as to their condition or the manner of supplying them would not probably produce danger of injury to person or property.

I draw particular attention to the fact that Lord Esher emphasises the necessity of goods having to be "used immediately" and "used at once before a reasonable opportunity of inspection." This is obviously to exclude the possibility of goods having their condition altered by lapse of time, and to call attention to the proximate relationship, which may be too remote where inspection even by the person using, certainly by an intermediate person, may reasonably be interposed. With this necessary qualification of proximate relationship, as explained in *Le Lievre* v. *Gould*, I think the judgment of Lord Esher expresses the law of England. Without the qualification, I think that the majority of the court in *Heaven* v. *Pender* was justified in thinking that the principle was expressed in too general terms. There will, no doubt, arise cases where it will be difficult to determine whether the contemplated relationship is so close that the duty arises. But in the class of case now before the court I cannot conceive any difficulty to arise. A manufacturer puts up an article of food in a container which he knows will be opened by the actual consumer. There can be no inspection by any purchaser and no reasonable preliminary inspection by the consumer. Negligently in the course of preparation he allows the contents to be mixed with poison. It is said that the law of England and Scotland is that the poisoned consumer has no remedy against the negligent manufacturer. If this were the result of the authorities, I should consider the result a grave defect in the law and so contrary to principle that I should hesitate long before following any decision to that effect which had not the authority of this House. I would point out that in the assumed state of the authorities not only would the consumer have no remedy against the manufacturer, he would have none against anyone else, for in the circumstances alleged there would be no evidence of negligence against anyone other than the manufacturer, and except in the case of a consumer who was also a purchaser no contract and no warranty of fitness, and in the case of the purchase of a specific article under its patent or trade name, which might well be the case in the purchase of some articles of food or drink, no warranty protecting even the purchaser-consumer. There are other instances than of articles of food and drink where goods are sold intended to be used immediately by the consumer, such as many forms of goods sold for cleaning purposes, when the same liability must exist. The doctrine supported by the decision below would not only deny a remedy to the consumer who was injured by consuming bottled beer or chocolates poisoned by the negligence of the manufacturer, but also to the user of what should be a harmless proprietary medicine, an ointment, a soap, a cleaning fluid or cleaning powder. I confine myself to articles of common household use, where everyone, including the manufacturer, knows that the articles will be used by persons other than the actual ultimate purchaser — namely, by members of his family and his servants, and, in some cases, his guests. I do not think so ill of our jurisprudence as to suppose that its principles are so remote from the ordinary needs of civilized society and the ordinary claims which it makes upon its members as to deny a legal remedy where there is so obviously a social wrong.

. . . .

(iii) Lloyds Bank Ltd. v. Bundy

[LORD DENNING M.R.:]

Broadchalke is one of the most pleasing villages in England. Old Herbert Bundy was a farmer there. His home was at Yew Tree Farm. It went back for 300 years. His family had been there for generations. It was his only asset. But he did a very foolish thing. He mortgaged it to the bank. Up to the very hilt. Not to borrow money for himself, but for the sake of his son. Now the bank have come down on him. They have foreclosed. They want to get him out of Yew Tree Farm and to sell it. They have brought this action against him for possession. Going out means ruin for him. He was granted legal aid. His lawyers put in a defence. They said that when he executed the charge to the bank he did not know what he was doing; or at any rate the circumstances were such that he ought not to be bound by it. At the trial his plight was plain. The judge was sorry for him. He said he was a 'poor old gentleman'. He was so obviously incapacitated that the judge admitted his proof in evidence. He had a heart attack in the witness box. Yet the judge felt he could do nothing for him. There is nothing, he said, 'which takes this out of the vast range of commercial transactions'. He ordered Herbert Bundy to give up possession of Yew Tree Farm to the bank.

Now there is an appeal to this court. The ground is that the circumstances were so exceptional that Herbert Bundy should not be held bound.

THE EVENTS BEFORE DECEMBER 1969

Herbert Bundy had only one son, Michael Bundy. He had great faith in him. They were both customers of Lloyds Bank at the Salisbury branch. They had been customers for many years. The son formed a company called MJB Plant Hire Ltd. It hired out earth-moving machinery and so forth. The company banked at Lloyds too at the same branch.

In 1961 the son's company was in difficulties. The father on 19th September 1966 guaranteed the company's overdraft for £1,500 and charged Yew Tree Farm to the bank to secure the £1,500. Afterwards the son's company got further into difficulties. The overdraft ran into thousands. In May 1967 the assistant bank manager, Mr. Bennett, told the son the bank must have further security. The son said his father would give it. So Mr. Bennett and the son went together to see the father. Mr. Bennett produced the papers. He suggested that the father should sign a further guarantee for £5,000 and to execute a further charge for £6,000. The farther said that he would help his son as far as he possibly could. Mr. Bennett did not ask the father to sign the papers there and then. He left them with the father so that he could consider them overnight and take advice on them. The father showed them to his solicitor, Mr. Trethowan, who lived in the same village. The solicitor told the father the £5,000 was the utmost that he could sink in his son's affairs. The house was worth about £10,000 and this was half his

---

[1974] 3 All E.R. 757 (C.A.) at 761–67.

assets. On that advice the father on 27th May 1969 did execute the further guarantee and the charge, and Mr. Bennett witnessed it. So at the end of May 1967 the father had charged the house to secure £7,500.

THE EVENTS OF DECEMBER 1969

During the next six months the affairs of the son and his company went from bad to worse. The bank had granted the son's company an overdraft up to a limit of £10,000, but this was not enough to meet the outgoings. The son's company drew cheques which the bank returned unpaid. The bank were anxious. By this time Mr. Bennett had left to go to another branch. He was succeeded by a new assistant manager, Mr. Head. In November 1969 Mr. Head saw the son and told him that the account was unsatisfactory and that he considered that the company might have to cease operations. The son suggested that the difficulty was only temporary and that his father would be prepared to provide further money if necessary.

On 17th December 1969 there came the occasion which, in the judge's words, was important and disastrous for the father. The son took Mr. Head to see his father. Mr. Head had never met the father before. This was his first visit. He went prepared. He took with him a form of guarantee and a form of charge filled in with the father's name ready for signature. There was a family gathering. The father and mother were there. The son and the son's wife. Mr. Head said that the bank had given serious thought whether they could continue to support the son's company. But that the bank were prepared to do so in this way. (i) The bank would continue to allow the company to draw money on overdraft up to the existing level of £10,000, but the bank would require the company to pay ten per cent of its incomings into a separate account. So that ten per cent would not go to reduce the overdraft. Mr. Head said that this would have the effect 'of reducing the level of borrowing'. In other words, the bank was cutting down the overdraft. (ii) The bank would require the father to give a guarantee of the company's account in a sum of £11,000 and to give the bank a further charge on the house of £3,500, so as to bring the total charge to £11,000. The house was only worth about £10,000, so this charge for £11,000 would sweep up all that the father had.

On hearing the proposal, the father said that Michael was his only son and that he was 100 per cent behind him. Mr. Head produced the forms that had already been filled in. The father signed them and Mr. Head witnessed them there and then. On this occasion, Mr. Head, unlike Mr. Bennett, did not leave the forms with the father; nor did the father have any independent advice.

It is important to notice the state of mind of Mr. Head and of the father. Mr. Head said in evidence:

> [The father] asked me what in my opinion Company was doing wrong and Company's position. I told him. I did not explain Company's accounts very fully as I had only just taken over.... [The son] said Company had a number of bad debts. I wasn't entirely satisfied with this. I thought the trouble was more deep-seated.... I thought there was no conflict of interest. I would think the [father] relied on me implicitly to advise him about the transaction as Bank Manager.... I knew he had no other assets except Yew Tree Cottage.

The father said in evidence:

> Always thought Mr. Head was genuine. I have always trusted him.... No discussion how business was doing that I can remember. I simply sat back and did what they said.

The solicitor, Mr. Trethowan, said of the father:

> [The father] is straightforward. Agrees with anyone.... Doubt if he understood all that Mr. Head explained to him.

So the father signed the papers. Mr. Head witnessed them and took them away. The father had charged the whole of his remaining asset, leaving himself with nothing. The son and his company gained a respite. But only for a short time. Five months later, in May 1970, a receiving order was made against the son. Thereupon the bank stopped all overdraft facilities for the company. It ceased to trade. The father's solicitor, Mr. Trethowan, at once went to see Mr. Head. He said he was concerned that the father had signed the guarantee.

In due course the bank insisted on the sale of the house. In December 1971 they agreed to sell it for £7,500 with vacant possession. The family were very disappointed with this figure. It was, they said, worth much more. Estate agents were called to say so. But the judge held that it was a valid sale and that the bank can take all the proceeds. The sale has not been completed, because the father is still in possession. The bank have brought these proceedings to evict the father.

(iii) Lloyds Bank Ltd. v. Bundy

THE GENERAL RULE

Now let me say at once that in the vast majority of cases a customer who signs a bank guarantee or a charge cannot get out of it. No bargain will be upset which is the result of the ordinary interplay of forces. There are many hard cases which are caught by this rule. Take the case of a poor man who is homeless. He agrees to pay a high rent to a landlord just to get a roof over his head. The common law will not interfere. It is left to Parliament. Next take the case of a borrower in urgent need of money. He borrows it from the bank at high interest and it is guaranteed by a friend. The guarantor gives his bond and gets nothing in return. The common law will not interfere. Parliament has intervened to prevent moneylenders charging excessive interest. But it has never interfered with banks.

Yet there are exceptions to this general rule. There are cases in our books in which the courts will set aside a contract, or a transfer of property, when the parties have not met on equal terms, when the one is so strong in bargaining power and the other so weak that, as a matter of common fairness, it is not right that the strong should be allowed to push the weak to the wall. Hitherto those exceptional cases have been treated each as a separate category in itself. But I think the time has come when we should seek to find a principle to unite them. I put on one side contracts or transactions which are voidable for fraud or misrepresentation or mistake. All those are governed by settled principles. I go only to those where there has been inequality of bargaining power, such as to merit the intervention of the court.

THE CATEGORIES

The first category is that of 'duress of goods'. A typical case is when a man is in a strong bargaining position by being in possession of the goods of another by virtue of a legal right, such as, by way of pawn or pledge or taken in distress. The owner is in a weak position because he is in urgent need of the goods. The stronger demands of the weaker more than is justly due, and he pays it in order to get the goods. Such a transaction is voidable. He can recover the excess: see *Astley v. Reynolds* and *Green v. Duckett*. To which may be added the cases of 'colore officii', where a man is in a strong bargaining position by virtue of his official position or public profession. He relies on it so as to gain from the weaker — who is urgently in need — more than is justly due: see *Pigot's Case* cited by Lord Kenyon C.J.; *Parker v. Bristol and Exeter Railway Co.* and *Steele v. Williams*. In such cases the stronger may make his claim in good faith honestly believing that he is entitled to make his demand. He may not be guilty of any fraud or misrepresentation. The inequality of bargaining power — the strength of the one versus the urgent need of the other — renders the transaction voidable and the money paid to be recovered back: see *Maskell v. Horner*.

The second category is that of the 'unconscionable transaction'. A man is so placed as to be in need of special care and protection and yet his weakness is exploited by another far stronger than himself so as to get his property at a gross undervalue. The typical case is that of the 'expectant heir'. But it applies to all cases where a man comes into property, or is expected to come into it, and then being in urgent need another gives him ready cash for it, greatly below its true worth, and so gets the property transferred to him: see *Evans v. Llewellin*. Even though there be no evidence of fraud or misrepresentation, nevertheless the transaction will be set side: see *Fry v. Lane* where Kay J. said:

> The result of the decisions is that where a purchase is made from a poor and ignorant man at a considerable undervalue, the vendor having no independent advice, a Court of Equity will set aside the transaction.

This second category is said to extend to all cases where an unfair advantage has been gained by an unconscientious use of power by a stronger party against a weaker: see the cases cited in Halsbury's Law of England and in Canada, *Morrison v. Coast Finance Ltd.* and *Knupp v. Bell*.

The third category is that of 'undue influence' usually so called. These are divided into two classes as stated by Cotton L.J. in *Allcard v. Skinner*. The first are these where the stronger has been guilty of some fraud or wrongful act — expressly so as to gain some gift or advantage from the weaker. The second are those where the stronger has not been guilty of any wrongful act, but has, through the relationship which existed between him and the weaker, gained some gift or advantage for himself. Sometimes the relationship is such as to raise a presumption of undue influence, such as parent over child, solicitor over client, doctor over patient, spiritual adviser over follower. At other times a relationship of confidence must be proved to exist. But to all of them the general principle obtains which was stated by Lord Chelmsford L.C. in *Tate v. Williamson*:

> Wherever the persons stand in such a relation that, while it continues, confidence is necessarily

reposed by one, and the influence which naturally grows out of that confidence is possessed by the other, and this confidence is abused, or the influence is exerted to obtain an advantage at the expense of the confiding party, the person so availing himself of his position will not be permitted to retain the advantage, although the transaction could not have been impeached if no such confidential relation had existed.

Such a case was *Tufton v. Sperni*.

The fourth category is that of 'undue pressure'. The most apposite of that is *Williams v. Bayley* where a son forged his father's name to a promissory note, and, by means of it, raised money from the bank of which they were both customers. The bank said to the father, in effect: 'Take your choice — give us security for your son's debt. If you do take that on yourself, then it will all go smoothly; if you do not, we shall be bound to exercise pressure.' Thereupon the father charged his property to the bank with payment of the note. The House of Lords held that the charge was invalid because of undue pressure exerted by the bank. Lord Westbury said:

> A contract to give security for the debt of another, which is a contract without consideration, is, above all things, a contract that should be based upon the free and voluntary agency of the individual who enters into it.

Other instances of undue pressure are where one party stipulates for an unfair advantage to which the other has no option but to submit. As where an employer — the stronger party — had employed a builder — the weaker party — to do work for him. When the builder asked for payment of sums properly due (so as to pay his workmen) the employer refused to pay unless he was given some added advantage. Stuart V-C said:

> Where an agreement, hard and inequitable in itself, has been exacted under circumstances of pressure on the part of the person who exacts it this Court will set it aside

see *Ormes v. Beadel*; *D & C Builders Ltd. v. Rees*.

The fifth category is that of salvage agreements. When a vessel is in danger of sinking and seeks help, the rescuer is in a strong bargaining position. The vessel in distress is in urgent need. The parties cannot be truly said to be on equal terms. The Court of Admiralty have always recognised that fact. The fundamental rule is:

> If the parties have made an agreement, the Court will enforce it, unless it be manifestly unfair and unjust; but if it be manifestly unfair and unjust, the Court will disregard it and decree what is fair and just.

See *Akerblom v. Price*, per Brett L.J. applied in a striking case, *The Port Caledonia and The Anna*, when the rescuer refused to help with a rope unless he was paid £1,000.

THE GENERAL PRINCIPLES

Gathering all together, I would suggest that through all these instances there runs a single thread. They rest on 'inequality of bargaining power'. By virtue of it, the English law gives relief to one who, without independent advice, enters into a contract of terms which are very unfair or transfers property for a consideration which is grossly inadequate, when his bargaining power is grievously impaired by reason of his own needs or desires, or by his own ignorance or infirmity, coupled with undue influences or pressures brought to bear on him by or for the benefit of the other. When I use the word 'undue' I do not mean to suggest that the principle depends on proof of any wrongdoing. The one who stipulates for an unfair advantage may be moved solely by his own self-interest, unconscious of the distress he is bringing to the other. I have also avoided any reference to the will of the one being 'dominated' or 'overcome' by the other. One who is in extreme need may knowingly consent to a most improvident bargain, solely to relieve the straits in which he finds himself. Again, I do not mean to suggest that every transaction is saved by independent advice. But the absence of it may be fatal. With these explanations, I hope this principle will be found to reconcile the cases. Applying it to the present case, I would notice these points.

1. The consideration moving from the bank was grossly inadequate. The son's company was in serious difficulty. The overdraft was at its limit of £10,000. The bank considered that their existing security was insufficient. In order to get further security, they asked the father to charge the house — his sole asset — to the uttermost. It was worth £10,000. The charge was for £11,000. That was for the benefit of the bank. But not at all for the benefit of the father, or indeed for the company. The bank did not promise to continue the overdraft or to increase it. On the contrary, they required the overdraft to be reduced. All that the company gained was a short respite from impending doom.
2. The relationship between the bank and the father was one of trust and confidence. The bank knew that the father relied on them

implicitly to advise him about the transaction. The father trusted the bank. This gave the bank much influence on the father. Yet the bank failed in that trust. They allowed the father to charge the house to his ruin.

3. The relationship between the father and the son was one where the father's natural affection had much influence on him.
4. He would naturally desire to accede to his son's request. He trusted his son. There was a conflict of interest between the bank and the father. Yet the bank did not realise it. Nor did they suggest that the father should get independent advice. If the father had gone to his solicitor — or to any man of business — there is no doubt that any of them would say: 'You must not enter into this transaction. You are giving up your house, your sole remaining asset, for no benefit to you. The company is in such a parlous state that you must not do it.'

These considerations seem to me to bring this case within the principles I have stated. But, in case that principle is wrong, I would also say that the case falls within the category of undue influence of the second class stated by Cotton L.J. in *Allcard v. Skinner*. I have no doubt that the assistant bank manager acted in the utmost good faith and was straightforward and genuine. Indeed the father said so. But beyond doubt he was acting in the interests of the bank — to get further security for a bad debt. There was such a relationship of trust and confidence between them that the bank ought not to have swept up his sole remaining asset into their hands — for nothing — without his having independent advice. I would therefore allow this appeal.

(iv) Harvard Presses Claim for Patent on Mouse: Genetically engineered rodent designed to develop cancer easily

Tom Spears

Genetically engineered lifeforms are totally different from any bred the conventional way, a lawyer for Harvard University says — and that should let their makers get patents in Canada.

Harvard wants to patent a type of laboratory mouse, one genetically engineered to get cancer easily. It's used by cancer researchers.

A crucial point, though, is whether a live mouse counts as an invention, and as a manufactured item. It has to be both to have a patent in Canada.

Canada's Federal Court has denied the application and yesterday Harvard argued its appeal of that decision in the Federal Court of Appeal.

Harvard's lawyer, David Morrow, said the Harvard mouse is implicitly different from genetically engineered crops such as corn, soybeans and canola.

"The genetically engineered mouse that emerges ... is one that would not have emerged but for man's intervention," he said.

"Man took the gene. Man put it in the plasmid (a piece of DNA). Man put it there," he told the three appeals judges.

"That's a huge difference," he said, from conventionally bred mice.

"That is qualitatively different, in my respectful submission, from just using what nature has already put in the field ... That (engineered) mouse has in it artificially introduced genes not found in nature."

Genetic engineering of this kind, he said, is a very different process from "selective breeding" — crossing different strains of crops, pets or livestock to try to find new and better ones.

Canada allows patenting of single-cells bio-engineered to do an industrial job, such as chewing up pollutants.

But Canada has never allowed patents on more complex life forms.

Government lawyer Rick Woyiwada said the mouse shouldn't be patentable because it has many

---

From *The Ottawa Citizen* (10 December 1999) A8. Reproduced by permission of The Ottawa Citizen.

characteristics that aren't manmade. Colour, behaviour, instincts and a long list of other traits have nothing to do with what Harvard's scientists build in, he said.

While the Harvard mouse has one special gene, this "is a very fine distinction between that animal and others of its kind."

Harvard asked Canada for the mouse patent in 1985. The commissioner of patents turned down the application 10 years later, and it's been the subject of litigation since then.

The U.S. has granted Harvard's mouse a patent.

For the first time, an environmental law firm was able to join the arguments yesterday.

The Canadian Environmental Law Association says patenting of higher life forms, such as mammals, isn't the kind of "article or thing made by hand" that patents are meant to cover.

The association also warned that the world's biological diversity would be threatened if humans can have patents, and therefore control, of higher life forms. Canada, it says, is bound by international convention to uphold biological diversity.

"Patents on genetic makeup of crops and livestock [ ] further concentrate economic power in large agricultural businesses," which would be against the public interest, they argued.

(v) Regulability of the Cyberspace

Lawrence Lessig

GOVERNORS

A state — call it "Boral" — doesn't like gambling, even though some citizens like to gamble. But the state is the boss; the people have voted; the law is as it is. Gambling in the state of Boral is illegal.

Then comes the Internet. With the Net wired into their phones, some citizens of Boral decide that Internet gambling is the next "killer app." Someone sets up servers that provide access to online gambling. The state doesn't like this business; the businessmen are just illegal gamblers. Shut down your servers, the attorney general warns, or we will lock you up.

Wise even if dishonest, the gamblers agree to shut down their servers in the state of Boral. But they don't exit the gambling business. Instead, they rent space on a server in an "offshore haven." This offshore web server hums away, once again making gambling available on the Net.

And just as available to people in Boral. For here's the important point: given the architecture of the Internet (at least as it was), it doesn't matter where in real space the server is set up. Access doesn't depend on geography. Nor, depending on how clever the gambling sorts are, does access require that the user know anything about who owns or runs the real server. The user's access can be passed through anonymizing sites that make it practically impossible in the end to know what went where.

The Boral attorney general faces a difficult problem. She may have moved the gamblers out of her state, but she hasn't succeeded in reducing gambling on the Net. She once would have had a group of people she could punish, but now she has made them essentially free from punishment. The world for this attorney general has changed. By going online, the gamblers moved into a world where behavior, so the argument goes, is no longer regulable.

Regulable. I am told there is no such word, though lawyers apparently do not know that fact. By "regulable" I mean simply that a certain behavior is capable of regulation. The term is comparative, not absolute — in some place, at some time, a certain behavior will be more regulable than at another place and in another time. My claim about Boral is simply that the Net makes gambling less regulable there than it was before the Net.

From *Code and Other Laws of Cyberspace* by Lawrence Lessig at 14, 19–20. Reproduced by permission of Basic Books, a member of Perseus Books, L.L.C.

Regulability

Regulability means the capacity of a government to regulate behavior within its proper reach. In the context of the Internet, that means the ability of the government to regulate the behavior of its citizens (and perhaps others as well) on the Net. My second story, about gambling in Boral, was thus about regulability, or more specifically, about the changes in regulability that cyberspace brings. Before the Internet, it was relatively easy for the attorney general of Boral to control gambling within her jurisdiction; after the Internet, when the servers moved outside of Boral, regulation became much more difficult.

For the regulator, this story captures the problem that cyberspace presents generally. The architecture of cyberspace makes regulating behavior difficult, because those whose behavior you're trying to control could be located in any place (meaning outside of your place) on the Net. Who someone is, where he is, and whether law can be exercised over him there — all these are questions that government must answer if it is to impose its will. But these questions are made impossibly difficult by the architecture of the space — at least as it was.

The balance of part 1 is about this question of regulability. I ask whether "unregulability" is necessary. Can we imagine a more regulable cyberspace? And is this the cyberspace we are coming to know?

B. Informal Modes of Regulation

(i) Non-Contractual Relationships in Business: A Preliminary Study

Stewart Macaulay

The Adjustment of Exchange Relationships and the Settling of Disputes

While a significant amount of creating business exchanges is done on a fairly noncontractual basis, the creation of exchanges usually is far more contractual than the adjustment of such relationships and the settlement of disputes. Exchanges are adjusted when the obligations of one or both parties are modified by agreement during the life of the relationship. For example, the buyer may be allowed to cancel all or part of the goods he has ordered because he no longer needs them; the seller may be paid more than the usual contract price by the buyer because of unusual changed circumstances. Dispute settlement involves determining whether or not a party has performed as agreed and, if he has not, doing something about it. For example, a court may have to interpret the meaning of a contract, determine what the alleged defaulting party has done and determine what, if any, remedy the aggrieved party is entitled to. Or one party may assert that the other is in default, refuse to proceed with performing the contract and refuse to deal ever again with the alleged defaulter. If the alleged defaulter, who in fact may not be in default, takes no action, the dispute is then "settled."

Business exchanges in non-speculative areas are usually adjusted without dispute. Under the law of contracts, if B orders 1,000 widgets from S at $1.00 each, B must take all 1,000 widgets or be in breach of contract and liable to pay S his expenses up to the time of the breach plus his lost anticipated

---

(1963) 28:1 American Sociological Review 55 at 60–67. Notes omitted.

profit. Yet all ten of the purchasing agents asked about cancellation of orders once placed indicated that they expected to be able to cancel orders freely subject to only an obligation to pay for the seller's major expenses such as scrapped steel. All 17 sales personnel asked reported that they often had to accept cancellation. One said, "You can't ask a man to eat paper [the firm's product] when he has no use for it." A lawyer with many large industrial clients said,

> Often businessmen do not feel they have "a contract"—rather they have "an order." They speak of "cancelling the order" rather than "breaching our contract." When I began practice I referred to order cancellations as breaches of contract, but my clients objected since they do not think of cancellation as wrong. Most clients, in heavy industry at least, believe that there is a right to cancel as part of the buyer-seller relationship. There is a widespread attitude that one can back out of any deal within some very vague limits. Lawyers are often surprised by this attitude.

Disputes are frequently settled without reference to the contract or potential or actual legal sanctions. There is a hesitancy to speak of legal rights or to threaten to sue in these negotiations. Even where the parties have a detailed and carefully planned agreement which indicates what is to happen if, say, the seller fails to deliver on time, often they will never refer to the agreement but will negotiate a solution when the problem arises apparently as if there had never been any original contract. One purchasing agent expressed a common business attitude when he said,

> if something comes up, you get the other man on the telephone and deal with the problem. You don't read legalistic contract clauses at each other if you ever want to do business again. One doesn't run to lawyers if he wants to stay in business because one must behave decently.

Or as one businessman put it, "You can settle any dispute if you keep the lawyers and accountants out of it. They just do not understand the give-and-take needed in business." All of the house counsel interviewed indicated that they are called into the dispute settlement process only after the businessmen have failed to settle matters in their own way. Two indicated that after being called in house counsel at first will only advise the purchasing agent, sales manager or other official involved; not even the house counsel's letterhead is used on communications with the other side until all hope for a peaceful resolution is gone.

Law suits for breach of contract appear to be rare. Only five of the 12 purchasing agents had ever been involved in even a negotiation concerning a contract dispute where both sides were represented by lawyers; only two of ten sales managers had ever gone this far. None had been involved in a case that went through trial. A law firm with more than 40 lawyers and a large commercial practice handles in a year only about six trials concerned with contract problems. Less than 10 per cent of the time of this office is devoted to any type of work related to contracts disputes. Corporations big enough to do business in more than one state tend to sue and be sued in the federal courts. Yet only 2,779 out of 58,293 civil actions filed in the United States District Courts in fiscal year 1961 involved private contracts. During the same period only 3,447 of the 61,138 civil cases filed in the principal trial courts of New York State involved private contracts. The same picture emerges from a review of appellate cases. Mentschikoff has suggested that commercial cases are not brought to the courts either in periods of business prosperity (because buyers unjustifiably reject goods only when prices drop and they can get similar goods elsewhere at less than the contract price) or in periods of deep depression (because people are unable to come to court or have insufficient assets to satisfy any judgment that might be obtained). Apparently, she adds, it is necessary to have "a kind of middle-sized depression" to bring large numbers of commercial cases to the courts. However, there is little evidence that in even "a kind of middle-sized depression" today's businessmen would use the courts to settle disputes.

At times relatively contractual methods are used to make adjustments in ongoing transactions and to settle disputes. Demands of one side which are deemed unreasonable by the other occasionally are blocked by reference to the terms of the agreement between the parties. The legal position of the parties can influence negotiations even though legal rights or litigation are never mentioned in their discussions; it makes a difference if one is demanding what both concede to be a right or begging for a favour. Now and then a firm may threaten to turn matters over to its attorneys, threaten to sue, commence a suit or even litigate and carry an appeal to the highest court which will hear the matter. Thus, legal sanctions, while not an everyday affair, are not unknown in business.

One can conclude that while detailed planning and legal sanctions play a significant role in some exchanges between businesses, in many business exchanges their role is small.

TENTATIVE EXPLANATIONS

Two questions need to be answered: (A) How can business successfully operate exchange relationships with relatively so little attention to detailed planning or to legal sanctions, and (B) Why does business ever use contract in light of its success without it?

Why Are Relatively Non-Contractual Practices So Common?

In most situations contract is not needed. Often its functions are served by other devices. Most problems are avoided without resort to detailed planning or legal sanctions because usually there is little room for honest misunderstandings or good faith differences of opinion about the nature and quality of a seller's performance. Although the parties fail to cover all foreseeable contingencies, they will exercise care to see that both understand the primary obligation on each side. Either products are standardized with an accepted description or specifications are written calling for production to certain tolerances or results. Those who write and read specifications are experienced professionals who will know the customs of their industry and those of the industries with which they deal. Consequently, these customs can fill gaps in the express agreements of the parties. Finally, most products can be tested to see if they are what was ordered; typically in the manufacturing industry we are not dealing with questions of taste or judgment where people can differ in good faith.

When defaults occur they are not likely to be disastrous because of techniques of risk avoidance or risk spreading. One can deal with firms of good reputation or he may be able to get some form of security to guarantee performance. One can insure against many breaches of contract where the risks justify the costs. Sellers set up reserves for bad debts on their books and can sell some of their accounts receivable. Buyers can place orders with two or more suppliers of the same item so that a default by one will not stop the buyer's assembly lines.

Moreover, contract and contract law are often thought unnecessary because there are many effective non-legal sanctions. Two norms are widely accepted. (1) Commitments are to be honored in almost all situations; one does not welsh on a deal. (2) One ought to produce a good product and stand behind it. Then, too, business units are organized to perform commitments, and internal sanctions will induce performance. For example, sales personnel must face angry customers when there has been a late or defective performance. The salesmen do not enjoy this and will put pressure on the production personnel responsible for the default. If the production personnel default too often, they will be fired. At all levels of the two business units personal relationships across the boundaries of the two organizations exert pressures for conformity to expectations. Salesmen often know purchasing agents well. The same two individuals occupying these roles may have dealt with each other from five to 25 years. Each has something to give the other. Salesmen have gossip about competitors, shortages and price increases to give purchasing agents who treat them well. Salesmen take purchasing agents to dinner, and they give purchasing agents Christmas gifts hoping to improve the chances of making a sale. The buyer's engineering staff may work with the seller's engineering staff to solve problems jointly. The seller's engineers may render great assistance, and the buyer's engineers may desire to return the favour by drafting specifications which only the seller can meet. The top executives of the two firms may know each other. They may sit together on government or trade committees. They may know each other socially and even belong to the same country club. The interrelationships may be more formal. Sellers may hold stock in corporations which are important customers; buyers may hold stock in important suppliers. Both buyer and seller may share common directors on their boards. They may share a common financial institution which has financed both units.

The final type of non-legal sanction is the most obvious. Both business units involved in the exchange desire to continue successfully in business and will avoid conduct which might interfere with attaining this goal. One is concerned with both the reaction of the other party in the particular exchange and with his own general business reputation. Obviously, the buyer gains sanctions insofar as the seller wants the particular exchange to be completed. Buyers can withhold part or all of their payments until sellers have performed to their satisfaction. If a seller has a great deal of money tied up in his performance which he must recover quickly, he will go a long way to please the buyer in order to be paid. Moreover, buyers who are dissatisfied may cancel and cause sellers to lose the cost of what they have done up to cancellation. Furthermore, sellers hope for repeats for orders, and one gets few of these from unhappy customers. Some industrial buyers go so far as to formalize this sanction by issuing "report cards" rating the performance of each supplier. The supplier rating goes to the top management of the seller organization, and these men can apply internal sanctions to salesmen, production supervisors or product designers if there are too many "D's" or "F's" on the report card.

While it is generally assumed that the customer is always right, the seller may have some counterbalancing sanctions against the buyer. The seller may have obtained a large downpayment from the buyer which he will want to protect. The seller may have an exclusive process which the buyer needs. The seller may be one of the few firms which has the skill to make the item to the tolerances set by the buyer's engineers and within the time available. There are costs and delays involved in turning from a supplier one has dealt with in the past to a new supplier. Then, too, market conditions can change so that a buyer is faced with shortages of critical items. The most extreme example is the post World War II gray market conditions when sellers were rationing goods rather than selling them. Buyers must build up some reserve of good will with suppliers if they face the risk of such shortage and desire good treatment when they occur. Finally, there is reciprocity in buying and selling. A buyer cannot push a supplier too far if that supplier also buys significant quantities of the product made by the buyer.

Not only do the particular business units in a given exchange want to deal with each other again, they also want to deal with other business units in the future. And the way one behaves in a particular transaction, or a series of transactions, will colour his general business reputation. Blacklisting can be formal or informal. Buyers who fail to pay their bills on time risk a bad report in credit rating services such as Dun and Bradstreet. Sellers who do not satisfy their customers become the subject of discussion in the gossip exchanged by purchasing agents and salesmen, at meetings of purchasing agents' associations and trade associations, or even at country clubs or social gatherings where members of top management meet. The American male's habit of debating the merits of new cars carries over to industrial items. Obviously, a poor reputation does not help a firm make sales and may force it to offer great price discounts or added services to remain in business. Furthermore, the habits of unusually demanding buyers become known, and they tend to get no more than they can coerce out of suppliers who choose to deal with them. Thus, often contract is not needed as there are alternatives.

Not only are contract and contract law not needed in many situations, their use may have, or may be thought to have, undesirable consequences. Detailed negotiated contracts can get in the way of creating good exchange relationships between business units. If one side insists on a detailed plan, there will be delay while letters are exchanged as the parties try to agree on what should happen if a remote and unlikely contingency occurs. In some cases they may not be able to agree at all on such matters and as a result a sale may be lost to the seller and the buyer may have to search elsewhere for an acceptable supplier. Many businessmen would react by thinking that, had no one raised the series of remote and unlikely contingencies, all this wasted effort could have been avoided.

Even where agreement can be reached at the negotiation stage, carefully planned arrangements may create undesirable exchange relationships between business units. Some businessmen object that in such a carefully worked out relationship one gets performance only to the letter of the contract. Such planning indicates a lack of trust and blunts the demands of friendship, turning a cooperative venture into an antagonistic horse trade. Yet the greater danger perceived by some businessmen is that one would have to perform his side of the bargain to its letter and thus lose what is called "flexibility." Businessmen may welcome a measure of vagueness in the obligations they assume so that they may negotiate matters in light of the actual circumstances.

Adjustment of exchange relationships and dispute settlement by litigation or the threat of it also has many costs. The gain anticipated from using this form of coercion often fails to outweigh these costs, which are both monetary and non-monetary. Threatening to turn matters over to an attorney may cost no more money than postage or a telephone call; yet few are so skilled in making such a threat that it will not cost some deterioration of the relationship between the firms. One businessman said that customers had better not rely on legal rights or threaten to bring a breach of contract law suit against him since he "would not be treated like a criminal" and would fight back with every means available. Clearly actual litigation is even more costly than making threats. Lawyers demand substantial fees from larger business units. A firm's executives often will have to be transported and maintained in another city during the proceedings if, as often is the case, the trial must be held away from the home office. Top management does not travel by Greyhound and stay at the Y.M.C.A. Moreover, there will be the cost of diverting top management, engineers, and others in the organization from their normal activities. The firm may lose many days work from several key people. The non-monetary costs may be large too. A breach of contract law suit may settle a particular dispute, but such an action often results in a "divorce" ending the "marriage" between the two businesses, since a contract action is likely to carry charges with at least overtones of bad faith. Many executives, moreover, dislike the prospect of being cross-examined in public. Some executives may dislike losing control of a situation by turning the decision-making power over to lawyers. Finally, the law of contract damages may not provide an adequate remedy even if the firm wins the suit; one may get vindication but not much money.

Why Do Relatively Contractual Practices Ever Exist?

Although contract is not needed and actually may have negative consequences, businessmen do make some carefully planned contracts, negotiate settlements influenced by their legal rights and commence and defend some breach of contract law suits or arbitration proceedings. In view of the findings and explanation presented to this point, one may ask why. Exchanges are carefully planned when it is thought that planning and a potential legal sanction will have more advantages than disadvantages. Such a judgment may be reached when contract planning serves the internal needs of an organization involved in a business exchange. For example, a fairly detailed contract can serve as a communication device within a large corporation. While the corporation's sales manager and house counsel may work out all the provisions with the customer, its production manager will have to make the product. He must be told what to do and how to handle at least the most obvious contingencies. Moreover, the sales manager may want to remove certain issues from future negotiation by his subordinates. If he puts the matter in the written contract, he may be able to keep his salesmen from making concessions to the customer without first consulting the sales manager. Then the sales manager may be aided in his battles with his firm's financial or engineering departments if the contract calls for certain practices which the sales manager advocates but which the other departments resist. Now the corporation is obligated to a customer to do what the sales manager wants to do; how can the financial or engineering departments insist on anything else?

Also one tends to find a judgment that the gains of contract outweigh the costs where there is a likelihood that significant problems will arise. One factor leading to this conclusion is complexity of the agreed performance over a long period. Another factor is whether or not the degree of injury in case of default is thought to be potentially great. This factor cuts two ways. First, a buyer may want to commit a seller to a detailed and legally binding contract, where the consequence of a default by the seller would seriously injure the buyer. For example, the airlines are subject to law suits from the survivors of passengers and to great adverse publicity as a result of crashes. One would expect the airlines to bargain for carefully defined and legally enforceable obligations on the part of the airframe manufacturers when they purchase aircraft. Second, a seller may want to limit his liability for a buyer's damages by a provision in their contract. For example, a manufacturer of air conditioning may deal with motels in the South and Southwest. If this equipment fails in the hot summer months, a motel may lose a great deal of business. The manufacturer may wish to avoid any liability for this type of injury to his customers and may want a contract with a clear disclaimer clause.

Similarly, one uses or threatens to use legal sanctions to settle disputes when other devices will not work and when the gains are thought to outweigh the costs. For example, perhaps the most common type of business contracts case fought all the way through the appellate courts today is an action for an alleged wrongful termination of a dealer's franchise by a manufacturer. Since the franchise has been terminated, factors such as personal relationships and the desire for future business will have little effect; the cancellation of the franchise indicates they have already failed to maintain the relationship. Nor will a complaining dealer worry about creating a hostile relationship between himself and the manufacturer. Often the dealer has suffered a great financial loss both as to his investment in building and equipment and as to his anticipated future profits. A cancelled automobile dealer's lease on his showroom and shop will continue to run, and his tools for servicing, say, Plymouths cannot be used to service other makes of cars. Moreover, he will have no more new Plymouths to sell. Today there is some chance of winning a law suit for terminating a franchise in bad faith in many states and in the federal courts. Thus, often the dealer chooses to risk the cost of a lawyer's fee because of the chance that he may recover some compensation for his losses.

An "irrational" factor may exert some influence on the decision to use legal sanctions. The man who controls a firm may feel that he or his organization has been made to appear foolish or has been the victim of fraud or bad faith. The law suit may be seen as a vehicle "to get even" although the potential gains, as viewed by an objective observer, are outweighed by the potential costs.

The decision whether or not to use contract — whether the gain exceeds the costs — will be made by the person within the business unit with the power to make it, and it tends to make a difference who he is. People in a sales department oppose contract. Contractual negotiations are just one more hurdle in the way of a sale. Holding a customer to the letter of a contract is bad for "customer relations." Suing a customer who is not bankrupt and might order again is poor strategy. Purchasing agents and their buyers are less hostile to contracts but regard attention devoted to such matters as a waste of time. In contrast, the financial control department — the treasurer, controller or auditor — leans toward more contractual dealings. Contract is viewed by these people as an organizing tool to control operations in a large organization. It tends to define precisely and to minimize the risks to which the firm is exposed. Outside lawyers — those with many clients — may share this enthusiasm for a more contractual method of dealing. These lawyers are concerned with preventive law — avoiding any possible legal difficulty. They see many unstable and unsuccessful exchange transactions, and so they are aware of, and perhaps overly concerned with, all of the things which can go wrong. Moreover, their job of settling disputes with legal sanctions is much easier if their client has not been overly casual about transaction planning. The inside lawyer, or house counsel, is harder to classify. He is likely to have some sympathy with a more contractual method of dealing. He shares the outside lawyer's "craft urge" to see exchange transactions neat and tidy from a legal standpoint. Since he is more concerned with avoiding and settling disputes than selling goods, he is likely to be less willing to rely on a man's word as the sole sanction than is a salesman. Yet the house counsel is more a part of the organization and more aware of its goals and subject to its internal sanctions. If the potential risks are not too great, he may hesitate to suggest a more contractual procedure to the sales department. He must sell his services to the operating departments, and he must hoard what power he has, expending it on only what he sees as significant issues.

The power to decide that a more contractual method of creating relationships and settling disputes shall be used will be held by different people at different times in different organizations. In most firms the sales department and the purchasing department have a great deal of power to resist contractual procedures or to ignore them if they are formally adopted and to handle disputes their own way. Yet in larger organizations the treasurer and the controller have increasing power to demand both systems and compliance. Occasionally, the house counsel must arbitrate the conflicting positions of these departments; in giving "legal advice" he may make the business judgment necessary regarding the use of contract. At times he may ask for an opinion from an outside law firm to reinforce his own position with the outside firm's prestige.

Obviously, there are other significant variables which influence the degree that contract is used. One is the relative bargaining power or skill of the two business units. Even if the controller of a small supplier succeeds within the firm and creates a contractual system of dealing, there will be no contract if the firm's large customer prefers not to be bound to anything. Firms that supply General Motors deal as General Motors wants to do business, for the most part. Yet bargaining power is not size or share of the market alone. Even a General Motors may need a particular supplier, at least temporarily. Furthermore, bargaining power may shift as an exchange relationship is first created and then continues. Even a giant firm can find itself bound to a small supplier once production of an essential item begins for there may not be time to turn to another supplier. Also, all of the factors discussed in this paper can be viewed as *components* of bargaining power — for example, the personal relationship between the presidents of the buyer and the seller firms may give a sales manager great power over a purchasing agent who has been instructed to give the seller "every consideration." Another variable relevant to the use of contract is the influence of third parties. The federal government, or a lender of money, may insist that a contract be made in a particular transaction or may influence the decision to assert one's legal rights under a contract.

Contract, then, often plays an important role in business, but other factors are significant. To understand the functions of contract the whole system of conducting exchanges must be explored fully. More types of business communities must be studied, contract litigation must be analyzed to see why the non-legal sanctions fail to prevent the use of legal sanctions and all of the variables suggested in this paper must be classified more systematically.

(ii) Bargaining in the Shadow of the Law: The Case of Divorce

Robert H. Mnookin

I wish to suggest a new way of thinking about the role of law at the time of divorce. It is concerned primarily with the impact of the legal system on negotiations and bargaining that occurs *outside* of court. Rather than regard order as imposed from above, I see the primary function of contemporary divorce law as providing a framework for divorcing couples themselves to determine their respective rights and responsibilities after dissolution. This process, by which parties to a marriage are empowered to create their own legally enforceable commitments, I shall call *"private ordering."*

Available evidence concerning how divorce proceedings actually work suggests that a re-examination from the perspective of private ordering is long overdue. "Typically the parties do not go to court at all until they have worked matters out and are ready for the rubber stamp." Both in the United States and England the overwhelming majority of divorcing couples resolve or settle the distributional questions concerning marital property, alimony, child support, and custody without bringing any contested issue to the court for adjudication.

This new perspective and the use of the term "private ordering" is not meant to suggest an absence of important social interests in how this process works, or in the fairness of the outcomes. The implicit policy questions are ones of emphasis and degree: to what extent should law permit and encourage divorcing couples to work out their own arrangements? Within what limits should parties be empowered to make their own law that they bring into existence by their agreement? What procedural or substantive safeguards are necessary because of various social interests? Nor is this new perspective meant to imply that the law and the legal system are unimportant. For divorcing spouses and their children, family law is inescapably relevant. The legal system affects *when* a divorce may occur; *how* a divorce must be procured; and *what happens* as a consequence of divorce. The primary purpose of this paper is to develop a framework for thinking about how the legal rules and procedures used in court for adjudicating disputes affect the bargaining process that occurs between divorcing couples *outside* the courtroom.

Before setting out together, let me provide you with a road map of where we are going. Our first stop involves an examination of the degree to which the law today authorises private ordering at the time of divorce. In other words, to what extent can a divorcing couple create their own legally enforceable commitments? In this context, I will also explain why I think the legal system should provide divorcing couples broad power through agreement to resolve the various questions that arise.

Secondly, against this background, I present a simple bargaining model to suggest how the legal system affects negotiations between spouses and their representatives at the time of divorce.

Finally, I will apply this framework to several issues that have dominated much of the academic discussion concerning family law during recent years:

1. The advantages and disadvantages of discretion conferring legal standards for child custody;
2. Goldstein, Freud and Solnit's proposed standard for visitation;
3. The role of lawyers in the divorce process; and
4. The role of courts in "undisputed" divorces.

Let us now turn to the question of the extent to which the law today sanctions private ordering. At the outset it is important to recall that a legal system might allow varying degrees of private ordering upon the dissolution of marriage. Until the no-fault revolution, the law concerning divorce did reflect a highly regulatory model that attempted to restrict private ordering. Couples had no formal power to end their marriage by mutual agreement. Divorce was granted only after an official inquiry by a judge, who had to determine whether there were "appropri-

---

(1979) 32 Current Legal Problems 65 at 65–70, 93–95, 96–102. Notes omitted. Reproduced by permission of Sweet & Maxwell Limited, Andover, Hampshire, U.K.

ate grounds," which were themselves very narrowly defined in terms of marital offences. If a divorce were granted, the State asserted broad power to impose distributional consequences, and to have continuing regulatory jurisdiction over the children and their relationship to their parents. Doctrines such as collusion, connivance and condonation were meant to curtail the degree to which parties themselves could through agreement bring about a divorce; and the procedural requirements reflected the view, in R.M. Jackson's words, that both the petitioner and the respondent were "suspicious characters." Obviously, the marital offence regime — even at its most restrictive — could not entirely eliminate collusion. Some divorcing spouses worked things out for themselves and then (with the help of their lawyers) staged a carefully rehearsed and jointly produced play for the court. Nonetheless, the legal system was structured to minimise private ordering.

Dramatic changes in divorce law during the past decade now permit a substantial degree of private ordering. The "no fault revolution" has made the fundamental decision of whether there shall be divorce largely a matter of private concern. Parties to a marriage can now explicitly create circumstances that will allow divorce. Indeed, the reality is that agreement between spouses is not even necessary — either spouse can unilaterally create the grounds for dissolution simply by separation for a sufficient period of time.

What about the parties' power to decide for themselves the consequences of divorce? Here the presence of children makes an important difference. Where the divorcing couple has no children, the law both in England and the United States largely recognises the power of the parties upon separation or divorce to make their own arrangements concerning marital property and alimony. A spousal agreement may be subject to some sort of judicial proceeding — or submission to a Registrar — but on both sides of the Atlantic the official review appears to be largely perfunctory. In some American states, a couple may if they choose make their agreement binding and final — i.e., not subject to later modification by a court after the divorce. In England, strictly speaking, this probably is not possible. Nonetheless, English courts are very slow after a divorce is granted to modify an agreement intended to be binding or an order issued with the consent of the parties.

Where there are minor children, existing law imposes substantial doctrinal constraints. For those allocational decisions that directly affect children — that is, child support, custody and visitation — parents lack the formal power "to make their own law." The court, exercising the state's *parens patrine* power, is said to have responsibility to determine who should have custody and on what conditions. Private agreements concerning these matters are possible, and common, but these agreements cannot bind the court which is said to have an independent responsibility for determining what arrangements best serve the child's welfare. Thus, the court has the power to reject a parental agreement, and order some other level of child support or some other custodial arrangement, if that is thought more desirable. Moreover, even if the parties' initial agreement is accepted by the court, the parties entirely lack the power to provide for finality. A court may at any time during the child's minority reopen and modify the initial decree in light of any subsequent change in circumstances. The parties entirely lack the power to deprive the court of this jurisdiction.

These limitations on parental power reflect a variety of policy concerns. They may acknowledge the fact that the child, although profoundly affected by the bargain, is not normally a meaningful participant in the negotiating process. A parental agreement concerning custody, visitation or support may not reflect the child's interests but instead the interests of the parents. A parent eager to escape an unhappy marriage may agree to custodial arrangements and levels of support that are less advantageous to the child than some feasible alternative. Judicial scrutiny and continual supervision of the elements of the separation agreement concerning the child might therefore be seen as a safeguard of the child's interests.

Available evidence concerning how the legal system in fact processes undisputed divorce cases involving minor children suggests that in fact parents have very broad powers to make their own deals. Typically separation agreements are rubber stamped even in cases involving children. A study of custody here in England suggests, for example, that courts rarely set aside an arrangement acceptable to the parents. Anecdotal evidence in America suggests that the same is true in the U.S.

That the legal system in fact gives parents broad discretion is less than surprising when one considers a number of factors. First, getting information is difficult when there is no dispute. There are usually very limited resources for a thorough or an independent investigation of the family's circumstances. Secondly, the applicable legal standards are extremely vague and give registrars or judges very little guidance as to what circumstances justify overriding a parental decision. Finally, there are obvious limitations on a court's practical power to control parental behaviour once they leave the courtroom. For all these reasons, it is not surprising that most courts behave as if their function in the divorce process is dispute settlement. Where there is no dispute, busy judges or registrars are typically quite willing to rubber stamp a private agreement, thus conserving resources for disputed cases.

Before proceeding, I should make clear the reasons I think law should give divorcing spouses broad powers to make their own agreement. When a couple can resolve distributional consequences of divorce without resort to court for adjudication, there are obvious and substantial savings. The cost of litigation, both private and public, is minimised. The pain of an adversarial proceeding is avoided. Recent findings from psychological studies suggest the desirability from a child's perspective in having parents agree on custodial arrangements. Moreover, through a negotiated agreement the parties can often avoid the risks and uncertainties of litigation which sometimes involve all or nothing consequences. Given the substantial delays that often characterise contested judicial proceedings, an agreement can often provide significant time-savings for the parties, thus allowing the spouses to proceed with their lives. Finally, a solution agreed to by the parties seems more likely to be consistent with their own preferences and accepted by them over time than a result that is simply imposed by a court.

For divorces where there are no minor children, divorcing couples should have very broad powers to make their own arrangements; significant limitations are inconsistent with the premises of no fault divorce. After all, who can better evaluate the comparative advantages of alternative arrangements than the parties themselves? In John Stuart Mill's words, each spouse "is the person most interested in his own well-being ... with respect to his own feelings and circumstances, the most ordinary man or woman has means of knowledge immeasurably surpassing those that can be possessed by anyone else." Courts should not, of course, enforce agreements that reflect fraud or overreaching. Nor do I wish to minimise the importance of appropriate standards for alimony and marital property for, in ways that I will describe shortly, these standards very much affect negotiated outcomes. Nonetheless, against a backdrop of fair standards, parties should be encouraged to settle for themselves these economic issues. The state should provide an efficient and fair mechanism for enforcing such agreements, and for settling disputes when the parties are unable to agree.

Where there are minor children, the state obviously has broader interests than simply dispute settlement. The state also has a responsibility for *child protection*. To acknowledge this responsibility, however, is not to define its limits. Indeed the critical questions concern the proper scope of the child protection function at the time of divorce, and the mechanisms that best achieve this goal.

For reasons I have spelled out at length elsewhere, the actual determination of what is in fact in a child's best interest is ordinarily quite indeterminate: it requires predictions beyond the capacity of the behavioural sciences. It also involves the imposition of values about which there appears to be little consensus in our societies today. Thus the fundamental question is: who decides on behalf of the child? To what extent should the child's parents be given the freedom to decide between themselves how responsibility for their children is to be allocated following divorce? I believe divorcing parents should be given considerable freedom to decide custody matters — subject only to the same minimum standards for child protection that the State imposes on *all* families with respect to neglect and abuse. A negotiated resolution is desirable from the child's perspective for several reasons. Since a child's social and psychological relationships with *both* parents ordinarily continue after the divorce, a process that leads to agreement between the parents is preferable to one that necessarily has a winner and a loser. A child's future relationship with each of his parents may be better maintained and his existing relationship less damaged by a negotiated settlement than by one imposed by a court after an adversarial proceeding. Moreover, the parents will know more about the child than the judge, since they have better access to information about the child's circumstances and desires. Indeed, given the basic indeterminacy of anyone knowing what is best for the child, having a privately negotiated solution by those who will be responsible for care after the divorce seems much more likely to match the parents' capacities and desires with the child's needs. These advantages suggest that courts should not second-guess parental agreements unless judicial intervention is required by the strict child-protection standard implicit in neglect laws.

If parents have the authority to decide, there can be no doubt that some parents will make mistakes. But so do judges. Parents (not the state) are primarily responsible for their children after divorce. Part of this responsibility involves attempting, themselves, to agree upon some allocation of responsibilities in the future. This is not to suggest that the State does not have an important responsibility to inform parents concerning the child's needs during and after divorce; nor does it mean that the State does not have an important interest in facilitating parental agreement. Nevertheless, the law in action (which acknowledges substantial parental power) strikes me as preferable to existing doctrine (which imposes substantial restrictions on parental power to decide for themselves).

Everyone may not share these premises concerning the desirability of private ordering. But no matter what one's thinking on these questions, the fact that most divorcing couples do not bring disputes to court for adjudication suggests the appropriateness of analysing how the legal system affects the bargaining behaviour of divorcing couples.

. . . .

An Evaluation of the Lawyer's Role

If one accepts the proposition that the primary function of the legal system should be to facilitate private ordering and dispute resolution, then several important questions come into sharp focus. To what extent does the participation of lawyers facilitate dispute resolution? Are there alternative procedures (in which lawyers play a lesser role) that are less costly and more fair? Many observers are very critical of the way some lawyers behave in divorce negotiations. Lawyers may "heat up" the process, make negotiations more adversarial and painful than they would otherwise be, and make it more difficult and costly for the spouses to reach agreement. Indeed, it may well be that lawyers more than lay people are prepared to adopt negotiating strategies involving threats, and the strategic misrepresentation of their client's true preferences in order to reach a more favourable settlement for the client. Ivan Illich has recently suggested that a broad range of illnesses are in fact "iatrogenic," i.e., induced and created by medical treatment and the health industry. The same charge might be laid on the legal profession. The participation of lawyers in the divorce process may on balance lead to more disputes and higher costs without improving the fairness of the outcomes.

There are also arguments that lawyers facilitate dispute settlement. The participation of lawyers may make negotiations more rational, may minimise the number of disputes, may increase the opportunities for resolution out of court, and may insure that the outcomes reflect the applicable legal norms. Professor Eisenberg has suggested how a pair of lawyers — each acting for his client — may make the process of negotiation in dispute settlement very much like adjudication, i.e., a process where "rules, precedents, and reasoned elaboration — may be expanded to determine outcome ..." Where each spouse has a lawyer, the lawyers

> are likely to find themselves allied with each other as well as with the disputants, because of their relative emotional detachment, their interest in resolving the dispute, and, in some cases, their shared professional values. Each therefore tends to take on a Janus-like role, facing the other as an advocate of that which is reasonable in the other's position.... Because a lawyer is both a personal advisor and a technical expert, each actor-disputant is likely to accept a settlement his lawyer recommends. Because of their training and the fact that typically they become involved only when formal litigation is contemplated, lawyers are likely to negotiate on the basis of *legal* principles, rules, and precedents. When these two elements are combined, the result is that paired legal affiliates typically function as a coupled unit which is strikingly similar to a formal adjudicative unit in terms of both input and output. Indeed, in terms of sheer number of dispute-settlements effected, the most significant legal dispute-settlement institution is typically not the bench, but the bar.

The perspective of private ordering exposes these various roles and raises the obvious question: what in fact do lawyers do in the process? Lawyers may serve various functions, and yet we know very little about how in fact lawyers behave. Obviously, lawyers are not of all one piece. Their styles differ. Some lawyers may prefer (and be more effective at) certain roles. Some lawyers are known within the profession as negotiators who strive to find middle ground acceptable to both sides; others are fighters, who love the courtroom battle. Research could usefully explore how much specialisation there is, and the extent to which clients (when they are choosing a lawyer at the time of divorce) have any notion at all of their lawyers' skills or tastes for these various roles. More generally, systematic empirical research might illustrate how often (and in what circumstances) lawyers facilitate dispute settlement at the time of divorce, and how often (and in what circumstances) they hurt.

This framework also suggests how timely it is to re-examine the question of why the legal profession should have a monopoly with respect to these roles, and the extent to which it does in fact have such a monopoly. How well are lawyers trained to perform these various roles? Other professionals or para-professionals might serve some of these functions as well as lawyers at a substantially lower cost. This is most obviously the case where there is no dispute, and the attorney's role is essentially that of "clerk." A recent study in Connecticut suggests that in most uncontested divorces, clients believe their lawyer did no more than fill out the necessary forms (a complaint, a claim for a hearing, and a decree) and made an appearance at a *pro forma* hearing. Moreover, the same study suggests that because the forms and procedures are complicated, do-it-yourself "divorce dissolution kits" (without additional lay assistance) pose rather little threat to the monopoly of the organised bar. Most people lack the time, confidence, or ability to navigate through the legal shoals themselves — even where they have no dispute with their spouse. This suggests that procedural reform aimed at simplifying the procedure for uncontested divorce could substantially reduce transaction costs in many cases.

. . . .

THE ROLE OF COURTS

Let us consider the role of courts in the divorce process from the perspective of private ordering. Obviously, the judicial system provides a mechanism for dispute settlement through adjudication where the parties have not been able to agree. But courts also play a role in a much larger number of cases than those where the dispute is adjudicated. Because each party knows the other can invoke the court's power to settle their differences, the presence of the judiciary exerts considerable pressure towards settlement. Indeed, anecdotal evidence suggests that courts often put pressure on the parties in disputed cases "to settle their own differences" through private negotiations, thus avoiding the need for adjudication.

One striking feature of the present day system, however, is the requirement that undisputed cases pass through court. With a narrow exception recently enacted in California, every American state requires a judicial proceeding to secure a divorce in all cases. From a historical perspective, this requirement is not surprising: it represented a regulatory mechanism to ensure that divorces were only granted in narrowly defined circumstances. Before the no-fault revolution, dispute settlement was not the primary function of divorce proceedings.

The no-fault revolution has now empowered either spouse unilaterally to create the circumstances for divorce. The state no longer purports to have an interest preventing re-marriage where either spouse wants to dissolve an earlier marriage. Ironically, however, the shell of the same administrative and regulatory mechanisms has been preserved. Indeed, this analysis suggests a policy question of substantial importance: where there is no dispute between the divorcing spouses concerning the allocation implications of their divorce, why should a judicial proceeding be required? Absent a dispute, why should a court have any role? Why require a costly legal transaction in court when the questions can be resolved by negotiations?

It would not be difficult to imagine the elimination of a judicial proceeding in undisputed divorce cases. Getting married obviously does not require judicial proceedings. Why should getting a divorce? The requirement of a judicial proceeding probably imposes significant transaction costs, both public and private. Because even uncontested divorces must go through court, parties may end up hiring a lawyer, even where the lawyer's function is basically that of a clerk. An appearance by a lawyer in court takes time — time for which the parties are charged. Moreover a judicial proceeding requires the use of judicial resources as well as the time of the parties themselves. Some countries have largely eliminated the requirement that undisputed divorces go through court; it certainly seems timely to examine the justifications for the requirement, and to ask whether there might not be alternatives that are preferable which cost less.

While the analysis that follows is necessarily preliminary, it is useful to identify and examine four arguments in defence of a judicial proceeding, in uncontested divorce cases.

Ceremonial Function

A judicial proceeding might be thought to serve a ceremonial function that re-confirms, both for the divorcing parties and the general public, the seriousness with which the state takes marriage and divorce. Rituals are important, and the court proceeding can be seen as a socially imposed divorce ritual. But as a ritual, the court proceeding for uncontested divorces, seems peculiar. The marriage ceremony itself is, after all, extremely simple, and does not require lawyers and a judge. Moreover, in most states, the parties themselves are not usually required to appear in court in order to procure a divorce. Their lawyers, instead, can appear for them. If the ritual were for the benefit of the parties, presumably their presence would be required. In all events, one can ask how well the existing requirement serves the ceremonial function? Is the purpose of the requirement ceremonial? Or is it more like a civil fine, imposed on a divorcing couple; a fine payable not to the treasury but to the divorce bar?

Review Ensures Fair Outcomes: Fairness between the Spouses

The requirement of judicial approval of post-marital agreements might be justified on the ground that the state has an interest in ensuring that the results of the bargaining process are fair, as between the spouses. A judicial proceeding might protect people from their own ignorance, and might also be thought to prevent unfair results arising from unequal bargaining capacity between the spouses. These arguments have a plausible air, but the reality of the present day system might suggest that they mean very little in practice. Courts typically rubber stamp an agreement reached between the parties. Moreover, there are reasons to doubt that the requirement of judicial review is very often necessary for these purposes. There may well be cases where one spouse (presumably the husband) is highly sophisticated in business matters, while the other spouse (the wife) is an innocent lamb being led to the slaughter. But typically married couples generally have similar educational and cultural backgrounds. Moreover, most individuals perceive very well their own financial interests and needs at the time of divorce.

If there are systematic biases in the process, a more appropriate safeguard would be to change the *substantive standards* concerning who gets what. For example, if it is thought that husbands systematically provide their wives with an insufficient share of the family's assets, or with inadequate alimony, after marriages of long duration where the wife has not worked, the *legal standards* can be changed to provide greater claims for the wife. Moreover, procedural mechanisms can then be developed that require review and a hearing only in those cases where the spousal agreement falls outside the norm (e.g., where marital property was divided very unequally, or where alimony claims were being waived). In practice today, I suspect judges or registrars attempt to identify such cases for intensive examination. At the present time, however, cases falling within the normal range must also pass through a judicial proceeding, with its attendant costs. A system where the state defines reasonable norms, and then permits couples to reach agreement outside the norms provided there were additional procedural safeguards, would seem both more effective and less costly.

Effect on Out-of-Court Settlements

It might be thought that the requirement that undisputed cases go to court, improves the private settlement process outside of court. Knowing that they will have to display their agreement to a judge, the parties (and their attorneys) may deal with each other in a fairer way and be more likely to reach an agreement reflecting the appropriate social norms. Behavioural scientists have suggested that the presence of an "audience" can affect bargaining. With respect to out-of-court negotiations, the judge represents both an "actual" audience and "abstract" audience. He is an actual audience in that parties know that eventually they may have to explain their agreement to a judge. This may mitigate extreme claims. The judge also represents an abstract audience as well, which symbolically represents the social interests in the child and various notions of honour, reputation, and history.

It is extremely difficult to evaluate this argument, and to know how the requirement of judicial proceedings in undisputed cases affects negotiations in such cases. A requirement that disputed cases alone would go before a court might be sufficient to bring the "audience" benefits to the process of negotiation. Moreover, it is possible that the requirement of judicial approval makes dispute settlement more not less difficult. For one thing, the requirement probably means that lawyers are more often involved in the process than would otherwise be the case. As earlier noted, it at least seems an open question whether having lawyers in the process facilitates dispute resolution in those case where the parties might otherwise reach agreement anyway. Moreover, there is always the possibility that in the occasional case where the judge does upset the agreement reached by the parties, the eventual outcome may on balance be no more desirable (or even less desirable) than would otherwise be the case.

Child Protection

Where a divorcing couple has minor children, the state has an important interest in child protection. The requirement of court review of private agreements relating to custody or child support might be justified on this ground. For one thing, from the child's perspective, the quality of negotiated agreements may be improved. Some parents might otherwise engage in divorce bargaining on the basis of preferences that reflected narrowly selfish interests, rather than concern for the child. The review requirement might serve as an important reminder to the parents of the social concern for their children, and may somehow constrain otherwise selfish behaviour. Even a selfish spouse may be more concerned about his reputation as a parent if there is some sort of public process. Especially in cases where there are children, the judge may represent an important "audience" whose unseen presence affects bargaining behaviour. Finally, although most parental agreements are approved after only superficial examination by the judge, some agreements are in fact disapproved: to the extent courts succeed in identifying arrangements that are disadvantageous to a child in a particular case and in imposing some better alternative, the child's welfare is obviously improved.

A variety of arguments can be made on the other side, however. For one thing, what evidence we have suggests that in operation courts rarely overturn parental agreements. Given the resources that are devoted to this task there is little reason to believe that the process today in fact operates as much of a safeguard where there is no parental dispute. Moreover, the process itself probably imposes not insubstantial transaction costs — both public (in terms of traditional resources expended) and private (in terms of the cost to the parties, the legal fees and time). These extra transaction costs might otherwise enure (at least in part) to the benefit of the children.

There are also reasons to think that, in the vast majority of cases, this review may well be unnecessary. For one thing, the custodial spouse will typically perceive very clearly the economic consequences for the child of any support arrangement that he or she agrees to. There is after all, considerable joint consumption between the custodial parent and the child. Moreover, child support payments (like alimony and the earnings of the custodial spouse) typically go into a single economic pot that supports both the custodial parent and the child. In other words, the economic interests of the child and the economic interests of the custodial parent substantially coincide.

A second safeguard — banal as it sounds — is that most parents care deeply for their children. No court proceeding can of course require parents to love their children, and prevent selfish calculation by a divorcing parent. Nevertheless, to the extent that divorcing parents do love their children there is every reason to think that they will in fact themselves be very concerned with making arrangements that are beneficial to the child. Perhaps there are good reasons not to trust parents with child-rearing responsibilities on or after divorce. That was certainly the implicit attitude during the heyday of the marital offence regime. But is it really appropriate today? Indeed, it is interesting to compare the review requirements imposed by law if the child's family is disrupted by divorce with the review requirements imposed if the family is disrupted by the death of one of the parents. American law permits a parent to disinherit his minor children. A decedent cannot, however, disinherit his spouse and in effect present day law trusts the surviving parent with child-rearing responsibility in the light of existing economic resources. With respect to any inheritance of any surviving spouse, there is no supervision imposed by operation of law on how he or she spends the inheritance, and there is no examination of what portion is spent on the child. Instead, the surviving parent is trusted to look after the child, subject of course to the minimum limitations imposed by the child neglect laws which apply to all parents.

The review requirement may, ironically, send an inappropriate set of signals to parents at the time of divorce: it may suggest to them that because of the divorce they are no longer trusted to be adequate parents, and that the state will now assume special responsibility for their children. Indeed, court review might conceivably induce more selfish behaviour on the part of parents who take the attitude that it is the court's job, not their own responsibility, to be concerned with the interests of their children. In fact, the state does not and cannot assume a broad role for child-rearing responsibility after divorce.

CONCLUSION

Viewing the process of dissolution from the perspective of private ordering does not make previously intractable family law problems disappear. If anything, the world seems even more complex, for analysis involves the examination of the effects of alternative rules and procedures on informal and formal bargaining outside of court about which we have little understanding. There is little existing theory to inform the enquiry. There now exists no bargaining theory that can yield accurate predictions of the expected outcomes, assuming different legal rules where rational self-interested parties are negotiating over money issues. Where there are minor children involved, the parents are not simply bargaining over money; they also must be necessarily concerned with allocating child-rearing responsibilities in the future. We have tried to suggest how the variability of parental preferences with respect to custody makes the task of analysing bargaining especially difficult. Furthermore, rational bargaining may be in short supply when a family is in the process of breaking up. Some divorcing spouses seem motivated by spite or envy, more than a careful assessment of self-interest in the light of available alternatives.

Where bargaining is motivated by emotional drives, the assessment of the effects of alternative legal rules seems even more speculative. Finally, it must sadly be reported that there has been little empirical work which has involved the systematic observation of how the process of private ordering in fact works today.

Given the absence of powerful theory or systematic data, this essay makes no claims at being definitive. It instead has suggested a theoretical perspective that permits a broader analysis of the probable consequences of family law rules and procedures. It also more sharply exposes a set of questions of enormous social importance. If one accepts the proposition that disputes settlement should be the primary goal of the legal system, the analysis does not imply that the state should simply withdraw all resources from the process, and leave it to the divorcing spouses to work things out on their own, unassisted by any professional help. Instead, this inquiry should underline the desirability of learning more about how alternative procedural mechanisms might facilitate dispute resolution during a typically difficult and painful time in the lives of parents and children alike.

The perspective certainly has implications far broader than family law. In a wide variety of contexts, individuals bargain in the shadow of the law. Few automobile accident claims are ever tried; most are settled out of court. Criminal prosecutions are typically resolved by a plea bargain, not an adjudication of guilt. Most administrative proceedings result in consent agreements not trials. In each of these contexts, the preferences of the parties, the entitlements created by law, transaction costs, and attitudes towards risk, will presumably substantially affect the negotiated outcomes. Indeed, I hope this essay will stimulate and encourage further work by others in a variety of contexts. Theoretical and empirical research concerning how people bargain in the shadow of law should provide us with a richer understanding of how the legal system affects behaviour, and allow a better appraisal of the consequences of reform proposals.

(iii) Profiting from Pollution: Canada promotes U.S.-style emissions sales to ease pain of cutting greenhouse gases

Andrew Duffy

On the Chicago Board of Trade, sulphur dioxide emissions can be bought and sold like so many pork bellies.

For the going rate of about $90 U.S., anyone can buy the legal right to emit one tonne of noxious gas into the atmosphere. Buyers — mostly electrical utilities — use them to comply with federal acid-rain standards or sell them for profit to other power plants. Speculators, too, have entered the picture, gambling on a bull market for the pollution credits first issued by the U.S. Environmental Protection Agency in 1990 as new air quality standards came into effect.

Emissions trading is a key part of the U.S. scheme to control acid rain that some countries, including Canada, want to adapt for the global campaign against greenhouse gases. Canada is banking heavily on some kind of emissions trading scheme to minimize the cost of any international deal.

More than 160 nations will meet in Kyoto, Japan, next month to finalize a binding treaty to stem the growth of gases that most scientists say are slowly warming the atmosphere. Entering the negotiations, Canada is in a difficult position compared with most industrialized countries.

Canadian emissions of carbon dioxide and other greenhouse gases have increased by about 13 per cent since 1990, the benchmark for new targets in Kyoto. During the same time, the vast majority of developed countries have managed to level or

---

From *The Ottawa Citizen* (21 November 1997) H1. Reproduced with permission of Southam News.

decrease their emissions. (Only the U.S. and Japan have experienced a steeper growth in emissions than Canada this decade.)

It means federal negotiators will be pushing for a flexible treaty since energy consumption in Canada will have to change considerably if the country is to reach its reductions goal. Central to their strategy will be a global emissions trading scheme.

"With emissions trading, it's not government saying, 'Reduce gases this way.' The marketplace determines how it will be done," says Avrim Lazar, assistant deputy minister of policy for Environment Canada.

"As a government, you can regulate, tax, or pay people to change. Or you can create a market for it. We think creating a market for it is more efficient."

Innovation, Mr. Lazar said, can be awakened by putting a price tag on inefficiency and waste. "That's why we're so keen on this. Rather than the heavy hand of government trying to say how we're going to to reduce emissions, the minds of the private sector kick in."

In the U.S., creating a market for sulphur dioxide has proven cost-effective in reducing acid rain.

The trading scheme put a value on pollution by assigning to each electric power company an emissions cap. If a power company exceeds its allowance, it can buy an emission "credit" from another firm through the commodity market. Companies that reduce emissions by paying for pollution controls can sell "credits" to off-set their costs.

Even if there's agreement to set up a trading scheme, it will be at least five years before one is developed. 'It won't be simple,' Avrim Lazar conceded. 'It will be a big challenge technically and politically.'

At the outset, industry leaders warned it would cost as much as $1,500 U.S. to remove one tonne of sulphur dioxide from the air.

But the private sector has proven itself adept at finding cheap and innovative ways to cut emissions when profits are at stake. The U.S. acid rain program is now 40 per cent ahead of schedule and is operating at a cost much lower than even the program's architects envisioned.

U.S. President Bill Clinton recently said the market-based scheme shows the world can meet the challenge posed by global warming without crippling economies.

"The lesson here is simple," he told a Washington audience. "Environmental initiatives, if sensibly designed, flexibly implemented, cost less than expected and provide unforeseen economic opportunities."

The U.S. program is being expanded to include other pollutants. In California, an inventive trading system is now in place for smog components. Under the scheme, for instance, four oil refineries gained credit for reducing 2,000 tonnes of pollution by buying and recycling 17,000 old cars, which the government said produced an equivalent amount of smog-causing emissions.

Meanwhile, Canadian officials are investigating the possibility of a joint trading system with the U.S. to fight smog. And in British Columbia, the government has launched the first attempt to use a market-based system to reduce greenhouse gases.

B.C.'s pilot project allows industries that reduce their carbon dioxide, nitrous oxide or methane levels to sell "ownership" of those emissions to another firm.

Most Canadian businesses welcome the initiative.

"Exploring these options now will help shape practical solutions which offer the best balance between environmental and economic benefits," said David Manning, president of the Canadian Association of Petroleum Producers.

Environmentalists are cautiously optimistic about the potential of emissions trading.

"It's a fine system in theory, but setting it up is the problem," said Robert Hornung, climate change director for the Pembina Institute.

Deciding which gases and which industries will be subject to an emissions cap — and how much each company will be allocated — are decisions fraught with political difficulty. It's also unclear whether developing countries will participate in the scheme, since they're reluctant to take on emission targets of any kind. Monitoring emissions worldwide to ensure obligations are met also poses a problem.

The federal government, however, remains intent on the scheme and wants to cast as wide a net as possible in Kyoto.

Mr. Lazar said a global market for emissions would make the trading system more complicated, but would give industry more options. A Canadian steel factory, for example, could meet its emissions cap by converting to natural gas from coal power. Or it could buy emission credits on the commodity market to meet its cap. Or it could invest directly in improving a dirty Russian factory to gain emission credits.

Still, even if there's agreement in Kyoto to set up a trading scheme, it will be at least five years before one is developed. "It won't be simple," Mr. Lazar conceded.

"It will be a big challenge technically and politically."

Politically, the scheme might be difficult to sell because it could result in huge amounts of money being transferred to Russia and Poland. Emissions in both countries have dropped significantly since 1990 — largely from the collapse of Communist-era industry — and they could have billions worth of "credits" to sell as a result.

And environmentalists fear the scheme could frustrate global emission reductions since the credits sold would be from out-of-service plants.

Mr. Lazar, however, believes the market-based system is the best way to marry economics and environmentalism.

"When you emit, what you're doing is using up a bit of the global commons. Until now that's been free. What we're saying is, if you're going to take this benefit from all of us, the community of humans who live on this planet, you'll pay for it so you don't squander it."

7 Dispute Resolution

A. The Disputes Resolution Spectrum

(i) The Mediator and the Judge

Torstein Eckhoff

Mediation consists of influencing the parties to come to agreement by appealing to their own interest. The mediator may make use of various means to attain this goal. He may work on the parties' ideas of what serves them best, for instance, in such a way that he gets them to consider their common interests as more essential than they did previously, or their competing interests as less essential. He may also look for possibilities of resolution which the parties themselves have not discovered and try to convince them that both will be well served with his suggestion. The very fact that a suggestion is proposed by an impartial third party may also, in certain cases, be sufficient for the parties to accept it (*cf.* Schelling, 1960, pp. 62, 63, 71 and 143 ff.). The mediator also has the possibility of using promises or threats. He may, for instance, promise the parties help or support in the future if they become reconciled or he may threaten to ally himself with one of them if the other does not give in. A mediator does not necessarily have to go in for compromise solutions, but for many reasons he will, as a rule, do so. The compromise is often the way of least resistance for one who shall get the parties to agree to an arrangement. As pointed out by Aubert (1963, p. 39) it may also contribute to the mediator's own prestige that he promotes intermediate solutions. Therewith he appears as the moderate and reasonable person with ability to see the problem from different angles — in contrast to the parties who will easily be suspected of having been onesided and quarrelsome since they have not managed to resolve the conflict on their own.

In order that both parties should have confidence in the mediator and be willing to co-operate with him and listen to his advice, it is important that they consider him impartial. This gives him an extra reason to follow the line of compromise (Aubert, 1963, p. 39, and Eckhoff, 1965, pp. 13–14). For, by giving both parties some support, he shows that the interests of one lie as close to his heart as those of the other. Regard for impartiality carries with it the consequence that the mediator sometimes must display caution in pressing the parties too hard. That the mediator, for instance, makes a threat to one of the parties to ally himself with the opponent unless compliance is forthcoming, may be an effective means of exerting pressure, but will easily endanger confidence in his impartiality. This can reduce his possibilities for getting the conflict resolved if threats do not work and it can weaken his future prestige as a mediator.

The conditions for a mediator are best in cases where both parties are interested in having the con-

---

Reproduced from *ACTA Acta Sociologica* (1966) 10: 158–66 by permission of Taylor & Francis, Oslo, Norway. Notes omitted.

flict resolved. The stronger this common interest is, the greater reason they have for bringing the conflict before a third party, and the more motivated they will be for co-operating actively with him in finding a solution, and for adjusting their demands in such a way that solution can be reached.

If the parties, or one of them, is, to begin with, not motivated for having the conflict resolved, or in any case not motivated to agree to any compromise, such motives must be *created* in him, for instance with the help of threats or sanctions. Cases may occur where the parties (or the unwilling one of them), may have a mediator forced upon them, and under pressure of persuasion from him or from the environment agree to an arrangement. But mediation under such circumstances presents difficulties, among other reasons, because it demands a balancing between the regard for impartiality and the regard for exertion of sufficient pressure. If the conditions for resolving the conflict by a judgement or administrative decision exist these will, as a rule, be more effective procedures than mediation in the cases described here.

That normative factors are considered relevant for the solution, can in certain cases be helpful during mediation. By referring to a norm (e.g., concerning what is right and wrong) the mediator may get the parties to renounce unreasonable demands so that their points of view approach each other. Even if the parties do not feel bound by the norms, it is conceivable that others consider it important that they be followed and that the mediator can therefore argue that a party will be exposed to disapproval if he does not accommodate.

The norms will be of special support for the mediator if the parties are generally in agreement on their content and are willing to submit to them, so that the reason that there is a conflict at all can be traced back to the fact that the norms do not cover all aspects of the difference. The remainder which is not covered will then have the features of a fairly pure conflict of interests where the norms have brought the points of departure nearer one another than they would otherwise have been.

If, however, the parties consider the norms as giving answers to the questions being disputed, but disagree on what the answers are, the possibilities for mediation will, as a rule, be weakened. In the first place, the probability that the conflict will at all be made the object of mediation is reduced, among other reasons, because bringing it before a judge will often be possible and more likely in these cases. Secondly, mediation which has been begun may be made difficult because of the parties' disagreement concerning the norms or the relevant facts. This is the more true the more inflexibly the opinions are opposed to each other and the more value-laden they are. The parties' resistance to compromising on questions of rights or truth makes itself felt also when the mediator appears in the arena. Perhaps the presence of a third party will make the parties even more set on asserting their rights than they otherwise would have been. The mediator can try to 'de-ideologize' the dispute by arguing that it is not always wise to 'stand on one's right' and that one should not 'push things to extremes', but go the 'golden middle road'. Sometimes he succeeds in this and manages to concentrate attention on the interest-aspects, so that the usual mediation arguments will have an effect. But it may also go the other way. The mediator lets himself be influenced by the parties to see the normative aspects as the most important, and ends up by judging instead of mediating. And even if he does not go so far, his opinions concerning norms and facts may inhibit his eagerness to mediate. In any case, it may be distasteful for him to work for a compromise if he has made up his mind that one of the parties is completely right and the other wrong.

Hoebel's survey (1954) of conflict-resolution in various primitive cultures confirms the impression that conditions are, generally speaking, less favourable for mediation than for other forms of conflict-resolution when the conflicts are characterized by disagreements about normative factors. Most of the third party institutions he describes have more in common with what I in this article call judgemental and administrative activity than with mediation. The only example in Hoebel's book of the development of a pure mediation institution for the resolution of disputes which have a strongly normative element, is found among the Ifugao-people in the northern part of Luzon in the Philippines. This is an agricultural people without any kind of state-form but with well developed rules governing property rights, sale, mortgage, social status (which is conditional on how much one owns), family relations, violation of rights, etc. Conflicts concerning these relations occur often. If the parties do not manage to solve them on their own they are regularly left to a mediator, who is called a *mokalun*. This is not a permanent office that belongs to certain persons but a task to which the person is appointed for the particular case. In practice the *mokalun* is always a person of high rank and generally someone who has won esteem as a head-hunter. He is chosen by the plaintiff, but is regarded as an impartial intermediary, not as a representative for a party. The parties are obligated to keep peace so long as mediation is in progress and they may not have any direct contact with each other during this period. The *mokalun* visits them alternately. He brings offers of conciliation and replies to these offers, and he tries, with the help of persuasion, and also generally with threats, to push through a conciliation. If he attains this he will receive good pay and increased prestige. If the mediation is not successful the conflict will remain unresolved and will perhaps result in homicide and blood feuds, for the *mokalun* has no authority to make decisions which are binding on the parties.

It is easy to point to features in the Ifugao culture which can have favoured the growth of such a method of conflict-resolution. On the one hand, there has obviously been a strong need to avoid open struggle within the local society, among other reasons, because the people were resident farmers who had put generations of work into terraces and irrigation works. On the other hand, there was no political leadership and no organized restraining power, and the conditions were therefore not favourable for conflict-resolution by judgement or coercive power. Nevertheless, it is noteworthy that the mediation arrangement functioned so well as it did, considering that it was applied to conflicts where divergent opinions of right and wrong were pitted against each other. It is natural to make a comparison with our present international conflicts, where the conditions are parallel to the extent that the danger for combat actions and the absence of other kinds of third party institutions create a strong need for mediation, but where the mediation institutions so far developed have been far less effective.

The *judge* is distinguished from the mediator in that his activity is related to the level of norms rather than to the level of interests. His task is not to try to reconcile the parties but to reach a decision about which of them is right. This leads to several important differences between the two methods of conflict-resolution. The mediator should preferably look forward, toward the consequences which may follow from the various alternative solutions, and he must work on the parties to get them to accept a solution. The judge, on the other hand, looks back to the events which have taken place (e.g., agreements which the parties have entered into, violations which one has inflicted on the other, etc.) and to the norms concerning acquisition of rights, responsibilities, etc. which are connected with these events. When he has taken his standpoint on this basis, his task is finished. The judge, therefore, does not have to be an adaptable negotiator with ability to convince and to find constructive solutions, as the mediator preferably should be. But he must be able to speak with authority on the existing questions of norms and facts in order to be an effective resolver of conflicts.

The possibility for judging in a dispute presupposes that the norms are considered relevant to the solution. The norms may be more or less structures. They may consist in a formal set of rules (e.g., a judicial system, the by-laws of an organization or the rules of a game), in customs or only in vague notions of what is right and just. The normative frame of reference in which a decision is placed does not have to be the same — and does not even have to exist — for all those who have something to do with the conflict. What one person perceives as a judgement another may perceive as an arbitrary command. If, however, *none* of those involved (the parties, the third party, the environment) applies normative considerations to the relationship because all consider it a pure conflict of interests, decision by judgement is excluded.

A decision may be a 'judgement' (in the sense in which the term is used here) even if the parties do not comply with it. But the greater the possibility that a judgement will be lived up to, the more suitable judgement will be as a method for conflict-resolution, and the better reason will the person who desires a solution have for preferring that procedure. It is therefore of significance to map out the factors which promote and hinder compliance to judgements.

The parties' interests in the outcome play an important role in this connexion. If the main thing for them is to have the dispute settled, and it is of secondary importance what the content of the solution is, it will require very little for them to comply with the judgement. If, on the other hand, there are strong and competing interests connected with the outcome, so that submission to the judgement implies a great sacrifice for one or both of the parties, the question of compliance is more precarious.

That one party (voluntarily or by force) submits to a judgement in spite of the sacrifice it means for him, may be due in part to norms and in part to the authority of the judge. There may be many reasons for the parties' respect for those *norms* on which the judge bases his decision; for instance, they may be internalized, or one fears gods' or people's punishment if one violates them, or one finds it profitable in the long run to follow them (e.g., because it creates confidence in one's business activities if one gains a reputation for law-abidance or because it makes the game more fun if the rules are followed). If the parties are sufficiently motivated to comply with the norms and give exhaustive answers to the question under dispute, then relatively modest demands are made on the judge's authority. If he is regarded as having knowledge of the norms and as having ability to find the facts, this will be sufficient to assure that his judgements are respected. Sometimes this is a simple assignment which many can fulfill. We may, for instance, take the case of two chess players who have not yet completely learned the rules of the game and who disagree as to whether it is permissible to castle in the present position. They ask a more experienced player who is present and comply without question to his decision because they consider it obvious that the rules should be followed and know that he is acquainted with them. But there are also cases where insight into norms, and perhaps also ability to clarify the factual relations in the matter, presuppose special expertise which only a few have. The kind of expertise required varies with the nature of the normative ideas. It may be, for instance, that contact with supernatural powers is considered to provide special prerequisites for finding out what is true and right, or it may be life-experience or professional studies. Monopolizing of insight may be a natural consequence of the fact that a norm system is large and cannot be taken in at a glance, but there are also many examples of systematic endeavours on the part of experts to prevent intruders from acquiring their knowledge.

If the parties are not sufficiently strongly motivated to comply with the norms which regulate their mutual rights and duties, or if they do not regard these as giving exhaustive answers to the matter of dispute, the judgement must appear as something more than a conveyance of information in order to command respect. The parties must, in one way or another, be bound or forced to adhere to it. One condition which may contribute to this is that, in addition to the primary norms which define the parties' mutual rights and obligations, there is also a set of secondary norms of adjudication which single out the judge as the proper person to settle the dispute and which possibly also impose upon the parties the duty to abide by his decision. That the judge is in this way equipped with *authority* is in many cases sufficient reason for the parties to consider themselves bound to live up to his decisions. But the establishment of authority often presupposes power, and even if the authority-relationship is established, it may sometimes be necessary to press through a decision by force. The power can reside with the judge, with someone he represents (e.g., the state) or with others who are interested in the decision being respected (e.g., the winning party or his relatives or friends). And it can have various bases: physical or military strength, control of resources on which the parties are dependent, powers of sorcery, etc. How *much* power is necessary depends partly on what other factors promote and hinder compliance, and partly upon the relative strength of the enforcing authority and the disobedient party.

That the parties and others have confidence in the judge's impartiality promotes compliance to judgements. It strengthens the belief that the decisions he makes are right and it facilitates enforcement by making the application of force more legitimate. As mentioned before, it is also important for the mediator to appear impartial, but the manner of showing impartiality is different for the two kinds of third parties. To a certain extent the judge can display that he gives equal consideration to both parties, for instance, by giving both the same possibilities for arguing and for presenting evidence. But he cannot, like the mediator, systematically endeavour to reach compromises, because the norms sometimes demand decision in favour of one of the parties. If he finds that one party is completely right he must judge in his favour, and the outcome of the case will not in itself be a testimony to his giving equal consideration to both.

But the judge has other possibilities for appearing impartial. Sometimes his person gives sufficient guarantee. He is, for instance, because of his high rank, his contact with supernatural powers or his recognized wisdom and strength of character regarded as infallible, or at least freed from suspicion of partisanship. The privilege of the judge to assume a retired position during the proceedings and not to engage in argumentation with the parties makes it easier to ascribe such qualities to him than to the mediator. Another significant factor is that there are, as a rule, small possibilities for checking the rightness of a judgement because this presupposes knowledge of both the system of norms and the facts of the particular case. To maintain a belief that certain persons are infallible can, nevertheless, present difficulties, especially in cultures characterized by democratization and secularization. To reduce or conceal the human factor in decision-making will therefore often be better suited to strengthening confidence in the decisions. Letting the judge appear as a 'mouthpiece of the law', who cannot himself exert any influence worth mentioning on the outcome of the cases, tends to remove the fear that his own interests, prejudices, sympathies and antipathies may have impact on his rulings.

(i) The Mediator and the Judge

Tendencies to overestimate the influence of the norms and underestimate the influence of the judge may also have other functions than strengthening confidence in the judge's impartiality. Firstly, these tendencies contribute to the transmission of authority from the norm system to the individual decisions. Secondly, the conditions are favourable for a gradual and often almost unnoticeable development of a norm system through court practice, so that the resistance to change is reduced. And thirdly, the judge will be less exposed to criticism and self-reproach when he (both in his own and others' eyes) avoids appearing as personally responsible for his decisions. This is important because it might otherwise involve great strain to make decisions in disputes where the parties' contentions are strongly opposed to each other, where there are perhaps great interests at stake for both, and where it may be extremely doubtful who is right (*cf.* Eckhoff and Jacobsen, 1960, especially pp. 37 ff.). It is therefore not surprising that many techniques have been used in the various judicial systems for the purpose of eliminating, limiting or concealing the influence of the judge. The use of ordeals and drawing of lots in the administration of justice (*cf.* Eckhoff, 1965, pp. 16–17; and Wedberg, 1935) may be mentioned as examples of this, and the same is true for the technique of judicial argumentation which gives the decisions the appearance of being the products of knowledge and logic, and not of evaluation and choice.

Judicial activity and formation of norms serve to support each other mutually. On the one hand, the judge is dependent on normative premises on which he can base his decisions. The greater the relevance attributed to them, and the stronger the ideological anchoring of the norm system, the more favourable are the conditions for conflict-resolution by judgement. On the other hand, the activity of judges can contribute to the spreading of knowledge about norms, to their increased recognition and authority, and to a gradual extension of the norm system to cover new types of conflict situations.

The activity of judging is in these respects quite different from the activity of mediating. As mentioned before, the task of the mediator becomes more difficult the more emphasis the parties place on the normative aspects of the conflict (presupposing that there is disagreement about these, as there usually will be in conflict situations). The mediator, therefore, must try to 'de-ideologize' the conflict, for instance, by stressing that interests are more important than the question of who is right and who is wrong, or by arguing that one ought to be reasonable and willing to compromise. The use of mediation in certain types of disputes may tend to create or reinforce the norm that willingness to compromise is the proper behaviour in conflict situations, and thereby to reduce the significance of such norms as judges base their decisions on.

The contrasts between the two types of third-party intervention make it difficult to combine the role of the judge and the role of the mediator in a satisfactory way. Indeed it does happen that a third party first tries to mediate between the parties and if that does not succeed, passes judgement. Also the reverse is conceivable: that a third party first passes judgement and then proceeds to mediate when he sees that the judgement will not be respected. But in both cases attempts to use one method may place hindrances in the way of the other. By mediating one may weaken the normative basis for a later judgement and perhaps also undermine confidence in one's impartiality as a judge; and by judging first one will easily reduce the willingness to compromise of the party who was supported in the judgement, and will be met with suspicion of partiality by the other.

When the establishment of new third-party institutions is sought, for instance, by a legislator who is looking for new ways of settling labour conflicts, or by those who are working for the peaceful adjustment of international conflicts, there may be a dilemma about which way to go. Should one go in for building up the norm system, and for strengthening the normative engagement with the aim of having as many conflicts as possible decided by judgement? Or ought one rather rely on 'de-ideologization' and mediation? In considering such questions it is important not to let oneself be led by superficial analogies but to take account of all the relevant factors. Regarding international conflicts, for instance, one must consider that there is no superior instance which is powerful enough to force a powerful state to obedience. This has the consequence that courts can hardly be effective organs for the resolution of conflicts where substantial interests are at stake. Mediation also presents difficulties, among other reasons because the parties often place great emphasis on the moral and legal aspects of the conflict, and have strongly divergent opinions concerning both norms and (perhaps especially) the relevant facts. But there is good reason to believe that the difficulties in mediation are, after all, easier to overcome and that endeavours should therefore go in the direction of reducing the normative engagement.

(ii) Alternative Dispute Resolution and the Ontario Civil Justice System

Allan Stitt, Francis Handy and Peter A. Simm

1. INTRODUCTION

The Civil Justice Review's First Report recognized that a modern civil justice system in Ontario must make available to the public both traditional court processes and Alternative Dispute Resolution (ADR) options. This paper will examine which ADR processes are appropriate for inclusion in Ontario's existing civil litigation framework, which legal proceedings are best suited for ADR, when in the litigation process ADR should be attempted, whether ADR should be mandatory or voluntary, whether court-connected ADR should be publicly funded, and whether court-connected ADR services should be provided by the public sector or the private sector.

This paper does not consider ADR in relation to specialized areas of civil disputes, since these topics are addressed in other forthcoming or recently-published studies.

The Terms of Reference of the Ontario Civil Justice Review state that:

> The members of the public require a more efficient, less costly, speedier and more accessible civil justice system. To achieve this objective ... this review is mandated to develop an overall strategy for the civil justice system in an effort to provide a speedier, more streamlined and more efficient structure which will maximize the utilization of public resources allocated to civil justice.
>
> ...
>
> Some issues which are to be considered in [the longer-range] aspect of the Review's mandate are the following:
>
> ...
>
> (d) the role of private industry in providing alternative methods for parties to resolve issues without resorting to the judicial process. This would include mediation, arbitration, and other alternative dispute resolution processes;
>
> (e) the role and obligations of litigants to avail themselves of the various resolution initiatives provided by the court prior to the entitlement to a trial.

With these goals in mind, we propose in this paper a system for integrating mediation into the civil litigation dispute resolution mainstream, so as to increase the flexibility of dispute resolution and give access to greater justice for a wider range of disputants.

One of the difficulties with examining ADR in a short paper is that ADR encompasses a spectrum of several different processes — from negotiation, to non-binding third-party intervention (such as mediation), to binding third-party intervention (such as arbitration). Our definitions for these terms are set out below in the section titled "The ADR Spectrum".

In this paper, we consider use of only non-binding processes that will contribute to the goals set out above and that are outside traditional litigation rules. We have therefore not looked at the possibility of having court-annexed binding arbitration programs for Ontario. No valid empirical basis exists for allocating cases for arbitration as opposed to litigation. Further, and more importantly, the litigation system already provides a binding mechanism for settling disputes. Therefore, in our view, arbitration programs are not fundamentally different from litigation, and may require procedural, rather than substantive changes to civil rules.

We have also not reviewed more creative use of options already existing in the rules of civil procedure, such as summary judgment, agreed statements of fact, requests to admit, and so on. We do not disagree that amendments to the rules of civil procedure or more creative use of the existing rules may be methods of contributing to more efficient and effective dispute resolution as well. For this paper, however, we have focused our efforts on non-binding mediation.

In its First Report, the Civil Justice Review states:

From *Rethinking Civil Justice: Research Studies for the Civil Justice Review*, Vol. 2 (Toronto: Ontario Law Reform Commission, 1996) at 451–457. Notes omitted. © Queen's Printer for Ontario, 1995. Reproduced with permission.

We believe that the State has an obligation to make available to its members the means by which their disputes may be resolved, peacefully, through the medium of independent, objective and fair third party intervention.

In Ontario, parties to litigation currently receive mandatory third-party intervention with their cases only at the pre-trial conference, and at trial. At pre-trials, judges, exercising their traditional function, give assessments of the likely outcome at trial, in the hope that this information will help the parties to settle.

As an American commentator, Wayne D. Brazil, has pointed out:

> One of organized society's most fundamental responsibilities is to provide means by which people can resolve disputes without violence. In other words, providing effective dispute-resolution processes is an essential public responsibility. It is because we recognize that fact, and because we are concerned that the formal adjudicatory process might not, in all circumstances, deliver the best dispute resolution services, that we are interested in having public courts explore the wisdom of sponsoring ADR programs.

We agree with this general statement, and wish to explore the wisdom of having public courts sponsor ADR programs in Ontario. This paper will examine the feasibility of incorporating mediation (which we define in this context only as third party assistance in a non-binding process) as part of the dispute-resolution process early in a civil proceeding that has been commenced in the Ontario court system. The goal of such a step would be to save judicial and administrative resources, reduce unnecessary confrontation, increase the substantive and procedural satisfaction of the users of the civil justice system, and produce outcomes that the parties want to implement.

2. EXECUTIVE SUMMARY

We recommend that Ontario adopt a system in which litigants in civil proceedings commenced in Ontario will be required to attend a mediation — a non-binding ADR process — after the close of pleadings and before discovery, as a prerequisite to proceeding with the litigation. At the mediation, the mediator should assist the parties to attempt to negotiate a resolution to the dispute by helping them determine their interests and generate creative options independent of their strict legal rights or a perceived outcome at trial.

We recommend that the mediators be drawn from a pre-approved private sector pool of mediators. The parties should be given the opportunity to choose their mediator. The pre-approval of mediators is not examined at any length in this paper.

In order to fund the mediation, we recommend that the government agree to contribute a nominal fixed sum (e.g. $200) toward the cost of the mediation if the parties settle the dispute at the mediation or within a short time thereafter. The parties should bear the balance of the cost of the mediation. If the parties do not settle within this time, they should bear all of the costs of the mediation themselves.

The model that we propose is similar to the model being used in Florida and Texas, where there is a requirement that parties go to private mediators before being permitted to proceed to trial. Parties in those two states are required to pay their own costs of the ADR process.

3. THE ADR SPECTRUM

(a) Introduction

Dispute resolution encompasses a number of processes, ranging from negotiation, to non-binding processes (such as mediation), to consensual binding forms of ADR (such as arbitration), to litigation. These processes frequently are described as a spectrum: they are often arranged to correlate with increasing cost and third-party involvement, decreasing control of the parties over the process, and, usually, increasing likelihood of having the relationship between the disputants deteriorate during and after the resolution of the dispute. Recently, the processes other than traditional litigation — i.e. those on the less costly and more party-controlled end of the spectrum — have been gathered under the term Alternative Dispute Resolution or ADR.

ADR is growing in importance as society and the legal profession grapple with the problems associated with traditional litigation. Faced with court overcrowding, rising demands on scarce public resources, escalating legal and emotional costs, and an increasingly long and arduous litigation process, disputants search for new processes that could resolve the issues in a way that makes sense for all involved. Some disputants want a binding decision imposed on them, but quickly, in private, with a minimum of monetary and emotional expense. Others want a less intimidating process where the parties have control over the decision, and can explore an increased number and range of available solutions ("expanding the pie"), rather than being confined to "win" or "lose" options. They want a process where they will have an opportunity to express their interests without fear that their legal rights will be harmed, and where their relationships will not be unnecessarily jeopardized by the very process of resolving the dispute.

In response to these needs and desires, ADR processes have developed both independently and as part of court programs. Many ADR processes can be considered as either forms of arbitration, in which a neutral provides a binding or non-binding decision about the likely outcome if the cases were to go to trial, or as forms of mediation, a non-binding process where a neutral third party assists the disputants to negotiate a resolution of the dispute. Whatever its specific features, an ADR process must be confidential to function effectively.

ADR is currently being used in Ontario in a number of areas. A summary of some of those uses is set out in Appendix "B" to this paper. Below, for the purposes of this paper only, we set out the attributes of the two primary techniques usually included in the term ADR: Arbitration and Mediation.

(b) Arbitration

In arbitration, as in litigation, a neutral third party (or a panel) makes a decision based on the merits of the dispute. The disputants can agree in advance to be bound by the decision of the neutral, or to treat the decision as advisory only. As in litigation, there may be witnesses who are examined and cross-examined, and ordinarily counsel make opening and closing arguments. Unlike litigation, however, there typically are no discoveries. Parties in an arbitration are able (with or without the arbitrator's assistance) to determine time limits both prior to and at the hearing, rules of evidence, whether witnesses should be sworn, the scope of pleadings (if there are to be any), and the level to which the arbitrator should be permitted to intervene in the hearing.

Although parties may opt out of some of its provisions, all arbitrations in Ontario are governed by the *Arbitration Act, 1991*, S.O. 1991, c. 17, as amended, while international arbitrations conducted in Ontario are subject to the International Commercial Arbitration Act, R.S.O. 1990, c. I.9. These cases are not part of the civil justice system in Ontario, and in this sense are truly alternative to litigation.

The parties may jointly select a single arbitrator, or have a court appoint the single arbitrator, or the parties may each appoint an arbitrator and have their two appointees agree on a third arbitrator (who will then chair the panel). If there is a panel rather than a single arbitrator, majority and minority decisions may be rendered.

Arbitration can have a number of advantages over traditional litigation. Firstly, hearings can be arranged quickly if the parties and arbitrator(s) are available. Secondly, because the parties set their own procedural rules, they can limit pleadings, discovery, number of witnesses, and time for examination, cross-examination, and oral argument. Therefore the parties can get a decision within months, weeks or sometimes days of the dispute arising.

With this control over the process, the parties can drastically decrease their costs and the time that they need to devote to resolving the dispute. Just as importantly, a quick resolution can avoid problems such as secondary disputes over the mitigation of damages, the loss of evidence, failure of memory of witnesses, and other complications that can arise when a trial takes place long after the events that caused the dispute. Further, the custom-tailored nature of procedural rules for the arbitration also enables the parties to agree on the admissibility of evidence, regardless of the admissibility of that evidence in court.

There is also a danger in litigation that the judge may be unfamiliar with the subject area in dispute. In arbitration, the parties can choose an arbitrator with expertise in the subject area and thereby increase the likelihood of receiving an informed decision. In her conclusions to her survey of the literature on private dispute-resolution mechanisms, Roehl states that: "Private dispute-resolution appears especially promising for complex, multi-party cases, and where narrow expertise is desirable from a neutral third party."

Finally, because appeal rights are limited for arbitrations, the decision of the arbitrator usually ends the process and resolves the dispute.

Disadvantages to arbitration do exist, however. Like litigation, arbitration calls for a decision to be made: there is no opportunity to adopt a creative solution which "expands the pie" and creates joint gains. There is still a winner and a loser in an arbitration, and a corresponding a priori uncertainty about the result, regardless of the arbitrator's expertise. At the end of an arbitration, relationships are often destroyed. Parties also have no opportunity during an arbitration to express their interests and to explain the problem as they see it (other than as allowed by their counsel in direct examination and by opposing counsel in cross-examination).

As well, once they are in the heat of a dispute, parties are often not amenable to resolving procedural issues amicably. The arbitrator may therefore have to resolve those issues for the parties; in such situations, the process can become as protracted as litigation.

Finally, although arbitration does impose a decision on the parties, it does not necessarily provide the parties with the procedural safeguards that have evolved in courts through the common and statute law. An inadequate or improperly conducted arbitration may lead therefore to subsequent litigation in the form of an appeal or judicial review, in a situation where substantive rights may already have been impaired.

(c) Mediation

Mediation is a process in which a neutral third party facilitates negotiations between disputing parties. The mediator has no power to impose a resolution: a resolution is achieved only if the parties agree to it. Generally, there are two forms of mediation: rights-based and interest-based.

In a rights-based mediation, a neutral third-party gives the parties his or her independent assessment of the merits of the case and the likely outcome. Rights-based mediation is therefore not readily distinguishable from non-binding arbitration. The parties are free to accept the assessment of the mediator, modify it, or reject it outright. A familiar example of rights-based mediation is the pre-trial conference. If given a choice, people with little or no experience with mediation may opt for rights-based mediation as the preferred form of dispute resolution. They may feel comfortable with a neutral third party opining on the merits of the dispute, and consequently may have difficulty seeing the utility of a neutral third party who does not provide an opinion on substance.

The other form of mediation — the form used at the Toronto ADR Pilot Project and the method that we advocate in this paper — is interest-based mediation. Interest-based mediation seeks to have the parties focus on their underlying interests rather than on the potential outcomes of litigation. The theories are often attributed to Roger Fisher, William Ury, Bruce Patton and Frank Sander of Harvard Law School.

An interest-based mediator attempts to determine why the parties take the positions they do on the issues, and encourages the parties to generate creative options to satisfy their interests. The mediator then focuses on objective criteria (often generated by the parties) to help the parties choose from among the options. The parties can then compare the creative options to their Best Alternative To a Negotiated Agreement (or BATNA). The mediator facilitates the process of the mediation and leaves the substantive issues to the parties and their counsel.

The advantages of interest-based mediation are numerous. Firstly, the parties have an opportunity to express their feelings, needs and interests in a way that does not exist at discovery, trial, or in a rights-based ADR process. Disputants sometimes find that after the cathartic experience of expressing interests, they are able to address the legal or monetary issues more easily.

Secondly, the parties have the opportunity to play a substantive role in shaping the solution ultimately achieved. The parties can look at all possible options, not only ones that a court or arbitrator could impose. Parties may come up with face-saving resolutions to the dispute that both sides can live with comfortably. They may also be able to combine a number or outstanding issues (whether or not part of a litigation proceeding) to create an elegant solution to outstanding problems, in a way that benefits all involved.

Thirdly, because the parties have control of the resolution that is achieved and must agree to it, the parties have a stake in abiding by the agreement to ensure that it works. Solutions achieved in mediations are therefore more likely to be honoured by the parties.

Next, mediation can be accomplished quickly. Mediations in civil cases rarely last longer than one day, and often can be completed in less than half a day. There is usually no need for production of documents, discovery, or any other court process prior to mediation. The resulting cost savings for the parties — in terms of legal fees and the saved opportunity cost as a result of the streamlined process — can therefore be very large if the mediation is successful.

Also, the mediation can be conducted in a non-adversarial and informal environment, in which the mediator attempts to make the parties feel comfortable with the process, so that the parties can concentrate their efforts on resolving outstanding issues.

Further, interest-based mediation, in stark contrast to litigation and arbitration, strives to improve or at least not to damage the relationship between the parties after the dispute is resolved. The trained interest-based mediator controls the process so that the parties can focus their energy on dealing with the issues, rather than on attacking each other. If the dispute can be resolved without harming the relationship, there may be an opportunity for parties to maintain their ability to deal with each other in the future, which may be important in many contexts, including, for example family, commercial or employment matters.

In addition, parties are generally satisfied with the results from interest-based mediation. A review of the empirical literature shows that "Both litigants and attorneys find mediation to be fair and satisfactory".

Finally, and perhaps most importantly, since mediation is a non-binding process, parties maintain their legal rights. If they are not satisfied with the resolution that they can achieve at the mediation, parties are free to continue along the litigation path. The mediation is conducted without prejudice.

[Note: In the preceding article the authors distinguish between "rights-based" mediation and "interest-based" mediation. Try to identify the difference between "rights" and "interests" in any conflict. See also the discussion of approaches to dispute settlement in contractual matters in Stuart MacAulay, "Non-Contractual Relationships in Business: A Preliminary Study," in Chapter 6B, reading (i), above. In this article MacAulay notes that most business people he interviewed preferred to keep all talk of lawyers and legal rights out of their efforts at informal dispute settlement, focussing instead on their "interests" in maintaining business relationships, or reducing costs or negative publicity.]

B. Adjudication

(i) The Judge and the Adversary System

Neil Brooks

THE ROLE OF THE JUDGE IN THE ADVERSARY SYSTEM

A thorough discussion of this subject would require an examination of the judge's role at each stage of the litigation process: at the pre-trial investigative stage; at the pre-trial procedural stages; at the trial; at the sentencing hearing; and at the hearing to determine law and policy. While the same principles may be applicable to each stage, the discussion in this paper will focus on the role of the trial judge in the conduct of the trial. The trial has a first claim on our attention since it is at this stage of the litigation process that all aspects of the adversary system bear most directly on the judge's role. Moreover, restricting the discussion in this way will permit, in the time available, a more detailed development of the central theoretical themes of the subject.

In determining the precise role that he will assume in discharging his responsibilities at trial, a judge will undoubtedly consider a wide range of factors: the peculiarities of his own temperament and abilities, the significance of the particular case to the parties and to the public, the complexity of the factual and legal issues raised by the case, and the effectiveness of the parties or their counsel in presenting the case. However, whatever other factors a judge might consider in defining the precise nature of the role he will play, the fact that he is an arbiter in an adjudicative proceeding that is adversarial in nature necessarily prescribes for him the parameters of his involvement in the proceeding. In this paper I will develop this theme by speculating about the justifications which have been or might be advanced supporting the adversary system, and then exploring

---

From Allen Linden, ed., *The Canadian Judiciary* (Toronto: Osgoode Hall Law School, 1976) at 89–118. Notes omitted. Reproduced by permission of Professor Neil Brooks.

the limitations that these justifications impose on the judge's role in conducting a judicial trial.

. . . .

Definition of "Adversary System"

The greatest impediment to clear thinking about the judge's role in the adversary system is the variety of meanings that are often assigned to the concept of the adversary system. Therefore, before examining the premises underlying the adversary system let me make clear the sense in which that concept is used in this paper by distinguishing it from various senses in which it is often misleadingly used.

The term is being used in this paper to refer generally to a procedural system in which the parties and not the judge have the primary responsibility for defining the issues in dispute and for carrying the dispute forward through the system. Thus, it should not be confused with what might more accurately be referred to as the adjudicative process. Adjudication is a method of settling disputes that is commonly contrasted with other methods of dispute resolution such as mediation, negotiation and conciliation. Used in this context, it refers characteristically to a means of resolving disputes in which some general principle or rule of law is applied to the facts that gave rise to the dispute and in which the parties involved are able to participate by presenting proofs and reasoned argument.

Professor Lon Fuller, who in a series of essays clarified the tasks for which adjudication because of its institutional framework was well-suited as a means of social ordering, argued that an adversary presentation is essential to adjudication. He postulated that the fundamental characteristic of adjudication is the opportunity it provides for the affected parties to participate in the decision-making by presenting proofs and arguments. He concluded that only the adversary system is capable of affording this requisite degree of participation. Whether or not these two concepts need to be so closely wed, it remains useful in analysing the judge's role to distinguish between them.

. . . .

[I]t is sometimes argued that the adversary system is deficient because it presents an all-or-nothing proposition — there are always winners and losers — and, as a consequence, the total satisfaction of the parties is often reduced. This is particularly the case in areas such as family law, labour law, or criminal law where the parties are part of a close social or economic relationship. Again the adversary system is here a victim because of its close association with adjudication. The attempt at the outset to adjudicate this kind of claim is more properly criticized.

. . . .

The adversary system, as that term is used by many proceduralists and as it will be used in this paper, embodies two distinct principles. The issues resolved by these two principles raise the two most basic questions that confront any adjudicative procedural system. The first issue is what should the respective functions of the parties and the judge be with reference to the initiation and content of the adjudication. The adversary system rests on the principle of party-autonomy. That is to say, that the parties have the right to pursue or dispose of their legal rights and remedies as they wish. The second issue is what should the respective functions of the parties and the judge be with reference to the progress of a dispute through the procedural system once initiated and defined. The adversary system rests on the principle of party-prosecution. This principle holds that the parties have the primary responsibility to choose without interference from the judge the manner in which they will go forward with their case and the proofs they will present for the judge's consideration in adjudicating the dispute.

Party-Autonomy

In defining the judge's role in the conduct of the trial it is, of course, the principle of party-prosecution that requires careful analysis. However, to place that examination in perspective, the principle of party-autonomy must be briefly examined. The principle of party-autonomy has two aspects. First, it limits the judge's function to disputes which have been presented to him. A judge plays a role only when a conflict has arisen between two or more parties, and at least one of them seeks the assistance of the judge in resolving the dispute. John Chipman Gray, in defining a judge, summarized this principle: "A judge of an organized body is a man appointed by that body to determine duties and the corresponding rights upon the application of persons claiming those rights." The authors of a casebook on civil procedure described the principle more prosaically: "Courts ought not to function as self-propelled vehicles of justice and right like King Arthur's knights in Good Humor trucks." Lon Fuller quotes a socialist critic of bourgeois law who caricatured this premise of the adversary system by asserting that courts in such a system "are like defective clocks; they have to be shaken to set them going". Fuller noted that, "[h]e of course added the point that the shaking costs money".

The second aspect of party-autonomy is that the parties have the sole responsibility for defining the dispute that they would like adjudicated. Thus, if the parties want the judge to decide one dispute, he will not insist on resolving another even though he perceives the other issue to be the real cause of the conflict between the parties.

Both aspects of party-autonomy are subject to qualifications. While the judge cannot initiate proceedings, he can prevent the parties from initiating certain proceedings. The courts have an important social function to perform by resolving disputes. Thus the judge can prevent parties from using the litigation process to resolve hypothetical or moot problems. He can judicially notice all facts that he considers beyond reasonable dispute and thus prevent the parties from consuming the time of the court by presenting evidence on clear factual issues. He can also prevent misuses of the process by a judicial screening of cases, he can give judgment on the pleadings or give a summary judgment. Indeed he is assisted in controlling the use of the court's process by counsel for the parties. Lawyers have a professional responsibility to ensure the claims and defences they put forward have merit and are related to a real conflict.

In criminal cases, the judge's role in controlling the issues disputed is even greater than his responsibility in civil cases. While the judge cannot control the criminal cases to reach his docket, nor find the accused guilty of a crime he is not charged with, nor insist that the Crown amend the indictment to add charges, he does not permit the accused or the Crown complete autonomy in defining the issues contested. For instance, he can prevent the Crown from initiating the case if he concludes that the Crown is abusing the process. There is also an increasing recognition of the judge's responsibility to examine the factual basis of a plea of guilty. In the United States a Presidential Commission has recently recommended that the guilty plea be abolished entirely because, among other things, it leaves too much of the public interest to the parties.

The limits of the principle of party-autonomy can, of course, only be defined by reference to the reasons why it is regarded as being an essential principle of the Anglo-American procedural system. Two justifications sometimes put forward fail to appreciate that party-autonomy is only a principle which defines the respective roles of the parties and the judge. In civil cases, it has been said that the principle of party-autonomy — that the judge only operates when the parties present him with a dispute to resolve — rests on the judgment that "the social interest in securing general observance of the rules of private law is sufficiently served by leaving their enforcement to the self-interest of the parties more or less directly affected." However, while this reason might explain why the state need not become involved in the enforcement of the civil law, it does not go directly to the issue of the roles of the parties and the judge in initiating actions. In many areas where there is an important public interest in the enforcement of the civil law, as in the enforcement of the criminal law, the state, through an administrative agency, might initiate actions enforcing the law. And yet, since it is not the judge who initiates such actions, the principle of party-autonomy would be satisfied.

Others have suggested that the principle of party-autonomy reflects a political ideology. Thurman Arnold asserted, "...the civil trial dramatizes the moral beauty of the noninterference of government in private affairs.... The whole ideology, and procedural organization of the civil trial is designed to insulate the court and the government from taking the initiative in enforcing or even protecting the civil rights of individuals". Thurman Arnold was at the time decrying the resistance to the New Deal and exploring its causes. He went on, "[t]his role of the civil trial as a symbol of individual freedom from active interference by the government makes it a most important factor in preserving conservative traditions in the face of new legislation". While party-autonomy may reflect a *laissez-faire* philosophy, Arnold's point goes to the role of the government generally in the enforcement of the civil law.

. . . .

Party-Prosecution
The second major premise of the adversary system, as that term is used by most proceduralists, is the principle of party-prosecution. This principle holds that the parties have the right and the responsibility to choose the manner in which they will go forward with their case and the proof they will present to support it. The judge's role is to passively evaluate the merits of the case as and when it is presented to him.

In the remainder of this paper I will explore the reasons why the principle of party-prosecution is adhered to at trial, and offer some general comments on the parameters that these reasons place upon the judge's intervention in the conduct of the case. The conclusion that I reach is that viewed in this way the adversary system does not impose as severe restraints on the judge's intervention as is often assumed, and that in appropriate cases the judge should, if he deems it necessary, play a much larger role in the conduct of the case. My argument will be a plea for more judicial activism in controlling the conduct of the trial.

The principle of party-prosecution at trial rests, in the main, upon two broad empirical assumptions. Firstly, that the legitimacy of adjudication as a means of social ordering is enhanced if it is conducted according to an adversarial presentation. Secondly, that more accurate fact-finding is likely to result if parties motivated by self-interest are given the responsibilities of investigating facts and presenting arguments, and if the decision-maker remains passive.

The Adversary System Increases the Acceptability of Adjudication

Every means of social ordering used by the state must be acceptable not only to those immediately affected by its particular sanctions but also to all those governed by the state. This need for legitimacy is particularly paramount in a free society with respect to adjudication since a judge's decision might be perceived, in some sense at least, to be undemocratic.

Legitimacy or acceptability is a derivative value. That is to say, a decision-making process will be acceptable to the extent that it meets all the criteria that people expect of that decision-making process. With respect to adjudication these expectations undoubtedly include such considerations as expediency, finality, inexpensiveness, and the protection of privacy and other social values. To the extent that the adversary system furthers these values it will render the adjudicative process more acceptable than would some other procedural device for finding the facts. But aside from these considerations, which are necessary attributes of any acceptable adjudicative proceeding, it is often argued that the adversary system has unique characteristics which render it in judicial trials a more acceptable procedure in our society than other methods of fact-finding. The reasons for the acceptability of the adversary system, if indeed it is more acceptable than other methods of fact-finding, must rest ultimately upon complex questions of political theory and psychology. I can only be suggestive here, in part repeating what others have speculated. Four reasons might be given as to why the adversary system is a more acceptable method of fact-finding in judicial trials than any other method.

Relationship to the Prevalent Political and Economic Theory

The adversary system yields greater satisfaction to the litigants and others because it is a procedure that is consistent with the prevalent social and political ideology of western society. An assertion made in the editorial page of a bar association journal illustrates this argument: "If you believe in the Anglo-Saxon common law tradition, that the individual is the important unit of our society, and the state exists to serve him, then it seems that the adversary system is preferable. If you hold a corporate view of society, that is to say, that the community is the important unit, and that the citizen must be primarily considered as a part of the corporate unit, then it seems you should champion the inquisitorial system...."

Jerome Frank is well known for linking the adversary system with economic theory. In his writings he repeatedly associated it with classic, *laissez-faire*, economic theory and unbridled individualism. Surprisingly, however, only recently has scholarship emerged in the English language which attempts to seriously study the influence of political and economic theory on judicial procedure. Naively, perhaps, the assumption has been made that procedure is value-free. Scholars who have turned their attention to this question in recent years seem to agree that at least at a very general and theoretical level there are connections between ideology and procedural choices. The connection may not be direct, nor empirically demonstrable. However, at least arguably, the adversary system can be seen as reflecting the political and economic ideology of classic English liberalism in three ways: by its emphasis upon self-interest and individual initiative; by its apparent distrust of the state; and, by the significance it attaches to the participation of the parties.

The adversary system legitimizes, indeed necessitates, a self-interested role for the parties. Thus one of its premises would appear to be consistent with the premise of the capitalist system of economic organization that if each individual strives to promote his self-interest an optimum allocation of resources will result. As Professors Neef and Nagel note, "...at the base of the adversary proceeding we encounter the old *laissez-faire* notion that each party will (or indeed can) bring out all the evidence favorable to his own side, and that if the accused is innocent (if his is the best case) he can act to 'outproduce' the presentation made by his competitors". With this competitive individualism at its base, if the party with the better case — that is the case that is correct on the facts — were to lose, that result would be satisfactory in an adversary system because he, not the system, would be the author of his defeat. Initiative is rightly rewarded, laziness or ignorance penalized. This justification for the adversary system is illustrated in a statement made in a commentary on the Japan *Code of Civil Procedure* that was enacted after World War II when Japan adopted the adversary system.

> [S]ince civil litigation is essentially a dispute concerning private rights, as a matter of course, the responsibility and duty to present proof rests with the parties; it is neither the responsibility nor the duty of the court.... When the necessary facts to maintain the allegation of a party cannot be proven, the disadvantage should be borne by such party, and it is sufficient grounds for the court to issue him an unfavorable determination. The disadvantage is a consequence invited by the party himself, over and beyond which the court should neither assist a party on one side nor interfere.

If this is one of the justifications for the adversary system then not many people today would likely perceive of it as placing very serious constraints on the judge's intervention in the trial. *Laissez-faire* theory is no longer taken as being determinative in the economic and social fields. It would be incongruous if its basic postulate was still the premise used to define the respective roles of the parties and the judge in a judicial trial.

A basic socialist value is a strong emphasis on collectivism. The interests of the state and the individual are assumed to coincide, state power is not distrusted. On the other hand, liberal political philosophy is premised on a distrust of the state and public officials. The adversary system can thus be viewed in a liberal state as a means of decentralizing power, and as an attempt to prevent abuses of political power. This view finds some support in the fact that the genesis of at least some rules of procedure and evidence can also be explained on the basis of a felt concern to decentralize power. Professor Friedman in his recent text, a *History of American Law*, notes that the law of evidence "...was founded in a world of mistrust and suspicion of institutions; it liked nothing better than constant checks and balances...." This concern in an adversary system to decentralize power was illustrated during the period of Jacksonian democracy in the United States when a serious effort was initiated to take many rights from the judge including not only the right to comment upon the evidence but also the right to summarize the evidence to the jury.

. . . .

Finally, the adversary system can be seen as being consistent with our prevalent political philosophy because it affords the parties the opportunity to participate in the making of decisions that affect their interests. Both psychological and theoretical literature in political philosophy support the view that the most acceptable type of decision in a democracy is personal choice. However, since it is clearly impossible to realize personal choice in many situations the best alternative is a system that assures to those affected by the decision some participation in the decisional process. A procedural system in which the judge assumes the primary responsibility for eliciting the proof, but permits the parties to assist in the proof-taking, would provide the parties a measure of participation in the decision-making process. However, Fuller argues that the adversary system "heightens the significance of ... participation" and thus "lifts adjudication toward its optimum expression". For this reason, he concludes that the adversary system is an essential characteristic of the adjudicative process.

The extent to which the judge's intervention in the trial, either in clarifying evidence or in calling for new evidence, impairs the parties' sense of participation is obviously an extremely complex question that cannot be explored in any detail here. In some instances, however, it might clearly be a consideration that leads the judge to the conclusion that he should not intervene. But in other situations his intervention in the form of asking questions might actually increase the meaningfulness of the parties' participation. Everyone has different cognitive needs and if the judge makes these needs known to the parties then it will make their participation more meaningful — obviously their participation will be meaningless unless the judge's understanding of the case is the meaning that they are attempting to convey to him. Also, even if the judge were to call additional proof, so long as he gives the parties the opportunity to test such proof and call rebutting proof their participation in the decision-making process would appear to remain meaningful.

(i) The Judge and the Adversary System

Cathartic Effect

Particularly in civil suits the adversary system might be a more acceptable procedure for fact-finding than the inquisitorial system because it satisfies the psychology of the litigants by legitimizing a courtroom duel which is a sublimation of more direct forms of hostile aggression. It has been suggested that there are psychological benefits in the "battle atmosphere" of adversary litigation. Charles Curtis in his book *It's Your Law* summarized this argument. He said:

> The law takes the position that we ought to be satisfied if the parties are; and it believes that the best way to get this done is to encourage them to fight it out, and dissolve their differences in dissention. We are still a combative people not yet so civilized and sophisticated as to forget that combat is one way to justice.

The use of the adversary system to satisfy the primeval competitive urges of the litigants might be suggested by its genealogy. The ancestry of the trial is of course the blood feud, trial by battle and individual or class acts of revenge. The justification for the adversary system is also apparent in the frequent analogy of the judicial trial to a sporting event. It leads lawyers to talk of tactics and strategy and to refer to the judge as an umpire. This view of the adversary process is most clearly perceived if the trial is regarded as a "game", using that word in the sense that it is used by game theorists. The "sporting theory of justice" describes the rules of the game. There has been a social disturbance and the game is played only to gain some relief or satisfaction.

The adversary system viewed as part of a game perhaps explains the system's acceptance of the result when a party loses on a technicality, even if his loss was due to a violation of one of the technical rules of evidence of procedure which regulate the game. If Justice is equated to the satisfaction of the litigants then the adversary system, which is directly responsible for this satisfaction, becomes an end in itself. The true facts of the case are less important than how well the parties play the game. Reasoning from this premise, Charles Curtis concluded:

> Justice is something larger and more intimate than truth. Truth is only one of the ingredients of justice. Its whole is the satisfaction of those concerned.... The administration of justice is no more designed to elicit truth than the scientific approach is designed to extract justice from the atom.

If this justification for the adversary system is correct then the judge's role in the trial would be a limited one. However, the basic premise of the argument is disputable. As one author posed the question: "Is the battle atmosphere of trial proceedings truly cathartic, in the sense of relieving tensions and aggressions that would otherwise find more destructive outlets, or does it instill an aggressive approach to problems that is incompatible with the need to compromise and co-operate in the vast majority of interpersonal contacts?" Unfortunately, no serious effort has been made to resolve this question by asking the ultimate consumers of the system—the litigants. Basing a judgement on common experience, however, most people would probably agree with Professor Garlan who wrote at the height of the legal realist movement, referring to the jurisprudential theory of what he called "sporting fairness":

> The game has become too brutal, too destructive of human life, too exhaustive to those who win, and too fatal for those who lose. Living begins to look more like a struggle, than a game. The participant's sense of humor and sense of balance are worn, and the sporting morale is breaking up into a fighting morale. The sides are too unequal for successful competition, and, in the eyes of the defeated, the game looks more like exploitation than competition.

While we know very little about the psychology of litigants, I suspect that most of them do not view social conflicts as social events. They come to court expecting justice, and unless the rules of substantive law are perverse, that means they expect their dispute to be resolved according to the law. A theory about the judge's role that begins by assuming that rules of evidence and procedure are simply rules of competition is therefore deficient.

Role of Counsel

A third aspect of the adversary system that might render it more acceptable than the inquisitorial system is the role played by counsel. It has been hypothesized that "[i]f parties perceive their adversary attorneys as having interests convergent with their own, they may begin to experience the comforting strength of belonging to a coalition the total purpose of which is to gain a favorable verdict at the expense of the opposing party". Also the lawyer will be a person who, in some sense, shares in the litigant's defeat. Certain institutional characteristics of the adversary system might encourage this coalition and the apparent identity of interest between the adversary lawyer and his client. However, assuming this to be true, intervention in the trial proceedings by the trial judge is unlikely to destroy in any way this coalition or this sense of shared purpose.

Appearance of Impartiality

Finally, the adversary system might be more acceptable than an inquisitorial system because it gives the tribunal the appearance of impartiality. Proponents of the Anglo-American procedural system attach great importance to the appearance of impartiality. While its importance cannot be denied, the intelligent control of the conduct of the trial need not leave a judge open to the charge of partiality. The possible appearance of impartiality is a matter a judge should consider when intervening, and to that extent it limits his intervention. For instance, if a judge calls a witness he must ensure that the parties have an opportunity to test the testimony of the witness and to call rebutting evidence or he might be open to the charge that he is shaping the record. If a witness is evasive in answering questions the judge must ensure that he does not appear hostile towards the witness. However, if the judge intervenes in a fair and dispassionate manner this consideration should not seriously impair his ability to intervene when he thinks it is necessary.

The Adversary System Increases the Accuracy of Fact-Finding

A second justification given for the adversary system is that it is a better fact-finding mechanism than the inquisitorial system. That is to say, given all the interests that must be balanced in a procedural system more accurate factual judgments about past events are likely to be achieved using the adversary system than using some other system. This justification rests, in turn, upon two premises. The first premise is that the adversary system will result in a more thorough investigation of the facts than the inquisitorial system. The second premise is that under the adversarial system the trier of fact is more likely to reach the correct decision because during the proceedings he will not acquire a bias towards one conclusion or the other. He will be able to remain completely disinterested in the outcome until all the proof has been elicited and the arguments made. In order to define the role of the judge in the adversary system these two premises must be explored in detail.

Parties Motivated by Self-Interest Are Likely to Be Most Diligent in Presenting and Critically Evaluating All the Evidence

The first premise of this justification for the adversary system is that in an adversary proceeding the judge will, when he makes his decision, be more informed as to the facts than a similarly situated judge in an inquisitorial system. This is so, it is argued, because parties who are given a free hand in pursuing their perceived self-interest are more likely than an official motivated only by official duty to transmit to the judge all evidence favorable to their case and to critically test all unfavourable evidence presented to him. Empirical studies have attempted to test whether this premise is correct. However, for purposes of defining the judge's role in the adversary system the premise must be accepted as true.

The parties do not have complete control over the presentation and testing of proof and this premise of the adversary system does not require them to have such control. Control is given to the parties to promote accurate fact-finding and to further achieve this end the parties are constrained in the conduct of their case by rules of procedure and evidence. The need for these rules arises because if this premise of the adversary system is to achieve its objective a number of factors must be present in the litigation of particular disputes. The rules are intended, in part, to ensure that these factors are present. If these factors are not present in a particular case the adversary system will not achieve its goal of accurate fact-finding; or if it is to achieve this end in their absence the judge may have to regulate his conduct accordingly. Thus the judge, in defining his role must be sensitive to the presence or absence of these factors. For purposes of clarity I will discuss these factors as assumptions of the premise that the adversary system is an accurate fact-finding mechanism because parties motivated by self-interest will present and critically test all relevant evidence.

ASSUMPTION 1: THE PARTIES ARE INITIALLY MOTIVATED

The first assumption that this premise of the adversary system makes is that the parties are initially motivated to seek out all the evidence favorable to their case. This obviously depends upon both parties being equally interested in the outcome of the case, that is, equally interested in pursuing their respective rights and remedies and in opposing the rights of the other party. If this is not the case, if one of the parties is not motivated to oppose the other party's case, the requisite factual investigation and presentation of proof will not take place. By way of illustration, one area where the parties may not be sufficiently interested in defending their legal rights, and in which, therefore, the adversary system breaks down, is in the area of divorce. A divorce cannot be granted under the *Divorce Act* unless the judge is satisfied that there has been no condonation or connivance on the part of the petitioner. But since both parties in a particular case may want to be divorced, neither will be motivated to bring such evidence forward. In England, in recognition of the lack of motivation on the part of the parties in a divorce case, and of the state's interest in ensuring that divorces are only granted where the law authorizes them, an officer called the Queen's Proctor has been appointed. His duty is to intervene in divorce cases and ferret out facts that might suggest a collusive divorce. In Canada, while a Queen's Proctor has been officially appointed in some provinces, he is seldom called upon to discharge his duties. However, section 9 of the *Divorce Act* would appear on a literal reading to require the judge to embark on his own investigation of the possibility of condonation or connivance in the undefended divorce cases.

ASSUMPTION 2: THE PARTIES WILL SUSTAIN THEIR MOTIVATION

A second assumption of this premise of the adversary system is that throughout the proceedings both parties will sustain their motivation to present all the evidence. A number of rules of evidence have been developed to encourage parties to diligently pursue all the evidence favorable to their side; at least these rules can, in part, be understood by reference to this need. The privilege against self-incrimination, for instance, is sometimes justified on this basis. By denying the police the right to compel the accused to incriminate himself the rule forces them to seek more reliable evidence. In the same way rules requiring the corroboration of certain witnesses who are generally assumed to be unreliable might be justified on the basis that they compel the Crown to search for additional independent evidence. It is interesting to note that these rules apply in the main against the prosecution in criminal cases — they encourage the police to seek additional evidence. Perhaps this is so because there is a fear that, at least in some cases, the prosecution motivated only by official duty, may not otherwise display the diligence in pursuing evidence that the adversary system demands.

A further rule of evidence that has the effect of encouraging the parties to independently investigate all evidence in their favour is the solicitor-client privilege — at least that part of it that the Americans call the work product rule. This rule, in general, prevents one lawyer or litigant from demanding disclosure, particularly before trial, of the other litigant's trial briefs, witness statements and related materials prepared or collected for use in the litigation. If a litigant could compel such disclosure there would be a great temptation for each litigant to rely on the other to do the investigations and to gather the necessary information. Eventually, litigants would become more and more reluctant to make an independent effort to collect information and to prepare arguments for trial. Thus, the rule contributes to the efficiency of the adversary scheme of litigation. Professor Maguire observed, "so long as we depend upon thorough advanced preparation by opposing trial counsel to accumulate the necessary information about law, fact and evidence, we must not let the drones sponge upon the busy bees. Otherwise it would not be long before all lawyers become drones".

As well as forming the basis of a number of rules of evidence and procedure this assumption of party-prosecution has a more direct implication in defining the judge's role. In a system that relies on party prosecution the judge cannot intervene to such an extent in the trial that the parties begin to rely upon him to search out the facts favourable to their case and thus become less diligent themselves in seeking out the facts. There is some evidence that this attitude on the part of litigants results when the court assumes a large responsibility for proof-taking. At least it is a concern that has been expressed in countries in which the judge assumes such a role. For example, in Japan, when the adversarial system was adopted in 1948 the commentators on the new *Code of Civil Procedure* noted that, "[e]xcessive interference by the Court dampens the zeal of the parties and instead — it being entirely impossible under the present trial system for the court completely to gather all evidence *ex officio* — produces a result which is accidental in nature. This is the reason why we thoroughly follow the doctrine of party presentation under the new constitution, in which the freedom and responsibility of the individual is made a fundamental principle."

In some cases a judge might justifiably be unwilling to intervene to correct an oversight or to call further proof in order to discipline a prosecutor in a criminal case for the inefficient presentation of a case. However, within the framework of the present Anglo-American trial increased intervention by the judge would likely have little impact on the parties' presentation of their case. The stakes in most cases are too high to risk leaving important proof-taking to the judge's initiative. Even if increased judicial intervention did not have the effect in some cases of weakening the parties' presentation of proof, there is the further question of "whether in the long run this is outweighed by benefits, such as helping the party represented by an ineffective lawyer".

ASSUMPTION 3: THE PARTIES HAVE EQUAL CAPACITY, SKILL AND RESOURCES

Party-prosecution, as a principle of the adversary system, rests on a third assumption: that each party has the ability, skill, and resources to search out the evidence favorable to his case and to present it to the court. Do the parties always have the capacity or ability to obtain access to all facts favourable to their case? The adversary system encourages parties to assume a self-interested role. While casting the parties into this role [ ] ensures that they will be diligent in presenting evidence favorable to their cause, it also legitimizes or at least would appear to sanction their suppressing evidence that is unfavorable to their case. This temptation laid before the parties is regarded by many as the greatest obstacle to accurate fact-finding in the adversary system. Professor Brett argued that because "...neither of the rival theorists ... [is] bound to put forward all the data in his possession — indeed ... each ... regard it as proper to suppress any 'inconvenient' or inconsistent observations of whose existence he ... [knows,] 'the adversary system' must be regarded as basically unscientific in approach, and unsound". He further asserted that Macaulay's justification of the adversary system that "we obtain the fairest decision when two men argue, as unfairly as possible, on opposite sides, for then it is certain that no important consideration will altogether escape notice", confuses an incentive to obtain contradictory evidence with the capacity or ability to obtain it. Jerome Frank also noted, in supporting his contention that the "fight" theory of litigation does not coincide with the "truth" theory, that "frequently the partisanship of the opposing lawyers blocks the uncovering of vital evidence or leads to a presentation of vital testimony in a way that distorts it". There is little a judge in any system can do to prevent the parties from suppressing or falsifying evidence. A number of rules of evidence and procedure, however, attempt to provide both parties with access to as much evidence as possible. While these rules do not bear directly on the judge's role they are important in increasing our understanding of the adversary system and thus at least indirectly the judge's role in it.

First, rules of pre-trial discovery assist the parties in obtaining evidence. In civil cases, these rules generally permit a party to question the other prior to the trial about his knowledge of the facts in the case. It has been argued that pre-trial discovery is inconsistent with the adversary system. However, this argument confuses means with ends. If one begins the analysis by looking at the reasons for the adversary system, the better view would appear to be that of Professor Goldstein who concluded the discovery "has as its object the harnessing of the full creative potential of the adversary process, bringing each party to trial as aware of what he must meet as his finances and his lawyer's energy and intelligence permit".

Another device used both by the common law and by the legislatures to overcome the danger that the parties will suppress evidence and thus render the adversary system self-defeating is the presumption. While presumptions are sometimes created for reasons of social policy, or in order to expedite proof-taking, many presumptions operate against the party who has the superior access to the proof with respect to a particular fact. Thus it forces him to come forward with evidence that his opponent would have difficulty obtaining. A simple illustration is the presumption that arises if a bailor proves that he delivered property to a bailee in good condition and that the property was returned to him in a damaged condition. Because the bailor is not likely to have access to evidence relating to the bailee's negligence the damage will be presumed, at common law, to have been caused by the negligence of the bailee. Thus the bailee will have to come forward with sufficient evidence to prove that the damage was not caused by his negligence. In another situation a higher than normal standard of proof is placed on a party because he has control over the proof. The prosecutor must prove beyond a reasonable doubt that a confession is voluntary before the confession is admissible in evidence. At least one justification for imposing this high standard of proof is that the accused's adversary, the prosecution, has the ability, to some extent, to control the proof that relates to the voluntariness of a confession. The police can usually take statements under circumstances in which there can be no doubt as to their voluntariness. The accused, if the burden were placed on him to prove involuntariness, would likely be able to produce only his own testimony as proof. If the burden on the Crown were to prove voluntariness only on the balance of probability, the confession would usually be admitted since the issue would resolve itself into the question of who is likely to be more credible, the police or the accused.

To assist a party in gaining access to all the evidence favorable to his case an adverse inference is drawn against a party who fails to disclose to the court evidence which is within his power to produce. This inference rests on the assumption that an "honest and fearless claimant" will produce all the evidence favorable to his case and over which he has control. Therefore if he fails to produce evidence over which he has control, it can be inferred that

(i) The Judge and the Adversary System

the evidence is unfavourable to his cause. As well as drawing an adverse inference against a party who fails to produce evidence over which he has control, conduct by a party which renders it difficult or impossible for the other party to produce certain evidence will be regarded by the court as an admission of guilt or liability against that party. "Spoliation" admissions might include such things as the destruction or concealment of relevant documents or objects, intimidation, or the fabrication of evidence.

Finally, to ensure that the party's strong sense of self-interest and stake in the trial [do] not result in the degeneration of the trial into fraud and deceit, interposed between the litigant and the process is a lawyer; a person who will, to a large extent, conduct the proceedings and who has a responsibility not only to the litigant, his client, but also to the process. While the exact nature of the lawyer's responsibility to the process is the subject of dispute, there is agreement that he has a responsibility in most cases to protect the process from evidence he knows to be falsified.

For this assumption of the adversary system to be operative both parties must also have equal resources to investigate and collect facts favorable to their case, and both must be of equal skill in presenting these facts and in testing the facts presented that are unfavorable to their case. If the adversaries do not have equal representation — if for instance the accused in a criminal trial is unable to avail himself of effective counsel — this premise, upon which the adversary system rests, will be impaired. But even when both parties are represented by counsel, the quality of the representation will obviously seldom be equal. What is the role of the judge if one party is not represented or if his representation is inadequate? In such a situation the adversary system will fail to achieve its objective. The judge should not hesitate to intervene. Whatever dangers arise when a judge intervenes in such a situation, they are outweighed by the serious danger that is present if he does not intervene. Professor Fleming James noted that "[a]nything that the law of procedure or the judge's role can do to equalize opportunity and to put a faulty presentation on the right track so that disputes are more likely to be settled on their merits, will in the long run bolster up rather than destroy the adversary system, and will increase the moral force of the decisions." Judge Breitel, in an article on judicial ethics, describes how, when he first went to the bench, he tried to be detached and disciplined in his conduct of the case — which he believed to reflect the ideal role of a judge in the adversary process. After several months, however, and after seeing numerous cases where the lawyers were not equal or were unequal to their task, he began, he says, "to feel revulsion and pangs of conscience". He concluded, "[p]assivity and silence in such a situation ceased to be an acceptable role. Indeed, it made the function and responsibility of being an umpire judge a distortion, an intolerable distortion of the whole process of the administration of justice". Canadian case authorities would appear to support the proposition that when the parties' representation is unequal, the judge has a responsibility to intervene to a greater extent than he otherwise would.

In many inquisitorial systems one of the principal justifications given for increasing the authority of the judge is the need to equalize the parties. The major innovation of the Austrian *Code of Civil Procedure* of 1895, which has had a great influence upon the legislation of many other European countries, was "...its emphasis on a more active role for the judge in both expediting the proceedings and of promoting the social aim of effective quality of the parties". Socialist scholars have contended that there is a reluctance in bourgeois jurisprudence to give the judge a stronger role precisely so that the weaker party can be manoeuvred by the system into a disadvantaged position.

A final aspect of this assumption of the adversary system is the necessity that both parties have the resources to carry out a thorough investigation of the facts. This, of course, is seldom the case. Jerome Frank suggested that in all cases there should be some kind of government intervention to help an impecunious litigant obtain evidence. In criminal cases the state's facilities for investigation are obviously far superior to those of the ordinary defendant. It might be possible to reduce this disparity by providing legal aid programs with the resources necessary to locate and investigate evidence favorable to the accused. A more efficient remedy, since it does not involve the costly duplication of investigative efforts, would be to place the results of government investigations in the hands of the defence. In the United States a rule of procedure that will have this result is emerging. Clearly if we do not wish to be accused of continuing to tolerate a system whose operations negate the reason for having it we will have to continue to move in this direction.

In some areas the adversary system might have to be completely abandoned because the potential parties are not likely to have sufficient resources to pursue their remedies. Where one spouse has been deserted, for instance, we assume that he or she will bring an action for maintenance. But because of the lack of resources this remedy is seldom pursued. The adversary system is simply not an adequate means of protecting civil rights in this area. Judicial intervention obviously cannot overcome this problem, and resort may be needed to administrative investigative bodies.

ASSUMPTION 4: THE PARTIES WILL BE GIVEN THE OPPORTUNITY TO TEST ADVERSE EVIDENCE

Party-prosecution assumes that each party will have the opportunity and the ability to thoroughly test the evidence unfavorable to his case. It assumes, also, that this testing of adverse evidence must be done by an adversary cross-examination as opposed to a dispassionate inquisitorial examination. Opinions on the utility of cross-examination are sharply divided. However, a judge presiding over an adversary proceeding must, to some extent at least, assume its efficacy. Numerous rules of evidence, the hearsay rule, the best evidence rule, and the opinion evidence rule, attempt to ensure that the parties will be given the opportunity to confront and cross-examine as effectively as possible the evidence that is introduced against them. But whatever the value of cross-examination in revealing and in testing evidence, it can present grave dangers to the process. In some cases it will have the effect of misleading the trier of fact. Cross-examination, even with the best of intentions on the part of the cross-examiner, may make reliable testimony look debatable, and clear information look confused. Witnesses on the witness stand, in a strange setting, compelled to give their testimony in an unnatural manner, and under the threat of a rigorous cross-examination, can very easily be led to say things that do not accurately represent their recollections. But more seriously, counsel might well use techniques in questioning a witness by which he deliberately attempts to force the witness to narrate his testimony in a way that gives a misleading impression as to his honest recollections.

Cross-examination has other costs of equal or greater significance, costs in terms of human dignity. Cross-examination sometimes results in the total humiliation and destruction of a witness without any corresponding benefits. But I have introduced here a value extrinsic to the adversary system, and I wish to discuss the judge's role only in terms of the assumptions of that system. The point is that if cross-examination is to achieve its purpose in the adversary system, the judge must ensure that it is not used as an instrument to distort and obscure testimony. That is not abandoning his role in the adversary system, it is assuming the responsibility of his role. Eliciting the testimony of children is an area, for instance, where there might be a need for strong intervention by the judge, perhaps to the point where all the questions directed to the child are asked through the judge. Harsh and critical cross-examination techniques can confuse the child to the point where he is unable to give intelligible answers.

The judge is also in a dilemma when cross-examination has proved to be ineffective, or when counsel declines to cross-examine a witness about whose perception of the event described, for instance, the judge is in serious doubt. Should he ask questions, the answer to which he feels might assist him in evaluating the witness's perception? The answer would appear obvious. While certain dangers arise when the judge asks questions, these dangers are overridden by the fact that if the questions are not asked, the adversary system will have failed to achieve its objective.

ASSUMPTION 5: ALL INTERESTS AFFECTED ARE REPRESENTED

Finally, the principle of party-prosecution assumes that all interests affected by the adjudication are represented by the parties. The adversary system depends upon the parties to bring forward the information upon which the judge will rely in reaching his decision. In reaching a decision the judge must reconcile all the competing interests affected by his decision. If he does not receive information about some of these interests because they are interests of no immediate concern to the parties before him the adversary system will be a defective method of fact-finding for that decision. The importance of this assumption can be illustrated by reference to two areas. In a custody proceeding the adversaries are commonly seen to be the parents of the child, both of whom will supply the court with information as to why they should take custody of the child. Both will obviously be arguing in their own perceived best interest. However, the real issue in the case is the best interest of the child. In such a situation it is possible that facts relevant to the real issue in the case will not be presented to the judge by the parties and if he is to reach a decision based on all relevant information, he will have to intervene in the fact-finding.

Another area in which the adversaries will not represent all the interests might be described broadly, if not with some circularity, as being the area of public interest law, such as environmental, consumer protection law. Again, in these areas, the wise judge might well call upon the intervention of third parties to represent those interests not represented by the immediate parties to the particular dispute. At the appellant level this is commonly done by means of asking for or inviting *amicus curiae* factums. Justice Thurgood Marshall of the United States Supreme Court recently called upon the organized bar to finance public interest law on the grounds that the practice of public interest law is a vital function of the adversary system since that system presupposes representation of all interests affected.

The Adversary System Counteracts Bias in Decision-Making

The second reason often given as to why the adversary system leads to more accurate fact-finding than an inquisitorial system is that the adversary system permits the judge to remain unbiased as between the parties throughout the proceedings. Bias is a word used in a wide variety of senses, many of which shade into each other. In this context, where important consequences are being drawn from the concept, it is particularly important to be clear about its meaning.

Bias in this context does not mean, as it commonly means in other contexts, a preconceived point of view about issues of law or policy, a personal prejudice against certain types of parties, or bias in the sense of being personally interested in the outcome of the case. No fact-finding mechanism can remove these types of biases. It refers to a bias or prejudgment that is acquired by a decision-maker because of the mechanism of fact-finding used. If the judge takes an active part in proof-taking, it could be argued that he might acquire a bias towards one party or the other for one of the following reasons:

1. If the judge questions a witness and the witness is evasive, disrespectful, hostile, or in some way does not live up to the expectations of the judge, the judge may become antagonistic towards the witness and therefore tend to discredit his testimony.
2. If the judge in proof-taking is responsible for having some important evidence revealed, he may tend to give too much weight to that evidence, either because he is overly impressed with the skilful manner in which the evidence was presented, or because it is important to him that his intervention is seen to have served a useful purpose.
3. The judge may, in his investigation, become so concerned about a detail of the case that the balance of the evidence will escape his careful attention. This is perhaps the kind of consideration that judges are concerned about when they assert that their ability to evaluate the credibility of a witness is impaired if they themselves become too involved in examining a witness. That is to say, as an investigator preoccupied with his own line of thought, the judge may unconsciously fail to explore important points, may amass so much detail that obvious truths are obscured, or may not carefully observe all of the diverse matters, such as demeanor evidence, that he should take into consideration in evaluating the probative value of testimonial proof.
4. A fourth source of bias that is not present in the adversary system, but which one might argue is present in the inquisitorial system, is the bias that is acquired when the judge is presented with a file of the evidence before the case is heard by him. In an inquisitorial system the judge will of course have had to study the documents contained in the file with some care if he is to be effective in carrying out the proof-taking at trial. There is an obvious danger that the information supplied in the file will bias the judge towards one side or the other. As Glanville Williams noted, "Our reaction to the French system is that it creates a danger that the point of view of the prosecution will communicate itself to the judge before the case has been heard."
5. Finally, it has been contended that the adversary system is an unbiasing fact-finding technique because it counteracts what psychologists call decision-maker bias. Decision-maker bias is acquired when a decision-maker himself investigates the facts upon which he is to rest his judgement. It arises because of the need when one begins to investigate facts to form certain tentative hypotheses about the reality that one is called upon to reconstruct. More or less imperceptibly, these preconceptions influence the course of the investigation. As well, facts which confirm the original hypothesis will make a strong imprint upon the mind, while facts that run counter to it are received with diverted attention. This bias, which arises from the process of fact-finding, is avoided in the adversary system, it is argued. It is avoided because, in the adversary system, the judge, since he is not responsible for the investigation, is able to avoid any judgment of the case until he has heard all the evidence.

While all of these kinds of bias may be present in an adversary proceeding, none of them should limit to any great extent, within the framework of our present trial, the judge's intelligent intervention in the case. A recognition of their presence should permit the judge to conduct the proceedings in a fashion that minimizes the dangers that might arise.

Conclusion

I suggested at the outset of this paper that the role of the judge, at least the limits of his intervention in the conduct of the trial, must be established by a careful reference to the premises of the adversary system. However, in some sense, that is only a starting point in defining his role. The adversary system is not a moral axiom. We do [not] maintain it for its own sake, and the values that we seek by use of the adversary system — the acceptability of the process, and accuracy in fact-finding — are only two of the process values that must be pursued in any system of adjudication. As well as these values, any procedural system designed to resolve disputes must strike a balance among many other process values such as finality, expedition, administrative efficiency, and the protection of the dignity of the participants. Interests extrinsic to the process must also be considered, for instance, the protection of important relationships, the control of governmental power, and the protection of the innocent in criminal cases. This is not the place to expand on these interests and their implications, I merely mention them, and the fact that they must be considered by the judge in defining his role in particular situations, in order to place the discussion in this paper in its larger context.

I do not intend to explore the specific instances where a judge might be called upon to intervene in a trial. However, I will make reference to one such instance to illustrate how the premises of the adversary system could form the guidelines upon which the judge relies in defining the extent of his intervention. If a judge decided that a person, whom neither party had called, could perhaps give relevant testimony, the following dangers, in terms of the adversary system, might arise if he called that person as a witness himself: it could weaken the motivating force of the parties in calling all evidence favorable to their case, they might become careless about calling evidence knowing that if they do not call the evidence the judge will, or they might not call a witness hoping that the judge will and thus give a witness favorable to them the appearance of objectivity; it might bias the trier of fact in favour of that witness's testimony, the judge might acquire a commitment to the witness's credibility because of his interest in making his efforts appear worthwhile, the jury might give a witness called by the judge undue weight because of the witness's apparent objectivity; it could give the judge the appearance of partiality, if the witness gives testimony adverse to the accused, for instance, the judge, who called the witness, might appear to be biased against the accused; it could render the judge's ultimate decision less acceptable to the parties, if they view his intervention as an unjustified intrusion in their private fight; or, it could lead to inaccurate fact-finding if the judge called the witness at a time which made it difficult for one of the parties to lead evidence rebutting the testimony, or at a time when it had the effect of weakening the persuasive force of one of the parties' case. As well as these considerations, when the judge calls a witness a number of purely pragmatic procedural considerations arise: who can examine, cross-examine and impeach the witness; if the judge questions the witness, how do the parties effectively object to any improper questions or other procedural errors; and, how does the judge, who does not likely have any detailed or even perhaps general knowledge about the proof in the case until it unfolds before him, know that his intervention is not going to simply waste time.

While I do not have time to explore each of these dangers, and others that might rise in specific contexts, in detail, it should be clear that they provide the judge a wide latitude in which to call witnesses in appropriate cases. A similar analysis could be done for each specific instance where a judge might intervene in a trial. Giving due considerations to the dangers that might be present in specific instances, if the judge thinks in a particular case it would be helpful, I see no reason why he should hesitate, for instance, to call his own witnesses, to question witnesses both to clarify and to develop additional evidence, to invite witnesses to give a narrative account of their testimony, to invite perhaps three or four witnesses to be sworn and take their evidence in a conference-room style, to intervene to protect witnesses from harassment and confusing questions, or to advise the parties in the presentation of their case so that they do not commit procedural errors.

In conclusion, there is undoubtedly considerable experience and knowledge of human nature captured in the adversary system. What I have attempted to do is re-examine the assumptions of the adversary system and review the judge's role in light of these assumptions. My conclusion is that the adversary system imposes on the judge as well as the parties an important and active role in the conduct of the trial. The adversary system is not an end in itself; it is a procedural device which we have adopted in the pursuit of more ultimate process values. The judge has responsibility not only to arrive at a decision but also to ensure that these process values are attained.

(ii) 'Fight' Theory vs. 'Truth' Theory

Judge Jerome Frank

There is one most serious handicap in litigation that has received little attention: With the ablest lawyer in the world, a man may lose a suit he ought to win, if he has not the funds to pay for an investigation, before trial, of evidence necessary to sustain his case. I refer to evidence not in the files of the other party and therefore not obtainable by "discovery" procedure. What I mean is this: In order to prove his claim, or to defend against one, a man may need to hire detectives to scour the country — even sometimes foreign countries — in order to locate witnesses who alone may know of events that occurred years ago, or to unearth letters or other papers which may be in distant places. Or, again, he may need the services of an engineer, or a chemist, or an expert accountant, to make an extensive — and therefore expensive — investigation. Without the evidence which such an investigation would reveal, a man is often bound to be defeated. His winning or losing may therefore depend on his pocketbook. He is out of luck if his pocketbook is not well-lined with money. For neither his lawyer nor any legal-aid institution will supply the needed sums. For want of money, expendable for such purposes, many a suit has been lost, many a meritorious claim or defense has never even been asserted.

Let me illustrate. Fisher, in his recent excellent book, *The Art of Investigation*, writes: "The percentage of witnesses who cannot be found if enough effort is exerted is infinitesimal. A famous investigator once said that the man who could not be found is the man at the bottom of the sea, and even then he must be at the bottom at its points of greatest depth. Anyone alive can be found if enough effort is put forth." That statement may be exaggerated. But you get the point: Suppose there is one man, John Brown, who alone could testify to a crucial event — such as that Sam Jones was in New York City on June 12, 1948. Brown is missing. He may be in China, India or Peru. If he can be found, and if he testifies, the plaintiff will win his suit; otherwise he will lose it. If the plaintiff can afford to pay enough to investigators to scour the world for the missing witness, he may be located. If the plaintiff is a man of means, he will hire such investigators. But if he has little money, he can't do so — and will lose his case which may involve all his worldly goods.

That is not true justice, democratic justice. This defect in our judicial system makes a mockery of "equality before the law," which should be one of the first principles of a democracy. That equality, in such instances, depends on a person's financial condition. The tragedy of such a situation is etched in irony when a man's impoverished condition has resulted from a wrong done him by another whom he cannot successfully sue to redress the wrong. Many of our state constitutions contain a provision that "every person ought to obtain justice freely and without being obliged to purchase it." But, as things stand, this is too often a provision in words only. For the advantage in litigation is necessarily on the side of the party that can "purchase justice" by hiring private assistance in obtaining evidence when his adversary cannot. Unless we contrive some method to solve the problem I have posed, we must acknowledge that, in a very real sense, frequently we are "selling justice," denying it to many under-income persons. It should shock us that judicial justice is thus often an upper-bracket privilege. Here we have legal *laissez-faire* at its worst.

From *Courts on Trial: Myth and Reality in American Justice* (Ewing, N.J.: Princeton University Press, 1949) at 94–99. Notes omitted. © 1949 Princeton University Press, 1977 renewed PUP. Reproduced by permission of Princeton University Press.

That brings me to a point which the fighting theory obscures. A court's decision is not a mere private affair. It culminates in a court order which is one of the most solemn of governmental acts. Not only is a court an agency of government, but remember that its order, if not voluntarily obeyed, will bring into action the police, the sheriff, even the army. What a court orders, then, is no light matter. The court represents the government, organized society, in action.

Such an order a court is not supposed to make unless there exist some facts which bring into operation a legal rule. Now any government officer, other than a judge, if authorized to do an act for the government only if certain facts exist, will be considered irresponsible if he so acts without a governmental investigation. For instance, if an official is empowered to pay money to a veteran suffering from some specified ailment, the official, if he does his duty, will not rely solely on the applicant's statement that he has such an ailment. The government officer insists on a governmental check-up of the evidence. Do courts so conduct themselves?

In criminal cases they seem to, after a fashion. In such cases, there is some recognition that so important a governmental act as a court decision against a defendant should not occur without someone, on behalf of the government itself, seeing to it that the decision is justified by the actual facts so far as they can be discovered with reasonable diligence. For, in theory at least, usually before a criminal action is begun, an official investigation has been conducted which reveals data sufficient to warrant bringing the defendant to trial. In some jurisdictions, indigent defendants *charged* with crime are represented by a publicly-paid official, a Public Defender — a highly important reform which should everywhere be adopted. And the responsibility of government for mistakes of fact in criminal cases, resulting in erroneous court judgments, is recognized in those jurisdictions in which the government compensates an innocent convicted person if it is subsequently shown that he was convicted through such a mistake.

In civil cases (non-criminal cases), on the whole a strikingly different attitude prevails. Although, no less than in a criminal suit, a court's order is a grave governmental act, yet, in civil cases, the government usually accepts no similar responsibilities, even in theory. Such a suit is still in the ancient tradition of "self help." The court usually relies almost entirely on such evidence as one or the other of the private parties to the suit is (a) able to, and (b) chooses to, offer. Lack of skill or diligence of the lawyer for one of those parties, or that party's want of enough funds to finance a pre-trial investigation necessary to obtain evidence, may have the result, as I explained, that crucial available evidence is not offered in court. No government official has the duty to discover, and bring to court, evidence, no matter how important, not offered by the parties.

In short, the theory is that, in most civil suits, the government, through its courts, should make orders which the government will enforce, although those court-orders may not be justified by the actual facts, and although, by reasonable diligence, the government, had it investigated, might have discovered evidence — at variance with the evidence presented — coming closer to the actual facts.

Yet the consequence of a court decision in a civil suit, based upon the court's mistaken view of the actual facts, may be as grave as a criminal judgment which convicts an innocent person. If, because of such an erroneous decision, a man loses his job or his savings and becomes utterly impoverished, he may be in almost as serious a plight as if he had been jailed. His poverty may make him a public charge. It may lead to the delinquency of his children, who may thus become criminals and go to jail. Yet in no jurisdiction is a man compensated by the government for serious injury to him caused by a judgment against him in a non-criminal case, even if later it is shown that the judgment was founded upon perjured or mistaken testimony.

I suggest that there is something fundamentally wrong in our legal system in this respect. If a man's pocket is picked, the government brings a criminal suit, and accepts responsibility for its prosecution. If a man loses his life's savings through a breach of a contract, the government accepts no such responsibility. Shouldn't the government perhaps assume some of the burden of enforcing what we call "private rights"?

Some few moves have been made in the right direction. In an English divorce court, an official, the King's Proctor, brings forward evidence, bearing on possible collusion, not offered by either contestant; some American states provide that the public prosecutor shall do likewise in divorce actions. In our own Domestic Relations Courts, government officers procure and present most of the evidence. Lawyers for any of the parties may cross-examine any witness, may offer additional evidence, and may argue about the applicable legal rules. The advantages of the adversary method are fully preserved, but the fighting spirit is much diminished. Under the *Chandler Act*, enacted in 1938, in certain types of cases relating to corporate reorganization, the SEC, at large public expense, uses its expert staff to obtain and

(ii) 'Fight' Theory vs. 'Truth' Theory

present to the court evidence which usually no private party could afford to procure; the judge and the private parties may treat this evidence like any other evidence, and the parties may introduce further supplementary or conflicting evidence.

Many of our administrative agencies have large and efficient staffs to conduct investigations in order to ferret out evidence put before those agencies in their own administrative proceedings. I know, from personal experience, that not much evidence escapes an agency like the SEC. Mr. Justice Jackson has said: "Such a tribunal is not as dependent as the ordinary court upon the arguments of skilled counsel to get at the truth. Skilled advocacy is neither so necessary to keep such a body informed nor is stupid or clever advocacy so apt to blur the merits of a controversy."

I do not suggest that courts, like such administrative bodies, conduct their own investigations through their own employees. I do suggest that we should consider whether it is not feasible to provide impartial government officials — who are not court employees, and who act on their own initiative — to dig up, and present to the courts, significant evidence which one or the other of the parties may overlook or be unable to procure. No court would be bound to accept that evidence as true. Nor would any of the parties be precluded from trying to show the unreliability of such evidence (by cross-examination or otherwise) or from introducing additional evidence. Trials would still remain adversary. As I concede that to use that device in all civil cases would lead to many complications, I do not urge that it be at once generally adopted. But I think experiments along those lines should now be made.

This proposal resembles somewhat the procedures long used in criminal cases on the European continent. Critics may oppose it on that ground, saying that we should not take over ideas from countries which have been less democratic than ours. To any such argument, Woodrow Wilson gave the answer: "But why should we not use such parts of foreign contrivances as we want if they may be in any way serviceable? We are in no danger of using them in a foreign way. We borrowed rice, but we do not eat it with chopsticks."

It will also be said that any such proposal is absurdly radical. Yet something of the sort was endorsed by President Taft, by no means a radical. More than thirty years ago he said: "Of all the questions ... before the American people I regard no one as more important than this, the improvement of the administration of justice. We must make it so that the poor man will have as nearly as possible an opportunity in litigating as the rich man, and under present conditions, ashamed as we may be of it, this is not the fact." Moreover, we now have public-utility commissions which, on behalf of private persons, bring rate-suits against utility companies. With that in mind, Willoughby wrote a book, published in 1927 by the conservative Brookings Institution, in which he proposed the appointment of a "public prosecutor of civil actions." If a complaint were made to the prosecutor, he would first try to settle the matter or to have the parties agree to submit the dispute to arbitration. Only if these efforts failed would he bring suit. No one would be obliged to retain prosecutor; his employment would be optional; and, if any action were brought on a person's behalf by the prosecutor, that person would be at liberty to retain a private lawyer to assist in the preparation for, and conduct of, the trial. That idea, I think, merits public discussion and consideration. Were it adopted, it should perhaps be supplemented to include a practice now adopted, in some states, by the Public Defender in criminal actions: That official is authorized to expend public funds to seek out and procure what he regards as essential evidence.

Statutes in some jurisdictions authorize the trial judge to call as a witness an expert selected by the judge. Judges might sometimes avail themselves of that power to help indigent or under-income litigants. But I believe that none of those statutes, as they now read, provides for payment by the government to judge-called experts in non-criminal suits. Moreover, those statutes will not meet the difficulties of a prospective litigant when making up his mind whether to bring or defend a suit. Nor do they permit expenditures for detectives and other investigators not regarded as "experts." Nevertheless, this expedient might be expanded so as partially to solve the problem I have presented.

None of these proposals, if adopted, would usher in the millennium. Official evidence gatherers, or public prosecutors of civil actions, will make mistakes, or become excessively partisan. The trial process is, and always will be, human, therefore fallible. It can never be a completely scientific investigation for the discovery of the true facts.

(iii) The Family Court

Peter H. Russell

Unlike the lower criminal courts which as an instrument of order have deep roots in colonial and British history, the family court is a distinctly modern, twentieth century institution. Its social genesis is the disintegration of the social bonds of family and community which has accompanied industrialization and urbanization. In the words of Judge Allard, "Family Courts have attempted to reflect the concern of the State for marriage and family life."

The family court represents the effort of the modern state to do what it can to preserve the family and when that effort fails, as it increasingly does, to provide a fair adjudication of disputes over the rights and duties of those directly affected. It is, then, at the centre of a fundamental revolution taking place in our society: the shift away from the nuclear, patriarchal family as the basic unit of the social fabric. The family court stands astride this river of social change. Its diagnostic and therapeutic services are dedicated to reducing conflict in deteriorating family relationships; its adjudicative services impose the sanctions of the state when traditional family responsibilities are not fulfilled.

Emergence of the Institution

The family court itself has become an instrument of social and political change. The patriarchal power structure within the traditional family is increasingly challenged by the values of a more egalitarian era. As the interests of wives and children gain the status of legally enforceable rights, the courts become the arenas for adjudicating disputes among family members. An Ontario family court judge, Stewart Fisher, makes the point eloquently:

> In my role as a Family Court judge it is not an unusual sight to see fathers whose backgrounds are patriarchal (and most are) stare in disbelief and often rage when I tell them what they can do and can't do within their own families. Recently in Ontario a man burst into tears and said "I can't believe that it has come to this, that a man can't beat his wife any more."

> In the past, the politics of the family predated and shaped the politics of the state. Today it seems that the egalitarian politics of the state have become the politics of the family.

In many respects today's family court and the social agencies attached to it are attempting to fill the vacuum created by the erosion of the traditional basis of family order.

Behind the emergence of the family court as a tribunal specializing in family-related disputes is a recognition of the limits of adjudication. Adjudication is concerned with establishing who is legally right and who is legally wrong with regard to a single issue. But disputes that arise within families that are or were living together usually are not the result of the wrongdoing of a single individual. The welfare of those involved will not be greatly enhanced simply by obtaining a verdict on a legal point in dispute. Family-related conflicts are likely to be prototypes of what Lon Fuller called polycentric disputes. Hence there is an assumption that the institution which deals with these disputes should be able to consider and, indeed, to treat not just the delinquent's crime, or the inter-spousal assault, or the father's failure to provide maintenance, but the whole situation. The family court, ideally, should deal with family-related disputes in a holistic manner so as to provide both justice and welfare. While this may be an ideal for family court enthusiasts, it is anathema to many members of the legal profession who are sceptical of the welfare professions and treasure the adversarial defence of legal rights.

. . . .

Adjudication versus Therapy

There is an emphasis in the work of family courts on treating the source of conflict and endeavouring to find resolutions to disputes which are best calculated to promote the welfare of those involved. Even where formal adjudication takes place, welfare is likely to be a primary consideration in determining legal rights. In child welfare cases,

---

From *The Judiciary in Canada: The Third Branch of Government* (Whitby, ON: McGraw-Hill Ryerson Limited, 1987) at 223–24, 231–33. Notes omitted. Reproduced by permission of the author.

(iii) The Family Court

for instance, where the state contests the right of parents to keep their children, the family court judge's findings on the needs of the children will be crucial in determining the rights of the parents. In domestic disputes concerning maintenance, custody, and access, court workers and judges are often predisposed toward making formal adjudication a last resort. In this setting the efforts of many judges are directed more toward facilitating and ratifying mediated settlements rather than rendering authoritative determinations of the litigants' rights.

The therapeutic objective of the family court is manifest in the relative informality which often characterizes its procedures, as well as in the cluster of support services usually associated with these courts. While there is a good deal of variation in the styles of family court judges, many are inclined to intervene in the hearing, question the litigants, and suggest compromise solutions. Some of these judges adopt this activist role even when, as increasingly is the case these days, both parties are represented by counsel. Most family courts have at least a minimal intake service to counsel complaining spouses on the appropriate course of conduct when they first make contact with the court. In a few of the larger courts, family counselling and conciliation services are available on the premises; elsewhere there is usually a referral system to outside counselling services. Family court judges often steer litigants and their children to clinics for psychiatric assistance and ask these clinics for information and advice when writing out dispositions. Probation officers, child welfare officials, and representatives of the social services ministry are frequent participants in court hearings.

In the contemporary debate about the family court the adjudicative and therapeutic dimensions of these courts are perceived to be in tension with one another. In the words of Judge Allard,

> Increasingly, it is seen that there are two pressures. There is pressure to formalize court procedures, to define roles and purposes in a precise manner, and in a more rigid way seek enforcement of traditional family duties. This position is supported by concern for traditional duty, for due process and a belief that the adversary type of proceeding best leads to a full and fair disposition of facts and, as a consequence, an appropriate decision. The other pressure is to avoid adversary approaches and to emphasize diagnosis and treatment to seek what is best for the family, to enquire as to the causes and cures and to make orders only where treatment fails.

This tension transfers into the debate over family court structures. Among those whose priority is formal adjudication and due process of law, there is a tendency to favour unification at the higher court level. The informality of the lower court and the intervention of their support services are looked upon with suspicion as paternalistic threats to the rights of the individual litigant. On the other hand, many who are accustomed to working in the setting of a provincial family court are wary of transferring jurisdiction upward to a superior court dominated by the legal profession and the adversary process. There is a fear that in this setting little use will be made of counselling and investigative services and that the concern for arriving expeditiously at practical solutions to domestic disputes and child welfare problems will be the victim of adhering rigorously to the requirements of formal litigation.

It is doubtful whether there is a single structural solution to establishing a proper balance between the therapeutic and adjudicative functions of a family court. In an examination of judicial technologies sponsored by the National Institute of Justice in the United States, three basic court processes are identified: procedural adjudication (the traditional trial process with its emphasis on due process); decisional adjudication (the handling of a large volume of routine matters); and diagnostic adjudication (the attempt to diagnose problems and prescribe effective remedies). While the report observes that diagnostic adjudication may be the emphasis of a court exercising family law jurisdiction, it concludes that "no court employs one process to the exclusion of all others" and that "a certain amount of tension among the three processes may be critical to ensuring that the multiple purposes of the courts are served." It would be unfortunate if the family court in Canada was to be captured by the ideology of either the overly confident social worker or the disputatious lawyer.

Fortunately, in the evolution of both the lower provincial family court and the higher section 96 court exercising family law jurisdiction, there is a convergence which suggests that either institution is capable of striking the balance needed in a well-functioning family court. The up-grading of the quality of judges appointed to the lower provincial courts, improvements in their physical and reporting facilities, the extension of legal aid to family law matters, and the establishment of official guardian's officers or children's advocates to represent children caught in the middle of domestic disputes have done much to make the provincial family court, where it exists, an appropriate forum in which to dispute complex issues of family law. On the other hand, among judges sitting on the higher trial courts there is increasing interest in alternative forms of dispute resolution, including procedures that facilitate pre-trial settlement. Superior courts in a number of jurisdictions have established mediation services to promote mutually agreeable solutions to disputed points of custody, access, support, and property ancillary to divorce proceedings. There is no reason in principle why courts at this level cannot maintain the diagnostic and counselling services required for the effective discharge of family court functions.

C. The Debate Over Use of Settlement-Based Dispute Resolution Processes

(i) Against Settlement

Owen M. Fiss

In a recent report to the Harvard Overseers, Derek Bok called for a new direction in legal education. He decried "the familiar tilt in the law curriculum toward preparing students for legal combat," and asked instead that law schools train their students "for the gentler arts of reconciliation and accommodation." He sought to turn our attention from the courts to "new voluntary mechanisms" for resolving disputes. In doing so, Bok echoed themes that have long been associated with the Chief Justice, and that have become a rallying point for the organized bar and the source of a new movement in the law. This movement is the subject of a new professional journal, a newly formed section of the American Association of Law Schools, and several well-funded institutes. It has even received its own acronym — ADR (Alternative Dispute Resolution).

The movement promises to reduce the amount of litigation initiated, and accordingly the bulk of its proposals are devoted to negotiation and mediation prior to suit. But the interest in the so-called "gentler arts" has not been so confined. It extends to ongoing litigation as well, and the advocates of ADR have sought new ways to facilitate and perhaps even pressure parties into settling pending cases. Just last year, Rule 16 of the *Federal Rules of Civil Procedure* was amended to strengthen the hand of the trial judge in brokering settlements: The "facilitation of settlement" became an explicit purpose of pre-trial conferences, and participants were officially invited, if that is the proper word, to consider "the possibility of settlement or the use of extrajudicial procedures to resolve the dispute." Now the Advisory Committee on Civil Rules is proposing to amend Rule 68 to sharpen the incentives for settlement: Under this amendment, a party who rejects a settlement offer and then receives a judgment less favorable than that offer must pay the attorney's fees of the other party. This amendment would effect a major change in the traditional American rule, under which each party pays his or her own attorney's fees. It would also be at odds with a number of statutes that seek to facilitate certain types of civil litigation by providing attorney's fees to plaintiffs if they win, without imposing liability for the attorney's fees of their adversaries if they lose.

The advocates of ADR are led to support such measures and to exalt the idea of settlement more generally because they view adjudication as a process to resolve disputes. They act as though courts arose to resolve quarrels between neighbors who had reached an impasse and turned to a stranger for help. Courts are seen as an institutionalization of the stranger and adjudication is viewed as the process by which the stranger exercises power. The very fact that the neighbors have turned to someone else to

---

Reproduced by permission of The Yale Law Journal Company and Fred B. Rothman & Company from Yale Law Journal, Vol. 93 (1984), pp. 1073-90. Notes omitted.

resolve their dispute signifies a breakdown in their social relations; the advocates of ADR acknowledge this, but nonetheless hope that the neighbors will be able to reach agreement before the stranger renders judgment. Settlement is that agreement. It is a truce more than a true reconciliation, but it seems preferable to judgment because it rests on the consent of both parties and avoids the cost of a lengthy trial.

In my view, however, this account of adjudication and the case for settlement rest on questionable premises. I do not believe that settlement as a generic practice is preferable to judgment or should be institutionalized on a wholesale and indiscriminate basis. It should be treated instead as a highly problematic technique for streamlining dockets. Settlement is for me the civil analogue of plea bargaining: Consent is often coerced; the bargain may be struck by someone without authority; the absence of a trial and judgment renders subsequent judicial involvement troublesome; and although dockets are trimmed, justice may not be done. Like plea bargaining, settlement is a capitulation to the conditions of mass society and should be neither encouraged nor praised.

THE IMBALANCE OF POWER

By viewing the lawsuit as a quarrel between two neighbors, the dispute-resolution story that underlies ADR implicitly asks us to assume a rough equality between the contending parties. It treats settlement as the anticipation of the outcome of trial and assumes that the terms of settlement are simply a product of the parties' predictions of that outcome. In truth, however, settlement is also a function of the resources available to each party to finance the litigation, and those resources are frequently distributed unequally. Many lawsuits do not involve a property dispute between two neighbors, or between AT&T and the government (to update the story), but rather concern a struggle between a member of a racial minority and a municipal police department over alleged brutality, or a claim by a worker against a large corporation over work-related injuries. In these cases, the distribution of financial resources, or the ability of one party to pass along its costs, will invariably infect the bargaining process and the settlement will be at odds with a conception of justice that seeks to make the wealth of the parties irrelevant.

The disparities in resources between the parties can influence the settlement in three ways. First, the poorer party may be less able to amass and analyze the information needed to predict the outcome of the litigation, and thus be disadvantaged in the bargaining process. Second, he may need the damages he seeks immediately and thus be induced to settle as a way of accelerating payment, even though he realizes he would get less now than he might if he awaited judgment. All plaintiffs want their damages immediately, but an indigent plaintiff may be exploited by a rich defendant because his need is so great that the defendant can force him to accept a sum that is less than the ordinary present value of the judgment. Third, the poorer party might be forced to settle because he does not have the resources to finance the litigation, to cover either his own projected expenses, such as his lawyer's time, or the expenses his opponent can impose through the manipulation of procedural mechanisms such as discovery. It might seem that settlement benefits the plaintiff by allowing him to avoid the costs of litigation, but this is not so. The defendant can anticipate the plaintiff's costs if the case were to be tried fully and decrease his offer by that amount. The indigent plaintiff is a victim of the costs of litigation even if he settles.

There are exceptions. Seemingly rich defendants may sometimes be subject to financial pressures that make them as anxious to settle as indigent plaintiffs. But I doubt that these circumstances occur with any great frequency. I also doubt that institutional arrangements such as contingent fees or the provision of legal services to the poor will in fact equalize resources between contending parties: The contingent fee does not equalize resources; it only makes an indigent plaintiff vulnerable to the willingness of the private bar to invest in his case. In effect, the ability to exploit the plaintiff's lack of resources has been transferred from rich defendants to lawyers who insist upon a hefty slice of the plaintiff's recovery as their fee. These lawyers, moreover, will only work for contingent fees in certain kinds of cases, such as personal-injury suits. And the contingent fee is of no avail when the defendant is the disadvantaged party. Governmental subsidies for legal services have a broader potential, but in the civil domain the battle for these subsidies was hard-fought, and they are in fact extremely limited, especially when it comes to cases that seek systemic reform of government practices.

Of course, imbalances of power can distort judgment as well: Resources influence the quality of presentation, which in turn has an important bearing on who wins and the terms of victory. We count, however, on the guiding presence of the judge, who can employ a number of measures to lessen the impact of distributional inequalities. He can, for example, supplement the parties' presentations by asking questions, calling his own witnesses, and inviting other persons and institutions to participate as *amici*. These measures are likely to make only a small contribution toward moderating the influence of distributional inequalities, but should not be ignored for that reason. Not even these small steps are possible with settlement. There is, moreover, a critical difference between a process like settlement, which is based on bargaining and accepts inequalities of wealth as an integral and legitimate component of the process, and a process like judgment, which knowingly struggles against those inequalities. Judgment aspires to an autonomy from distributional inequalities, and it gathers much of its appeal from this aspiration.

. . . .

THE LACK OF A FOUNDATION FOR CONTINUING JUDICIAL INVOLVEMENT

The dispute-resolution story trivializes the remedial dimensions of lawsuits and mistakenly assumes judgment to be the end of the process. It supposes that the judge's duty is to declare which neighbor is right and which wrong, and that this declaration will end the judge's involvement (save in that most exceptional situation where it is also necessary for him to issue a writ directing the sheriff to execute the declaration). Under these assumptions, settlement appears as an almost perfect substitute for judgment, for it too can declare the parties' rights. Often, however, judgment is not the end of a lawsuit but only the beginning. The involvement of the court may continue almost indefinitely. In these cases, settlement cannot provide an adequate basis for that necessary continuing involvement, and thus is no substitute for judgment.

The parties may sometimes be locked in combat with one another and view the lawsuit as only one phase in a long continuing struggle. The entry of judgment will then not end the struggle, but rather change its terms and the balance of power. One of the parties will invariably return to the court and again ask for its assistance, not so much because conditions have changed, but because the conditions that preceded the lawsuit have unfortunately not changed. This often occurs in domestic-relations cases, where the divorce decree represents only the opening salvo in an endless series of skirmishes over custody and support.

The structural reform cases that play such a prominent role on the federal docket provide another occasion for continuing judicial involvement. In these cases, courts seek to safeguard public values by restructuring large-scale bureaucratic organizations. The task is enormous, and our knowledge of how to restructure on-going bureaucratic organizations is limited. As a consequence, courts must oversee and manage the remedial process for a long time — maybe forever. This, I fear, is true of most school desegregation cases, some of which have been pending for twenty or thirty years. It is also true of antitrust cases that seek divestiture or reorganization of an industry.

The drive for settlement knows no bounds and can result in a consent decree even in the kinds of cases I have just mentioned, that is, even when a court finds itself embroiled in a continuing struggle between the parties or must reform a bureaucratic organization. The parties may be ignorant of the difficulties ahead or optimistic about the future, or they may simply believe that they can get more favorable terms through a bargained-for agreement. Soon, however, the inevitable happens: One party returns to court and asks the judge to modify the decree, either to make it more effective or less stringent. But the judge is at a loss: He has no basis for assessing the request. He cannot, to use Cardozo's somewhat melodramatic formula, easily decide whether the "dangers, once substantial, have become attenuated to a shadow," because, by definition, he never knew the dangers.

The allure of settlement in large part derives from the fact that it avoids the need for a trial. Settlement must thus occur before the trial is complete and the judge has entered findings of fact and conclusions of law. As a consequence, the judge confronted with a request for modification of a consent decree must retrospectively reconstruct the situation as it existed at the time the decree was entered, and decide whether conditions today have sufficiently changed to warrant a modification in that decree. In the *Meat Packers* litigation, for example, where a consent decree governed the industry for almost half a century, the judge confronted with a request for modification in 1960 had to reconstruct the "danger" that had existed at the time of the entry of the decree in 1920 in order to determine whether the danger had in fact become a "shadow." Such an inquiry borders on the absurd, and is likely to dissipate whatever savings in judicial resources the initial settlement may have produced.

Settlement also impedes vigorous enforcement, which sometimes requires use of the contempt power. As a formal matter, contempt is available to punish violations of a consent decree. But courts hesitate to use that power to enforce decrees that rest solely on consent, especially when enforcement is aimed at high public officials, as became evident in the *Willowbrook deinstitutionalization case* and the recent *Chicago desegregation case*. Courts do not see a mere bargain between the parties as a sufficient foundation for the exercise of their coercive powers.

Sometimes the agreement between the parties extends beyond the terms of the decree and includes stipulated "findings of fact" and "conclusions of law," but even then an adequate foundation for a strong use of the judicial power is lacking. Given the underlying purpose of settlement — to avoid trial — the so-called "findings" and "conclusions" are necessarily the products of a bargain between the parties rather than of a trial and an independent judicial judgment. Of course, a plaintiff is free to drop a lawsuit altogether (provided that the interests of certain other persons are not compromised), and a defendant can offer something in return, but that bargained-for arrangement more closely resembles a contract than an injunction. It raises a question which has already been answered whenever an injunction is issued, namely, whether the judicial power should be used to enforce it. Even assuming that the consent is freely given and authoritative, the bargain is at best contractual and does not contain the kind of enforcement commitment already embodied in a decree that is the product of a trial and the judgment of a court.

JUSTICE RATHER THAN PEACE

The dispute-resolution story makes settlement appear as a perfect substitute for judgment, as we just saw, by trivializing the remedial dimensions of a lawsuit, and also by reducing the social function of the lawsuit to one of resolving private disputes: In that story, settlement appears to achieve exactly the same purpose as judgment — peace between the parties — but at considerably less expense to society. The two quarrelling neighbors turn to a court in order to resolve their dispute, and society makes courts available because it wants to aid in the achievement of their private ends or to secure the peace.

In my view, however, the purpose of adjudication should be understood in broader terms. Adjudication uses public resources, and employs not strangers chosen by the parties but public officials chosen by a process in which the public participates. These officials, like members of the legislative and executive branches, possess a power that has been defined and conferred by public law, not by private agreement. Their job is not to maximize the ends of private parties, nor simply to secure the peace, but to explicate and give force to the values embodied in authoritative texts such as the Constitution and statutes: to interpret those values and to bring reality into accord with them. This duty is not discharged when the parties settle.

In our political system, courts are reactive institutions. They do not search out interpretive occasions, but instead wait for others to bring matters to their attention. They also rely for the most part on others to investigate and present the law and facts. A settlement will thereby deprive a court of the occasion, and perhaps even the ability, to render an interpretation. A court cannot proceed (or not proceed very far) in the face of a settlement. To be against settlement is not to urge that parties be "forced" to litigate, since that would interfere with their autonomy and distort the adjudicative process; the parties will be inclined to make the court believe that their bargain is justice. To be against settlement is only to suggest that when the parties settle, society gets less than what appears, and for a price it does not know it is paying. Parties might settle while leaving justice undone. The settlement of a school suit might secure the peace, but not racial equality. Although the parties are prepared to live under the terms they bargained for, and although such peaceful coexistence may be a necessary precondition of justice, and itself a state of affairs to be valued, it is not justice itself. To settle for something means to accept less than some ideal.

I recognize that judges often announce settlements not with a sense of frustration or disappointment, as my account of adjudication might suggest, but with a sigh of relief. But this sigh should be seen for precisely what it is: It is not a recognition that a job is done, nor an acknowledgment that a job need not be done because justice has been secured. It is instead based on another sentiment altogether, namely, that another case has been "moved along," which is true whether or not justice has been done or even needs to be done. Or the sigh might be based on the fact that the agony of judgment has been avoided.

There is, of course, sometimes a value to avoidance, not just to the judge, who is thereby relieved of the need to make or enforce a hard decision, but also to society, which sometimes thrives by masking its basic contradictions. But will settlement result in avoidance when it is most appropriate? Other familiar avoidance devices, such as *certiorari*, at least promise a devotion to public ends, but settlement is controlled by the litigants, and is subject to their private motivations and all the vagaries of the bargaining process. There are also dangers to avoidance, and these may well outweigh any imagined benefits. Partisans of ADR — Chief Justice Berger, or even President Bok — may begin with a certain satisfaction with the *status quo*. But when one sees injustices that cry out for correction — as Congress did when it endorsed the concept of the private attorney general and as the Court of another era did when it sought to enhance access to the courts — the value of avoidance diminishes and the agony of judgment becomes a necessity. Someone has to confront the betrayal of our deepest ideals and be prepared to turn the world upside down to bring those ideals to fruition.

THE REAL DIVIDE

To all this, one can readily imagine a simple response by way of confession and avoidance: We are not talking about *those* lawsuits. Advocates of ADR might insist that my account of adjudication, in contrast to the one implied by the dispute-resolution story, focuses on a rather narrow category of lawsuits. They could argue that while settlement may have only the most limited appeal with respect to those cases, I have not spoken to the "typical" cases. My response is twofold.

First, even as a purely quantitative matter, I doubt that the number of cases I am referring to is trivial. My universe includes those cases in which there are significant distributional inequalities; those in which it is difficult to generate authoritative consent because organizations or social groups are parties or because the power to settle is vested in autonomous agents; those in which the court must continue to supervise the parties after judgment; and those in which justice needs to be done, or to put it more modestly, where there is a genuine social need for an authoritative interpretation of law. I imagine that the number of cases that satisfy one of these four criteria is considerable; in contrast to the kind of case portrayed in the dispute-resolution story, they probably dominate the docket of a modern court system.

Second, it demands a certain kind of myopia to be concerned only with the number of cases, as though all cases are equal simply because the clerk of the court assigns each a single docket number. All cases are not equal. The *Los Angeles desegregation case*, to take one example, is not equal to the allegedly more typical suit involving a property dispute or an automobile accident. The desegregation suit consumes more resources, affects more people, and provokes far greater challenges to the judicial power. The settlement movement must introduce a qualitative perspective; it must speak to these more "significant" cases, and demonstrate the propriety of settling them. Otherwise it will soon be seen as an irrelevance, dealing with trivia rather than responding to the very conditions that give the movement its greatest sway and saliency.

Nor would sorting cases into "two tracks," one for settlement, and another for judgment, avoid my objections. Settling automobile cases and leaving discrimination or antitrust cases for judgment might remove a large number of cases from the dockets, but the dockets will nevertheless remain burdened with the cases that consume the most judicial resources and represent the most controversial exercises of the judicial power. A "two track" strategy would drain the argument for settlement of much of its appeal. I also doubt whether the "two track" strategy can be sensibly implemented. It is impossible to formulate adequate criteria for prospectively sorting cases. The problems of settlement are not tied to the subject matter of the suit, but instead stem from factors that are harder to identify, such as the wealth of the parties, the likely post-judgment history of the suit, or the need for an authoritative interpretation of law. The authors of the amendment to Rule 68 make a gesture toward a "two track" strategy by exempting class actions and shareholder derivative suits, and by allowing the judge to refrain from awarding attorney's fees when it is "unjustified under all of the circumstances." But these gestures are cramped and ill-conceived, and are likely to increase the workload of the courts by giving rise to yet another set of issues to litigate. It is, moreover, hard to see how these problems can be avoided. Many of the factors that lead a society to bring social relationships that otherwise seem wholly private (e.g., marriage) within the jurisdiction of a court, such as imbalances of power or the interests of third parties, are also likely to make settlement problematic. Settlement is a poor substitute for judgement; it is an even poorer substitute for the withdrawal of jurisdiction.

For these reasons, I remain highly skeptical of a "two track" strategy, and would resist it. But the more important point to note is that the draftsmen of Rule 68 are the exception. There is no hint of a "two track" strategy in Rule 16. In fact, most ADR advocates make no effort to distinguish between different types of cases or to suggest that "the gentler arts of reconciliation and accommodation" might be particularly appropriate for one type of case but not for another. They lump all cases together. This suggests that what divides me from the partisans of ADR is not that we are concerned with different universes of cases, that Derek Bok, for example, focuses on boundary quarrels while I see only desegregation suits. I suspect instead that what divides us is much deeper and stems from our understanding of the purpose of the civil law suit and its place in society. It is a difference in outlook.

Someone like Bok sees adjudication in essentially private terms: The purpose of lawsuits and the civil courts is to resolve disputes, and the amount of litigation we encounter is evidence of the needlessly combative and quarrelsome character of Americans. Or as Bok put it, using a more diplomatic idiom: "At bottom, ours is a society built on individualism, competition, and success." I, on the other hand, see adjudication in more public terms: Civil litigation is an institutional arrangement for using state power to bring a recalcitrant reality closer to our chosen ideas.

We turn to the courts because we need to, not because of some quirk in our personalities. We train our students in the tougher arts so that they may help secure all that the law promises, not because we want them to become gladiators or because we take a special pleasure in combat.

To conceive of the civil lawsuit in public terms as America does might be unique. I am willing to assume that no other country — including Japan, Bok's new paragon — has a case like *Brown v. Board of Education* in which the judicial power is used to eradicate the caste structure. I am willing to assume that no other country conceives of law and uses law in quite the way we do. But this should be a source of pride rather than shame. What is unique is not the problem, that we live short of our ideals, but that we alone among the nations of the world seem willing to do something about it. Adjudication American-style is not a reflection of our combativeness but rather a tribute to our inventiveness and perhaps even more to our commitment.

(ii) For Reconciliation

Andrew Wolfe McThenia and Thomas L. Shaffer

Professor Owen Fiss, in his recent comment, *Against Settlement,* weighs in against the Alternative Dispute Resolution (ADR) movement. He brings to the discussion his often stated preference for adjudication, which he views as "a tribute to our inventiveness," to be encouraged because it is a forum for the articulation of important public values. Fiss argues that the entire movement for alternatives to litigation is misplaced. He understands that the movement's claim to legitimacy turns on the inefficiency of the legal system and on popular dissatisfaction with law as a means for maintaining order, and he challenges this claim.

Fiss attacks a straw man. In our view, the models he has created for argument in other circumstances have become mechanisms of self-deception not only for him but for most of those who write about alternatives to litigation. His understanding that the plea of ADR advocates is based on efficiency reduces the entire question to one of procedures. Fiss's argument rests on the faith that justice — and he uses the word — is usually something people get from the government. He comes close to arguing that the branch of government that resolves disputes, the courts, is the principal source of justice in fragmented modern American society.

Fiss's view that the claims of ADR advocates arise from a popular dissatisfaction with law reduces the issue to one of order. As his first stated understanding reduces justice to statism, this understanding reduces justice (or, if you like, peace) to a tolerably minimum level of violence in the community. In our view, an appropriate engagement of the Fiss attack on ADR must go all the way back to these two characterizations in his argument against ADR and in favor of court-dominated dispute resolution. We are not willing to let him frame the issue.

Reproduced by permission of The Yale Law Journal Company and Fred B. Rothman & Company from Yale Law Journal, Vol. 94 (1985), pp. 1660–68. Notes omitted.

Certain themes recur in the ADR literature. Many advocates of ADR make efficiency-based claims. And a plea for ending the so-called litigation explosion, and for returning to law and order, runs through the rules-of-procedure branch of the ADR literature. But the movement, if it is even appropriate to call it a single movement, is too varied for Fiss's description. Rather than focusing on the substance of claims made for ADR, Fiss has created a view of the function of courts that he can comfortably oppose.

In an earlier and provocative article, Fiss called for both a recognition and an affirmation of the expanded role of courts in modern America. He urged an explicit recognition that "[a]djudication is the social process by which judges give meaning to our public values." Further, he argued that a new form of adjudication, "structural reform," be celebrated as "a central—maybe the central—mode of constitutional adjudication." To develop his thesis and to meet Professor Lon Fuller's arguments on the limits of adjudication, Fiss resorted to modelling. He contrasted his preferred view of adjudication, "structural reform," with what he described as a "traditional" model of adjudication. Although it is not clear whether he understood the *substance* of the two types of adjudication to be fundamentally different, he clearly viewed the *form* of structural reform litigation as "breathtakingly different" from the "dispute resolution" or "traditional" model of adjudication.

While Fiss was initially content to construct contrasting models of adjudication simply in order to accentuate his position and argue against Fuller's, he has in more recent writings asserted that one of these models, that of traditional dispute resolution, has a life of its own, a life that has "long dominated the literature and our thinking." In fact, Fiss's later positive description of structural reform continues to flower, while his negative description of traditional adjudication has become abstract and lifeless. Fiss's response to the imperfections of life that lay bare the difficulties with his model of structural reform has been, it seems to us, to provide a shrill description of traditional judicial dispute resolution.

Fiss's description of traditional dispute resolution is a story of two neighbors "in a state of nature" who each claim a single piece of property and who, when they cannot agree, turn to "a stranger" to resolve their dispute. He asserts that traditional dispute resolution depicts a sociologically impoverished universe, operates in a state of nature where there are no public values or goals except a supposed "natural harmony" of the *status quo*, and calls on the exercise of power by a stranger. That was never Fuller's position. Nor do we find much support in the literature or in reality for such a view of traditional adjudication. If there ever was such a world we expect it was "nasty, brutish and short." However, we don't really believe that traditional adjudication ever bore much resemblance to that story. Yet this is the view of the world that Fiss attributes to the advocates of ADR; his attack on ADR is premised on that notion.

Models are, of course, human creations. The good ones contain elements of the creator's perception of the world and of the reality he seeks to perceive. They are designed to invite conversation and to appeal to the reader in a search for understanding. They are abstractions; but to be effective, they must have some connection either with the creator's view of reality or with what he wants the world to be like. Fiss's model of structural reform is, in this way, an effective model. While it may not depict the world that many of us observe, it does reflect his view of the world he wishes he could find. It reflects, we suspect, more his hope than his actual belief. We honor that. The model is rich. It leads to conversation and debate.

But Fiss's model of traditional dispute resolution is flat; it is only an abstraction, and is therefore also a caricature. It has no relation to the world as it is; it does not appeal to the reader as a convincing way to understand adjudication or its alternatives. It does not permit one to express hope in alternatives to adjudication.

In any event, after setting up his "state of nature" model of dispute resolution, Fiss attributes that view of the world to the advocates of ADR. He understands pleas to consider alternatives to current means of resolving disputes as turning on the inefficiency of traditional adjudication (his negative model), and popular dissatisfaction with it. He equates the ADR movement with those who urge settlement more than judgment and who seek a "truce more than a true reconciliation." He argues that settlement is "a capitulation to the conditions of mass society," a capitulation that "should be neither encouraged nor praised." He assumes that the ADR movement is one that wants peace at any price and treats settlement as "the anticipation of the outcome of trial," that is, trial in his stranger-judge, negative model of adjudication.

Fiss is against settlement because he views the matters that come before courts in America, and that are inappropriate for ADR, as including cases in which: (1) there are distributional inequities; (2) securing authoritative consent or settlement is dif-

(ii) For Reconciliation

ficult; (3) continued supervision following judgment is necessary; and (4) there is a genuine need for an authoritative interpretation of law. Fiss characterizes disputes in this limited way — as arguments between two neighbors, one of whom has vastly superior bargaining power over the other. It is then easy for him to prefer litigation to settlement, because litigation is a way to equalize bargaining power.

The soundest and deepest part of the ADR movement does not rest on Fiss's two-neighbors model. It rests on values — of religion, community, and work place — that are more vigorous than Fiss thinks. In many, in fact most, of the cultural traditions that argue for ADR, settlement is neither an avoidance mechanism nor a truce. Settlement is a process of reconciliation in which the anger of broken relationships is to be confronted rather than avoided, and in which healing demands not a truce but confrontation. Instead of "trivializing the remedial process," settlement exalts that process. Instead of "reducing the social function ... to one of resolving private disputes," settlement calls on substantive community values. Settlement is sometimes a beginning, and is sometimes a postscript, but it is not the essence of the enterprise of dispute resolution. The essence of the enterprise is more like the structural injunction, about which Fiss has written so eloquently, than like an alternative to the resolution-by-stranger described by his negative model.

The "real divide" between us and Fiss may not be our differing views of the sorts of cases that now wind their way into American courts, but, more fundamentally, it may be our different views of justice. Fiss comes close to equating justice with law. He includes among the cases unsuited for settlement "those in which justice needs to be done, or to put it more modestly, where there is a genuine social need for an authoritative interpretation of law." We do not believe that law and justice are synonymous. We see the deepest and soundest of ADR arguments as in agreement with us: Justice is not usually something people get from the government. And courts (which are not, in any case, strangers) are not the only or even the most important places that dispense justice.

Many advocates of ADR can well be taken to have asked about the law's response to disputes, and alternatives to that response, not in order to reform the law but in order to locate alternative views of what a dispute is. Such alternatives would likely advance or assume understandings of justice (or, if you like, peace) that are also radically different from justice as something lawyers *administer*, or peace as the absence of violence. They assume not that justice is something people get from the government but that it is something people give to one another. These advocates seek an understanding of justice in the way Socrates and Thrasymachus did in the *Republic*: Justice is not the will of the stronger; it is not efficiency in government; it is not the reduction of violence; Justice is what we discover — you and I, Socrates said — when we walk together, listen together, and even love one another, in our curiosity about what justice is and where justice comes from.

Most of us who have gone to college know something about Socrates. Many more of us who grew up in the United States know something about Moses and Jesus. It is from Torah and Gospel, more than from Plato, that we are most likely to be able to sketch out radical alternatives to the law's response to disputes. As a matter of fact, our religious culture contains both a theoretical basis for these alternatives and a way to apply theory to disputes.

In the Hebraic tradition (as in the Islamic), scripture is normative. Judaism, for example, does not merely seek to follow Torah; it loves Torah, it finds life in Torah, it celebrates Torah as one might celebrate the presence of a lover, or of a loving parent, or of a community that nourishes peace — commitment to common well being, and even a feeling of being well. (Salvation is not too strong a word for it.) Justice is the way one defines a righteous life; justice does involve according other persons their due but, more radically, in the Hebraic view, it involves loving them. Such a justice is the product of piety, to be sure, but not piety alone; it is the product of study, of reason, and of attending to the wise and learning from them how to be virtuous. *Quare fidem intellectum*.

The Christian side of the Hebraic tradition has, or should have, all of this. It also has a unique procedure established in St. Matthew's Gospel — a *system* backed up by stern condemnation of Christians who turn from the Gospel and seek instead the law's response to disputes. In this system — as well as Judaism — the religious community claims authority to resolve disputes and even to coerce obedience. The procedure involves, first, conversation; if that fails, it involves mediation; if mediation fails, it involves airing the dispute before representatives of the community. If the dispute goes so far as judgment, the system — as is also the case in Judaism — permits pressure: "[I]f he refuses to listen to the community, treat him like a pagan or a tax collector. I tell you solemnly, whatever you bind on earth shall be considered bound in heaven; whatever you loose on earth shall be considered loosed in heaven."

Thus, the procedure gives priority to restoring the relationship. Hebraic theology puts primary emphasis on relationships, a priority that is political and even ontological, as well as ethical, and therefore legal. And so, most radically, the religious tradition seeks not *resolution* (which connotes the sort of doctrinal integrity in the law that seems to us to be Fiss's highest priority) but *reconciliation* of brother to brother, sister to sister, sister to brother, child to parent, neighbor to neighbor, buyer to seller, defendant to plaintiff, *and judge to both*. (The Judge is also an I and a Thou.) This view of what a dispute is, and of what third parties seek when they intervene in disputes between others, provides an existing, traditional, common alternative to the law's response. The fact seems to be that this alternative has both a vigorous modern history and a studiable contemporary vitality (Jerrold Auerbach to the contrary notwithstanding).

Contemporary manifestations of the Hebraic tradition claim adherence to a moral authority that is more important than the government. The Torah is the wisdom of God, the Gospel is the good news that promises a peace the world cannot give. From one perspective, theology makes such religious views of dispute and resolution seem peripheral. That impression is deceptive, though: In the aggregate these views of what a dispute is are consistent with one another and, as such, consistent with the moral commitments of most people in America. The numbers of people in this country who might find them so is not declining; it is increasing. "In the aggregate" is an appropriate consideration, as one assays radical alternatives to the law's response to disputes, because there is substantial commonality among the practitioners of this radical Hebraic alternative. Religious systems of reconciliation rest on a substantively common theology and on a substantively common argument that, contrary to the implications of Fiss's view of justice, the government is not as important as it thinks it is.

Professor David Trubek ends a recent and pessimistic essay on alternative dispute resolution with a paradox: "[N]o one," he says, "really seems to believe in law any more." The "elites" who complain of a litigation explosion — Chief Justice Warren Burger and others "who champion alternatives" — "question the law's efficacy." But so do those who criticize the law as political and oppressive, most notably scholars in the Critical Legal Studies movement. The elites exalt an informalism they don't believe in, Trubek says; and the radicals exalt a formalist they distrust. Apparently the new legal-process school — or at least one of its eloquent spokesmen, Owen Fiss — still believes in law. Fiss's writing on structural reform is powerful. It may not reflect the way the world actually is, but it is a statement of hope. And that is important in an age of nihilism. But we suspect those who believe in law and in nothing else; we hope Fiss is not among them. Informalism of the Chief Justice's formulation may deserve distrust. But informalism has some contemporary manifestations — many of them resting on the most ancient and deepest of our traditions — that deserve trust and even celebration. These manifestations too are statements of hope. Suggestions for alternatives to litigation need to be critically examined — no doubt many of them are hollow. What they do not need, and what the legal community does not need, is an argument that reduces these alternatives to a caricature.

(iii) Unpacking the 'Rational Alternative': A Critical Review of Family Mediation Movement Claims

Martha J. Bailey

INTRODUCTION

The family mediation movement marches ahead, making its way with claims that are problematic on both theoretical and methodological grounds. These claims include the following:

1. family law cases are inherently unsuited to adjudication and are inherently suited to mediation;
2. mediation reduces the hostilities of divorce;
3. joint custody and mediation as a means of achieving that custody results are in the best interests of children;

(1989) 8 C.J.F.L. at 61–62, 70–76, 86–94. Notes omitted. Reproduced by permission of Martha J. Bailey, Associate Professor, Faculty of Law, Queen's University, and the Canadian Journal of Family Law.

4. mediation costs less than litigation;
5. higher levels of support result from mediation;
6. parties are more likely to comply with a mediated agreement; and
7. mediation empowers the parties by allowing them to fashion their own arrangements.

Family mediation proponents are not, of course, unanimous on these issues, but the majority of those in the movement adopt all or most of these positions. This paper critically examines these claims with reference to representative examples of the mediation literature.

. . . .

MEDIATION REDUCES HOSTILITIES

Divorce is an Emotional Not a Legal Issue

Mediation proponents have created a discourse in which divorce is an emotional problem which should be within the exclusive jurisdiction of the helping professions:

> [A]ll the available evidence suggests that the adversarial system is poorly suited to the resolution of disputes between divorcing spouses. The judicial emphasis on discovery of facts using proper legal procedure, and the reliance by lawyers on tactics designed to win, fits poorly with the emotional processes which underpin conflict over substantive issues, it is neither willing nor able to grapple with key emotional issues and, for this reason, is fundamentally unsuited to the resolution of divorce cases.

Of course many disputes other than family law cases involve emotionally charged conflicts — intentional torts are only one obvious example. Yet we are not concerned about the court's failure to "grapple with" the emotional aspects of such cases. The court is not expected to — the plaintiff seeks legal redress from the court and obtains help with emotional problems, if required, elsewhere.

Proponents assume that emotional conflicts in family law cases are particularly acute and that the legal issues will not be satisfactorily resolved unless hostilities are resolved in mediation. This claim is not supported by the research (discussed below), and is closely related to the assumption that couples continue to have close and informal contact after separation, and that their relationships must therefore be healthy. Having successfully transformed divorce into a restructuring rather than a termination of family ties, the helping professions now stress the importance of resolving emotional issues to ensure the success of the post-divorce relationships.

Mediators have an interest in promoting the ideology of family system preservation because of the expanded employment opportunities this ideology ensures. When divorce was considered a pathology, those in the "helping professions" were employed to counsel reconciliation. Under the current no-fault divorce regime, social workers have moved away from the goal of formal reconciliation and have moved toward "reconciling" couples to a continuing post-divorce relationship involving joint custody. Robert J. Levy notes that the mediation

> 'movement' has been swelled by those who were previously employed by the custody investigation 'movement', the conciliation court 'movement', the compulsory marriage counseling at divorce 'movement' — in short, by persons who may have professional careers riding on widespread acceptance of the 'mediation alternative'.

While stressing the emotionally charged nature of divorce and criticizing the legal system for its failure to deal with those issues, many mediators fail to provide adequate legal safeguards for the parties. For example, Irving and Benjamin, who scorn "[t]he judicial emphasis on the discovery of facts using proper legal procedure", state that "unlike the adversary system which assumes that people will lie and builds in a series of procedures to detect it, mediation has no such procedures". Financial disclosure should not be required but "encouraged", say the authors, by overcoming the "trust vacuum" in which most separating couples operate. "Feeling states" and "goals" must also be disclosed, they argue, and this aspect is presented as having as much importance as financial disclosure.

The approach advocated by Irving and Benjamin benefits those who wish to hide assets and disadvantages their partners. Eschewing legal safeguards and making trust the issue run counter to accepted negotiation practice. For example, Roger Fisher and William Ury, in a standard text on negotiation, suggest "making the negotiation proceed independent of trust. Do not let someone treat your doubts as a personal attack.... A practice of verifying factual assertions reduces the incentive for deception, and your risk of being cheated". Women, who are almost always the claimants in family law cases, are put at particular risk if trust is betrayed in the mediation process. Irving and Benjamin have no answer to this problem other than to say that the courts are available as a "backup" and that failure to make full disclosure "is likely an issue which an evolving mediation profession will need to address". The ability of the mediation profession to address the issue of disclosure is impaired by its characterization of separation as an emotional issue and its rejection of procedural safeguards because of their legalizing effect.

Reducing Hostilities

Many mediators claim that litigation exacerbates hostilities and that mediation reduces the emotional tensions between parties, often expressing particular concern about the detrimental impact of litigation on children. These advocates often fail to distinguish between the causes and effects of family dissolution and litigation in their effects on children. For example, Bennett Wolff advocates mediation with the argument that, "The harmful effects of the adversary process most seriously impact the children, especially the younger ones. They may not possess an adequate psychic capacity to intellectually understand divorce and to appropriately tolerate their intense feelings generated by the family breakup". Of course the effects on children of divorce do not in themselves support either mediation or litigation as a preferred procedure.

Mediation advocates also fail to note that, even if litigation in itself were shown to be emotionally harmful, in some cases it may well be less detrimental to the child than any available alternative. For example, the side effects of litigation are probably less damaging to a child than being delivered into the custody of an abusive parent who will not give up the claim for custody. Perhaps the alleged trauma of litigation is less detrimental to children than the reality of living in poverty pursuant to an inadequate settlement which many children are currently experiencing. This is not to say that litigation assures adequate child support, only that it may be the only possibility of getting some financial assistance when dealing with a recalcitrant spouse.

Mediators' criticisms of the adversary system, described in Department of Justice research as "highly polemical and simplistic", often involve the assertion of "the advantages of mediation by juxtaposing it with litigation or a court battle". They suggest that "litigation" inevitably involves the hotly contested trials and fail to acknowledge that litigation usually involves a settlement which is processed through the courts. When mediation advocates do compare mediation with negotiations between lawyers, a more common method of resolving family law cases than either mediation or trials, the polemic against the adversary system is continued by mediators against lawyers. For example Irving and Benjamin claim:

> The win-lose mentality of adversarial proceedings promote and support the use of pressure tactics, manipulation, the concealment or distortion of facts as well as competitive strategies as necessary and justifiable means of winning. The tendency for lawyers to promote increased conflict between spouses and to prohibit them from seeking nonadversarial solutions is well known.

Research in both Canada and the United States has found that this adversarial portrait of lawyers is inaccurate, that the attitudes of mediators and lawyers toward settlement are similar, and that the outcomes of mediation are probably very similar to those achieved by lawyers in negotiation.

Often mediation advocates do not consider non-mediated negotiated settlements at all, but implicitly impute the disadvantages of full-scale litigation to the "adversary system" in general, and suggest that mediation is the only "rational alternative". Mediation research, which tends to be conducted by mediation proponents, often underrepresents or excludes uncontested cases from the sample groups, and this research is used to support claims about family law cases in general and in favour of mandatory mediation. Yet the vast majority of cases are settled, and in most divorces the respondent does not even file an answer. The research used by proponents to support the claim that the adversary system increases hostility between parents and that mediation alleviates hostility suffers this deficiency.

For example, Irving and Benjamin conducted a study at the Provincial Court (Family Division) in Toronto over a ten month period in 1978–79. They studied only couples who agreed to participate in court-connected counselling or other parties who used the court system. Of their original study sample of 193 couples, only ninety remained to completion. Half of the sixty-one couples who had reached agreement were contacted for one year follow-up interviews — the couples who had not reached agreement were not contacted. Of those contacted, sixteen couples and nine individuals, a total of forty-one persons, gave follow-up interviews. Of these forty-one persons, twenty-one reported that their overall family situation had "improved in the year following counselling". Irving and Benjamin also report that the majority felt that marital conflict existing when the couple first went to court was reduced and had "positive feelings" about counseling. On the basis of this data, the authors claim, *inter alia*, to have "highlight[ed] the qualitative aspects of divorce litigation, namely, the intense and prolonged emotional turmoil typically associated with it. To the extent that such turmoil clouds judgment and intensifies hostility, it can often prolong conflict and worsen an already traumatic situation". One wonders how they can make this claim in view of their small sample size, equivocal results and, most importantly, the lack of any court control group.

Kathryn Dunlop did include a court control group in her study, which looked at forty-nine persons who had reached agreement in mediation at the Frontenac Family Referral Service in Kingston, and nineteen persons who used the court process. Her findings that a higher percentage of mediation clients perceived an improvement in their problems, an increased ability to discuss problems with their partners, and an improved relationship with their children are of limited value as far as proving a causal link to mediation because of her selection of only couples who had reached agreement in mediation.

Pearson and Thoennes included couples who did not reach agreement in mediation in their Denver comparison of mediating couples who reached agreement, mediating couples who did not reach agreement, those who rejected mediation and a control group using court process. They found that a lower percentage of those who unsuccessfully mediated showed an improvement in their relationship with their spouse than of those who rejected mediation or the control group. Those who mediated successfully, that is, reached an agreement, showed the most improvement. Because they excluded uncontested cases from their study, however, their study gives an exaggerated picture of the contentiousness of custody cases and cannot support claims regarding the general population of family law cases.

The research project completed by the Department of Justice, which was more comprehensive than any other study of mediation and notable for having *not* been conducted by persons in the mediation business, also includes an overrepresentation of both mediated and contested cases, but at least notes that such cases "comprise a minority of all cases dealt with in family courts". The study also addresses the effects of such overrepresentation on research results and does include some uncontested cases in its sample. This study refutes the claim that litigation (in the sense of court processing of contested and uncontested cases) exacerbates hostilities and harms children and found, not only a low level of conflict between divorcing couples, but also a correlation between higher levels of conflict and the use of mediation:

About 43 percent of the men and 52 percent of the women described their present relationship as friendly, cordial or at least business-like, with respect to the children. In contrast, about 21 percent of the men and 16 percent of the women said that the present relationship was tense or hostile. Nor does mediation seem to have an impact in the anticipated direction. In all, about 47 percent of the men and women who did not use mediation described their relationship as friendly, cordial or business-like, compared with about 37 percent of those who attended mediation. It must be kept in mind, however, that those who chose to mediate their case were sometimes those who started out with the most conflict and were attempting to work out a shared parenting arrangement.

This study also found that few ex-spouses experienced post-divorce parenting problems — 13.4 percent of the men and 19.7 percent of the women. Those who had attended mediation were slightly more likely to be experiencing post-divorce parenting problems than those who had not. Although this study did not include assessments of children, these results do provide some evidence in rebuttal of mediators' unsubstantiated claims about the hostility generated by litigation and its negative effects on children.

. . . .

COSTS

Irving and Benjamin make a typical argument of mediation advocates: "On average mediation clients, both public and private, pay hundreds of dollars less for service than those who have their divorce processed through the courts". They base this claim, however, at least in part on the Denver study of court-connected custody mediation conducted by Pearson and Thoennes which excluded uncontested cases. The relatively low costs of having uncontested divorces, which form the large majority of cases "processed through the courts", were not included in their calculations.

Even the cost savings Pearson and Thoennes did find are equivocal. Those who reached agreement in mediation paid an average of $1,630 in legal fees, but those who mediated without reaching agreement paid an average of $2,000 as compared with $1,800 for those who rejected mediation, information not mentioned by Irving and Benjamin. The nonmediation control group's average legal fees were $2,360, but it should again be noted that uncontested cases were excluded from the study.

The Canadian Department of Justice study found that mediation does not reduce legal costs, but results in higher legal fees. Women who mediated paid an average of $1,599 in legal fees compared with $1,214 for those who did not, a difference of $385, and men who mediated paid an average of $2,019 in legal fees compared with $1,511, a difference of $508. The argument that those who went to mediation would have had even higher legal costs if they had not mediated because of the more contentious nature of their cases was also contradicted by the study:

> [I]n general, where clients said that no matters were ever in dispute, the average legal fees were estimated at $658, compared with an average of $1,758 when one or matters [sic] were, at least initially, in dispute. Those with nothing to dispute and who, nevertheless, attended mediation estimated their legal fees at $937, compared with $627 for those who did not attend mediation. Where matters were initially in dispute, the mediation group estimated legal fees at $2,071, compared with $1,582 for non-mediation clients, a difference of $489. When legal fees are broken down by clients' assessments of whether the case was contested or uncontested, they are still higher for those in the mediation group.

The Ontario Association for Family Mediation (OAFM) lobbies for mandatory court-connected mediation, arguing that "litigation is often prohibitively expensive for most families". Family Mediation Canada continues to assert that "Research has found that mediation is typically less costly from both a financial and emotional aspect than litigation." Yet the evidence shows that mediation is not less expensive for the parties.

Mediation may reduce government costs of processing family law cases. Mediation services cost less per hour than court time, and some studies show that mediated cases require less court time and therefore result in a savings for government. Some mediation advocates assume cost savings to government on the basis of high settlement rates in mediation, without examining settlement rates of nonmediated cases or undertaking any other cost analysis. The Department of Justice study did not reveal a significant saving in court time resulting from mediation. In the Winnipeg portion of the study, the judges and lawyers interviewed on this question were divided as to whether mediation led to a saving in court time. The study of Saskatoon, St. John's, and Montreal found that mediation clients were somewhat more likely to spend less than an hour in court — 77 percent versus 56 percent of nonmediated cases. A slightly higher percentage of mediated cases, however, returned to court at least once — 36 percent versus 31 percent of nonmediated cases.

At this point the evidence as to whether mediation reduces the use of court time is equivocal, and existing data will have to be examined in light of the developing role of courts in the mediation process. Mr. Justice Zuber, in his report on court reform in Ontario, has recommended that judges be trained in mediation, and specifically suggests that judges in family law cases may take on the role of mediator. If judges become further involved in the process, the costs of mediation will change because of the different salary levels of judges and those currently providing mediation services. Of course, other changes to the current structure of mediation services may also affect costs.

SUPPORT OUTCOMES

There is some evidence that mediation results in higher support awards. The Department of Justice study found that support awards in mediated cases are about 22 percent higher than in nonmediated cases. When this figure is adjusted for income, because of the relative affluence of those who use mediation, there is a somewhat smaller but still very significant difference. There are, however, two *caveats* relating to this evidence on mediation. First, the three sites from which the Department of Justice figures are drawn show very disparate results. In Montreal, the only research site offering comprehensive mediation, support in the mediated cases was 28 percent higher than in nonmediated cases; in Saskatoon the difference was 11 percent; and in St. John's support levels in mediated cases were 4.5 percent *below* those in nonmediated cases. Support levels may be affected by, *inter alia*, the method of mediation. The Department of Justice study notes connection between higher support levels in Montreal and the comprehensive mediation offered at the site. Other variables may also affect support results.

The second point is that the higher levels of support resulting from mediation, "though no doubt important to the well-being of these families, are not large enough to offset the wider inequalities which result in an impoverished situation for many women and their children following divorce and separation". Women may achieve somewhat higher support but in most cases not enough to lift them and their children out of poverty. However, because in mediation "the ultimate authority belongs to the disputants", responsibility is shifted to the women who "agree" to continuing but slightly reduced poverty.

With regard to this last point, it is useful to look at the context in which family mediation has developed — a society with a growing belief in the inefficiency of government, and the efficiency of the marketplace in allocating resources. The current reaffirmation of the efficiency of the private marketplace has been paralleled by a growing belief in the efficiency of private ordering of family disputes. Michael Ignatieff's analysis of the reemphasis on the free market may also be applied to the current trend toward private family ordering:

> Market signals are more accurate and more responsible predictors than government-backed planning based on social science indicators ... [but] there was a further specifically political attraction in the market model besides its predictive plausibility. One of the crucial functions of the market solution — denationalization, privatization — has been to take distributional conflicts out of the political arena.

Similarly, private ordering appears to remove distributional conflicts between separating couples from the government's area of responsibility. To draw on Ignatieff's point, the efficiency arguments on behalf of mediation may simply mask the evasion of responsibility for distributional outcomes.

COMPLIANCE

Mediation is supposed to increase compliance in making support payments by giving the parties a sense of participation and a strong commitment to the mediated agreement and by reducing the "anger, feelings of loss, sense of injustice and separation from their children that many divorcing fathers experience". The OAFM lobbies for mandatory mediation with the claim that 85 percent of support orders are not complied with, but has not shown that mediation improves compliance rates.

In their Denver mediation study, Pearson and Thoennes found that, at two to three month and six month follow-ups after the court order, the compliance rate was highest for those who reached agreement in mediation. The lowest compliance rate, however, was among those who had mediated but did not reach agreement — compliance rates were higher for those who rejected mediation and for the control group. Compliance rates for uncontested cases were not included in their study.

The Department of Justice study found that, overall, mediation did not have a positive impact on compliance with support orders. In Montreal the compliance rate was much higher among those who mediated (97% versus 66%), but in Saskatoon and St. John's there was no significant difference between mediated and nonmediated cases, and in Winnipeg, where custody mediation is mandatory, there is a greater likelihood of default among those who reached full or partial agreement in mediation than among those who did not.

The research on this issue is ambiguous. It appears that some forms of mediation may positively affect compliance while others do not, but the relevant variables are not clear. There is not sufficient evidence at this point to make the general claim that mediation leads to greater compliance.

EMPOWERMENT

John Stuart Mill made the argument that men and women should be allowed to govern themselves as far as possible because they are in the best position to determine their own cases:

> [W]ith respect to his own feelings and circumstances the most ordinary man or woman has means of knowledge immeasurably surpassing those that can be possessed by anyone else. The interference of society to overrule his judgement and purposes in what only regards himself must be grounded on general presumptions which may be altogether wrong and, even if right, are as likely as not to be misapplied to individual cases, by persons no better acquainted with the circumstances of such cases than those are who look at them merely from without.

Mill acknowledged, however, that, "In the conduct of human beings towards one another it is necessary that general rules should for the most part be observed in order that people may know what they have to expect". He also said "As soon as any part of a person's conduct affects prejudicially the interests of others, society has jurisdiction over it, and the question whether the general welfare will or will not be promoted by interfering with it becomes open to question."

The increasing tension is between the efficiency of self-rule and the duty of not injuring others is expressed in Post-Mill liberalism's seemingly schizophrenic support for growing government intervention accompanied by expressions of renewed allegiance to the principle of liberty. Modern family law seems to be a quintessential expression of this schizophrenia because it seeks to create a near-comprehensive scheme for marriage dissolution, yet simultaneously gives the parties freedom to disregard it and fashion their own scheme. On the one hand we have rules governing marriage dissolutions "in order that people may know what they have to expect", and on the other hand we encourage the parties to exercise their freedom to dissolve their marriage in a way that suits them. One interpretation of this schizophrenia is that family law acknowledges the potentially prejudicial effect of marriage dissolution on one or both parties and society's jurisdiction over it by the enunciation of rules, but, by permitting parties to ignore these rules, family law stops short of claiming complete jurisdiction on the grounds of general welfare.

Mediation proponents have taken up Mill's argument concerning the benefits of individual autonomy:

> The ultimate authority in mediation belongs to the participants themselves, and they may fashion a unique solution that will work for them without being strictly governed by precedent [or] being unduly concerned with the precedent they may set for others. They may, with the help of their mediator, consider a comprehensive mix of their needs, interests, and whatever else they deem relevant regardless of rules of evidence or strict adherence to substantive law. Unlike the adjudicatory process, the emphasis is not on who is right or wrong or who wins and who loses, but rather upon establishing a workable solution that meets the participant's [sic] unique needs. Mediation is a win/win process.

The typographical error in this quoted passage is ironic because, for the most part, mediation proponents have failed to address the distinction between self-rule and what one might call "couple-rule". The parties may have incompatible interests and wishes. One party's judgment may be overruled, to use Mill's terms, not directly by society, but by the other party. Granting the parties control over the outcome will not necessarily result in a solution that is best for each of the parties, but "may enable one party to enforce a solution which would not have been tolerated by an even-handed outsider." Mediation is touted as allowing the couple the freedom to make their own standards of fairness. To the extent that the weaker party's standards are overruled by the other's, this freedom claim is untenable.

Clients are said to be empowered by their freedom to determine their own cases in accordance with their personal standards of fairness. The relationship between this freedom or autonomy and the existing legal framework, however, has not been fully explained. Robert H. Mnookin and Lewis Kornhauser make the point that divorce settlements take place "in the shadow of the law", that is, are affected by and reflect to some degree existing procedural and substantive laws. According to Mnookin and Kornhauser, private ordering does not delegalize settlements, but only dejudicializes them. The extent to which the law does or should affect settlements, however, is not clear.

Mediators themselves have not come to terms with the problem of the extent to which legal norms should limit the "autonomy" of the parties. Not all mediators have been legally trained, and some may be unaware of likely legal outcomes. The OAFM's *Code of Conduct* requires the mediator to advise participants if the mediator believes that the agreement being reached is unreasonable, but does not correlate reason with legal norms. Perhaps because of their claim that parties may set their own standards of fairness, mediators express confusion about the meaning of substantive fairness and their role, if any, in ensuring same.

Mediation purportedly allows couples to decide their own standard of fairness in financial matters, but deviation from legal standards may result in injury to one of the parties. Mnookin and Kornhauser, while suggesting that judicial review of divorce settlements is usually unnecessary, have said that cases of unequal bargaining power could be addressed by judicial review of settlements falling outside a broad range of norms. Setting a high threshold for intervention, however, is problematic because gender inequality will reduce the *de facto* legal entitlements of women to that which a court will not overturn.

Other mediation proponents take a more cavalier attitude toward the place of law in mediation. Leonard Marlow argues that divorce mediation "rejects the idea that ... legal rules and principles embody any necessary wisdom or logic. In fact, it views them as being arbitrary principles, having little to do with the realities of a couple's life and not superior to the judgments that the couple could make on their own". Marlow suggests that mediators not feel bound by legal rules which are "limiting factors", and yet at times useful to the mediator "as an intervention of strategy to achieve a desired result". The desired result is "a fairer agreement than the law would provide". It is apparently the mediator who decides what is fair, and "from his [the mediator's] standpoint, the problem is that the expectations created by these rules and principles will produce an agreement between the parties that is not fair". Marlow does not explain why the values of a mediator should be preferable to those of a judge or legislator, or why the parties should give away their legal bargaining counters and put their trust in individual mediators' notions of fairness.

Neither the high threshold for intervention recommended by Mnookin and Kornhauser, nor the substitution of the mediator's notions of fairness for law suggested by Marlow are satisfactory to women who, as the less advantaged parties, rely on legal entitlements. The ideal of the parties achieving their own standard of fairness is unlikely to be reached in a situation of inequality.

Mediators also claim to correct power imbalances between the parties. They have failed, however, to recognize and address a basic issue of mediation — systemic power imbalances. Family mediation generally deals with a dispute between a man and a woman, so the issue of gender inequality must be addressed. Some mediators acknowledge that women are usually the "weaker" party, even that this "weakness" is caused by conformity to current social norms; but, consistent with the liberal discourse in which mediation is situated, addressing this problem is seen as being in conflict with the ideal of neutrality. Their insight that women happen to be the weaker party leads them, at best, to a case-by-case approach of "helping" women on an individualized basis rather than to a political analysis that would call into question the initial premises of mediation.

Other mediators discuss inequality of bargaining power in a gender neutral way, suggesting that disparities in power are solely the result of personal characteristics of individuals and unrelated to gender. Still others accept the argument of fathers' rights groups that women have more power than men, at least with regard to custody. Regardless of the model or individual mediator's approach, the rule is to treat psychological, economic, and emotional imbalances as personal matters to be addressed on an individualized basis rather than as existing within a framework of systemic imbalance.

CONCLUSION

The growth of the family mediation movement has been sustained by claims which are open to question. Supporters of mediation — mediators, fathers' rights groups, the three branches of government — should address the problems with the research if they hope to establish the legitimacy of the movement and avoid charges of self-interest. Mediation is a method of dispute resolution we may want to use, but only with a clearer understanding of its problems and possibilities.

(iv) The ADR Explosion — The Implications of Rhetoric in Legal Reform

Laura Nader

THE SHIFT OF LEGAL TRADITION FROM JUSTICE TO HARMONY

From 1960 to the present, law reform discourse in the United States has shifted from a concern with justice and root causes to a concern with harmony and efficiency, from debates over right and wrong to programs of treatment and a public debate over "too much litigation." The process whereby ideologies that are forces of change are shaped through discourse is an interesting one, and goes far beyond the law to include the links between law, business, and community constituencies. The sixties have been described as confrontative, a time when many social groups felt encouraged to come forward with their agendas: civil rights, consumer rights, environmental rights, women's rights, and American Indian rights. It was also a period of sharp critique of law and lawyers in relation to issues of rights and remedies. The law was declared unsatisfactory in dealing with the explosion of rights consciousness (Cahn and Cahn 1966).

(1988) 8 Windsor Y.B. Access Just. 269 at 271–73, 280–82, 286–87. References omitted. Reproduced by permission of the author.

Two reform agendas emerged: those who thought that Americans might improve legal services (Wasserstein and Green 1970; Danzig 1973), and those who thought that Americans were becoming too litigious and who sought to remedy what they saw as a confrontational mode (Burger 1976, Wahrhaftig 1978, and Shonholtz 1978). Solutions were proposed to meet the needs of these various and often opposing constituencies, and although there were a plethora of experiments, the sum total began to be known as Alternative Dispute Resolution.

Alternative dispute resolution usually encompasses programs that emphasize non-judicial means for dispute handling: the focus is commonly on mediation and arbitration. Alternative dispute resolution came to be known as informal justice, a justice that promoted compromise rather than win or lose, that replaced confrontation with harmony and consensus, war with peace. It was hoped that such alternatives would be efficient, speedy and inexpensive. Law schools that had been staunchly training lawyers in the adversarial method in the 1960s and early 1970s were made to feel shame for encouraging parties to dispute, and they were encouraged, at least in terms of updating their curriculum, to include training in alternative dispute resolution mechanisms.

Throughout this period there gradually came a change in the manner of thinking about rights and justice. The production of harmony, the rebellion against law and lawyers — often by lawyers themselves — the movement against the contentious, and the movement to control litigation were constructed. Ironically, the work of social critics and legal reformers was used to construct an ideology that is directed to control the very people the liberal reformers wanted to have access to law. By means of harmony ideology, potential plaintiffs are conditioned to treatment. The elements of control that evolved are far more pervasive than the direct extension of state control (Hofrichter 1977 and 1982, Abel 1982, and Harrington 1985). Harmony ideology has become embedded in the way we look at the world more generally. It is commonly accompanied by an intolerance for conflict and an intention to prevent, not the causes of discord but the expression of it. An intolerance for strife seeks to rid the society of those who complain — "love it, or leave it," and by various means to create consensus, homogeneity, agreement. The harmony model was to effect a dampening of controversy thus protecting the courts from the "garbage cases." The rationalization for how well harmony works was often sought in the anthropological literature (Gibbs 1963, Nader 1969), but the expression of the reform agenda was by means of public rhetoric.

It was at the Roscoe Pound Conference: "Perspectives on Justice in the Future," held in St. Paul, Minnesota in 1976, that the turning point was declared (Levin and Wheeler, eds. 1979). In St. Paul harmony and efficiency ideologies both came to replace the litigation, justice model. The St. Paul Pound Conference was to adumbrate a cultural shift that had ramifications for social relations, for the structural problems of inequality, for solutions to needed procedural reform. The event was what anthropologists have called a key social drama.

. . . .

EXAMINING ALTERNATIVE DISPUTE RESOLUTION

It is important to consider the various critics of the alternative reform movement before mentioning the consequences of reform and the breadth of impact of ADR. The critical literature is abundant, a small portion of which is cited here. Some critics sought to examine the political transformation of law with the advent of informal justice (Abel, ed. 1982; Tomasic and Feeley 1982); others (or even the same scholars) examined the central arguments for alternatives, seeking to separate myth and rhetoric from substantiated evidence.

In one study of justice systems in seven industrial democracies (Johnson and Drew 1978) (USA, Canada, England-Wales, France, Italy, Sweden, and West Germany) some interesting information appears: U.S. judicial manpower is smaller than all but two of the countries; over the 13-year period studied (1960–73), the U.S. spent half as much per capita on its courts than West Germany and 20% less than Sweden; more money has been spent in the U.S. proportionately on police and prosecution than on courts and this is in contrast to *all* the countries studied; public investment in legal aid in the U.S. is much lower than in England, Sweden, and Canada; and after controlling for population growth, litigation measured by civil findings or dispositions have remained relatively stable in the U.S., while comparable to the rate per 1,000 population in England, Sweden, and West Germany. The overall conclusion of the Johnson and Drew study was that compared with six European industrial democracies, the U.S. system of justice has inadequate public investment. A series of critiques followed.

Richard Abel's book on *The Politics of Informal Justice* (1982) is an early pivotal critique and the questions he asks are designed to understand the contours and the significance of the change:

> Do the following phenomena have anything in common: the attack on professionals, the state, and bureaucracy; calls to deregulate the economy; the advocacy of decentralization; demands for the decriminalization and delegalization of private behavior (drug use, divorce); deinstitutionalization (in education, care of the mentally ill, restraint and punishment of the delinquent and criminal); the preference for informality in hearing complaints and processing disputes? What is it that is really changing.... Is the ambit of state control contracting or expanding? What impact will these changes have on fundamental social, economic, and political structures? Or is it all a lot of talk, with minimal significance for anyone except those who manage the legal system?

An article in the *Yale Law Journal* (Fiss, 1984) turns the ADR argument around and argues that the purpose of lawsuits is more than resolving disputes; law has a public function of using state power to bring reality closer to our chosen ideals. A *Harvard Law Review* article (Alschuler, 1986) argues that the crisis in our courts "may be a product of an inadequate supply of adjudication rather than of the excessive litigiousness of our society" (*id*.: 1818). Two widely influential articles appeared to further question the assumption of a litigation explosion. Marc Galanter in 1983 ("Reading the Landscape of Disputes: What We Know and Don't Know [and Think We Know] About Our Allegedly Contentious and Litigious Society,") and in 1986 a follow-up article, ("The Day After the Litigation Explosion"), examines the numbers. In the first piece Galanter concludes his analysis with the observation that there is no litigation explosion, although litigation had become a symbolic presence, feeding perceptions of a litigation explosion because of changes in governmental activity, in the organization of legal work, and in the relation of media to law. According to Galanter, the evidence that Justice Burger and others present for the litigation explosion consists of the growth in filings in federal courts, the growth in size of the legal profession, accounts of monster cases that seem atrocious, and "war stories" from managers who complain about litigation impairing their effectiveness. The majority of dispute cases taken to court are disposed of by abandonment, withdrawal, or settlement without full-blown adjudication. Most civil cases in American courts are settled as in automobile injury claims cases, and an increase in filings is not equivalent to increased litigation rates. While warning of the problems of cross-cultural comparison, Galanter finds that per capita use of regular civil courts in the U.S. was comparable to that of England, Ontario, Australia, Denmark, and New Zealand in 1975, and somewhat higher than Germany and Sweden and far higher than Japan, Spain, and Italy. In the end, he concludes that the "litigation explosion" is more an item of elite folklore than an objective fact. In his follow-up article Galanter continues to unravel fact from fiction to understand why some people have concluded that Americans are increasingly litigious, showing for example, how some product liability cases, as with asbestos or the Dalkon Shield cases come in and out of the system, swelling the case loads when they come in, but presenting no indication that Americans are increasingly litigious. Further on he notes that increased filings in federal court originate from businesses suing one another over contract disputes rather than from citizens attacking corporate defendants. The articles are thoughtful analyses which leave the reader to wonder how it came about that a vast reform movement could be built on folk sociology.

Richard Hofrichter (n.d.) sees these new dispute arrangements as representing a significant restructuring within the capitalist state, a relatively new type of political domination or hegemony. The transformation in state power which he refers to as the informal state, is embedded in the practices of everyday life. He sees the alternative movement as an alternative to politics and community organization in general. But while the critics continue to examine ADR and its consequences the movement proceeds at full speed relatively untouched.

. . . .

DISCUSSION

Over the past decades anthropologists of law and legal historians have observed that with the development of Third World colonialism, harmony ideology replaced feuds and wars, a form of pacification. With the development of the new nation-states in the Third World the harmony ideology, so commonly associated with the colonial period, was being replaced by the adversary model. In the old nation states of Europe and the New World the situation appeared to be moving in the opposite direction. In 1969 Wilhelm Aubert reported that Norway had moved toward a harmony model and away from the adversarial one, and a decade later in the 1970s the harmony model was also center stage in the United States. The concern with compromise, with mediation, with court avoidance was widely broadcast. These observations indicate that cultural values underlying the disputing processes change over time and circumstance and extant evidence suggests that they are profoundly political. The question remains. Are we seeing strategies of pacification that were common to colonial situations of indirect rule being applied to the U.S. population?

The political context of the 1960s and early 1970s was one of active public political activity in the United States and elsewhere. Power was what people spoke about—who has it, who does not, and what are the responsibilities that accompany both public and private power. The late 1970s and the 1980s have been subdued and apathetic by comparison. The conservative resolution, ushered in even prior to the Reagan revolution, stifled discussion of power by means of indirect controls and, I contend, by means of harmony ideologies. Even party politics is touched. In a July 12, 1987 article in the *Los Angeles Times*, political writer Ronald Brownstein wrote about the dispassionate politics toward which the bulk of the Democratic field is drifting: "This campaign is witnessing the full emergence of post-confrontational Democrats—pragmatic candidates who tend to be less polarizing, less critical of business interests and inclined toward solving difficult problems with compromises that avoid creating clear winners and losers.... What is occurring, particularly on economic issues is the Hands-Across-Americanization of Democratic politics ... building their appeal on the premise that everyone shares the same goals and need only be encouraged to hold hands and work together to solve the nation's problems." The issue for Brownstein is whether this soft post-confrontational mode will submerge confrontational Democratic politics.

When theorists speak about hegemony as a form of cultural control, they are speaking of constructed culture that moves out from a center to effect change incrementally. By itself the concept of cultural control leads neither to explanation nor to understanding. On the other hand, Gramsei's idea of hegemony is useful in forcing us to look at the institutions through which dominant belief systems are transmitted (Greer 1982). Concepts like the informal state, or economic government help us to visualize the motivation of organizations and professions who seek control through pacification. But the struggle from pacification or the struggle for freedom and autonomy may better utilize concepts such as class or community. When "over-litigiousness" and declining productivity are presented as a causal relationship, corporate interests are at hand. When debate in government is considered a negative, government interest is at hand. A departing Securities and Exchange Chairman, John Shad, was recently interviewed by the *Washington Post*. Upon the occasion of his leaving the commission after a six-year fight against insider trading he was asked: "What has been your biggest disappointment at the commission?" His response was quoted: "I think there is an awful lot of adversarial debate going on here, which I don't really think is the way to improve the securities laws. It gets politicized when it shouldn't. This is not a political agency ... the job could be done better with a recognition of our common interests and objectives rather than just the idea of constant criticism" (*id*., June 14, 1987). "Constant criticism" has become a disease for some while others believe that a clash of ideas and views is what fuels a political democracy. The serious study of harmony is only now underway. For the most part harmony has been taken as a given, a prima facie assumption not examined in terms of purpose or consequence. In examining harmony ideology in relation to the ADR explosion its function as pacification stands out as a challenge to the idea of rule of law.

In China to rule by law is to admit the loss of virtue and the inability of a rule of men. In Islam, justice can only be attained by establishing the rule of God. The rule of law is one of the philosophic and political cornerstones of Western society. We might well ponder the implications of a rhetoric of consensus, homogeneity and agreement that is incompatible with litigation in light of the idea of a rule of law as the principle of order in society, and rethink the limits and possibilities of both harmony and adversarial legal traditions in relation to equal and unequal power distribution, and relation to a future law reform movement which is preventive.

(v) Water Disputes in Ontario: Environmental Dispute Resolution and the Public Interest

Dianne Saxe

INTRODUCTION

This chapter examines the opportunities to use ADR in managing public and private disputes over water taking and drainage in Ontario, Canada. It describes the environmental and legal context for these disputes. The two key statutes, the Drainage Act and the Ontario Water Resources Act, present an almost complete contrast in philosophy and structure. A comparison between the two illustrates limits and opportunities for classic mediation, and for related processes that may go by the same name but have dramatically different dynamics.

THE ENVIRONMENTAL CONTEXT

Canada in general (and Ontario in particular) is well supplied with water. Snow is heavy, rains frequent. There are thousands of lakes and rivers, and groundwater is abundant. Nevertheless, there are hundreds of disputes a year over water, particularly in the Southern areas of the province where the population is concentrated.

One typical problem arises when a high volume water user, such as a fruit or vegetable grower dependent on irrigation, draws down the water supply that his neighbour depends on. During the hot months of mid-summer when surface watercourses are depleted, heavy water use by some may leave those downstream with only a muddy rivulet. When the neighbourhood depends on groundwater, increased pumping rates by one farmer can lower the water table below the bottom of his neighbours' wells, thus depriving them of water for irrigation, or even for drinking and bathing.

Disputes over water management also arise between very different users: quarry operations and their neighbours are a classic example. In Southern Ontario, surface deposits of high quality rock and aggregate have often been exhausted. The quarries which continue to operate are often digging below the water table. This requires them to 'dewater' the quarry, pumping out groundwater as fast as it flows in. Sometimes that is very fast: quarries of sand and gravel are often located on glacial eskers which contain significant aquifers. To dispose of the water, quarry operators pump it into nearby lakes, streams or sewers, thus creating a massive transfer of water from groundwater to the surface. The deeper the quarry digs, the more it depresses the water table and the more it may interfere with nearby wells. In theory, the diverted waters could provide a replacement water supply, but this rarely works in practice. Surface waters are much more susceptible to contamination than groundwater, and the homes and farms that depend on groundwater wells rarely have direct access to them.

Too much water can cause as much trouble as too little. Proper drainage is essential to the productivity of woodlots and fields, and to protect buildings and roads from flooding. Typically, water draining from one home or farm must flow over several of its neighbours before reaching a water course. Changes in the drainage, grading, or uses of upstream properties can have dramatic impacts on the volume and velocity of water reaching downstream properties, causing flooding or erosion. If the downstream property attempts to protect itself by damming or controlling the flow of water, heavy rains may backup and flood the upstream property. In both cases, a great deal of money may be at stake.

In unusually dry or wet years, these interests come into particularly sharp conflict. In addition, changes in the availability of water have important implications for local ecosystems. There is considerable dispute over who has the right and the responsibility to speak for these ecosystems, and over how their interests are to be balanced with human ones.

. . . .

From Julie MacFarlane, ed., *Rethinking Disputes: The Mediation Alternative* (Toronto: Emond Montgomery, 1997) at 233–34, 235–37, 241–48, 250–51. Notes omitted. Reproduced by permission of the publisher.

THE DRAINAGE ACT

The Drainage Act is a statute of key importance to rural dwellers, although almost unknown by urbanites. Its goals are:

- to facilitate land drainage and development, by allowing the objections of some landowners to be overridden;
- to fairly allocate the cost of drainage works;
- to offset the adverse impacts of drainage works through appropriate compensation;
- a more recent goal, to temper human desires for the economic benefits of drainage with some consideration of the importance of natural water courses and wetlands to the natural environment.

Section 2 of the Act allows drainage questions to be resolved privately, by agreement, by anyone willing to pay for it. Two or more owners of land may enter a written agreement for the construction, financing and maintenance of any drainage works. The agreement must state the lands to be drained, the costs of the drainage works and what portion must be paid by each land owner. The agreement may then be registered against the title of those lands and stays in effect indefinitely. The Act makes no provision for resolving disputes which may arise in the course of time over the operation of the drainage works, nor how the agreement would be affected by subdivision of any of the lands, or changes in the volume of water.

The rest of the Act establishes detailed procedures to drain lands where not all the owners agree on what should be done or on how it should be paid for. These procedures are initiated by the landowner(s) who want(s) their land drained. For small projects costing less than $7,500, a single landowner may requisition a drainage evaluation from his or her municipality. Larger projects are commenced by public petitions, or, in the case of drainage for agriculture or roads, by civil servants.

THE ENGINEER

Once a request for drainage is initiated, the first review is a technical one: can the lands be drained effectively, and what would it cost? This review is conducted by 'the engineer', a professional engineer or surveyor appointed by the municipality. It is the engineer's job to examine the site, meet with the landowners, and prepare a detailed report to the municipal council on the costs and benefits of the project.

The engineer has substantial powers and responsibilities. She/he may enter private property and plant stakes and benchmarks, and it is a serious offence to obstruct him/her. The engineer has the initial say in every detail of the drainage works, from where each hole or trench is to be dug to where the removed soil shall be put. Typically, it is the engineer who assesses the impact on the environment, landowners' claims to compensation, and the overall balance of costs and benefits of the project. It is also the engineer who assesses who should pay what part of the project cost.

The heavy emphasis placed upon the engineer in the Drainage Act reflects a time when society had greater faith in science and experts to resolve our problems. Today, this faith has been substantially eroded. An engineer or surveyor may be well equipped to measure the lands affected, to design drainage works, to predict the effect on water levels and to estimate their costs, but there is little in their training that assists them to balance the competing desires of a developer and a naturalist, to fairly allocate costs, or to help different parties to find common ground.

In fulfilling all of these tasks, the engineer does not work for the landowners concerned. Instead, she/he is engaged in a public duty on behalf of the municipality, and must report to the municipality everything that she/he learns. As the Act puts it:

> The engineer shall, to the best of the engineer's skill, knowledge, judgment and ability, honestly and faithfully, and without fear of, favour to or prejudice against any person, perform the duty assigned to the engineer in connection with any drainage works and make a true report thereon.

The rest of the Act sets out a complex set of procedures for review of the engineer's report and of any decisions that the council makes as a result. Council decisions may be variously appealed to the 'court of revision', the 'referee', the specialised Ontario Drainage Tribunal, and/or the courts. Different aspects of a single dispute can be appealed to different bodies. Different parties have different rights of appeal at different stages in the process.

It is apparent from this elaborate structure of appeals that drainage questions have long been a fertile source of disputes. Drainage can have a major impact on the productivity and profitability of a farm, and on the comfort and convenience of its inhabitants. Drainage cases have been known both to cause and to feed on a variety of social and domestic tensions. Sometimes they split families and communities, and linger on, causing resentment, for many years. These divisions and resentments can be exacerbated by the statutory dispute resolution process, which can be both lengthy and costly.

In years of average weather, the government receives approximately 500 drainage complaints a year. Most are resolved informally but about 10% result in public hearings. The Drainage Review Board, which hears most of them, is an administrative tribunal originally set up to provide a simple, speedy and inexpensive alternative to the courts. Over the years, it has become more and more like a court and is no longer simple, speedy or cheap. There are now hundreds of drainage appeals each year.

For these very reasons, all interested parties have a great deal at stake when the engineer makes his/her report. It is not surprising that the engineers experience strong pressure from the parties to make the recommendations that one side or another would prefer. On technical issues, engineers have the advantage of specialised training with which to stand their ground. However, an engineering degree is of no particular assistance in resolving the social, domestic, and emotional questions which often permeate drainage cases.

As a result, many drainage cases just won't go away, even after a technological 'solution' has been found; the parties may continue to call the engineers, and remain unsatisfied, years after their report is made. Having heard much praise of mediation, the drainage engineers in Ontario requested that they be trained as mediators. The relevant government ministry (Agriculture, Food and Rural Affairs) eventually decided to fund two days of training.

. . . .

PRIVATE v PUBLIC DISPUTES

The essential difference between a private mediation and the Drainage Act 'engineer's report' is that private mediations deal with private disputes; drainage engineers deal with disputes that are, in some senses, public. In a previous paper on environmental ADR, I proposed that *private disputes* could be defined as those which, if not resolved, could result in a civil lawsuit between (and controlled by) two or more parties. Examples include: disputes between vendors and purchasers over the cost of cleanup of contaminated land; disputes between landlords and tenants; disputes between lenders and borrowers; and disputes between fuel companies and their customers.

In contrast, the key characteristic of a *public dispute* is that it affects the public interest. Therefore, the parties are generally not entitled to resolve it in complete privacy, and their own desires are not the only relevant factors. There may be large numbers of actual or potential parties. In addition, the 'public' is a necessary party. How the public is to be represented, and how its needs for notice and accountability can be met, are frequently critical issues in the use of ADR for public disputes. In general, these disputes have quite different characteristics:

Private Disputes	Public Disputes
The essential issue between the parties is a private one that affects no one else, eg, a private environmental dispute relates to responsibility for an environmental problem or its resolution, not to the degree of harm to the environment which should be allowed or continue.	The essential issue between the parties affects the public interest, eg a public environmental dispute relates to how a key public resource shall be used or protected.
The parties are legally entitled to compromise their dispute. That is, the parties own their dispute, and can resolve it as they see fit.	The parties do not have exclusive ownership of their dispute, precisely because of the public interest that is affected.
All of the parties can readily be identified. Generally, there is a limited number of parties. If not, there is a judicial procedure for allowing some parties to represent others (eg class actions).	There may be numerous unidentified or self-identified parties. Determining who are proper parties can be difficult and contentious, especially if there is a dispute about who represents the 'public interest', the 'environment', etc.
Government in its role as regulator or as prosecutor is not directly involved.	Government is involved, generally as an ultimate decision-maker who is not a party to the dispute and who is exercising a statutory power of decision, namely an administrative tribunal or regulator.
There is no legal requirement that the general public be consulted as to the resolution of the dispute.	The general public often has a right to be consulted or at least informed.
There is no legal requirement for a public hearing.	There may be a requirement for a public hearing.

Many characteristics of a public dispute cannot be readily accommodated in a classic private mediation:

- Mediation means that the parties bargain with each other. A regulator with a statutory power of decision will not, and perhaps cannot lawfully, make a bargain on how to exercise that power. It certainly cannot do so in private.
- In a public dispute, the ultimate decision-maker is usually unwilling to come to the table and treat the other parties as equals. Those who do come to the table must usually report back to someone.
- Parties are usually unwilling to make concessions without gaining something of value in exchange. In public disputes where the ultimate decision-maker is not at the table, all that can be obtained in exchange for a concession is an agreement to make a recommendation, which the ultimate decision maker may ignore. The parties therefore have less to offer each other, and a greater risk of giving up something without ultimately receiving something in return.
- The confidentiality which is generally essential in a mediation, (eg to permit safe disclosure of weakness, and exploration of possible solutions) is incompatible with the public disclosure and consultation required of a decision on a matter of public interest.
- There is no obvious mechanism for public participation in a classic private mediation process.
- How can a mediation, which depends upon the consent of the parties, define who the parties should be?
- A mediation is not the legal equivalent of a public hearing.

Drainage disputes are often, at least to some extent, 'public' disputes. How, then, can ADR be best used to help resolve them?

MEDIATION BEFORE PETITION

Classic private mediation is possible at the earliest stages of a drainage project, before it legally becomes a 'public dispute'. That is, mediation could take place prior to invoking any of the statutory remedies under the Drainage Act. The goal of the mediation would be to finally resolve the dispute without government action, either through a mutual decision not to drain, or through a mutual agreement between directly affected landowners on what to drain and how to pay for it.

The Drainage Act provides for such agreements in s 2. These agreements do not require the approval of the municipality, nor a public engineer's report. No tax powers are used to enforce their funding, and the elaborate structure of the Drainage Act does not apply to them. Thus, the mediation itself could take place entirely outside the statutory framework and therefore would be a true private mediation.

Private mediation may also play a useful role in handling disputes that fall outside the Drainage Act. For example, the Drainage Act does not provide a mechanism for determining claims for compensation that arise *after* a drainage project has been completed. These must be resolved by common law claims in the civil courts. The best known case of this type is *Scarborough Golf and Country Club v City of Scarborough*. At the time, Scarborough was a rapidly growing suburb of Toronto. As fields and woodlots were replaced by roads and subdivisions, rain water and snow melt ran off faster and with greater force. That, in turn, increased the erosion of local creek banks. In this case, one of the creeks wound through a local golf course. The increased water volume and velocity caused so much erosion that it widened the stream and changed its course, seriously compromising some holes of the golf course. The golf course sued the City for allowing the creek to be altered in this way. Years later, after a very lengthy trial, it was awarded $3,076,146 plus pre-judgment interest and costs.

Private mediation of such disputes should have numerous advantages for the parties:

- *Control*: the parties themselves would determine the issues that they required resolved. The parties would retain control of the process, and could not be forced to accept any settlement without their consent. The mediator would owe no duties to any third parties. If the parties to the mediation agreed on the resolution to the dispute, the resolution would be final and binding and would not require the approval of any third party.
- *Choice of mediator*: the parties themselves would choose the mediator and pay for his or her services; thus they could reasonably demand and expect to receive rapid, responsive service.
- *Confidentiality*: the parties could keep the dispute, and even the fact that there was a dispute, strictly confidential.
- *Effectiveness*: because the mediation would take place early in the development of the dispute, a high success rate seems likely, thus achieving substantial savings for the parties to the dispute and for the regulatory agencies who would otherwise be drawn into it.

In fact, private mediation of drainage disputes has rarely occurred, although there are dozens of mediators actively seeking environmental work. There are significant barriers to the employment of private mediators for such disputes, including:

- lack of awareness of mediation among the agricultural and rural community;
- substantial difficulties in locating competent mediators, especially in the absence of a clear accreditation process;
- lack of technical qualifications to understand the issues among general purpose mediators;
- lack of mediation qualifications among the drainage engineers who understand the technical issues;
- lack of appropriate physical facilities and
- fear of high, unpredictable costs.

ASSOCIATION-SPONSORED PRIVATE MEDIATION

One way to overcome these barriers may be to offer mediation under the aegis of a popular rural organisation such as the Ontario Federation of Agriculture or the Food and Vegetable Growers Association. Such associations could set up mediation panels for the various regions of the province, consisting of experienced mediators with specialised training in drainage and hydrogeology. Due to the substantial bargaining power of large associations, they should be able to negotiate attractive rates for the mediations on a fixed fee basis. A mediation program of this type would have the greatest likelihood of acceptance by the agricultural community.

Pamphlets distributed through association offices could advise the farming community of the availability of the service and its cost. The pamphlet could contain a simple mediation agreement, which could be dropped off or mailed together with the necessary cheque to the association. The association would take a small part of the fee and in exchange would make arrangements to obtain a mediator and an appropriate meeting space. With a sufficient roster, it ought to be possible to schedule a mediation within days or weeks. Urgent cases, such as an immediate shortfall of irrigation or drinking water, could be given particular priority.

If the mediation is successful, the parties could consult a lawyer to prepare the formal agreement or could pay a further fee to the mediator or to the association to have such an agreement prepared for them. If the mediation is unsuccessful, the parties could request the mediator to prepare a report outlining the issues; this would help to clarify the dispute in any subsequent proceedings.

MEDIATION BEFORE A PUBLIC HEARING

At the other end of the spectrum, some form of mediation could be made available as part of the proceedings of the Drainage Review Board. Once filed with the Board, cases could be referred to a mediator at the option of any party or at the direction of the Board itself. If mediation has not been tried earlier in the dispute, it could well be useful at this stage. In a sense, the goal of mediation is a return to the original objectives of the Drainage Review Board itself, namely to resolve disputes in a simple, inexpensive, expeditious manner, preferably without lawyers.

'Mediation' of public proceedings before administrative tribunals can undoubtedly be useful. I use the word 'mediation' here, as tribunals typically do, to refer to the effort, guided by a neutral, to assist the parties to agree. However, it would be more accurate to describe this process as 'facilitation'. A skilled facilitator, using interest-based bargaining, can help reduce the parties to bridge their differences, and to design solutions that can be recommended to the ultimate decision-maker. She/he can avoid some hearings and greatly shorten others, by helping each party to recognise and articulate its own underlying interests and to seek common ground with those of the other stakeholders. Misunderstandings are often resolved, and many questions answered, by the simple exchange of information. In many cases, mediation is the first face-to-face opportunity for the parties to seek common ground since the dispute arose. However, 'mediation' at this stage is not the same as it would have been before the petition was issued. By the time a drainage dispute has reached the Board, it has generally become a public dispute. The ultimate decision-maker is the Board, not the parties themselves. The Board has an obligation to ensure that the public interest is protected, no matter what the parties prefer. In this sense, the immediate parties no longer own their dispute, and no longer have unfettered right to settle. This is particularly the case where a tribunal must conclude its proceedings by issuing a permit.

The powers and responsibilities of a Board have both positive and negative effects upon the prospects for a mediated settlement. In terms of advantages, there is no difficulty in identifying the parties to the mediation and in getting them to take the dispute seriously: they are the parties to the dispute before the Board. Where mediation is a standard feature of an administrative proceeding, parties who are generally unfamiliar with mediation must give it serious consideration. In the notoriously conservative agricultural and legal communities, such 'compulsory' consideration is key to more general acceptance of mediation.

The parties do not have the burden of finding a mediator, of designing a mediation agreement or of determining the appropriate process. All of this is done for them by the tribunal. The very fact that a hearing is approaching changes the legal options of the parties. Under tribunal rules, they must shortly disclose their whole case to each other; this means they must be well-prepared and makes it less attractive to hold back information.

Cost is also a significant factor affecting parties' willingness to attempt mediation. Administrative tribunals have generally provided mediators to the parties free of charge, in order to save the much greater expense of a publicly funded hearing. The costs and uncertainty of a hearing also begin to come home to the parties once a hearing is approaching and they must pay their lawyer to prepare for it.

On the other hand, the actual negotiations in a tribunal-annexed mediation are much more difficult than in a private mediation. Bargaining is more difficult where the actual decision-maker (here, the panel of tribunal members assigned to the dispute) is not at the table. Parties are usually unwilling to make concessions without gaining something of value in exchange. In these mediations, all that can be obtained in exchange for a concession by one or more parties is an agreement to make a recommendation, which the ultimate decision-maker(s) may reject. The parties therefore have less to offer each other, and a greater risk of giving up something without ultimately receiving something in return.

In private mediations, confidentiality is often the key factor that allows the parties to agree. It is confidentiality which permits parties to safely explore areas of weakness, make conditional concessions and explore possible solutions. Board-annexed mediations can provide very limited confidentiality, for at least three reasons:

- the neutral is typically either a member of the decision-making tribunal, or an employee of that tribunal;
- any mediated solution must be reported to the Board, which must be persuaded that it is in the public interest; and
- there are often one or more organisations as parties that cannot obtain authority to agree without making a full report to their members.

The close relationship between the neutral and the Board can make a 'mediation' no more than an introduction to the hearing. Nothing can be said to the 'neutral' in confidence; everything said or done by any party may be taken into account by the tribunal in its final decision. The behaviour of the parties at the 'mediation' may be reported to the decision-maker, who may let it affect their ultimate decision. Will a party that gives up too little in 'mediation' be branded by the tribunal as unreasonable? Will a party that offers too much in 'mediation' encourage the tribunal to include its 'concession' in the final result, even if that party did not obtain the concession it was seeking in exchange?

Thus, a substantial tension is set up. The success of mediation typically depends upon its informality and confidentiality; the parties are free to be open with one another because what they say cannot be used against them. Typically, the parties are also powerfully driven by the opportunity to obtain a certain result now rather than hope for a more favourable but less certain result later on. Board requirements for transparency and for the ultimate right of decision powerfully undermine both of these motivations.

Moreover, cases reach the Drainage Review Board only after the dispute has festered for a long time and the parties have hardened their positions by moving through a series of earlier appeals. This could also have an adverse effect upon the likelihood that mediation would be useful at this stage in the dispute.

. . . .

DISPUTES BETWEEN NEIGHBOURS

When water disputes arise between neighbours, the Ontario Water Resources Act provides no mechanism to resolve them. Accordingly, aggrieved water users turn to the courts and seek common law remedies. The leading case over excessive water taking is *Pugliese v National Capital Commission*. In that case, the National Capital Commission constructed a new sewer main in a residential area. In order to keep the excavation dry, they decided to lower the ground water table by more than 10 metres. Contractors 'dewatered' the area by pumping out large volumes of groundwater, far exceeding 50,000 litres per day, for a year and a half, all without the benefit of an OWRA permit. This caused the ground under more than one hundred neighbouring houses to subside, causing damage estimated at $2,000,000.

The homeowners successfully sued the Commission for this damage. The courts ruled that every person has a common law obligation to exercise their right to take water reasonably so as to avoid harming their neighbours. They also agreed that the statutory threshold of 50,000 litres per day (without a permit) was the presumptive measure of what was reasonable. However, it is noteworthy that, even in the 1970's, the courts took four years to resolve a single preliminary motion; it took much longer before the plaintiffs actually received money to repair their homes.

Could ADR be used to help manage disputes such as this? Once the *Pugliese* dispute had ripened into a full-scale lawsuit, it was framed as a private, common law action, and all that was at stake was money. Such actions are frequently resolved through normal private mediation, if neither party needs to set a precedent. In *Pugliese*, there would have been some challenges due to the large number of plaintiffs, but these same challenges arose in the court and can be overcome.

There might have been a much earlier opportunity to use mediation; during the construction project itself. If the neighbours had realised at that time that their houses were settling, and had brought their concerns to the City's attention, it might have been possible to change the system of dewatering and prevent serious damage to the homes.

Timely awareness may not occur where homes slowly subside, but everyone notices when their water runs out. This points to another opportunity for technically qualified mediators or facilitators: to resolve disputes between neighbouring water users. In dry years, when water demand is high, disputes over fair water use are urgent and cannot wait for the outcome of litigation. To date, government officials working for the Director have tried to resolve these disputes. Their technical skills are not in doubt, but they have often found it a difficult and frustrating task. Informal mediation or facilitation skills would help them to better understand and manage the human side of these conflicts.

However, like the engineer under the Drainage Act, the Director (and his/her subordinates) are not neutral facilitators of a process of negotiations. The Director can control the result. She or he has a mandate to protect water quantity, and the statutory power to issue, alter and revoke water permits. Thus, if neighbours cannot agree, the Director can promptly intervene and force a change. No one else can do so. Even if the neighbours do agree, the Director may override their decision in order to protect public and private interests in water, including those of wildlife. Confidentiality is limited, because government officials are accountable to the Director, to their Minister, to the public and to the courts for the way they exercise their statutory powers.

Officials with such powers should not be described as mediators; mediators, if desired, would have to work outside the regulatory structure. Therefore, attempts to better manage these disputes should focus on improving the conflict management skills of the technically qualified staff of the Director. If funds permit, this can be supplemented by a panel of independent mediators who will be available for private mediations on request.

In summary, the minimalist legislative scheme for disputes over water taking, which relies on the broad discretion of a regulator and not on the rights of parties, dramatically reduces both opportunities to use mediation and regulators' interest in doing so. However, there is an opportunity to reduce disputes by providing mediation-like, conflict-resolution skills to the front line staff who deal with water-taking issues.

(vi) Understanding the Critiques of Mediation: What Is All the Fuss About?

Neil Sargent

The essential claim I am making in this paper is that it is difficult, if not impossible, to discuss the topic of 'critical perspectives on mediation' in any coherent way as if there is a comprehensive set of critiques

---

Unpublished. Notes omitted.

of mediation which can be talked about in the same breath, or listed in one extended paragraph. Instead, I argue that there is a range of critiques of mediation which start from very different theoretical positions, which view the role and functioning of the formal justice system from quite different perspectives, and which have very different implications for the development of mediation theory and practice.

On the one hand, there is a strong liberal consensus critique of mediation which critiques the advocates of mediation for their supposed emphasis on the quantity of justice over the quality of justice. Within this liberal consensus critique, mediation and other forms of Alternative Dispute Resolution, or ADR, are often described as offering, at best, a commitment to 'second class justice'. It may be, according to even some of the liberal critics of mediation and ADR, that there is a place for mediation and informal justice in relation to some types of disputes for which mediation might be appropriate. But, according to this liberal critique, we must never lose sight of the fact that the formal justice system, with its commitment to the rule of law, the requirements of due process, and the adversarial trial process, provides the only true measure of justice within the liberal, democratic state.

It is worth observing that even many advocates for an increased role for mediation and other ADR initiatives articulate their support for this position in terms which are not inconsistent with this liberal critique of mediation. In other words, the liberal critique always insists that a clear hierarchy of the forms of justice be drawn, with mediation and other ADR initiatives being seen as supplements to the existing formal justice system, but never as a substitute or alternative to the formal justice system. In consequence, here the language of mediation existing "in the shadow of the law", as Mnookin and Kornhauser put it, is very clearly articulated.

In addition to the liberal consensus critique of settlement and mediation there is an equally strong contingent of critics of mediation who frame their critique of mediation and informal justice from within a conflict perspective which differs radically from the liberal consensus critique in its view of the ideological function of law within liberal democracy. Rather than viewing the formal justice system as a reflection of a shared liberal democratic value system, the conflict perspective begins from the assumption that conflict, rather than consensus, characterizes the structured inequalities of social, economic and political relations within capitalist societies. Consequently, here the emphasis of the critique of mediation is not so much the liberal consensus view of the inadequate promise of mediation as it is with what a conflict theorist might refer to as the false promise of mediation.

Thus, critics such as Richard Abel and Laura Nader have pointed to the insidious nature of the state sponsored community justice movement, which seems to provide a means of empowerment for communities which have been traditionally marginalized by the formal justice system. They warn that the promise of increased community control over the forms of justice is a trojan horse, by means of which the liberal state seeks to gain entrance within the walls of those very communities which are capable of providing sites of resistance to capitalist liberal hegemony, precisely because they have been so marginalized. Community justice models, which provide a means by which such communities will effectively police themselves according to standards and values established outside their own milieu, offer a very powerful mechanism of informal social control to the liberal state, which is all the more effective because it is voluntary, and thus avoids the social, economic and political costs of more direct, coercive forms of social control.

A primary concern in much of this literature is that the ideology of mediation and informal justice operate to neutralize social conflict by privatizing and individualizing conflict and making it appear that all conflicts can be resolved through consensual processes such as mediation, rather than through more confrontational forms of political action. Nader argues that the 'harmony ideology' associated with mediation and other forms of alternative dispute resolution functions to suppress legitimate social conflict. According to Nader, the theory of harmony justice which undergirds the alternative dispute resolution movement views conflict as "dysfunctional and threatening to the social order". For Nader, however, social conflict is rational and to be expected in a society in which access to economic, legal and political power is unevenly distributed. Indeed, social conflict may be a way to expose inequalities and make claims to social justice. In this context, Nader views official expressions of state support for harmony justice models with suspicion, as part of a legitimizing ideology which is aimed at defusing and depoliticizing forms of societal conflict which otherwise have the potential to challenge the status quo.

In some respects it seems as if the conflict critique of community mediation and harmony ideology provides an inverted mirror image of the liberal consensus critique of mediation and ADR. Different

(vi) Understanding the Critiques of Mediation: What Is All the Fuss About?

sides of the same coin, neither critique seems to recognize mediation as a form of justice having any identity, any history, or any integrity in its own right. Thus, conflict theorists like Auerbach and Harrington also tend to see the informal justice system as existing 'in the shadow of the law'. But here that shadow is a more ominous presence. The formal legal system retains all of its power and authority, while the informal justice system looks after the minor dispute processing; all the while reinforcing, rather than challenging, the legitimacy of the existing set of power relations within capitalist society.

Alongside the liberal and conflict critiques of mediation there is also a significant camp of feminist critics of mediation, who raise the question whether mediation (and by implication other forms of alternative dispute resolution) is capable of addressing imbalances of power between the participants in mediation. The focus of much of this feminist critique of mediation has been directed to the particular context of divorce mediation; although there has also been a significant degree of concern expressed in the feminist literature over attempts to promote mediation as an alternative to formal criminal proceedings in the context of violence against women.

In its concern with the family as a site of oppression against women, the feminist critique of mediation differs from both of the preceding liberal and conflict positions. And yet, at the same time, the feminist critique of mediation also has affinities with each of the above critiques. Thus, many feminist commentators have pointed to the lack of due process safeguards for women in mediation; as well as to a risk that women's hard won substantive legal rights in the area of family property and support entitlements may be sacrificed within the mediation process in the interest of reaching a 'consensual' mediated agreement between participants who are often in very unequal bargaining positions. In this sense, the feminist critique of divorce mediation bears more than a passing resemblance to the liberal critique of settlement as an inadequate alternative to the formal justice system, one that is less concerned with protecting the legal rights and procedural interests of the participants than is the adversarial trial process.

At the same time, feminist critics have also pointed to the ideological dimensions of the divorce mediation movement in suppressing and depoliticizing conflicts over systemic gender inequalities within 'the family'. Thus, Pickett argues that the 'familial ideology' of divorce mediation constructs the 'private' emotional nature of family disputes as being illfitted to the adversarial forum of the court system; thereby succeeding in transforming feminist struggles over the legal norms governing property and custody entitlements on family breakdown into individualized disputes which are suited to therapeutic treatment by divorce mediators. In this context, Pickett's critique of the ideological function of divorce mediation in legitimizing the existing 'gendered' structure of power relations within the nuclear family bears an obvious relation to many conflict theorists' critique of 'harmony justice'. Divorce mediation is presented as a trojan horse which women accept at their peril.

In conclusion, two themes seem to emerge out of this brief discussion of the critiques of mediation. We could categorize them as emphasizing on the one hand, the inadequate promise of mediation, and on the other the false promise of mediation. Both themes are concerned with the problem of power. However, they appear to address the problem of power in very different ways. The liberal critique of mediation assumes that the procedural requirements of due process within the formal justice system provide an appropriate (and sufficient) mechanism for redressing imbalances of power between litigants. Indeed, within the liberal conception of justice, law occupies a privileged institutional position as a protector of the interests of the weak against those of the strong.

However, seen from a conflict perspective, (and from many feminists' perspective) the liberal ideal of justice is just that, an ideal, which operates to legitimize the unequal structure of class, gender and race relations within capitalist and patriarchal society. From this critical perspective, mediation also functions to legitimize the status quo, rather than to pose any real challenge to it. However, in some respects mediation is seen as being even more ideologically 'dangerous' than the formal justice system, because it appears to hold out the promise of individual 'empowerment' to those who feel disempowered by the formal justice system. As a result, many conflict and feminist critics of mediation are forced into the position of becoming reluctant defenders of the formal justice system as the 'least worst alternative' available for pursuing claims to social justice. It is one of the ironies of this field of study that from a certain distance it is hard to tell the liberal and the conflict and the feminist critics of mediation apart.

8 People in the Legal Process: Access to "Justice"

A. Who Uses the Law and Why?

(i) Why the "Haves" Come Out Ahead: Speculation on the Limits of Legal Change

Marc Galanter

This essay attempts to discern some often general features of a legal system like the American by drawing on (and rearranging) commonplaces and less than systematic gleanings from the literature. The speculative and tentative nature of the assertions here will be apparent and is acknowledged here wholesale to spare myself and the reader repeated disclaimers.

I would like to try to put forward some conjectures about the way in which the basic architecture of the legal system creates and limits the possibilities of using the system as a means of redistributive (that is, systematically equalizing) change. Our question, specifically, is, under what conditions can litigation be redistributive, taking litigation in the broadest sense of the presentation of claims to be decided by courts (or court-like agencies) and the whole penumbra of threats, feints, and so forth, surrounding such presentation.

For the purposes of this analysis, let us think of the legal system as comprised of these elements:

- A body of authoritative normative learning — for short, RULES
- A set of institutional facilities within which the normative learning is applied to specific cases — for short, COURTS
- A body of persons with specialized skill in the above — for short, LAWYERS
- Persons or groups with claims they might make to the courts in reference to the rules, etc. — for short, PARTIES

Let us also make the following assumptions about the society and the legal system:

- It is a society in which actors with different amounts of wealth and power are constantly in competitive or partially cooperative relationships in which they have opposing interests.
- This society has a legal system in which a wide range of disputes and conflicts are settled by court-like agencies which purport to apply pre-existing general norms impartially (that is, unaffected by the identity of the parties).
- The rules and the procedures of these institutions are complex; wherever possible disputing units employ specialized intermediaries in dealing with them.
- The rules applied by the courts are in part worked out in the process of adjudication (courts devise interstitial rules, combine diverse rules, and apply old rules to new situations). There is a living tradition of such rule-work and a system of

(1975) 9 *Law and Society Review* at 95–151. Notes omitted. Reproduced by permission of the Law and Society Association.

communication such that the outcomes in some of the adjudicated cases affect the outcome in classes of future adjudicated cases.

- Resources on the institutional side are insufficient for timely full-dress adjudication in every case, so that parties are permitted or even encouraged to forego bringing cases and to "settle" cases, — that is, bargain to a mutually acceptable outcome.

- There are several levels of agencies, with "higher" agencies announcing (making, interpreting) rules and other "lower" agencies assigned the responsibility of enforcing (implementing, applying) these rules. (Although there is some overlap of function in both theory and practice, I shall treat them as distinct and refer to them as "peak" and "field level" agencies.)

- Not all the rules propounded by "peak" agencies are effective at the "field level," due to imperfections in communication, shortages of resources, skill, understanding, commitment and so forth. (Effectiveness at the field level will be referred to as "penetration.")

A TYPOLOGY OF PARTIES

Most analyses of the legal system start at the rules end and work down through institutional facilities to see what effect the rules have on the parties. I would like to reverse that procedure and look through the other end of the telescope. Let's think about the different kinds of parties and the effect these differences might have on the way the system works.

Because of differences in their size, differences in the state of the law, and differences in their resources, some of the actors in the society have many occasions to utilize the courts (in the broad sense) to make (or defend) claims; others do so only rarely. We might divide our actors into those claimants who have only occasional recourse to the courts (one-shotters or OS) and repeat players (RP) who are engaged in many similar litigations over time. The spouse in a divorce case, the auto-injury claimant, the criminal accused are OSs; the insurance company, the prosecutor, the finance company are RPs. Obviously this is an oversimplification; there are intermediate cases such as the professional criminal. So as we ought to think of OS-RP as a continuum rather than as a dichotomous pair. Typically, the RP is a larger unit and the stakes in any given case are smaller (relative to total worth). OSs are usually smaller units and the stakes represented by the tangible outcome of the case may be high relative to total worth, as in the case of injury victim or the criminal accused. Or, the OS may suffer from the opposite problem: his claim may be so small and unmanageable (the shortweighted consumer or the holder of performing rights) that the cost of enforcing them outruns any promise of benefit. See Finklestein (1954: 284–86).

Let us refine our notion of the RP into an "ideal type", if you will — a unit which has had and anticipates repeated litigation, which has low stakes in the outcome of any one case, and which has the resources to pursue its long-run interests. (This does not include every real-world repeat player; that most common repeat player, the alcoholic derelict, enjoys few of the advantages that may accrue to the RP [see below]. His resources are too few to bargain in the short run or take heed of the long run.) An OS, on the other hand, is a small unit whose claims are too large (relative to size) or too small (relative to the cost of remedies) to be managed routinely and rationally.

We would expect an RP to play the litigation game differently from an OS. Let us consider some of his advantages:

1. RPs, having done it before, have some advance intelligence; they are able to structure the next transaction and build a record. It is the RP who writes the form contract, requires the security deposit, and the like.

2. RPs develop expertise and have ready access to specialists. They enjoy economies of scale and have low start-up costs for any case.

3. RPs have opportunities to develop facilitative informal relations with institutional incumbents.

4. The RP must establish and maintain credibility as a combatant. His interest in his "bargaining reputation" serves as a resource to establish "commitment" to his bargaining positions. With no bargaining reputation to maintain, the OS has more difficulty in convincingly committing himself in bargaining.

5. RPs can play the odds. The larger the matter at issue looms for OS, the more likely he is to adopt a minimax strategy (minimize the probability of maximum loss). Assuming that the stakes are relatively smaller for RPs, they can adopt strategies calculated to maximize gain over a long series of cases, even where this involves the risk of maximum loss in some cases.

6. RPs can play for rules as well as immediate gains. First, it pays an RP to expend resources

in influencing the making of the relevant rules by such methods as lobbying. (And his accumulated expertise enables him to do this persuasively.)

7. RPs can also play for rules in litigation itself, whereas an OS is unlikely to. That is, there is a difference in what they regard as a favorable outcome. Because his stakes in the immediate outcome are high and because by definition OS is unconcerned with the outcome of similar litigation in the future, OS will have little interest in that element of the outcome which might influence the disposition of the decision-maker next time around. For the RP, on the other hand, anything that will favorably influence the outcomes of future cases is a worthwhile result. The larger the stake for any player and the lower the probability of repeat play, the less likely that he will be concerned with the rules which govern future cases of the same kind. Consider two parents contesting the custody of their only child, the prizefighter vs. the IRS for tax arrears, the convict facing the death penalty. On the other hand, the player with small stakes in the present case and the prospect of a series of similar cases (the IRS, the adoption agency, the prosecutor) may be more interested in the state of the law.

Thus, if we analyze the outcomes of a case into a tangible component and a rule component, we may expect that in case 1, OS will attempt to maximize his tangible gain. But if RP is interested in maximizing his tangible gain in a series of cases 1 ... n, he may be willing to trade off tangible gain in any one case for rule gain (or to minimize rule loss). We assumed that the institutional facilities for litigation were overloaded and settlements were prevalent. We would then expect RPs to "settle" cases where they expected unfavorable rule outcomes. Since they expect to litigate again, RPs can select to adjudicate (or appeal) those cases which they regard as most likely to produce favorable rules. On the other hand, OSs should be willing to trade off the possibility of making "good law" for tangible gain. Thus, we would expect the body of "precedent" cases — that is, cases capable of influencing the outcome of future cases — to be relatively skewed toward those favorable to RP.

Of course it is not suggested that the strategic configuration of the parties is the sole or major determinant of rule-development. Rule-development is shaped by a relatively autonomous learned tradition, by the impingement of intellectual currents from outside, by the preferences and prudences of the decision-makers. But courts are passive and these factors operate only when the process is triggered by parties. The point here is merely to note the superior opportunities of the RP to trigger promising cases and prevent the triggering of unpromising ones. It is not incompatible with a course of rule-development favoring OSs (or, as indicated below, with OSs failing to get the benefit of those favorable new rules).

In stipulating that RPs can play for rules, I do not mean to imply that RPs pursue rule-gain as such. If we recall that not all rules penetrate (i.e., become effectively applied at the field level) we come to some additional advantages of the RPs.

8. RPs, by virtue of experience and expertise, are more likely to be able to discern which rules are likely to "penetrate" and which are likely to remain merely symbolic commitments. RPs may be able to concentrate their resources on rule-changes that are likely to make a tangible difference. They can trade off symbolic defeats for tangible gains.

9. Since penetration depends in part on the resources of the parties (knowledge, attentiveness, expert services, money), RPs are more likely to be able to invest the matching resources necessary to secure the penetration of rules favorable to them.

It is not suggested that RPs are to be equated with "haves" (in terms of power, wealth and status) or OSs with "have-nots." In the American setting most RPs are larger, richer and more powerful than are most OSs, so these categories overlap, but there are obvious exceptions. RPs may be "have-nots" (alcoholic derelicts) or may act as champions of "have-nots" (as government does from time to time); OSs such as criminal defendants may be wealthy. What this analysis does is to define a position of advantage in the configuration of contending parties and indicate how those with other advantages tend to occupy this position of advantage and to have their other advantages reinforced and augmented thereby. This position of advantage is one of the ways in which a legal system formally neutral as between "haves" and "have-nots" may perpetuate and augment the advantages of the former.

Digression on Litigation-Mindedness

We have postulated that OSs will be relatively indifferent to the rule-outcomes of particular cases. But one might expect the absolute level of interest in rule-outcomes to vary in different populations: in some there may be widespread and intense concern with securing vindication according to official rules that overshadows interest in the tangible outcomes of disputes; in others rule outcomes may be a matter of relative indifference when compared to tangible outcomes. The level and distribution of such "rule mindedness" may affect the relative strategic position of OSs and RPs. For example, the more rule minded a population, the less we would expect an RP advantage in managing settlement policy.

But such rule mindedness or appetite for official vindication should be distinguished from both (1) readiness to resort to official remedy systems in the first place and (2) high valuation of official rules as symbolic objects. Quite apart from relative concern with rule-outcomes, we might expect populations to differ in their estimates of the propriety and gratification of litigating in the first place. Such attitudes may affect the strategic situation of the parties. For example, the greater the distaste for litigation in a population, the greater the barriers to OSs pressing or defending claims, and the greater the RP advantages, assuming that such sentiments would affect OSs, who are likely to be individuals, more than RPs, who are likely to be organizations.

It cannot be assumed that the observed variations in readiness to official tribunals is directly reflective of a "rights consciousness" or appetite for vindication in terms of authoritative norms. Consider the assertion that the low rate of litigation in Japan flows from an undeveloped "sense of justiciable rights" with the implication that the higher rate in the United States flows from such rights-consciousness. But the high rate of settlements and the low rate of appeals in the United States suggest it should not be regarded as having a population with great interest in securing moral victories through official vindication. Mayhew (1973: 14, Table I) reports a survey in which a sample of Detroit area residents were asked how they had wanted to see their "most serious problem" settled. Only a tiny minority (0% of landlord-tenant problems; 2% of neighborhood problems; 4% of expensive purchase problems; 9% of public organization problems; 31% of discrimination problems) reported that they sought "justice" or vindication of their legal rights: "most answered that they sought resolution of their problems in some more or less expedient way."

Paradoxically, low valuation of rule-outcomes in particular cases may co-exist with high valuation of rules as symbolic objects. Edelman (1967: chap. 2) distinguishes between remote, diffuse, unorganized publics, for whom rules are a source of symbolic gratification and organized, attentive publics directly concerned with the tangible results of their application. Public appetite for symbolic gratification by the promulgation of rules does not imply a corresponding private appetite for official vindication in terms of rules in particular cases. Attentive RPs on the other hand may be more inclined to regard rules instrumentally as assets rather than as sources of symbolic gratification.

We may think of litigation as typically involving various combinations of OSs and RPs. We can then construct a matrix such as Figure 1 and fill in the boxes with some well-known if only approximate American examples. (We ignore for the moment that the terms OS and RP represent ends of a continuum, rather than a dichotomous pair.)

On the basis of our incomplete and unsystematic examples, let us conjecture a bit about the content of these boxes:

Box I: OS vs. OS

The most numerous occupants of this box are divorces and insanity hearings. Most (over 90 percent of divorces, for example) are uncontested. A large portion of these are really pseudo-litigation, that is, a settlement is worked out between the parties and ratified in the guise of adjudication. When we get real litigation in Box I, it is often between parties who have some intimate tie with one another, fighting over some unsharable good, often with overtones of "spite" and "irrationality." Courts are resorted to where an ongoing relationship is ruptured: they have little to do with the routine patterning of activity. The law is invoked ad hoc and instrumentally by the parties. There may be a strong interest in vindication, but neither party is likely to have much interest in the long term state of the law (of, for instance, custody or nuisance). There are few appeals, few test cases, little expenditure of resources on rule-development. Legal doctrine is likely to remain remote from everyday practice and from popular attitudes.

Box II: RP vs. OS

The great bulk of litigation is found in this box — indeed every really numerous kind except personal injury cases, insanity hearings, and divorces. The law is used for routine processing of claims by parties

(i) Why the "Haves" Come Out Ahead: Speculation on the Limits of Legal Change

FIGURE 1
A TAXONOMY OF LITIGATION BY STRATEGIC CONFIGURATION OF PARTIES

		Initiator, Claimant	
		One-shotter	**Repeat Player**
Defendant	**One-shotter**	Parent v. Parent (Custody) Spouse v. Spouse (Divorce) Family v. Family Member (Insanity Commitment) Family v. Family (Inheritance) Neighbor v. Neighbor Partner v. Partner OS vs OS I	Prosecutor v. Accused Finance Co. v. Debtor Landlord v. Tenant I.R.S. v. Taxpayer Condemnor v. Property Owner RP vs OS II
	Repeat Player	Welfare Client v. Agency Auto Dealer v. Manufacturer Injury Victim v. Insurance Company Tenant v. Landlord Bankrupt Consumer v. Creditors Defamed v. Publisher OS vs RP III	Union v. Company Movie Distributor v. Censorship Board Developer v. Suburban Municipality Purchaser v. Supplier Regulatory Agency v. Firms of Regulated Industry RP vs RP IV

for whom the making of such claims is a regular business activity. Often the cases here take the form of stereotyped mass processing with little of the individuated attention of full-dress adjudication. Even greater numbers of cases are settled "informally" with settlement keyed to possible litigation outcome (discounted by risk, cost, delay).

The state of the law is of interest to the RP, though not to the OS defendants. Insofar as the law is favorable to the RP it is "followed" closely in practice (subject to discount for RP's transaction costs). Transactions are built to fit the rules by creditors, police, draft boards and other RPs. Rules favouring OSs may be less readily applicable, since OSs do not ordinarily plan the underlying transaction, or less meticulously observed in practice, since OSs are unlikely to be as ready or able as RPs to invest in insuring their penetration to the field level.

Box III: OS vs. RP

All of these are rather infrequent types except for personal injury cases which are distinctive in that free entry to the arena is provided by the contingent fee. In auto injury claims, litigation is routinized and settlement is closely geared to possible litigation outcome. Outside the personal injury area, litigation in Box III is not routine. It usually represents the attempt of some OS to invoke outside help to create leverage on an organization with which he has been having dealings but is now at the point of divorce (for example, the discharged employee or the cancelled franchisee). The OS claimant generally has little interest in the state of the law; the RP defendant, however, is greatly interested.

Box IV: RP vs. RP

Let us consider the general case first and then several special cases. We might expect that there would be little litigation in Box IV, because, to the extent that two RPs play with each other repeatedly, the expectation of continued mutually beneficial interaction would give rise to informal bilateral controls. This seems borne out by studies of dealings among businessmen and in labour relations. Official agencies are invoked by unions trying to get established and by management trying to prevent them from getting established, more rarely in dealings between bargaining partners. Units with mutually beneficial relations do not adjust their differences in courts. Where they rely on third parties in dispute-resolution, it is likely to take a form (such as arbitration or a domestic tribunal) detached from official sanctions and applying domestic rather than official rules.

However, there are several special cases. First, there are those RPs who seek, not furtherance of tangible interests, but vindication of fundamental cultural commitments. An example would be the organizations which sponsor much church-state litigation. Where RPs are contending about value differences (who is right) rather than interest conflicts (who gets what) there is less tendency to settle and less basis for developing a private system of dispute settlement.

Second, government is a special kind of RP. Informal controls depend upon the ultimate sanction of withdrawal and refusal to continue beneficial relations. To the extent that withdrawal of future association is not possible in dealing with government, the scope of informal controls is correspondingly limited. The development of informal relations between regulatory agencies and regulated firms is well known. And the regulated may have sanctions other than withdrawal which they can apply; for instance, they may threaten political opposition. But the more inclusive the unit of government, the less effective the withdrawal sanction and the greater the likelihood that a party will attempt to invoke outside allies by litigation even while sustaining the ongoing relationship. This applies also to monopolies, units which share the government's relative immunity to withdrawal sanctions. RPs in monopolistic relationships will occasionally invoke formal controls to show prowess, to give credibility to threats, and to provide satisfactions for other audiences. Thus we would expect litigation by and against government to be more frequent than in other RP vs. RP situations. There is a second reason for expecting more litigation when government is a party. That is, that the notion of "gain" (policy as well as monetary) is often more contingent and problematic for governmental units than for other parties, such as businesses or organized interest groups. In some cases courts may, by proffering authoritative interpretations of public policy, redefine an agency's notion of gain. Hence government parties may be more willing to externalize decisions to the courts. And opponents may have more incentive to litigate against government in the hope of securing a shift in its goals.

A somewhat different kind of special case is present where plaintiff and defendant are both RPs but do not deal with each other repeatedly (two insurance companies, for example.) In the government/monopoly case, the parties were so inextricably bound together that the force of informal controls was limited; here they are not sufficiently bound to each other to give informal controls their bite; there is nothing to withdraw from! The large one-time deal that falls through, the marginal enterprise — these are staple sources of litigation.

Where there is litigation in the RP vs. RP situation, we might expect that there would be heavy expenditure on rule-development, many appeals, and rapid and elaborate development of the doctrinal law. Since the parties can invest to secure implementation of favorable rules, we would expect practice to be closely articulated to the resulting rules.

On the basis of these preliminary guesses, we can sketch a general profile of litigation and the factors associated with it. The great bulk of litigation is found in Box II; much less in Box III. Most of the litigation in these Boxes is mass routine processing of disputes between parties who are strangers (not in mutually beneficial continuing relations) or divorced — and between whom there is a disparity in size. One party is a bureaucratically organized "professional" (in the sense of doing it for a living) who enjoys strategic advantages. Informal controls between the parties are tenuous or ineffective; their relationship is likely to be established and defined by official rules; in litigation, these rules are discounted by transaction costs and manipulated selectively to the advantage of the parties. On the other hand, in Boxes I and IV, we have more infrequent but more individualized litigation between parties of the same general magnitude, among whom there are or were continuing multi-stranded relationships with attendant informal controls. Litigation appears when the relationship loses its future value; when its "monopolistic" character deprives informal controls of sufficient leverage and the parties invoke outside allies to modify it; and when the parties seek to vindicate conflicting values.

LAWYERS

What happens when we introduce lawyers? Parties who have lawyers do better. Lawyers are themselves RPs. Does their presence equalize the parties, dispelling the advantage of the RP client? Or does the existence of lawyers amplify the advantage of the RP client? We might assume that RPs (tending to be larger units) who can buy legal services more steadily, in larger quantities, in bulk (by retainer) and at higher rates, would get services of better quality. They would have better information (especially where restrictions on information about legal services are present). Not only would the RP get

FIGURE 2
A TYPOLOGY OF LEGAL SPECIALISTS

		Lawyer		
		Specialized by Party	**Specialized by Field and Party**	**Specialized by Field**
Client	RP	• "House Counsel" or General Counsel for Bank, Insurance Co. etc. • Corporation Counsel for Government Unit	• Prosecutor • Personal Injury Defendant • Staff Counsel for NAACP • Tax • Labour/Management Collections	• Patent
	OS	• "Poverty Lawyers" • Legal Aid	• Criminal Defense • Personal Injury Plaintiff	• Bankruptcy • Divorce

more talent to begin with, but he would on the whole get greater continuity, better record-keeping, more anticipatory or preventive work, more experience and specialized skill in pertinent areas, and more control over counsel.

One might expect that just how much the legal services factor would accentuate the RP advantage would be related to the way in which the profession was organized. The more members of the profession were identified with their clients (i.e., the less they were held aloof from clients by their loyalty to courts or an autonomous guild) the more the imbalance would be accentuated. The more close and enduring the lawyer-client relationship, the more the primary loyalty of lawyers is to clients rather than to courts or guild, the more telling the advantages of accumulated expertise and guidance in overall strategy.

What about the specialization of the bar? Might we not expect the existence of specialization to offset RP advantages by providing OS with a specialist who in pursuit of his own career goals would be interested in outcomes that would be advantageous to a whole class of OSs? Does the specialist become the functional equivalent of the RP? We may divide specialists into (1) those specialized by field of law (patent, divorce, etc.), (2) those specialized by the kind of party represented (for example, house counsel). and (3) those specialized by both field of law and "side" or party (personal injury plaintiff, criminal defense, labour). Divorce lawyers do not specialize in husbands or wives, nor real estate lawyers in buyers or sellers. But labour lawyers and tax lawyers and stockholders-derivative-suit lawyers do specialize not only in the field of law but in representing one side. Such specialists may represent RPs or OSs. Figure 2 provides some well-known examples of different kinds of specialists.

Most specializations cater to the needs of particular kinds of RPs. Those specialists who service OSs have some distinctive features:

First, they tend to make up the "lower echelons" of the legal profession. Compared to the lawyers who provide services to RPs, lawyers in these specialties tend to be drawn from lower socio-economic origins, to have attended local, proprietary or part-time law schools, to practise alone rather than in large firms, and to possess low prestige within the profession. (Of course the correlation is far from perfect; some lawyers who represent OSs do not have these characteristics and some representing RPs do. However, on the whole the difference in professional standing is massive).

Second, specialists who service OSs tend to have problems of mobilizing a clientele (because of the low state of information among OSs) and encounter "ethical" barriers imposed by the profession which forbid solicitation, advertising, referral fees, advances to clients, and so forth.

Third, the episodic and isolated nature of the relationship with particular OS clients tends to elicit a stereotyped and uncreative brand of legal services. Carlin and Howard (1965: 385) observe that:

> The quality of service rendered poorer clients is ... affected by the non-repeating character of the matters they typically bring to lawyers (such as divorce, criminal, personal injury): this combined with the small fees encourages a mass processing of cases. As a result, only a limited amount of

time and interest is usually expended on any one case since there is little or no incentive to treat it except as an isolated piece of legal business. Moreover, there is ordinarily no desire to go much beyond the case as the client presents it, and such cases are only accepted when there is a clear-cut cause of action; i.e., when they fit into convenient legal categories and promise a fairly certain return.

Fourth, while they are themselves RPs, these specialists have problems in developing optimizing strategies. What might be good strategy for an insurance company lawyer or prosecutor — trading off some cases for gains on others — is branded as unethical when done by a criminal defense or personal injury plaintiff lawyer. It is not permissible for him to play his series of OSs as if they constituted a single RP.

Conversely, the demand of routine and orderly handling of a whole series of OSs may constrain the lawyer from maximizing advantage for any individual OS. Rosenthal (1970: 172) shows that "for all but the largest [personal injury] claims an attorney loses money by thoroughly preparing a case and not settling it early."

For the lawyer who services OSs, with his transient clientele, his permanent "client" is the forum, the opposite party, or the intermediary who supplies clients. Consider, for example, the dependence of the criminal defense lawyer on maintaining cooperative relations with the various members of the "criminal court community." Similarly, Carlin notes that among metropolitan individual practitioners whose clientele consists of OSs, there is a deformation of loyalty toward the intermediary.

> In the case of those lawyers specializing in personal injury, local tax, collections, criminal, and to some extent divorce work, the relationship with the client ... is generally mediated by a broker or business supplier who may be either another lawyer or a layman. In these fields of practice the lawyer is principally concerned with pleasing the broker or winning his approval, more so than he is with satisfying the individual client. The source of business generally counts for more than the client, especially where the client is unlikely to return or to send in other clients. The client is then expendable: he can be exploited to the full. Under these conditions, when a lawyer receives a client ... he has not so much gained a client as a piece of business, and his attitude is often that of handling a particular piece of merchandise or of developing a volume of a certain kind of merchandise.

The existence of a specialized bar on the OS side should overcome the gap in expertise, allow some economies of scale, provide for bargaining commitment and personal familiarity. But this is short of overcoming the fundamental strategic advantages of RPs — their capacity to structure the transaction, play the odds, and influence rule-development and enforcement policy.

Specialized lawyers may, by virtue of their identification with parties, become lobbyists, moral entrepreneurs, proponents of reforms on the parties' behalf. But lawyers have a cross-cutting interest in preserving complexity and mystique so that client contact with this area of law is rendered problematic. Lawyers should not be expected to be proponents of reforms which are optimum from the point of view of the clients taken alone. Rather, we would expect them to seek to optimize the clients' position without diminishing that of lawyers. Therefore, specialized lawyers have an interest in a framework which keeps recovery (or whatever) problematic at the same time that they favour changes which improve their clients' position within this framework. (Consider the lobbying efforts of personal injury plaintiffs and defense lawyers.) Considerations of interest are likely to be fused with ideological commitments: the lawyers' preference for complex and finely-tuned bodies of rules, for adversary proceedings for individualized case-by-case decision-making. Just as the culture of the client population affects strategic position, so does the professional culture of the lawyers.

INSTITUTIONAL FACILITIES

We see then that the strategic advantages of the RP may be augmented by the advantages in the distribution of legal services. Both are related to the advantages conferred by the basic features of the institutional facilities for the handling of claims: passivity and overload.

These institutions are passive, first, in the sense that Black refers to as "reactive" — they must be mobilized by the claimant — giving advantage to the claimant with information, ability to surmount cost barriers, and skill to navigate restrictive procedural requirements. They are passive in a further sense that once in the door the burden is on each party to proceed with his case. The presiding official acts as umpire, while the development of the case, collection of evidence and presentation of proof are left to the initiative and resources of the parties. Parties are treated as if they were equally endowed with economic resources, investigative opportunities and legal skills (*Cf.* Homberger [1971: 641]). Where, as is usually the case, they are not, the broader the delegation to the parties, the greater the advantage conferred on the wealthier, more experienced and better organized party.

The advantages conferred by institutional passivity are accentuated by the chronic overload which typically characterizes these institutions. Typically there are far more claims than there are institutional resources for full dress adjudication of each. In several ways overload creates pressures on claimants to settle rather than to adjudicate:

(a) by causing delay (thereby discounting the value of recovery);
(b) by raising costs (of keeping the case alive);
(c) by inducing institutional incumbents to place a high value on clearing dockets, discouraging full-dress adjudication in favour of bargaining, stereotyping and routine processing;
(d) by inducing the forum to adopt restrictive rules to discourage litigation.

Thus, overload increases the cost and risk of adjudicating and shields existing rules from challenge, diminishing opportunities for rule-change. This tends to favour the beneficiaries of existing rules.

Second, by increasing the difficulty of challenging going practice, overload also benefits those who reap advantage from the neglect (or systematic violation) of rules which favour their adversaries.

Third, overload tends to protect the possessor — the party who has the money or goods — against the claimant. For the most part, this amounts to favoring RPs over OSs, since RPs typically can structure transactions to put themselves in the possessor position.

Finally, the overload situation means that there are more commitments in the formal system than there are resources to honour them — more rights and rules "on the books" than can be vindicated or enforced. There are, then, questions of priorities in the allocation of resources. We would expect judges, police, administrators and other managers of limited institutional facilities to be responsive to the more organized, attentive and influential of their constituents. Again, these tend to be RPs.

Thus, overloaded and passive institutional facilities provide the setting in which the RP advantages in strategic position and legal services can have full play.

RULES

We assume here that rules tend to favour older, culturally dominant interests. This is not meant to imply that the rules are explicitly designed to favour these interests, but rather that those groups which have become dominant have successfully articulated their operations to pre-existing rules. To the extent that rules are evenhanded or favour the "have-nots," the limited resources for their implementation will be allocated, I have argued, so as to give greater effect to those rules which protect and promote the tangible interest of organized and influential groups. Furthermore, the requirements of due process, with their barriers or protections against precipitate action, naturally tend to protect the possessor or holder against the claimant. Finally, the rules are sufficiently complex and problematic (or capable of being problematic if sufficient resources are expended to make them so) that differences in the quantity and quality of legal services will affect capacity to derive advantages from the rules.

Thus, we arrive at Figure 3 which summarizes why the "haves" tend to come out ahead. It points to layers of advantages enjoyed by different (but largely overlapping) classes of "haves" — advantages which interlock, reinforcing and shielding one another.

ALTERNATIVES TO THE OFFICIAL SYSTEM

We have been discussing resort to the official system to put forward (or defend against) claims. Actually, resort to this system by claimants (or initiators) is one of several alternatives. Our analysis should consider the relationship of the characteristics of the total official litigation system to this use *vis-à-vis* the alternatives. These include at least the following:

1. Inaction — "lumping it," not making a claim or complaint. This is done all the time by "claimants" who lack information or access or who knowingly decide gain is too low, cost too high (including psychic cost of litigating where such activity is repugnant). Costs are raised by lack of information or skill, and also include risk. Inaction is also familiar on the part of official complainers (police, agencies, prosecutors) who have incomplete information about violations, limited resources, policies about *de minimus*, schedules of priorities, and so forth.

2. "Exit" — withdrawal from a situation or relationship by moving, resigning, severing relations, finding new partners, etc. This is of course a very common expedient in many kinds of trouble. Like "lumping it," it is an alternative to invocation of any kind of remedy system — although its presence as a sanction may be

8. People in the Legal Process: Access to "Justice" — A. Who Uses the Law and Why?

FIGURE 3
WHY THE "HAVES" TEND TO COME OUT AHEAD

Element	Advantages	Enjoyed by
Parties	• ability to structure transaction • specialized expertise, economies of scale • long-term strategy • ability to play for rules • bargaining credibility • ability to invest in penetration	• repeat players, large, professional*
Legal Services	• skill, specialization, continuity	• organized, professional*, wealthy
Institutional Facilities	• passivity • cost and delay barriers • favorable priorities	• wealthy, experienced, organized • holders, possessors • beneficiaries of existing rules • organized, attentive
Rules	• favorable rules • due process barriers	• older, culturally dominant • holders, possessors

* in the simple sense of "doing it for a living"

important to the working of other remedies. The use of "exit" options depends on the availability of alternative opportunities or partners (and information about them), the costs of withdrawal, transfer, relocation, development of new relationships, the pull of loyalty to previous arrangements — and on the availability and cost of other remedies.

3. Resort to some unofficial control system — we are familiar with many instances in which disputes are handled outside the official litigation system. Here we should distinguish (a) those dispute-settlement systems which are normatively and institutionally appended to the official system (such as settlement of auto-injuries, handling of bad checks) from (b) those settlement systems which are relatively independent in norms and sanctions (such as businessmen settling disputes *inter se*, religious groups, gangs).

What we might call the "appended" settlement systems merge imperceptibly into the official litigation system [Figure 4]. We might sort them out by the extent to which the official intervention approaches the adjudicatory mode. We find a continuum from situations where parties settle among themselves with an eye to the official rules and sanctions, through situations where official intervention is invoked, to those in which settlement is supervised and/or imposed by officials, to full dress adjudication. All along this line the sanction is supplied by the official system (though not always in the manner prescribed in the "higher law") and the norm or rules applied are a version of the official rules, although discounted for transaction costs and distorted by their selective use for the purpose of the parties.

From those "appended" systems of discounted and privatized official justice, we should distinguish those informal systems of "private justice" which invoke other norms and other sanctions. Such systems of dispute-settlement are typical among people in continuing interaction such as an organized group, a trade, or a university. In sorting out the various types according to the extent and the mode of intervention of third parties, we can distinguish two dimensions: the first is the degree to which the applicable norms are formally articulated, elaborated, and exposited, that is the increasingly organized character of the norms. The second represents the degree to which initiative and binding authority are accorded to the third party, that is, the increasingly organized character of the sanction. Some conjectures about the character of some of the common types of private systems are presented in Figure 5.

(i) Why the "Haves" Come Out Ahead: Speculation on the Limits of Legal Change

FIGURE 4
"APPENDED" DISPUTE-SETTLEMENT SYSTEMS

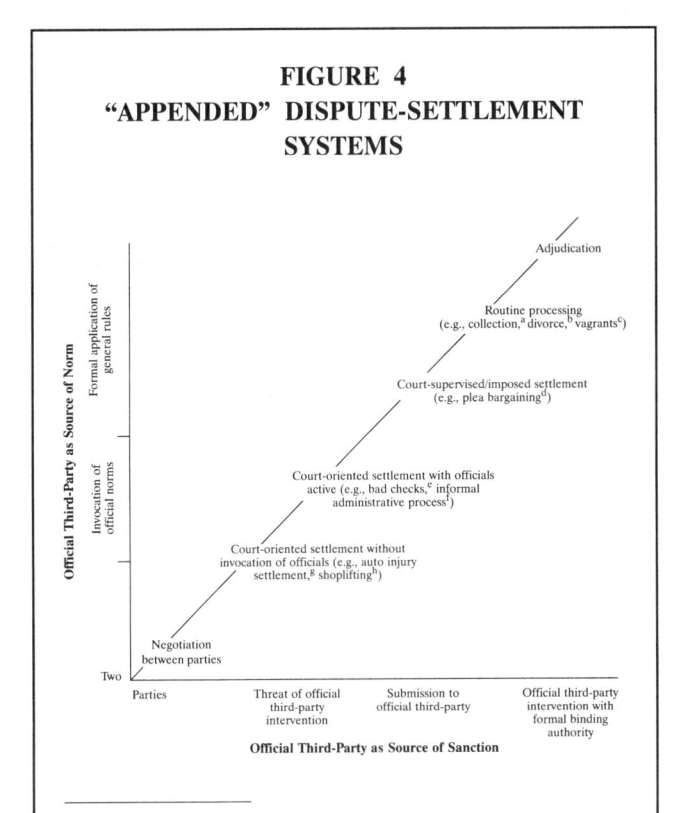

a. Jacob (1969).
b. O'Gorman (1963); Virtue (1956).
c. Foote (1956); Spradley (1970).
d. Newman (1966: chap 3); McIntyre and Lippman (1970).
e. Beutal (1957: 287 ff.); *cf.* the operation of the Fraud and Complaint Department at McIntyre (1963: 470–71).
f. Woll (1970); *cf.* the "formal informal settlement system" of the Motor Vehicles Bureau, described by Macaulay (1966: 153 ff.).
g. Ross (1970).
h. Cameron (1964: 32–34).

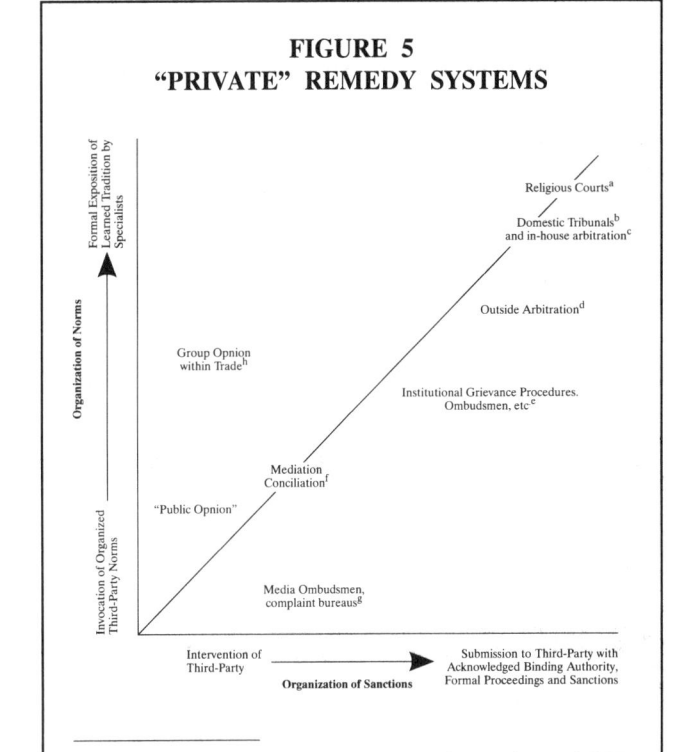

FIGURE 5
"PRIVATE" REMEDY SYSTEMS

a. *Columbia J. of Law and Social Problems* (1970, 1971); Shriver (1966); Ford (1970: 457–79).
b. E.g., "The International Air Transport Association" (*New York Times*, Nov. 8, 1970); professional sports leagues and associations (*N.Y. Times*, Jan. 15, 1971).
c. Mentschikoff (1961: 859).
d. Bonn (1972); Mentschikoff (1961: 856–57).
e. Gellnorn, 1966; Anderson (1969; chaps IV, V).
f. E.g., labour-management (Simkin [1971: chap. 3]); MacCallum (1967).
g. E.g., newspaper "action line" columns, Better Business Bureaus
h. Macaulay (1963: 63–64); Leff (1970a: 29 ff.)

Our distinction between "appended" and "private" remedy systems should not be taken as a sharp dichotomy but as pointing to a continuum along which we might range the various remedy systems. There is a clear distinction between appended systems like automobile injury or bad check settlements and private systems like the internal regulation of the mafia (Cressey, 1969: Chaps. VIII, IX; Ianni, 1972), or the Chinese community. The internal regulatory aspects of universities, churches, and groups of businessmen lie somewhere in between. It is as if we could visualize a scale stretching from the official remedy system through ones oriented to it through relatively independent systems based on similar values to independent systems based on disparate values.

Presumably it is not accidental that some human encounters are regulated frequently and influentially by the official and its appended systems while others seem to generate controls that make resort to the official and its appended systems rare. Which human encounters are we likely to find regulated at the "official" end of our scale and which at the "private" end? It is submitted that location on our scale [Figure 6] varies with factors that we might sum up by calling them the density of the relationship. That is, the more inclusive in life-space and temporal span a relationship between parties, the less likely it is that

269

FIGURE 6
A SCALE OF REMEDY SYSTEMS FROM OFFICIAL TO PRIVATE

Remedy Systems

Official	Appended			Private	
Adjudication	Routine processing	Structurally Interstitial (Officials Participating)	Oriented to Official	Articulated to Official	Independent	Oppositional
	Collections Divorce	Plea bargaining, bad check recovery	Auto injury settlement	Businessmen	Churches, Chinese community	Gangs	Mafia, Revolutionaries

Examples

those parties will resort to the official system and more likely that the relationship will be regulated by some independent "private" system. This seems plausible because we would expect inclusive and enduring relationships to create the possibility of effective sanctions; and we would expect participants in such relationships to share a value consensus which provided standards for conduct and legitimized such sanctions in each case of deviance.

The prevalence of private systems does not necessarily imply that they embody values or norms which are competing or opposed to those of the official system. Our analysis does not impute the plurality of remedy systems to cultural differences as such. It implies that the official system is utilized when there is a disparity between social structure and cultural norm. It is used, that is, where interaction and vulnerability create encounters and relationships which do not generate shared norms (they may be insufficiently shared or insufficiently specific) and/or do not give rise to group structures which permit sanctioning these norms.

Figure 7 sketches out such relationships of varying density and suggests the location of various official and private remedy systems. It restates our surmise of a close association between the density of relationships and remoteness from the official system. We may surmise further that on the whole the official and appended systems flourish in connection with the disputes between parties of disparate size which give rise to the litigation in Boxes II and III of Figure 1. Private remedy systems, on the other hand, are more likely to handle disputes between parties of comparable size. The litigation in Boxes I and IV of Figure 1, then seems to represent in large measure the breakdown (or inhibited development) of private remedy systems. Indeed, the distribution of litigation generally forms a mirror image of the presence of private remedy systems. But the mirror is, for the various reasons discussed here, a distorting one.

From the vantage point of the "higher law" what we have called the official system may be visualized as the "upper" layers of a massive "legal" iceberg, something like this:

Adjudication
Litigation
Appended Settlement Systems
Private Settlement Systems
Exit Remedies/Self Help
Inaction ("lumping it")

The uneven and irregular layers are distinct although they merge imperceptibly into one another. As we proceed to discuss possible reforms of the official system, we will want to consider the kind of impact they will have on the whole iceberg.

We will look at some of the connections and flows between layers mainly from the point of view of the construction of the iceberg itself, but aware that flows and connections are also influenced by atmospheric (cultural) factors such as appetite for vindication, psychic cost of litigation, lawyers' culture and the like.

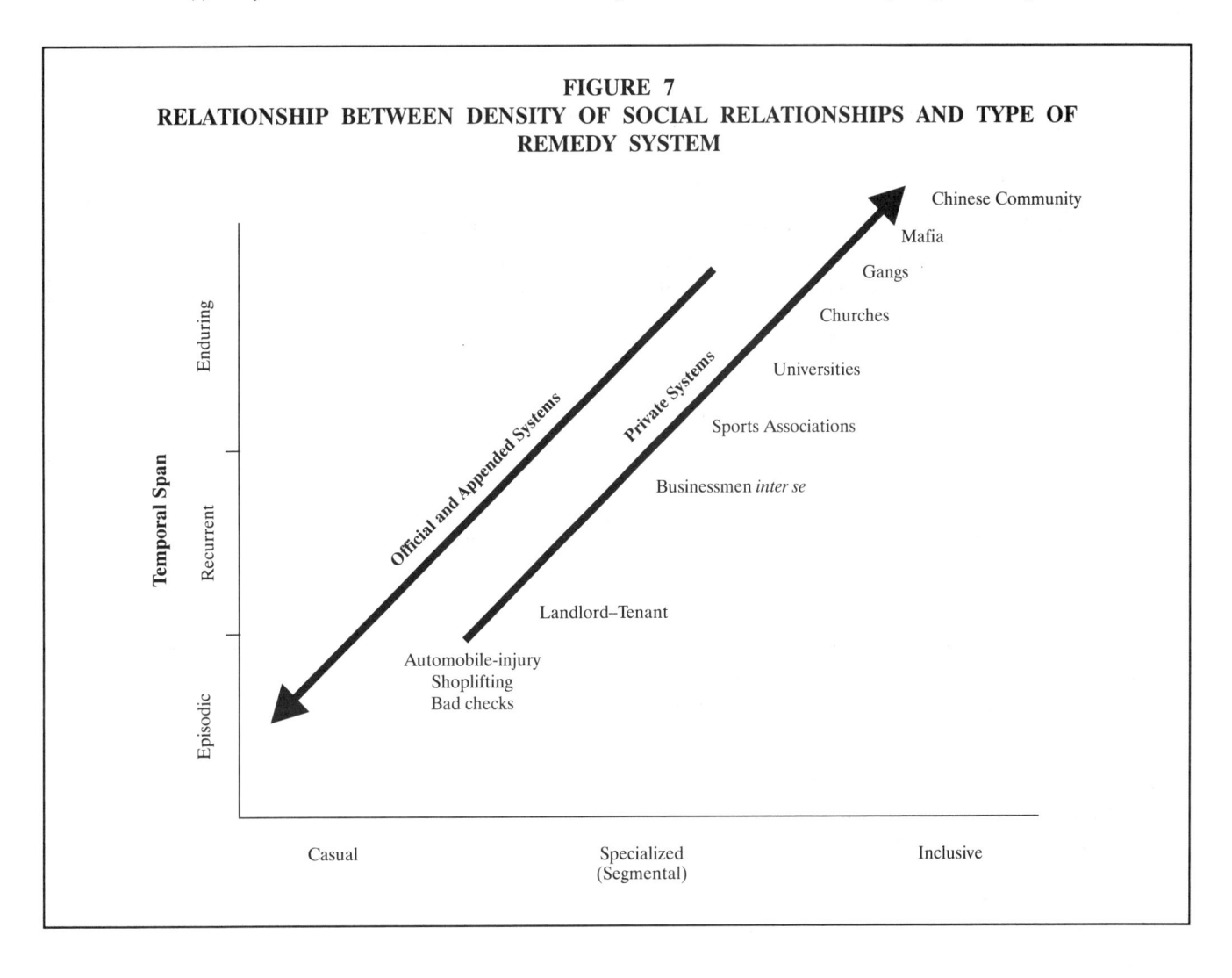

(i) Why the "Haves" Come Out Ahead: Speculation on the Limits of Legal Change

FIGURE 7
RELATIONSHIP BETWEEN DENSITY OF SOCIAL RELATIONSHIPS AND TYPE OF REMEDY SYSTEM

Temporal Span: Enduring, Recurrent, Episodic

Chinese Community
Mafia
Gangs
Churches
Universities
Sports Associations
Businessmen *inter se*
Landlord–Tenant
Automobile-injury
Shoplifting
Bad checks

Official and Appended Systems / *Private Systems*

Casual — Specialized (Segmental) — Inclusive

STRATEGIES FOR REFORM

Our categorization of four layers of advantage (Figure 3) suggests a typology of strategies for "reform" (taken here to mean equalization conferring relative advantage on those who did not enjoy it before.) We then come to four types of equalizing reform:

1. rule-change
2. improvement in institutional facilities
3. improvement of legal services in quantity and quality
4. improvement of strategic position of have-not parties

I shall attempt to sketch some of the possible ramifications of change on each of these levels for other parts of the litigation system and then discuss the relationship between changes in the litigation system and the rest of our legal iceberg. Of course such reforms need not be enacted singly, but may occur in various combinations. However, for our purposes we shall only discuss, first, each type taken in isolation and then, all taken together.

Rule-Change

Obtaining favorable rule changes is an expensive process. The various kinds of "have-nots" (Figure 3) have fewer resources to accomplish changes through legislation or administrative policy making. The advantages of the organized, professional, wealthy and attentive in these forums are well-known. Litigation, on the other hand, has a flavour of equality. The parties are "equal before the law" and the rules of the game do not permit them to deploy all of their resources in the conflict, but require that they proceed within the limiting forms of the trial. Thus, litigation is a particularly tempting arena to "have-nots," including those seeking rule change. Those who seek change through the courts tend to represent relatively isolated interests, unable to carry the day in more political forums.

Litigation may not, however, be a ready source of rule-change for "have-nots." Complexity, the need for high inputs of legal services and cost barriers (heightened by overloaded institutional facilities) make challenge of rules expensive. OS claimants, with high stakes in the tangible outcome, are unlikely to try to obtain rule changes. By definition, a test case — litigation deliberately designed to procure rule-change — is an unthinkable undertaking for an OS. There are some departures from our ideal type: OSs who place a high value on vindication by official rules or whose peculiar strategic situation makes it in their interest to pursue rule victories. But generally the test-case involves some organization which approximates an RP.

The architecture of courts severely limits the scale and scope of changes they can introduce in the rules. Tradition and ideology limit the kinds of matters that come before them: not patterns of practice but individual instances, not "problems" but cases framed by the parties and strained through requirements of standing, case or controversy, jurisdiction, and so forth. Tradition and ideology also limit the kind of decision they can give. Thus, common law courts for example, give an all-or-none, once-and-for-all decision which must be justified in terms of a limited (though flexible) corpus of rules and techniques. By tradition, courts cannot address problems by devising new regulatory or administrative machinery (and have no taxing and spending powers to support it); courts are limited to solutions compatible with the existing institutional framework. Thus, even the most favorably inclined court may not be able to make those rule-changes most useful to a class of "have-nots."

Rule-change may make use of the courts more attractive to "have-nots." Apart from increasing the possibility of favorable outcomes, it may stimulate organization, rally and encourage litigants. It may directly redistribute symbolic rewards to "have-nots" (or their champions). But tangible rewards do not always follow symbolic ones. Indeed, provision of symbolic rewards to "have-nots" (or crucial groups of their supporters) may decrease capacity and drive to secure redistribution of tangible benefits.

Rule-changes secured from courts or other peak agencies do not penetrate automatically and costlessly to other levels of the system, as attested by the growing literature on impact. This may be especially true of rule-change secured by adjudication, for several reasons:

1. Courts are not equipped to assess systematically the impact or penetration problem. Courts typically have no facilities for surveillance, monitoring, or securing systematic enforcement of their decrees. The task of monitoring is left to the parties.
2. The built-in limits on applicability due to the piecemeal character of adjudication. Thus a Mobilization for Youth lawyer reflects:
   > ...What is the ultimate value of winning a test case? In many ways a result cannot be clear-cut ... if the present welfare-residency laws are invalidated, it is quite possible that some other kind of welfare-residency law will spring up in their place. It is not very difficult to come up with a policy that is a little different, stated in different words, but which seeks to achieve the same basic objective. The results of test cases are not generally self-executing.... It is not enough to have a law invalidated or a policy declared void if the agency in question can come up with some variant of that policy, not very different in substance but sufficiently different to remove it from the effects of the court order.
3. The artificial equalizing of parties in adjudication by insulation from the full play of political pressures — the "equality" of the parties, the exclusion of "irrelevant" material, the "independence" of judges — means that judicial outcomes are more likely to be at variance with the existing constellation of political forces than decisions arrived at in forums lacking such insulation. But resources that cannot be employed in the judicial process can reassert themselves at the implementation stage, especially where institutional overload requires another round of decision making (what resources will be deployed to implement which rules) and/or private expenditures to secure implementation. Even where "have-nots" secure favorable changes at the rule level, they may not have the resources to secure the penetration of these rules. The impotence of rule-change, whatever its source, is particularly pronounced when there is reliance on unsophisticated OSs to utilize favorable new rules.

Where rule-change promulgated at the peak of the system does have an impact on other levels, we should not assume any isomorphism. The effect on institutional facilities and the strategic position of the parties may be far different then we would predict from the rule-change. Thus, Randall's study of movie censorship shows that liberalization of the rules did not make censorship boards more circumspect; instead, many closed down and the old game between censorship boards and distributors was replaced by a new, rougher game between exhibitors and local government-private group coalitions.

Increase in Institutional Facilities

Imagine an increase in institutional facilities for processing claims such that there is timely full-dress adjudication of every claim put forward — no queue, no delay, no stereotyping. Decrease in delay would lower costs for claimants, taking away this advantage of possessor-defendants. Those relieved of the necessity of discounting recovery for delay would have more to spend on legal services. To the extent that settlement had been induced by delay (rather than insuring against the risk of unacceptable loss), claimants would be inclined to litigate more and settle less. More litigants without stereotyping would mean more contests, including more contesting of rules and more rule change. As discounts diminished, neither side could use settlement policy to prevent rule-loss. Such reforms would for the most part benefit OS claimants, but they would also improve the position of those RP claimants not already in the possessor position, such as the prosecutor where the accused is free on bail.

This assumes no change in the *kind* of institutional facilities. We have merely assumed a greater quantitative availability of courts of the relatively passive variety typical of (at least) "common law" systems in which the case is "tried by the parties before the court..." (Homberger, 1970: 31). One may imagine institutions with augmented authority to solicit and supervise litigation, conduct investigations, secure, assemble and present proof; which enjoyed greater flexibility in devising outcomes (such as compromise or mediation); and finally which had available staff for monitoring compliance with their decrees. Greater institutional "activism" might be expected to reduce advantages of party expertise and of differences in the quality and quantity of legal services. Enhanced capacity for securing compliance might be expected to reduce advantages flowing from differences in ability to invest in enforcement. It is hardly necessary to point out that such reforms could be expected to encounter not only resistance from the beneficiaries of the present passive institutional style, but also massive ideological opposition from legal professionals whose fundamental sense of legal propriety would be violated.

Increase in Legal Services

The reform envisaged here is an increase in quantity and quality of legal services to "have-nots" (including greater availability of information about these services). Presumably this would lower costs, remove the expertise advantage, produce more litigation with more favorable outcomes for "have-nots," perhaps with more appeals and more rule challenges, more new rules in their favour. (Public defender, legal aid, judicare, and prepayment plans approximate this in various fashions.) To the extent that OSs would still have to discount for delay and risk, their gains would be limited (and increase in litigation might mean even more delay). Under certain conditions, increased legal services might use institutional overload as leverage on behalf of "have-nots." Our Mobilization for Youth attorney observes:

> ...if the Welfare Department buys out an individual case, we are precluded from getting a principle of law changed, but if we give them one thousand cases to buy out, that law has been effectively changed whether or not the law as written is changed. The practice is changed; the administration is changed; the attitude to the client is changed. The value of a heavy case load is that it allows you to populate the legal process. It allows you to apply remitting pressure on the agency you are dealing with. It creates a force that has to be dealt with, that has to be considered in terms of the decisions that are going to be made prospectively. It means that you are not somebody who will be gone tomorrow, not an isolated case, but a force in the community that will remain once this particular case has been decided.
>
> As a result ... we have been able, for the first time to participate along with welfare recipients ... in a rule-making process itself... (Rothwax, 1969: 140–41).

The increase in quantity of legal services was accompanied here by increased coordination and organization on the "have-not" side, which brings us to our fourth level of reform.

Reorganization of Parties

The reform envisaged here is the organization of "have-not" parties (whose position approximates OS) into coherent groups that have the ability to act in a coordinated fashion, play long-run strategies, benefit from high-grade legal services, and so forth.

One can imagine various ways in which OSs might be aggregated into RPs. They include (1) the membership association-bargaining agent (trade unions, tenant unions); (2) the assignee-manager of fragmentary rights (performing rights associations like ASCAP); (3) the interest group-sponsor (NAACP, ACLU, environmental action groups). All of these forms involve upgrading capacities for managing claims by gathering and utilizing information, achieving continuity and persistence, employing expertise, exercising bargaining skill and so forth. These advantages are combined with enhancement of the OS party's strategic position either by aggregating claims that are too small relative to the cost of remedies (consumers, breathers of polluted air, owners of performing rights); or by reducing claims to manageable size by collective action to dispel or share unacceptable risks (tenants, migrant workers). A weaker form of organization would be (4) a clearing-house which established a communication network among OSs. This would lower the costs of information and give RPs a stake in the effect OSs could have on their reputation. A minimal instance of this is represented by the "media ombudsman", — the "action line" type of newspaper column. Finally, there is governmentalization — utilizing the criminal law or the administrative process to make it the responsibility of a public officer to press claims that would be unmanageable in the hands of a private grievant.

An organized group is not only better able to secure favorable rule changes, in courts and elsewhere, but is better able to see that good rules are implemented. It can expend resources on surveillance, monitoring, threats, or litigation that would be uneconomic for an OS. Such new units would in effect be RPs. Their encounters with opposing RPs would move into Box IV of Figure 1. Neither would enjoy the strategic advantages of RPs over OSs. One possible result, as we have noted in our discussion of the RP v. RP situation, is delegalization, that is, a movement away from the official system to a private system of dispute-settlement; another would be more intense use of the official system.

Many aspects of "public interest law" can be seen as approximations of this reform. (1) The class action is a device to raise the stakes for an RP, reducing his strategic position to that of an OS by making the stakes more than he can afford to play odds on, while moving the claimants into a position in which they enjoy the RP advantages without having to undergo the outlay for organizing. (2) Similarly, the "community organizing" aspect of public interest law can be seen as an effort to create a unit (tenants, consumers) which can play the RP game.

(3) Such a change in strategic position creates the possibility of a test-case strategy for getting rule-change. Thus, "public interest law" can be thought of as a combination of community organizing, class action and test-case strategies, along with increase in legal services.

REFORM AND THE REST OF THE ICEBERG

The reforms of the official litigation system that we have imagined would, taken together, provide rules more favorable to the "have-nots." Redress according to the official rules, undiscounted by delay, strategic disability, disparities of legal services and so forth could be obtained whenever either party found it to his advantage. How might we expect such a utopian upgrading of the official machinery to affect the rest of our legal iceberg?

We would expect more use of the official system. Those who opted for inaction because of information or cost barriers and those who "settled" at discount rates in one of the "appended" systems would in many instances find it to their advantage to use the official system. The appended systems, insofar as they are built on the costs of resort to the official system, would either be abandoned or the outcomes produced would move to approximate closely those produced by adjudication.

On the other hand, our reforms would, by organizing OSs, create many situations in which *both* parties were organized to pursue their long-run interest in the litigation arena. In effect, many of the situations which occupied Boxes II and III of Figure 1 (RP v. OS, OS v. RP) — the great staple sources of litigation — would now be moved to Box IV (RP v. RP). We observed earlier that RPs who anticipate continued dealings with one another tend to rely on informal bilateral controls. We might expect then that the official system would be abandoned in favour of private systems of dispute-settlement.

Thus we would expect our reforms to produce a dual movement: the official and its appended systems would be "legalized" while the proliferation of private systems would "delegalize" many relationships. Which relationships would we expect to move which way? As a first approximation, we might expect that the less "inclusive" relationships currently handled by litigation or in the appended systems would undergo legalization, while relationships at the more inclusive end of the scale (Figure 7) would be privatized. Relationships among strangers (casual, episodic, non-recurrent) would be legalized; more dense (recurrent,

(i) Why the "Haves" Come Out Ahead: Speculation on the Limits of Legal Change

inclusive) relationships between parties would be candidates for the development of private systems.

Our earlier analysis suggests that the pattern might be more complex. First, for various reasons a class of OSs may be relatively incapable of being organized. Its size, relative to the size and distribution of potential benefits, may require disproportionately large inputs of coordination and organization. Its shared interest may be insufficiently respectable to be publicly acknowledged (for instance, shoplifters, homosexuals until very recently). Or recurrent OS roles may be staffed by shifting population for whom the sides of the transaction are interchangeable. (For instance, home buyers and sellers, negligent motorists and accident victims.) Even where OSs are organizable, we recall that not all RP v. RP encounters lead to the development of private remedy systems. There are RPs engaged in value conflict; there are those relationships with a governmental or other monopoly aspect in which informal controls may falter; and finally there are those RPs whose encounters with one another are non-recurring. In all of these we might expect legalization rather than privatization.

Whichever way to movement in any given instance, our reforms would entail changes in the distribution of power. RPs would no longer be able to wield their strategic advantages to invoke selectively the enforcement of favorable rules while securing large discounts (or complete shielding by cost and overload) where the rules favored their OS opponents.

Delegalization (by the proliferation of private remedy and bargaining systems) would permit many relationships to be regulated by norms and understandings that departed from the official rules. Such parochial remedy systems would be insulated from the impingement of the official rules by the commitment of the parties to their continuing relationship. Thus, delegalization would entail a kind of pluralism and decentralization. On the other hand, the "legalization" of the official and appended systems would amount to the collapse of species of pluralism and decentralization that are endemic in the kind of (unreformed) legal system we have postulated. The current prevalence of appended and private remedy systems reflects the inefficiency, cumbersomeness and costliness of using the official system. This inefficient, cumbersome and costly character is a source and shield of a kind of decentralization and pluralism. It permits a selective application of the "higher law" in a way that gives effect at the operative level to parochial norms and concerns which are not fully recognized in the "higher law" (such as the right to exclude low status neighbors, or police dominance in encounters with citizens). If the insulation afforded by the costs of getting the "higher law" to prevail were eroded, many relationships would suddenly be exposed to the "higher law" rather than its parochial counterparts. We might expect this to generate new pressures for explicit recognition of these "subterranean" values or for explicit decentralization.

These conjectures about the shape that a "reformed" legal system might take suggest that we take another look at our unreformed system, with its pervasive disparity between authoritative norms and everyday operations. A modern legal system of the type we postulated is characterized structurally by institutional unity and culturally by normative universalism. The power to make, apply and change law is reserved to organs of the public, arranged in unified hierarchic relations, committed to uniform application of universalistic norms.

There is, for example, in American law (that is, in the higher reaches of the system where the learned tradition is propounded) an unrelenting stress on the virtues of uniformity and universality and a pervasive distaste for particularism, compromise and discretion. Yet the cultural attachment to universalism is wedded to and perhaps even intensifies diversity and particularism at the operative level.

The unreformed features of the legal system then appear as a device for maintaining the partial dissociation of everyday practice from these authoritative institutional and normative commitments. Structurally, (by cost and institutional overload) and culturally (by ambiguity and normative overload) the unreformed system effects a massive covert delegation from the most authoritative rule-makers to field level officials (and their constituencies) responsive to other norms and priorities than are contained in the "higher law." By their selective application these field level communities produce regulatory outcomes which could not be predicted by examination of the authoritative "higher law."

Thus its unreformed character articulates the legal system to the discontinuities of culture and social structure: it provides a way of accommodating cultural heterogeneity and social diversity while propounding universalism and unity; of accommodating vast concentrations of private power while upholding the supremacy of public authority; of accommodating inequality in fact while establishing equality at law; of facilitating action by great collective combines while celebrating individualism. Thus "unreform" — that is, ambiguity and overload of rules, overloaded and inefficient institutional facilities, disparities in the supply of legal services, and disparities in the strategic position of parties — is the foundation of the "dualism" of the legal system. It permits unification and universalism at the symbolic level and diversity and particularism at the operating level.

IMPLICATIONS FOR REFORM

We have discussed the way in which the architecture of the legal system tends to confer interlocking advantages on overlapping groups whom we have called the "haves." To what extent might reforms of the legal system dispel these advantages? Reforms will always be less total than the utopian ones envisioned above. Reformers will have limited resources to deploy and they will always be faced with the necessity of choosing which uses of those resources are most productive of equalizing change. What does our analysis suggest about strategies and priorities?

Our analysis suggests that change at the level of substantive rules is not likely in itself to be determinative of redistributive outcomes. Rule change is in itself likely to have little effect because the system is so constructed that changes in the rules can be filtered out unless accompanied by changes at other levels. In a setting of overloaded institutional facilities, inadequate costly legal services and unorganized parties, beneficiaries may lack the resources to secure implementation; or an RP may restructure the transaction to escape the thrust of the new rule. (Leff, 1970b; Rothwax, 1969: 143; *Cf.* Grossman, 1970). Favorable rules are not necessarily (and possibly not typically) in short supply to "have-nots;" certainly less so than any of the other resources needed to play the litigation game. Programs of equalizing reform which focus on rule-change can be readily absorbed without any change in power relations. The system has the capacity to change a great deal at the level of rules without corresponding changes in everyday patterns of practice or distribution of tangible advantages. (See, for example, Lipsky, 1970: chap. 4, 5). Indeed, rule-change may become a symbolic substitute for redistribution of advantages. (See Edelman, 1967: 40).

The low potency of substantive rule-change is especially the case with rule-changes procured from courts. That courts can sometimes be induced to propound rule-changes that legislatures would not make points to the limitation as well as the possibilities of court-produced change. With their relative insulation from retaliation by antagonistic interests, courts may more easily propound new rules which depart from prevailing power relations. But such rules require even greater inputs of other resources to secure effective implementation. And courts have less capacity than other rule-makers to create institutional facilities and re-allocate resources to secure implementation of new rules. Litigation then is unlikely to shape decisively the distribution of power in society. It may serve to secure or solidify symbolic commitments. It is vital tactically in securing temporary advantage or protection, providing leverage for organization and articulation of interests and conferring (or withholding) the mantle of legitimacy. The more divided the other holders of power, the greater the redistributive potential of this symbolic/tactical role. (Dahl, 1958: 294).

Our analysis suggests that breaking the interlocked advantages of the "haves" requires attention not only to the level of rules, but also to institutional facilities, legal services and organization of parties. It suggests that litigating and lobbying have to be complemented by interest organizing, provisions of services and invention of new forms of institutional facilities.

The thrust of our analysis is that changes at the level of parties are most likely to generate changes at other levels. If rules are the most abundant resource for reformers, parties capable of pursuing long-range strategies are the rarest. The presence of such parties can generate effective demand for high grade legal services — continuous, expert, and oriented to the long-run — and pressure for institutional reforms and favorable rules. This suggests that we can roughly surmise the relative strategic priority of various rule changes. Rule changes which relate directly to the strategic position of the parties by facilitating organization, increasing the supply of legal services (where these in turn provide a focus for articulating and organizing common interests) and increasing the costs of opponents for instance, authorization of class action suits, award of attorneys fees and costs, award of provisional remedies — these are the most powerful fulcrum for change. The intensity of the opposition to class action legislation and autonomous reform-oriented legal services such as California Rural Legal Assistance indicates the "haves" own estimation of the relative strategic impact of the several levels.

The contribution of the lawyer to redistributive social change, then, depends upon the organization and culture of the legal profession. We have surmised that court-produced substantive rule-change is unlikely in itself to be a determinative element in producing tangible redistribution of benefits. The leverage provided by litigation depends on its strategic combination with inputs at other levels. The question then is whether the organization of the profession permits lawyers to develop and employ skills at these other levels. The more that lawyers view themselves exclusively as courtroom advocates, the less their willingness to undertake new tasks and form enduring alliances with clients and operate in forums other than courts, the less likely they are to serve as agents of redistributive change. Paradoxically, those legal professions most open to accentuating the advantages of the "haves" (by allowing themselves to be "captured" by recurrent clients) may be most able to become (or have room for, more likely) agents of change, precisely because they provide more licence for identification with clients and their "causes" and have a less strict definition of what are properly professional activities.

(ii) Legal Victory Still Leaves Rosa Becker Out in Cold

William Marsden

Money was the operative word, but revenge was what Rosa Becker really wanted.

Revenge for being tossed out on her fanny by her common-law husband Lothar Pettkus, who showed his appreciation for their 18 years by throwing $3,000 on the floor and suggesting she "get lost."

Rosa thought: That's no way to say goodbye. Not after 18 years (during which she literally cleaned and tied his shoes and ran their business).

So, in 1974, she sued for half of all Pettkus's property, and her revenge turned into one of the most celebrated palimony cases in Canadian history.

In 1980, all nine judges of the Supreme Court of Canada awarded her half of a bee farm the couple built up and half-interest in three properties — setting a legal precedent that the late Chief Bora Laskin believed would settle the matrimonial-property issue.

Her victory was front-page news. Editorials applauded. Her lawyer, Gerald Langlois, predicted a $150,000 settlement for the beekeeping business and other properties. Then the excitement died — and now only law books remember Rosa Becker.

She still has not got her revenge.

Eleven years after she launched her suit and five years after the Supreme Court ruled, she has not received one cent from Lothar Pettkus.

Alone in a 9-room farmhouse in Franklin Centre near Ormstown, where she is paid $3,000 a year plus room and board to clean and cook for a dairy farmer and his farmhand, Becker, 58, reflects on Canadian justice:

"It's weird. I don't understand it."

Lothar Pettkus is 52, 5-foot-11, 200 lbs., strong. He likes hunting moose, is an excellent shot, keeps German shepherds, has thin blond hair, blue eyes.

By his calculation, Rosa Becker has lied 460 times to the Supreme Court of Canada in 1980 and 68 times to the Supreme Court of Ontario during a 1982 trial to divide up the property. He's trying to persuade the Ontario ombudsman to investigate his allegations.

"She was lying so badly that she had the (Supreme Court of Canada) judges convinced that this is the truth and it's definitely not the truth," Pettkus says.

(Judge K.A. Flannigan of the Ontario Supreme Court told Lothar Pettkus at a hearing in 1982: "It's the truth because the court found it to be true." But that hasn't stopped Lothar Pettkus.)

Convinced that the courts have been tricked by Rosa and her lawyer and their "lies," he decided that he cannot become a party to the Supreme Court ruling.

"A person who is perjuring herself with her lawyer — I should be party to a criminal act?" he asks rhetorically.

"I am just an innocent citizen sitting back and watching what the law is doing to people like me."

He might prove that, while you can't fight city hall, you sure can fight the Supreme Court of Canada.

Every move Rosa Becker makes, he thwarts, Becker's lawyer Langlois said.

From *Montreal Gazette* (February 16, 1985) at B5. Reproduced by permission of The Gazette, Montreal.

He has exhausted seven lawyers and wielded every available weapon in the justice system to counter the Supreme Court ruling, he said.

Since the Supreme Court judgment, there have been 21 motions, judgments, affidavits, appeals and court orders issued concerning this case and the division of property — and still no money for Rosa Becker.

Court appearances are catfights, with Pettkus at times attempting to retry the case.

At a 1982 hearing into the division of property, Pettkus, between lawyers, represented himself and was questioning Becker about rent received from a West Hawkesbury, Ont., property they owned:

Rosa Becker: In the beginning it was $80 and then it gone up to $100.

Lothar Pettkus: Your honour, that's not true. At the beginning it was $40 and she says April the 14th, this year, that she paid $80. What was the truth now? Tell your honour the truth.

Becker: It was never $40. It was always $80 and then $100 but never $40.

Pettkus: You don't know if it's $80, you don't know if it was $40 and you don't know if it's $100, because you're so confused you can't answer the question proper.

Becker: Can you blame me for being confused after eight years with you in court?

Q: You took me to court.

A: No. I had no choice.

Q: Establish what was paid for in 1980. When you left...

A: I don't care anymore. You want it, shove it, shove it. I'm sick and tired. (Witness leaves courtroom.)

Rosa Becker, small, missing some front teeth, remembers when she first met Lothar Pettkus 30 years ago in the spring of 1955.

It was at a German Club dancehall near the Windsor Hotel. She was 28. He was 22. She earned $28 a week in a lace factory. He earned $75 a week as a garage mechanic.

She thought his tall brushcut made his face "look a mile long." They moved in together. He saved his money. They spent hers.

"Things happen in life that you can't explain and that's one of those things," she said without malice.

He said he "fell into her trap" and stayed for almost 20 years.

In 1960, they bought a 125-acre farm for $5,000, which he paid for out of his savings.

In 1971 and 1973, they purchased properties in East and West Hawkesbury in Ontario, where they moved their beekeeping business.

By that time, they were making as much as $30,000 profit a year. She played a major part in every aspect of the business. Everything was in his name.

But Judge Omer H. Chartrand of the Ontario District Court ruled that Rosa Becker's contribution was in the form of "risk capital invested in the hope of seducing a younger defendant into marriage."

He awarded her 40 empty beehives (which without bees are worthless) and $1,200.

The Court of Appeals ruled in 1978 that Chartrand had undervalued Becker's contributions. It gave her half the assets, valued as of 1974 when the two broke up. The Supreme Court agreed and implied that Chartrand's reference to risk capital "lacked gallantry."

The task then was to evaluate the assets as of 1974, apply interest and give Becker her share.

That process, which normally might take a year, is still not over.

Court judgments so far would put Becker's total claim on Pettkus at about $95,000.

In November 1983, Pettkus offered Becker a deal. He would pay her $46,408.90 if she would allow the Hawkesbury properties to be transferred to Pettkus's wife Monique.

Becker refused because she realized this would leave Pettkus without assets and make it impossible for her to receive the balance owing.

Eric Williams, Pettkus's latest lawyer, points to this offer as an example of Pettkus's willingness to settle. "I'll bet you 99 to one she doesn't get better than that offer," he said, adding that Pettkus has always been willing to settle the matter fairly.

Langlois said he attempted to freeze Lothar Pettkus's bank accounts but found only $12. Pettkus said his wife owns everything now.

Indeed, Monique Pettkus is claiming half her husband's interest in the beekeeping business and the East Hawkesbury property where she and Pettkus live with about 550 beehives. This claim will be fought out in court Feb. 21.

When Langlois tried last fall to seize the beehives, Pettkus's wife went to court and appealed the seizure, claiming that the hives are hers. That trial will be heard in March.

When the bees were seized by the court in November, Pettkus refused to feed them. By the time a court order could be obtained demanding that he feed and maintain the hives (valued at $50 each), most of the bees were dead, Monique told *The Gazette*. Without the bees, the business is worthless.

The only cash available is the $69,000 received from the sale last fall of the two Hawkesbury properties. The money is being held by the court.

By this June, Becker's half with interest will total $32,785.10. But all of that will go to pay her legal fees, which Langlois estimates total about $35,000. She also has to pay half the sheriff, appraisal and real-estate broker fees of about $10,000.

There's a good chance she will get all the $69,000, said Langlois. But it will take a fight, perhaps another year.

"That's the tragedy of this whole thing," Langlois said. "He (Pettkus) is ready to pay whatever amount to whatever lawyers it takes and it's clear that he doesn't intend to pay anything to Rosa Becker.

"She has been given the benefit of these judgments but the law has afforded protection to Pettkus on the realization of the funds."

Williams argues that Becker is trying to get blood out of a stone. "No matter how you cut it, the man is not rich."

Rosa Becker has visions. Ghosts tell her things.

They tell her her lawyer is conspiring with Lothar Pettkus.

"They (the visions) are always true and I know that makes Gerry Langlois uneasy about me," she said.

In 1983, she asked the Law Society of Upper Canada to investigate Langlois. They did and found "absolutely no evidence of professional misconduct."

She has also asked Chief Justice Brian Dickson of the Supreme Court of Canada to intervene on her behalf. He has refused.

"I can understand Rosa's frustration," Langlois said. He knows about her visions.

In December, he sent Rosa Becker a letter suggesting that he withdraw from the file since she has lost confidence in him.

Meanwhile, he is preparing her next court appearance and his bill.

And she's thinking she might take her case to the World Court. Still seeking revenge.

Last month, the Supreme Court of Canada decided that the entire question of division of matrimonial property needed another look. It decided to hear an appeal from Mary Sorochan, 69, of Two Hills, Alberta.

"After 40 years of common-law marriage, she received nothing from her estranged husband, who argued that he owned their 190-hectare farm before she came on the scene.

She wants recognition for her help in maintaining the farm.

[Note: This case is an example of Galanter's observation that rule changes do not necessarily get implemented at what he calls the field level. After 11 years of legal proceedings, including a victory in Supreme Court of Canada, she still had not received any tangible financial outcome as a result of her court battles.]

(iii) Access to the Courts

G. Brodsky and S. Day

This chapter discusses standing to sue, intervenor status, and funding for litigation. The first two are legal issues. When a court deals with standing and intervenor status, it determines who will be recognized as a proper participant in a case. Despite uncertainty about the courts' approach and some important unresolved issues, recent decisions hold out hope that women and other disadvantaged groups may not be barred from participation by narrow rulings. However, even if disadvantaged groups are assisted by a generous approach to standing, their access will be severely restricted if adequate

---

From G. Brodsky, and Shelagh Day, "Access to the Courts" in *Canadian Charter Equality Rights for Women: One Step Forward or Two Steps Back?* (Ottawa: Canadian Advisory Council on the Status of Women, 1989) at 131–40. Reproduced by permission of Canadian Advisory Council on the Status of Women (CACSW), Ottawa, Ontario.

money and resources are not available to support Charter equality rights litigation.

Questions of access are crucial because they determine who can make their voices heard in the courts and who can participate in shaping the interpretations of the new equality guarantees.

RELAXED RULES OF STANDING

There has been a recent relaxation of the rules governing standing, or who the courts will recognize as a party. Traditionally, no person, except an Attorney General, could bring a constitutional challenge unless they were directly affected by the impugned law in a more significant way than were other citizens. But in the past decade, courts have shown increasing flexibility about that requirement. The decision of the Supreme Court of Canada in the case of *Borowski* radically altered the law of standing.

Joseph Borowski was granted standing to challenge section 251 of the *Criminal Code*, a law that was totally inapplicable to him, on the basis of alleged violations of fetal rights under the *Canadian Bill of Rights*. The effect of the standing decision in *Borowski* is that a court challenge may be brought by a citizen who is not affected directly by legislation where there is "no other reasonable and effective manner in which the issue may be brought before the court."

Another example of the relative ease with which constitutional challenges may be initiated arises in the context of criminal prosecutions. Anyone charged with a criminal offence is permitted to challenge the constitutional validity of the law under which she/he has been charged, even if the alleged infringement is not directly applicable to the accused. An implication for women of this broad rule of standing becomes apparent in the context of a sexual assault trial such as that of *R. v. W.D.C.G.* in which a male accused was permitted to argue that section 149(1) of the *Criminal Code* should be struck down because only a "female person" could be a victim of the crime. The accused was not himself suffering from any lack of legislative protection, nor was he being penalized because of his sex. Section 149(1) said:

> Everyone who indecently assaults a female person is guilty of an indictable offence and is liable to imprisonment for five years.

Although the New Brunswick Court of Appeal upheld the law on the basis that it did not penalize men but rather singled out a particular group for protection, the Court did not question the standing of the accused to raise the sex equality challenge, which had the potential to affect all women in Canada.

Further, the principle that a person may challenge legislation on behalf of other persons as part of his or her defence against a lawsuit is apparently not restricted to criminal prosecutions. For example, in *Shewchuk v. Ricard* where the issue was liability of a putative father for child maintenance under a provincial statute, Jerry Ricard, the putative father, was permitted to challenge the legislation on the grounds of underinclusiveness, even though he was not a member of the excluded class. Ricard argued that sections of the *Child Paternity and Support Act* should be struck down because a father who is left with an "abandoned" child in his arms (which Ricard was not) does not have the same remedies open to him to obtain support from the child's mother, as the mother does to obtain support from the child's father.

Third parties have been permitted to make fair trial challenges pursuant to section 11(d) of the Charter, in trials that are not even their own. For example, in the Ontario Court of Appeal, as a result of a sexual assault trial, Canadian Newspapers Co. (a publishing conglomerate) was able to invoke the Charter's fair trial guarantee to challenge a provision of the *Criminal Code* protecting persons who are sexually assaulted from having their names publicized against their will. Canadian Newspapers Co. was not a party in the sexual assault proceeding, and at no point was it suggested that the fair trial rights of the accused had been violated. Despite this, the Ontario Court of Appeal permitted Canadian Newspapers Co. to argue that fair trial rights had been violated.

As these cases indicate, relaxing the rules of standing has made challenging women's protections easier; it is not yet clear, however, whether it will also make it easier to represent women who are not in a position to initiate challenges on their own.

In some cases, parties directly affected by inequality are too isolated and too threatened to act on their own behalf. This may be the case, for example, with domestic workers, the majority of whom are women of colour, in Canada on temporary permits. Many of them are reluctant to challenge their poor working conditions and their lack of protection in Canadian labour law. Legitimately, they fear reprisals and deportation. Standing rules should be broad enough to allow another party, such as an advocacy organization, to initiate a challenge in circumstances like these.

Despite the recent relaxation of the rules of standing, however, it is still not clear that non-profit societies will be able to initiate section 15 challenges on women's behalf when there is no directly harmed woman willing or able to be the named plaintiff. Depending on the courts' approach to this issue, groups like INTERCEDE, or the Women's Legal Education and Action Fund (LEAF) may not be able to obtain standing, because section 15 says "every individual has the right to equality", and the courts seem to agree that "individual" does not include corporations.

Corporations do not have equality rights according to most of the courts that have ruled on this issue so far. We believe this is the correct position for the courts to take, because constitutional equality guarantees are not needed to secure the rights of corporations. However, it will be important for the future of equality rights litigation that, when courts make decisions about standing under section 15, they distinguish between not-for-profit societies seeking to bring forward public interest issues on behalf of members of disadvantaged groups and for-profit corporations litigating in their own interests.

Given that many cases affecting but not involving women can be initiated, women's ability to get before the courts themselves is crucial.

A GENEROUS APPROACH TO PUBLIC INTEREST INTERVENORS

Because there has been a general relaxation of the rules governing who can initiate a constitutional case, it is important to establish a similar relaxation of the rules governing who can intervene as well as a generous approach to public interest intervenors.

Inherent Jurisdiction

The power of the courts to hear representations from intervenors is based on their inherent jurisdiction to accept assistance from an *amicus curiae*, that is, a friend of the court. In addition to the powers vested in the courts by virtue of their inherent jurisdiction to allow interventions, most jurisdictions have statutory rules giving the courts wide discretion to grant or deny leave to prospective intervenors.

Automatic Rights of Attorneys General

In contrast to the general principle that decisions concerning intervenor status are discretionary, rules governing many courts give provincial and federal Attorneys General automatic rights of notice and participation in constitutional cases. The imbalance between citizen and state representation permitted by the special rules for Attorneys General has not gone unnoticed. One academic commentator has said:

> There is a certain irony to this in the context of Charter litigation, since the participation of Attorneys General, who will normally (though not always) be united in seeking to uphold the constitutional validity of the challenged legislation, tends to "stack the deck" in favour of government. If the primary purpose of the Charter is to give Canadians a vehicle for asserting rights *against* government, it seems strange that governments that were not initially parties to the litigation should be provided with an automatic vehicle for conveying their message to the courts, while those interested in presenting a non-governmental perspective must depend on the willingness of the courts to let their voices be heard. (Emphasis in original.)

The fact that Attorneys General have automatic rights of intervention is one consideration in favour of a generous approach to interventions by public interest intervenors in constitutional cases.

Public Participation in Charter Litigation

There may be some private law disputes, involving the routine application of established legal principles, that do not have much impact on anyone other than the parties to the dispute. However, this is never the case with Charter litigation. The superordinate status of the Charter means that every time a Charter challenge is brought, laws may be changed. In addition, the Charter is so new that the meaning of its provisions is being tested constantly. It has been argued by the Canadian Civil Liberties Association and others that it is contrary to democratic principles for courts to interpret and apply the Charter, which will affect the lives of all Canadians, without the benefit of representations from a variety of perspectives. These are additional reasons for the courts to take a liberal approach to public interest interventions in Charter cases.

The idea that public interest intervenors have a role to play in Charter cases involving important questions of interpretation was accepted by Justice Lamer in the case of *Mark Andrews* at the Supreme Court of Canada. As previously indicated, this case is the first equality rights case to be heard by the Supreme Court of Canada. Though Andrews, being white, British, and a male law graduate, is certainly not disadvantaged, his case has been identified as critical for those who are. Justice Lamer granted intervenor status to LEAF, the Coalition of Provincial Organizations of the Handicapped (COPOH), and the Canadian Association of University Teachers (CAUT), saying in his order:

> ...it is apparent that the Judgement of the Court of Appeal of British Columbia as it now stands is determinative of more issues than that of whether the restrictive bylaw of access to the legal profession to Canadian citizens only is in violation of Section 15 of the Charter. I am accordingly granting these motions to intervene ...

The Rights of Intervenors

The rights of a public interest intervenor are usually thought to be less than that of a party. For example, an intervenor will not ordinarily be permitted to add to the evidence or expand the grounds of an appeal. Such restrictions may be appropriate for public interest intervenors in a case such as *Mark Andrews*, where the concern of the intervenors was not with the resolution of the dispute but with the manner in which the Charter is interpreted. However, in a case such as *Schachter* — where the intervenor, LEAF, was advocating a particular resolution of the issues before the court and where women would be directly affected by the outcome of the case, possibly even to a greater extent than the parties themselves — it was appropriate that the intervenor be accorded party rights. In *Schachter*, LEAF was granted intervenor status with all the rights of a party.

Interventions by Feminist Organizations Are Needed

There is a further argument that gives a feminist organization with expertise in the area of equality a particularly strong claim to intervenor status in Charter cases. In view of the overwhelming number of male-initiated sex equality cases and the nature of the arguments being made both by their advocates and by counsel for the Attorneys General, it seems doubtful that many Canadian judges will ever be exposed to models of equality that could actually do something positive for women if women are not permitted to intervene in equality cases initiated by men.

The extent of the courts' willingness to hear from disadvantaged groups when they are not parties may well determine the direction of equality rights jurisprudence. There is no way to ensure that the courts will breathe real life into the Charter's equality guarantees. But if only those interpretations espoused by Attorneys General, defence lawyers, and professional groups are before them, the courts' view will be very limited. The equality guarantees cannot be given the full meaning and impact required by a purposive approach unless the courts listen to the voices of those who are disadvantaged.

Trends Concerning the Granting of Intervenor Status

Traditionally, a prospective intervenor had to demonstrate a direct legal interest, such as a proprietary interest, in the subject matter of the dispute. Even in the mid-1980s, it was apparently quite difficult to obtain intervenor status in the Supreme Court of Canada. But the recent trend in Canada seems to be away from a restrictive approach. It is evident from at least one case that the Charter itself has encouraged courts to re-evaluate their traditional view of intervenors. Justice Addy of the Federal Court of Appeal said:

> The narrow view found in common law jurisprudence to the effect that only parties with a triable interest in the actual issues raised in the pleadings have a right to be heard, was developed and established long before administrative law as we know it today really came into being and thus became subject to judicial control and intervention to any extent. A completely different situation now exists especially in Canada where the supervisory role granted to our Courts has been largely extended by reason of the Charter of Rights, as well as by the proliferation of boards and commissions.

In 1987, LEAF was granted intervenor status by the Supreme Court of Canada, courts of appeal, and the Federal Court.

However, women have not been successful in obtaining intervenor status in all jurisdictions and at all court levels. On November 10, 1986, LEAF's application for intervenor status in the case of *Klachefsky v. Brown* was rejected by Justice Huband of the Manitoba Court of Appeal, with costs against LEAF.

The background of the case argued strongly for court assistance from a feminist intervenor. In the court below, a child custody order had been varied in favour of a father because he had a new wife who would be available to the children 24 hours a day whereas their mother, who was starting a new job, would have to rely on child-care services. LEAF sought leave to intervene, with the consent of the children's mother, to argue that if women's equality is to be obtained, child-care services cannot be con-

(iii) Access to the Courts

sidered inferior to care at home in the absence of specific evidence that it is so. Concerning the intervenor application in the Court of Appeal, Justice Huband said:

> Counsel for the wife is entirely capable of raising and ventilating any issue relative to the *Charter of Rights and Freedoms* should counsel consider that such an argument would advance the cause of her client.

There is a problem with Justice Huband's reasoning. It does not necessarily follow that arguments relevant to women as a group will be raised by an individual woman's lawyer, no matter how capable she/he might be. In particular, if a lawyer suspects that a court will be impatient or uncomfortable about hearing equality rights arguments, her/his sense of duty to her/his client will likely cause her/him to refrain from making such arguments because they would *not* "advance the cause of the client". Indeed, counsel for Ms. Brown did not make equality rights arguments before the Manitoba Court of Appeal, even though she had been agreeable to the arguments being added by an intervenor. Ultimately, the Manitoba Court of Appeal ruled in favour of Ms. Brown, saying that the trial judge had committed a palpable error by placing undue emphasis on the fact that Ms. Brown was going to require paid child-care services.

Roininen is another case in which an intervenor application by a feminist organization was refused. The central question in that case was whether the child apprehension powers of the Superintendent of Child Welfare permitted the apprehension of a fetus *in utero*. The British Columbia Superintendent of Child Welfare had used these powers while Sandy Roininen was in labour in order to force her to undergo a caesarian section. The authorities had set out to test the scope of their legislative power when they apprehended her fetus *in utero*. With the consent of Sandy Roininen, LEAF sought leave to intervene in the subsequent legal proceedings to present relevant Charter issues to the Court. The application of the prospective intervenor before Judge Davis of the British Columbia Provincial Court was denied, on the basis that a provincial court lacks jurisdiction to permit an intervention and, further, that LEAF did not fall within a class of "other persons the court considers appropriate" to participate in a child apprehension hearing.

Judge Davis then proceeded to uphold the initial apprehension order without any discussion about women's rights to refuse medical treatment, arguing that it was simply a case of what was best for the safety and well-being of a child, not a case of women's rights. Need we say more about why the Court required the assistance of an intervenor? The judge's inability to see that state-ordered cutting into women's bodies raises issues of women's rights calls to mind words of Justice Wilson concerning men's perspective on abortion:

> It is probably impossible for a man to respond, even imaginatively, to such a dilemma not just because it is outside the realm of his personal experience (although this is, of course, the case) but because he can relate to it only by objectifying it, thereby eliminating the subjective elements of the female psyche which are at the heart of the dilemma.

Having said that the courts should take a generous approach to would-be intervenors, it must be acknowledged that the courts' discretion to permit non-party participation in court cases is open to manipulation by those with nothing different to present to the court but who merely wish to reinforce the position of one of the parties. If such an agenda is made apparent to the court, intervenor status will be denied. In *Borowski*, Justice Matheson of the Saskatchewan Court of Queen's Bench denied Campaign Life Canada (CLC) permission to intervene because

> ...it was quite apparent that CLC intended, if granted permission to intervene, to substantially support the position advocated by the plaintiff.

If the agenda of a prospective intervenor is disguised, however, it may be possible to obtain intervenor status, notwithstanding a duplicative position. Five years after Campaign Life's application for intervenor status in *Borowski* was refused in the Saskatchewan Court of Queen's Bench, R.E.A.L. Women of Canada (an anti-feminist organization) obtained intervenor status in the *Borowski* appeal at the Supreme Court of Canada. The public position of R.E.A.L. Women on abortion does not differ in any appreciable way from that espoused by Borowski in the case. The group's position is that the "human rights of the unborn" take precedence over women's freedom of choice. This is also Borowski's position. Of course the final test of R.E.A.L. Women's legitimacy as an intervenor in the *Borowski* case will be whether the group adds anything that is useful to the Court.

Ironically, in documents supporting its application for intervenor status in this case, R.E.A.L. Women espoused equality for women, even though the organization opposes the introduction of many of the laws and programs requisite to that equality.

This should not be surprising. Equality is a term of our Constitution. This means that fighting it openly is difficult, whereas manipulating its meaning may be possible. As the equality rights movement in Canada gains momentum, instances of its detractors using the language of equality rights to justify the continued oppression of disadvantaged groups will no doubt become increasingly common. Already affirmative action programs are criticized as being a kind of reverse discrimination, and those opposed to legal protections for lesbians and gay men complain that human rights laws interfere with their liberty and their freedom of religion. It is to be hoped the courts will look with a critical eye upon the submissions of any intervenor, or indeed of any party, who uses the language of equality to advocate limits on women's freedoms and access to resources.

ACCESS: THE PRACTICAL QUESTIONS

Can women and other disadvantaged groups really use the equality rights guaranteed in the Charter, or do they, in practice, remain beyond their reach?

The figures given in Chapters Three and Five, documenting women's participation in equality rights litigation in the first three years, demonstrate dramatically the seriousness of the access problem. Women simply do not have the money, resources, and power necessary to use the law that is there to protect and support them.

Developing the cases to challenge the many inequalities experienced by women and others is a major task. The cases are difficult and complex. It is rarely simple discrimination on the face of legislation that women need to challenge, but rather laws and policies that have an adverse impact, despite their apparent neutrality. Interventions are equally complex because they often concern difficult and important interpretive issues. Because the Charter guarantees are so new, every equality case is a crucial one, and it is important to describe the scope and nature of each sex equality issue as fully as possible for the courts. As we have said earlier, Canadian courts are not familiar with equality issues. This means that every equality-seeker who litigates now must also be an educator. To do this work well requires extensive research, knowledgeable counsel, access to experts, and informed litigants.

This case development is expensive and time-consuming, requiring a special expertise that few activists or lawyers in Canada have acquired thus far. Few women in Canada who act alone have the money or the resources to engage in Charter litigation.

The irony of this situation is that those with the greatest need for the equality guarantees have the least access to them. As described in earlier chapters, corporations and men have better access to the use of equality guarantees than women and other disadvantaged groups.

Public funding is essential if women are to have any meaningful access to the exercise of their Charter rights. A constitutional guarantee of equality is a hollow promise if only the wealthy and advantaged can use it.

The federal government has taken one step to increase access for equality-seekers. In 1985, it established the Court Challenges Program, which is administered by the Canadian Council on Social Development. Litigants with equality cases challenging a federal law or program can apply to the Court Challenges Program for financial support. The program can supply up to $35,000 per court level for lawyers' fees, case research, and disbursements.

Unfortunately, this public funding scheme has some severe shortcomings:

FUNDING IS AVAILABLE ONLY FOR CHALLENGES TO FEDERAL LAWS AND POLICIES.

No money is available to support challenges to provincial laws or policies through this program, and no provincial governments have made similar funds available, with one limited exception. Health, education, the terms and conditions of employment, and social services are provincial matters because of the constitutional division of powers between the federal and provincial governments. These are crucial issues for women, but no funding is available to support challenges in these areas.

$35,000 PER COURT LEVEL FOR ALL EXPENSES IS NOT ENOUGH TO COVER THE DEVELOPMENT OF COMPLEX CASES.

Lawyers' fees are high, and extensive work is required to develop cases properly. Sophisticated statistical and demographic evidence is needed in some cases. Historical, sociological, and economic studies are needed in others.

In addition, cases for women and other disadvantaged groups cannot be seen as simply individual. Every case will affect other women and perhaps other groups. This means that the preparation of any equality case has an importance beyond its particular factors and beyond the situation of the particular litigant. In these circumstances, the capacity to do thorough and wide-ranging research and to involve

(iii) Access to the Courts

those with specialized knowledge and first-hand experience about particular equality issues is essential. The $35,000 ceiling is an improper limit for disadvantaged litigants.

FUNDING IS AVAILABLE ONLY FOR LAWYERS' FEES AND CASE-RELATED RESEARCH.

If the Charter's equality rights are to be used by disadvantaged groups in anything more than a purely haphazard fashion, resources and money are required to allow the development of expertise and litigation capacity. As already stated, equality cases are, by their very nature, not individual in scope. Well-developed cases require knowledge of the patterns of inequality for the whole group, where a particular case fits into this pattern, and what agreements will best serve the equality interest of the group as a whole.

While knowledge of the key issues for each group and the patterns of inequality from which it suffers exists in advocacy organizations for disadvantaged groups, the expertise to turn that information into legal arguments and developed cases does not.

After studying the experience of women in the United States, women in Canada decided that meaningful access to the use of the new equality guarantees would require founding an organization dedicated specifically to the task of developing strategic equality rights litigation for women. In April 1985, women founded the Women's Legal Education and Action Fund (LEAF), an organization designed to assist women to exercise their new equality rights. As references throughout this report indicate, LEAF has been significantly involved in the Charter sex equality litigation to date.

Recently, organizations representing disabled persons have taken the same decision and founded the Canadian Disability Rights Council. EGALE (Equality for Gays and Lesbians Everywhere) is also developing a litigation capacity, and groups representing racial and ethnic minorities, prisoners, and people with low incomes are considering how they can support effective litigation on behalf of their members.

For groups that have experienced longstanding disadvantage and powerlessness, meaningful access to the use of the equality guarantees requires more than money for lawyers' fees. It requires money to develop awareness, information, and expertise in their communities and to arrange consultation between groups. Without this vital education, research, and consultation, there is likely to be little equality rights litigation that truly represents the interests of women and other disadvantaged groups. As long as governments do not recognize this, any funding schemes they design will continue to perpetuate the inequity between the advantaged and the disadvantaged in terms of their access to the courts.

THE COURT CHALLENGES PROGRAM IS A FIVE-YEAR PROGRAM; ITS MANDATE RUNS OUT IN MARCH 1990.

Those who apply for funds to the Court Challenges Program are being informed now that the program cannot pay for any litigation expenses after March 1990. Because litigation is often lengthy, litigants cannot be certain that actions they begin now will be completed by that time. In effect, women and other disadvantaged groups are being advised that they cannot rely any longer on the Court Challenges Program, even for support for cases within its mandate.

CONCLUSION

Thus, with all these difficulties, women and other disadvantaged groups struggle to gain access to the law, while institutions, including governments, universities, and hospitals, spend public dollars without restriction to oppose them.

The issue of access is the most basic one, and the state of access is, at present, shocking. There is only one source of funds to support equality rights litigation, and its mandate is too narrow, its funding levels too restricted, its design too unimaginative, and its future too uncertain to provide real access to the exercise of equality rights in Canada. It is to women's credit and to the credit of other disadvantaged Canadians that with so few resources and from such an unequal position, they are still struggling to make their voices heard in the courts.

The following chapter discusses the inadequacy of the theory of formal equality as an interpretive foundation for the Charter's equality guarantees. But the practical issue of access to the courts makes evident the failure of what formal equality offers. Currently, the law allows the advantaged and the disadvantaged alike to pursue their equality claims in court. Nothing in the law bars the disadvantaged: formal equality exists. However, the practical barriers are all too real. Women's disadvantage, their lack of money, resources, and power mean that they do not have equal access to the use of the very guarantees that are designed to advance their equality.

(iv) Naken, The Supreme Court and What Are Our Courts For?

W.A. Bogart

Class actions are not a clarion call to reckless social change. Their effect is not nearly so dramatic as some on either side of the question would maintain. They are, nevertheless, a useful device for litigating issues which affect large numbers of people. Since the 1960s there has been pressure to use them for many reasons, but a dominant one is the simple fact that they mirror societal structure. As much as many of us may yearn for it, the day when we could conduct ourselves as fiercely independent atoms is gone. Large entities — corporations, government, unions — have seen to that. When these entities act, their conduct affects many people. When they act wrongly the question is what means should be available to obtain redress so that the remedy will be sufficient to counter the widespread injury that has been inflicted. Class actions are no universal solution, but properly designed they can be an effective means to achieve redress for widespread harm by allowing access to the court for the many claims of those injured and by providing an efficient means to litigate so that related issues do not have to be decided repeatedly.

. . . .

THE FUNCTION OF OUR COURTS

Introduction

Classically, we have thought of civil litigation's prime function as dispute resolution. Private parties have a difference and come to court — to a neutral, passive, aloof judge — to have their differences resolved by a finding of liability or non-liability. The whole process is both initiated and controlled by the parties as the hallmark of the adversarial process.

These essential characteristics determine the other attributes of the traditional lawsuit. First, it is bipolar — two parties, with one the winner, the other the loser — unless they choose to settle. Secondly, the process is retrospective since it focusses upon the past conduct of the parties as the factual basis of the suit. Thirdly, rights and remedies are closely connected. Fourthly, the lawsuit is self-contained; the judgment only affects the parties before the court other than through *stare decisis*. The prototypical lawsuit may be between businessmen in a suit where damages are claimed. But lawsuits for damages for a car accident or for a breach of trust would also conform to the traditional model.

True, the traditional lawsuit sometimes does not conform strictly to the model just described. Admittedly, rules relating to joinder of parties and claims, counterclaims and third party proceedings could serve to extend its range. But this enlargement is confined to a limited number of parties and kinds of issues. Similarly, forms of equitable relief such as injunctions and specific performance require the presence of the court to ensure that there is continuing compliance with, for example, an injunction when its terms so require. But the courts' suspicion of these remedies is, in large part, due to their concern about being involved on an ongoing basis. In any event the terms of these remedies are usually narrow and well defined. It is a comparatively easy task to know whether or not the court's orders are being carried out.

. . . .

The New Model of Litigation

In the United States a new form of litigation with an altered role for the court is now widely recognized, though its desirability remains deeply controversial. These lawsuits have been given a variety of titles — "managerial", "complex", "structural", "public law". Nevertheless, while these descriptions are meant to convey differing emphasis and varying degrees of approval, there are common aspects which have emerged.

In essence the new model involves a challenge to the policy of some large entity — most frequently

---

From W.A. Bogart, "Naken, The Supreme Court and What Are Our Courts For?" (1984) 9 Can. Bus. L.J. at 280–81, 299–308. Notes omitted. Reproduced by permission of Professor W.A. Bogart and Canadian Business Law Journal.

that of government but also of corporations. This principal feature determines other attributes which, it will be noted, are in marked contrast to the features of the traditional model. Firstly, the party structure and the matter in controversy are much less well defined and can change throughout the litigation. Secondly, the orientation of the lawsuit is prospective, particularly in relation to non-monetary relief. Thirdly, the relief, as it is forward looking, is not necessarily logically derived from the right established and is often established on the basis of some negotiating process. Fourthly, the relief described in points two and three requires continuing, and active, judicial involvement and the relief, because it is against some policy, governmental or corporate, will have far-ranging impact. The vehicle for this kind of litigation is frequently the class action.

It would be surprising if the new model did not spark debate centring upon the changed role of the judge. No longer neutral, passive, and aloof, he or she is, at least sometimes, the main player. Supporters of the model see it as "stirring the deep and durable demand for justice in our society". Detractors see the judge reduced to little more than a broker and negotiator presiding over intractable tasks such as institutional reform "constantly descending to the level of the litigants, as an examiner, patient or hectoring, as counselor and advisor [and] as insistent promoter of settlements".

As is often the case, the state of the law in Canada in this area trails significantly that of the United States. However, one can point to a number of developments which suggest that there are alterations being made to the traditional model of litigation. And, as with any situation of following rather than leading, there is the opportunity to examine what is occurring here and to influence its direction based on what has already happened to those who have gone before.

To some extent litigation is changing simply because it is becoming more complicated. These complications, while making the lawsuit more protracted and difficult (and more expensive), cause relatively limited departures from the traditional model. For example, commercial litigation is often now more complicated but the complexity arises from the highly technical issues in the dispute and the sometimes vast numbers of documents generated in the relationship between the parties, rather than the introduction of a multitude of parties and wide variation of interests within the litigation.

However, complexities in other forms of litigation do arise from the nature of the parties involved and the rights sought to be enforced. For example, in derivative suits a shareholder normally sues in respect of a wrong done to a corporation. But the interests of the other shareholders, aligned in interest with the suing shareholder, are affected by the suit, which cannot be initiated without the court's permission or settled without its consent. Furthermore, the nature of wrongs done to corporations often involves complicated corporate transactions and this too can add an additional dimension to derivative suits.

Litigation conducted by an individual suing to enforce a "public right", which arises from harm done that affects a large group of people and yet no one of them particularly, will also depart from the traditional model. These cases, which have had a history as checkered as class actions, are often referred to as standing cases since the plaintiff's right to bring these suits is often challenged precisely because he has been harmed to no greater extent than other members of the public. Here the interests of a large group, many of whom will not actually be parties to the litigation, will have to be asserted by individuals and these actions will have to be monitored to ensure that the group's interests are taken into account. In addition, apart from the complexity inherent in deciding liability issues, the courts and the parties will expend substantial effort in fashioning an appropriate remedy for the harm done on a mass scale. There may be a variety of representations made by the group in respect of the kind and scope of the remedy that should be fashioned.

Nevertheless, it is the class action which represents the greatest departure from the traditional model of litigation. The nature of the right asserted based upon a mass harm, the representation of absentee members whose interests may not coincide in all respects and the need to protect those interests, the assessment and distribution of monetary relief in innovative ways as well as the fashioning of other relief, sometimes on the basis of competing representations within the class, and the procedural aspects of class actions such as the motion for certification, are all factors which can make the class action, both in appearance and performance, a clear departure from the traditional model of litigation.

Defining the Role of the Court in the New Litigation

If one accepts the basic proposition that we need a mechanism to challenge the actions of large entities, then it follows that we must be prepared to accept procedural changes that will allow such challenges to be made effectively. Unless one is prepared to create a totally new adjudicative body or adopt some other far-ranging solution, it seems to follow that the court's role will be altered as it begins to deal with this new form of litigation.

In contrast, to reject the need for effective challenge to the activities of large entities would, it seems to me, only breed confusion and frustration in a citizenry which already feels hopelessly at odds with much of the workings of society during the last part of the 20th century. Even if such frustration is not the stuff of revolutions, at a minimum the widely held perception of our courts as anachronistic and unresponsive may spread. More damaging may be the belief that the rules of litigation really do favour institutions and are less concerned with the enforcement of rights by individuals.

To me the only realistic alternative is to develop new rules and standards which will allow this new form of litigation to proceed. In this Estey J.'s judgment in *Naken* is disappointing because it displays so little interest in the problems and issues raised by cases like *Naken*. Such an attitude does little to deflect the trenchant criticisms about the Supreme Court's lack of capacity or willingness to engage in far-ranging analysis of difficult problems. Nevertheless, one clear effect of the Supreme Court's decision in *Naken* is to signal the Legislatures that change, if it is to come, must come through them.

In attempting to define the role of the court in class action litigation the recommendations of the Ontario Law Reform Commission in its *Report on Class Actions* offers a significant basis for discussion. The commission has attempted to steer a middle course between, on the one hand, a passive court that does little to control litigation and, on the other hand, an active court which, in perception at least, dominates it.

The key to its recommendations is to give the court a more developed role but one which is defined by specific guidelines. For example, a critical stage of the class action is the certification hearing during which the court decides whether or not the action should proceed as a class action. In Chapter 10 of the report, the commission makes recommendations about the certification hearing, the timing of it, the means by which evidence is placed before the court in the hearing and the powers of the court when it hears the certification application. In addition, the court would be empowered to allow or refuse certification and to make all amendments to the proceedings required by its order. The court could also amend a certification order and, subsequently, set the order aside if satisfied that the action was no longer one which should be a class action.

In order to control the class action during and from certification to trial of the common questions general management powers are recommended for the court. These powers most closely resemble some of the pre-trial powers exercised by "activist" judges in the United States. While there are many differences, the vital one is that in the commission's model one judge would take all pre-trial motions and interlocutory proceedings, including the certification hearing, but another judge would preside at the trial of the common questions. The trial judge would also supervise any proceedings after the hearing of the common questions, for example, if the class were successful but hearings were necessary to determine individual questions. Thus the function of "managing" the litigation during the pre-trial phase and actually adjudicating the merits of the action at trial would be separated. The lack of separation of these functions is a main criticism of those concerned with the activist stance of courts in the United States. Central to this potential for greater involvement by the court is a provision which states:

> 15. The court, upon the application of a party or upon its own motion, may make any order under this Act and all appropriate orders determining the course of the action for the purpose of ensuring the fair and expeditious determination thereof, including an order to prevent undue repetition or complication in the action, and the court may impose such terms and conditions upon the parties as it considers proper.

In making the recommendation concerning broader management powers the commission recognized the dual rationale of the need to protect the interest of absentees and to deal with the complexity inherent in many class actions. However, the commission was careful to point out that its guiding philosophy was not to depart from the adversarial model of litigation. It simply wished to equip the court with sufficient power to allow it to deal properly with this new form of expanded and complex litigation while, at the same time, permitting as much independence and freedom to the parties as possible.

CONCLUSION

For those who see the potential of class actions there is clearly an agenda of issues to be discussed concerning their structure so that their intended purposes are achieved and abuses avoided. Issues such as design of a certification mechanism, whether class actions should play a deterrence function, calculation and distribution of monetary claims, the role of class members, and costs, are only a selection of issues which merit reflection. For me the effect of class actions upon the court and how we should design the mechanism both to allow the court to adjust to this new form of litigation and to be sufficiently innovative in managing it is the most fascinating aspect. To what extent will we need to become part of the debate about the appropriate function of courts in the new litigation which now seems so much a part of the American legal culture and how will we solve the issue to which this debate gives rise?

Notwithstanding the complexities and controversies surrounding them, I believe those who reject class actions will have a hard road. If the basis of rejection is the lack of need for such a procedure, I think they will have a difficult time demonstrating that there are not widespread harms that require a means of redress. If they acknowledge these harms but simply object to class actions as the means of redress they will then have to suggest a suitable and adequate alternative. Thinking about such alternatives will be a fascinating exercise and we should not hesitate to do so. However, in the end I believe it is the class action — the *ad hoc* collectivity which organizes its members for a specific purpose and limited time — which will best answer the needs of group action at the end of the 20th century.

(v) Class Actions Seen Ideal in Handling Mass-termination Claims

Randall Scott Echlin

Class action lawsuits are getting a lot of attention. One major area where judges have allowed class actions to proceed is in employment disputes, particularly involving terminations of many workers.

Lawyers for plaintiffs have viewed the class action approach as an effective way to deal with common claims, particularly among lower level, lesser paid employees. Judges have agreed and are allowing these types of class actions to proceed.

First, a little background. The media regularly report on class action lawsuits involving hundreds, if not thousands, of plaintiffs and often millions of dollars. But the vast majority of these actions have occurred in the United States.

In Canada, only three provinces permit class actions — Ontario, Quebec and British Columbia. Quebec has had legislation allowing such proceedings for nearly a quarter of a century; British Columbia and Ontario more recently jumped on the bandwagon.

Legislation was enacted to provide a procedure for the fair and efficient resolution of common claims that otherwise would not be economically viable for people to pursue on their own.

But these actions have only recently grown in popularity. Experience is still limited, and judges have taken a cautious, pragmatic approach to deciding which cases should proceed as class actions.

What's required to constitute a class action? In Ontario, there appear to be five prerequisites:

- Is there a proper claim?
- Is there a "class" that could be represented by a plaintiff — an identifiable group of employees?
- Are there common issues in the claims of the class members?
- Is a class action the preferable procedure for the resolution of the common issue?
- Is there a plaintiff who could fairly and adequately represent the interests of the class? Has this representative plaintiff produced a plan for the proceeding? Or does this person have an interest in conflict with those of the other class members?

Before a class proceeding in an employment dispute can proceed, the employees' counsel must bring a court application for "certification" before a

---

From "Employment Law," *The Globe and Mail* (24 January 2000). Reproduced with permission.

judge. These types of motions deal with how the action is to proceed. In short, the court determines the ground rules.

In any such application, the onus is always on the defendant company to show that there is a better way of doing things.

The goals of proceeding through a class action are: to process cases with multiple litigants; to improve the access to the courts for those who would find the cost disproportionate to the claim; and to modify behaviour of wrongdoers.

Lawyers, judges and employees are rapidly coming to the conclusion that this type of proceeding is an ideal way to handle claims arising from mass terminations.

A recent and relatively high-profile class action suit was brought against K mart Canada Co. when Hudson's Bay Co. purchased the chain and closed down 31 stores. This resulted in about 3,000 to 4,000 employees being dismissed.

The presiding judge initially ruled that the class members had been dismissed without cause and were entitled to reasonable notice of termination.

He created a comprehensive scheme for resolving each individual damage claim. This blueprint "litigation plan" involved the plaintiffs sending an offer to K mart. The company could accept or reject the offer, or make a counteroffer.

If the parties could not agree at that point, a "mini-hearing" was scheduled before lawyers in various localities. In the end, the results of these hearings would be reported back to the court for approval and implementation.

The K mart case may well become a model for how to handle large actions. If a class proceeding is run effectively, there can be huge saving in the legal costs of prosecuting and defending lawsuits for both plaintiffs and defendants.

A similar employment-related action was also brought by approximately 65 Becker employees against Silcorp Ltd. when, after a takeover, nearly three dozen stores were closed.

It should be noted that a class action proceeding is generally not available to employees in the unionized work force. Their remedies are available under an applicable collective agreement.

While hundreds of class actions are going on at any given time, as well as dozens of employment-related class proceedings, the majority of smaller downsizings do not involve a large enough class or significant enough dollars to merit such proceedings.

There is no doubt that such actions are entirely appropriate when an employer refuses to pay even its minimum statutory obligations to its departing employees.

If nothing else, the spectre of a class action lawsuit may well influence employers to do the right thing. The best course of action for any employer contemplating a restructuring with a significant number of redundancies is to prepare reasonable settlement packages for all involved.

If they do not, the force of this litigation hammer may be brought to bear upon them.

B. Access to Justice for the Poor

(i) Legal Services and the Poor

R.J. Gathercole

Justice is open to all — like the Ritz Hotel.

Making legal services accessible to the poor is an issue that has long confronted the legal profession, although significant developments in legal aid have taken place only in the last two decades. There had been relatively little discussion of whether the poor really are in dire need of lawyers' services; rather

---

From Robert G. Evans and Michael J. Trebilcock, eds., *Lawyers and the Consumer Interest: Regulating the Market for Legal Services* (Toronto: Butterworth & Co. (Canada) Ltd., 1982) 407 at 407–18, 423, 426–29. Notes omitted. Reproduced by permission of the editors.

lawyers assume that the poor, like the rest of society, need these services almost as much as food, clothing, shelter and medical attention.

Nor have lawyers been modest about what legal services — as provided by lawyers — can accomplish for the poor. Reginald Heber Smith in his classic work, *Justice and the Poor*, published in 1919 and generally regarded as the motivating force of the American legal aid movement, wrote "In vast tracts of the civil law and in all of the criminal law related to the more severe crimes, equality in the administration of justice can be had only by supplying attorneys to the poor." If more legal aid offices were opened and existing staff increased, "that part of the denial of justice which is traceable solely to the inability of the poor to employ counsel will be completely overcome."

Forty-six years later, E. Clinton Bamberger Jr., a young Baltimore attorney who attended an A.B.A. conference to learn about the new neighbourhood legal offices being established in the United States and found himself recruited as the first Director of Legal Services in the Office of Economic Opportunity (O.E.O.) — the central office of the "War on Poverty" — went even further than Smith.

> We cannot be content with the creation of systems rendering free legal assistance to all the people who need it but cannot afford a lawyer's advice. Our responsibility is to marshal the forces of law and the strength of lawyers to combat the causes and effects of poverty. Lawyers must uncover the legal causes of poverty, remodel the systems which generate the cycle of poverty, and design new social, legal and political tools and vehicles to move poor people from deprivation, depression and despair to opportunity, hope and ambition.

These high expectations of what lawyers could accomplish for the poor were not restricted to the United States. In a 1971 study prepared for the National Council of Welfare, a leading Canadian legal aid activist wrote:

> At the lowest level of abstraction, a legal services programme can at least assist in mitigating the surface attributes of poverty. As a service provided to the poor at no cost, it has a redistributive effect. The nature of the day-to-day legal care provided would lessen at least the effect of poverty. Illegal evictions, consumer fraud, and abuses of official discretion, all wrongs to which the poor are particularly vulnerable, could be vigilantly monitored and often remedied. As well, efforts directed at law reform might succeed in gaining even more widespread relief.

> ...

> The lawyer's business is to assist his client in analysing alternatives. He is expected to be partial, to act as the advocate of those with interests to pursue. This work, carried on in a way which encouraged the participation of the individual and the group in the work involved in the pursuit of grievances could offer the poor an opportunity to come to grips, perhaps for the first time, with problems heretofore beyond reach.

> ...

> At first, through their lawyers, but later with progressively less and less assistance, the poor could make articulate and knowledgeable inputs into decision-making processes which affect their lives. This new access to the levers of policy-making might be an important first step in the efforts of the poor to gain some control of their own lives. The degree to which this control can be achieved is the degree to which a legal services programme can contribute to the alteration of the structure of poverty in this country.

It is almost 15 years since these goals of the legal aid movement were articulated. During that time virtually every Canadian province that did not already have one, has developed a legal aid program to provide at least the services envisioned by Smith. A Legal Services Corporation has been established in the United States as an outgrowth of the legal services work started in the O.E.O. and the United Kingdom has made some significant, if somewhat overdue improvements in its legal aid services. Nevertheless, the poor in each of these countries are at best only marginally better off for all of these efforts and even the relatively limited goals articulated by Reginald Heber Smith 60 years ago have not been achieved. It is doubtful that they will be in the foreseeable future.

What went wrong? Although the leaders of the legal aid movement in Canada, and elsewhere, were motivated by the best intentions and a genuine desire to help alleviate the problems of the poor, they did not and perhaps could not fully understand their problems. Contrary to their expectations, the fundamental problems of the poor are not susceptible to traditional legal solutions. They are not the traditional middle class legal problems that lawyers are familiar with. As Bernard Veney, Executive Director of the National Clients' Council in the United States put it:

> The problems of low-income people are different from the problems of other people; and their cases must be handled differently. Most attorneys in private practice do not have, as a matter of routine, the skills necessary to practice law for poor people ... low-income people have lives of constant crisis. What may be a casual matter for

someone who has options is a life and death matter for a low-income person because one of the characteristics of poverty is the *absolute lack of options*. That lack of options may mean that to meet one crisis, people do something that is going to cause another crisis further down the line.

So it is not enough just to handle the legal matter that is there on the surface. Unless you are skilled at recognizing this problem, and skilled at recognizing what the possible remedies are, skilled enough to resolve the initial crisis but also take care of the longer-range crisis, you haven't done anything for low-income people.

Most legal aid programs, even if not so designed originally, have tended to develop according to the interests and priorities of lawyers providing the services rather than those of their clients. Legal services are traditionally provided on a one-to-one, private enterprise basis. The legal profession is generally identified with, and identifies itself with the *status quo*. Lawyers cannot accept the fact that the problems of the poor can only be solved through a fundamental restructuring of traditional institutions, not by suing someone in a court of law. While the motivations ascribed by one observer to the early development of legal aid in the United Kingdom (that "[it] was produced to justify ideologically the operations of the legal system, which was primarily concerned with property interests, by giving the appearance of making equal access to the legal system available to the lower classes") may not be applicable to recent developments in legal aid, the fact remains that the legal profession remains identified in the minds of the poor with the source of their problems rather than with the solution. An equally important consideration is that governments have consistently underfunded legal services, partly because the poor are not a powerful political constituency but also because government departments and agencies are prime targets of legal aid lawyers. Both of these factors will be discussed more fully later. First, a brief history of the development of legal aid is necessary.

JUDICARE VERSUS LEGAL SERVICES

Civil legal aid has generally followed one of the two models — Judicare or legal services. The Judicare model utilizes members of the private bar as the prime deliverers of legal services. They are paid on a fee-for-service basis, usually in accordance with a specified tariff. The administrative responsibility for most Judicare plans is assigned to the legal profession. The underlying philosophy of Judicare is to provide the poor with access to the same services as are available to the rest of society. Judicare plans tend to concentrate on providing legal assistance for serious criminal offences and for civil actions in superior courts. For example, 41% of the Ontario legal aid budget in 1978 was spent on criminal offences and 27% on divorce and other civil matters. There were only 184 small claims and 578 review board cases out of a total of more than 24,000 civil cases. There were insufficient welfare, landlord-tenant, or unemployment insurance cases to justify a separate heading in the annual report. Judicare's emphasis on litigation stresses a "problem solving" rather than "problem preventing" approach. The emphasis is on ensuring that the poor are accorded their "day in court" rather than on substantive reform of existing laws and institutions.

The legal services model did not become a significant alternative to Judicare until the 1960s and early 1970s. This model stresses the use of full-time salaried lawyers and non-legal personnel operating from offices located in low-income communities, generally of the "storefront" variety. Emphasis is placed on providing legal services in areas of prime concern to the poor — welfare, housing, unemployment insurance, workers' compensation, small claims, domestic disputes — providing assistance to groups and organizations in the community, education programs and law reform activities such as lobbying and test case litigation.

The stated philosophy of the legal services movement is that the goal of legal aid should be nothing less than the eradication of poverty. Poverty is a question of power — or, more particularly, lack of it — and the role of the lawyer is to assist the poor person to gain the power to change the institutions, both private and public, which contribute to his poverty and control his life. Case-by-case legal services must be provided but only within this overall framework. In jurisdictions that have adopted the legal services model, administration of legal aid is generally the responsibility of an independent board or commission rather than the legal profession.

For years proponents of the two models carried on a sometimes heated debate over their respective merits. Questions of cost-effectiveness, the efficacy of professional control and whether lawyers had any role to play in social change were argued at great length. Generally, the traditional bar and most politicians tended to support the development of Judicare, professional administrative control and limitations on law reform and lobbying activities by legal aid lawyers. Legal services lawyers criticized Judicare for its adherence to traditional legal solutions and its failure to deal with the "real" problems of the poor.

However, it became apparent that neither approach had all the answers and both had important strengths and weaknesses. As a result, most jurisdictions have developed mixed civil legal aid systems, albeit with the emphasis on one of the two models.

. . . .

Canada, as it often does, has borrowed extensively from both the United States and the United Kingdom. Legal aid in Canada falls within provincial constitutional jurisdiction as part of the administration of justice, although the federal government does provide financial assistance to the provinces for legal aid in criminal matters based on a negotiated formula which can vary from province to province. All provinces, with the exception of Prince Edward Island and New Brunswick, have well-developed legal aid programs. Most have a mixed Judicare and legal services system. Quebec, Saskatchewan and Nova Scotia have adopted legal services as the basic model with a limited Judicare component. The other provinces have adopted the Judicare model.

Both the Manitoba and British Columbia plans have a legal services component. Ontario has a fairly extensive network of legal services offices (approximately 40 throughout the province as of September 1980). They initially developed outside the Ontario Legal Aid Plan, are not referred to in the *Legal Aid Act* and have, at best, only the grudging support of the Law Society of Upper Canada. Funding of these offices is now provided for by regulation, amounting to $4.75 million for the 1980–81 fiscal year, and they now are part of the Ontario Legal Aid Plan under the general supervision of the Clinical Funding Committee which allocates their funding and closely monitors their operations. For example, it is empowered by regulation to require a clinic to employ a solicitor and to train personnel to an approved standard.

The Ontario Legal Aid Plan arose from the report of a joint committee of the Law Society and the government of Ontario released in March 1965. This report drew heavily on the English experience in recommending a Judicare plan to be operated by the Law Society and made no reference at all to the American experience. On the other hand, the Quebec Plan, established in 1972 and the Saskatchewan Plan, established in 1974 adopted the American legal services model which by then was well established. Service under both plans is provided primarily by full-time salaried lawyers. However, the Quebec plan has a more significant Judicare component, and is less community based than the Saskatchewan plan. The boards of directors of the Quebec offices (or "bureaux") are appointed by the Commission de Services Juridiques which administers the plan while boards of the Saskatchewan clinics are elected by the communities for which they operate. The Saskatchewan Plan also has a specific mandate to undertake law reform and related activities. Other provinces have drawn from the Ontario, Quebec and Saskatchewan plans for inspiration depending upon the political views of each provincial government and its susceptibility to the pressures of the provincial bar.

The legal services offices established in Ontario, British Columbia and Manitoba, also imitated the American experience. The first such office in Ontario, Parkdale Community Legal Services, located in a low income area of Toronto, was one of four such offices funded by the federal Department of Health and Welfare on the basis of a study which strongly supported the American approach. Parkdale also received funding from the Council for Legal Education in Professional Responsibility, a branch of the Ford Foundation, which also funded a number of legal services offices in the United States affiliated with law schools as Parkdale was with Osgoode Hall Law School of York University.

The early development of legal aid in Canada produced some tension between the proponents of Judicare and the supporters of the legal services movement. This was particularly true in Ontario, where Judicare was well established and the Law Society was particularly powerful. After a decade or more of relatively peaceful co-existence, however, the clear consensus is that both models are needed. The traditional bar has overcome its initial paranoia about legal services offices, in part because the fundamental social changes that they feared and legal services lawyers hoped for have not materialized, and in part because legal services offices have created work for private lawyers, both through direct referral and through bringing legal action against their clients. Legal services lawyers, on the other hand, have come to accept that the private bar has a role to play in legal aid, both because of its special expertise and its ability to take cases where legal services lawyers might have conflicts of interest.

THE INADEQUACIES OF LEGAL AID

"Comprehensive" legal aid plans have existed for a decade or more, but the fact remains that the poor still have, at best, only limited access to legal services. One main reason is that legal aid is funded from public monies and governments have failed to provide more than minimal funding. This is partly because the poor do not constitute an effective political constituency, but also because the most effective legal aid programs are continually engaged in fighting government agencies. Accordingly, politicians react with, at best, grudging support and, at worst, outright hostility.

. . . .

A recent Canadian example is the decision of the Saskatchewan government in June 1978 to require the legal services offices in that province to cease their practice of referring criminal cases to private lawyers under the Judicare component of the Saskatchewan plan, while concentrating themselves on the provision of the civil legal aid. The legal services lawyers felt that the demands for services could best be met by utilizing the experience of the private bar in criminal matters and developing their own expertise in civil matters, such as housing and welfare. The government, however, stated that budgetary restraints were necessary and money could be saved if the offices did the criminal work themselves because using private lawyers cost more. This, of course, meant that legal services lawyers would be spending most of their time on criminal matters and would have to neglect what they considered to be the more important civil cases. It was not clear whether the government was motivated solely by financial concerns or whether it wanted to limit the effectiveness of legal services offices. After the Saskatoon Legal Assistance Clinic threatened to close rather than comply with the government's directive, the government backed down and agreed to conduct a review of the province's legal aid system. However, the government appears to have succeeded in the end. The 1979–80 *Annual Report* of the Saskatchewan Community Legal Services Commission showed that the number of criminal cases completed by the private bar in the fiscal year dropped to 505 from 2,562 the previous fiscal year. Private bar civil cases also were reduced from 281 to 120.

Governments continue to refuse to fund legal aid adequately. In 1977 Clinton Bamberger claimed that it would cost $500 million to provide basic minimum legal services to the poor in the United States. This represented 5 lawyers for every 10,000 poor people, compared to the ratio in the general population of 14 lawyers for every 10,000 persons. This year, after years of inflation the Legal Services Corporation budget is still under $300 million, with no chance of any increase in the next few years.

In Canada the situation is no better. In Ontario, legal aid is funded through the Ministry of the Attorney General. The Ministry's entire budget represents less that 1% of the provincial budget ($165.5 million out of $17.1 billion in 1980–81). The legal aid component is $43.3 million or about 26% of that total, but a portion of that amount (about $8 million) is received from the federal government as a contribution towards the provision of criminal legal aid. In other words 1/4 of 1% of the provincial budget is allocated to legal aid. The legal aid expenditure in Quebec ($32 million in the 1978–79 fiscal year) has not increased significantly in the past few years. New Brunswick continues to refuse to establish a civil legal aid program mainly for financial reasons. Similar situations exist in other provinces.

Even with adequate funding however, there are inherent weaknesses in existing legal aid programs which result in seriously inadequate access of the poor to legal services. The main weakness is the emphasis on individual case service. This results in a curative rather than a preventive approach to legal problems. It also means that available legal aid resources cannot begin to cope with the potential caseload let alone undertake effective law reform, lobbying or other group-oriented activities.

The emphasis on case-by-case service of both Judicare and legal services plans results from different factors. The Judicare approach is predicated on this type of service delivery. The legal profession is organized on a free enterprise, single lawyer, single client basis and Judicare seeks to apply this approach in delivering legal services to the poor. Legal services offices, however, have to some extent been forced to emphasize individual cases by funding agencies. While lawyers' training and interests and client demand are also important factors, the requirements of funding agencies that individual services be stressed is the predominant reason for the "caseload crisis" faced by most legal services offices. The evaluation of a legal services office is based on its caseload. This is easier to measure than more nebulous factors such as acceptance in the community, long-term interests of clients and law reform. It is also easier to persuade politicians that public money is being properly used if something concrete, e.g., a thousand cases handled, has resulted from the expenditure.

There are other inadequacies in both legal aid models which have to be considered. Judicare suffers from the underlying assumption that all the poor need is access to the same services that lawyers traditionally provide. Not only does this ignore the specific legal problems of the poor, most of which are substantively different than those of the middle class, but reliance on the private bar also creates particular problems. Most law offices are physically and psychologically inaccessible to the poor. They are located some distance from most poor communities and are designed to appeal to traditional clients. Most poor people find this a completely foreign environment, adding to the pressures of dealing with lawyers. The poor person also identifies the private bar with the "other side" — landlords, finance companies, government agencies — that represent the source of his problem.

The private lawyer lacks expertise in the legal problems of the poor. The intricacies of social welfare legislation, for example, are not easily grasped by handling one or two such cases a year. Conflicts of interest can and do arise between the poor and other existing or potential clients of the lawyer (for example in landlord-tenant and debtor-creditor cases). There is an inability to identify patterns and to organize strategies to deal with underlying problems. Most Judicare plans lack effective research components resulting in a great deal of duplication of effort, as individual lawyers continue to re-invent the wheel. The Ontario Legal Aid plan, in existence for some 13 years, has only recently created a research facility and then only because it was one of the conditions imposed by the provincial Attorney General for his support of a tariff increase.

The method of payment — fee for service, usually in accordance with an established tariff — also limits the coverage which can be provided by Judicare. It is not acceptable politically or economically to expend $500 of public funds in an attempt to recover $50 in unpaid welfare benefits, to sue for $200 in Small Claims Court or to force a landlord to effect small but necessary repairs or to cease harassing tenants. Legal aid assistance is therefore given only in very special cases. In Ontario, for example, clients are entitled to legal aid services for indictable criminal matters and for civil cases brought in the "higher" courts. In other civil cases the test is whether a person of modest means would retain a lawyer in the circumstances. Given the present level of legal fees, the answer is usually negative. The result is that Judicare plans tend to concentrate on providing services for serious criminal cases, traditional civil lawsuits (e.g., motor vehicle accidents, collections) and divorce and other family matters. The Ontario Legal Aid Plan, a representative Judicare plan, shows a very high proportion of certificates granted for these types of cases. In his oft-quoted article "Practicing law for Poor People," Stephen Wexler pointed out that "poor people are not just like rich people without money. Poor people do not have legal problems like those of private plaintiffs and defendants in law school casebooks." Judicare plans are premised on the opposite assumption and limit themselves to providing services for those "casebook" problems.

Outside of the United States, most legal services programs came into being because of the deficiencies of Judicare and were specifically tailored to deal with the particular problems of the poor. The salaried lawyers employed in these offices were expected to — and did — develop an expertise in these areas. In jurisdictions where legal services were the basic delivery model, such as the United States and Quebec, provision was made for a substantial research component to assist lawyers in the field and to identify particular problem areas which might require collective action. Emphasis was also supposed to be placed on law reform activities, both judicial and legislative.

However, as noted above, the emphasis in legal services programs as in their Judicare counterparts has been on the provision of individual case services. Although the type of case emphasized has been somewhat different than in Judicare programs, the fact remains that the essential service provided is the same — problem-solving on a one-to-one basis rather than preventive services on a collective basis as was the hope of many of the early proponents of the legal services movement.

. . . .

If the legal profession as presently structured, even if supplemented by trained non-legal personnel, cannot adequately deal with the problems of the poor, what is the answer? The assumption is that increased access to lawyers and traditional legal services will benefit the poor. In fact that is not the case. The poor need services which will assist them in dealing effectively with their problems; this cannot be done on a case-by-case basis. While there is, and will continue to be, a huge demand for individual case service, the resources do not presently exist to fill that demand and alternative approaches must be considered.

. . . .

Community organization must also be a priority. An effective tenants' organization prepared to utilize techniques such as rent strikes is more effective in enforcing a landlord's repair obligations than any number of individual court cases, particularly given the problems of enforcement. The welfare bureaucracy is more likely to respond to the immediate pressure of an organized welfare group than to the strictures of a court. When a welfare cheque is not forthcoming on time, this type of pressure, unlike a time-consuming application to a court, can bring quick results. In 1972 Stephen Wexler argued that only effective community organizing could give the poor power to effect change. The passage of time has only proven the validity of this argument.

New methods of dispute resolution are also required. Traditional methods are slow, costly and ineffective. Too much emphasis is placed on due process rather than on effective decision-making. Procedures need to be streamlined and simplified so that individuals can effectively represent themselves. More emphasis should be placed on providing official assistance to persons appearing before tribunals. This would reduce the need for lawyers and allow more effective participation by the individuals concerned.

These changes would have serious ramifications for the legal profession. Lawyers are not necessarily the most effective lobbyists and they are certainly not trained to be organizers. They are trained to provide specific services to individual clients. This means that the lawyer's role in providing services to the poor is limited. Most bar associations and professional governing bodies have opposed any developments along these lines, suggesting that the profession could not operate effectively in the type of service system.

The provision of legal services to the poor should be the responsibility of persons, both lawyers and non-lawyers, specifically trained for that purpose. How should they be trained? There is no scope in this chapter for a discussion of the problems in legal education but there is no doubt that law schools have a dismal record of training lawyers to serve the poor. Law school curricula emphasize traditional legal subjects, with the special legal problems of the poor being dealt with in one or two courses with such titles as "Poverty Law" and "Law and the Poor", a phenomenon that caused Wexler to remark that "[these courses] serve a useful function by making it crystal clear that the remainder of the curriculum deals with law and the rich; they do little, however, to change the law schools' treatment of legal problems, or their perception of the proper roles and concerns of a lawyer." The calendar of the People's Law School of Los Angeles, California, a law school whose aim is "the development and training of lawyers dedicated to the struggle for social change in the communities of oppressed peoples", puts it more graphically:

> In the past, traditional legal institutions have mass-produced lawyers whose concept of lawyering consisted of joining an elite organization dedicated to maintaining the national socio-economic *status quo*, as well as the lawyer's superior position in it, by serving the rich or acting as legal functionaries of the state.... Existing law schools, at their worst, destroy the development of socially-conscious students, and at their best allow only a limited development of skills by a highly motivated and often select group. Traditional legal education almost uniformly teaches the skills which are required to serve the establishment; the non-establishment student, if not an outcast, is nevertheless segregated with a small group concerned with what are institutionally considered the marginal interests of society: the areas of poverty, civil rights, labour and criminal law.

Specially trained people are needed to serve the interests of the poor. If the law schools are not prepared to meet this challenge, other institutions will, and the law schools will be limited to providing training to a limited portion of the legal services community.

In any legal aid system it is crucial that the poor have some control over the nature of the services to be provided. Most legal services plans recognize this and provide for representation of the client community on the board of directors of each legal services clinic. Invariably, however, client representation is limited to one-half or less. Sometimes express provision is made for lawyers and legal staff to form a majority of the board of directors; sometimes the client representation is specifically restricted, but, in either case, the poor are allowed only to participate in, but not control, the decision-making process. Given lawyers' ability and propensity to control meetings, it is unlikely that lawyers' influence would be seriously diminished even if non-lawyers had a majority on any board.

. . . .

Codes of Professional Conduct also support lawyer control. A lawyer is responsible for the conduct of any case he undertakes; he must take instructions from his individual client. Any attempt by outsiders, such as boards of directors, to interfere in a case must be resisted. Additionally, a lawyer is under a duty of confidentiality. He cannot disclose details of any case to outsiders without the express consent of the client or in other very limited circumstances. Therefore any attempt by a client-controlled board of directors to determine what cases should or should not be undertaken by lawyers in its employ, or how a particular case should be handled (e.g., whether it should be settled in the interest of the individual client or carried through to litigation in the hope of obtaining a favourable decision which might benefit a broader community) must, under the present Codes, be resisted by a lawyer. Meaningful client input into the determination of the services to be provided and the manner of their provision seems possible by non-legal personnel not subject to the same professional constraints. This is not to say that these constraints are necessarily wrong in every case; only that they do militate against effective client control of legal services.

In the final analysis, whether the poor are to receive effective services from the legal profession either through the provision of traditional services by the established bar or through a more sophisticated and responsive model, depends on whether governments and the people they represent are prepared to make that commitment. Even if the legal profession were to change fundamentally its outlook on legal aid and itself make a profound commitment to providing adequate services to the poor (an admittedly unlikely development) this would not be enough. To date, few, if any, governments or societies have shown any such inclination. There are too many vested interests to overcome. Governments, the economically and politically powerful, and the legal profession, have no immediate interest in alleviating the plight of the poor. Until we are prepared to accept that fundamental changes are required, we will continue to provide, always grudgingly, inadequate legal assistance. The underlying problems will continue to be ignored. The poor, it seems, will always be with us and justice will continue to be identified with the Ritz Hotel.

(ii) Small Claims Courts: A Review

Iain Ramsay

INTRODUCTION

Small claims courts are often regarded as important symbols for the justice system. Dubbed "The People's Court" by the media, many writers argue that since this is the court most often encountered by the ordinary person,*1* it is an important symbol for the legitimacy of the justice system.

Several objectives have been hitched to the star of small claims court reform throughout their history. The idea of access to justice — in the 1900s for the wage earner and tradesperson — in the 1970s for the consumer — is often associated with this court. But the court has also been conceived as a laboratory for testing new ideas in dispute settlement, such as mediation and arbitration, providing an alternative to the adversary system of the higher courts. Small Claims Courts have been one focus for the intellectual and political movement of alternative dispute resolution. Within this framework, it has been argued that these courts might contribute to "solving problems" rather than merely "deciding" disputes, becoming a positive force within communities. The court has also been viewed as providing a channel for diverting claims from higher courts, hopefully providing a partial solution to the perceived problems of caseloads in higher courts. The greatest continuity in the role of small claims courts in Canada has however been its role as a low-cost cog in the process of debt collection by business against individuals.

It is clear that there are a variety of objectives which may be attributed to the court: dispute settlement[;] social problem solving[;] effective debt enforcement[;] access to justice. These differing objectives may lead to different prescriptions for reform and make it difficult to make simple judgments about success or failure in relation to these courts.

From *Rethinking Civil Justice: Research Studies for the Civil Justice Review*, vol. 2 (Toronto: Ontario Law Reform Commission, 1996) at 491–93, 501–502, 504–507. Notes omitted. © Queen's Printer for Ontario, 1995. Reproduced with permission.

An important modern perspective on these courts has been to view them as part of the "Access to Justice" movement. The institution of small claims courts is one response to the "problem" of the small claim, which has often been conceptualized as that of achieving a forum for the vindication of the rights and resolving the dispute of the ordinary individual where the costs (economic, psychological, legal costs) of the existing system of litigation are prohibitive. Cappelletti and Garth argue that the characteristics of such a forum should be "speed, relative informality, an active decision maker and the possibility of litigating effectively without attorneys". The introduction of small claims courts represents institutional change to make individualized legal justice more accessible to the ordinary individual. But it should be recognized at the outset that the small claims "problem" may be addressed in many ways. Substantive rule changes or public enforcement may reduce or prevent the occurrence of disputes: self-help remedies may reduce the need for third party intervention: developing party capability (e.g. through class actions, public substitute actions) may be a further alternative. Moreover, small claims courts now compete with a variety of other private and quasi-public redress mechanisms in the area of consumption activity. A rational approach to policy cannot view the court in isolation from these mechanisms.

Canada presents a number of models of small claims courts. Most of these courts grew out of earlier Small Debt Court and it was only in the 1970s that a significant effort was made to rethink the role of these courts. The Ontario model presents a court which is essentially a modified version of the higher courts. There are no restrictions on business filings, or corporate claims, lawyers and agents may appear for the parties, the rules of evidence are relaxed and there are restrictions on costs. Quebec, following US precedents, was the first jurisdiction to enact a specific small claims court and remains the only Canadian jurisdiction where the court meets almost all the reform ideals outlined by Cappelletti and Garth. Under the *Loi favorisant l'accès à la justice* of 1971 lawyers were barred from the court, business corporations could not use the court, judges may mediate as well as adjudicate, are empowered to use the procedure most appropriate to the case and the court provides a conciliation service to litigants. The rules envisage an active role for the judge and there is no appeal. The court currently has a jurisdiction of $3000.

. . . .

Jurisdiction of Small Claims Court

Since 1993 the Small Claims Court has jurisdiction in any action for the payment of money or recovery of property where the value does not exceed $6000. This limit is established by regulations made under s. 53(1)(c) of the *Courts of Justice Act*. There is no restriction on who may bring an action and both corporations and individuals may file claims in the court. The broad terms of its jurisdiction will cover many actions in contract and tort including defamation, wrongful dismissal, consumer and business claims.

It is important, however, to note those situations where the court does not have jurisdiction. Landlord/Tenant issues in relation to eviction and repairs are addressed elsewhere, issues of discrimination are under the jurisdiction of the Ontario Human Rights Commission, employment standards are addressed by the Employment Standards tribunal, issues of social security by the Social Assistance Review Board. Unionized employees will take grievances concerning employment to arbitration rather than the courts. Complaints concerning government agencies may be channelled to the Ombudsman who received approximately 31,000 complaints in 1994–95. Many issues associated with the welfare state have bypassed the courts as the primary adjudicator and administrative tribunals may be a more significant dispute settlement mechanism than the courts for the average individual. This obvious but important point is sometimes overlooked in evaluating the small claims court. In addition, many of these tribunals may be more "legalized" than the small claims court and it might be useful to compare the small claims courts process with tribunals rather than the higher courts.

. . . .

Fees

There is a fee of $35 for filing and $20 for serving a small claim under $1000, $50.00 and $20 for claims over $1000, and no fee for filing a defense. The court carries out service of the documents unless the plaintiff is represented by a solicitor. The court serves the claim on behalf of the plaintiff.

Process: Pre-Trial: Adjudication

If a claim is defended then in many areas of Ontario there will be a pre-trial hearing, which is heard before a referee (a court employee), a part-time judge or a judge. If there is a trial then the vast majority of trials will be before deputy judges.

These are not full-time judges but lawyers appointed by the regional senior judge with the approval of the Attorney General. There are approximately 380 of these judges who sit approximately one day each month. They may be appointed for up to a three year, renewable, term. They are paid a per diem rate of $235. There are no province-wide guidelines or criteria for appointment, no measures to train or evaluate their performance and no guidelines on conflicts of interest.

Costs

Costs are limited generally to 15 percent of the amount claimed. There are limited possibilities for night sittings for cases under $500 in Toronto which could reduce litigants costs through lost wages. The court may provide and pay for a court interpreter for a French language trial. For other languages the parties have to bring their own interpreter.

Enforcement of Judgments

Judgments obtained in the small claims court may be enforced by the small claims court bailiff. The most common means of enforcement is the use of garnishment orders, but seizure of personal property is used in a minority of cases. Where a judgment remains unpaid creditors may request an examination hearing of the debtor concerning the reason for non-payment and the debtor's ability to satisfy the judgment. This is an increasingly common form of enforcement activity.

. . . .

Type of Case Brought before the Small Claims Court

The majority of actions in small claims courts are debt actions brought by businesses against individuals. In those courts where corporations may not sue, such as Quebec, it would appear that debt collection by unincorporated businesses and professionals continues to represent the majority of cases. There are also significant numbers of cases between businesses. Apart from debt claims, the balance of the caseload consists of landlord actions for arrears of rent, consumer claims, tort actions, and employment actions.

Many studies of the 60s and 70s indicated that consumer claims, defined as individuals bringing a consumer claim against a business, made up a small percentage of the total claims filed with the court, perhaps at most 10% of disputed cases. It became almost a part of conventional wisdom to view the small claims courts as a court "colonized" by business repeat-players suing individuals for debt. The court appeared to have failed in its promise to provide consumers and other individuals with an accessible forum for redress, seemingly confirming the McRuer Commission's conclusion that it functioned as a "statutory collection system".

Vidmar challenged these findings in a study of the small claims court in Middlesex County drawing data from cases in 1980. His study is the only major published study of an Ontario Small Claims court [Hildebrandt *et al* is described as an exploratory study]. His data indicated that of the total number of claims filed (Sample size 2079) 25% never proceeded beyond filing a statement of claim, 54% resulted in a default judgment and 21% of cases were contested. Of the default judgment cases, 75% were by a business against a consumer and 16% a business against a business. Of disputed cases, 22% were a business versus an individual, 11% a consumer versus a business, 27% a business versus a business and 12% an individual versus an individual. The median amount claimed in the default case was $279.

Vidmar argued that previous research had underestimated the number of consumer cases because they had only counted as consumer cases those situations where a consumer appeared as plaintiff. When cases where a consumer defended by withholding payment are added, consumer cases comprised 33% of all disputed cases. In addition, he introduced the concept of "partial liability". He argued that a typical situation was where a consumer withholds payment for renovations because of dissatisfaction with some aspect of performance. The consumer is willing to pay a percentage of the bill but not the total bill. At trial the plaintiff might not recover the total amount, possibly the amount which the consumer was willing to pay. Judgment will be recorded for the plaintiff, therefore inviting coding as "plaintiff win", but the plaintiff may have lost, if her claim was for $900, and the defendant had been willing to pay $600 and judgment was given for $600. The judgment would be a vindication of the rights of the defendant consumer.

Vidmar drew a picture of the typical consumer case:

> Consider some cases where the consumer was the defendant. A service station claimed for car repairs; the defendant argued that she had been overcharged on labor ... A real estate firm claimed for a brokerage fee, but the consumer said the plaintiff had failed to provide the service ... a tile company sued for an unpaid

account, but the defendant asserted that the work was inferior and that in addition the final account exceeded the original estimate ... Consider cases where the consumer was plaintiff ... The plaintiff's boat was destroyed when wind blew down the defendant bailees shed ... A consumer had a new roof installed and paid upon completion, but when it rained the roof leaked; the roofer asserted that the water damage had occurred before repairs were made ... the underlying nature of the disputes was similar.

He concluded that in disputed cases individuals seemed to succeed as often as business whether as plaintiffs or defendants, business plaintiffs in disputed cases tended to be small business and although businesses were more likely to be repeat players and be represented by lawyers, there was no association between these factors and dispute outcomes.

Vidmar's study underlines a distinction which may be drawn between the two major businesses of the court; debt-collection resulting in default judgment and disputed cases before the court. Unfortunately, his study did not investigate in any detail the default judgment cases, or the demographic characteristics of those using the court. Having noted that limitation, his analysis does provide us with some pause before drawing a blanket conclusion that the small claims court is solely a tool for the "haves".

Demographic Profile of Users

Studies of small claims courts have tended to focus on the demographics and experiences of plaintiffs. Existing studies in Canada, the US, and elsewhere indicate that it is middle income, better educated, male, individuals who bring cases as plaintiffs in small claims courts. Studies of the court have often obtained small and unreliable samples of defendants, or simply neglected to study defendants, in particular those who were involved in default actions. This is of policy significance since defendants and default defendants are also users of the court and by finding out more about their circumstances and their reasons for default we might learn about the role of the court process in the process of debt collection.

In order to gain some insight into the demographics of default judgment defendants we can turn to studies which have looked at the court process as part of a study of debt collection. These provide some data to fill the gaps in the court studies. The profile of an individual taken to judgment for debt [indicates] that the majority are in blue-collar occupations, have lower than average incomes, have less post-secondary education than the general population and rent rather than own. Most have been unable to pay the debt because of a change in life circumstances such as unemployment or the loss of a partner's income.

It might be hypothesized that there are class differences between differing "users" of the court. The majority of those involved in disputed cases may be drawn more from the ranks of the middle class. Those who are defendants in default judgment cases may however be drawn more from the working class and those in more precarious economic positions in our society. This latter category may overlap with issues of gender and race, given that statistical data indicate the precarious position of single parent families headed by women and the likelihood that lower income and new immigrant groups are often the targets of fraudulent selling practices. This hypothesis gains strength from the consultations carried out for the Civil Justice Review. There was a significant distinction between differing groups' perception of satisfaction with the small claims court. Business groups and middle class consumer groups thought that the existing court system was satisfactory, while poverty groups indicated that courts were intimidating for their clients and that reforms such as full time inquisitorial judges and a duty counsel would make small claims more effective for the poor. Minority groups were concerned about language barriers, judges lack of knowledge of the problems faced by minority groups and a general lack of confidence of minority groups in the civil justice system.

(iii) The Development of Prepaid Legal Services in Canada

C.J. Wydrzynski

THE ISSUES: COST AND ACCESS

Recently, increased examination of the cost of legal services and the quality of access to legal service providers has spawned a host of suggested reforms to the current system for delivery of legal services. These reforms fall generally within a number of categories. Some reforms which may lower cost and improve access include more economic law office management, changes in substantive and procedural law to allow for more systematic resolution of legal problems, increased efficiency of judicial and administrative decision-making processes, liberalization of the ethical norms which regulate and authorize law practice and even increased or improved government regulation to improve competition in the interest of the consumer. All of these methods offer logical alternatives which should be carefully analyzed. Others, such as government-sponsored comprehensive judicare, suggest fundamental alterations of our present educational and occupational foundations, by amplifying the government's role and seeking to transfer the cost of legal services to the general public through taxes. In a similar manner, improvements to the legal aid structure are more appropriately identified as social concerns or governmental welfare assistance. Generally, all suggested reforms seek to eliminate existing impediments to optimal use of legally trained personnel: to reduce the cost of legal services to the consumer and improve access to those who dispense legal services.

The problems of cost and access can be affected by many of these methods, but many improvements offer a piecemeal, although important, approach to the basic concerns. None of the methods is comprehensive in its approach to the overall improvement of client-access and client-cost issues. Each option offers improvements over the existing mechanisms, but few seek to provide a total relief package for a broad group within the community.

The concept of prepaid legal services is designed to provide an alternative, comprehensive mechanism which addresses the issues of cost and access directly. Its scope is extensive and directed toward a large segment of the currently underserviced population. Prepaid legal service plans incorporate many of the schemes suggested above and such plans probably will encourage other reforms. Such plans offer one alternative, although a highly useful one, for certain groups in society to organize an economically sound method to apportion costs and help to reduce the random and irregular nature of access to capable lawyers.

Essentially, the concept of prepaid legal services can be seen as a self-help mechanism for the consumer. It allows consumers to design an appropriate cost model to fit their needs and to structure an access model which will provide the desired degree of availability of lawyers to the group, given the circumstances and the context in which a group must operate. It is by virtue of such an arrangement that actual consumer needs can be determined. Other forms of analysis engage in speculation about these questions. They tend to exclude the consumer from their perspective, or decide for them what they want in the "public interest". Prepaid legal service plans, within limits, tend to leave this choice where it ought to be left: with those who have the greatest interests at stake.

Prepaid legal service plans are designed largely for a specific economic group within society: the middle-income earner. While there are many statistics to show that middle-income wage earners are a prime group experiencing both cost and access problems, economic common sense dictates that cost and access should be a greater problem for this group than the most affluent in society. As well, the development of provincial legal aid schemes has placed the indigent client in a relatively better cost-access position than the middle-income earner. Historically, the middle-income individual has been provided with the fee-for-service access model. The many inherent problems of this model have been recognized and reforms such as specialization and advertising have been suggested as providing some relief, while remaining generally within this model.

From Robert G. Evans and Michael J. Trebilcock, eds., *Lawyers and the Consumer Interest: Regulating the Market for Legal Services* (Toronto: Butterworth & Co. (Canada) Ltd., 1982) 199 at 199–204. Notes omitted. Reproduced by permission of the editors.

Given the generally negative public perception of the legal profession and lack of knowledge about legal problems and legal rights, it is safe to suggest that alternative mechanisms to the fee-for-service model may narrow the gap between the legal system and a large segment of the population which it attempts to serve. Most importantly, the prepaid model leaves the precise form of the remedy within the hands of those who are experiencing the problems. While proper regulation and ethical standards must be maintained, and political choices must also be made, it is not unwarranted to let the consumers have a large degree of independence in choosing an appropriate model to fit their needs.

THE PREPAID MODEL

Prepaid legal service plans relate directly to the cost of legal services because essentially they are a means to finance or budget legal service costs for the individual consumer. No precise definition can be formulated to illustrate the myriad forms of the model but the following can be helpful:

> ...any system or arrangement whereby payment is made in advance for legal services that may be needed later if such services are within the type of benefits provided by the plan.

The many types of available financing for prepayment and intermarriage with a realistic scope of benefits provide flexibility in plan structure.

Prepayment of costs is a typical method for providing against future needs. The operative principle is group liability for individual costs: a spreading of the expense or cost of legal services over the members of the group. While the individual alone may be unable to sustain the costs of legal services because of limited financial resources, the enhanced power of a group of similarly interested individuals to finance individual members' costs is self-evident. Annual individual cost could be less than the cost of individual legal services used in any particular year. Of course, this assumption depends on annual utilization rates. Efficient funding of a plan makes such predictions essential. Basically, simple principles of budgeting and insurance can be applied by middle-income persons to the legal services market.

A considerable and often excruciating debate has raged concerning whether prepaid legal service plans are really a form of insurance or prepayment. The mixture of fortuitous (insurance) and non-fortuitous (prepayment) events often covered by prepaid legal plans has caused this dilemma. In a practical sense, this debate is somewhat meaningless in that plans do in fact cover both types of activity. Whether the applicable principle is true risk-bearing or simple budgeting does not undermine the advantages of group affiliation for the average consumer.

Public funds need not be used directly to help solve this cost dilemma for the average citizen. While some governmental encouragement of plans might be induced by an equitable taxation format, basically, the mechanism is self-induced and self-funded. Unaided resources can command much greater influence and resolve common problems through group affiliation. Collective activity to resolve individual problems is a standard method of social organization. It is precisely the recognition of this fundamental principle that allowed the growth of prepaid plans in the United States.

Sufficient group interest can be generated from commonly recognizable units or organizations within society. The union hall, the credit union, the church, a tenants' association, a co-operative and many others provide recognizable communities of interest which can provide the framework and administrative expertise necessary to operate a legal services plan for its members. The community of interest need not be narrow, although this adds an element of economic predictability as to the type of legal services a relatively homogenous group may require. On the other hand, insurance companies have shown an interest in circumscribing the parameters of a group simply on the basis of its desire to prepay for legal services. The community of interest is identified by a willingness to pay the premium cost, and individual policies might be sold to persons unattached to any group. However, the existence of a "group" is an obvious asset in plan administration.

There are many variations of prepaid legal services plan models. The models can vary on many levels: basic design and organizational features, how the plan is sponsored, who makes the administrative decisions, and how the service providers are regulated. Creative planning can design a model which fits the cost and access needs of the member-clients with efficiency and quality, and which maintains the professional character of the services provided.

For example, the scope of available benefits can be relatively narrow or very extensive, depending on the commitment of available resources and the premium levels. Services which are covered by any particular plan will depend on the nature and character of the group to be served. Utilization rate would be an additional element in the cost calculus. Costs can be estimated for each individual plan and reasonable predictions are possible.

(iii) The Development of Prepaid Legal Services in Canada

When there is a large enough subscription group, prepaid legal services compare favourably in cost to similar mechanisms used by other professions to deliver their services — for example, prepaid dental or optical plans. The relatively low individual subscriber cost insures that those with unmet legal needs are provided with a reasonable method to meet those needs. At the least, prepaid legal plans should be attractive as a fringe benefit.

For those who are establishing Canada's first plans today, adoption of a meaningful schedule of benefits and exclusions can present serious problems of choice. Actuarial data relating to legal fees have not been developed with any degree of sophistication in this country. Appropriate financial levels of coverage for particular legal tasks have to be worked out through practical experience.

Since most plans are aimed at the middle-income individual, certain typical legal problems of such a group can be identified. These would include preparation of wills, uncontested divorces, landlord and tenant problems, real estate purchases, applications for various government benefits, consumer purchases, and general legal advice. Different types of coverage must be worked out for each group's needs.

In addition to the relatively predictable routinized services, plans can be structured to encompass problems which display greater elements of "risk". Criminal and civil defense as well as plaintiff civil actions, or total family law and estate planning services can be built into a specific plan. It would seem that plans can incorporate both the prepayment principle for routinized legal services and the traditional concept of insurance for protection against unforeseen risks which could lead to financial catastrophe. On the whole, prepaid plans can be viewed as a financing or budgeting mechanism, rather than the traditional risk-spreading device. However, plans would seem to provide a genuine service that at least tends to bridge the gap toward traditional risk-spreading. For example, consumers may tend to doubt the need for insurance as protection against an unforeseen legal catastrophe, but may tend to see the value in a telephone advice service as part of the structure of their plan.

In addition, there are cost-saving mechanisms which can be used to tailor a plan further to available resources. These include maximum charges for services, deductibles, hourly rates and specific exclusions. For example, in some types of plans, "adverse selection", or inclusion of high risk individuals within the covered group, may present a threat to the financial stability of the plan. Exclusion of pre-existing legal problems or a time delay before the plan becomes effective may be used to counteract such difficulties.

While the scope of coverage is a major problem to be resolved with any proposed plan, the method chosen to link the lawyer and client also presents a number of alternatives. Traditionally, the two basic structures are described as the open panel and the closed panel models. In open panel plans the beneficiary may choose any lawyer in the community to provide the services by his or her plan. The plan would eventually pay the lawyer directly for the services provided to the members, or allow the members to be reimbursed for their out-of-pocket expenses. Except for the fact that a third party — the plan — is paying the costs incurred, the traditional manner in which the client selects a lawyer and in which the lawyer's services are rendered remains largely undisturbed. Wide geographic distribution of a plan's members or a membership which experiences frequent interjurisdictional legal problems may make this type of access system desirable. In fact, many forms of regulation would make this system mandatory. The thrust of this model is to indemnify member costs while remaining close to the fee-for-service mechanism.

At the opposite end of the spectrum is the closed panel model, in which the group retains one or more lawyers to represent, often exclusively, the members of the group. A staff of full-time salaried lawyers, members of a single law firm or a limited number of private practitioners might be chosen to provide the services. The member's freedom of choice of lawyer is limited by this type of structure, but it has been shown to be an efficient model in the union-sponsored, consumer group or co-operative setting. It is especially useful in controlling costs, due to the direct availability of price control, peer evaluation techniques, paraprofessional components and a centralized administration to standardize data collection and claims procedures. The approach is largely viewed as provision of a service rather than indemnification of costs.

Many variations of these open and closed panel models are possible. In fact, pure versions of either type are unusual in practice. For example, a partially open or partially closed system of lawyer selection might be used, in which lawyers participate in the plan if they agree to fee levels established by it. Only lawyers who agree to this condition would be eligible to provide services to plan members. The beneficiary would thus have a wider choice available than in the strict closed plan system, but would have less choice than a wholly open panel would provide.

Even in open panel systems some form of informal referral system arises in practice.

It should be noted that the terms "open" and "closed" are not terms of art with specific meanings. The definitions vary with context and with need. Nor is the latter a limitation on "choice" and the former a protection of "free choice". When compared with the relevant choice available in the fee-for-service market, both improve access and the labels attached to relevant provider schemes tend to become less useful. The key issue should be to provide flexibility for the consumer.

(iv) Paralegals Fill Gaps in Legal Service Delivery Ontario Task Force Discussion Paper Argues

Don Brillinger

Evidence gathered by Ontario's special task force on paralegals during the past 10 months suggests that independent paralegals should be allowed to operate "in some fashion with appropriate safeguards for the public interest."

In a discussion paper released last month, the task force says research indicates that Ontario's growing paralegal industry seems to be filling "some gaps in the system of legal service delivery" in the province and appears "to be filling an important public need."

"Most consumers seem to be satisfied with the quality of service they have obtained through independent paralegals. There is also some evidence that the fees charged by independent paralegals are lower than those charged by the legal profession for comparable work," the discussion paper says.

It adds that, "[o]n the whole, while there have been some inappropriate acts carried out by paralegals, the perception of the level of complaints has been exaggerated."

But while the task force says it recognizes independent paralegals should be subject to some form of regulation, it suggests that such controls should be implemented cautiously.

"We are mindful that to establish a costly and cumbersome regulatory scheme would be to defeat some of the potential benefits of greater access to legal services at a reasonable cost which would be possible through the recognition of independent paralegals.

"We think that the regulatory system chosen should be the least intrusive necessary to ensure a consistent and competent level of services being offered to the public," the paper says.

"Independent paralegals should be viewed as legal technicians provided with the capacity to service the public in a very specific manner in areas of lesser complexity and lower risk. The independent paralegal must also be educated to have the ability to recognize when a particular legal problem must be referred to a fully qualified lawyer," the paper adds.

The task force was created last summer by Attorney General Ian Scott to study the role of paralegals in Ontario and to recommend whether or not paralegals should be able to provide legal services to the public.

Chaired by University of Windsor president Ronald Ianni, it has spent the past 10 months gathering empirical research about the scope of paralegal activity in the province. It also has received more than 60 written submissions from paralegal organizations, law societies and other parties, and has met privately with legal and paralegal groups to explain its mandate and procedures.

The discussion paper outlines some of the task force's preliminary findings, and is intended to focus proceedings at a series of public hearings the group began holding across Ontario earlier this month.

The paper says the "phenomenon" of independent paralegals — those who work without direct supervision by lawyers — "is widespread throughout

---

From *The Lawyer's Weekly* (30 June 1989). Reproduced with permissions of Butterworths Canada Ltd.

(iv) Paralegals Fill Gaps in Legal Service Delivery Ontario Task Force Discussion Paper Argues

the province and is continuing to grow and attract new members to its ranks."

Consumers appear to be satisfied with paralegals, whose fees seem to be lower than those charged by lawyers "for comparable work," the discussion paper notes.

"...Members of the public are using the services of independent paralegals, especially with regard to the more routine and 'lower risk' legal services where form filling or minimal expertise is necessary."

Overall, the "perception" of the number of complaints about paralegals appears to be "exaggerated," the paper says, adding that the task force has "uncovered no generalized abuse of clients by independent paralegals."

Still, "there are definite concerns about the lack of education and training of most independent paralegals," of whom "very few have been operating for more than a couple of years."

Turning to the various options it could recommend to the attorney general, the task force says it does not favour retaining the *status quo*, "whereby independent paralegals are allowed to be gainfully employed as agents before some minor courts and administrative agencies, but not to provide any other legal services.

"Because of the concern expressed about the competence of the service being provided by independent paralegal agents, almost no individual or group which has made its views known to the task force has argued for retention of the present state of affairs. At the very least, independent paralegal agents should be trained and minimally regulated in some fashion.

"The task force is in agreement with these basic sentiments," the paper says, "and cannot see how the people of Ontario would be served by continuing on the current path. There is much confusion in the minds of the public concerning the legitimate role of paralegals in the legal services marketplace. Retaining the *status quo* would only perpetuate the present confused state."

The task force also does not favour allowing paralegals to operate *only* under lawyers' supervision.

"This, in effect, would be to retain the legal status of the present situation, without expanding the range of services available to the public through independent paralegals."

Similarly, it is "not inclined to recommend the abolition of those agents currently appearing within minor courts and tribunals that have received the approval of the Court of Appeal in the *POINTTS* decision. Indeed, these activities appear to be filling an important public need."

(In *R. v. Lawrie and POINTTS Ltd.*, the Ontario Court of Appeal said paralegals may act as paid agents in traffic law prosecutions and certain other minor proceedings without violating *Law Society Act* prohibitions against the unauthorized practice of law. See: *Lawyers Weekly*, March 27, 1987.)

"Furthermore," says the paper, "should such agents and paralegals be allowed to carry out these limited activities, subject to some form of educational requirements and regulation, it would appear illogical to preclude paralegals from carrying out other technical tasks with similar or lesser skill requirements.

"This would involve setting out specific areas of practice, and establishing education and training programs relevant to these areas of practice. It would be necessary to appoint an individual with the responsibility of overseeing the activities of independent paralegals generally, and managing a regulatory scheme," the paper points out.

Finally, the task force warns that enacting a "costly and cumbersome" regulatory scheme could defeat the benefits of allowing paralegals to provide the public with legal services at a reasonable cost.

9 The Personnel of Law

A. Lawyers: Education and Training

(i) Legal Education as Training for Hierarchy

Duncan Kennedy

Law schools are intensely political places despite the fact that they seem intellectually unpretentious, barren of theoretical ambition or practical vision of what social life might be. The trade-school mentality, the endless attention to trees at the expense of forests, the alternating grimness and chumminess of focus on the limited task at hand, all these are only a part of what is going on. The other part is ideological training for willing service in the hierarchies of the corporate welfare state.

To say that law school is ideological is to say that what teachers teach along with basic skills is wrong, is nonsense about what law is and how it works; that the message about the nature of legal competence, and its distribution among students, is wrong, is nonsense; that the ideas about the possibilities of life as a lawyer that students pick up from legal education are wrong, are nonsense. But all this is nonsense with a tilt; it is biased and motivated rather than random error. What it says is that it is natural, efficient, and fair for law firms, the bar as a whole, and the society the bar services to be organized in their actual patterns of hierarchy and domination.

Because students believe what they are told, explicitly and implicitly, about the world they are entering, they behave in ways that fulfill the prophecies the system makes about them and about that world. This is the linkback that completes the system: students do more than accept the way things are, and ideology does more than damp opposition. Students act affirmatively within the channels cut for them, cutting them deeper, giving the whole a patina of consent, and weaving complicity into everyone's life story.

. . . .

The Formal Curriculum: Legal Rules and Legal Reasoning

The intellectual core of the ideology is the distinction between law and policy. Teachers convince students that legal reasoning exists, and is different from policy analysis, by bullying them into accepting as valid in particular cases arguments about legal correctness that are circular, question-begging, incoherent, or so vague as to be meaningless. Sometimes these are just arguments from authority, with the validity of the authoritative premise put outside discussion by professorial fiat. Sometimes they are policy arguments (e.g., security of transaction, business certainty) that are treated in a particular situation as though they were rules that everyone accepts but

---

From *The Politics of Law: A Progressive Critique* 3rd edition by David Kairys at 54, 60–62, 64–66, 73–75. Copyright © 1998 by David Kairys. Reproduced by permission of Basic Books, a member of Perseus Books, L.L.C.

that will be ignored in the next case when they would suggest that the decision was wrong. Sometimes they are exercises in doctrinal logic that wouldn't stand up for a minute in a discussion between equals (e.g., the small print in a form contract represents the "will of the parties").

Within a given subfield, the teacher is likely to treat cases in three different ways. There are the cases that present and justify the basic rules and basic ideas of the field. These are treated as cursory exercises in legal logic. Then there are cases that are anomalous — "outdated" or "wrongly decided" because they don't follow the supposed inner logic of the area. There won't be many of these, but they are important because their treatment persuades students that the technique of legal reasoning is at least minimally independent of the results reached by particular judges and is therefore capable of criticizing as well as legitimating. Finally, there will be an equally small number of peripheral or "cutting-edge" cases the teacher sees as raising policy issues about growth or change in the law. Whereas in discussing the first two kinds of cases the teacher behaves in an authoritarian way supposedly based on his objective knowledge of the technique of legal reasoning, here everything is different. Because we are dealing with "value judgments" that have "political" overtones, the discussion will be much more freewheeling. Rather than every student comment being right or wrong, all student comments get pluralist acceptance, and the teacher will reveal himself to be mildly liberal or conservative rather than merely a legal technician.

The curriculum as a whole has a rather similar structure. It is not really a random assortment of tubs on their own bottoms, a forest of tubs. First, there are contracts, torts, property, criminal law, and civil procedure. The rules in these courses are the ground rules of late-nineteenth-century laissez-faire capitalism. Teachers teach them as though they had an inner logic, as an exercise in legal reasoning, with policy (e.g., commercial certainty in the contracts course) playing a relatively minor role. Then there are second- and third-year courses that expound the moderate reformist program of the New Deal and the administrative structure of the modern regulatory state (with passing reference to the racial egalitarianism of the Warren Court). These courses are more policy oriented than first-year courses, and also much more ad hoc.

Liberal teachers teach students that limited interference with the market makes sense and is as authoritatively grounded in statutes as the ground rules of laissez-faire are grounded in natural law.

But each problem is discrete, enormously complicated, and understood in a way that guarantees the practical impotence of the reform program. Conservative teachers teach that much of the reform program is irrational or counter-productive or both, and would have been rolled back long ago were it not for "politics." Finally, there are peripheral subjects, like legal philosophy or legal history, legal process, clinical legal education. These are presented as not truly relevant to the "hard" objective, serious, rigorous analytic core of law; they are a kind of playground or finishing school for learning the social art of self-presentation as a lawyer.

It would be an extraordinary first-year student who could, on his own, develop a theoretically critical attitude toward this system. Entering students just don't know enough to figure out where the teacher is fudging, misrepresenting, or otherwise distorting legal thinking and legal reality. To make matters worse, the most common kind of liberal thinking the student is likely to bring with her is likely to hinder rather than assist in the struggle to maintain some intellectual autonomy from the experience. Most liberal students believe that the liberal program can be reduced to guaranteeing people their rights and to bringing about the triumph of human rights over mere property rights. In this picture, the trouble with the legal system is that it fails to put the state behind the rights of the oppressed, or that the system fails to enforce the rights formally recognized. If one thinks about law this way, one is inescapably dependent on the very techniques of legal reasoning that are being marshalled in defense of the status quo.

This wouldn't be so bad if the problem with legal education were that the teachers *misused* rights reasoning to restrict the range of the rights of the oppressed. But the problem is much deeper than that. Rights discourse is internally inconsistent, vacuous, or circular. Legal thought can generate equally plausible rights justifications for almost any result. Moreover, the discourse of rights imposes constraints on those who use it that make it difficult for it to function effectively as a tool of radical transformation. Rights are by their nature "formal," meaning that they secure to individuals legal protection for as well as from arbitrariness — to speak of rights is precisely *not* to speak of justice between social classes, races, or sexes. Rights discourse, moreover, presupposes or takes for granted that the world is and should be divided between a state sector that enforces rights and a private world of "civil society" in which individuals pursue their diverse goals. This framework is, in itself, a part of the problem rather than of the solution. It makes it difficult even to conceptualize radical proposals such as, for example, decentralized democratic worker control of factories.

Because it is incoherent and manipulable, traditionally individualist, and willfully blind to the realities of *substantive* inequality, rights discourse is a trap. As long as one stays within it, one can produce good pieces of argument about the occasional case on the periphery where everyone recognizes value judgments have to be made. But one is without guidance in deciding what to do about fundamental questions and fated to the gradual loss of confidence in the convincingness of what one has to say in favor of the very results one believes in most passionately.

Left liberal rights analysis submerges the student in legal rhetoric but, because of its inherent vacuousness, can provide no more than an emotional stance against the legal order. It fails liberal students because it offers no base for the mastery of ambivalence. What is needed is to think about law in a way that will allow one to enter into it, to criticize it without utterly rejecting it, and to manipulate it without self-abandonment to *their* system of thinking and doing.

. . . .

Incapacitation for Alternative Practice

Law schools channel their students into jobs in the hierarchy of the bar according to their own standing in the hierarchy of schools. Students confronted with the choice of what to do after they graduate experience themselves as largely helpless: they have no "real" alternative to taking a job in one of the firms that customarily hire from their school. Partly, faculties generate this sense of student helplessness by propagating myths about the character of the different kinds of practice. They extol the forms that are accessible to their students; they subtly denigrate or express envy about the jobs that will be beyond their students' reach; they dismiss as ethically and socially suspect the jobs their students won't have to take.

As for any form of work outside the established system — for example, legal services for the poor and neighborhood law practice — they convey to students that, although morally exalted, the work is hopelessly dull and unchallenging, and that the possibilities of reaching a standard of living appropriate to a lawyer are slim or nonexistent. These messages are just nonsense — the rationalizations of law teachers who

long upward, fear status degradation, and above all hate the idea of risk. Legal services practice, for example, is far more intellectually stimulating and demanding, even with a high caseload, than most of what corporate lawyers do. It is also more fun.

Beyond this dimension of professional mythology, law schools act in more concrete ways to guarantee that their students will fit themselves into their appropriate niches in the existing system of practice. First, the actual content of what is taught in a given school will incapacitate students from any other form of practice than that allotted graduates of that institution. This looks superficially like a rational adaptation to the needs of the market, but it is in fact almost entirely unnecessary. Law schools teach so little, and that so incompetently, that they cannot, as now constituted, prepare students for more than one career at the bar. But the reason for this is that they embed skills training in mystificatory nonsense and devote most of their teaching time to transmitting masses of ill-digested rules. A more rational system would emphasize the way to learn law rather than rules, and skills rather than answers. Student capacities would be more equal as a result, but students would also be radically more flexible in what they could do in practice.

A second incapacitating device is the teaching of doctrine in isolation from practice skills. Students who have no practice skills tend to exaggerate how difficult it is to acquire them. There is a distinct lawyers' mystique of the irrelevance of the "theoretical" material learned in school, and of the crucial importance of abilities that cannot be known or developed until one is out in the "real world" and "in the trenches." Students have little alternative to getting training in this dimension of things after law school. It therefore seems hopelessly impractical to think about setting up your own law firm, and only a little less impractical to go to a small or political or unconventional firm rather than to one of those that offer the standard package of postgraduate education. Law schools are wholly responsible for this situation. They could quite easily revamp their curricula so that any student who wanted it would have a meaningful choice between independence and servility.

A third form of incapacitation is more subtle. Law school, as an extension of the educational system as a whole, teaches students that they are weak, lazy, incompetent, and insecure. And it also teaches them that if they are willing to accept extreme dependency and vulnerability for a probationary term, large institutions will (probably) take care of them almost no matter what. The terms of the bargain are relatively clear. The institution will set limited, defined tasks and specify minimum requirements in their performance. The student/associate has no other responsibilities than performance of those tasks. The institution takes care of all the contingencies of life, both within the law (supervision and backup from other firm members; firm resources and prestige to bail you out if you make a mistake) and in private life (firms offer money but also long-term job security and delicious benefits packages aimed to reduce risks of disaster). In exchange, you renounce any claim to control your work setting or the actual content of what you do, and agree to show the appropriate form of deference to those above and condescension to those below.

By comparison, the alternatives are risky. Law school does not train you to run a small law business, to realistically assess the outcome of a complex process involving many different actors, or to enjoy the feeling of independence and moral integrity that comes of creating your own job to serve your own goals. It tries to persuade you that you are barely competent to perform the much more limited roles it allows you, and strongly suggests that it is more prudent to kiss the lash than to strike out on your own.

. . . .

For committed liberal students, there is another possibility, which might be called the denunciatory mode. One can take law school work seriously as time serving and do it coldly in that spirit, hate one's fellow students for their surrenders, and focus one's hopes on "not being a lawyer" or on a fantasy of an unproblematically leftist legal job on graduation. This response is hard from the very beginning. If you reject what teachers and the student culture tell you about what the first-year curriculum means and how to enter into learning it, you are adrift as to how to go about becoming minimally competent. You have to develop a theory on your own of what is valid skills training and what is merely indoctrination, and your ambivalent desire to be successful in spite of all is likely to sabotage your independence. As graduation approaches, it becomes clearer that there are precious few unambiguously virtuous law jobs even to apply for, and your situation begins to look more like everyone else's, though perhaps more extreme. Most (by no means all) students who begin with denunciation end by settling for some version of the bargain of public against private life.

I am a good deal more confident about the patterns that I have just described than about the attitudes toward hierarchy that go along with them.

My own position in the system of class, sex, and race (as an upper-middle-class white male) and my rank in the professional hierarchy (as a Harvard professor) give me an interest in the perception that hierarchy is both omnipresent and enormously important, even while I am busy condemning it. And there is a problem of imagination that goes beyond that of interest. It is hard for me to know whether I even understand the attitudes toward hierarchy of women and blacks, for example, or of children of working-class parents, or of solo practitioners eking out a living from residential real-estate closings. Members of those groups sometimes suggest that the particularity of their experience of oppression simply cannot be grasped by outsiders, but sometimes that the failure to grasp it is a personal responsibility rather than inevitable. Often it seems to me that all people have at least analogous experiences of the oppressive reality of hierarchy, even those who seem most favored by the system — that the collar feels the same when you get to the end of the rope, whether the rope is ten feet long or fifty. On the other hand, it seems clear that hierarchy creates distances that are never bridged.

It is not uncommon for a person to answer a description of the hierarchy of law firms with a flat denial that the bar is really ranked. Lawyers of lower-middle-class background tend to have far more direct political power in the state governments than "elite" lawyers, even under Republican administrations. Furthermore, every lawyer knows of instances of real friendship, seemingly outside and beyond the distinctions that are supposed to be so important, and can cite examples of lower-middle-class lawyers in upper-middle-class law firms, and vice versa. There are many lawyers who seem to defy hierarchical classification, and law firms and law schools that do likewise, so that one can argue that the hierarchy claim that everyone and everything is ranked breaks down the minute you try to give concrete examples. I have been told often enough that I *may* be right about the pervasiveness of ranking, but that the speaker has never noticed it himself, himself treats all lawyers in the same way, regardless of their class or professional standing, and has never, except in an occasional very bizarre case, found lawyers violating the egalitarian norm.

When the person making these claims is a rich corporate lawyer who was my prep school classmate, I tend to interpret them as a willful denial of the way he is treated and treats others. When the person speaking is someone I perceive as less favored by the system (say, a woman of lower-middle-class origin who went to Brooklyn Law School and now works for a small, struggling downtown law firm), it is harder to know how to react. Maybe I'm just wrong about what it's like out there. Maybe my pre-occupation with the horrors of hierarchy is just a way to wring the last ironic drop of pleasure from my own hierarchical superiority. But I don't interpret it that way. The denial of hierarchy is false consciousness. The problem is not whether hierarchy is there, but how to understand it, and what its implications are for political action.

(ii) Task Force Reports on Women in the Courts: The Challenge for Legal Education

Elizabeth M. Schneider

The Role of the Law Schools

Law schools play a critical role in shaping and socializing our attitudes toward the law, the legal profession generally, and appropriate styles of lawyering. Law schools transmit out first messages about what is permissible in the law. Many present law school faculty members went to law school when there were few women students and almost no women faculty — when law school was a largely male institution. Only in the last fifteen years have women been in law schools in significant numbers. Women law teachers are still a minority on the faculty of many law schools. However, at schools such as Brooklyn Law School and a few others there are a sufficient number of women law teachers (more than twenty at Brooklyn) to constitute a real critical mass, and many of the women play leadership roles within the law school community.

The inclusion of women as law students and the presence of women on law school faculties have been important in many ways. In particular, women law faculty are important role models who send the message that women are a serious and important part of the profession. There are too few women faculty members at most schools and many who are on law faculties are not in tenure-track positions. They are clustered in clinical or legal writing jobs that frequently demand the most challenging work, but for less pay, long-term security, or status than other faculty members receive. Yet the numbers have had an impact. Last year, for example, some first-year students in my section of Civil Procedure had three or four women teachers in their first year. Many told me how important it was for them to see women teaching the basic first-year courses. They understood the positive message that the law school was sending.

To acknowledge that increasing numbers of women in law schools is important in shaping attitudes toward the profession is not to suggest that numbers alone are sufficient. Numbers are only a start; they are *necessary* to begin to affect attitudes, but they are not *sufficient*. The task force reports dramatically document that numbers alone cannot change attitudes. The increasing numbers of women have had little impact on the pervasiveness of gender bias in the profession. And despite the statistical increase in women students and faculty, gender bias in legal education persists.

The increasing numbers of women law students and law teachers and their developing sensitivity to issues of concern to women stimulated the process of examination of gender bias in legal education that began while I was a student at NYU Law School. In 1972 I attended a historic conference, the Symposium on the Law School Curriculum and the Legal Rights of Women sponsored by the AALS, the first that I am aware of on gender bias in legal education. Presentations were made on many traditional areas of the law. The focus was on the need to integrate issues concerning women within the basic structure of American legal education, rather than simply relying on the Women and the Law courses that were then developing to remedy serious omissions

---

(1988) 38 J. Legal Educ. 87 at 88–95. Notes omitted. Reproduced by permission of the Association of American Law Schools, Vanderbilt University Law School, Nashville, Tennessee.

in the curriculum as a whole. Until a few years ago, however, the effort begun in 1972 to integrate women's issues into the curriculum had not developed very far.

Recently, law teachers around the country, mostly women, have begun to address these issues. Much of the most exciting work in legal education is now focusing on the problem of how to remedy gender bias in its many forms. The New York Task Force urges education in all the areas of inequity that it documents. The education that many law students now receive in law schools still omits many of these areas. Women and men in legal education concerned with these issues are beginning to meet the challenge of the task force reports, although we are still largely talking to each other. Work is now focusing on analysis of curriculum content and on casebooks in traditional, particularly first-year courses. We are beginning not only to examine overt bias and omission of women's issues in courses but to explore the traditional pedagogy of legal education that leaves many women students feeling alienated and devalued. We are now also studying what actually goes on in the classroom — all the explicit and implicit ways that women are told that their ideas and perspectives are not equally valuable, but that the law is for men. Some have begun to examine the impact of gender on career choices, professional development, and professional socialization, and are urging law schools to address the issues raised, for example, by recent articles documenting the fact that women are leaving the legal profession. In continuing legal education programs and the judicial education programs that schools such as CUNY Law School have developed, these issues are also being addressed. Let us look at some of these areas more closely.

Curriculum and Casebooks

In a number of substantive areas women in legal education have begun to explore gender bias in curriculum and casebooks, both biased coverage and omission of issues of concern to women. This work was begun at the 1972 AALS Conference and has now focused on the first-year curriculum. In 1983 Professors Nancy Erickson of Ohio State Law School and Nadine Taub of Rutgers Law School-Newark initiated a project on sex bias in the teaching of criminal law, responding to complaints by students in many law schools concerning the treatment of women's issues in criminal law. Their study analyzes the leading casebooks used in the field and surveys curriculum coverage. When completed, the report will be widely circulated to criminal law teachers and will provide supplementary course materials and suggestions for remedying gender bias. Similar work is going on in torts, property, and contracts. A developing literature is analyzing gender bias in doctrine, casebooks and curriculum content. For example, the Torts section of the AALS and the Women in Legal Education section jointly sponsored a program at the AALS Annual Meeting in 1987 on gender bias in Torts. The Women and the Law Project at American University Law School is dedicated to examining the problem of gender bias in the law school curriculum, particularly the first-year curriculum, and to coordinate these efforts. The efforts are just beginning — much more needs to be done to ensure that the entire range of issues raised in the New York Task Force Report is included within curricula and course materials in all law school courses.

The Classroom

Course materials are not the only focus. Classroom dynamics are an additional area of study. A special workshop at the 1986 AALS Annual Meeting, sponsored by the Society of American Law Teachers (SALT) and various AALS sections, focused on Racism, Sexism, and Heterosexism in the Classroom. Women, minority, and gay students spoke movingly of the way in which they were made to feel unwelcome and were ignored or demeaned in the classroom. These students experienced legal education as excluding their own distinctive voices. Women students at Harvard and Yale Law Schools, for example, have written open letters to their faculties to confront and correct classroom attitudes and behaviours that they believe make women feel like outsiders in the classroom and ultimately in the legal profession.

I certainly remember this from my own law school experience. In my first year another woman student and I made a presentation to the NYU Law School faculty, on behalf of NYU Law Women, to complain of gender bias in the classroom. A study undertaken by faculty members at Yale Law School is examining this problem and analyzing its impact on professional socialization of women into law. Many students recount that they perceive a difference in the reception of their concerns in classes taught by women or minorities. For example, some of my third-year students in Women and the Law say it is the first class in which they have spoken. The burden for eliminating these problems must not be left for women and minorities to carry alone.

Legal Education, Lawyering, and Professional Development

Recent efforts to consider gender bias also look at the traditional structure of legal education and its impact on women. Many women students complain that traditional modes of legal education and models of lawyering are inappropriate, adversarial, and incorporate stereotypes of male aggressiveness as the norm. The New York Task Force Report documents the dilemma that these stereotypes pose for women lawyers when they do attempt to represent clients vigorously — they are punished for being too aggressive. Research is being undertaken to investigate whether women's lawyering styles have a different cast, modeled after Carol Gilligan's well-known work in differences in male and female moral development, *In a Different Voice*. Many law teachers concerned with these issues are exploring the possibility of more dialogic, collaborative, and experiential educational approaches that attempt to empower and activate students rather than break and destroy them. These concerns intersect with modern efforts in legal education to include more experiential learning, clinical teaching, and simulation. Our work seeks to help students integrate both heart and mind in addressing legal problems and to encourage the possibility of more self-critical and self-reflective styles of lawyering, sensitive to the dilemma of stereotyped roles.

Legal Education and Scholarship

The New York Task Force Report documents that judges and legal decision-makers have not been sufficiently educated on issues of concern to women, such as gender bias in family law, criminal law, and other areas of the law. There is a clear need for law schools to encourage faculty to do more scholarly work on gender bias, not just in traditional women's rights areas or family law, but in the law broadly. This need contrasts with the implicit or explicit message which many women law faculty members have been given by deans and other members of their faculties: "Don't write on women's issues or soft topics like family law." Documentation by the task force reports of the way in which legal education has not been sufficiently responsive to women also suggests the need to recognize feminist jurisprudence as an important topic of scholarship generally. Feminist jurisprudence began with feminist legal scholars addressing issues that have largely been of concern to women. However, feminist legal theory has now been recognized as a significant approach to legal analysis and legal problem solving in general.

Legal Profession

In addition, the New York Task Force Report documents the need to investigate the impact on the profession and on women of the increasing numbers of women moving into the legal profession. The section of the Report which documents the problems which women attorneys face in practice has important implications for the legal profession generally, and for legal education. It suggests that it is important for the law schools to integrate discussion of gender bias in practice into clinical courses, trial advocacy courses, and into general discussion of ethics and strategy in more traditional courses as well. In addition it suggests that placement officers study the career paths of both men and women graduates and provide programs that are sensitive to issues which women may face in practice.

The Challenge of the Task Force Reports: The Work Ahead for Legal Education

The task force reports place the burden on the law schools. The devastating picture of treatment of women in the courts that the New York Task Force paints requires that the legal education community respond. In response to the New York Task Force Report, there have been some beginning efforts. In October 1986 the Metropolitan Women Law Teachers Association, an organization of women law teachers in the New York area, held a program addressing a range of issues on gender bias in legal education. In December of that year, the New York State Department of Education sent a letter to the deans of all New York state law schools asking for information concerning the implementation of the Report. The letter received a range of responses from law school deans. The Department of Education report summarizing these responses was issued in July 1987. This report has been circulated to the deans of all New York State law schools, but no further action has been taken.

The New York Task Force Report demonstrates that law schools must deal affirmatively with issues of gender bias within their own institutions. Professional development workshops and faculty fora should be instituted by deans and given institutional priority. Gender bias should be a topic of serious attention and discussion within law schools. It is an important issue that should be addressed by the AALS. The AALS should provide leadership to stimulate law school deans to take more institutional initiative. The publication of the present symposium issue of the *Journal of Legal Education* can assist in these efforts.

The task force reports present an important challenge for legal education. Law schools can play a central role in changing gender bias. The question is whether they will meet the challenge. Legal education must be reconstructed to remedy the problems discussed in the task force reports. The law schools will be successful only when all law school graduates are not only knowledgeable about and sensitive to women's concerns in the law but have eradicated gender bias in their own practice.

B. Control over Access to the Profession

(i) Rogue Lawyer Runs Out of Arguments: Bruce Clark's in-your-face fight for native rights has led the once-acclaimed legal mind to be found guilty of conduct unbecoming of a solicitor

Paul Mckay

Bruce Clark, the renegade lawyer who spent two decades cultivating militant native clients across Canada with arguments dating back to the 1700s, has used up his ninth legal life.

Ten days ago, he was disbarred in Ontario. The ruling effectively kills the Canadian courtroom career of the only lawyer on the planet to combine a banker's suit, PhD, conehead haircut, Star Wars glasses, and self-penned writs to arrest judges hearing his cases.

A disciplinary panel, reviewing Mr. Clark's 1997 convictions for contempt of court and resisting a police officer (during a court hearing for five charged in the 1995 Gustafsen Lake armed stand-off in British Columbia) found him ungovernable and guilty of "conduct unbecoming a barrister and solicitor."

The Law Society of Upper Canada panel also cited scathing accounts of his courtroom conduct from Supreme Court Justice Antonio Lamer, a dismal 0-for-40 record in native land claim cases he argued, his 16-month flight from Canada while facing criminal charges, and his claim that virtually all of Canada's judges, police and governments are guilty of treason and genocide against native peoples.

But in the murky world of guerrilla politics, Mr. Clark's disbarment may enhance his hallowed status among a minority of native activists. A self-declared exile and "fugitive for justice" who moved to the rural town of Granville, New York, last year, he refused to attend his Ontario disbarment hearing.

Instead, he filed a sheaf of papers constituting what one respected aboriginal historian has called "a never-ending argument in search of a client."

They relate to a 1704 British Privy Council judgment on the legality of land expropriations against the Mohegan Indians in what was then the British colony of Connecticut. It ruled that British colonial courts were intrinsically biased against aboriginal peoples in land claims cases, and that just decisions could only be made by a special constitutional court created in the name of the Queen of England.

That court was never convened. The Mohegans lost their land. And the 1704 Privy Council ruling was decisively forgotten as the British colonized much of North America during the next two centuries.

Mr. Clark, who unearthed the case during research for his PhD in law in Scotland, immediately seized on the potential legal implications: much of North America may have been illegally seized from aboriginal peoples. And if that were established as a matter of law, native treaties, forced reservation status, and land claim settlements covering most of

---

From *The Ottawa Citizen* (4 April 1999) A3. Reproduced with the permission of The Ottawa Citizen.

the continent and hundreds of native bands, were potentially void.

It was an argument many aboriginal leaders wanted to hear. Mr. Clark quickly gained near-celebrity status on both sides of the Canada-U.S. border for his startling legal discovery. Many were impressed by his flashes of legal brilliance, personal charm, and unwavering commitment to native rights. He is the author of two authoritative books on aboriginal law.

Even his critics agree he gave up a lucrative law practice, huge home and private airplane in the 1970s to champion the native cause — at one time from the very log cabin the Indian imposter Grey Owl used as part of his own mythology. Since 1995, Mr. Clark, his wife Margaret, three children and a menagerie of pets have lived in impoverished circumstances, often smuggled like illegal aliens into native villages from northern New Brunswick to the B.C. coast.

But some native rights activists and native lawyers who were once allies of Mr. Clark became adversaries after he repeatedly lost land claim cases, ignited courtroom fracases, and aligned himself with militants who set up armed barricades and attempted to serve subpoenas, make arrests or seize historical documents in the name of "aboriginal courts" conceived by Mr. Clark.

The more charitable critics say Mr. Clark is the biggest liability to the legal merits of the 1704 case because that message has become inseparable from an obsessive, in-your-face messenger with a taste for martyrdom.

"A lot of aboriginal people agree with his arguments, but not with his tactics," says David Nahwegahbow, an Anishnabe (Ojibway) lawyer in Ottawa who is president of the Indigenous Bar Association of Canada. "He hurts the arguments in the long run. He has divided communities."

Those less charitable say his embattled image and charismatic promises of sweeping legal victories have derailed a dozen land claim settlements — and helped escalate land-claim legal costs in Canada — by splitting native band loyalties and triggering competing claims.

Recently, he filed a surprise case on behalf of a dissident native faction in northern Ontario. The 1704 case is cited as the leading legal grounds for the lawsuit. It pits Mr. Clark and a militant minority against the Ontario and federal governments — as well as the elected Longlac chief and council.

"He's a dangerous item. He ends up creating internal turmoil. That's happened like clockwork in every community he's gone to," says, Peter Di Gangi, an Ottawa-based researcher and policy analyst who has advised native groups across Canada since 1981. Several have been convulsed with bitter in-fighting triggered by Mr. Clark's tactics, he says.

"He's been bad for public optics, for (native) relations with governments, and for native communities themselves. Whenever he leaves, there's a mess to clean up."

The bottom line, Mr. Nahwegahbow says, is that Mr. Clark hasn't won a single land claim case on behalf of native clients during the past two decades. Meanwhile, the Supreme Court of Canada's landmark Delgamuukw decision has affirmed aboriginal rights to self-government and land use across Canada — and effectively achieved much of what Mr. Clark's native apostles could have hoped to attain from a favourable ruling on the 1704 Connecticut case.

Ironically, Mr. Clark once briefly represented one of the 75 Gitskan chiefs who fought the Delgamuukw case through two decades of setbacks and appeals before the Supreme Court ruled in their favour. Stuart Rush, an aboriginal lawyer in Vancouver who was lead counsel on the case, say he and native leaders were appalled by Mr. Clark's guerrilla tactics.

"We were arguing the case at appeal when Bruce Clark showed up, out of the blue, and purported to arrest the four Appeal Court judges for genocide and crimes against aboriginal people," recalls Mr. Rush. "One judge ordered him taken away by the bailiff. We will never know what effect that had (the appeal was lost, but superseded by the Supreme Court decision), but it sure left a bad impression."

Mr. Rush contends that Canadian courts at all levels have properly dismissed Mr. Clark's 1704 legal argument, because it demands that aboriginal title claims be adjudicated at a non-existent court in England — and ignores the Canadian Constitution.

"His whole argument is misplaced and wrong in law. Canada is the only place this can be settled. Yet some of his native clients have gone to jail because of a vain, discreditable argument. He wasn't helping them."

Mr. Clark also argued — and lost — the original Temagami land claim case in Northern Ontario. He left after new lawyers were hired to salvage the land claim on appeal, then returned to advise a small faction of militant dissidents to pursue a competing land claim case.

It has gone nowhere. So have attempts to win similar land claim efforts in the Maritimes, northern Quebec, the upper Ottawa Valley, British Columbia, and in the U.S.

In September 1995, Mr. Clark finally got a chance to argue his 1704 case at the Supreme Court of Canada. He used most of 45 minutes to excoriate Chief Justice Lamer — and the Canadian judicial system — for fraud, chicanery, treason and genocide. It took a mere two minutes for the court to dismiss his case.

"I must say, Mr. Clark, that in my 26 years as a judge I have never heard anything so preposterous and presented in an unkind way," said Chief Justice Lamer. "To call the judges of the Supreme Court of Canada and the 975 High Court judges of Canada accomplices to genocide is something preposterous. I do not accept that and think you are a disgrace to the bar ... The various documents filed in this court, the Supreme Court of British Columbia, and the Court of Appeal are, in large part, an utter farrago of nonsense."

Only three days later, Mr. Clark burst into a courtroom in north central British Columbia, pushing a cart laden with papers relating to the 1704 case. He demanded to represent five native people charged in the Gustafsen Lake standoff. When the judge resisted his arguments, Mr. Clark threw a stack of legal papers at him, and was tackled by police while condemning the hearing as a "kangaroo court."

That scene triggered charges of contempt and resisting arrest. Mr. Clark fled Canada for Amsterdam, where he publicly vowed never to return. (Sixteen months later he returned to Canada. He was convicted on both charges, lost an appeal on the contempt charge, and was sentenced to three months in jail).

Improbably, his fugitive status increased his cachet among some militant natives, but also within pockets of arch-conservative, anti-government activists such as Parliament Hill crusader Glen Kealey and white supremacist defender Doug Christie.

The 1995 criminal charges were laid against Mr. Clark two months after a disciplinary panel of the Law Society of Upper Canada recommended that he be disbarred for professional conduct charges dating back to 1992. The evidence in that hearing was virtually identical to that used in the 1999 hearing in which he lost his legal licence to practice.

But in 1995, Mr. Clark had an extraordinary ally in Clayton Ruby, a left-wing Toronto lawyer and native rights advocate. He almost single-handedly reversed the initial Law Society recommendation, defending Mr. Clark as a merely over-zealous champion of an oppressed native minority. Mr. Ruby co-authored a report which concluded that while Mr. Clark was guilty on three counts of professional misconduct, he deserved only a formal reprimand.

"I read that report carefully," says Mr. Di Gangi, who works directly with native groups across Canada. "Clayton Ruby didn't look at the damage Mr. Clark did to the communities. He ignored the impacts on (Mr. Clark's) own native clients."

Nevertheless, Mr. Ruby's defence of Mr. Clark was adopted by the Law Society governors. Then Mr. Clark refused to appear for his reprimand, leaving no doubt in letters to the Law Society that he was resolutely unrepentant. That prompted a new Law Society panel to review his case and overturn the 1995 reversal engineered by Mr. Ruby, an influential Law Society governor.

Mr. Clark, who could not be contacted for a *Citizen* interview, still has no apparent misgivings about the scrappy tactics, courtroom confrontations and single-minded conviction which has underpinned his crusade. In a final letter to the Law Society he concluded:

"I really don't belong with your crowd. I have nothing further to say. I am content with the matter being disposed of in absentia. I have no further desire to appeal before the committee. I am asking this committee of its own motion to recommend that (the Law Society governors) commission an inquiry of the Law Society's ongoing treason and fraud and complicity in genocide."

(ii) *Regina* v. *Lawrie and POINTTS Ltd.*

BLAIR J.A.: The question in this case is whether a paid agent acting for persons charged with traffic offences under the *Highway Traffic Act*, R.S.O. 1980, c. 198, pursuant to s. 51(1) of the *Provincial Offences*

(1987) 32 C.C.C. (3d) 549 (Ont. C.A.).

Act, R.S.O. 1980, c. 400, can be prosecuted for acting as a barrister or solicitor under s. 50(2) of the *Law Society Act*, R.S.O. 1980, c. 233.

The respondents, Brian Lawrie (Lawrie) and Pointts Limited (the Company) were separately charged in a private prosecution initiated by the Law Society of Upper Canada with unlawfully acting as barristers or solicitors contrary to s. 50 of the *Law Society Act*. (Pointts is an acronym for Provincial Offences Information and Traffic Ticket Service.) The charges were dismissed by His Honour Judge Kerr of the Provincial Court whose decision was affirmed on appeal by the Honourable Judge Moore of the District Court [58 O.R. (2d) 535, 29 C.C.C. (3d) 160]. This appeal is brought pursuant to leave granted by a judge of this court under s. 114 of the *Provincial Offences Act*.

Lawrie is not a barrister or solicitor. He is a retired policeman with considerable experience in the conduct of traffic cases under the *Provincial Offences Act*. He incorporated the company for the purpose of representing persons charged with traffic offences under the *Highway Traffic Act*. Each customer or client is required to sign a form appointing the company as agent to act on his or her behalf "within the meaning of the *Provincial Offences Act*". Lawrie controls the company. At the time of trial, two former police officers were also employed by the company and represented its clients in proceedings under the *Provincial Offences Act*.

The relevant provisions in the *Law Society Act* are:

> **50.**(1) *Except where otherwise provided by law*, no person, other than a member whose rights and privileges are not suspended, shall act as a barrister or solicitor or hold himself out as or represent himself to be a barrister or solicitor or practise as a barrister or solicitor.
>
> (2) Every person who contravenes any provision of subsection (1) is guilty of an offence and on conviction is liable to a fine of not more than $1,000. (Emphasis added.)

The prosecution was conducted under the *Provincial Offences Act*, which provides:

> **51.**(1) A defendant may appear and act personally or by counsel or *agent*.
>
> ...
>
> (3) The court may bar any person from appearing as an agent who is not a barrister and solicitor entitled to practise in Ontario if the court finds that the person is not competent properly to represent or advise the person for whom he appears as agent or does not understand and comply with the duties and responsibilities of an agent. (Emphasis added.)

The learned trial judge found that both respondents had acted as barristers or solicitors within the meaning of s. 50(1) of the *Law Society Act*. This finding was challenged by the respondents in this appeal but, since it is amply supported by the evidence, it should not be disturbed. The respondents were charged only with acting as barristers or solicitors and not with holding themselves out or practising as barristers or solicitors which are the other activities prohibited by s. 50(1).

Nevertheless, the trial judge acquitted both respondents. He held that the *Provincial Offences Act* permitted them to act as agents and that, consequently, they fell within the exceptions that were "otherwise provided by law" in s. 50(1) of the *Law Society Act*. He said [at p. 537 O.R., p. 162 C.C.C.]:

> On all the evidence, bearing in mind that in the opinion of this court s. 48(1) of the *Provincial Offences Act*, that is, the burden section, means the burden is only upon the defence to satisfy a court on the balance of probabilities that an authorization, exception, exemption, or qualification operates in his favour, that Mr. Lawrie has done that in this case as has Pointts Limited. They have satisfied the burden cast upon them of showing that this exemption is provided for by the various sections of the *Provincial Offences Act*, certainly not expressly, but impliedly, and as a result, the defendant Lawrie and the defendant Pointts Limited must receive the benefit of the doubt on these informations, and the charges will be dismissed.

Judge Moore, affirming the trial judge's decision, went further and concluded that a new trade or profession of paralegals had been created by the *Provincial Offences Act*. After reviewing a number of statutes, which authorized the appearance of agents, he had this to say [at pp. 542–3 O.R., pp. 167–8 C.C.C.]:

> [T]he Legislature ... has provided a number of exceptions to the long-standing prohibition of ... others acting and practising as lawyers. In saying that, I mean that the various Acts of Legislature I have referred to above [permit] agents to appear and act and represent others in provincial court, and in some cases surrogate and district court. This legislation does not just permit an appearance in place of a defendant. It also permits an appearance with and for a defendant. No prohibition or restriction was brought to my attention which prevents the same person appearing as agent for a different person on numerous occasions or even receiving renumeration for so doing.

The Legislature has thus created a new trade or calling, that is to say, the calling of para-legals.

. . . .

Appearances through agents, who are not barristers or solicitors, are permitted by other statutes. These include the *Landlord and Tenant Act*, R.S.O. 1980, c. 232, s. 118(1), dealing with residential tenancies; the *Courts of Justice Act*, 1984 (Ont.), c. 11, s. 79, dealing with the Provincial Court (Civil Division) which is now responsible for small claims; the *Construction Lien Act*, 1983 (Ont.), c. 6, s. 69(5), dealing with lien claims not exceeding $200; the *Coroners Act*, R.S.O. 1980, c. 93, s. 41(2), dealing with coroners' inquests; and the *Statutory Powers Procedure Act*, R.S.O. 1980, c. 484, s. 23(3), dealing with appearances before administrative tribunals. With the exception of the *Statutory Powers Procedure Act*, these statutes permit the employment of agents only in relatively minor matters. All the statutes except the *Construction Lien Act, 1983* and the *Coroners Act* contain a provision similar to s. 51(3) of the *Provincial Offences Act* empowering the court or tribunal to bar any agent who is found not competent to represent or advise the person for whom the agent appears or who does not understand and comply with the duties and responsibilities of an agent.

There are other cases where persons, who are not qualified lawyers, are authorized by statute or permitted in practice to act as counsel or solicitors. The Crown makes use of agents under the *Crown Attorneys Act*, R.S.O. 1980, c. 107, s. 7, which provides for the appointment of provincial prosecutors under the *Provincial Offences Act* who are not members of the bar. The *Police Act*, R.S.O. 1980, c. 381, s. 57, enables police officers to act as prosecutors and they are considered agents under s. 1(h) of the *Provincial Offences Act*. Students are employed by the Ministry of the Attorney-General primarily to prosecute traffic offences under the *Provincial Offences Act*, as are students-at-law articled with the Attorney-General's office. Law students, who have completed one year of their law course, may appear in some legal aid matters handled by Student Legal Aid Societies: R.R.O. 1980, Reg. 575, s. 80, under the *Legal Aid Act*, R.S.O. 1980, c. 234. Under para. 12 of the rules of the law society made pursuant to s. 62(1) of the *Law Society Act*, articled students-at-law are permitted to appear in various proceedings.

Rule 20 of the Law Society's Rules of Professional Conduct permits delegation of many tasks by lawyers to employees who are not lawyers or articled students. The delegable tasks include conveyancing, drafting corporate and commercial documents, administration of estates and trusts, and research and preparation of documents in litigation. The rule states that "[g]enerally speaking a non-lawyer shall not attend on examinations or in court except in support of a lawyer also in attendance". The rule makes an exception for appearances by law clerks employed by only one lawyer or law firm in a variety of cases. These include appearances as agents where statutes or regulations permit non-lawyers to appear and on routine adjournments in Provincial Court. Law clerks may also attend on routine examinations in uncontested matters, *ex parte* or consent orders before a master and the taxation of costs.

The common thread that runs through these examples of employment of law students and non-lawyers is that their work is done under the direction and supervision of lawyers who are responsible to clients and the public for the work's proper performance. Moreover, the work is done by salaried employees whose renumeration, unlike that of lawyers, is fixed and not related to fees charged for specific services.

The position of the respondents in this case is different. They operate their own business independent of any direction or supervision by qualified lawyers. The respondents, when acting as agents under the *Provincial Offences Act*, perform the same services as lawyers and, like them, are paid on a fee-for-service basis. They are not barred, as the legal profession is, from carrying on their business through corporations. As recently as 1980 "The Report of the Professional Organizations Committee", April, 1980, at p. 69, reported that law clerks appearing before the committee did not seek independent status: see also "The Market for Legal Services: Paraprofessionals and Specialists", Working Paper No. 10 of the Professional Organizations Committee. It is the growth since that report of the independent paralegal business carrying on lawyer-like activities free from the direction and supervision of the legal profession that elevates the public importance of this case.

Agents have been authorized to act in some proceedings for more than a century. They were first permitted in small claims matters before Division Courts in 1872: "An Act to empower all persons to appear on behalf of others in the Divisional Courts in the Province of Ontario", 1872 (Ont.), c. 8, s. 1, and in mechanics' lien proceedings in 1910: *Mechanics and Wage-Earners Lien Act*, 1910 (Ont.), c. 69, s. 37(7). As previously mentioned they have acted in summary conviction proceedings under

(ii) Regina v. Lawrie and POINTTS Ltd.

the *Criminal Code* since 1906. Their appearance before coroners' inquests was authorized by the *Coroners Act*, 1972 (Ont.), c. 98, s. 33, and their limited participation in proceedings in the *Landlord and Tenant Act* dates from 1975: *Landlord and Tenant Amendment Act*, 1975 (Ont.) (2nd Sess.), c. 13, s. 6. The first statutory reference to their appearance before administrative tribunals was in the *Statutory Powers Procedure Act*, 1971 (Ont.), c. 47, s. 23(3), but it is known that laymen appeared as advocates before such tribunals prior to that date.

Despite the long participation of agents in judicial proceedings, they have been the subject of only one reported decision and little has been written about them. In *R. v. Duggan* (1976), 31 C.C.C. (2d) 167, this court held that right of audience of an agent was confined to the court which was specifically authorized by statute. Thus an agent authorized by s. 735(2) of the *Criminal Code* to appear in a summary conviction court was not entitled to appear on an appeal from conviction before the County Court. MacKinnon A.C.J.O. stated at p. 169:

> It is clear that s. 50 does not allow, unless otherwise provided, non-barristers or solicitors to practise in the Courts, and non-barristers have not been permitted over the years to represent parties in either civil or criminal proceedings in the County or Supreme Court. When the Legislature, which is competent in this field, wished to make exceptions to s. 50 they did so in clear terms, as for example, s. 100 of the *Small Claims Courts Act*, R.S.O. 1970, c. 439:
>
> > "100. A barrister of solicitor, or any other person not prohibited by the judge, may appear at the trial or hearing of an action as agent for a party thereto."

(see also: the *Mechanics' Lien Act*, R.S.O. 1970, c. 267, s. 38(8).) It is of some historical interest to note that over a hundred years ago, in considering the predecessor section of s. 50(1) it was held that it was contrary to law and public policy to permit a person who was not a barrister to appear as an advocate in a County Court: *Re Brooke* (1864), 10 *U.C.L.J.* 49.

One is entitled, in my opinion, to take judicial notice of the extent of the business carried on in this province by persons acting as agents under the *Provincial Offences Act* quite apart from those performing other paralegal services. While it is the view of the law society that agents are not entitled to operate a business for reward, the obvious fact is that they do and have done so for many years. Writing in 1971 about the encroachment on the legal profession, Mark M. Orkin observed: "[T]he 'small claims' field of practice is no longer financially attractive for most lawyers, hence the emergence of division court 'agents', non-lawyers who openly carry on this type of business." (Orkin, Mark M. "Professional Autonomy and the Public Interest: A Study of the Law Society of Upper Canada", D.Jur. dissertation, York University, 1971 at p. 182.)

The hiring of agents as a common practice in provincial offence proceedings is acknowledged in the leading textbook on the *Provincial Offences Act*: see Drinkwater and Ewart, *Ontario Provincial Offences Procedure* (1980), note 46 at p. 57. It is beyond dispute that paid agents are employed in proceedings before administrative tribunals or under the *Construction Lien Act*. The fact that agents do carry on business for reward does not, of course, determine the legal question whether they are authorized to do so under the *Law Society Act*. It does, however, place this case in its proper context. It is not an isolated occurrence but appears rather to be an example of a reasonably common practice.

It is not the role of this court to determine whether, as a matter of policy, the operations of the respondents serve the public interest. It is obvious from the business they have attracted that they are providing an unmet need for service to the public. While no reflection of any kind was made in this case on the respondents, there must be concern about the absence of any control over the education, qualification, competence and probity of all agents. They deal with serious matters because penalties of up to six months imprisonment apply to some offences under the *Highway Traffic Act*. No provision exists for disciplining or supervising agents and protecting the public from financial loss arising from improper performance of their responsibilities by way of an insurance scheme like that of the law society.

It has been observed many times that the prohibition against the unauthorized practice of law is not merely to protect qualified lawyers from infringement of their right to practise their profession. Its primary purpose is to protect the public as Robertson C.J.O. stated in *R. ex rel. Smith v. Ott*, [1950] O.R. 493 at p. 496, 97 C.C.C. 302 at p. 302, [1950] 4 D.L.R. 426 at p. 426:

> To protect the public against persons who, for their own gain, set themselves up as competent to perform services that imperatively require the training and learning of a solicitor, although such persons are without either learning or experience to qualify them, is an urgent public service.

See also *R. ex rel. Smith v. Mitchell*, [1952] O.R. 896 at p. 903, 104 C.C.C. 247 at p. 250, [1953] 1 D.L.R. 700 at p. 703, *per* Laidlaw J.A. It is the responsibility of the Legislature to resolve these issues of policy. The task of this court is to determine whether, on a proper construction of the relevant statutes, they prohibit what the respondents were doing.

If only s. 50 of the *Law Society Act* had to be considered, there would be little difficulty in deciding that the respondents are not prohibited from carrying on the business of acting as agents for a fee under the *Provincial Offences Act*. I can find nothing in the Act that limits the exception in s. 50 of the *Law Society Act* of persons "otherwise authorized" to friends and relatives acting as agents without remuneration. Absent a specific limitation to this effect in the *Law Society Act*, the court could not read such a restriction into the statute.

. . . .

It is ironic that there is lack of clarity in the statutes governing the legal profession and their application to the respondents. I commend for the Legislature's attention to the clarification of this legislation and also the status of agents and other paralegals which is now a matter of considerable public discussion.

For the foregoing reasons, I would dismiss the appeals with costs.

Appeal dismissed.

(iii) Debate Heating Up over Paralegals' Role

Margot Gibb-Clark

Paralegal Maureen Boldt and the body that regulates Ontario lawyers faced off last week in the latest round of a long-running legal slugfest.

Ms. Boldt, of North Bay, Ont., has already pleaded guilty — in April, 1998 — to the unauthorized practice of law. She formally agreed to stop, but the Law Society of Upper Canada alleges she's still at it.

A city councillor who once had Ontario Premier Mike Harris interceding on her behalf, Ms. Boldt says what she is doing is mediating agreements in areas such as uncontested divorces.

A judge of the Ontario Superior Court last week set a new trial for April, turning down the law society's request for an injunction to stop her working in the meantime.

Ms. Boldt's battle symbolizes a larger debate about paralegal services that has continued on and off for years and seems to be picking up speed again.

Independent paralegals say they can offer some uncomplicated services more cheaply and better than lawyers.

Lawyers say there may be some good paralegals. But they say because the profession is unregulated and has no formal education requirements, others can fleece clients or get them into serious trouble.

Brian Lawrie, a paralegal and a former policeman, agrees that "you cannot replace the qualified, educated lawyer — you just can't in complex cases."

"We don't hold ourselves out as capable to do those types of things," says Mr. Lawrie, who heads Pointts, a company that specializes in handling traffic cases in Ontario, Manitoba and Alberta. "But what we do say is that you don't need a neurosurgeon to come and put a stitch in the end of your finger."

Canadian Bar Association president Eugene Meehan also picks up on the neurosurgery image. "Electrical impulses control the brain, but we don't let electricians do neurosurgery," he says.

The official position of his 36,000-member organization is that legal services should only be offered by lawyers, Ottawa-based Mr. Meehan says. "What it's really about is protection of the public."

In Mr. Lawrie's mind, whenever lawyers talk about public interest, "if you replace the word 'public' by 'self,' it still makes sense."

These arguments have gone back and forth for more than a dozen years with no resolution, either

From *The Globe and Mail* (24 January 2000) M1. Reproduced with permission from The Globe and Mail.

(iii) Debate Heating Up over Paralegals' Role

for lack of political will or because the two sides couldn't agree on what paralegals should be allowed to do.

Now Ontario's Attorney General has asked retired Supreme Court of Canada Justice Peter Cory to act as "facilitator" in bringing the two sides to some resolution by May.

At the same time, Ontario's law society has commissioned independent research to get more evidence about the background of people working in the field and about potential problem areas.

A decision last year by the Ontario Court of Appeal refuelled the interest. "A person who decided to sell T-shirts on the sidewalk needs a licence and is subject to government regulation," a three-judge panel says.

"That same person can, however, without any form of government regulation, represent a person in a complicated criminal case where that person may be sentenced to up to 18 months imprisonment."

Manitoba has legislation limiting the areas in which paralegals can practice, but nowhere in Canada are there education requirements or mandatory liability insurance, even though Mr. Lawrie, among others, are covered.

This leaves the door open to scam artists and to others who are overconfident about their abilities, lawyers contend.

"It's a particular problem for vulnerable, poor consumers or for people from ethnic communities," says Ajit John, the lawyer in charge of unauthorized practice complaints for Ontario's law society.

The law society cites the example of an Ontario man who two years ago handed his uncontested divorce case to a paralegal who kept stalling, asking for more money and claiming rules for filing the papers had changed.

The date for the man's remarriage in the Philippines was approaching and he went to meet his intended, assured that things would be resolved in time. But finally he had to delay his wedding and come back to Canada to get the divorce redone.

Yet Mr. Lawrie says he spent 10 years as a policeman watching people arrive in traffic court with valid arguments, then lose their cases. They were unrepresented and didn't know the procedures, he says, but it doesn't take a fully trained lawyer to know how to handle such issues.

Paralegals should be allowed to work in areas such as traffic offences, small claims court and some immigration matters that are subject to reviews or appeals, he says. These are areas where errors are readily correctable. "Much of it is conveyer-belt stuff."

A 10-year-old study by the late University of Windsor law professor Ron Ianni suggested permissible areas of practice for paralegals. They included small claims court, traffic offences, landlord-tenant disputes and some immigration matters.

Disputes over territory arise in areas such as real estate law — which has been an important part of many small-town practices — and in wills and estates.

Tasks that on the surface seem to be mere filling out of forms, such as writing a will or incorporating a company, often need an understanding of law, says lawyer Graham Nichols of Markham, Ont. "I can't imagine anyone not having a few questions about the rights and obligations of directors. You get what you pay for."

However, the day-to-day reality is that despite the Canadian Bar Association's position, a number of law firms — including Mr. Nichols' — do hire outside paralegals.

Mr. Nichols has one on staff and uses a freelancer as well. "In a small practice, you can't do everything," he says. "It's nice to be able to refer clients to people with other expertise." That may include accountants, appraisers, specialist lawyers and paralegals, he says.

Courses have sprung up at community colleges, such as Toronto's Seneca College, to train paralegals. The teachers are lawyers, and outsiders such as the law society's Mr. John take part as speakers.

"I'm looking forward to the day we get regulated," says Tom McLean, 28, who began work last spring for Toronto law firm Fireman Regan after graduating from Seneca. Until regulation comes, he prefers to be called a court agent. "When you say paralegal, there are a lot of bad connotations."

As for Ms. Boldt, the North Bay paralegal says she pleaded guilty to unauthorized practice of law under duress. She says she understood the law society would work with her in developing regulations for the paralegal profession.

New she vows to appeal if she loses in April. "My whole intention is to see what Justice Cory [the province's facilitator] decides, and not have the law society decide what the legislation is for him."

(iv) Franchising Paralegals

Ian McGugan

After the appeal court decided *Law Society of Upper Canada v. Brian Lawrie*, the price-tag for a POINTTS franchise went from $2,000–$10,000 to $30,000–$50,000.

One morning as he waited to present evidence in traffic court, Constable Brian Lawrie had a moment of insight. Presiding over the court was a non-lawyer who had been appointed a justice of the peace.

The prosecutor, like Const. Lawrie, was a Metro Toronto police officer. "Since no-one else in the courtroom was a lawyer," he recalls, "I began to wonder why lawyers were the only ones to defend a case."

With that question, Mr. Lawrie, 39, launched himself on a collision course with the Canadian legal establishment. Tired of the regimented life of a police officer, he had been contemplating a career in business.

After quitting the force in February 1983, and spending several unsatisfying months as an executive with a family-owned bakery, he remembered this courtroom inspiration.

In a city where about 3,500 policemen hand out 1,650 traffic tickets every day, why not defend people accused of traffic offences?

Mr. Lawrie believed there had to be room for a paralegal service that could offer drivers a cheaper alternative to lawyers.

He knew that many lawyers were reluctant to handle traffic cases, regarding them as a time-wasting, unprofitable nuisance. Given their lack of interest and his own wealth of police experience as a witness, Mr. Lawrie felt well qualified to be a courtroom defender.

Five years as a policeman in his native England, followed by another 10 years in Toronto, provided him with a detailed knowledge of the ins and outs of traffic law.

He quickly found, however, that banks weren't interested in lending money to an untried business with no tangible assets.

Undaunted, he raised $15,000 from relatives, and in May 1984, launched POINTTS Ltd. — a name derived from **P**rovincial **O**ffences **I**nformation and **T**raffic **T**icket **S**ervice.

Mr. Lawrie's formula remains as it was then. Potential clients pay nothing for an opinion on the merits of their case. If a client chooses to go to court, POINTTS charged a flat fee of $225 to represent those accused of minor offences, such as failing to halt at a stop sign, driving without a seatbelt or a minor speeding infraction.

The charge jumps to $375 for major offences, including careless driving, driving while under suspension or any incident involving an accident.

Mr. Lawrie estimates his fee to be one-third of what most lawyers charge. And, unlike lawyers' hourly billing, POINTTS's one-time fee covers any number of court appearances.

But how do you promote a business that doesn't already exist? A classified ad in the tabloid *Toronto Sun* brought two clients, Mr. Lawrie says.

Aware that he couldn't explain his concept in the short glib manner of advertisers, he "bugged the life out of the city staffs" of the three Toronto Daily newspapers to do a feature story on his innovative new business.

One day in July, a reporter bit: the article appeared in the Sunday business section. "That really ignited a booster rocket under this thing," Mr. Lawrie says.

Other newspapers called to get matching stories, as did interviewers from the CBC and local television and radio stations. And, at last, clients flooded in.

Nevertheless, Mr. Lawrie worried about his acceptance by the judiciary.

"My first court appearance was in the same court I used to appear in as a witness," he recalls.

Former police colleagues were friendly but sceptical. "When the justice of the peace came in, I was really nervous, and he had a quizzical look on his face when he saw me on the other side [opposite the prosecution]," Mr. Lawrie says.

"I went through the whole thing dry-mouthed, but I won the case."

At first, Mr. Lawrie represented clients himself. But by November, he had more cases than he could handle.

From *The Lawyer's Weekly* (30 June 1989) at 17, 31. Copyright Ian McGugan. Reproduced by permission of the author.

(iv) Franchising Paralegals

The enthusiastic response convinced him he could franchise the idea to other former police officers across the country.

He established POINTTS Advisory Ltd. as the franchisor and, after selling his first franchise for $2,000 in January 1985, he appeared well on his way. First-year revenues were $36,000, and because he was working from his home, he had few expenses.

Then came an unexpected blow. The Law Society of Upper Canada accused him, early in 1985, of unlawfully acting as a barrister and solicitor.

Mr. Lawrie found himself in a legal battle he had not anticipated. He won the initial case, then had to fight on as the law society appealed to the District Court and then to the Ontario Court of Appeal. Both decided in Mr. Lawrie's favour.

The two-year battle left Mr. Lawrie with a $120,000 legal bill, but failed to stop new POINTTS offices from popping up across Ontario.

The company grew from two franchises at the end of 1985 to 14 in 1986, generating franchise fees and royalties of $160,000 — 75 per cent of which went to pay Mr. Lawrie's legal bills.

Franchises now pay $30,000–$50,000 for an outlet ($2,000–$10,000 before the Ontario Court of Appeal decision), depending on the size of their territory.

All are former police officers with at least 10 years' experience, a prerequisite Mr. Lawrie uses to market the reliability of his service.

Once in business, they pay a nine per cent royalty on gross revenues and contribute five per cent to co-operative advertising expenses.

POINTTS guarantees them exclusive rights to their franchise territory and provides start-up expertise, management advice, on-going educational seminars and a computerized accounting service.

While Mr. Lawrie declines to reveal average franchise profits, he does say "no-one is earning less than he did as a policeman." (The Ontario Provincial Police force pays $41,300 annually to constables with three years or more of experience.)

As POINTTS gained in visibility and reputation, imitators set up similar operations. To maintain his edge, Mr. Lawrie expanded.

He opened company-owned offices in Vancouver at the end of 1986 and in Alberta in May 1987. By the end of 1987, 24 POINTTS franchises raked in a total of $1.4 million in revenues and paid $200,000 in fees and royalties to their franchiser, POINTTS Advisory.

But legal societies continued to resist. In January 1988, B.C.'s law society won an injunction to close POINTTS's Vancouver office on the familiar ground that POINTTS agents were unlawfully acting as lawyers.

In Alberta, the provincial law society recently asked the attorney general to ban paralegals like POINTTS from representing drivers accused of traffic offences.

Mr. Lawrie believes he will emerge victorious in both provinces. Some members of the Alberta legislature hint that they will introduce a Bill to regulate (but not ban) paralegals, a proposal Mr. Lawrie welcomes.

Indeed, because of the standards he applies to his own franchises, POINTTS has obtained "errors and omissions" insurance — the equivalent of malpractice insurance in the medical profession — similar to that carried by lawyers.

By the end of 1988, the POINTTS network grew to 34 franchisees, who collectively made $2.5 million in revenues.

POINTTS Advisory earned fees and royalties of $340,000, but again legal costs and expenditures related to the development of the franchise network cancelled out profit.

"You have to invest a tremendous amount of time and money in making it a secure business that will be around in a few years," explains Mr. Lawrie.

"Even more so because of the natural scepticism of policemen, who come in with one eyebrow raised asking what kind of scam this guy is running."

Mr. Lawrie's battle with the Law Society of Upper Canada also continues: He is suing the society for malicious prosecution. The case is still before the courts.

POINTTS's growing ranks of competitors share Mr. Lawrie's belief that the market for traffic ticket defenders is still largely untapped, and that paralegals are here to stay.

"I think there's room for all of us," says Brian Stanley, a partner in Not Guilty, a Brampton, Ont.-based company that has been offering services similar to POINTTS's for the past two years.

"The industry is growing quickly as consumers become more aware, and it's only going to grow more in the future."

The question is how much of the market POINTTS will be able to claim.

Mr. Stanley and partner John Burd, both former police officers, give high marks to Mr. Lawrie's operation. But they rejected the idea of running a POINTTS franchise, largely because they didn't want to be limited to one franchise area.

Mr. Lawrie is counting on his company's marketing clout and size to help him fend off rivals. His current strategy emphasizes keeping ahead of the competition with aggressive expansion over the next few years through the western and Maritime provinces.

He opened a Winnipeg office in March and plans a Nova Scotia office later in the year. While the Manitoba Law Society has already made efforts to block his way, he's confident he can carry the day in court.

But one of his most significant claims to legitimacy is success. After representing more than 20,000 Ontario drivers over the past five years, POINTTS claims an impressive record.

In four out of five speeding cases, for example, the company has won an acquittal or succeeded in having the charge withdrawn or reduced.

"That's really not that surprising," says Mr. Lawrie. "There's no one who is likely to know the traffic code better than a former police officer who's had to deal with it day in and day out for years."

C. The Organization of Legal Practice

(i) Specialization and the Legal Profession

Alvin Esau

INTRODUCTION

Pressures for Change

Lawyers have often reminded themselves of the need to be responsive to changing needs in fulfilling the self-regulating mandate of the legal profession to focus on the public interest. This challenge appears to have become particularly urgent in our time as increasing pressures for change from both inside and outside the profession are converging around a number of often interrelated and difficult issues which have found their way to the top of the profession's agenda for consideration.

Informed Access to Legal Services

The increasing growth and complexity of the law in substance and range, coupled with the increasing demands made by people for participation, protection, and equal rights within the legal process has led to increasing demands for legal services. We have witnessed in response a growing emphasis on legal aid plans aimed at providing essential legal services for those who cannot afford to pay for them. The provision of legal aid is still a very live issue for the legal profession due to such continuing problems as funding and the formulation of the most appropriate form of delivery system. However, the pressure for change appears to have shifted now to the legal needs of the majority of the population, namely the middle income groups. There appears to be some evidence that the general public has difficulty knowing when a legal problem exists, or how to find a lawyer to help, and that a segment of the public fears the size of legal fees or has a general distrust or even fear of lawyers. A recent survey in the United States revealed that even though adult Americans experience an average of 3.3 "serious legal problems" during their lives, a third of the public has never used a lawyer and another 28.9% has used a lawyer only once. This survey also revealed that 79.2% of all respondents agreed that "[a] lot of people do not go to lawyers because they have no way of knowing which lawyer is competent to handle their particular problem". As well, the survey revealed that over 60% of the respondents, including both people who have used and those who have not used lawyers, thought that lawyers cost too much.

That middle income groups in Canada have difficulty making informed choices about legal services and how much they cost, given traditional professional advertising rules, was recently documented in the *Canadian Consumer*. From inside the profession, Stuart Thom, the Treasurer of the Law Society

---

(1979) 9 Man. L.J. 255 at 255–63, 265–73. Notes omitted. Reproduced by permission of the author.

of Upper Canada, confirmed that the public needs more knowledge about the availability and kinds of the legal services:

> The large corporation or institution with sophisticated personnel in charge of its affairs usually has a well-established legal connection. The average man or woman who as a rule seeks legal assistance only occasionally and for some immediate specific reason such as buying a house, because of an accident, to get a divorce, is not so equipped. The questions the occasional clients have to ask and try to get answered are "How do I get in touch with a lawyer who will do the work I want done?", "How do I know he will be any good?", "How much will he charge me?". The legal profession hasn't done much, in fact it has done very little, to help people answer these questions.

At the same time that these claims are made about unmet needs for legal services there appears to be a serious and growing problem finding articling positions and jobs for the increasing number of law school graduates. Thus pressure for change to provide better access to legal services is increased by the perception that a "job gap" should not exist when there is a "need gap" to fill.

Quality of Legal Services

Delay and neglect continue to be frequent complaints lodged against lawyers by their clients, and there is a rise in the number of successful malpractice suits against lawyers. Much of the pressure which has made the competency issue of such current concern, however, has come from within the legal fraternity itself. For example, Chief Justice Warren Burger of the United States Supreme Court has expressed the opinion on several occasions that up to one-half of the attorneys practising before the courts are incompetent as trial advocates. Professor Irving Younger, a former New York State Court judge, has stated:

> Perhaps half of the lawyers who tried cases before me showed an inadequate grasp of the law of evidence, the law of procedure, and trial technique. Some — perhaps 10% — were total strangers to those interesting subjects. The remaining 40% did not know enough about them to do a workmanlike job. Usually they stumbled through somehow — because the lawyer on the other side was just as bad, or the judge helped, or the jury managed to figure the case out despite the lawyer. This state of affairs is inexcusable.

Chief Justice Irving Kaufman of the United States Court of Appeals has stated that many attorneys lack competency as well as integrity, and one judge went so far as to say that only two percent of the lawyers appearing before him were competent.

Whether or not incompetence has reached such a [crisis] proportion can certainly be debated with regard to trial skills, and in non-trial aspects of lawyering as well, but in this period of both rapid change and increased complexity within many areas of the law, the problem of what the profession's response to the incompetency problem should be, is a current issue of utmost importance occupying a great deal of the profession's attention, not only in the United States but also in Canada.

The Delivery and Cost of Legal Services

Related to the need for informed access to quality legal services, is the issue involving the method of delivering these services and their cost. The suitability of the traditional delivery system of the sole practitioner or small law firm has been challenged by demands for prepaid and group legal services plans, by demands for special community legal clinics utilizing a high degree of standardization procedures and paraprofessional services, and by "public interest" law firms. Furthermore, demands for change in the method of delivering legal services are related to concurrent demands for change in the legal process such as legalization of certain conduct, no-fault laws, law reform proposals aimed at simplified and understandable legal forms and procedures, and the utilization of less formal mechanisms of dispute resolution.

. . . .

THE CONCEPT OF SPECIALIZATION

One of the most debated proposals aimed at responding to the challenge of providing more informed access to competently performed, efficiently delivered, reasonably priced legal services is the demand for some formal regulation of specialization within the legal profession. This paper will outline the developments on this front in the United States and Canada and raise some of the specific problems involved in the formal regulation of specialization. First, however, some comments on *de facto* specialization, and the assumed positive goals and possible negative effects of specialization must be presented as a background to understanding the developments taking place.

De Facto Specialization

Leaving aside for a moment the problems of defining what it means to be a "specialist", it is at least common knowledge within the legal profession that some lawyers only handle certain matters and not others, or spend most of their time on certain matters. It is also common knowledge in the profession that the growth of large law firms is often based on teamwork within the context of a high degree of individual specialization.

Generally, a poll of Wisconsin lawyers found that 55% of the respondents indicated that their practices were more than 50% in one given field. A random survey of 125 Toronto lawyers in 1971 found that 72% were restricting their practice and that 58% of the lawyers were spending more than 70% of their time in one field of law or spending their full time in one or two fields. On a provincial basis, the MacKinnon Committee in Ontario found that of 4,411 lawyers responding to a questionnaire in 1972, approximately 50% said they specialized rather than engaged in general practice. According to a 1969 California survey, two out of three lawyers in that State considered themselves specialists, and four out of five lawyers called themselves specialists. A 1975 Illinois State Bar Association survey found that 48% of the lawyers in that State said they engaged in specialized practice only, while 51% called themselves general practitioners who also had one or more specialties.

While surveys may not help establish the actual amount of *de facto* specialization that exists, and until there is a consensus as to what the definition of "specialization" is, one can conclude at least that many lawyers do not hold themselves out as willing to help every potential client who happens to call. Thus, the issue is not whether specialization should exist in the profession, since it already does; but rather the issue is whether it should be encouraged and formally regulated and what the approach to that regulation should be.

There are undoubtedly many factors leading to the *de facto* narrowing of legal practice. Commonly noted is that with the increasing complexity of society, there is an increasing complexity in the law and an increasing difficulty in keeping up with legal developments in many areas. Some typical expressions in favor of narrowing practice are as follows:

> If a lawyer truly tries to be proficient in a great number of fields, he must necessarily spend a fantastic number of hours in understanding those fields before he can move forward in them. When he develops a particular subject as his field, he can much more expeditiously accomplish the work to his own benefit, as well as to the benefit of his client, so that his time is utilized in the most efficient manner.
>
> Concentration of experience enables lawyers to provide better legal services in their speciality in less time with consequent savings to their clients.
>
> New developments, procedures and problems in every field of practice are generated continuously by the courts, legislatures, administrative agencies and special bar groups. Many popular and active fields of legal practice did not even exist forty years ago. The volume of current material in the form of advance sheets, services, synopses, summaries, articles, journals and the like are so numerous and voluminous that no practitioner can possibly read it all. It is unrealistic to expect any modern lawyer to stay abreast of all the developments in all the areas of law or to be competent in all fields of general practice.
>
> Since most lawyers simply cannot maintain more than a nodding acquaintance with most areas of the law, we have witnessed the growth of an informal system of legal specialization.
>
> Few practitioners today can hope, claim, or even pretend to be master of every field of the law — the day of the true general practitioner who handles every matter himself without referring to or consulting with others who have more particularized knowledge and experience is a thing of the past.

The connection between competence and specialization, then, appears to be a leading factor in the development of *de facto* specialization. Competence, furthermore, is a dimension of professional ethics, and thus to some degree *de facto* narrowing of practice is encouraged by our Code of Professional Conduct. Even the general practitioner may not be so "general" after all. Chapter II of the Code dealing with "Competency and Quality of Service" has the following rule:

> (a) The lawyer owes a duty to his client to be competent to perform the legal services which the lawyer undertakes on his behalf.
> (b) The lawyer should serve his client in a conscientious, diligent and efficient manner and he should provide a quality of service at least equal to that which lawyers generally would expect of a competent lawyer in a like situation.

The commentary after the rule includes the following provision:

> It follows that the lawyer should not undertake a matter unless he honestly believes that he is competent to handle it or that he can become

competent without undue delay, risk or expense to his client. If the lawyer proceeds on any other basis he is not being honest with his client. This is an ethical consideration and is to be distinguished from the standard of care which a court would invoke for purposes of determining negligence.

If becoming competent in a matter without undue delay, risk, or expense is an increasingly difficult problem, then one may conclude that *de facto* specialization is not only a present reality but may well substantially increase in the future.

One factor, however, which may be pointing away from a substantial increase in *de facto* specialization is the greater number of lawyers who are not able to stay with the law firms they articled in or find jobs with established law firms and thus move immediately into setting up their own independent practices, alone or in association with lawyers in the same position. This growth of independent practice by very recently licensed lawyers may lead to a greater number of general practitioners, unable economically to restrict their practices to a few fields, at least for many years. How are the Code provisions noted above accepted by these lawyers who may have a considerable lack of confidence and experience in many areas of the law, but who must nevertheless gain experience and confidence by taking cases if their independent practices are going to survive? What reforms, if any, should be undertaken by the legal profession to be fair both to young lawyers caught in a "job squeeze" and to the public who deserve high quality legal services?

Aside from the difficulty of being "omnicompetent" as one factor leading to *de facto* specialization, a variety of other factors could be cited, including a lawyer's own special interests in certain fields; or a lawyer's innate aptitude, or lack thereof, in particular skills like advocacy or negotiation; or the lawyer's sensitivity to perceived economic, political, or moral status attributed to certain kinds of firm or being employed for the particular needs of a certain group or individual, in government or industry.

The Definitional Problem

Any movement from the existence of *de facto* specialization to some formal regulation of specialization, including the provision for advertising to the public of the availability of specialists, must first deal with the fact that no consensus appears to exist as to what "specialization" really means.

. . . .

...How one chooses to define specialization — as expertise or concentration, in specialized areas or in all areas — may depend on the goal to be accomplished by the regulatory scheme.

Assumed Positive Goals of Specialization

While the existence, and perhaps increase, of *de facto* specialization may by itself further certain sought-after goals, the formal regulation of specialization may both accelerate the movement toward these goals as well as add to or modify them. At this stage, however, one must still make assumptions and speculate about the effects of formal regulation schemes because sophisticated evaluations of existing formal regulation programs have not been completed. The most recent report of the A.B.A. Committee on Specialization stated: "No data exists now, or will exist in the foreseeable future, which provides definitive answers to the access, quality and cost implications of specialization regulation." Until we have more data on the effects of formal regulation we are left with a number of assumed effects which may be considered worthwhile if achieved by regulation. These assumed effects are related directly to the demands for change cited earlier.

Improved Quality of Legal Service

The A.B.A. Committee on Specialization formulated a list of possible "pros and cons" of specialization. Of the sixteen items on the "pro" list, at least eight items related to the argument that specialization improves the quality of legal services:

1. The certified specialist will become more proficient in solving problems in his specialized field.
2. Other lawyers will become more proficient in solving legal problems.
3. The overall quality of legal services to the public will improve.
...
6. The quality of solutions to legal problems on an individual basis will improve.
7. Specialized services will be made available to the general practitioner.
...
14. Specialists will recognize a legal problem or solution overlooked by a general practitioner.
15. Law schools will be encouraged to offer in depth courses in the areas of specialization certification.
16. Because quality of legal work will be improved, there will be less load on court dockets.

How could a formal regulation scheme arguably lead to this effect of increased quality of service and competency of lawyers, individually and generally? As noted earlier, incentives to narrow practice may help lawyers to keep up with developments in their chosen areas and help lawyers gain substantial experience in certain matters which should lead to increased skill and familiarity in handling them. The primary function of a formal regulation scheme should be to encourage greater numbers of lawyers to move from generalist practice and thus generally raise the level of competence in the profession. With the advertising of the availability of specialized legal services, matters calling for special expertise will more likely be channelled away from nonspecialists to the specialists and thus these matters will be better handled and the overall quality of legal services will be higher than in the present situation where some of these matters would be handled by generalists wanting work. Setting high standards and testing for experience, skill, and knowledge as entrance requirements for the formal certification or recognition of specialists may serve to weed out those who do not deserve to be called specialists and generally encourage achievement to reach the standards set, all of which may serve to improve standards of legal practice. Furthermore, periodic mandatory recertification requirements may serve to maintain high standards of competence over time. The formal regulation of specialization may encourage development and utilization of specialized C.L.E. programs and special post-graduate university educational programs all of which would help lawyers become more competent and maintain such competency. The formal regulation of specialization may provide general practitioners with more knowledge about the availability of specialists than they now have, and thus, a greater number of referrals may result with a consequent rise in the general quality of legal service.

These propositions about increased competency depend obviously on what form the scheme of regulation would take. As well, the effects of specialization on competency must be taken together with the effects of the many other factors bearing on the competency issue.

Informed Access to Legal Services

Professor Reed, commenting on the view that formal regulation of specialization coupled with informational advertising, might increase informed rather than random access to legal services, noted that: "If I've got trouble with my head and I want to see a psychiatrist, I can find out who one is. I don't have to call some doctor and say, 'Do you know anything about psychiatry, Doctor?'" Similarly, demands for the formal regulation of specialization in California arose originally, not out of a perceived competency problem, but out of the suggestion of a Committee on Group Legal Services which urged the certification of specialists as a possible alternative or adjunct to meeting the needs of the public for informed access to legal services.

More informed access is accomplished through a formal regulation scheme providing some method whereby lawyers who meet certain standards can hold themselves out to the public as specialists in a certain field or fields of law. Again the achievement of this goal will depend on what form the specialization scheme takes, what fields of law are chosen, how many lawyers will meet the standards set or attempt to meet them and thus be able to participate in the program, how quickly the program can be implemented, and so forth.

The definitional problem of what it means to be a "specialist" may well depend on which goal is primarily pursued, increased access to legal services or increased quality. Whether the focus is, or should be primarily on access, may depend on the policies adopted or lacking regarding other factors that aim at public knowledge of the availability and kind of legal services.

Efficient Delivery and Lower Cost of Legal Services

Another assumed positive goal of the regulation of specialization is that the specialist can spend much less time on matters because the substantial experience gained by concentration should lead to increased efficiency. Decreased costs should also result because the client would not have to pay for as many research hours and perhaps in some situations with high volume, the lawyer may even have standardized procedures and paralegal services, which will lower the cost for the client. Of course, in all of this, the specialist, it is argued, will still be able to earn more than the generalist.

Public Trust and Legal Ethics Improved

Clients generally may be more satisfied with results achieved when specialists are used, so the public image of the legal profession may improve. The formulation of special standards of ethics and increased discussion of the special ethical problems encountered within certain areas of practice may lead to heightened sensitivity toward ethical dimensions of practice.

(i) Specialization and the Legal Profession

Controlled Advertising

While the formal regulation of specialization may *encourage* advertising to achieve the goal of informed access to legal services, the formal regulation of specialization may also serve to *control* advertising. If lawyers will be allowed to advertise fields of law in which they are willing to accept cases, then some formal regulation of specialization may serve to minimize the problem of misrepresentation to consumers of implied special expertise that results from such advertising in the absence of a specialization scheme. The most recent report of the A.B.A. Committee on Specialization noted that the changes made in advertising policy have resulted in an increased demand for regulation of specialization as "One step toward increasing the accuracy of information which the public and the bar will have about the lawyers who have appropriate qualifications to help with particular problems." Such regulation, of course, requires the formulation of generally accepted labels, definitions and quality standards if it is going to be successful in providing accurate information to the public. Specialization regulation might have the effect of allowing only those who are likely to be *able* to take problems in certain fields and not just *willing* to take them, to advertise such actual or implied competence.

Less "Unauthorized Practice"

The Alberta Law Society Committee reporting on specialization noted:

> If the public does not have specialist legal assistance available, there is a likelihood it will turn to other professions and groups for assistance in some fields. An example given is that a great deal of the work in tax matters formerly done by the legal profession is now done by chartered accountants. Similarly, in real estate transactions the parties may not use a lawyer at all or, at any event only in a late stage of the transaction. The specialist doing a volume of such work as a routine, can offer superior service at a lower fee.

Possible Negative Effects of Specialization

The formal regulation of specialization may be criticized without necessarily pointing to a list of possible negative effects that must be balanced against the assumed positive effects listed above. Rather the criticism can proceed by asserting that the positive effects cannot be attained by formal regulation anyway. For example, it may be argued that setting standards and testing for competency cannot achieve a measure of quality assurance because standards cannot be formulated that objectively measure competence in any case, and that furthermore, the cost to the consumer of legal services will rise with specialization, not fall.

The criticism of formal regulation might proceed as well with the assertion that the need to examine possible positive and negative effects is unnecessary because there is no public demand for specialized legal services in the first place. Those groups in need of specialized service have the legal connections to serve them in the present situation, and the public simply needs competent generalists and more information about their services. This, of course, begs the question again as to what the definition of a "specialist" should be.

If a critic, however, does accept that positive goals may be furthered by formal regulation, the argument may be made that the negative effects may outweigh the positive effects. What these negative effects are will depend on what form the regulation takes in the light of what priority of goals is emphasized and what concept of specialization is adopted.

Overspecialization Dangers

Beneath the surface of the pressures for change in the legal profession there appears to be a tension between two value clusters which might broadly be labelled "consumerism" and "humanism." While these two movements are certainly not opposing systems of thought, there are points of tension discernible between them. On one hand, the consumer movement appears to favor developments that provide legal services very much like the supply of goods in a supermarket. Standardization of forms and procedures, check-list interviews, pre-advertised fees, labelled services, and the like, are indicative of this consumer movement stressing efficiency, low cost, and accessibility. On the other hand, there is a movement, most visible in legal education, but also discernible from both within and without the profession, stressing the need for greater awareness and aptitude on the part of lawyers in handling the relational aspects of legal practice. Legal educators stress the need to be sensitive to the whole person, to see the client as a person not simply as a problem, to have greater sensitivity to the interaction of nonlegal aspects with the legal aspects of a client's problems, to be sensitive to feelings in the interviewing and counselling process, and generally to concentrate on the lawyer-client relationship rather than on commercial dimensions of law practice. These humanistic values may be difficult to pursue within the delivery systems arising out of the consumer movement.

Perhaps a third force, partly related to humanism, might be labelled "traditionalism" which views many of the proposed changes in the legal profession with scepticism. Related to both the humanistic and traditionalistic forces are criticisms of the formal regulation of specialization focusing on a series of dangers brought about by over-specialization. The bad joke is told about the old doctor who was talking to the young doctor, who was just going into a specialty. The old doctor said, "I hear you are not going to be an ear, nose, and throat doctor like your daddy. You are just going to take the nose?" "Oh no," said the young man, "just the left nostril." The legal profession has traditionally viewed itself as being the architect of democracy, a prime source of wise leadership at all levels of policy making, with the capacity for a broad vision applied to human problems. Thus, a mass movement toward narrow practice is feared by some lawyers. The following comments are indicative:

> In some ways, it seems that as we get better and better at more restricted assignments, we are valued less and less on matters of general importance.
>
> A specialist loses touch with the many problems which present themselves in the general practice of law; specialists are generally ignorant of matters outside their specialty; a narrow and confined approach to overall problems tends to hasten the disintegration of a free society which needs generalists as well as specialists; and, the well-rounded lawyer can more easily see the interrelated problems of a client and can thus better serve him.
>
> The principal and overriding defect of most certification/recognition proposals is their acceptance of the theory of *expertise*. That concept is delusive because technical experts tend to destroy the integrity of any discipline of which they are a part. In the legal profession, more likely than not, they will substitute the ways of the expert for the traditional qualities of the generalist lawyer: reflection, comprehension, discrimination, imagination, inspiration, wisdom, fortitude and tenacity.
>
> [S]pecialization, of necessity, tends to segmentize the law and, to some extent, emphasizes the mechanics of law as distinguished from a broad sense of justice acquired from familiarity with the legal problems of people of different walks of life in a variety of situations.

While some specialization of the "specialist area" or "specialist problem" variety giving rise to a number of "lawyer's lawyers" might be acceptable to these critics, any movement in the direction of full scale encouragement of narrow practice is viewed as leading to a dehumanized, less creative, overly technical profession. As one commentator, speaking about the virtues of a country lawyer, expressed it, "He will sometimes sacrifice efficiency to solve individual problems individually."

Is this just naive, romantic traditionalism or is there something here which must be taken seriously? After all, legal education continues to be based on a broad exposure to many doctrinal fields and some orientation to the "seamless web" view of law. Is it really true, however, that most general practitioners perform such a variety of work that their skill of legal analysis is particularly creative and that their understanding of legal principles is likely to be sharper than that of the lawyer concentrating on a few areas? Or is broad perspective more likely to result from a willingness to study with focused intensity the policies, practices, theories, and principles both legal and non-legal interacting on a particular area of practice? How can we have omnicompetent judges, however, if they are to be picked from a profession which will be largely specialized? Must we have a great number of specialized courts as well? Our perception of the importance of these questions may depend partly on how narrow or broad the recognized specialty fields will be. A formal regulation scheme which encourages very wide participation by formulating attainable standards, and allowing lawyers a number of specialty designations from many broadly defined fields, including perhaps even a catch-all "general practice" field, would hardly mean a mass movement away from generalist practice, even if lawyers called themselves specialists. But, how meaningful would such a scheme be? Similarly, support for such a scheme might affect our perception of the importance of possible negative effects on those who choose to remain nonspecialists.

General Practitioners May Be Hurt

The formal regulation of specialization may accelerate the movement of business from the sole practitioners and small firms to the large law firms. Even if specialists do not have a monopoly in their field, and lawyers are allowed to take on whatever they feel willing to do, in reality the market forces with formal regulation may result in an inability to practice in as broad a way as one might prefer. It has been suggested that the regulation of specialization will tend inevitably to the next step of a monopoly. Professor Mindes writes:

> The desire of specialists to distinguish themselves from other less "professional" practitioners is the key to the internal processes that lead a group to want to separate itself from the rest and also to its subsequent course after separation is achieved.

(i) Specialization and the Legal Profession

...

> A distinctive identity increases the feeling of commonality with others in the specialty and increases the psychological, social, and professional distance from other members of the bar. Contacts within the group increase, and those with other lawyers decrease. A special language develops by stages, as do special techniques and attitudes. The in-group feeling of "we" against "they" grows, and this in turn leads to more isolation of the specialty group.

Professor Mindes suggests the final step would be a monopoly by specialists of the right to practice in their area.

A formal regulation scheme may have the further effect of implying to the public that a nonspecialist is not special and therefore not competent or important, and so public confidence in the nonspecialist may fall. Furthermore, a traditional concept is that law is a "seamless web" and that problems may result from clients self-diagnosing which specialist is needed. The validity and weight of some of these criticisms may depend on how generalists are related to the specialists in a formal regulation scheme.

The problem of possible negative effects on the nonspecialist is most often countered by the argument that formal regulation schemes include provisions relating to the referral of business from nonspecialist to specialist which protect the nonspecialist. "Anti-pirating" provisions could be formulated so that the specialist would be prevented from providing services to the referred client beyond the confines of the referral. The client would still "belong," as it were, to the generalist. This argument does not of course counter the argument that many clients will, or should, self-diagnose which lawyer they need, this being part of the goal of more informed access to legal services, which may lead to a movement of business from the generalist to the specialist.

The A.B.A. Committee on Specialization in 1969 suggested that formal regulation may, nevertheless, help rather than hinder the sole practitioner or small firm to compete with the large firm:

> The most frequently voiced objection to regulation of specialization presented to our committee was its supposed harmful effect upon the sole practitioner and the small partnership in rural areas. Everyone agrees that the big firm lawyer already has the benefits of specialized practice. It was argued that large law firms in general are not adversely affected by the failure of the bar to regulate specialization, because a large law firm usually has little difficulty in making the availability of the specialized services of its individual lawyers collectively known to its prospective clients, and that regulation would only encourage clients to leave general practitioners to go to those large conglomerates of legal specialists. The committee did not accept that argument as we believe that experimentation may demonstrate that regulation of legal specialization tends to equate the sole practitioner and small law firm with the large firm in making specialized services available to their respective clients.
>
> Realistically, one of the principal reasons for the success of large law firms is that they have had no difficulty in communicating to the public that they offer specialized services, and that the collective abilities of their lawyers enable them to be specialists in every field of the law. Many lawyers argue that the official recognition of specialists would enable general practitioners more easily to obtain qualified specialists to assist them in situations where they may occasionally need such specialized legal services. Certainly, the committee believes that it would aid those lawyers in informing the public that specialized legal services can be made available by general practitioners as well as by large law firms. If experimentation does show that it enables the small practitioner more effectively to compete with the large law firms, regulated specialization may be the means whereby the ultimate survival of the independent sole practitioner is insured.

That ever present ghost of definition haunts us again with the statement made above that "specialized legal services can be made available by general practitioners."

(ii) Styles of Legal Work

Edwin M. Schur

Another avenue to an understanding of the law in action involves studying the organization and routine work patterns of the legal profession. As was mentioned earlier, some of the current sociological interest in the legal system developed out of research focused on the general analysis of occupations and professions. From this standpoint a broad array of sociological concepts may be applicable to analyzing the positions and work of the individuals who man the legal order — ranging from "professional self-image" to occupational "role set," from "recruitment" and "socialization" to colleague relationships and possible "role conflicts." Similarly, at least for other than lone practitioners, organization theory may be relevant, with such concepts as "bureaucracy," organizational "commitment," and organizational "goals" coming into play.

It has been suggested, by at least one legal critic, that research along these lines may produce an overly narrow concentration on certain small-scale and mundane aspects of the realm of law. Thus, it is argued that law is much more than simply what lawyers do and further that the lawyer's role is, in some essential aspects, not at all like other occupational and professional roles. Hazard states that "the term 'lawyer' refers less to a social function than to a type of training, a type which in fact is shared by people doing a bewildering variety of tasks." The same writer also insists that for full understanding of legal work one must recognize that with respect to any important legal problem "there is a long, a rich and a demanding intellectual culture." Certainly it is true, and most sociologists accept the fact, that lawyers operate in a great many different settings, that any conception of *the* lawyer (believed to apply to the entire profession) would be misleading. Likewise, sophisticated social analysts are aware of both the relevant heritage of legal philosophy and the significant technical formulations embodied in the legal system. Yet these factors do not vitiate an investigation of law as a profession. Such research represents one of a number of complementary, rather than mutually exclusive, approaches to the study of legal institutions. Nor is it an absolute prerequisite for such research that the sociologist have extensive training in the law. Clearly, some familiarity with legal substance and procedure will be of great help to the investigator. At the same time, it should be kept in mind that to require of the researcher lengthy formal and technical training in the discipline or occupational field to be investigated would greatly hamper sociological research in any number of fields, such as the sociology of science, of medicine, of religion, and indeed the social analysis of any occupation or profession. There is no greater need for specialized knowledge in studying the legal profession than in these other instances. Of course, a very good argument can be made for better communication and more cooperative interaction between sociologists and lawyers; cross-disciplinary team research will often provide a useful means of averting some of the problems just mentioned.

We have already seen that there is a very real social stratification within the legal profession, and that the lawyer's general standing and specific work patterns may be partly determined by his social background and type of legal education. The interplay between the numerous variables involved here is complex, but the overall relationship between recruitment and professional role is well summarized in the following statement: "Social background prescribes two major career contingencies: level of technical skill and access to clients." Whereas all lawyers theoretically share a common body of technical knowledge and special skills, as well as a dual commitment to serve the client (in a personal and confidential relationship) and the public (as "servant of the court"), in practice there is an enormous amount of variation not only in what particular types of lawyers do but also in how they relate to their clients and other individuals and agencies and in how they view their professional roles. If we examine actual work situations, a few dominant patterns emerge.

The Large Law Firm

The major law firms maintain a position of considerable power in modern American society. They

From Edwin M. Schur, *Law and Society: A Sociological View* (New York: Random House, 1968) at 163–71. Reproduced by permission of author.

wield a substantial influence in the business community and on public policy in general. Members of such firms tend to be held in high social esteem. Under these circumstances, it is probably not surprising that the large, well-established firms tend to recruit as new members individuals of relatively high socioeconomic status. Members of large firms are much more likely than are members of small firms or individual practitioners to be Protestant; to have fathers who were in business, managerial or professional positions; to have attended an Ivy League or other high-quality college; and to have attended (and done well at) one of the major, nationally known law schools or at least some other full-time, university-connected law school (as compared with nonuniversity-connected and night law schools). In particular, a man who obtains top grades (and is on the "law review," the prestigeful and influential student-edited journal) at the top, nationally known schools (primarily Harvard, Yale, and Columbia) may be "ticketed for life as a first-class passenger on the escalator for talent." As David Riesman goes on to comment, there is a "self-confirming myth" in legal education, in which the law-review men get the top jobs, make the contacts, and gain the experience necessary for advancement, and hence attain a success that "proves" that the law-school marking system (which, in the first year, determines law-review membership) is an accurate indicator of talent. At an early point in their training, such men gain a high level of confidence and the conviction that they are destined for important jobs.

This conviction is usually upheld through their work experience in the large firms. As one observer puts it, "What the Wall Street lawyers do in their professional capacity is nothing less than to provide prudential and technical assistance in the management of the private sector of the world economy." Surveys reveal significant differences in work patterns and clientele between large-firm lawyers on the one hand and small-firm members and individual practitioners on the other. The former are more likely than the latter to serve business clients (mainly large corporations in the field of heavy industry and finance) and wealthy, Protestant, individual clients, to have an overwhelming concentration of work in the areas of business and probate law, to spend much less time in court, and to deal with federal and appellate courts (rather than local ones) when such contact does occur. There is also a pronounced pattern of higher income for lawyers in the larger firms.

At the very top of the bar's status hierarchy, in the major New York firms described in Smigel's *The Wall Street Lawyer*, the lawyer deals almost exclusively with the corporate and financial problems of big business. Here too, the incoming lawyer gains membership in a substantial organization, which is impressive is its own right. He finds himself part of an establishment that may occupy three or four floors of a downtown office building and that may comprise as many as 50 to 150 lawyers and up to 250 nonprofessional staff. The firm is likely to have a long and renowned history, an atmosphere all its own, and an almost tangible aura of importance. Lawyers in the firm hold positions within a well-elaborated hierarchy — as reflected in the distribution of income and general prestige and in the allocation of status symbols, such as office space, secretaries, and so forth, and of professional tasks and responsibilities. Although the young lawyer's initial work may be of a segmental or highly specialized variety, not involving direct contact with clients and perhaps dealing with only one small facet of a broader matter, he is likely at once to be impressed by the wealth and power of the clients and the sizable nature of their business transactions. Nor is he dealt with as a mere underling. He has been hired for his demonstrated competence and his potential for leadership in the profession and in many respects he is treated as a colleague, albeit a junior one.

Work in such a setting is not, of course, without its difficulties. Some lawyers feel that the firms engender too early and too great specialization; most of the large firms have separate departments, officially or unofficially, to deal with such areas of work as corporate law, tax law, litigation, and so on. Others find troublesome the very keen competition for advancement to full partnership. Then too, some lawyers may be concerned that the work in the impersonal, bureaucratic setting seems to have little relation to the ideal of the lawyer as a "free professional," as a free-wheeling and confidential advisor to trusting clients. A few of the lawyers may even be defensive about the close ties between Wall Street firms and big business and conscious of the fact that the bulk of their work contributes little to protecting the underdog, an important theme in popular conceptions of the lawyer's role. And notwithstanding the firms' attempts to maintain a spirit of colleagueship, the fact that they are salaried employees who must in the last analysis take orders is disturbing to some. Finally, the pervasive pressures to conform — personally, socially, and even politically — may cause irritation.

For most of its members most of the time, however, the large law firm provides good earnings, excellent experience, and satisfying work. The prospect of a partnership holds out the possibility of a really sizable income combined with enormous prestige and entrée to the inner circles of the corporate and financial worlds. And for those not destined to achieve partnership, or for those who may be dissatisfied with the firm for one reason or another, there is the possibility of using their positions in the large firm as a stepping stone to other favorable situations — in industry, government, teaching, or in somewhat smaller but still very successful law firms.

INDIVIDUAL PRACTICE

Sharply contrasting with the situation of the elite, large-firm lawyer, is that of the typical individual practitioner in a large city. As we have already seen, there are significant differences between lawyers in the two types of practice, both in social background and in the kinds of work they do and the success they achieve. The lone practitioner is likely to be the son of an immigrant, who has worked his way up; he is likely to have attended either a "proprietary" or a Catholic night law school and not to have completed college, which at one time was not always a requirement for admission to such law schools. At least at the lower levels of individual practice, he is earning a precarious living, and his clientele tends to be a transient one of lower-income individuals. His legal work involves mainly small-scale and routine business matters and litigation between individuals. His contact with agencies and courts (the latter being particularly frequent) tends to be at the local level. As Jerome Carlin points out in *Lawyers on Their Own*, an important study of individual practice in Chicago, these men constitute something like a "lower class" of the metropolitan bar. Their practice consists largely of "those residual matters (and clients) that the large firms have not pre-empted" — such as matters too inconsequential (financially or otherwise) for such firms to handle, and "the undesirable cases, the dirty work, those areas of practice that have associated with them an aura of influencing and fixing and that involve arrangements with clients and others that are felt by the large firms to be professionally damaging. The latter category includes local tax, municipal, personal injury, divorce, and criminal matters."

Carlin distinguishes between upper-level and lower-level individual practitioners; the former may have a more stable and secure small-business clientele for whom they perform a wider range of less routine services. It is primarily the lower-level, solo practitioners who are bogged down in the dirty work of the law, whose financial circumstances are perilous, and for whom getting business represents a continuous battle.

At the outset, many lawyers trying to establish practices of their own are closely tied to the local neighbourhood, a situation that few find satisfactory. As a fairly successful neighbourhood practitioner told Carlin:

> People don't look at the neighbourhood lawyer as on the same professional level as the lawyer in the Loop — but on the same level as service people, real estate and insurance brokers, and similar types of nonprofessional categories. He's looked at more as a neighbourhood businessman rather than as a professional. Doctors don't have that problem; you don't consider Loop doctors to be on a completely different level.

Going beyond the neighbourhood, the solo lawyer seeks contact with potential clients through membership in a range of communal organizations, which usually have an ethnic or religious basis. Politics is also seen as a useful means of extending one's clientele, as well as developing helpful court and other official contacts. But often these methods are insufficient, and it becomes necessary to rely on individuals who, for one reason or another may be in a position to channel legal business in his direction. As Carlin notes, such a "broker" (between lawyer and client) may be "another lawyer, an accountant, a real estate or insurance broker or agent, a building contractor, a doctor, a policeman, bondsman, precinct captain, garage mechanic, minister, undertaker, plant personnel director, foreman, etc." Personal injury cases often are referred by a variety of individuals who may serve as "runners"; waitresses and bar girls may refer divorce matters, policemen criminal matters. At the same time, and especially in connection with wills, business, and real-estate matters, these lawyers face continuous and increasingly strong competition from nonlegal sources, such as banks, real-estate brokers, and accountants. These competitors often have the edge both in specialized skill and visibility; and as Carlin points out, the lawyer cannot today claim exclusive access to the agencies that process the matters in question.

Apart from the sheer difficulty of earning a decent living under these circumstances, the less successful of the individual practitioners experience a generalized and severe status dilemma. Whereas "law appeared to provide the easiest and cheapest avenue to professional status ... they find that access to the higher status positions is all but closed to them and that the positions they do manage to achieve are often marginal, their practice residual, and their foothold in the profession precarious." Not only is much of their work relatively insignificant by the dominant standards of the profession, but they have very little contact (and virtually no sense of real colleagueship) with the more successful, large-firm lawyers. Individual practitioners rarely attain positions of leadership in the bar, and in fact they are not even as likely as large-firm lawyers to maintain membership in the leading professional associations, often finding it more valuable to be active in the smaller, ethnic bar associations. While solo lawyers can at least pride themselves on being their own boss, most seem to recognize that this independence is a very mixed blessing.

Of course it must be kept in mind that the "Wall Street lawyer" and the lower-level individual practitioner represent the extreme points of a continuum along which legal practices vary. In between are numerous gradations involving membership in a variety of middle-sized and small firms, many of which are very successful and handle a considerable range of interesting legal work. Also, it should be noted that there certainly are some individuals who practice on their own and attain a high degree of success, both financially and in terms of professional standing. This attainment may occur particularly when a lawyer develops a reputation for great skill in a highly specialized field, such as patent law, literary property, civil liberties, or even matrimonial or criminal law. Indeed, all of the comments made thus far concerning stratification within the metropolitan bar must be recognized as reflecting statistical regularities only. They refer to large classes of individual instances, and to each generalization there are undoubtedly specific exceptions.

Furthermore, the major studies of legal practice have concentrated almost exclusively on lawyers in the largest metropolitan centers. As Carlin mentions, "In comparison with the highly stratified metropolitan bar, the smaller city bar has over the years remained a fairly homogeneous professional community." Attributing this homogeneity partly to the absence of huge "law factories," he noted that (in 1958) there were no firms with as many as fifteen lawyers in American cities of less than 200,000 population, and very few with more than five or six lawyers. Similarly, there has been virtually no sociological analysis of the position and functions of the small-town lawyer. Legal practice in such a setting undoubtedly varies a good deal from that of the lone practitioner in the metropolis. It is quite possible that some lawyers in small towns may be able satisfactorily to combine the independence of individual practice with a considerable measure of financial success and professional and social standing within the local community. Other varieties of legal work — including positions in government agencies, in prosecutor's and legal-aid offices, and as "house-counsel" on corporation staffs — also deserve further attention from researchers. Undoubtedly each type of legal practice has its peculiar recruitment and work patterns, compensations, drawbacks, strains, and dilemmas.

(iii) Law Firm Mergers: A Case of Greed or Survival?

Kirk Makin

The once-genteel pursuit of the law is running smack into the realities of the late twentieth century. Unbridled competition, globalization and the cult of greed have changed the face of law firms — and of the lawyers who work in them.

Professional courtesy and camaraderie are failing. Raiding and merger mania are replacing the old, relaxed atmosphere that was borne of a steady, reliable clientele.

"More than ever before, lawyers are working harder, getting richer, and enjoying it less," says Toronto lawyer Morris Gross. "I think the senior people in the profession have not done enough about it. You get lots of talk about fancy hardware or saving time and making money. But nobody is saying: 'What are we doing to ourselves?'"

The most dramatic sign is growth. Across the civil law landscape, firms are expanding almost

From *The Globe and Mail* (5 May 1990) at D1, D8. Reproduced by permission of The Globe and Mail.

uncontrollably. Suddenly, mega-firms dot the downtown centres. A significant proportion of the country's medium-sized firms — those with 10 to 70 lawyers — are gone.

"It is happening at a pace we cannot even keep track of," said Gerald Riskin, vice-president of Edmonton's Edge Consulting Associates.

The overhead for medium firms has proven too great and their range of services too limited to attract large clients. The result is the death of the firm or a merger into a mega-firm — usually involving 200 to 500 lawyers whose work is largely directed by rather anonymous management committees. Colleagues in the same firm barely recognize one another in the hallways.

"They have gotten bigger and they have gotten worse," said Mr. Gross, a senior partner in a mid-sized firm determined to survive. He said that mid-sized firms are obligated to find "niches" in which they can specialize.

Even large and venerable old firms such as Toronto's McCarthy and McCarthy have been erased by merger. The hybrid of that merger, McCarthy and Tetrault, had 450 lawyers. Fasken Martineau Walker is Canada's largest firm — for the moment. It boasts 480 lawyers. Yet even these numbers appear modest next to the granddaddy of United States firms — 1,200-lawyer Baker & McKenzie.

Most self-respecting mega-firms now have branches not only in large Canadian cities, but also in New York and London. One has expanded into Moscow. The reasons [is] that they need this enhanced flexibility to offer clients a full range of services. However, Mr. Riskin says many are doing it for strictly "defensive purposes."

The firms live in constant fear of being eclipsed. "People get worried that if you do not follow along in expanding and growing, you will be seen as lagging behind other firms," said a partner in a mega-firm.

But there is a logic behind the fear. There is an increasing need to offer clients all services under one roof. These services might include active litigation and advice on taxation, real estate, competition law.

To be sure, the pool of clients is shrinking. More corporations are creating their own in-house counsel departments to deal with their legal needs. Para-legals and no-fault insurance schemes have also carved away some of their terrain.

Indeed, many observers think a vicious shakedown is bound to occur eventually, leaving a Big Eight of mega-firms.

Patrick McKenna, president of Edge Consulting, said the trend will only get worse. "Our fear is others may see it as a bandwagon to gang onto and that they are like sheep — following in the same footsteps without a client base to follow," he said.

Mega-firms are competing feverishly for clients with deep pockets. They compete just as hard when it comes to stocking their firms with fresh talent. Raiding has come into vogue, either directly or through head hunters. By attracting a leading light in a particular field of law, a firm can quickly become known as a specialist in that field.

There are about 37,000 lawyers in Canada. Still, firms compete furiously for the best young prospects coming out of law school. Like college athletes, the students are wooed and drafted before they can explain the difference between a tort and a torte.

The human factor is the great unknown in this rapid growth — from the perspective of both the client and the employee. Clients of large firms may feel they are being served by an anonymous monolith. They inevitably get less personal attention from senior partners.

Corporate clients may also become leery of going to a firm so large that it probably represents competitors.

The cost can be just as high on the other end — within the merging firms. "There is a cultural clash when two firms of professionals operate in very different ways," Mr. McKenna said. "Not everyone is willing to go along with the impersonalization of these large firms."

It all adds up to a profession-wide identity crisis. At law conferences and in the pages of legal journals, one frequently runs into lawyers anguishing over the evolution of law from a calling to a cold-hearted, isolated business. Have they become overwhelmed by the "greed is good credo" that has swept other areas of business? Are they being carried along by forces beyond their control?

"I prefer to call it something other than greed," Mr. Gross said. "I think there is a status in making $350,000 per year. It filters down from the top. If you are a senior lawyer not making $350,000, you are made to feel somewhat inadequate."

The money and status-seeking leave them vulnerable to raiding. "You make them offers they simply can't refuse," Mr. Gross said.

A junior member of a large firm who asked for anonymity said: "More and more, the legal profession has become a competitive and cutthroat business. You have to spend more time on marketing and generating business than on practising law. The pressure is on to prove you can generate business for yourself and others in the firm."

The lawyer said that subtle pressure is usually applied to get lawyers in a firm to join business clubs, lunch with clients frequently, teach, and speak in seminars to get their names in front of the public.

In some firms, lawyers are expected to tabulate the time they spend on glad-handing. Their salaries may be docked if they do not do enough.

The supersonic pace is not appealing to everyone. Some fresh-faced young lawyers are burning out before they are 30, worn down by disillusionment, ridiculous demands and working hours. "We are finding that in the last year or two, some of the most promising lawyers have woken up and said: 'Gee, is this what I fought to get into law school for? I am just not going to sell my soul,'" said Mr. Gross.

In a recent paper prepared for the Canadian Bar Association (Ontario), lawyers Ronald Manes and Valerie Edwards spoke of this fear. Many lawyers practise in "a climate of anxiety," they said, worrying about making a costly mistake, losing an important client, being embarrassed in court, not being able to make ends meet "and, most ominously, about losing control and no longer being able to cope."

The starkest evidence of this is the sensitive issue of billable hours — the accumulation of work hours for which a client can actually be billed an hourly fee.

At some firms, each lawyer's billable hours are posted at the end of the month. "At the end of the year, you find out what everyone else made, which puts even greater pressure on you," said one lawyer.

Mr. Gross tells of a young lawyer at a megafirm who had not been home for a weekday dinner in two years. His wife was distraught. Mr. Gross went to a senior partner he knew at the firm to suggest something was wrong. "His response was: 'What's wrong with that? If you want to make megabucks, the only way to do it is to put in megahours.'" He was, I think, rather proud of it.

"They are all aping what has gone on in New York," said Mr. Gross. "A few years ago in New York, they had 1,500 hours and people thought that was terrible. Now they have 2,500 hours and people think that is insanity."

"Large Toronto firms are making it clear that if you are not doing 2,000 hours, you are not going to make it here. This is an absolute outrage. You cannot do that without giving up a major portion of your private life."

In the past year, Canadian Bar Association President John Jennings and Supreme Court of Canada Judge John Sopinka have both publicly deplored the profession's obsession with increasing billable hours.

Mr. Justice Sopinka said many firms think nothing of demanding their lawyers work up to 10 hours a day, six days a week for 48 weeks of the year.

"I think it's time to send a warning," Mr. Jennings said in a speech. "I think the pressure of the bottom line has made us become legal technicians. The bottom line: how we worship it, how we pamper it, how we follow its every wish, its every demand, no matter how irrational or how unhealthy."

The concept of billable hours recognizes little but the ability to make money. It may actually discourage technological efficiency, experience and thoughtfulness. Indeed, some lawyers think straight fees per transaction or contingency fees will eventually replace the increasingly-ridiculous billing system.

(iv) Societies Keep Legal Ads' Volume Turned Low

Margot Gibb-Clark

On the heels of a B.C. decision to forbid ads suggesting lawyers are aggressive, Ontario has rebuffed attempts to strike down a ban on those comparing prices or services.

"Lawyer will do deal for 10 per cent less than the competition."

That's the kind of advertising you rarely see in Canada's conservative legal industry, although many consumers would welcome it.

From *The Globe and Mail* (29 May 2000) M1. Reproduced with permission from The Globe and Mail.

In Ontario, where comparative ads are banned, some senior lawyers think they would be a popular innovation.

Consumers should get this kind of information to help them make choices, says Gavin MacKenzie, co-chairman of a task force that has just spent two years re-examining all the rules governing Ontario lawyers.

Across the country, legal regulators are wrestling with changes in their industry that are putting pressure on traditional advertising constraints.

Law firms face new competitors in accounting outfits and paralegals. Clients are also changing, becoming more educated or more sophisticated. What's considered acceptable in advertising is shifting.

But many lawyers are resisting these changes, saying that law is a profession first and a business second. And they are still carrying the day. British Columbia decided recently to forbid ads suggesting lawyers are aggressive.

Ontario tried to allow ads comparing prices or services, but the attempt ran off the rails late last week at a meeting of the Law Society of Upper Canada.

The law society had figured it was time to reconsider its ban on comparative ads. It is anachronistic and was enacted more for the benefit of lawyers than of the public, says Mr. MacKenzie, one of about 40 benchers elected to govern Ontario lawyers. "It's a relic of a guild mentality."

In the B.C. debate over aggressive advertising, industry officials weren't reacting to any particular ad, says B.C. Law Society president Karl Warner. However, Vancouver lawyer Ted Ewachniuk did once use grizzly bear images in his marketing. The lawyer proudly refers to himself as "Go-For-The-Throat Ewachniuk."

"Most benchers were of the view that baring the teeth does nothing to engender resolution of a dispute," Mr. Warner says.

The rule on aggressiveness grew out of discussion in an ethics committee about what was acceptable for a lawyer to say in testimonials, he says.

Another B.C. lawyer, Lawrence Pierce, says ads calling him aggressive and tenacious actually quoted a Supreme Court of British Columbia registrar's ruling. "I see that as a major challenge to my right to free speech," the personal injury lawyer said in an interview.

In Ontario, the task force's comparative-pricing proposal drew a flood of letters from other lawyers who thought it was a bad idea. Most of the letter-writers were lawyers practicing real estate law.

"Comparison advertising is the dirtiest and most negative form of advertising in the marketplace today," said one letter from Alan Silverstein of Concord, Ont.

"It pits an aggressive firm [likely with deep pockets] against an innocent victim, whose only crime is to charge a different price than its competitor. Comparison advertising also assumes the identical product is being marketed — apples and apples, not apples and oranges."

Changing the rule would lead to an explosion of tacky advertising and further tarnish lawyers' collective image, another letter argued.

Bob Aaron, president of the Ontario Real Estate Lawyers Association and himself a law society bencher, had sparked the controversy by sending a letter to the 1,400 members of his group. He said that if the change were allowed, it would encourage deep price cutting and discourage lawyers from providing quality services.

Residential real estate deals are the bread and butter of small law practices. It is also an area where clients tend to pay more attention to price than to the quality of services offered, lawyers say.

Fierce competition in recent years from firms who use law clerks to do much of their work has led to heavy fee-chopping. "I'm now charging 25 per cent less than I did in 1988 for the same work or more work," Mr. Aaron said in an interview.

Toronto criminal lawyer Paul Copeland doesn't think that's always a bad idea. "My view is that it's in the public interest to have lower legal fees," he says. "Some lawyers make far too much. Fees of $500 an hour are sort of obscene — though people do pay them."

That's true, retorts Brad Wright, who has a general solicitor's practice in Nepean, Ont., but they are the tiny minority in the profession. "Most of our [firm's] bills are in the range of hundreds of dollars. It's the rare account that exceeds $1,000."

Craig Carter, a lawyer with a big Toronto firm and head of the Canadian Bar Association's real estate section, says "competition is good, but there comes a point when it has to erode the quality of service or drive people out of the business."

The issue provoked lively discussion at a meeting of Ontario benchers last week. "I don't want this to be seen as a real estate issue," Mr. Aaron told his colleagues. "It is profession-wide issue." It would affect lawyers with family law and criminal practices and probably most small firms outside the cities, he said.

The current rule allowing lawyers to advertise their own prices or services was fine, he said, "but don't say you're cheaper than Torys or better than Fasken." That would destroy the image of the legal profession within six months, he predicted.

It could also force lawyers to make promises they may not be able to keep, said Todd Ducharme of Toronto. Criminal or family law clients are often unsophisticated and, in such emotionally charged situations, it is unfair to ask them to judge comparative advertising, he said.

Well-known libel lawyer Julian Porter supported Mr. Aaron. Allowing comparative ads would be too great a risk, he said. For one thing, it would be almost impossible for the law society — which regulates members' behaviour — to effectively prosecute improper price comparisons. "We'll have a slew of cases that don't work."

Late Thursday afternoon, the 28 benchers who remained after a long day's meeting voted down the idea of allowing comparative ads. Only Mr. MacKenzie and Mr. Copeland were in favour. Two abstained.

So consumers will have to continue doing their own research on prices and services.

(v) Turning Lawyers into Gamblers Is a Bad Bet

Alan Hutchinson

The Ontario government is floating plans to bring lawyers' contingency fees to the province. While some say this will unleash the full venality of U.S.-style law practice on Canada, others argue the move will improve people's access to justice without committing more public money to lawyers' pockets. In fact, Queen's Park's [plan] to introduce contingency fees is just a case of whistling in the face of the gale. If the government wants to make real progress on improving access to justice, it should tackle the real problems — clogged courts, high legal fees, and monopolistic legal services, to mention a few. Contingency fees are not only potentially problematic, they're as likely to benefit lawyers as citizens.

Contingency fees are an arrangement between lawyers and their clients, usually plaintiffs, that the lawyer will not charge a fee unless the legal action is successful — in which case, the lawyers will receive a percentage of the proceeds, typically 33 per cent, as their fee. The basic dynamic is that, for carrying the risk of receiving no fee, lawyers should get a bonus if they succeed. Because the lawyers are financially implicated, the argument is that they will work harder and produce larger returns for their client, without involving public funding.

Such contingency-fee arrangements for litigation are currently illegal in Ontario (except in recently introduced class actions); the old offences of maintenance and champerty (fancy words for having a stake in the outcome of litigation) remain Ontario law. The tradition behind this principle was that it is improper for lawyers or any other persons to "gamble" on the outcome of a case lest it cloud legal judgment and lead to ethical improprieties — that is, if a lawyer suspected a strong case would require minimum work, she might tell a client that it was labour-intensive to justify her high percentage. Queen's Park seems to have overcome such scruples.

There are two major reasons why Queen's Park's latest innovation is more about show than go. First, the rest of Canada has had contingency fees for quite a while. Not only has U.S.-style law practice not taken hold, the problems of poor clients gaining access to justice remain largely unimproved. Aggressive lawyering is as much cultural as it is rule-based. Ontario lawyers still like to pretend theirs is a vocation rather than a business. And even though there has been a greater appetite for legal sport in recent years, Canadians are simply not as litigious as Americans. Second, contingency fees already exist in fact. It's estimated that, in about two-thirds of personal injury cases, lawyers only get paid if they win; that's because it's difficult to expect a grievously injured plaintiff to bear the further financial burden of a losing lawsuit. After all, the reason the plaintiffs are suing in the first place is because they have little or no money to deal with the tragedy that has

From *The Globe and Mail* (7 June 2000) A13. Reproduced by permission of the author.

befallen them. Lawyers, therefore, are already making economic calculations about risk and reward in deciding what claims to pursue and which clients to represent. There's no reason to believe that the hope of fat contingency fees would prompt lawyers to take greater risks on weak cases than they do now.

Still, whatever the dubious ethics of contingency fees, there is little to recommend the current situation in which lawyers are paid win or lose. It creates little incentive for lawyers to refuse weak cases or end them quickly. For many poor plaintiffs, contingency fees will be welcomed, as it will mean they get more opportunity to obtain legal services.

The problem is not so much with contingency fees themselves as their scope for abuse. Much will depend on the kind of regulation, if any, that is introduced. Instead of allowing lawyers to dictate their own terms, it would be better to set limits on the percentage they can charge — say, a fifth to a quarter of the total settlement (U.S. lawyers sometimes go as high as 40 per cent). Or we could require some general correlation between the work done and the fee received. In this way, it might be possible to balance the stark imbalance of power between lawyers and those less-advantaged clients who probably will enter into such arrangements. Nova Scotia has struck such a compromise.

Many believe that the real reasons certain kinds of worthy claims are discouraged in Ontario is the way the province's legal system allocates costs. Winners receive a large part of their costs from losers — which means that losers must not only pay their own lawyers' bill, but a large part of their opponents' lawyers' bill (half to two-thirds). This, of course, is a massive disincentive for people deciding whether to sue. Even under a contingency fee arrangement, a losing party will still have to pay some share of the winner's costs.

It's estimated that on a claim for $30,000 (with legal costs for each side running at a conservative $10,000 each), a plaintiff stands to gain no more than about $26,000 if he or she wins (the $30,000 claim minus $4,000 for the share of the plaintiff's lawyer's outstanding bill) and, if he or she loses, be in the hole for more than $16,000 (the plaintiff's own costs and a significant share of the winning party's bill). In the hope that the plaintiff may take home $26,000, he or she must be prepared to lose another $16,000 on top of the $30,000 that may not be recovered.

In such circumstances, it is not surprising that many people settle for much less than they might otherwise be entitled to or simply walk away altogether. On the other hand, some defendants are leveraged in to settling cases for much more than they feel the claim is worth to avoid the Draconian sanctions of losing the case. Either way, litigation is less about substantive justice and more about raw economics. And one in which lawyers tend to be too often the real winners.

The introduction of contingency fees is a no-cost (and a likely no-change) strategy for the provincial government. But if Queen's Park is serious about improving access to justice, it must tackle deeper causes. If it were to do so seriously, it would need to revitalize legal aid, or preferably to get a handle on lawyers' fees; this might involve confronting the Law Society's monopoly over the admission and regulation of lawyers. Any of these reforms are highly unlikely in today's political climate. But until they take place, the government would do well to look at the whole regime for fixing costs in civil litigation.

D. Juries

(i) Justice and the Jury

W. Neil Brooks and Anthony N. Doob

The jury has been described as serving one of two separate functions. It can be seen as an institution designed to ensure the accuracy of fact finding in the adjudication of disputes,

---

(1975) 31 *Journal of Social Issues* at 171–82. Notes/References omitted. Reproduced by permission of Blackwell Publishers.

(i) Justice and the Jury

applying to the facts of the dispute the law as given by the judge; or it can be seen as an institution which has the right to construe or ignore a relevant rule of law in a case in which its application would not be in accord with the notions of justice and fairness prevailing in the community. After a short review of some of the views taken on each of these sides, we consider the kinds of extra-legal factors that appear to influence jury decisions.

An important function of the legal process is settling controversies by adjudicating competing claims. Characteristically, judicial dispute resolution involves the application of a relevant and fixed rule of law to the factual conflict situation that is found to exist between two contesting parties. To be an effective means of social ordering in a democratic society the application of rules of law must obviously result in decisions that are morally acceptable to the community at large. That is to say, the outcome of adjudication must correspond with shared notions of what is equitable and fair between the parties to the dispute, whether one party is the state and the other a private person, or whether both are private parties.

Rules of law, however, have another important function. They permit social intercourse by serving as guidelines on the basis of which people may plan their affairs, knowing the consequence of different courses of action. To achieve this purpose, rules of law must be formulated at a level of generality that permits each rule to govern the consequence of recurrent factual situations. The necessity on the one hand for general fixed rules of law to regulate social action and the necessity on the other hand for rules that will result in the just resolution of all disputes poses a dilemma for the legal system. A general rule can be formulated that guides behavior and that results in the just resolution of most disputes controlled by it. However, a fact situation will inevitably arise in which, because of the particular equities between the parties to the dispute, a disposition of the case in accord with the relevant rule of law will result in an outcome that does not correspond with the community's notion of fairness, since a judge's decision in a particular case gives rise to a precedent that controls the disposition of all similar cases. Attempts by judges to interpret a general rule of law to reach a just decision in a case in which the equities between the parties are peculiar might cause injustices in future cases: "Hard cases make bad law" is a well known legal adage. A judicial institution that is capable, at least in theory, of resolving the tension between the need for general rules of law and the need to resolve each dispute equitably is the jury.

The proper role of the jury has been the subject of extended and often vigorous debate in legal and political literature. The jury may be seen and defended as fundamentally a political institution which has the right to construe or ignore a relevant rule of law in a case in which its application would not be in accord with the notions of justice and fairness prevailing in the community. This view has been advocated by a number of eminent legal scholars.

Wigmore, the great evidence scholar, urged that the jury's role was to supply "that flexibility of legal rules which is essential to justice and popular contentment" (1929, p. 170). Justice Holmes suggested:

> One reason why I believe in our practice of leaving questions of negligence to the jury is that jurors will introduce into their verdict a certain amount — a very large amount, so far as I have observed — of popular prejudice, and thus keep the administration of the law in accord with the wishes and feelings of the community. (1889, pp. 459–460)

Dean Pound noted that "Jury lawlessness is the great corrective of law in its actual administration" (1910, p. 36). As stated in a Columbia Law Review paper: "Respect for the law is increased when law operates with scrupulous firmness, but with the leaven of charity that is added when the jury acts as the conscience of the community" ("Trial by Jury," 1969, p. 471). The relative importance that is often placed on the jury's role in construing the law in a particular case is illustrated by a statement made in 1789 by Thomas Jefferson: "Were I called upon to decide whether the people had best be omitted in the legislative or judicial departments, I would say it is better to leave them out of the legislative. The execution of the laws is more important than the making of them" (cited in Howe, 1939). Indeed Lord Devlin went so far as to declare: "Each jury is a little parliament. The jury sense is the parliamentary sense" (1956, p. 114).

On the other hand, the jury may be viewed simply as an institution designed to ensure the accuracy of fact finding in the adjudication of disputes, its task being to apply to the facts of the dispute before it, as the jurors find them, the law as given to them by the judge in his instructions. If the general rule of law they are asked to apply appears to result in a harsh or unjust decision in the particular case, that is of no consequence to them in reaching their verdict. Indeed the United States Supreme Court in a case in 1895 (*Sparf & Hansen v. United States*) expressly held that the jury was bound to follow the judge's instructions on the law. The court reasoned that certainty and uniformity in the application of the law was more important than flexibility in individual cases.

Throughout history the legal system has been ambivalent about which of these two roles the jury should assume. When jury trials first emerged in England in the twelfth century, juries were required to apply the law to the facts of the dispute, of which they were assumed to have personal knowledge. If a jury returned a verdict that was found to be wrong they were subject to punishment (Thayer, 1898). However, by the seventeenth century the prevailing view appeared to be that the jury could consider in reaching their verdict the peculiar equities in the case before them. Lord Hale, discussing the function of the jury in 1665, stated, "It is the conscience of the jury that must pronounce the prisoner guilty or not guilty" (cited in Scheflin, 1972). Five years later the judges in Bushnell's Case (1670) held that there was no recourse against the jury for acquitting a person even though the judge or a subsequent jury concluded that the jury's decision was not decided according to the law. Even though it was taken as established that the jury was not accountable for its verdict, and that a verdict of acquittal by the jury was final, several American judges in the middle and late nineteenth century returned to the theoretical position that the jury's only role was to determine the propositions of fact in dispute. The jury, they argued, had no right to refuse to apply the strict letter of the law. These cases are discussed in Howe (1939), in the Yale Law Journal ("The Changing Role," 1964) and in Scheflin (1972). Within the past five years, however, there appears to have been a return to the common law position of the sixteenth century. The decisions in a number of cases, including several Supreme Court of United States decisions have assumed, and several judges have noted, that an important function of the jury is to consider the conscience of the community in reaching its verdict ("Trial by Jury," 1969).

In two states, Indiana and Maryland, the jury's right to nullify the law is given constitutional status, and juries in those states are instructed that they may ignore the strict application of the law. The state of Kansas was considering a constitutional amendment requiring that the following instruction be given to juries:

> It is difficult to draft legal statements that are so exact that they are right for all conceivable circumstances. Accordingly, you are entitled to act upon your conscientious feelings about what is a fair result in this case. (Scheflin, 1972, p. 206)

Whatever role the jury has in theory, in practice it is clear that the jury can ignore the strict application of the law and respond to the unique aspects of each case that comes before it. The jury deliberates in secrecy, they do not give reasons for their verdict, they are in no way accountable for their verdict, their decisions do not establish a precedent that is binding on future cases, and in criminal cases if the jury acquits the accused their decision is final. Indeed the jury's right to determine the facts gives them an almost unlimited discretion in returning whatever verdict they choose. As chief Justice Hughes (cited in Broeder, 1954) in 1931 remarked, "An unscrupulous administrator might be tempted to say, 'Let me find the facts for the people of my country and I care little who lays down the general principles'." Lord Devlin has observed, "I do not mean that they [the jury] often deliberately disregard the law. But if they think it is too stringent, they sometimes take a merciful view of the facts" (1959, p. 21). Indeed the jury's power to ignore the strict application of a relevant rule of law in itself has been construed as the right to do so in certain cases (Kadish and Kadish, 1971).

The jury's right to ignore the law may be supported as an effective means of protecting individuals from the oppressive or unjust use of governmental power. However, whether the rules controlling the jury should permit it wide latitude in deciding a particular case, or indeed if we should retain the jury, because of the need for the exercise of an equitable jurisdiction to mitigate rigid rules in particular cases, depends upon how the jury exercises that function. This empirical question is of overriding importance in the debate on the jury in general. Kalven, coauthor of one of the most definitive studies done to date on the jury, has remarked, "Debate about the merits of the jury system should center far more on the value and propriety of the jury's sense of equity, of its modest war with the law, than on its sheer competence" (1964, p. 1702).

Those who oppose the jury on the ground that it is lawless contend that the jury exercises its "equitable" jurisdiction on the basis of prejudices and biases, such as race or physical attractiveness, that are not in accord with acceptable community notions of equity. They argue that jury verdicts result not only in a lack of uniformity in the law but also in malicious decisions and invidious discrimination (Frank, 1949). Those who support the jury and the exercise by it of an equitable jurisdiction, argue that the extra-legal factors that might influence it in reaching its verdict are factors that should be considered by a rational decision maker in reaching a just decision.

Studies of Jury Decision-Making

A few years ago if disputants over the jury were to join on this issue their supporting arguments could only be based on conjecture and isolated personal experiences. In 1954 Broeder observed with respect to the jury's law dispensing function that "we do not know how well it works; the verdict is a seal of secrecy which the law has thus far refused to open" (p. 412). Although the jury's deliberations are still shrouded in secrecy, the use of various methods of empirical research has yielded some data on the extra-legal variables that influence the jury's decision-making process. These studies permit us to draw some tentative conclusions about the basis upon which the jury exercises its equitable jurisdiction.

In the remainder of this paper we will review a few recent studies which illustrate the kinds of extra-legal factors that appear to influence jury decisions. Even this impressionistic review should reveal the direction in which the jury appears to exercise its equitable jurisdiction and thus enable us to draw a tentative conclusion about whether it is a useful social institution for imparting justice into one aspect of societal decision making. But more importantly, it will hopefully illustrate the importance of research on jury decision-making in studying the justice motive (Lerner, 1970; Mysliwiec, 1974).

Common experience suggests that the jury's verdict is likely to be influenced by the personal characteristics of the parties in the dispute, such as their physical attractiveness, character, and race. Empirical studies tend to confirm this commonsense judgment. Efran (1974) found that when subjects were asked to judge a student who was accused of cheating, physically attractive defendants were less likely to be seen as guilty than were unattractive defendants. In this case, attractiveness was manipulated by giving subjects a picture of the hypothetical defendant, one group receiving a photo of an attractive person, the other receiving a photo of an unattractive person. Efran found that students drawn from a similar population generally reported that they did not feel that the defendant's physical attractiveness should influence such decisions. This same bias in favor of physically attractive persons was reflected in a study done by Dion (1972). She found that a transgression by an unattractive child was seen by adults as more serious than was an identical transgression committed by an attractive child.

The attractiveness of a person's personality also affects decisions made by laymen about another's culpability. In a jury simulation experiment, Landy and Aronson (1969) found that on a charge of causing death by criminal negligence the jury recommended a shorter prison term for a defendant who was described as being happily married, regularly employed, and friendly with everyone than they did for a person described as being a janitor, a two-time divorcé, and an ex-convict. Although this was a study in which the simulated jurors were asked to give a judgment about sentencing, it seems likely that the jurors would also consider such facts in deciding on the guilt or innocence of the defendant. Indeed, in view of the danger that if the jury hears about the "bad" character of the accused they might be less careful about determining the certainty of his guilt before convicting, the law tries to keep this information from them. In no Anglo-American jurisdiction can evidence of the accused's bad character be led by the prosecution for the purpose of tending to prove that the accused committed the crime with which he is charged, even though it is sometimes undoubtedly relevant for that purpose.

In apparent conflict with the concern reflected by this rule is the rule whereby if an accused takes the witness stand in his own defense, evidence of his previous criminal convictions can be led by the prosecution. In such a situation, the judge must instruct the jury that this evidence of bad character can be used by them only in evaluating the accused's credibility as a witness. The jury must expressly be told not to infer from the criminal record that the accused is a bad person and therefore is more likely to have committed the crime with which he is charged. Simulations (Doob and Kirshenbaum, 1972; Hans, 1974) and correlational findings from reports of cases (Kalven and Zeisel, 1966) support the conclusion that such instruction is futile. An accused person with previous criminal convictions stands a much greater chance of being convicted of a crime than does a person with no such history.

Race is another personal characteristic that in some jurisdictions has clearly influenced juries in reaching their verdicts. Studies have demonstrated that it is a factor taken into account by the jury in the sentencing process (Bullock, 1961; Thornberry, 1973), and interviews with actual jurors reveal that it is a recurrent topic of conversation throughout their deliberations (Broeder, 1965a).

In criminal cases, the personal characteristics of the victim as well as the accused appear to influence the jury in reaching their verdict. Brooks, Doob, and Kirshenbaum (Note 1), in a jury simulation of a rape case, showed that jurors thought that it was less justified to convict a man of raping a woman who had a history of prostitution than it was to convict a man (on identical evidence) of raping a woman of chaste character. There was no evidence whatsoever that people thought that the defendant who was accused of raping the prostitute was less likely to have done it; rather it seemed that they simply felt that, given the amount of evidence that existed and the circumstances surrounding the rape, the person ought not to be convicted if the victim were "only" a prostitute. Similarly, Landy and Aronson (1969) found that people recommended longer sentences for someone who had been found guilty of killing (through criminal negligence) a "good" person than they did if the victim were a "bad" person.

The consequence of their decision, although in law irrelevant, is another factor which the jury considers in doing individual justice. In a criminal case, the consequence might be that the defendant will be incarcerated as a result of the decision or, in a few cases, could be executed. Vidmar (1972) and Hester and Smith (1973) have both shown that these consequences do indeed affect jury decision making. Where a jury sees that a consequence might be very severe, they seem less likely to come to a decision that might lead to such a severe result. Similarly, in civil actions the relative ability of the parties to absorb a financial loss is considered by the jury. In cases in which a simulated jury was told that the defendant had liability insurance, the average damages awarded rose considerably. Correspondingly, the jury takes into account any collateral benefits mitigating the loss (Kalven, 1958).

A study based on personal interviews with actual jurors about the deliberation in the jury room revealed that in a civil suit the plaintiff's family responsibilities influenced the jury both in finding liability and in awarding damages (Broeder, 1965b). The government of the province of Prince Edward Island, sensitive to the "deep pocket" philosophy sometimes adopted by jurors in doing individual justice, has recently moved to abolish the jury in civil suits where the government is the defendant (Charlottetown *Guardian*, 1973).

In criminal cases such as assault or various sexual offences, the victim though legally blameless may be partially responsible for the criminal act. The jury, however, is likely to consider the whole situation surrounding the particular crime in coming to a "just" (though not strictly legal) decision. Kalven and Zeisel (1966) found that in cases in which there was some degree of victim precipitation the jury was less likely to convict the accused or at least more likely to convict him of a lesser offense. In the past, a similar result was often revealed by juries in civil cases. Until recently, in many jurisdictions, if the plaintiff contributed to an accident to any degree, he was completely barred from any recovery no matter how negligent the defendant had been in causing the damages. In such cases, rather than bar the plaintiff completely, the jury would take a "merciful view of the facts," and adjust the size of their verdict to correspond to the comparative negligence of the parties (Ulman, 1933).

Kalven and Zeisel (1966) also cite a number of cases where the jury seemed to acquit the defendant because he had suffered enough, even though he might technically be guilty. Thus, for example, it would seem that a jury is less likely to convict a man on a charge of causing death by criminal negligence when it was the defendant's wife who was killed (through his negligence) and the defendant himself was permanently and totally paralyzed in the accident.

Finally, in criminal cases, although only the accused is on trial, the jury in reaching a decision appears to consider whether the state "deserves" to win. If the police have used grossly unfair methods in obtaining evidence against the accused, or if the accused is being singled out for prosecution among many who appear to be equally guilty of the crime, the jury is less likely to convict (Kalven and Zeisel, 1966).

Discretion and Extra-legal Factors

The argument is often made that to ensure certainty and equal treatment there should be no discretion in the legal process. If injustices result from decisions in particular kinds of cases, then it is the rules of substantive law that should be changed. The rules should not be subverted by ignoring them or by applying them liberally. While many rules of law are in need of reform, it is doubtful whether any system in which fixed rules were applied rigidly, untempered by considerations of justice and fairness in individual cases, could maintain its legitimacy. Kalven has asserted that "we have a sense that many of the jury's most interesting deviations would be exceedingly hard to codify and incorporate by rule" (1964, p. 1071).

The legal system recognizes this need to take into account the peculiar facts of each case. Prosecutors have a broad and largely unreviewable discretion in deciding whether to prosecute a suspected offender. In exercising their discretion, they undoubtedly consider many of the factors reviewed above.

Another place in the criminal justice system where most of this kind of information can legally affect the court's decisions is in the sentencing of a convicted defendant. Indeed, many of the factors that are specifically excluded from the trial of an accused are to be taken into account in determining the proper disposition for a convicted person. Thus such factors as the defendant's criminal record, his standing in the community, his occupational status, etc., often form a critical part of the presentence report on which the judge bases his sentencing decision. The American Law Institute's Model Penal Code states:

> The presentence investigation shall include an analysis of the circumstances attending the commission of the crime, the defendant's history of delinquency or criminality, physical and mental condition, family status and background, economic status, education, occupation and personal habits and any other matters that the probation officer deems relevant or the Court directs to be included. (American Law Institute, 1962, p. 118)

In Canada, recent legislation has given further recognition to the fact that these extra-legal factors should be considered in "doing justice." Where the maximum penalty for a crime is imprisonment of ten years or less, the judge can avoid some of the effects of a guilty verdict by granting an absolute or conditional discharge. The effect of this is that even though the man has been found guilty of a crime, a conviction is not registered. The intent behind the legislation appears to be to encourage a judge to find the defendant guilty or not guilty on the basis of the relevant facts, and then allow himself to be influenced by the totality of the circumstances surrounding the case in his decision to grant or not grant a discharge. (For a more complete description see Greenspan, 1973).

The Jury's Function

The question of whether we should retain the jury because of its ability to dispense justice in individual cases thus depends on the answer to two distinct questions: (a) does the jury exercise discretion in ways that are considered to be just, and (b) in view of the other stages in the legal process where such discretion can be exercised by both the prosecutor and the judge, is there any need for the additional institution of the jury. With respect to the first question, it appears, for instance, that in a shoplifting case, if the defendant is a person of some stature and will lose his job if convicted, the jury is likely to find that he has learned his lesson and that the consequences are too serious to warrant conviction. If the prosecutor does not prosecute the ringleader of a gang, but instead calls him as a witness against his underlings, the jury is likely to protest that this is unfair and acquit the accused. If the accused was seriously injured in an accident in which his beloved wife was killed because of his criminal negligence, the jury is likely to find that he has suffered enough. But law dispensing by the jury appears to cut both ways. The fact that minority groups have historically been unfairly subjected to jury lawlessness cannot be doubted. Furthermore, many people would argue that the fact that the accused is a nice fellow, a good looking woman, a cripple, or employed, or that his or her victim is insufferable, should not affect the disposition of the case.

It would appear, not surprisingly, that the jury injects into the legal process notions of fairness that are shared by the average person. However, they are not able to rise above the prejudices and biases held by the same people. Although empirical research is important in demonstrating the subtleties of jury equity, even when all of the evidence has been collected an important value judgment remains.

If the jury, however, is to perform a function different from that of the prosecutor in exercising his discretion to charge and the judge in exercising his discretion on sentencing, it would appear essential that the jury be representative of the community so that the breadth of community values be represented on the jury. Indeed if the juries were truly representative of the community, perhaps many of the present prejudices that influence the jury would be removed from their deliberations. In this regard, it is interesting that at present a heated battle is being fought over whether the jury should be reduced from the traditional twelve members to six (Note 2). If the jury is reduced in size, then the case for retaining it because of the injection into the legal process of community values would appear to be greatly weakened.

(ii) *Morgentaler, Smoling and Scott* v. *The Queen*

Defence Counsel's Address to the Jury

In his concluding remarks to the jury at the trial of the appellants, defence counsel asserted:

> The judge will tell you what the law is. He will tell you about the ingredient of the offence, what the Crown has to prove, what the defences may be or may not be, and you must take the law from him. But I submit to you that it is up to you and you alone to apply the law to this evidence and you have a right to say it shouldn't be applied.

The burden of his argument was that the jury should not apply s. 251 if they thought that it was a bad law, and that, in refusing to apply the law, they could send a signal to Parliament that the law should be changed. Although my disposition of the appeal makes it unnecessary, strictly speaking, to review Mr. Manning's argument before the jury, I find the argument so troubling that I feel compelled to comment.

It has long been settled in Anglo-Canadian criminal law that in a trial before judge and jury, the judge's role is to state the law and the jury's role is to apply that law to the facts of the case. In *Joshua v. The Queen*, [1955] A.C. 121 at p. 130 (P.C.), Lord Oaksey enunciated the principle succinctly:

> It is a general principle of British law that on a trial by jury it is for the judge to direct the jury on the law and in so far as he thinks necessary on the facts, but the jury, whilst they must take the law from the judge, are the sole judges on the facts.

The jury is one of the great protectors of the citizen because it is composed of 12 persons who collectively express the common sense of the community. But the jury members are not expert in the law, and for that reason they must be guided by the judge on questions of law.

The contrary principle contended for by Mr. Manning, that a jury may be encouraged to ignore a law it does not like, could lead to gross inequities. One accused could be convicted by a jury who supported the existing law, while another person indicted for the same offence could be acquitted by a jury who, with reformist zeal, wished to express disapproval of the same law. Moreover, a jury could decide that although the law pointed to a conviction, the jury would simply refuse to apply the law to an accused for whom it had sympathy. Alternatively, a jury who feels antipathy towards an accused might convict despite a law which points to acquittal. To give a harsh but I think telling example, a jury fueled by the passions of racism could be told that they need not apply the law against murder to a white man who had killed a black man. Such a possibility need only be stated to reveal the potentially frightening implications of Mr. Manning's assertions. The dangerous argument that a jury may be encouraged to disregard the law was castigated as long ago as 1784 by Lord Mansfield in a criminal libel case, *R. v. Shipley* (1784), 4 Dougl. 73 at pp. 170–1, 99 E.R. 774 at p. 824:

> So the jury who usurp the judicature of law, though they happen to be right, are themselves wrong, because they are right by chance only, and have not taken the constitutional way of deciding the question. It is the duty of the Judge, in all cases of general justice, to tell the jury how to do right, though they have it in their power to do wrong, which is a matter entirely between God and their own consciences.
>
> To be free is to live under a government by law.... Miserable is the condition of individuals, dangerous is the condition of the State, if there is no certain law, or, which is the same thing, no certain administration of law, to protect individuals, or to guard the State.
>
> ...
>
> In opposition to this, what is contended for? —That the law shall be, in every particular cause, what any twelve men, who shall happen to be the jury, shall be inclined to think; liable to no review, and subject to no control, under all the prejudices of the popular cry of the day, and under all the bias of interest in this town, where thousands, more or less, are concerned in the publication of newspapers, paragraphs, and pamphlets. Under such an administration of law, no man could tell, no counsel could advise, whether a paper was or was not punishable.

[1988] 1 S.C.R. 30, 44 D.L.R. 4th. 385 at 417–19, Dickson C.J.C.

I can only add my support to that eloquent statement of principle.

It is no doubt true that juries have a *de facto* power to disregard the law as stated to the jury by the judge. We cannot enter the jury room. The jury is never called upon to explain the reasons which lie behind a verdict. It may even be true that in some limited circumstances the private decision of a jury to refuse to apply the law will constitute, in the words of a Law Reform Commission of Canada working paper, "the citizen's ultimate protection against oppressive laws and the oppressive enforcement of the law" (Law Reform Commission of Canada, Working Paper 27, *The Jury in Criminal Trials* (1980). But recognizing this reality is a far cry from suggesting that counsel may encourage a jury to ignore a law they do not support or to tell a jury that it has a *right* to do so. The difference between accepting the reality of *de facto* discretion in applying the law and elevating such discretion to the level of a right was stated clearly by the United States Court of Appeals, District of Columbia Circuit, in *U.S. v. Dougherty*, 473 F. 2d 1113 (1972), *per* Leventhal J., at p. 1134:

> The jury system has worked out reasonably well overall, providing "play in the joints" that imparts flexibility and avoid[s] undue rigidity. An equilibrium has evolved — an often marvelous balance — with the jury acting as a "safety valve" for exceptional cases, without being a wildcat or runaway institution. There is reason to believe that the simultaneous achievement of modest jury equity and avoidance of intolerable caprice depends on formal instructions that do not expressly delineate a jury charter to carve out its own rules of law.

To accept Mr. Manning's argument that defence counsel should be able to encourage juries to ignore the law would be to disturb the "marvelous balance" of our system of criminal trials before a judge and jury. Such a disturbance would be irresponsible. I agree with the trial judge and with the Court of Appeal that Mr. Manning was quite simply wrong to say to the jury that if they did not like the law they need not enforce it. He should not have done so.

Conclusion

Section [251] of the *Criminal Code* infringes the right to security of the person of many pregnant women. The procedures and administrative structures established in the section to provide for therapeutic abortions do not comply with the principles of fundamental justice. Section 7 of the Charter is infringed and that infringement cannot be saved under s. 1.

(iii) Are Selection Experts Stacking Juries?

Michael Crawford

Choosing Juries Now a Scientific Exercise

On November 8, 1984, a jury of 12 people in Toronto acquitted Dr. Henry Morgentaler and two other doctors of criminal charges of conspiracy to procure a miscarriage.

As controversial as the verdict was the way in which the jury was chosen. Helping defence lawyer Morris Manning eliminate potentially biased jurors were two American jury selection experts who used body language and verbal cues to detect prejudice.

As in any jury trial, the jurors had been chosen from a panel of citizens drawn at random from the community. But, the use of jury consultants in this explosively controversial case prompted anti-abortion lobbyists to cry "the jury was stacked."

Scientific jury selection experts are a new breed of psychologists and sociologists who are bringing the behavioral sciences into the courtroom. The Morgentaler case has brought the infant profession of scientific jury selection under the scrutiny of the Canadian public for the first time.

From *National* (February 1985) at 30. Reproduced by permission of the Canadian Bar Association.

While jury selection experts are becoming commonplace in many American courtrooms, they have been used only rarely in Canadian cases. Some people say they are not better than witch-doctors when it comes to picking juries, while others claim they can turn a losing case into a winner. The truth likely lies somewhere in between.

Scientific jury selection techniques grew out of the trials of American radicals and Vietnam war protestors in the early 1970's. Young, radical social scientists wanted to ensure their colleagues had a fair trial. The list of those early cases reads like a history of radical causes of the last decade, including the trials of black rights activist Angela Davis, militant Indians at Wounded Knee and the prisoners at riot-torn Attica prison.

There were many wins in the early cases. The grand-daddy of scientific jury selection, who played a role in most of those cases, was New York Sociologist Jay Schulman. Said Schulman: "I would say in these major political cases or quasi-political cases in America we have won seven out of 10, and the usual batting average in a Federal court in America is you lose eight or nine out of 10."

Schulman was brought to Canada in 1983 for the trial of the Squamish Five, a group of terrorists accused of planting bombs in British Columbia. A community opinion survey in Vancouver was used to convince the judge that massive pre-trial publicity had created prejudices among potential jurors in the community and extensive questioning of prospective jurors was permitted.

The techniques of the jury selection consultants were eventually applied to other types of cases. By the mid-seventies, the techniques had captivated the interest of large American corporate law firms. The techniques which had been used in criminal trials of radicals could be applied just as easily in civil cases, particularly those involving millions of dollars. For highly complex cases, such as the anti-trust lawsuit involving International Business Machines in 1978, the jury selection experts offered invaluable advice on how the jury would interpret legal arguments.

Said Schulman: "Almost no important civil case in this country goes to trial without the use of jury work, and only 14 years after it began."

There are three main techniques used by jury selection experts. The first and most powerful is the community opinion poll. Prior to the trial, the jury selection consultant surveys a random sample of citizens to detect attitudes or prejudices which might somehow affect the case. The survey results can be used to change the lawyer's trial tactics and also to design a profile of the "ideal juror" for the case at hand.

In one American murder trial involving millionaire T. Cullen Davis, the researchers not only surveyed the community by telephone, they also checked car bumper stickers, the upkeep of yards and steel bars on home windows to draw conclusions about community attitudes and prospective jurors.

The second technique is the pre-trial simulation or mock jury. The lawyer presents his evidence and witnesses before a number of mock juries chosen by the consultant as being representative of the community where the trial will be held. The deliberation of each jury is video-taped for later consideration by the consultant and the lawyer. Weak arguments are dropped and complex points are simplified before the case actually goes to trial.

In one U.S. case, a railroad company being sued for the wrongful death of a young boy, found through mock juries that the verdict could go either way. Rather than risk a larger court-imposed settlement, the company settled before trial.

The third technique involves the jury selection expert sitting beside the lawyer in court, observing the verbal and non-verbal behaviour of each prospective juror. A rigid posture, folded arms or lack of eye contact are all cues to beliefs and attitudes.

An offshoot of the in-court technique, known as the "shadow jury," was used in the IBM case. After the jury was chosen, the consultants hired people who were demographically representative to the real jury to sit in the courtroom and give daily feedback on who was winning and what arguments they did or did not understand. The shadow jury allowed the IBM lawyers to change their strategies throughout the trial, always having some idea what jurors were thinking.

Lawyers in both the United States and Canada can use these techniques in the jury selection process by rejecting jurors in either of two ways. If a prospective juror displays obvious bias or is unable to deliver a fair verdict for some other reason, such as not understanding the language of the trial, a "challenge for cause" can be used to eliminate potential jurors. The Canadian jury selection system is unique in that a challenge for cause is decided by two potential jurors who are selected by the judge from the jury panel. In a sense, the jury selects itself when a challenge for cause is prompted.

In addition, each lawyer has a very limited number of "peremptory challenges" which can be used to reject a potential juror without giving any reasons. In Canada, peremptory challenges can number from four to 20 for each defendant in a criminal trial.

(iii) Are Selection Experts Stacking Juries?

The number of peremptory challenges vary in civil trials from province to province.

In criminal cases in Canada, the Crown also has up to 48 "stand-asides," which place prospective jurors in limbo.

The differences in the Canadian jury selection process have slowed the introduction of the scientific selection methods here. In Canada, the questioning of prospective jurors is not a right and the judge has to be convinced there is widespread prejudice in order to ask questions. In most trials, if bias isn't obvious or readily admitted by a prospective juror, a lawyer has few chances to discover otherwise.

The first use of any sort of modern jury selection techniques in Canada occurred in London, Ontario in 1979. A widely-publicized fraud trial involving a building products company which had cheated little old ladies upset the community. The defendant in that same trial was coming up in court on subsequent charges and the lawyer wanted a change of venue. He asked Neil Vidmar, a psychology professor at the University of Western Ontario, to perform a community opinion survey.

Said Vidmar of that first case: "We learned that large numbers of people had knowledge about the case, detailed knowledge; large numbers of people said any defendant that had any connection with that prior case they would automatically find guilty."

Vidmar has since become one of Canada's most prominent experts on jury selection techniques. He is also an unrelenting critic and realist about what jury selection experts can do.

Said Vidmar: "It's not really a question of what does not work, but what claims are made for it. For example, much claim has gone for the body language research. There are certain linguistic or kinesetic cues, body posture, that show some rough indications, but it does not tell much about personality, and in fact, is much over-rated. I think that the polling is the most useful technique. I think that the jury simulation is probably the second most useful."

However, Vidmar notes that a combination of all of the techniques together can be a powerful tool for a lawyer, sharpening his presentation skills and helping him understand the type of people sitting on the jury. But, Vidmar says these techniques are really only useful in certain types of trials.

"Where there's massive pre-trial publicity, where there are emotional issues, where there are political issues, or where one has a reason to believe that the evidence is so close that the jury could go either way, that is the instance where we find that the jury selection technique would be most useful" said Vidmar.

Even in those cases which are perfectly suited to sophisticated selection techniques, all of the experts agree the methods are only one factor in the outcome of the case. The nature of the evidence presented, the lawyer's presentation of the case or the lack of proof presented by the other lawyer, can all affect the verdict.

Vidmar says they cannot stack juries: "The jury selection experts are not that good. What they do is eliminate the most prejudiced persons from the jury." He notes the other side in the case would most likely reject jurors favoring the opposition.

In the Morgentaler case, Vidmar said: "I would point out something. Dr. Morgentaler was acquitted three times in Quebec in 1973, 1974 and 1975 by juries that had not in any way been selected by jury selection experts ... should the jury selection experts get all of the credit for the acquittal or is it something about the nature of the law itself and the way juries respond?"

Canadian lawyers will, no doubt, consider using the techniques more often now. While the Canadian legal system is, in many ways, vastly different from the American system, there are similarities and modified versions of jury selection techniques which would work well in Canada.

At this moment, Canada is at crossroads. Before Canadians decide whether to follow the American example, Osgoode Hall law professor Louise Arbour suggests two questions must be dealt with. Prof. Arbour says there must be in-depth research into the way jurors make their decisions, whether they are influenced by their personalities and prejudices or if they decide on the evidence and law.

But more importantly, Arbour says we have to decide if we want juries to merely be a fact-finding neutral process or if we expect them to be the ultimate democratic test of the wisdom and the fairness of legislation.

Said Arbour: "If that's the function we want them to perform, to prevent convictions that would be harsh and unjust, then I think maybe our selection process is no longer adequate, maybe we'd have to know about who they are, the people who will pass that judgment."

(iv) *R. v. Williams*

McLACHLIN J.:

INTRODUCTION

Victor Daniel Williams, an aboriginal, was charged with the robbery of a Victoria pizza parlour in October, 1993. Mr. Williams pleaded not guilty and elected a trial by judge and jury. His defence was that the robbery had been committed by someone else, not him. The issue on this appeal is whether Mr. Williams has the right to question (challenge for cause) potential jurors to determine whether they possess prejudice against aboriginals which might impair their impartiality.

The *Criminal Code*, R.S.C. 1985, c. C-46, s. 638, provides that "an accused is entitled to any number of challenges on the ground that ... a juror is not indifferent between the Queen and the accused," The section confers discretion on the trial judge to permit challenges for cause. The judge should do so where there is a realistic potential of juror partiality. The evidence in this case established widespread racial prejudice against aboriginals. I conclude that in the circumstances of this case, that prejudice established a realistic potential of partiality and that the trial judge should have exercised his discretion to allow the challenge for cause.

HISTORY OF THE PROCEEDINGS

The First Trial

At his first trial, Williams applied to question potential jurors for racial bias under s. 638 of the Code. In support of his application, he filed materials alleging widespread racism against aboriginal people in Canadian society and an affidavit which stated, in part, "[I] hope that the 12 people that try me are not Indian haters." Hutchison J. ruled that Williams had met the threshold test and allowed potential jurors to be asked two questions:

1. Would your ability to judge the evidence in the case without bias, prejudice or partiality be affected by the fact that the person charged is an Indian?

2. Would your ability to judge the evidence in the case without bias, prejudice, or partiality be affected by the fact that the person charged is an Indian and the complainant is white?

On a number of occasions, Hutchison J. allowed additional questions to clarify responses to the first two questions. Forty-three panel members were questioned and 12 were dismissed for risk of bias. The Crown applied for a mistrial on the basis of procedural errors, including use of the same two jurors on all the challenges, coupled with "unfortunate publicity" of the jury selection process. The accused objected, arguing that the Crown was seeking a new trial in order to obtain reversal of the challenge for cause ruling. The trial judge replied that he doubted this would happen, given the case law, and granted the Crown's application for a mistrial.

. . . .

Criminal Code, R.S.C., 1985 c. C-46

638.(1) A prosecutor or an accused is entitled to any number of challenges on the ground that

...

(b) a juror is not indifferent between the Queen and the accused;

...

(2) No challenge for cause shall be allowed on a ground not mentioned in subsection (1).

Canadian Charter of Rights and Freedoms

7. Everyone has the right to life, liberty and security of the person and the right not to be deprived thereof except in accordance with the principles of fundamental justice.

11. Any person charged with an offence has the right

...

(d) to be presumed innocent until proven guilty according to law in a fair and public hearing by an independent and impartial tribunal;

15.(1) Every individual is equal before and under the law and has the right to the equal protection and equal benefit of the law without discrimina-

[1998] 1 S.C.R. 1128.

tion and, in particular, without discrimination based on race, national or ethnic origin, colour, religion, sex, age or mental or physical disability.

ANALYSIS

What Is the Rule?

The Prevailing Canadian Approach to Jury Challenges for Lack of Indifference between the Crown and the Accused

The prosecution and the defence are entitled to challenge potential jurors for cause on the ground that "a juror is not indifferent between the Queen and the accused." Lack of "indifference" may be translated as "partiality," the term used by the Courts below. "Lack of indifference" or "partiality," in turn, refer to the possibility that a juror's knowledge or beliefs may affect the way he or she discharges the jury function in a way that is improper or unfair to the accused. A juror who is partial or "not indifferent" is a juror who is inclined to a certain party or a certain conclusion. The synonyms for "partial" in Burton's Legal Thesaurus (2nd ed. 1992), at p. 374, illustrate the attitudes that may serve to disqualify a juror:

> bigoted, ... discriminatory, favorably disposed, inclined, influenced, ... interested, jaundiced, narrow-minded, one-sided, partisan, predisposed, prejudiced, prepossessed, prone, restricted, ... subjective, swayed, unbalanced, unequal, uneven, unfair, unjust, unjustified, unreasonable.

The predisposed state of mind caught by the term "partial" may arise from a variety of sources. Four classes of potential juror prejudice have been identified — interest, specific, generic and conformity: see Neil Vidmar, "Pretrial prejudice in Canada: a comparative perspective on the criminal jury" (1996), 79 Jud. 249, at p. 252. Interest prejudice arises when jurors may have a direct stake in the trial due to their relationship to the defendant, the victim, witnesses or outcome. Specific prejudice involves attitudes and beliefs about the particular case that may render the juror incapable of deciding guilt or innocence with an impartial mind. These attitudes and beliefs may arise from personal knowledge of the case, publicity through mass media, or public discussion and rumour in the community. Generic prejudice, the class of prejudice at issue on this appeal, arises from stereotypical attitudes about the defendant, victims, witnesses or the nature of the crime itself. Bias against a racial or ethnic group or against persons charged with sex abuse are examples of generic prejudice. Finally, conformity prejudice arises when the case is of significant interest to the community causing a juror to perceive that there is strong community feeling about a case coupled with an expectation as to the outcome.

Knowledge or bias may affect the trial in different ways. It may incline a juror to believe that the accused is likely to have committed the crime alleged. It may incline a juror to reject or put less weight on the evidence of the accused. Or it may, in general way, predispose the juror to the Crown, perceived as representative of the "white" majority against the minority-member accused, inclining the juror, for example, to resolve doubts about aspects of the Crown's case more readily: see Sheri Lynn Johnson, "Black Innocence and the White Jury" (1985), 83 Mich. L. Rev. 1611. When these things occur, a juror, however well intentioned, is not indifferent between the Crown and the accused. The juror's own deliberations and the deliberations of other jurors who may be influenced by the juror, risk a verdict that reflects, not the evidence and the law, but juror preconceptions and prejudices. The aim of s. 638 of the Code is to prevent effects like these from contaminating the jury's deliberations and hence the trial: see *R.* v. *Hubbert* (1975), 29 C.C.C. (2d) 279 (Ont. C.A.). The aim, to put it succinctly, is to ensure a fair trial.

The practical problem is how to ascertain when a potential juror may be partial or "not indifferent" between the Crown and the accused. There are two approaches to this problem. The first approach is that prevailing in the United States. On this approach, every jury panel is suspect. Every candidate for jury duty may be challenged and questioned as to preconceptions and prejudices on any sort of trial. As a result, lengthy trials of jurors before the trial of the accused are routine.

Canada has taken a different approach. In this country, candidates for jury duty are presumed to be indifferent or impartial. Before the Crown or the accused can challenge and question them, they must raise concerns which displace that presumption. Usually this is done by the party seeking the challenge calling evidence substantiating the basis of the concern. Alternatively, where the basis of the concern is "notorious" in the sense of being widely known and accepted, the law of evidence may permit a judge to take judicial notice of it. This might happen, for example, where the basis of the concern is widespread publicity of which the judge and everyone else in the community is aware. The judge has a wide discretion in controlling the challenge process, to prevent its abuse, to ensure it is fair to the prospective juror as well as the accused, and to prevent the trial from being unnecessarily delayed by unfounded challenges for cause: see Hubbert, *supra*.

. . . .

Identifying Evidentiary Threshold

. . . .

(1) The Assumption that Prejudice Will Be Judicially Cleansed

Underlying the Crown's submissions (as well as the judgments of Esson C.J. and the Court of Appeal) is the assumption that generally jurors will be able to identify and set aside racial prejudice. Only in exceptional cases is there a danger that racial prejudice will affect a juror's impartiality. In contrast, the defence says that jurors may not be able to set aside racial prejudices that fall short of extreme prejudice. Is it correct to assume that jurors who harbour racial prejudices falling short of extreme prejudice will set them aside when asked to serve on a jury? A consideration of the nature of racial prejudice and how it may affect the decision-making process suggests that it is not.

To suggest that all persons who possess racial prejudices will erase those prejudices from the mind when serving as jurors is to underestimate the insidious nature of racial prejudice and the stereotyping that underlies it. As Vidmar, *supra*, points out, racial prejudice interfering with jurors' impartiality is a form of discrimination. It involves making distinctions on the basis of class or category without regard to individual merit. It rests on preconceptions and unchallenged assumptions that unconsciously shape the daily behaviour of individuals. Buried deep in the human psyche, these preconceptions cannot be easily and effectively identified and set aside, even if one wishes to do so. For this reason, it cannot be assumed that judicial directions to act impartially will always effectively counter racial prejudice: see Johnson, *supra*. Doherty J.A. recognized this in *Parks, supra*, at p. 371:

> In deciding whether the post-jury selection safeguards against partiality provide a reliable antidote to racial bias, the nature of that bias must be emphasized. For some people, anti-black biases rest on unstated and unchallenged assumptions learned over a lifetime. Those assumptions shape the daily behaviour of individuals, often without any conscious reference to them. In my opinion, attitudes which are engrained in an individual's subconscious, and reflected in both individual and institutional conduct within the community, will prove more resistant to judicial cleansing than will opinions based on yesterday's news and referable to a specific person or event.

Racial prejudice and its effects are as invasive and elusive as they are corrosive. We should not assume that instructions from the judge or other safeguards will eliminate biases that may be deeply ingrained in the subconscious psyches of jurors. Rather, we should acknowledge the destructive potential of subconscious racial prejudice by recognizing that the post-jury selection safeguards may not suffice. Where doubts are raised, the better policy is to err on the side of caution and permit prejudices to be examined. Only then can we know with any certainty whether they exist and whether they can be set aside or not. It is better to risk allowing what are in fact unnecessary challenges, than to risk prohibiting challenges which are necessary: see *Aldridge* v. *United States*, 283 U.S. 308 (1931), at p. 314, and *Parks, supra*.

. . . .

This Court rejected the argument that prejudice based on pre-trial publicity could be cured by the safeguards in the trial process in *Sherratt, supra*, at p. 532, per L'Heureux-Dubé J.:

> While it is no doubt true that trial judges have a wide discretion in these matters and that jurors will usually behave in accordance with their oaths, these two principles cannot supersede the right of every accused person to a fair trial, which necessarily includes the empanelling of an impartial jury.

The same may be said of many forms of prejudice based on racial stereotypes. The expectation that jurors usually behave in accordance with their oaths does not obviate the need to permit challenges for cause in circumstances such as the case at bar, where it is established that the community suffers from widespread prejudice against people of the accused's race.

. . . .

Racial prejudice against the accused may be detrimental to an accused in a variety of ways. The link between prejudice and verdict is clearest where there is an "interracial element" to the crime or a perceived link between those of the accused's race and the particular crime. But racial prejudice may play a role in other, less obvious ways. Racist stereotypes may affect how jurors assess the credibility of

(iv) R. v. Williams

the accused. Bias can shape the information received during the course of the trial to conform with the bias: see *Parks*, *supra*, at p. 372. Jurors harbouring racial prejudices may consider those of the accused's race less worthy or perceive a link between those of the accused's race and crime in general. In this manner, subconscious racism may make it easier to conclude that a black or aboriginal accused engaged in the crime regardless of the race of the complainant: see Kent Roach, "Challenges for Cause and Racial Discrimination" (1995), 37 Crim. L.Q. 410, at p. 421.

Again, a prejudiced juror might see the Crown as non-aboriginal or non-black and hence to be favoured over an aboriginal or black accused. The contest at the trial is between the accused and the Crown. Only in a subsidiary sense is it between the accused and another aboriginal. A prejudiced juror might be inclined to favour non-aboriginal Crown witnesses against aboriginal accused. Or a racially prejudiced juror might simply tend to side with the Crown because, consciously or unconsciously, the juror sees the Crown as a defender of majoritarian interests against the minority he or she fears or disfavours. Such feeling might incline the juror to resolve any doubts against the accused.

Ultimately, it is within the discretion of the trial judge to determine whether widespread racial prejudice in the community, absent specific "links" to the trial, is sufficient to give an "air of reality" to the challenge in the particular circumstances of each case. The following excerpt from *Parks*, *supra*, at pp. 378–79, per Doherty J.A., states the law correctly:

> I am satisfied that in at least some cases involving a black accused there is a realistic possibility that one or more jurors will discriminate against that accused because of his or her colour. In my view, a trial judge, in the proper exercise of his or her discretion, could permit counsel to put the question posed in this case, in any trial held in Metropolitan Toronto involving a black accused. I would go further and hold that it would be the better course to permit that question in all such cases where the accused requests the inquiry.
>
> There will be circumstances in addition to the colour of the accused which will increase the possibility of racially prejudiced verdicts. It is impossible to provide an exhaustive catalogue of those circumstances. Where they exist, the trial judge must allow counsel to put the question suggested in this case.

. . . .

"Concrete" evidence as to whether potential jurors can or cannot set aside their racial prejudices can be obtained only by questioning a juror. If the Canadian system permitted jurors to be questioned after trials as to how and why they made the decisions they did, there might be a prospect of obtaining empirical information on whether racially prejudiced jurors can set aside their prejudices. But s. 649 of the Code forbids this. So, imperfect as it is, the only way we have to test whether racially prejudiced jurors will be able to set aside their prejudices and judge impartially between the Crown and the accused, is by questioning prospective jurors on challenges for cause. In many cases, we can infer from the nature of widespread racial prejudice, that some jurors at least may be influenced by those prejudices in their deliberations. Whether or not this risk will materialize must be left to the triers of impartiality on the challenge for cause. To make it a condition of the right to challenge [for] cause is to require the defence to prove the impossible and to accept that some jurors may be partial.

. . . .

This raises the question of what evidentiary standard is appropriate on applications to challenge for cause based on racial prejudice. The appellant appears to accept the standard of widespread racial prejudice in the community. Interveners, however, urge a lower standard. One suggestion is that all aboriginal accused should have the right to challenge for cause. Another is that any accused who is a member of a disadvantaged group under s. 15 of the *Charter* should have the right to challenge for cause. Also possible is a rule which permits challenge for cause whenever there is bias against the accused's race in the community, even if that bias is not general or widespread.

A rule that accords an automatic right to challenge for cause on the basis that the accused is an aboriginal or member of a group that encounters discrimination conflicts from a methodological point of view with the approach in *Sherratt*, *supra*, that an accused may challenge for cause only upon establishing that there is a realistic potential for juror partiality. For example, it is difficult to see why women should have an automatic right to challenge for cause merely because they have been held to constitute a disadvantaged group under s. 15 of the *Charter*. Moreover, it is not correct to assume that membership in an aboriginal or minority group always implies a realistic potential for partiality. The relevant community for purposes of the rule is the community from which the jury pool is drawn. That community may or may not harbour prejudices against aboriginals. It likely would not, for example, in a community where aboriginals are in a majority position. That said, absent evidence to the contrary, where widespread prejudice against people of the accused's race is demonstrated at a national or provincial level, it will often be reasonable to infer that such prejudice is replicated at the community level.

On the understanding that the jury pool is representative, one may safely insist that the accused demonstrate widespread or general prejudice against his or her race in the community as a condition of bringing a challenge for cause. It is at this point that bigoted or prejudiced people have the capacity to affect the impartiality of the jury.

. . . .

In my view, the rule enunciated by this Court in *Sherratt*, *supra*, suffices to maintain the right to a fair and impartial trial, without adopting the United States model or a variant on it. Sherratt starts from the presumption that members of the jury pool are capable of serving as impartial jurors. This means that there can be no automatic right to challenge for cause. In order to establish such a right, the accused must show that there is a realistic potential that some members of the jury pool may be biased in a way that may impact negatively on the accused. A realistic potential of racial prejudice can often be demonstrated by establishing widespread prejudice in the community against people of the accused's race. As long as this requirement is in place, the Canadian rule will be much more restrictive than the rule in the United States.

In addition, procedures on challenges for cause can and should be tailored to protect the accused's right to a fair trial by an impartial jury, while also protecting the privacy interests of prospective jurors and avoiding lengthening trials or increasing their cost.

. . . .

At the stage of the actual challenge for cause, the procedure is similarly likely to be summary. The trial judge has a wide discretion in controlling the process to prevent its abuse, to ensure that it is fair to the prospective juror as well as to the accused, and to avoid the trial's being unnecessarily prolonged by challenges for cause: see Hubbert, *supra*. In the case at bar, Hutchison J. at the first trial confined the challenge to two questions, subject to a few tightly controlled subsidiary questions. This is a practice to be emulated. The fear that trials will be lengthened and rendered more costly by upholding the right to challenge for cause where widespread racial prejudice is established is belied by the experience in Ontario since the ruling in *Parks*, *supra*. The Criminal Lawyers' Association (Ontario), an intervener, advised that in those cases where the matter arises, an average of 35–45 minutes is consumed. The Attorney General for Ontario did not contradict this statement and supports the appellant's position.

CONCLUSION

Although they acknowledged the existence of widespread bias against aboriginals, both Esson C.J. and the British Columbia Court of Appeal held that the evidence did not demonstrate a reasonable possibility that prospective jurors would be partial. In my view, there was ample evidence that this widespread prejudice included elements that could have affected the impartiality of jurors. Racism against aboriginals includes stereotypes that relate to credibility, worthiness and criminal propensity. As the Canadian Bar Association stated in Locking up Natives in Canada: A Report of the Committee of the Canadian Bar Association on Imprisonment and Release (1988), at p. 5:

> Put at its baldest, there is an equation of being drunk, Indian and in prison. Like many stereotypes, this one has a dark underside. It reflects a view of native people as uncivilized and without a coherent social or moral order. The stereotype prevents us from seeing native people as equals.

. . . .

In these circumstances, the trial judge should have allowed the accused to challenge prospective jurors for cause. Notwithstanding the accused's defence that another aboriginal person committed the robbery, juror prejudice could have affected the trial in many other ways. Consequently, there was a realistic potential that some of the jurors might not have been indifferent between the Crown and the accused. The potential for prejudice was increased by the failure of the trial judge to instruct the jury to set aside any racial prejudices that they might have against aboriginals. It cannot be said that the accused had the fair trial by an impartial jury to which he was entitled.

I would allow the appeal and direct a new trial.

E. The Judges

(i) The Meaning and Scope of Judicial Independence

Bora Laskin

...I hope I do not abuse this privilege if I strike a serious note in this address. It would please me better if I could banter and amuse, which I may assure you is not beyond my capacity. But special reasons, to which I will come shortly, impel me to speak more soberly on a subject of fundamental importance to the judicial office. That subject is the meaning and scope of judicial independence. I would have thought that its meaning would have been well understood over the years in which the Judges have exercised their judicial roles. I would have thought that there was a clear public understanding that Judges cannot be measured in the same way as other holders of public office or any members of the public. In my understanding, and in that of most of the members of the legal profession and members of the Bench, Judges are expected to abstain from participation in political controversy. Obviously, considering the storm that has brewed early this year on the Berger affair, I was somewhat mistaken. The limited public role of the Judge, one perfectly clear to me, seems to have been misunderstood or forgotten, even by lawyers, let alone by members of the press and of the public.

A fundamental principle has pervaded the judicial role since it took root in the reign of Queen Anne. It was established — not without fits and starts — that Judges would no longer hold office at the pleasure of the Crown, at the pleasure of the government. They would have the security of tenure, once assigned to their position, and would hold office during good behaviour to the age of retirement. Their duration in judicial office would no longer depend on governmental whim, and they could be removed only for judicial misbehaviour.

What this imported, as it evolved over the years, was the separation of the executive and the judiciary; no admixture of the one with the other; no mixture of the judiciary in politics or political controversy; correspondingly, no intermeddling of the executive with the judiciary; each branch was to be independent of the other, left alone to carry on its separate duties. For the Judges, they had utmost freedom of speech in the discharge of their judicial functions. Unbelievably, some members of the press and some in public office in this country, seem to think that freedom of speech for the Judges gave them the full scope of participation and comment on current political controversies, on current social and political issues. Was there ever such ignorance of history and of principle?

A Judge, upon appointment — and I am speaking here of appointments which cover all members of our provincial and federal superior courts as well as the Supreme Court of Canada — takes a prescribed oath of office. It is a short oath which is common to all superior court Judges, being as follows:

> I do solemnly and sincerely promise and swear that I will duly and faithfully, and to the best of my skill and knowledge, execute the powers and trust reposed in me as ...
>
> So help me God.

But it is invested with all the authority and surrounded by all the limitations that are imported by the principle of judicial independence and that are spelled out in the *Judges Act*, the federal statute which defines the judicial office.

What does the *Judges Act* say about the judicial office? It says quite clearly that a Judge may not, directly or indirectly, engage in any occupation or business other than his judicial duties. There is a limited exception for him or her to act as commissioner or arbitrator or adjudicator or referee or conciliator or mediator, if so appointed in respect of a federal matter by the federal Government; and similarly, if so appointed by the provincial government in respect of a provincial matter. These are short-term, temporary assignments not intended to give a Judge

---

From F.L. Morton, ed., *Law, Politics and the Judicial Process in Canada* (Calgary: University of Calgary Press, 1985) at 115–20. Reproduced by permission of the editor.

a regular assignment to carry out a non-judicial role. Two recent illustrations of the distinction may be mentioned. A few years ago, the Government of Canada wished to appoint a Judge as Deputy Minister of an executive department. He was unwilling to accept unless he retained his security as Judge. The Government was prepared to go along. I felt it my duty as Chief Justice to protest and did so vigorously, pointing out that it was either the one position or the other, but not both.

A Judge who wishes to accept an executive appointment could not remain a Judge at the same time. In the case I mentioned, the Judge put more store on his judicial position than on the proposed executive position. The matter was accordingly dropped. The same thing happened a little later in Ontario when the provincial government wished to appoint an Ontario Supreme Court Judge as Chairman of the provincial Workman's Compensation Board. Again, I protested; if the Judge wished to accept the provincial appointment, he should resign from the Bench; he could not be both Judge and non-judicial or executive functionary. The principle was accepted and the matter was abandoned.

These instances concerned permanent appointments to governmental positions. The authorized exceptions to allow governments to appoint Judges to special assignments as, for example, by order-in-council or by a limited inquiry, do not involve Judges in executive government or in governmental operations. They are asked to perform a particular service, with generally a short-term duration, although some inquiries like the MacKenzie Valley Pipeline and the McDonald Inquiry into the R.C.M.P. did go on for some years.

I am myself not a great supporter of the use of Judges to carry out short-term assignments at the behest of a government, federal or provincial. Apart from anything else, it is not always convenient to spare a particular Judge, given the ever increasing workload of all Courts. Moreover, there is always the likelihood that the Judge will be required to pass on policy, which is not within the scope of the regular judicial function. But I recognize that governments will continue to ask Judges (generally with the consent of their Chief Justice) to perform these limited tasks. The important thing to remember is that these short-term assignments are not intended to establish a career for the Judge in the work he or she carried out. The Judge is expected to make his or her report to the particular government and to regard the assignment as completed without any supplementary comment. Any comment or action is for the government; the Judge himself or herself is *functus*,

done with the matter. This has been the general behaviour of Judges who have accepted and carried out special or particular government assignments. Whatever has been the value of the inquiry must rest in what it says — the Judge is certainly not intended to be a protagonist, however enamored he or she may become of the work. Nor is the Judge intended to make a career of the special assignment.

There has been a large increase in the number of federally-appointed Judges in the last decade. Indeed, there are now 466 superior court Judges throughout Canada and 232 county and district court Judges. I do not take account of provincial court Judges who are appointed by provincial governments. The increase in the number of federally-appointed Judges increased the burden of judicial administration, the need to monitor complaints (which are inevitable, even if in most cases misconceived) and the need also to provide outlets for judicial conferences. It was beyond the capacity of Parliament to provide for these matters and they also raised sensitive matters engaging the independent position of the Judges.

In 1971, a new policy was introduced by Parliament to govern supervision of judicial behaviour or, I should say, alleged misbehaviour....

...The Canadian Judicial Council came into being in October, 1971 and has had a considerable amount of business in the past decade. It has exercised its powers of inquiry and investigation with great care, seeking on the one hand to satisfy complaints against alleged judicial misbehaviour and on the other hand to protect the reputation of the Judge against unfounded allegations. The most common type of complaint received against Judges has to do with objections to their judgments. Laymen have misconceived the role of the Council: it is not a court of appeal to rectify decisions alleged to be in error; for that there are established appeal courts, and the Council repeatedly has to tell complainants that the recourse is an appeal, not an invocation of the powers of the Canadian Judicial Council.

Since the Canadian Judicial Council has a statutory mandate to conduct inquiries into alleged judicial misbehaviour, it can hardly ignore a responsible complaint. In the Berger case, the complaint was made by a long-serving superior court Judge. Was the Canadian Judicial Council to ignore it? At least, it had the obligation to consider whether the complaint merited investigation, that it was not merely frivolous. Those members of the press who became engaged with the complaint in Justice Berger's support seemed entirely ignorant of the mandate of the Canadian Judicial Council. They appeared to be of

(i) The Meaning and Scope of Judicial Independence

the view that a Judge's behaviour was for him to measure, that it was not open to the Canadian Judicial Council to investigate, let alone admonish a Judge in respect of a complaint against objectionable behaviour. This was clearly wrong and could have been established by some modest inquiry.

My mention of the Berger case is not to reopen an issue which is closed. It is only to set the record straight on the statutory function and duty of the Canadian Judicial Council, whoever be the subject of a complaint to it. In view of the obvious misunderstanding to which the Berger incident gave rise, it seemed important to me that I, as Chairman, should underline the role and duty of the Canadian Judicial Council, however distasteful it may seem to be to assess the behaviour of a fellow Judge. I would have welcomed, as I always do, the balance provided by the media, by the press, and I regret that it was unfortunate that they did not discharge that responsibility on this occasion.

There was one respect in which members of the press, and indeed some public "bodies" and members of Parliament, showed their ignorance of judicial propriety. It was said that pursuit of the complaint against Justice Berger was an interference with his freedom of speech. Plain nonsense! A Judge has no freedom of speech to address political issues which have nothing to do with his judicial duties. His abstention from political involvement is one of the guarantees of his impartiality, his integrity, his independence. Does it matter that his political intervention supports what many, including the press, think is a desirable stance? Would the same support be offered to a Judge who intervenes in a political matter in an opposite way? Surely there must be one standard, and that is absolute abstention, except possibly where the role of a Court is itself brought into question. Otherwise, a Judge who feels so strongly on political issues that he must speak out is best advised to resign from the Bench. He cannot be allowed to speak from the shelter of a Judgeship.

In the Berger case, the Judge's intervention was on critical political and constitutional issues then under examination by the entire Canadian ministerial establishment. No Judge had a warrant to interfere, in a public way, and his conviction, however well intended, could not justify political intervention simply because he felt himself impelled to speak. To a large degree, Judge Berger was reactivating his McKenzie Valley Pipeline inquiry, a matter which was years behind him and should properly be left dormant for a political decision, if any, and not for his initiative in the midst of a sensitive political controversy.

The Canadian Judicial Council — one member of Parliament accused us of being engaged in a witch hunt — was badly served by those who, obviously, did no homework on the Council's role and on its obligation. There was another matter which seemed rather shabby, also the result of failure to do any homework. It was indicated, quite explicitly in some news quarters, that the Canadian Judicial Council acted because the Prime Minister had complained of the Judge's intrusion into the political sphere when the Prime Minister was giving a press interview in Vancouver. The record on this matter is quite clear. The written complaint against Judge Berger was addressed to me under dates of November 18 and 19, 1981, and delivered to me, from Ottawa, on those days. The next day, November 20, 1981, I sent a memorandum to the Executive Secretary of Council asking that the complaints — there were two successive ones — be referred for consideration by the Executive Committee. So far as the Canadian Judicial Council was concerned, the complaint had become part of our agenda. The interview of the Prime Minister did not take place until November 24, 1981. It is therefore mere mischief making to suggest that the Canadian Judicial Council was moved to action by the Prime Minister.

The Berger inquiry, as I have said, is behind us, and I regret that I found it necessary to say as much as I did about it. However, the Canadian Judicial Council, which does not and cannot reach out publicly to the media, deserves to have its record cleared. This would not have been necessary if we had been better served by the press throughout the whole affair. A matter like the Berger case is not likely to recur; the Canadian Judicial Council has signalled the danger of recommended removal from office if it should recur. As it was, the Council took a placating view and administered an admonishment in the following terms:

1. The Judicial Council is of the opinion that it was an indiscretion on the part of Mr. Justice Berger to express his views as to matters of a political nature, when such matters were in controversy.

2. While the Judicial Council is of the opinion that Mr. Justice Berger's actions were indiscreet, they constitute no basis for a recommendation that he be removed from office.

3. The Judicial Council is of the opinion that members of the judiciary should avoid taking part in controversial political discussions except only in respect of matters that directly affect the operation of the Courts.

In view of the obfuscation that surrounded the Berger case, there are a number of propositions that must be plainly stated. First, however personally compelled a Judge may feel to speak on a political issue, however knowledgeable the Judge may be or think he or she be on such an issue, it is forbidden territory. The Judge must remain and be seen to remain impartial. Compromise which would impair judicial independence and integrity is out, if the Judge is to remain in judicial office. Second, no federally-appointed Judge can claim immunity from examination by the Canadian Judicial Council of complaints (unless obviously frivolous) lodged against the Judge; nor against the decision of the Canadian Judicial Council to investigate the complaints through a formal inquiry. Third, the Canadian Judicial Council is not limited to recommending removal or dismissal; it may attach a reprimand or admonishment without either recommending removal or abandoning the complaint. Only if it gets to removal does it become necessary, in the case of a superior court Judge, to engage the Minister of Justice and Parliament, whose approval on a recommended removal must be sought. Fourth, Judges who are objects or subjects of a complaint are entitled to a fair hearing, to appear before the Council or before an appointed committee or to refuse to appear (as Justice Berger did refuse). Refusal to appear does not paralyse the Council, and did not in the Case under discussion....

(ii) Judicial Inquiries

Stephen Bindman

> Should judges be removed from their normal duties to investigate social ills?

Sex. Drugs. Free refrigerators. Hardly the stuff of which a typical day on the bench is made, yet Canada's most senior judges are being called upon more than ever to investigate these and other pressing social crises.

There are now seven judicial inquiries at work across the country, probing everything from drugs in amateur sports to sexual abuse in a Newfoundland orphanage to the problems of natives in the justice system.

And that has rekindled debate about whether it is proper for judges to be taken away from their ordinary duties to head royal commissions of inquiry into controversial political and social questions.

The advocates say no one is better suited for the job—judges are excellent fact finders, totally independent and generally respected in the community.

The critics, including the Canadian Bar Association, say appointments to royal commissions compromise the independence of judges and leave already overburdened courts even more shorthanded.

"You have to use judges because nobody else will do. Judges are the only figures in our society who command that kind of public respect," says Toronto civil rights lawyer Clayton Ruby, who is representing Donald Marshall at a Nova Scotia inquiry into his 11-year wrongful imprisonment.

"But they're overused. Governments are using judges to solve difficult problems that they ought to be taking direct responsibility for. They want to be seen to be doing something but clearly want to put an issue off for a year. That's the classic use of royal commissions and it's wrong."

Calling on judges to at least temporarily take the heat off the politicians is nothing new.

Between Confederation and 1982, almost 800 separate inquiries were called by provincial governments—on everything from public accountancy in Saskatchewan (1953) to tree farm licenses in British Columbia (1960) to lunatic asylums in Quebec (1888) to suspicious baby deaths at Toronto's Hospital for Sick Children (1984).

There have also been 446 royal commissions appointed by the federal government since 1867—though not all were headed by sitting judges.

From *The Ottawa Citizen* (8 July 1989). Reproduced by permission of Southam News.

"Scandals aren't unusual in Canadian politics and using a judicial inquiry to deal with a scandal is almost the norm rather than the exception," said University of Toronto political science professor Peter Russell.

"You've got the opposition crying for it and I think the government finds it reasonably convenient if the scandal can't be swept under the rug."

Royal commissions are also costly.

The Parker commission, which investigated conflict-of-interest allegations against former industry minister Sinclair Stevens, cost the Canadian taxpayer more than $3 million. The budget for the Dubin drug probe has been set at about $3.7 million.

But some observers say the costs are even greater — the independence of the judiciary.

In 1985, a study by the Canadian Bar Association recommended judges not be allowed to sit on most commissions unless the subject matter makes the choice of a judge "particularly appropriate."

"When judges are too frequently seen to be working with the government, even if merely as commissioners, there will be a natural tendency for the public to see judges as not completely independent of the government," said the study, headed by former Supreme Court of Canada justice Louis-Philippe de Grandpré.

Two years later, a second bar report recommended Supreme Court justices not be allowed to sit on commissions because of the potential disruption to the country's top court.

In their response, all of the Supreme Court justices of the day agreed, except Willard Estey who left the bench for more than a year in 1985 when he headed a one-man inquiry into the collapse of two western banks.

However, in a recent speech, Mr. Justice John Sopinka, a newcomer to the country's highest court but a frequent commission participant as a lawyer, said judges shouldn't necessarily turn down inquiry appointments.

Sopinka noted there is some room for concern "because of the potential for conflict between policy-making functions" and a judge's future responsibilities.

(Since 1793, the U.S. Supreme Court has refused all extra-judicial assignments.)

Russell said it is particularly inappropriate for judges to be dragged into inquiries into purely political matters, such as reviewing the behaviour of cabinet ministers.

The political scientist also said most courts are already backlogged and "I resent the judgement of politicians that these scandals are more important things for judges to work on than the cases the judges have."

"I also don't buy the theory that only judges have public respect. I think there are people in other walks of life, including such things as chartered accountancy, the business world, universities, who have equal credentials."

But Mr. Justice David Marshall, head of the new Canadian Judicial Centre at the University of Ottawa, said judges should accept appointments to royal commissions.

"Who else is going to do it? When you look around in our society, there aren't very many independent adjudicators. Judges are in a unique position. We're paid to be independent, we're not allowed to accept money from any other source."

"There really isn't anybody else in society that has that independence. They're men and women who presumably will not be turned by future promise of office or money. They should be the least corruptible."

Ottawa lawyer David Scott, who was counsel to the inquiry examining the Sinclair Stevens controversy, said the work a judge does while a commissioner isn't really that much different from regular judging.

"Most of these things are basically fact-finding exercises and there is no one better equipped to find facts than a judge. That's what they do every day of their life."

Former justice minister Ray Hnatyshyn said the "political realities" of the Canadian parliamentary system require that in most cases a judge be appointed.

Judges are so appealing because they have secure tenure and they must sever all their political connections when they are appointed to the bench, Hnatyshyn said.

Queen's University law professor Gordon Bale says judges who become commissioners should also be able to lobby for the changes they suggest in their reports.

"I don't think it should be a one-way street. If the politicians involve the judges in inquiries and the judges acquire expertise in this particular area, I think the country deserves to have the benefit of this even after their report is submitted."

Canada would probably not have a national health scheme today had former Supreme Court Justice Emmett Hall not been such an outspoken advocate after he headed a 1961 royal commission into health services, the professor said.

(iii) Stupid Judge Tricks

Sandra Martin

Why do our upholders of justice go off the rails? Incompetence, prejudice, ignorance and declining mental faculties are a few obvious explanations. But most often they trip up when they venture into the treacherous territory of social commentary.

Judges are people, like the rest of us, until they don their judicial robes and enter courtrooms. Then they are expected to rise above human frailties and become impartial triers of facts and arbiters of disputes. Mostly, but not always, they succeed.

When they fail, we are outraged. Martin Friedland, author of a 1995 report on judicial independence and accountability for the Canadian Judicial Council, says that's because we put them on a pedestal and expect them to operate with great integrity instead of seeing them as "real people who sometimes get drunk or do stupid things."

The passing of the Charter of Rights and Freedoms in 1982 gave judges both more visibility and more power to make rulings that have wide applications in social and public policy. Some of those decisions have sparked controversy — not only in academic debates but in the media and on political platforms. Psychiatrist Vivian Rakoff says judges are caught in a curious sort of contradiction. "They are given an elevated position in which they must express themselves with regard to the law," he says, "but they also think that gives them permission to talk about anything."

So why do judges sometimes go off the rails? Incompetence, prejudice, ignorance and declining mental faculties are a few obvious explanations. Typically, though, they tend to trip up when they veer from a strict interpretation of the law and venture into the treacherous territory of social and cultural commentary. Lest you thought for a second that the recent boner by Mr. Justice John McClung of the Alberta Court of Appeal was an isolated incident, herewith a lineup of gaffes from the past:

1. Mr. Justice Jean Bienvenue of the Quebec Superior Court berated a Trois-Rivières jury in 1995 for being "idiotic and incompetent" for finding a woman guilty of only second-degree murder after she had killed her husband by slashing his throat with a razor. Then he delivered full-bore invective against the defendant in pronouncing sentence: "When women ascend the scale of virtues, they reach higher than men; and I have always believed this. But it is also said, and this, too, I believe, that when they decide to degrade themselves, they sink to depths to which even the vilest man could not sink."

He continued: "Alas, you are indeed the image of these women so famous in history: the Delilahs, the Salomes, Charlotte Corday, Mata Hari and how many others who have been a sad part of our history and have debased the profile of women. You are one of them, and you are the clearest living example of them that I have seen." But he didn't stop there: "At the Auschwitz-Birkenau concentration camp in Poland, which I once visited, horror-stricken, even the Nazis did not eliminate millions of Jews in a painful or bloody manner. ... They died in the gas chambers, without suffering."

Judge Bienvenue also commented on the short skirt worn by a reporter covering the trial and asked the bailiff for a bottle of vodka while the jury was deliberating.

2. Judge Jocelyn Moreau-Bérubé told a court in Tracadie-Sheila, N.B., in 1998, that there were few "honest people" in the province's francophone Acadian peninsula. She also wondered aloud whether she was surrounded by crooks in her neighbourhood.

3. Judge Monique Dubreuil angered the Haitian community in Montreal in 1998 when she sentenced two men, whom she said were "immature" and not a threat to society, to an 18-month suspended sentence for sexual assault. She explained her leniency by saying that the victim was not a juvenile and that the men, who were of Haitian origin, came from a culture where rape is accepted. "The absence of regret of the two accused seems to be related more to the cultural context, particularly with regard to relations with women than a veritable problem of a sexual nature," she said in her ruling.

From *The Globe and Mail* (12 March 1999) D2. Reproduced with permission of The Globe and Mail.

(iii) Stupid Judge Tricks

4. In a 1997 wrongful-dismissal suit against the owners of a McDonald's franchise in Milton, Ont., Mr. Justice Casimir Herold of the Ontario Court's General Division criticized "the goop that they put on Big Macs, the patented stuff," on the grounds that it "makes you sleepy, especially if you are a bookkeeper or an area manager." He impugned the defence lawyer's credibility by saying that some of his responses should be filed under the heading "the moon is made out of green cheese," and suggested he had either shredded some pertinent documents or had put them in "somebody's hamburger."

5. Criticizing the complainant in the Ewanchuk case because she "did not present herself [to the defendant] in a bonnet and crinolines" is not the first time that Judge McClung's rash judicial pen has gotten him into trouble. In 1996, he wrote the Alberta Court of Appeal judgment in a majority decision reversing a lower court ruling that the government should change the Individual Rights Protection Act to prohibit discrimination based on sexual orientation. "Rightly or wrongly, the electors of the province of Alberta, speaking through their parliamentary representatives, have declared that homosexuality ... is not to be included in the protected categories of the IRPA," he wrote in determining that a private Christian college had the right to fire Delwin Vriend from his job as a lab assistant because he is gay.

By ignoring the issue of sexual orientation in its human-rights legislation, the province was neither encouraging nor condoning discrimination, Judge McClung argued and therefore was not violating the Charter of Rights and Freedoms. "When they choose silence, provincial legislatures need not march to the Charter drum."

6. Mr. Justice Marcel Joyal of the Federal Court criticized his employer — Parliament — when he was presiding over a 1998 Toronto hearing in which Ted Weatherill, then head of the Canada Labour Relations Board, was seeking an injunction to prevent the federal cabinet from firing him. Mr. Weatherill had spent close to $150,000 on food and travel during his eight years at the CLRB. When then labour minister Lawrence MacAulay told the House of Commons that Mr. Weatherill would be fired for his extravagance, MPs stood up and applauded. In the subsequent hearing, Judge Joyal compared Parliament's treatment of Mr. Weatherill to the cheering crowds gathered at the guillotine during the French Revolution. "I don't know if I have the right to intervene. But it left a bad taste in my mouth," he said.

7. Martha and Joseph Sorger, both Holocaust survivors living in Toronto, sued the Bank of Nova Scotia, one of its branch managers and a lawyer acting for the bank for failing to perform their fiduciary duties. Halfway through the 1996 trial, the lawyer for the plaintiffs tried to obtain a mistrial because Mr. Justice Joseph Potts of the Ontario Court's General Division frequently interrupted testimony, gave the impression that he had made up his mind before hearing testimony, was rude and anti-Semitic. At one point, he allegedly interrupted Mrs. Sorger's evidence by saying: "Jesus Christ, it's like pulling hen's teeth." When the Sorgers' lawyer asked for an adjournment so they could observe the High Holidays, Judge Potts replied: "You're one of those, too?"

8. Mr. Justice Kerr Twaddle of the Manitoba Court of Appeal lessened the sentence of a man convicted of having sex with a 13-year-old girl from nine months in prison to a curfew and community service on these grounds: "She was apparently more sophisticated than many her age and was performing many household tasks, including babysitting the accused's children." Judge Twaddle described the relationship with the accused as "entirely inappropriate and criminal," but he argued that the victim was not coerced. "The girl, of course, could not consent in the legal sense, but nonetheless was a willing participant," he concluded.

9. In 1996, Mr. Justice Allyre Sirois of the Saskatchewan Court of Queen's Bench observed during a bail hearing for a man who beat his former girlfriend unconscious after she asked him to turn down the television set that "it takes two to tango." In 1993, at a dangerous-offender hearing, Judge Sirois referred to a prostitute who had been assaulted at knifepoint as belonging to "a different caste"; the year before, he told a woman who had been assaulted at the age of 12 that she had to accept some responsibility for the event.

10. During the 1987 trial of a Sri Lankan man accused of soliciting sexual services from a female police officer posing as a prostitute, Ontario Judge J.S. Climans advised the accused to "write back to Sri Lanka and get yourself a girlfriend. All she needs is a boat and she can come in."

11. Quebec Judge Denys Dionne observed during a trial in 1989 in Longeuil that: "Rules are like a woman, they are made to be violated."

12. Quebec Judge Raymonde Verreault cited "extenuating circumstances" when she handed down a 23-month sentence in 1994 to a man who had repeatedly sodomized his stepdaughter from the time she was 9 until 11. The victim did not have any "permanent scars" from the sexual assaults, according to Judge Verreault, because the attacker had respected the values of her Muslim faith and had "spared her virginity" by not engaging in vaginal intercourse. Besides, the girl may have encouraged the accused because she "harboured hatred" against her mother.

13. Quebec Judge René Crochetière ruled in 1993 that there was not enough evidence to bring a man to trial for threatening to kill his live-in lover. On leaving the crowded courtroom, the alleged victim said to the judge: "If I get killed, it will be your fault." To which he replied: "I would like to tell everyone here that, if ever this man kills this woman, it won't stop me from sleeping and I won't die — don't worry, I won't get depressed, either. It isn't my responsibility."

14. Manitoba Judge Frank Allen offered the following advice in 1989 to a 19-year-old man accused of beating a female acquaintance: "There isn't any woman worth the trouble you got yourself into." In a 1984 sexual-assault trial, the same judge observed: "You would have to be living in a vacuum, totally without wordly experience at all, not to know in many cases women are first to resist and later give in to persuasion and sometimes their own instinct."

(iv) Will Women Judges Really Make a Difference?

Justice Bertha Wilson

When I was appointed to the Supreme Court of Canada in the Spring of 1982 a great many women from all across the country telephoned, cabled or wrote to me rejoicing in my appointment. "Now", they said, "we are represented on Canada's highest court. This is the beginning of a new era for women." So why was I not rejoicing? Why did I not share the tremendous confidence of these women? The reasons form the theme of my lecture this evening.

First of all, of course, came the realization that no-one could live up to the expectations of my well-wishers. I had the sense of being doomed to failure, not because of any excess of humility on my part or any desire to shirk the responsibility of the office, but because I knew from hard experience that the law does not work that way. Change in the law comes slowly and incrementally; that is its nature. It responds to changes in society; it seldom initiates them. And while I was prepared — and, indeed, as a woman judge anxious — to respond to these changes, I wondered to what extent I would be constrained in my attempts to do so by the nature of judicial office itself.

In the literature which is required reading for every newly appointed judge it is repeatedly stated that judges must be both independent and impartial, that these qualities are basic to the proper administration of justice and fundamental to the legitimacy of the judicial role. The judge must not approach his or her task with pre-conceived notions about law or policy, with personal prejudice against parties or issues, or with bias toward a particular outcome of a case. Socrates defined the essential qualities of a judge in the following manner. "Four things belong to a judge; to hear courteously; to answer wisely; to consider soberly and to decide impartially."

In Winters' *Handbook for Judges*, there is a section devoted to the essential qualities of a judge and these are defined as integrity and independence, impartiality, flexibility, creativity, responsibility and common sense. The late Justice Frankfurter was quoted as stating:

> To practise the requisite detachment and to achieve sufficient objectivity no doubt demands of judges the habit of self-discipline and self-criticism, incertitude that one's own views are incontestable and alert tolerance toward views not

---

From The Fourth Annual Barbara Betcherman Memorial Lecture, Osgoode Hall Law School, February 8, 1990. Notes omitted. Reproduced by permission of the author.

(iv) Will Women Judges Really Make a Difference?

shared. But these are precisely the presuppositions of our judicial process. They are precisely the qualities society has a right to expect from those entrusted with ... judicial power.

In an article entitled "The Virtue of Impartiality" the late Judge Shientag of the Appellate Division of the New York Supreme Court discusses the difficulty in attaining impartiality and states that the term implies an appreciation and understanding of the differing attitudes and viewpoints of those involved in a controversy. He quotes Lord MacMillan's description of the difficulty judges face in this regard:

> The judicial oath of office imposes on the judge a lofty duty of impartiality. But impartiality is not easy of attainment. For a judge does not shed the attributes of common humanity when he assumes the ermine. The ordinary human mind is a mass of prepossessions inherited and acquired, often none the less dangerous because unrecognized by their possessor. Few minds are as neutral as a sheet of plate glass, and indeed a mind of that quality may actually fail in judicial efficiency, for the warmer tints of imagination and sympathy are needed to temper the cold light of reason if human justice is to be done.

And later Lord MacMillan issues the following warning:

> [The judge] must purge his mind not only of partiality to persons, but of partiality to arguments, a much more subtle matter, for every legal mind is apt to have an innate susceptibility to particular classes of arguments.

Many have criticized as totally unreal the concept that judges are somehow super-human, neutral, above politics and unbiased, and are able to completely separate themselves from their personal opinions and pre-dispositions when exercising their judicial function. For example, Lord Justice Scrutton doubted that complete impartiality was possible. He said:

> This is rather difficult to attain in any system. I am not speaking of conscious impartiality; but the habits you are trained in, the people with whom you mix, lead to your having a certain class of ideas of such a nature that, when you have to deal with other ideas, you do not give as sound and accurate judgments as you would wish. This is one of the great difficulties at present with Labour. Labour says: "Where are your impartial Judges? They all move in the same circle as the employers, and they are all educated and nursed in the same ideas as the employers. How can a labour man or a trade unionist get impartial justice?" It is very difficult sometimes to be sure that you have put yourself into a thoroughly impartial position between two disputants, one of your own class and one not of your class. Even in matters outside trade-unionist cases ... it is sometimes difficult to be sure, hard as you have tried, that you have put yourself in a perfectly impartial position between the two litigants.

In his text on *The Politics of the Judiciary*, Professor Griffith caused a furore in legal and judicial circles in the United Kingdom when he questioned whether the English judiciary were capable of impartiality. He stated that for a judge to be completely impartial he or she would have to be like a political, economic and social eunuch and have no interests in the world outside the court. Because this is impossible, Griffith concludes that impartiality is an ideal incapable of realization. He says of the English judiciary:

> These judges have by their education and training and the pursuit of their profession as barristers acquired a strikingly homogeneous collection of attitudes, beliefs, and principles which to them represents the public interest.

The public interest, in other words, is perceived from the viewpoint of their own class. Chief Justice Nemetz has suggested that the views of Professor Griffith may have some validity in Canada too, more particularly, Professor Griffith's view that judicial attitudes towards political and social issues reflect the lack of a proper understanding of the views of labour unions, minorities and the under-privileged.

Judge Rosalie Abella, Chair of the Ontario Law Reform Commission, also doubts that judicial impartiality is a realistic requirement. She emphasizes in her article "The Dynamic Nature of Equality" that "every decision-maker who walks into a court room to hear a case is armed not only with the relevant legal texts but with a set of values, experiences and assumptions that are thoroughly embedded."

Judge Shientag refers to the fact that many judges believe that they have acted with the cold neutrality of an impartial judge when in fact they have completely failed to examine their prejudices and biases. He points out that the partiality and prejudice with which we are concerned is not overt, not something tangible on which the judge can put his or her finger. Yet many judges by failing to appreciate this are lulled into a false sense of security. Judge Shientag emphasizes that progress will only be made when judges recognize this condition as part of the weakness of human nature and then "[h]aving admitted the liability to prejudice, unconscious for the most part, subtle and nebulous at times, the next step is to determine what the judge, with his trained mind, can do to neutralize the incessant play of these obscure yet potent influences." Judge Shientag concludes that "the judge who realizes, before listening to a case, that all men have a natural bias of mind and that thought is apt to be coloured by predilection, is more likely to make a conscientious effort at impartiality and dispassionateness than one who believes that his elevation to the bench makes him at once the dehumanized instrument of infallible logical truth."

But what, you may be asking, has all this got to do with my subject: "Will women judges really make a difference?" Well, I think it has a great deal to do with it and whether you agree with me or not will probably depend on your perception of the degree to which the existing law reflects the judicial neutrality or impartiality we have been discussing. If the existing law can be viewed as the product of judicial neutrality or impartiality, even although the judiciary has been very substantially male, then you may conclude that the advent of increased numbers of women judges should make no difference, assuming, that is, that these women judges will bring to bear the same neutrality and impartiality. However, if you conclude that the existing law, in some areas at least, cannot be viewed as the product of judicial neutrality, then your answer may be very different.

Two law professors at New York University, Professor John Johnston and Professor Charles Knapp, have concluded, as a result of their studies of judicial attitudes reflected in the decisions of judges in the United States, that United States judges have succeeded in their conscious efforts to free themselves from habits of stereotypical thought with regard to discrimination based on colour. However, they were unable to reach a similar conclusion with respect to discrimination based on sex and found that American judges had failed to bring to sex discrimination the judicial virtues of detachment, reflection and critical analysis which had served them so well with respect to other areas of discrimination. They state:

> "Sexism" — the making of unjustified (or at least unsupported) assumptions about individual capabilities, interests, goals and social roles solely on the basis of sex differences — is as easily discernible in contemporary judicial opinions as racism ever was.

Professor Norma Wikler, a sociologist at the University of California, has reviewed a number of other studies of judicial attitudes by legal researchers and social scientists and states that these confirm that male judges tend to adhere to traditional values and beliefs about the "natures" of men and women and their proper roles in society. They have found overwhelming evidence that gender-based myths, biases and stereotypes are deeply embedded in the attitudes of many male judges as well as in the law itself. They have concluded that particularly in areas of tort law, criminal law and family law, gender difference has been a significant factor in judicial decision-making. Many have concluded that sexism is the unarticulated underlying premise of many judgments in these areas and that this is not really surprising having regard to the nature of the society in which the judges themselves have been socialized.

A number of strategies have been tried in the United States for the elimination of gender bias from the courts — legislative reform, enhanced legal representation of women litigants, increased numbers of women lawyers and judges. These measures have been accompanied by an intensive educational program aimed at judges right across the country. Women judges and women lawyers in the United States played a very active role in the creation of this program. They were able to persuade substantial numbers of their male peers that gender bias, like all other forms of bias they had worked so hard to eradicate, violated the core principle of judicial impartiality and neutrality and posed an increasing threat in the seventies and eighties to the maintenance of public confidence in the judiciary.

As might be anticipated, a direct frontal attack on gender bias in the courts and especially the institution of an educational program for judges on this subject, was highly controversial and would probably have died on the vine but for the support of a substantial number of the country's leading male judges and educators who recognized the profound changes that were taking place in the society including a major redefinition of the roles of men and women.

Professor Wikler has been one of the moving forces behind the United States program to sensitize judges to the problem of gender bias. She reports some modest indicators of success of the program, although she acknowledges that it is too early to assess the long term effects. She reports that requests for speakers and material generated from courses and workshops indicate a growing interest as does also the positive evaluation by judges themselves of the courses presented. Even more gratifying, attorneys practising in States where the program has been actively promoted report a noticeable increase in judicial sensitivity to gender bias. Program materials have been cited in the courts and quoted in the judgments. Judicial Conduct Commissions are disciplining

(iv) Will Women Judges Really Make a Difference?

judges for gender biased behaviour such as sexist remarks to women lawyers and litigants and inappropriate comments in rape cases. Professor Wikler concludes that one very important goal has been achieved: gender bias is now a subject which judges and judicial educators think and care about.

Another development in the United States has been the establishment of judicially appointed Task Forces to investigate the extent to which gender bias exists in the judiciary. The first of these Task Forces was created in New Jersey in 1982 and, as stated by Chief Justice Wilentz, was mandated to "investigate the extent to which gender bias exists in the New Jersey judicial branch, and to develop an educational program to eliminate any such bias". Since 1982 over twenty other States have created Task Forces. Lynn Hecht Schafran, in her article "The Success of the American Program", reports that the Task Forces have significantly enhanced judicial education programs and have created a level of public awareness that generates its own pressures for reform.

Schafran identifies four reasons why a judicially appointed Task Force is important as opposed to other groups outside the court system focussing on particular concerns. The first is that a gender bias Task Force is able to look at a broad range of issues and demonstrate a pattern of gender bias that manifests itself throughout the judicial system. The second reason is credibility. She explains this critical reason in the following manner:

> When a coalition of rape crisis counsellors asserts that rape victims are ill-treated in court, or a women's bar association claims that women attorneys are denied a fair share of appointments to challenging and lucrative civil and criminal cases, these charges are heard as the claims of special interest groups. When a blue ribbon panel appointed by a state's chief justice makes these same charges, people listen. There was little in what the New Jersey and New York Task Forces reported that numerous women's rights organizations and feminists' legal commentators have not been saying for years, but the task force reports twice made the front page of the New York Times.

The third reason relates to the administration of the Task Force. The Chief Justice of the State is in a position to authorize funds, compel co-operation, endorse and propose reforms and ensure their implementation, and support judicial education on the subject. A final reason in favour of the Task Force route to reform is that such a task force brings together judges, lawyers, law professors, and community activists to study an issue which many of them do not initially appreciate is an issue at all. Schafran reports that Task Force members from New Jersey and New York "who start out with no knowledge of gender bias in the courts, or even a conviction that the idea is nonsense, emerge from the data collection process convinced that the problem is real and has deeply serious implications for the administration of justice."

So, where do we stand in Canada on this matter? Well, as you might expect, feminist scholars in Canada have over the past two decades produced a vast quantity of literature on the subject, some of it, in my view, very insightful, very balanced and very useful, and some of it very radical, quite provocative and probably less useful as a result. But all of it, it seems to me, is premised, at least as far as judicial decision-making is concerned, on two basic propositions, one that women view the world and what goes on in it from a different perspective from men, and two that women judges, by bringing to bear that perspective on the cases on which they sit, can play a major role in introducing judicial neutrality and impartiality into the justice system.

Let me say right away from my own experience as a judge of fourteen years' standing, working closely with my male colleagues on the bench, that in my view there are probably whole areas of the law on which there is no uniquely feminine perspective. This is not to say that the development of the law in these areas has not been influenced by the fact that the lawyers and the judges have all been men. But rather that the principles and the underlying premises are so firmly entrenched and, in my opinion, so fundamentally sound that no good would be achieved by attempting to re-invent the wheel, even if the revised version did have a few more spokes in it. I have in mind areas such as the law of contract, the law of real property and the law applicable to corporations. In some other areas of the law, however, I think that a distinctly male perspective is clearly discernible and has resulted in legal principles that are not fundamentally sound and should be revisited as and when the opportunity presents itself. Canadian feminist scholarship has, in my view, done an excellent job of identifying those areas and making suggestions for reform. Some aspects of the criminal law in particular cry out for change since they are based on presuppositions about the nature of women and women's sexuality that in this day and age are little short of ludicrous.

But how do we handle the problem that women judges, just as much as their male counterparts, are subject to the duty of impartiality? As we said at the outset, judges must not approach their task with pre-conceived notions about law and policy. They must approach it with detachment and, as Lord MacMillan said, purge their minds "not only of partiality to persons but of partiality to arguments." Does this then foreclose any kind of "judicial affirmative action" to counteract the influence of the dominant male perspective of the past and establish judicial neutrality through a countervailing female perspective? Is Karen Selick, writing recently in the Lawyers Weekly, correct when she argues that offsetting male bias with female bias would only be compounding the injustice? Does the nature of the judicial process itself present an insuperable hurdle so that the legislatures rather than the courts must be looked to for any significant legal change?

I think in part this may be so. Certainly, the legislature is the more effective instrument for rapid or radical change. But I see no reason why the judiciary cannot exercise some modest degree of creativity in areas where modern insights and life's experience have indicated that the law has gone awry. However, and I think this is extremely important, it will be a Pyrrhic victory for women and for the justice system as a whole if changes in the law come only through the efforts of women lawyers and women judges. The Americans were smart to realize that courses and workshops on gender bias for judges male and female are an essential follow-up to scholarly research and learned writing. In Canada we are just beginning to touch the fringes.

The first national, interdisciplinary conference on the relationship between judicial neutrality and gender equality was held in Banff, Alberta, in May of 1986. At the conference judges, academics, practising lawyers and experts in anthropology, political science, sociology and social welfare examined judicial behaviour in equality related matters. The judicial acceptance of traditional stereotypes concerning women was noted as well as its impact in Canada on important areas of constitutional equality litigation, family law, criminal law, tort law and human rights.

Mr. Justice Rothman of the Quebec Court of Appeal, one of the speakers at the conference, endorsed the approach adopted in the United States to counteract gender bias through nation-wide educational programs for judges and the creation of judicial task forces. In his perception, women face the same kind of discrimination in Canada as they do in the United States and we should be working to change the old attitudes *now*. He suggested that conferences and seminars for newly appointed judges would be a good place to start but, in addition, courses on gender bias should be part of the continuing education programs for judges at all stages of their careers. Justice Rothman added that it is not, however, going to be enough to sensitize judges to equality issues if lawyers are not sensitized to them as well!

The Canadian Judicial Council and the Canadian Judicial Centre have both recognized the need for judicial education in this area and will include gender issues in their summer seminars for judges this year. I understand that the Centre hopes to subsequently present the program in a number of locations across the country and the course materials will be available to all Canadian judges. I heartily endorse this initiative. It is, in my view, a significant first step towards the achievement of true judicial neutrality. But it is only a first step and there is a long way to go.

Coming back then to the question whether the appointment of more women judges will make a difference. Because the entry of women into the judiciary is so recent, few studies have been done on the subject. Current statistics, however, show that just over nine percent of federally appointed judges are women and it is reasonable to assume that more and more women will be appointed to the Bench as more and more women become licensed to practise law. Will this growing number of women judges by itself make a difference?

The expectation is that it will; that the mere presence of women on the bench will make a difference. In an article entitled "The Gender of Judges", Suzanna Sherry, an Associate Law Professor at the University of Minnesota, suggests that the mere fact that women are judges serves an educative function and helps to shatter stereotypes about the role of women in society that are held by male judges and lawyers as well as by litigants, jurors and witnesses.

Judge Gladys Kessler, former President of the National Association of Women Judges in the United States, defends the search for competent women appointees to the bench. She says:

> But the ultimate justification for deliberately seeking judges of both sexes and all colors and backgrounds is to keep the public's trust. The public must perceive its judges as fair, impartial and representative of the diversity of those who are being judged.

Justice Wald has expressed similar sentiments. She believes that women judges are indispensable to the public's confidence in the ability of the courts to respond to the legal problems of all classes of citizens.

Diane Martin, a criminal lawyer writing in the Lawyers Weekly, sees another way in which the presence of women on the bench is helpful and constructive. It is easier, she says, for women lawyers to appear as counsel before a woman judge. She says the "difference is that you are 'normal' — you and the judge have certain shared experiences and a shared reality that removes, to a certain extent, the need to 'translate' your submissions into 'man talk' or a context that a male judge will understand." The woman judge does not see you as "out of place" or having "something to prove by appearing in a courtroom arguing a case before her."

For women counsel, appearing in front of a woman judge also decreases the risk of sexist comments and inappropriate efforts at humour. The courtroom treatment of women litigants, witnesses and lawyers was examined by the New Jersey and New York task forces. The New York Task Force found that "[w]omen uniquely, disproportionately, and with unacceptable frequency must endure a climate of condescension, indifference, and hostility". The New Jersey Task Force found strong evidence that women are often treated differently in courtrooms, in judges' chambers and at professional gatherings. As Justice Rothman pointed out at the Banff conference, there is no excuse for a judge allowing himself or anyone else in his courtroom to make unprofessional or inappropriate references to gender. He saw as a possible solution the appointment of more women judges and more courteous and sensitive male judges!

Some feminist writers are persuaded that the appointment of more women judges will have an impact on the process of judicial decision-making itself and on the development of the substantive law. As I mentioned earlier, this flows from the belief that women view the world and what goes on in it from a different perspective from men. Some define the difference in perspective solely in terms that women do not accept male perceptions and interpretations of events as the norm or as objective reality. Carol Gilligan, a Professor of Education at Harvard University, sees the difference as going much deeper than that. In her view women think differently from men, particularly in responding to moral dilemmas. They have, she says, different ways of thinking about themselves and their relationships to others.

In her book, *In a Different Voice*, Gilligan analyses data she collected in the form of responses from male and female participants in a number of different studies. These responses, she submits, support her central thesis that women see themselves as essentially connected to others and as members of a community while men see themselves as essentially autonomous and independent of others. Gilligan makes no claim about the origins of the differences she describes. She does, however, use the psychoanalytical work of Dr. Nancy Chodorow as a starting point. Chodorow postulates that gender differences arise from the fact that women do the mothering of children. Because the gender identity of male children is not the same as their mothers, they tend to distance and separate themselves from their mothers' female characteristics in order to develop their masculinity. Female children, on the other hand, define themselves through attachment to their mothers. Masculinity is therefore, according to Gilligan, defined through separation and individualism while femininity is defined through attachment and the formation of relationships. The gender identity of the male, she submits, is threatened by relationships while the gender identity of the female is threatened by separation.

Gilligan's work on conceptions of morality among adults suggests that women's ethical sense is significantly different from men's. Men see moral problems as arising from competing rights; the adversarial process comes easily to them. Women see moral problems as arising from competing obligations, the one to the other, because the important thing is to preserve relationships, to develop an ethic of caring. The goal, according to women's ethical sense, is not seen in terms of winning or losing but rather in terms of achieving an optimum outcome for all individuals involved in the moral dilemma. It is not difficult to see how this contrast in thinking might form the basis of different perceptions of justice.

I think there is merit in Gilligan's analysis. I think it may in part explain the traditional reluctance of courts to get too deeply into the circumstances of a case, their anxiety to reduce the context of the dispute to its bare bones through a complex system of exclusionary evidentiary rules. This is, it seems to me, one of the characteristic features of the adversarial process. We are all familiar with the witness on cross-examination who wants to explain his or her answer, who feels that a simple yes or no is not an adequate response, and who is frustrated and angry at being cut off with a half truth. It is so much easier to come up with a black and white answer if you are unencumbered by a broader context which might prompt you, in Lord MacMillan's words, to temper the cold light of reason with the warmer tints of imagination and sympathy.

It may explain also the hostility of some male judges to permitting intervenors in human rights cases. The main purpose of having intervenors is to broaden the context of the dispute, to show the issue in a larger perspective or as impacting on other groups not directly involved in the litigation at all. But it certainly does complicate the issues to have them presented in polycentric terms.

Professor Patricia Cain of the University of Texas in an article entitled "Good and Bad Bias: A Comment on Feminist Theory and Judging" says:

> What we want, it seems to me, are lawyers who can tell their client's story, lawyers who can help judges to see the parties as human beings, and who can help remove the separation between judge and litigant. And, then, what we want from our judges is a special ability to listen with connection before engaging in the separation that accompanies judgment.

Obviously, this is not an easy role for the judge — to enter into the skin of the litigant and make his or her experience part of your experience and only when you have done that, to judge. But I think we have to do it; or at least make an earnest attempt to do it. Whether the criticism of the justice system comes to us through Royal Commissions, through the media or just through our own personal friends, we cannot escape the conclusion that in some respects our existing system of justice has been found wanting. And as Mr. Justice Rothman says — the time to do something about it is *now*.

One of the important conclusions emerging from the Council of Europe's Seminar on Equality between Men and Women held in Strasbourg last November is that the universalist doctrine of Human Rights must include a realistic concept of masculine and feminine humanity regarded as a whole, that human kind *is* dual and must be represented in its dual form if the trap of an asexual abstraction in which "human being" is always declined in the masculine is to be avoided. If women lawyers and women judges through their differing perspectives on life can bring a new humanity to bear on the decision-making process, perhaps they *will* make a difference. Perhaps they will succeed in infusing the law with an understanding of what it means to be fully human.

(v) *R. v. S. (R.D.)*

Present: Lamer C.J. and La Forest, L'Heureux-Dubé, Sopinka, Gonthier, Cory, McLachlin, Iacobucci and Major JJ.

APPEAL from a judgment of the Nova Scotia Court of Appeal (1995), 145 N.S.R. (2d) 284, 418 A.P.R. 284, 102 C.C.C. (3d) 233, 45 C.R. (4th) 361, dismissing an appeal from a judgment of the Nova Scotia Supreme Court (Trial Division), [1995] N.S.J. No. 184 (QL), allowing an appeal from acquittal by Sparks F.C.J. with oral reasons December 2, 1994, with supplementary written reasons, [1994] N.S.J. No. 629 (QL). Appeal allowed, Lamer C.J. and Sopinka and Major JJ. dissenting.

The reasons of La Forest and Gonthier JJ. were delivered by GONTHIER J.:

I have had the benefit of the reasons of Justice Cory, the joint reasons of Justices L'Heureux-Dubé and McLachlin and the reasons of Justice Major. I agree with Cory J. and L'Heureux-Dubé and McLachlin JJ. as to the disposition of the appeal and with their exposition of the law on bias and impartiality and the relevance of context. However, I am in agreement with and adopt the joint reasons of L'Heureux-Dubé and McLachlin JJ in their treatment of social context and the manner in which it may appropriately enter the decision-making process as well as their assessment of the trial judge's reasons and comments in the present case.

The following are the reasons delivered by L'HEUREUX-DUBÉ and McLACHLIN JJ.:

I. INTRODUCTION

We have read the reasons of our colleague, Justice Cory, and while we agree that this appeal must be allowed, we differ substantially from him in how we reach that outcome. As a result, we find it necessary to write brief concurring reasons.

[1997] 3 S.C.R. 484, aff'g (1995) 145 N.S.R. (2d) 284, 418 A.P.R. 284, 102 C.C.C. (3d) 233, 45 C.R. (4th) 361, aff'g [1995] N.S.J. No. 184 (QL).

(v) R. v. S. (R.D.)

We endorse Cory J.'s comments on judging in a multicultural society, the importance of perspective and social context in judicial decision-making, and the presumption of judicial integrity. However, we approach the test for reasonable apprehension of bias and its application to the case at bar somewhat differently from our colleague.

In our view, the test for reasonable apprehension of bias established in the jurisprudence is reflective of the reality that while judges can never be neutral, in the sense of purely objective, they can and must strive for impartiality. It therefore recognizes as inevitable and appropriate that the differing experiences of judges assist them in their decision-making process and will be reflected in their judgments, so long as those experiences are relevant to the cases, are not based on inappropriate stereotypes, and do not prevent a fair and just determination of the cases based on the facts in evidence.

We find that on the basis of these principles, there is no reasonable apprehension of bias in the case at bar. Like Cory J. we would, therefore, overturn the findings by the Nova Scotia Supreme Court (Trial Division) and the majority of the Nova Scotia Court of Appeal that a reasonable apprehension of bias arises in this case, and restore the acquittal of R.D.S. This said, we disagree with Cory J.'s position that the comments of Judge Sparks were unfortunate, unnecessary, or close to the line. Rather, we find them to reflect an entirely appropriate recognition of the facts in evidence in this case and of the context within which this case arose — a context known to Judge Sparks and to any well-informed member of the community.

II. THE TEST FOR REASONABLE APPREHENSION OF BIAS

The test for reasonable apprehension of bias is that set out by de Grandpré J. in *Committee for Justice and Liberty* v. *National Energy Board*, [1978] 1 S.C.R. 369. Though he wrote dissenting reasons, de Grandpré J.'s articulation of the test for bias was adopted by the majority of the Court, and has been consistently endorsed by this Court in the intervening two decades: see, for example, *Valente* v. *The Queen*, [1985] 2 S.C.R. 673; *R.* v. *Lippé*, [1991] 2 S.C.R. 114; *Ruffo* v. *Conseil de la magistrature*, [1995] 4 S.C.R. 267. De Grandpré J. stated, at pp. 394–95:

> ...the apprehension of bias must be a reasonable one, held by reasonable and right-minded persons, applying themselves to the question and obtaining thereon the required information....
>
> [T]hat test is "what would an informed person, viewing the matter realistically and practically — and having thought the matter through — conclude. Would he think that it is more likely than not that [the decision-maker], whether consciously or unconsciously, would not decide fairly."
>
> The grounds for this apprehension must, however, be substantial and I ... refus[e] to accept the suggestion that the test be related to the "very sensitive or scrupulous conscience".

As Cory J. notes at para. 92, the scope and stringency of the duty of fairness articulated by de Grandpré depends largely on the role and function of the tribunal in question. Although judicial proceedings will generally be bound by the requirements of natural justice to a greater degree than will hearings before administrative tribunals, judicial decision-makers, by virtue of their positions, have nonetheless been granted considerable deference by appellate courts inquiring into the apprehension of bias. This is because judges "are assumed to be [people] of conscience and intellectual discipline, capable of judging a particular controversy fairly on the basis of its own circumstances": *United States* v. *Morgan*, 313 U.S. 409 (1941), at p. 421. The presumption of impartiality carries considerable weight, for as Blackstone opined at p. 361 in Commentaries on the Laws of England, Book III, cited at footnote 49 in Richard F. Devlin, "We Can't Go On Together with Suspicious Minds: Judicial Bias and Racialized Perspective in R. v. R.D.S." (1995), 18 Dalhousie L.J. 408, at p. 417, "the law will not suppose a possibility of bias or favour in a judge, who is already sworn to administer impartial justice, and whose authority greatly depends upon that presumption and idea". Thus, reviewing courts have been hesitant to make a finding of bias or to perceive a reasonable apprehension of bias on the part of a judge, in the absence of convincing evidence to that effect: *R.* v. *Smith & Whiteway Fisheries Ltd.* (1994), 133 N.S.R. (2d) 50 (C.A.), at pp. 60–61.

Notwithstanding the strong presumption of impartiality that applies to judges, they will nevertheless be held to certain stringent standards regarding bias — "a reasonable apprehension that the judge might not act in an entirely impartial manner is ground for disqualification": *Blanchette* v. *C.I.S. Ltd.*, [1973] S.C.R. 833, at pp. 842–43.

In order to apply this test, it is necessary to distinguish between the impartiality which is required of all judges, and the concept of judicial neutrality. The distinction we would draw is that reflected in the insightful words of Benjamin N. Cardozo in The Nature of the Judicial Process (1921), at pp. 12–

13 and 167, where he affirmed the importance of impartiality, while at the same time recognizing the fallacy of judicial neutrality:

> There is in each of us a stream of tendency, whether you choose to call it philosophy or not, which gives coherence and direction to thought and action. Judges cannot escape that current any more than other mortals. All their lives, forces which they do not recognize and cannot name, have been tugging at them — inherited instincts, traditional beliefs, acquired convictions; and the resultant is an outlook on life, a conception of social needs.... In this mental background every problem finds its setting. We may try to see things as objectively as we please. None the less, we can never see them with any eyes except our own.
>
> ...
>
> Deep below consciousness are other forces, the likes and the dislikes, the predilections and the prejudices, the complex of instincts and emotions and habits and convictions, which make the [person], whether he [or she] be litigant or judge.

Cardozo recognized that objectivity was an impossibility because judges, like all other humans, operate from their own perspectives. As the Canadian Judicial Council noted in Commentaries on Judicial Conduct (1991), at p. 12, "[t]here is no human being who is not the product of every social experience, every process of education, and every human contact". What is possible and desirable, they note, is impartiality:

> ... the wisdom required of a judge is to recognize, consciously allow for, and perhaps to question, all the baggage of past attitudes and sympathies that fellow citizens are free to carry, untested, to the grave.

True impartiality does not require that the judge have no sympathies or opinions; it requires that the judge nevertheless be free to entertain and act upon different points of view with an open mind.

III. THE REASONABLE PERSON

The presence or absence of an apprehension of bias is evaluated through the eyes of the reasonable, informed, practical and realistic person who considers the matter in some detail (Committee for Justice and Liberty, supra.) The person postulated is not a "very sensitive or scrupulous" person, but rather a right-minded person familiar with the circumstances of the case.

It follows that one must consider the reasonable person's knowledge and understanding of the judicial process and the nature of judging as well as of the community in which the alleged crime occurred.

A. The Nature of Judging

As discussed above, judges in a bilingual, multiracial and multicultural society will undoubtedly approach the task of judging from their varied perspectives. They will certainly have been shaped by, and have gained insight from, their different experiences, and cannot be expected to divorce themselves from these experiences on the occasion of their appointment to the bench. In fact, such a transformation would deny society the benefit of the valuable knowledge gained by the judiciary while they were members of the Bar. As well, it would preclude the achievement of a diversity of backgrounds in the judiciary. The reasonable person does not expect that judges will function as neutral ciphers; however, the reasonable person does demand that judges achieve impartiality in their judging.

It is apparent, and a reasonable person would expect, that triers of fact will be properly influenced in their deliberations by their individual perspectives on the world in which the events in dispute in the courtroom took place. Indeed, judges must rely on their background knowledge in fulfilling their adjudicative function. As David M. Paciocco and Lee Stuesser write in their book The Law of Evidence (1996), at p. 277:

> In general, the trier of fact is entitled simply to apply common sense and human experience in determining whether evidence is credible and in deciding what use, if any, to make of it in coming to its finding of fact. [Emphasis in original.]

At the same time, where the matter is one of identifying and applying the law to the findings of fact, it must be the law that governs and not a judge's individual beliefs that may conflict with the law. Further, notwithstanding that their own insights into human nature will properly play a role in making findings of credibility or factual determinations, judges must make those determinations only after being equally open to, and considering the views of, all parties before them. The reasonable person, through whose eyes the apprehension of bias is assessed, expects judges to undertake an open-minded, carefully considered, and dispassionately deliberate investigation of the complicated reality of each case before them.

It is axiomatic that all cases litigated before judges are, to a greater or lesser degree, complex. There is more to a case than who did what to whom, and the questions of fact and law to be determined in any given case do not arise in a vacuum. Rather, they are the consequence of numerous factors, influenced by the innumerable forces which impact on them in a particular context. Judges, acting as finders of fact, must inquire into those forces. In short, they must be aware of the context in which the alleged crime occurred.

Judicial inquiry into the factual, social and psychological context within which litigation arises is not unusual. Rather, a conscious, contextual inquiry has become an accepted step towards judicial impartiality. In that regard, Professor Jennifer Nedelsky's "Embodied Diversity and the Challenges to Law" (1997), 42 McGill L.J. 91, at p. 107, offers the following comment:

> What makes it possible for us to genuinely judge, to move beyond our private idiosyncracies and preferences, is our capacity to achieve an "enlargement of mind". We do this by taking different perspectives into account. This is the path out of the blindness of our subjective private conditions. The more views we are able to take into account, the less likely we are to be locked into one perspective.... It is the capacity for "enlargement of mind" that makes autonomous, impartial judgment possible.

Judicial inquiry into context provides the requisite background for the interpretation and the application of the law. For example, in a case involving alleged police misconduct in denying an accused's right to counsel, this Court inquired not simply into whether the accused had been read their *Charter* rights, but also used a contextual approach to ensure that the purpose of the constitutionally protected right was fulfilled: *R. v. Bartle*, [1994] 3 S.C.R. 173. The Court, placing itself in the position of the accused, asked how the accused would have experienced and responded to arrest and detention. Against this background, the Court went on to determine what was required to make the right to counsel truly meaningful. This inquiry provided the Court with a larger picture, which was in turn conducive to a more just determination of the case.

An understanding of the context or background essential to judging may be gained from testimony from expert witnesses in order to put the case in context: *R. v. Lavallee*, [1990] 1 S.C.R. 852, *R. v. Parks* (1993), 15 O.R. (3d) 324 (C.A.), and *Moge v. Moge*, [1992] 3 S.C.R. 813, from academic studies properly placed before the Court; and from the judge's personal understanding and experience of the society in which the judge lives and works. This process of enlargement is not only consistent with impartiality; it may also be seen as its essential precondition.

A reasonable person far from being troubled by this process, would see it as an important aid to judicial impartiality.

B. The Nature of the Community

The reasonable person, identified by de Grandpré J. in Committee for Justice and Liberty, supra, is an informed and right-minded member of the community, a community which, in Canada, supports the fundamental principles entrenched in the Constitution by the Canadian Charter of Rights and Freedoms. Those fundamental principles include the principles of equality set out in s. 15 of the Charter and endorsed in nation-wide quasi-constitutional provincial and federal human rights legislation. The reasonable person must be taken to be aware of the history of discrimination faced by disadvantaged groups in Canadian society protected by the Charter's equality provisions. These are matters of which judicial notice may be taken. In Parks, supra, at p. 342, Doherty J.A., did just this, stating:

> Racism, and in particular anti-black racism, is a part of our community's psyche. A significant segment of our community holds overtly racist views. A much larger segment subconsciously operates on the basis of negative racial stereotypes. Furthermore, our institutions, including the criminal justice system, reflect and perpetuate those negative stereotypes.

The reasonable person is not only a member of the Canadian community, but also, more specifically, is a member of the local communities in which the case at issue arose (in this case, the Nova Scotian and Halifax communities). Such a person must be taken to possess knowledge of the local population and its racial dynamics, including the existence in the community of a history of widespread and systemic discrimination against black and aboriginal people, and high profile clashes between the police and the visible minority population over policing issues: Royal Commission on the Donald Marshall Jr. Prosecution (1989); *R. v. Smith* (1991), 109 N.S.R. (2d) 394 (Co. Ct.). The reasonable person must thus be deemed to be cognizant of the existence of racism in Halifax, Nova Scotia. It follows that judges may take notice of actual racism known to exist in a particular society. Judges have done so with respect to racism in Nova Scotia. In *Nova Scotia (Minister of Community Services) v. S.M.S.* (1992), 110 N.S.R. (2d) 91 (Fam Ct.), it was stated at p. 108:

[Racism] is a pernicious reality. The issue of racism existing in Nova Scotia has been well documented in the Marshall Inquiry Report (sub. nom. Royal Commission on the Donald Marshall, Jr., Prosecution). A person would have to be stupid, complacent or ignorant not to acknowledge its presence, not only individually, but also systemically and institutionally.

We conclude that the reasonable person contemplated by de Grandpré J., and endorsed by Canadian courts is a person who approaches the question of whether there exists a reasonable apprehension of bias with a complex and contextualized understanding of the issues in the case. The reasonable person understands the impossibility of judicial neutrality, but demands judicial impartiality. The reasonable person is cognizant of the racial dynamics in the local community, and, as a member of the Canadian community, is supportive of the principles of equality.

Before concluding that there exists a reasonable apprehension of bias in the conduct of a judge, the reasonable person would require some clear evidence that the judge in question had improperly used his or her perspective in the decision-making process; this flows from the presumption of impartiality of the judiciary. There must be some indication that the judge was not approaching the case with an open mind fair to all parties. Awareness of the context within which a case occurred would not constitute such evidence; on the contrary, such awareness is consistent with the highest tradition of judicial impartiality.

IV. APPLICATION OF THE TEST TO THE FACTS

In assessing whether a reasonable person would perceive the comments of Judge Sparks to give rise to a reasonable apprehension of bias, it is important to bear in mind that the impugned reasons were delivered orally. As Professor Devlin puts it in "We Can't Go On Together with Suspicious Minds: Judicial Bias and Racialized Perspective in R. v. R.D.S.", supra, at p. 414:

> Trial judges have a heavy workload that allows little time for meticulously thought-through reasoning. This is particularly true when decisions are delivered orally immediately after counsel have finished their arguments.

(See also *R.* v. *Burns*, [1994] 1 S.C.R. 656, at p. 664.)

It follows that for the purposes of this appeal, the oral reasons issued by judge Sparks should be read in their entirety, and the impugned passages should be construed in light of the whole of the trial proceedings and in light of all other portions of the judgment.

Judge Sparks was faced with contradictory testimony from the only two witnesses, the appellant R.D.S., and Constable Stienburg. Both testified as to the events that occurred and were subjected to cross-examination. As trier of fact, Judge Sparks was required to assess their testimony, and to determine whether or not, on the evidence before her, she had a reasonable doubt as to the guilt of the appellant R.D.S. It is evident in the transcript that Judge Sparks proceeded to do just that.

Judge Sparks briefly summarized the contradictory evidence offered by the two witnesses, and then made several observations about credibility. She noted that R.D.S. testified quite candidly, and with considerable detail. She remarked that contrary to the testimony of Constable Stienburg, it was the evidence of R.D.S. that when he arrived on the scene on his bike, his cousin was handcuffed and not struggling in any way. She found the level of detail that R.D.S. provided to have "a ring of truth", and found him to be "a rather honest young boy". In the end, while Judge Sparks specifically noted that she did not accept all the evidence given by R.D.S., she nevertheless found him to have raised a reasonable doubt by raising queries in her mind as to what actually occurred.

It is important to note that having already found R.D.S. to be credible, and having accepted a sufficient portion of his evidence to leave her with a reasonable doubt as to his guilt, Judge Sparks necessarily disbelieved at least a portion of the conflicting evidence of Constable Stienburg. At that point, Judge Sparks made reference to the submissions of the Crown that "there's absolutely no reason to attack the credibility of the officer", and then addressed herself to why there might, in fact, be a reason to attack the credibility of the officer in this case. It is in this context that Judge Sparks made the statements which have prompted this appeal:

> The Crown says, well, why would the officer say that events occurred the way in which he has relayed them to the Court this morning. I am not saying that the Constable has misled the court, although police officers have been known to do that in the past. I am not saying that the officer overreacted, but certainly police officers do overreact, particularly when they are dealing with non-white groups. That to me indicates a state of mind right there that is questionable. I believe that probably the situation in this particular case is the case of a young police officer who overreacted. I do accept the evidence of [R.D.S.]

that he was told to shut up or he would be under arrest. It seems to be in keeping with the prevalent attitude of the day.

At any rate, based upon my comments and based upon all the evidence before the court I have no other choice but to acquit.

These remarks do not support the conclusion that Judge Sparks found Constable Stienburg to have lied. In fact, Judge Sparks did quite the opposite. She noted firstly, that she was not saying Constable Stienburg had misled the court, although that could be an explanation for his evidence. She then went on to remark that she was not saying that Constable Stienburg had overreacted, though she was alive to that possibility given that it had happened with police officers in the past, and in particular, it had happened when police officers were dealing with non-white groups. Finally, Judge Sparks concluded that, though she was not willing to say that Constable Stienburg did overreact, it was her belief that he probably overreacted. And, in support of that finding, she noted that she accepted the evidence of R.D.S. that "he was told to shut up or he would be under arrest".

At no time did Judge Sparks rule that the probable overreaction by Stienburg was motivated by racism. Rather, she tied her finding of probable overreaction to the evidence that Constable Stienburg had threatened to arrest the appellant R.D.S. for speaking to his cousin. At the same time, there was evidence capable of supporting a finding of racially motivated overreaction. At an earlier point in the proceedings, she had accepted the evidence that the other youth arrested that day, was handcuffed and thus secured when R.D.S. approached. This constitutes evidence which could lead one to question why it was necessary for both boys to be placed in choke holds by Constable Stienburg, purportedly to secure them. In the face of such evidence, we respectfully disagree with the views of our colleagues Cory and Major JJ. that there was no evidence on which Judge Sparks could have found "racially motivated" overreaction by the police officer.

While it seems clear that Judge Sparks did not in fact relate the officer's probable overreaction to the race of the appellant R.D.S., it should be noted that if Judge Sparks had chosen to attribute the behaviour of Constable Stienburg to the racial dynamics of the situation, she would not necessarily have erred. As a member of the community, it was open to her to take into account the well-known presence of racism in that community and to evaluate the evidence as to what occurred against that background.

That Judge Sparks recognized that police officers sometimes overreact when dealing with non-white groups simply demonstrates that in making her determination in this case, she was alive to the well-known racial dynamics that may exist in interactions between police officers and visible minorities. As found by Freeman J.A. in his dissenting judgment at the Court of Appeal (1995), 145 N.S.R. (2d) 284, at p. 294:

> The case was racially charged, a classic confrontation between a white police officer representing the power of the state and a black youth charged with an offence. Judge Sparks was under a duty to be sensitive to the nuances and implications, and to rely on her own common sense which is necessarily informed by her own experience and understanding.

Given these facts, the question is whether a reasonable and right-minded person, informed of the circumstances of this case, and knowledgeable about the local community and about Canadian Charter values, would perceive that the reasons of Judge Sparks would give rise to a reasonable apprehension of bias. In our view, they would not. The clear evidence of prejudgment required to sustain a reasonable apprehension of bias is nowhere to be found.

Judge Sparks' oral reasons show that she approached the case with an open mind, used her experience and knowledge of the community to achieve an understanding of the reality of the case, and applied the fundamental principle of proof beyond a reasonable doubt. Her comments were based entirely on the case before her, were made after a consideration of the conflicting testimony of the two witnesses and in response to the Crown's submissions, and were entirely supported by the evidence. In alerting herself to the racial dynamic in the case, she was simply engaging in the process of contextualized judging which, in our view, was entirely proper and conducive to a fair and just resolution of the case before her.

V. CONCLUSION

In the result, we agree with Cory J. as to the disposition of this case. We would allow the appeal, overturn the findings of the Nova Scotia Supreme Court (Trial Division) and the majority of the Nova Scotia Court of Appeal, and restore the acquittal of the appellant R.D.S.

(vi) Antonio Lamer: Should Judges Hold Their Tongues? — The Chief Justice worries that, by keeping silent, judges are helping misconceptions to spread

Antonio Lamer

From my vantage point as Chief Justice of Canada, it strikes me that the place of the judiciary in our constitutional democracy has been a matter of considerable public debate and controversy, particularly over the past year. I see this in the editorials I read, the coverage that is given to judgments of my court and other courts and, indeed, in the public statements and debates of members of Parliament, senators and members of provincial legislatures.

And all that is fine.... It is natural, indeed desirable, for the roles of our various public institutions, including the courts, to be the subject of lively debate. There is only one aspect of the current discussion I wish to comment on.

Let me begin by reminding you of something you all know. The enactment in 1982 of a constitutionally entrenched Charter of Rights and Freedoms changed the *kind* of constitutional cases the courts have been faced with and, in that sense, changed their role. It did not really create a new *function* for the judiciary, since Canadian courts have always had the power to tell elected officials when they have gone too far. What has happened is that the basis on which the courts can, indeed must, do this has broadened considerably. There is no doubt that the judiciary was drawn into the political arena to a degree unknown prior to 1982.

Since 1982, judges as a whole have been subject to increasing criticism, especially of course in respect of controversial decisions made under the Charter. By no means would I ever suggest that this kind of criticism should be stifled. Of course not. It is valuable and healthy to our democracy. But, because of other factors I will come to in a moment, it causes me to wonder whether we now have to rethink another aspect of the attitude to be taken by the judiciary. In particular, I wonder whether judges, or maybe through their Chief Justices, should be rolling up the sleeves of their judicial robes and involving themselves in these public discussions more directly.

I am not saying that the judiciary should or should not be participating in public debates. I merely wish to raise the question for your consideration, perhaps over the next year....

I am sure it seems peculiar to the public that the judges simply make their decisions and then remain mute while the rest of society reacts to them. The public hardly ever hears any reaction from the judges. From the judges' point of view, it is certainly frustrating sometimes to stand by when there are errors made, whether innocent or deliberate, by those who write about or comment on judicial decisions. But our judicial tradition has been that judges generally do not comment on judgments or, for that matter, on any issue in the public domain touching them.

I confess that there have been times when I felt a particularly strong urge to comment publicly about a judgment of my court, for example, such as when the inconvenience of the requirement to obtain a warrant is described without any mention of the existence of telewarrants, which are available over the phone in a few minutes. There have been other times when I wished I could say something, in the public interest, about a piece of legislation before Parliament, such as a bill affecting judicial salaries and benefits. But our tradition, and it is a strong one, is one of silence on such matters. I have always thought that this was proper — that the judiciary should keep silent lest it sacrifice its independence or, at least, the perception of impartiality.

But lately I have begun to wonder whether that tradition of silence continues to be appropriate. And my main concern is not for the judges who are criticized in the press or by public figures. Rather, it seems to me that judicial silence sometimes means that the public misses out on a full understanding of what the courts are doing and why. Public debate on issues that come before the courts and, indeed, on

---

From *The Globe and Mail* (25 August 1998) A17. Quoted from remarks made on Sunday by Antonio Lamer, Chief Justice of the Supreme Court of Canada, to the Canadian Bar Association in St. John's. Reproduced by permission of the author.

the role of the judiciary itself is not as full as it should be because the perspective of the judiciary is usually absent.

It used to be the case that, while judges themselves were silent, the judicial perspective was supplied by the law officers of the Crown and by the bar. Accordingly, the tradition of judicial silence was paired with an equally strong tradition of support from other quarters. The purpose, of course, was not to defend every decision made by a judge but to explain, where necessary, the issues before the court, the basis on which the judge made the decision and any other necessary concepts to aid public understanding of the judicial role.

It appears to me, however, that the latter tradition of support for the judiciary has faded somewhat, which leads me to wonder whether the tradition of judicial silence itself should be revisited. I do not blame anyone for this state of affairs. It strikes me that it may be another inevitable by-product of the Charter. Perhaps as judicial decisions have become more entwined with political issues, the more difficult it has become for public figures and lawyers themselves to speak up. There is a political risk in their doing so. But the consequence is that the judiciary has no voice and no champion. In turn, public understanding of such fundamental concepts as judicial review under the Constitution and judicial independence is, I fear, fast eroding.

I admit that I do not have a clear solution to offer. I would be certainly reluctant to see judges enter the political fray. There would be enormous risks in this. On the other hand, I worry that there is also a risk in having judges hold their tongues. Perhaps there is some other solution....

I hope that you will agree with me that it is, at least, a matter worthy of discussion in the public interest.

(vii) Gavels, Microphones Don't Mix: Judicial decisions may be political, but judges don't need to act like politicians

Astutely, the Chief Justice of the Supreme Court of Canada has identified the next big political flashpoint on the fall horizon.

Populists in the Reform Party and in Premier Ralph Klein's Alberta are spoiling for battle against "judicial activism" — the perceived encroachment of judges on political decisions in Canada. Chief Justice Antonio Lamer is appropriately alert to the challenge.

But less wisely, Chief Justice Lamer has mused about a way to respond to this looming showdown between populists and judges. So you think the Supreme Court has too loud a voice in politics? Curiously, the Chief Justice believes that the solution may lie in further amplifying and broadcasting that voice.

"I wonder whether judges, or maybe through their chief justices, should be rolling up the sleeves of their judicial robes and involving themselves in these public discussions more directly," he said Sunday in a speech to the Canadian Bar Association's annual conference.

It is a strange proposition indeed to suggest that people would want more of the Supreme Court's thinking lobbed into the political arena in Canada. Critics of the court's power have not been asking to hear more from the judges in politics, but less.

Chief Justice Lamer wonders whether someone should be speaking on the court's behalf, if the August judiciary is going to be kicked around by the Reform Party, editorial writers and court critics. "The judiciary has no voice and no champion," he said, lamenting the loss of vocal support from lawyers and "law officers of the Crown."

Although we can admire the Chief Justice's understandable desire to defend his institution, we urge caution. When the fortress is under siege, it's foolhardy to mount the defence by dragging your leaders out from behind the walls.

The walls in this case are the walls of silence, the code that prevents judges from publicly dis-

---

From "Editorial," *The Globe and Mail* (26 August 1998) A14. Reproduced with permission from The Globe and Mail.

cussing their rulings after they are released. These walls exist to ensure that the Supreme Court speaks through its rulings, not its individual personalities. If Chief Justice Lamer and his colleagues truly believe that the Supreme Court is in danger of being misunderstood in its increasingly activist role, there are other solutions.

Most obviously, they can do their best to explain their rulings better. Chief Justice Lamer should note that the uprising against the court's power rests largely on the rulings, not on the individual judges. Clearly, the current Supreme Court is up to the challenge of explaining itself more fully — in print. The recent ruling on Quebec's secession rights, for example, was deft in execution and accessible in style.

The rulings, let's not forget, represent the collected wisdom and opinions of the judges. Once a judge starts venturing out to do a "just-what-was-meant" on the ruling, whether on television or in speeches, it's almost inevitable that two things will happen: (1) he will start treading into questions not covered by the ruling; and (2) the judge will start speaking for himself instead of the court as a whole.

If Chief Justice Lamer and his eight colleagues truly believe that Canadians need to hear more from them, the time for their views to be aired is before their rulings — not after the fact — with more open selection processes for judges. The last thing Canada needs is nine more unelected political voices crowding to be heard around a microphone.

10   Law and Social Transformation

(i) Doing Justice to "British Justice": Law, Ideology and Canadian Historiography

Greg Marquis

> In days of yore, from Britain's shore,
> Wolfe, the dauntless hero came,
> And planted firm Britannia's flag
> On Canada's fair domain.
> Here may it wave, our boast, our pride;
> And joined in love together
> The Thistle, Shamrock, Rose entwine,
> The Maple Leaf forever!
>
> Maple Leaf, our emblem dear, the Maple Leaf forever!
> God save our Queen, and heaven bless, the Maple leaf forever!
>
> At Queenston's Heights and Lundy's Lane
> Our brave forefathers, side by side,
> For freedom, homes and loved ones dear,
> Firmly stood and nobly died;
> And those dear rights which they maintained
> We swear to yield them never;
> Our watchword ever more shall be
> The Maple Leaf forever!
>   Alexander Muir, "The Maple Leaf Forever"

In an era when Canada had only a handful of progressive labour lawyers and no mainstream national civil liberties organization, the Communist-organized Canadian Labour Defence League raised funds, attracted thousands of members and defended trade unionists and leftists in the courts. In 1933 the CLDL held a convention in Toronto to discuss matters such as the recent Red Scare. The convention's report attempted to explain the League's failure to exploit local issues such as police corruption, political scandals and the notorious section 98 of the Criminal Code, on the basis of radical organizers' distaste for "humanitarianism" or "sentimentalism": "For instance, many workers still believe in 'British justice' and 'Democratic rights.' We should make effective use of demands on these very questions, thus drawing the workers into the struggle against the [police] terror." The report was addressing a thorny issue for early twentieth-century Canadian socialists, the popular legitimacy of the rule of law, which was an important, if often latent and ambiguous dimension of political culture. The standard sloganeering of the *Worker* and the *Young Worker*, organs of the Communist Party, was that legal rights were a bourgeois sham. Hence workers arrested on picket lines or at public meetings were considered political prisoners, and the police, the judiciary and the bar were enforcers of class justice. The treatment of elements of the Toronto labour and socialist movements by the police and courts in the 1920s and 1930s lent credibility to such an instrumentalist view of the legal order. The CLDL 1933 report nonetheless advised organizers to remain sensitive to the superstitions of the masses regarding the rule of law:

> Often, because we feel we are 'advanced', 'people on a higher level', etc., we do not take into account the moods, sentiments, and traditions of the workers, and arguing that they are 'bad' traditions, we therefore either ignore them or evoke resentment through tactics sneering at these traditions.

A speech given at the Canadian Law in History Conference, Carleton University in June of 1987. Reproduced by permission of the author.

The CLDL anecdote serves as the springboard for this paper, which will discuss Canadian Criminal justice historiography and research possibilities. Two major suggestions are made. First, that historians in a number of fields would benefit from examining popular attitudes towards and expectations of legal authority. The second point is that much of the "new history" of the last fifteen years, particularly social and working-class history in the process of reinterpreting or rejecting liberal historiography, has emphasized coercion and control by the dominant classes and ignored or neglected the question of the popular legitimacy of state institutions. According to an influential interpretation in legal history, the dominant classes, acting through the state, with varying degrees of success, have indoctrinated the masses with these "moods, sentiments and traditions." This interpretation must yield to a more sophisticated approach sensitive to the complexities and ambiguities of popular attitudes towards the law.

Perhaps because intellectual history, which traditionally relies on elite sources, is not currently fashionable, we rely on assumptions, rather than systematic examination of popular ideologies in Canada's past. The law and its administration were not remote for nineteenth-century British North Americans, but part of their orientation towards local affairs, government and the Empire. Justice, in the form of the constable, the alderman, the justice of the peace or the stipendiary magistrate, was a highly visible if decentralized sign of the state. The law was viewed as an instrument of control as well as a vehicle for political and social change — not merely by great men, but by much of the ignorant populace. It is significant, for example, that the Patriote Party of Lower Canada responded to popular rural demands by advocating magistrates appointed by the people. Lloyd Kramer, in a recent article that attempts to find common ground between social and intellectual history, suggests one solution in the mentalité methodology developed by French historians who explore "the unconscious, deep structural aspects of human thought and behaviour" found "in popular culture, beliefs, ritual and ideologies." In like manner Robert Gordon has suggested that legal historians should

> treat legal forms as ideologies and rituals whose 'effects' — effects that include people's ways of sorting out social experience, giving it meaning, grading it as natural, just and necessary, or as contrived, unjust and subject to alteration — are in the realm of consciousness.

The challenge is to reconstruct a "demotic intellectual history" to complement the institutional approach of much criminal justice historiography. I have adopted the nineteenth-century term "British justice," which links law and legal institutions to political culture, to suggest a promising category of analysis for such inquiries.

The English Inheritance

Any study of Canadian attitudes towards the law and uses of the legal system must begin with the English cultural heritage, particularly the powerful view of British institutions as the bulwark of liberty. An 1880 Ontario government publication, for example, promised prospective immigrants from the old country no less than "All the protection and safety that British law can ensure." One has but to recall former generations of Canadian school textbooks for a glimpse of these Whiggish ideals. To date these sentiments have been explored mainly by intellectual historians, in their most exaggerated form, in the writings and speeches of late nineteenth- and early twentieth-century Canadian imperialists. According to Carl Berger, Canadian imperialism combined an awareness of Canadian nationality and "an equally decided desire to unify and transform the British Empire so that this nationality could attain a position of equality within it." Historians should now turn to the hypothesis that emotional attachment to British institutions, which included a particular view of history, was not confined to the middle and upper classes but influenced the social experience of the urban and rural masses.

In the British constitutionalist tradition legal rights were not separated from political rights; both had been wrested from a tyrannical monarchy. Although these ancient rights and privileges were for most of British history ignored or honoured selectively, the culture of constitutionalism stressing the benefits of English law was an important ideological force in the eighteenth- and nineteenth-century British world. As Anne Pallister has demonstrated, the key to this tradition was veneration of an idealized past that included emotive symbols such as Magna Carta:

> The equation of law and liberty, the belief that the law of England protects rather than restricts the freedom of the individual, which is the central feature of the Charter, still lies at the heart of English political and legal thought and practice; and the Charter provides a standard of political ethos against which official action in its effects upon the individual can be measured.

Magna Carta and other symbols, moreover, became "the property of both conservative constitutionalists and radical agitators." These traditions were evident in the independence movements of Britain's rebellious eighteenth-century North American colonies, whose leaders were well versed in Whig history and ritualistic invocations of freedom as the birthright of Englishmen. By 1760, American Whigs were reaching back into history, appropriating national myths such as the Norman Yoke, Magna Carta and the Glorious Revolution, to legitimize their constitutional dispute with Britain. Similarly, despite national differences among Great Britain, the United States and Canada, the Victorians praised the spirit of Magna Carta as the heritage of all English-speaking peoples.

The rhetoric of British liberty can be interpreted in more than one way. A Marxist might explain that the great constitutional struggles that captivated Whig historians represented a debate of limited parameters, involving factions of the dominant classes, one representing landed property, the other commercial and industrial capitalism. That legal ideology can be used to buttress the status quo should come as no surprise. Douglas Hay, in an influential article, has argued that the law replaced monarchy as the principal ideology legitimizing the eighteenth-century English state. In Hay's functionalist interpretation, elite management of ideology is the key to state power. An earlier article, "Patrician Society, Plebeian Culture", by E.P. Thompson examined eighteenth-century paternalist relations and the importance of law as "public theatre" in maintaining the hegemony of the state. Although the law was used as an ideological weapon to reinforce class relations, it was not, in the opinion of Thompson, merely an instrument for maintaining control and consent. The ideology of the dominant classes could also become the rallying cry of popular resistance:

> And finally, far from the ruled shrugging off this rhetoric as hypocrisy, some part of at least was taken over by the plebeian crowd, of the 'free-born Englishman', with his inviolable privacy, his *habeas corpus*, his equality before the law.

Thus various social groups could combine self-interest with a vision of constitutional rights, often in a utopian frame of reference.

. . . .

Conclusion

How then, should we do justice to British justice? First, by attempting to recover a potentially rich and complex symbolic tradition that linked law to political culture. Second, by recognizing that the law's class instrumentality co-existed with a degree of popular legitimacy. The interaction of state ideology and institutions on the one hand and popular attitudes and responses on the other is a promising research area. Historians must develop strategies for evaluating both popular resistance to and the popular legitimacy of the legal order. This will not be *the way* to do legal history or a new organizing principle for social history, but a possible corrective to the internal focus of legal historiography and the "great man" focus of intellectual historiography. Legal historians cannot afford to ignore the legal consciousness of the masses, however vulgarized it may be. British justice and its meanings may also prove useful in social history where there will be increasing interest in ambiguity and less in conflict and control. Working-class historians, if they are to retain their claim of being on the cutting edge, must come to grips with these traditions. Inquiries along these lines will face methodological obstacles, notably the challenge of gauging the opinions of the common people, but they will broaden our conception of law, society and the state.

(ii) Interest Group Litigation and Canadian Democracy

Gregory Hein

Interest Groups in Court
The Debate

Anyone who wants to understand judicial politics in Canada has to consider the efforts of organized interests. Groups are at the centre of most policy debates, trying to persuade an audience of elected officials, bureaucrats, editorialists and ordinary citizens to accept rival positions. The stakes are

---

From (2000) 6:2 *Choices* in the *Courts and Legislatures* series (Montreal: Institute for Research on Public Policy) at 3–5, 8–10, 11, 25–26. Notes omitted. Reproduced by permission.

higher when they enter the courtroom. Organizations shoulder the burden of representing thousands of individuals, hundreds of unions scattered across the country, or entire industries. Some use impressive resources to mobilize the law, deploying teams of lawyers and expert witnesses. Advocates who want to reform society urge courts to make the bold decisions that infuriate critics of judicial activism. Instead of asking conventional legal questions, they often present novel arguments that stretch the boundaries of law.

Canadians can no longer ignore interest group litigation because it affects the style and substance of our political life. Though a specialized activity practiced by lawyers and discussed by legal scholars, it has become an important strategy for interests trying to shape public policy. Stories about court challenges are reported in the media every week and interest groups participate in most of the cases: civil libertarians guard free expression with vigilance, even if their efforts help men who produce and consume child pornography; disabled people refuse to accept laws that ignore their needs; feminists take on defence lawyers who attack Criminal Code measures designed to counter sexual assault; pro-choice activists and pro-life groups return to court to argue about the presence or absence of fetal rights; gays and lesbians pursue an ambitious campaign to stop discrimination based on sexual orientation; First Nations assert Aboriginal treaty rights; hunters enter the courtroom to oppose measures that restrict the use of guns; groups that promote law and order denounce judges for paying too much attention to the rights of the criminally accused and too little attention to the victims of violent crimes. Unions enter the judicial system to help workers and corporations challenge regulations that frustrate their ability to maximize profits. Their adversaries also litigate. Environmentalists and economic nationalists try to enforce laws that discipline the free market.

Canadians who find these efforts unsettling identify several concerns. Organizations raise difficult moral, economic and political questions, but courts are not designed to sustain public discussions on complex issues. The most controversial claims pit courts against legislatures by asking judges to reject choices made by elected officials. Political life is pulled into our judicial system by groups that generate a steady stream of cases, but without confirmation hearings we know little about the men and women elevated to the Supreme Court. We know even less about superior court judges who also exercise broad powers. These fears are expressed by those who think that litigation can undermine the struggle for a better society and by those who insist that democracy is threatened by organizations that encourage judicial activism.

The debate in the 1980s was initiated by critical legal scholars and neo-Marxists who refused to believe that courts would be transformed into brash agencies of social change. Their assessment was scathing. The Charter cannot create a forum of principle elevated above the fray of politics, they argued, because courts are not immune from the public pressures, economic realities and ideological contests that affect legislatures. Citizens have new guarantees, but they are grandiose declarations that will not alter the allocation of power and the distribution of wealth. What did these sceptics predict? The barriers impeding access to legal remedies would not wither away. Working people would fail to win dramatic victories because too many judges are guided by values that favour corporate interests. Feminists so determined to win in court would soon discover grave dangers — their resources would be depleted and their adversaries would use the Constitution to attack the welfare state. After discovering the limits of litigation, activists trying to build a just society would see that Parliament is the real engine of reform.

The debate in the 1990s has been dominated by scholars and politicians on the right. According to their account, activists on the left have been wildly successful because so many judges are "removed from reality." These interests flood the courts because they cannot win the support of legislative majorities: most voters find their demands radical and dogmatic. We are told that gays and lesbians want to impose values that will undermine the traditional family. Aboriginal peoples are determined to establish title over huge tracts of land and secure access to lucrative resources just by presenting flimsy oral histories. Feminists promote an interpretation of equality that leads to "reverse discrimination." Civil libertarians, by guarding the rights of alleged criminals, make it more difficult for police and prosecutors to secure law and order. For critics on the right, these "special interests" belong to a coalition which could be called the "court party." They bring the claims that fuel the growth of judicial power. Instead of trying to build public support for their ideas, these activists urge the Supreme Court to expand social services and benefits, alter the meaning of Aboriginal treaties written centuries ago, bolster regulatory regimes or repair legislative omissions. This use of litigation diminishes Canadian democracy, we are told, because it allows members of the court party to circumvent the legislative process.

(ii) Interest Group Litigation and Canadian Democracy

This study offers an alternative argument by marshalling a large body of empirical data. The account advanced by conservative critics is incomplete and misleading. While warning us about "zealous" activists who invite judicial activism, they never tell us that courts are filled with a broad range of interests that express a wide array of values. Litigants talk to judges about child custody, labour disputes, income tax policy, advertising laws, medical procedures that cause harm, and the dangers of hazardous substances. This diversity exists because successive generations of Canadians have asked courts and governments to create new opportunities to participate in the judicial system and the legislative arena. We will see that critics on the right are correct when they argue that social activists are eager to pursue legal strategies. However, their interpretation ignores the economic interests that also appreciate the benefits of litigation. Corporations exert a surprising degree of pressure by asking judges to scrutinize the work of elected officials.

At the heart of this argument is an important analytical distinction designed to help us understand the strategic choices that groups make. The propensity to litigate is elevated by *stable characteristics*. Interests will be more inclined to mount court challenges when they have impressive legal resources, collective identities energized by rights, and normative visions that demand judicial activism. Strategic choices are also affected by *changing circumstances* that can make litigation seem attractive or even essential. Interests take advantage of interpretive opportunities, counter immediate threats that can be addressed by judges, and move policy battles into the courtroom when their political resources have been eroded.

The evidence below suggests that Aboriginal peoples, Charter Canadians, civil libertarians, and new left activists have the greatest potential to influence public policy through litigation because they are pulled and pushed into the courtroom by both stable characteristics and changing circumstances. These interests can be called *judicial democrats* because a provocative idea is embedded in their legal arguments and political appeals — judicial review can enhance democracy. Finding deficiencies that weaken our system of government, they believe that the courts should listen to groups that lack political power, protect vulnerable minorities and guard fundamental values, from basic civil liberties forged by the common law tradition to ecological principles that have emerged in the past century.

This study also reveals that corporations do not have the stable characteristics that elevate the propensity to litigate. However, they do confront the changing circumstances that make legal action a compelling strategic manoeuvre. Businesses enter the courtroom to counter hostile actions, to block investigating government agencies and when their political resources have been depleted.

. . . .

Interest Group Litigation before the Charter

. . . .

...For more than a century, few organizations entered the courtroom to affect public policy. It was possible to have a complete understanding of Canadian politics without ever thinking about interest group litigation. The labour movement concentrated on the party system because courts did little to help workers; relying on the assumptions of classical liberalism, judges allowed market forces to settle most issues. Activists who wanted to solve social problems pressured legislators and devised novel strategies in order to change public attitudes, but few imagined that litigation could be turned into an instrument of reform. While achieving some of their objectives in court, corporations lobbied cabinet ministers and senior officials because they appreciated the importance of elite accommodation and the power of bureaucracies.

Interest Group Litigation after the Charter

This study reveals that a transformation has occurred. Interest group litigation is now an established form of collective action. Organizations [presented] 819 claims between 1988 and 1998. They appear as parties or intervenors in 30 percent of the disputes considered by the Federal Court and the Supreme Court. Figure 1 records the frequency of participation.

Groups from every category pursue legal strategies. This single finding is remarkable — we now find the same mix of political players trying to influence courts and governments. But if there has been an important change, we also find elements of continuity. Court dockets are still laden with corporations. They [brought] 468 legal actions, far more than the other interests. Companies engage in civil litigation against private parties, and challenge regulations governing banking, federal elections, international trade, environmental protection and the pharmaceutical industry. Groups representing professionals [participated] in 32 cases. They try to win higher salaries as employees and as experts they talk to judges about a range of issues, including the principles that guide child custody disputes and criminal investigations. Very few of their challenges try to alter major public policies. The unions and advocacy groups that represent labour interests [brought] 58 claims. They back members alleging gender discrimination, fight for higher salaries, counter measures that undermine collective bargaining, try to escape criminal contempt charges and assert the right to strike.

The big change is that courts now hear from interests that struggled for decades to win access. For more than a century, courts and governments in Canada maintained barriers that discouraged or even prevented litigation. The Indian Act was amended in 1927 to stop Aboriginal peoples from bringing legal claims. Although this restriction was lifted in 1951, the Supreme Court did not begin to recognize and protect Aboriginal rights until 1973, when it considered a case brought by the Nisga'a. Steep obstacles were preserved by the common law. Rules on standing, proof, evidence, and costs reflected a clear preference. Judges wanted to sift through intrinsic evidence to settle discrete legal questions raised by two parties engaged in a live controversy. Applicants who could demonstrate a direct stake in a dispute were allowed to exercise their private rights. Citizens who organized to address public problems were usually sent away.

. . . .

Figure 1 reveals that litigation is now an important strategy for groups that once confronted these obstacles:

- Aboriginal peoples [launched] 77 claims between 1988–98. First Nations take on the federal government when it fails to act in their best interests; they secure title to land by asserting Aboriginal rights and challenge laws that fail to respect treaty rights.
- Charter Canadians are just as active: 80 legal arguments [were] presented to oppose measures restricting abortion services, to chastise provincial governments for breaching language rights, to reveal racism in the criminal justice system, and to overturn election laws that discriminate against the mentally ill.
- Civil libertarians [participated] in 40 cases that attack policies impairing democratic rights, fundamental freedoms and guarantees that protect the criminally accused.
- New left activists [brought] 37 claims. They enter the courtroom in order to protect delicate ecosys-

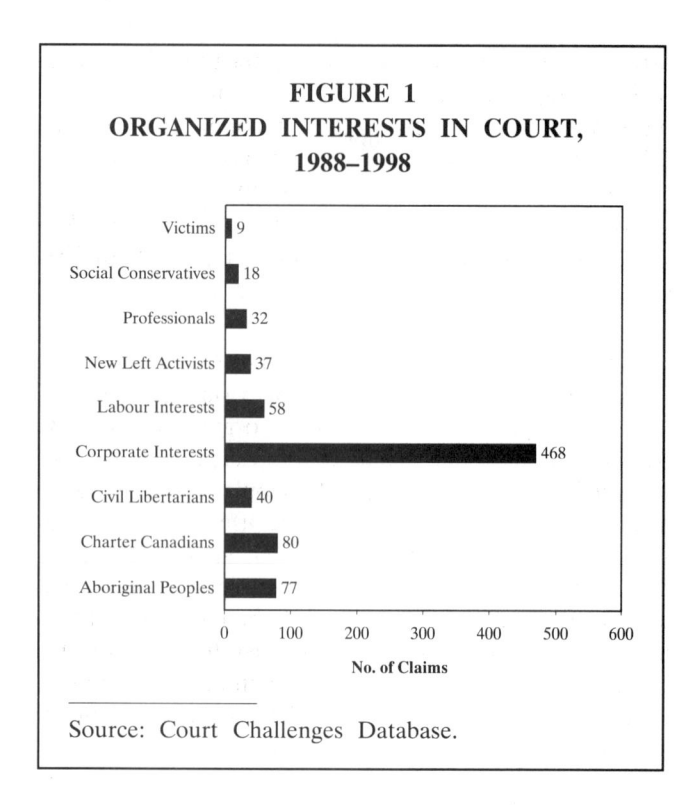

FIGURE 1
ORGANIZED INTERESTS IN COURT, 1988–1998

Group	No. of Claims
Victims	9
Social Conservatives	18
Professionals	32
New Left Activists	37
Labour Interests	58
Corporate Interests	468
Civil Libertarians	40
Charter Canadians	80
Aboriginal Peoples	77

Source: Court Challenges Database.

tems, help poor people facing arrest, overturn policies that exclude homosexuals, and counter measures that limit demonstrations.
- Social conservatives [brought] fewer claims, only 18. The most controversial claims try to persuade courts to recognize fetal rights. Unlike their American allies and their Canadian adversaries, social conservatives have not formed any legal advocacy groups; these are specialized organizations designed to fight legal campaigns. In the early 1990s, the Canadian Rights Coalition was established to take on doctors who dared to perform abortions, but it soon disappeared.
- Organizations that represent victims [brought] even fewer court challenges, only nine. They usually participate outside the courtroom. Most legal claims are brought by individuals who allege negligence or breach of trust to win compensation. Class actions are also orchestrated to counter threats that harm hundreds of victims.

. . . .

The Supreme Court has also introduced changes that have encouraged interest group litigation. The law of standing has been liberalized in stages. The old common law rule favoured property owners and corporations trying to protect private rights and filtered out citizens who wanted to address public problems. Under the new rule, applicants who ask a serious legal question and demonstrate a "genuine interest" can win access if certain conditions are satisfied. The Supreme Court has also relaxed the requirements for intervening. Groups with a record of advocacy displaying expertise in a particular area usually receive permission to appear as friends of the court.

The Legal Status of Participants

Looking at evidence from the Court Challenges Database, we can find out how organizations participate. A clear pattern emerges. Corporations, professionals, unions, Aboriginal peoples, and victims usually participate as parties because they tend to seek "private" benefits for partners, shareholders, or members. Figure 2 reveals that litigants with this legal status present 81 percent of their claims. Standing is not a barrier because it is easy to demonstrate a direct stake in a dispute. These interests do intervene when they are represented by advocacy groups that want to influence public policy.

We find the very opposite in Figure 3. Charter Canadians, civil libertarians, new left activists, and social conservatives usually participate as intervenors because they tend to seek "public" benefits. Litigants with this legal status present 78 percent of their claims. Most appear before the Supreme Court. Groups that take this route have to accept several constraints. Intervenors cannot file motions, submit evidence, call witnesses, cross-examine or appeal decisions. These limitations do not discourage public interests because they appreciate the advantages of this form of intervention. Not confined to a specific set of facts, intervenors are free to develop bold claims that dissect complicated social problems. Instead of wasting time and money participating as parties, intervenors can be selective. They can monitor thousands of cases moving up the levels of our judicial system. By appearing before the Supreme Court, interests seeking diffuse public benefits can build precedents, shape public policy and counter hostile actions — without exhausting their resources.

. . . .

Critics troubled by active courts want to restore the relative calm we once enjoyed by resurrecting "traditional judicial review." What do they propose? The Supreme Court has to bring back the old standing requirements, discourage interests from intervening, consider only narrow legal questions raised by live controversies and question the value of extrinsic

FIGURE 2
THE LEGAL STATUS OF INTERESTS SEEKING PRIVATE BENEFITS

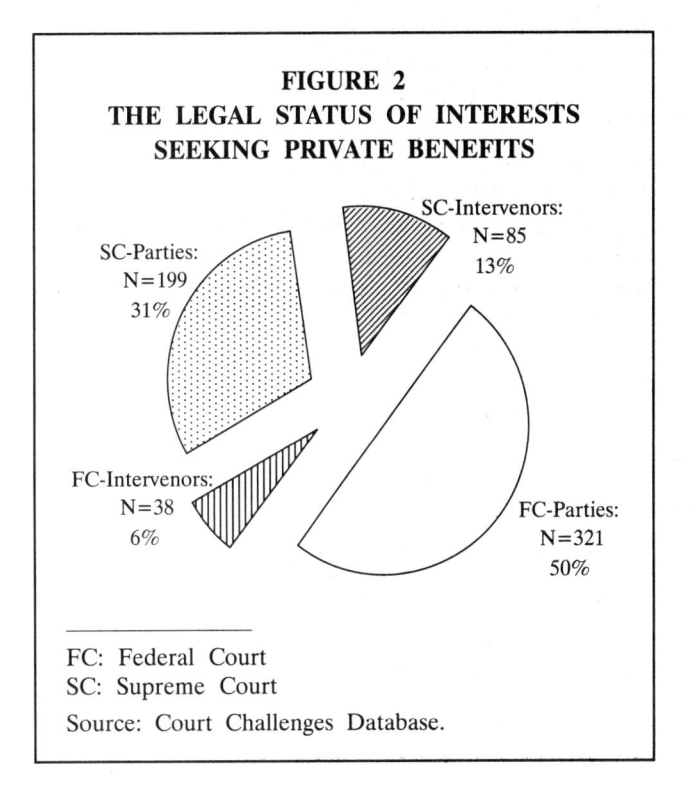

SC-Intervenors: N=85, 13%
SC-Parties: N=199, 31%
FC-Intervenors: N=38, 6%
FC-Parties: N=321, 50%

FC: Federal Court
SC: Supreme Court
Source: Court Challenges Database.

FIGURE 3
THE LEGAL STATUS OF INTERESTS SEEKING PUBLIC BENEFITS

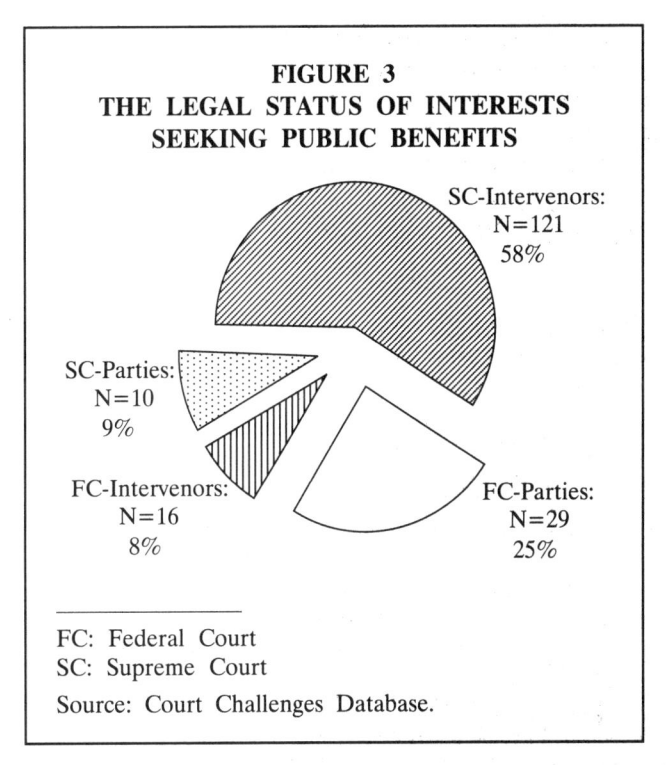

SC-Intervenors: N=121, 58%
SC-Parties: N=10, 9%
FC-Intervenors: N=16, 8%
FC-Parties: N=29, 25%

FC: Federal Court
SC: Supreme Court
Source: Court Challenges Database.

evidence. They resent judges who allow political adversaries to clutter the courtroom, evaluate policy alternatives with misplaced confidence and try to settle future disputes in a single decision. Conservative critics believe that prudence should replace arrogance. It is too easy for judges to advance their personal preferences, they insist, if the "living tree metaphor" can be invoked as a license to alter the meaning and scope of enumerated guarantees. The Supreme Court has to remember the primary purpose of a liberal democratic constitution: to protect individuals by placing limits on the state. Legal remedies should not increase the presence of the state. Judges should never punish governments for failing to act by filling perceived omissions. They should also resist the temptation to expand services, benefits, regulatory regimes and Aboriginal treaties.

This argument can sound appealing, especially when the Supreme Court delivers a decision that divides the country. Still, the measures that conservative critics propose have a distinct bias that Canadians should know about. Resurrecting traditional judicial review would filter out certain interests and values. Returning to the old rules governing standing and intervenor status would hurt public interests unable to demonstrate a direct stake in a dispute. Excluding extrinsic evidence would make it more difficult for litigants who want to trace the adverse effects of a law. Freezing the meaning and scope of constitutional guarantees would leave judges unable to address new social problems that create discrimination. If courts only placed limits on the state, litigation would be a poor strategy for citizens who want to bolster regulatory regimes or expand social services. Taken together, these obstacles would hinder interests concerned about racism, homophobia, gender inequality, environmental degradation, poverty, the lives of the disabled and the plight of Aboriginal peoples. Traditional judicial review would not, however, frustrate litigants advancing conventional pecuniary claims and legal action would still be an effective strategy for interests that want to resist state intervention.

Although constrained courts would cause fewer disruptions, we would pay a price. Litigation would help corporations but not groups trying to address public problems. Critics of judicial activism stumble here. They want to stop social reformers from seeking the legal remedies that businesses have always requested. Seen from this perspective, the current relationship between citizens, legislators, and judges is attractive because it meets a basic requirement of democracy that many Canadians embrace. Nations composed of diverse interests should not have institutions that respond to some and ignore others.

(iii) Social Control, State Autonomy and Legal Reform: The Law Reform Commission of Canada

Ross Hastings and R.P. Saunders

There is a general agreement among social scientists that law serves a strategic purpose as a formal expression of the dominant values of a society, as a mechanism for the resolution of conflicts and the coercion of rule-breakers, or as a tool in the education or "civilizing" of the general public. In this sense, it is impossible to study the forms and uses of law apart from the wider social relations and structural arrangements from [ ] which it emerges. However, this notion can be operationalized in very different ways. On the one hand, functionalists are more likely to view law as expressing the outcome of a relatively open negotiation process between competing interest groups and to focus their analysis on the consequences of law for the overall welfare of a given social system. On the other hand, Marxists emphasize the class-based material and ideological interests which are served by the law at a given social and political conjuncture. The common thread in these otherwise incompatible positions is a view of the law as emerging within current social relations and social structures and as contributing to their preservation or transformation.

. . . .

This excerpt is reproduced with permission of the Publisher from *State Control: Criminal Justice Politics in Canada*, edited by R.S. Ratner and John L. McMullan. Copyright University of British Columbia Press 1987. All rights reserved by the Publisher. References omitted.

(iii) Social Control, State Autonomy and Legal Reform: The Law Reform Commission of Canada

The present paper focuses on an aspect of the specific case of the reform of criminal law in Canada. The process, content, and consequences of legal reform can only be adequately understood in the context of the wider role of the state in general and of the issues of ideology and social control in particular. Our focus will be on the work of the Law Reform Commission of Canada (LRCC), which is one of the key state agencies involved in the current project of the Canadian government to rewrite the Canadian Criminal Code. We wish to establish the LRCC's contribution to this process and the degree to which this is related to the relative autonomy of the LRCC in particular and the criminal justice system in general.

The movement of the Canadian state towards the creation of a law reform agency began in the late 1960's, culminating in 1971 with the formation of the Law Reform Commission of Canada. The commission was intended to be a response, and in part a solution, to the conflict and social disjunctures which marked the 1960's. According to John Turner, Minister of Justice at the time, this period was an "age of confrontation": "we are witnessing today what has been called a 'crisis of legitimacy' or as some would have it a 'crisis of authority.' All our institutions ... are being challenged" (1971, p. 2). In the face of this crisis, Turner nevertheless argued that "revolution" can be made possible through law, and that "law is not just a 'technical body' of rules; it is the organizing principle for the reconfiguration of society. Law is not just an agency of social control; it articulates the values by which men seek to live" (*ibid.*).

The LRCC was thus designed to contribute to the challenge of coming to grips with social conflict and social change. There was a recognition that the old order was giving way to a new, more heterogeneous and more fragmented society, one in which the law would be called upon to provide "the means by which multiple sets of values can co-exist and develop" (Burke, 1971; p. 5). The goal was to codify, rationalize, and rethink the law in order to adapt our legal instruments to the task of constructing a more harmonious world.

The formal mandate of the LRCC directed it to engage in both the technical task of systematizing and rationalizing the law and the broader sociopolitical task of reform. More specifically, the LRCC was authorized to make recommendations on:

1. the removal of anachronisms and anomalies in the law;
2. the reflection in and by the law of the distinctive concepts and institutions of the common and civil law systems in Canada and the reconciliation of differences and discrepancies in the expression and application of the law arising out of differences in these concepts and institutions;
3. the elimination of obsolete laws; and
4. the development of new approaches to and new concepts of the law in keeping with and responsive to the changing needs of modern Canadian society and individual members of that society (Law Reform Commission Act, 1970, s. 11).

This mandate, particularly in its directive to develop new orientations to the law, justifies an analysis of the results of over a decade of LRCC work.

. . . .

In order to accomplish this analysis, we will discuss the contributions of the LRCC to the current project of revising and rewriting the Canadian Criminal Code, focusing on three major issues. First, we will discuss the internal division of labour and the working process adopted by the LRCC in its attempt to accomplish its mandate. This general description will permit an appreciation of the broad scope of the task assigned to the LRCC, and will allow us to identify some of the main groups who participate in the work of legal reform.

. . . .

The LRCC and the Work of Reform

Despite its high level of funding and its original intentions to engage in fundamental research and consult broadly during the process of legal reform, the LRCC is relatively little known outside the legal profession. For this reason, a brief description of the organization and its working procedures is useful.

In order to fulfill its mandate, the LRCC has structured its tasks so as to best reflect the various potential areas of law reform within the federal jurisdiction. This had led to a division of the work of the LRCC into four major research projects:

1. the Substantive Criminal Law Project, which is responsible for the writing of a new code of substantive criminal law;

2. the Criminal Procedure Project, which is involved in the production of a code of criminal procedure;
3. the Protection of Life Project, which is engaged in the examination of a broad range of medico-legal matters, including issues relating to pollution, the environment, and consumer products; and
4. the Administrative Law Project, which is concerned with research into the general relationship between law and administrative agencies. (LRCC, 1984, pp. 17–18)

Each project is headed by a project co-ordinator and is under the overall direction of an individual commissioner (*ibid.*, p. 5). For the purposes of our study, we have focused our attention solely on the work of the Substantive Criminal Law Project. There are two reasons for this. First, it is this project which is most directly responsible for the production of the *content* of criminal law within the law reform process. As such, its work will best illustrate the positions adopted by the LRCC on both the general aims of criminal law in Canadian society and the process of criminal law reform. Second, the government of Canada is currently engaged in a long-term project of rewriting the Criminal Code. The Department of Justice has placed a high priority on the production of this code; as a result, the work of the LRCC has taken on an increased importance.

During its first years of operation, the LRCC produced its work in several stages:

> First, the publication by a project group of a study paper (which does not express the views of the commission) inviting comments, then, of a commission working paper, written in the light of public reaction to the study paper and again inviting comment, and, finally, publication of a report to the Minister of Justice for his consideration and for tabling in Parliament. (Barnes, 1975, p. 84)

The working procedure of the LRCC changed, however, with more emphasis placed on the working paper itself. Moreover, in practice, the direction and spirit of the criminal law working papers have been substantially the same as those of the reports which followed them.

In the actual preparation and production of its paper and reports, the LRCC and, more particularly, the Criminal Law Project, uses various research techniques. Four methods have been identified: 1) philosophical enquiry; 2) the comparative method; 3) empirical research; and 4) consultation (*ibid.*, p. 72). The first, philosophical enquiry, is a "search for values." We will focus on this issue later in this chapter, for it is the discussions of values and the purpose of criminal law which we find the most illustrative of the orientation of the LRCC. Using the comparative method, the LRCC has focused on the bi-jural nature of the Canadian system and has examined other common law and civil law systems (*ibid.*, p. 76). The goal of the LRCC in its empirical research is to "discover the actual living law, the law that really governs Canadian people." Even from a conventional perspective, however, this research has been found to be "sporadic" at best (*ibid.*, pp. 76–77). But a more fundamental criticism can be made of the type of empirical research into criminal law in which the LRCC engages. This criticism relates to the restricted methodology which the LRCC uses and is discussed later in this chapter. The consultation process of the LRCC in the production of its working papers and reports is a relatively narrow one. While the LRCC has at times attempted to involve the wider public in the law reform process, the response has been generally unsatisfying. An early example of the failure of an attempt at broad-based public involvement is the Ottawa Pilot Project (which was basically a series of public information meetings in 1974) which excited little public response (*ibid.*, pp. 85–85). In contrast, the regular consultations in which the LRCC engages are much more important and influential. They involve representatives of five groups: judges, defence lawyers, police chiefs, law teachers, and crown counsel (LRCC, 1984; pp. 19–20). It is evident from this list that the consultation process is a relatively closed one, involving as it does only certain (usually legal) professionals in the criminal justice system. This bias towards the legal profession is evident as well in the background of the majority of the members of the Substantive Criminal Law Project. Not surprisingly, this restricted participation is not without consequence for the findings or recommendations of the LRCC.

. . . .

In the long run, however, this may not be too important. The new Canadian Constitution and the emerging tendency for key political and legal issues to be resolved in the courts will probably shift the real axis of legal reform from the LRCC to the Supreme Court. Time goes on — the LRCC probably will not.

(iv) The Role of Law in Social Transformation: Is a Jurisprudence of Insurgency Possible?

Stephen Brickey and Elizabeth Comack

Contemporary Marxist theorizing on law has produced a number of different ways of conceptualizing the class character of law within a capitalist society. The main focus of these approaches has largely been on the role of law in maintaining and reproducing an unequal, exploitative system. As a consequence, the issue, even the possibility of using law as a mechanism for securing substantial social change has been downplayed and, in some cases, precluded.

The purpose of this paper is to argue for a rethinking of law, especially in terms of its potential as an agent for social transformation. The discussion will be divided into two main sections. The first involves theoretical considerations. Problems encountered with existing approaches to law *vis-à-vis* their implications for change will be examined and the direction in which a theoretical reformulation might proceed will be outlined. The second involves practical considerations. Here the focus will be on the kinds of legal strategies and particular forms and conditions of law that could be extended or developed in order to move in the direction of a socialist society.

. . . .

Toward a Theoretical Reformulation

It is not our intention to deny the insights to be gained from current Marxist theorizing on law. Much has been accomplished, for example, in the way of clarifying the class character of law under capitalism. Nor is it our intention to deny the significance of law as a mechanism of class domination. In this regard, we would agree with writers like Picciotto that the rule of law — to the extent that it has bourgeois limitations and characteristics — must and should be transcended. The question remains, however, as to *how* that is to be accomplished. Neither instrumentalism nor structuralism offers much hope for law as a mechanism for social transformation. Even those writers who are sensitive to the changing forms of state and law under advanced capitalism offer little guidance in the way of concrete strategies or proposals for bringing about substantive change. As a result, we are left with the uneasy feeling that social transformation must await the 'revolution,' but are given no real indication as to how that will be possible.

In contrast, we would argue that law offers an important (although by no means the sole) source for realizing substantive social change. Implicit in this position is a particular conception of law. As opposed to instrumentalism, we take law to have a distinctly social character; that is, more than just a 'tool' or an external set of rules imposed on individuals, law emerges out of distinct social and historical conditions. In contrast to the structuralist tendency toward 'overdetermination,' we would suggest that emphasis be placed on the role of social actors in the constitution and reproduction of legal order. Following this, the legal sphere can be viewed as an arena of struggle which engages individuals of different classes and political positions.

We would also argue that there are some very good reasons for not abandoning the law. First, if we turn our backs on law, then, as Young suggests, we are left in a position whereby we are denied *any* of the protections afforded by the law — however limited they may be.

Second, although several writers have objected to the discourse of rights as an inappropriate form for generating liberating practices, the fact remains that the very terms of political argument and debate in advanced capitalist societies are unavoidably legalistic. As Hunt remarks:

> All political issues involve, usually quite directly, appeals to rights; whether it be the 'right to work' or 'the right to a fair profit,' 'a woman's right to choose' or 'the right to life,' politics and political demands invoke appeals to rights, or to the analogous language of 'freedom.' So persistent is this appeal to rights that it makes little or no sense to dismiss this reality as some on

---

(1987) 2 Revue canadienne droit et societe/Canadian Journal of Law and Society 97 at 97, 102–14. Notes omitted. Reproduced by permission.

the left seek to do, by arguing that "rights" are merely ideological masks disguising naked interests.

In this respect, despite its 'bourgeois character,' rights discourse at the very least offers the potential of facilitating the mobilization of political action among subordinate groups.

Third, the tendency for those on the left to deny the possibility of 'legal justice' has left the door wide open for other interpretations. As a result, the right has been given relatively free reign in defining the terms and parameters of 'law and order' issues. The increasing prominence of right wing law and order campaigns, coupled with the emergence of the new law and order state, with its reduction of welfare services and legal encroachments on civil liberties and legal rights, only showcases the need to mount a defense and extension of existing rights and liberties. Indeed, if (as the structuralists suggest) 'crime control' and related issues are an important source of legitimation for the status quo, then there is all the more reason to formulate a Marxist dialectical position which justifies the defense of legal rights and civil liberties.

Finally, to view the law as irrelevant in the attempt to secure social transformation denies the significance of the rights struggles of women, Natives, youth, prisoners and other subordinated segments of society. It promotes a narrow conception of class struggle in that, as Sumner notes, it excises the class character of these conflicts and reduces the struggle of the working class to the economic claims of an urban, white, male labour aristocracy. In effect, it amounts to the 'colonization' of subordinate fractions of the working class by a dominant fraction. Not to give significance to these types of rights struggles also suggests that social transformation may result in a classless society, but it would still be sexist, racist and ageist.

The question remains, then, as to what direction theoretical reformulation should proceed in order to fashion an approach which incorporates, rather than abandons, law as a potential agent for social transformation?

If the law is too narrowly conceived as simply a mechanism of class rule, then it can be easily dismissed as a 'fraud'; as an empty set of guarantees of equity and fairness that have somehow been sold to an unwitting public. Such a narrow conception of law misses some important considerations, not the least of which is that justice *is* often seen to be done. In order to maintain the appearance of equity and fairness, the law must live up to its own claims. As Thompson notes:

If the law is evidently partial and unjust, then it will mask nothing, legitimate nothing, contribute nothing to any class's hegemony. The essential precondition for the effectiveness of law, in its function as ideology, is that it shall display an independence from gross manipulation and shall seem to be just. It cannot seem to be so without upholding its own logic and criteria of equity; indeed, on occasion, by actually *being* just.

Mandel offers further clarification in the distinction he makes between two opposing senses of the rule of law. The first, which he labels 'democratic,' is essentially the one invoked by Thompson. It "stresses the inhibitions placed on official power ... by clear rules strictly adhered to ... [rules which] contribute in content to real equality and freedom." The second, which Mandel labels the "juridical," is best described by Pashukanis's analysis of the legal form under capitalism. It "stresses those characteristic features which work to strengthen the *status quo* of unequal social power...." One of the main insights to be gained from this distinction is that there is an inherent *tension* built into the law. This tension is further reflected in the fact that law is *both* a means of coercive and ideological domination; of force *and* consent. As an ideological form, the law acts as a legitimizer of capitalist social relations — it presents those relations in a certain light. Yet, at one and the same time, it too must be legitimized. The law requires an ideological base without which it is simply 'naked power.'

In order to win the consent of the dominated classes to the capitalist order — in order to mediate class relations — the law has to take into account interests other than those of the dominant class. In this sense, "law is not simply imposed upon people, but is also a *product* and *object of* and provides an arena which circumscribes class (and other types of) struggle." Indeed, the rights enshrined in law (universal suffrage, right to form a union, right to strike and so on) were not simply handed down by a benevolent state, but were the outcome of progressive struggles by the subordinate classes.

Thus, as Thompson and others have shown, if the law is to be a legitimizer of capitalist social relations, then the rhetoric and rules of law must be more than 'sham.' Law must provide some protection against the arbitrary use of state power. It must live up to its own claims of equity and fairness. While one need not go so far as to suggest, as Thompson does, that the rule of law is an 'unqualified good' that should be defended at all costs (especially given its 'juridical' sense), the recognition of the tension built into law does open up a number of theoreti-

(iv) The Role of Law in Social Transformation: Is a Jurisprudence of Insurgency Possible?

cal possibilities concerning its implications for social transformation. Specifically, law is no longer viewed exclusively as a weapon of class rule, as an abstract, homogeneous entity whose functions can be generalized across different historical periods and circumstances. Instead, the function of law can differ, depending upon the relative strength of social forces that struggle around and within the legal order. Such an assertion involves working at a different level of abstraction than most structuralist accounts.

As Hall and Scraton note, if we rely on Marx's writings in *Capital*, which discuss the 'laws of motion' of a capitalist economy at a very high and abstract level (generalizing these laws across historical periods and societies), then law will be assigned a more 'fixed' and determined role within capitalism. If, however, we rely on the more historical writings of Marx, in which he takes account of the whole social formation — including its political, legal and ideological aspects — then the role of law is treated more problematically. This latter viewpoint allows us to break with the notion of a 'necessary' or 'functional' fit between law and the economic interests of capital. Instead we are left with a very contradictory picture. To quote Hall and Scraton:

> There is no historical guarantee that capital must prevail, and no certainty that it can prevail on its own terms, outside the limits imposed by contestation and struggle. The outcomes of particular struggles, sometimes waged within and about the law, sometimes against it, will have real and pertinent effects on how particular historical struggles develop. Law, in this sense, is constitutive of (i.e., it creates) the very conditions of historical development and struggle, and does not merely reflect them.

What we would advocate, therefore, is a theoretical approach to law that moves beyond both a narrow conception of the relations between base and superstructure, and the more fixed and deterministic view of law as operating to the permanent advantage of capital. Such an approach must be materialist and dialectical. It must also be sensitive to the historically specific and contradictory nature of the bourgeois legal form and the system in which it operates.

An appropriate starting point for such an approach is the Marxist conception of social formation. 'Social formation' connotes that certain elements and forms of politics, culture and law are organic to a particular mode of production at a given phase of its development. Without their establishment and maintenance, such a mode of production cannot survive. Once established, however, a capitalist mode of production generates its own internal contradictions. These contradictions will be expressed not only in the economic form (at the point of production), but also in the forms of politics, culture and law which correspond to it. Moreover, these internal contradictions will generate particular legal forms of resistance, which will emerge alongside economic, political and cultural forms. To quote Sumner: "Like feudalism, capitalism must breed its successor in legal forms ... before it leaves the scene." As such, the task — both theoretical and practical — is to determine what forms and principles of law we should develop and extend *now* as a precondition for a socialist transformation.

A general strategy for realizing this task is the development of what Tigar and Levy refer to as a "jurisprudence of insurgency." Jurisprudence can be defined as a "process by which legal ideology is created and elaborated." Following this, "jurisprudence of insurgency" can be used to refer to "a certain kind of jurisprudential activity in which a group challenging the prevailing system of social relations no longer seeks to reform it but rather to overthrow it and replace it with another."

If capitalist legality contains the seeds of a socialist legality, then one step toward the development of a jurisprudence of insurgency would be to explore the limits of the dominant legal ideology in order to gauge how much can be accomplished within those limits. This would involve, as Tigar and Levy note, the use of the assumptions of the governing class to one's own advantage. In short, given the tension built into law, the aim would be to grasp the contradictions inherent in the bourgeois legal form — to work *through* law — in order to alter the very nature of that legal form. Rather than dismissing the rule of law, therefore, we need to consider what effect pushing the 'democratic' sense of the rule of law to its full limit and extent would have on undermining the social relations of capitalism. It is this kind of strategy that we will explore in the remainder of this paper.

Practical Considerations

In approaching the task of assessing the role of law in social transformation, we start from the premise, documented in Tigar and Levy's analysis of European society between the eleventh and nineteenth centuries, that legal change did not simply go through a single stage of transformation in the movement from feudalism to capitalism. Rather, the process was one of an increasing number of small, incremental legal changes that gave increasing power and legitimacy to the fledgling capitalist class. Consistent with this premise, we do not expect law to be either the vanguard or the consequence of the transformation from capitalist to socialist society. We would argue, instead, that it will be one of many strategic areas where existing tension within the system can be used to push the contradictions that result from the structure of capitalism.

Before delineating those legal activities that best represent a jurisprudence of insurgency, we readily admit the difficulty in attempting to predict what will be the most 'progressive' avenues of legal reform. The advantage of retrospective analysis — like that conducted by Tigar and Levy — is that one can discern the significance of small legal changes over historical periods by examining the diverse consequences these changes had over time. When trying to forecast how current legal changes may facilitate future substantive changes in society, one is blind to all of the potential consequences these changes may produce. If, however, historical analysis has any value, it is in the extent to which it enables us to make prescriptive statements, even tentative ones, on how to transform the existing system.

The central issue to be addressed is one of specifying the criteria by which legal reforms are to be evaluated. More specifically, what kinds of legal reform could be defined as insurgent in terms of their orientation or consequence? How do we distinguish, for example, between reforms which aim only for a greater participation of individuals within the capitalist order (i.e., demanding a "bigger share" of the capitalist pie) from those which aim to transform the very basis of that order?

Structuralists have premised their scepticism about law on the observation that equality is limited to the legal sphere (i.e., it does not extend to the economic sphere of capitalist society). It is in this respect that principles like "equality of all before the law" or "blind justice" are viewed as a major source of legitimation for the system of structured or economic inequality. However, several writers have argued that this position with its ritual invocation of the Anatole France quote, lets the law off too lightly since the law is applied in anything but an equal manner. This recognition of the inequalities in the legal order has led to a number of suggestions for reform.

Mandel, for example, in his analysis of Canadian sentencing law, notes that a central feature of sentencing practices is the recognition of varying punishment according to the offender's 'character,' in particular, the offender's relation to the productive apparatus. By taking into account such factors as educational attainment, employment record and one's "good standing in the community" in the determination of sentence, the law operates to the advantage of one class over another. High status offenders, by virtue of their class position, are perceived as requiring (even deserving) less punishment to ensure their continued conformity. Hence, by varying punishment according to class, the law has the net effect of preserving the status quo of inequality, dominance and subordination. In light of this analysis, Mandel suggests that if sentencing was based solely on the utilitarian principle of general deterrence, that is, the protection of individuals from the harmful effects of crime at the least social cost, punishment would then be based entirely on the conduct sought to be prevented, and not on the "character" (i.e., class) of the offender.

What would be the effect of such a reform? Mandel suggests that it would represent a move in the direction of the 'neutral' state which liberals claim exists in modern democratic societies, that is, the system would be more 'just' in the sense that punishment would no longer vary by class. In this respect, such a reform strategy is laudable to the extent that it would mitigate the unequal treatment to which members of the subordinate classes are subjected by the legal system.

Yet, what of the structuralist argument that equality in sentencing practices would only reinforce the system of economic inequality and hence further legitimate that system? On the one hand, removing the class-based nature of punishment (i.e., viewing dominant class members as 'deserving' of lesser punishment) would eliminate one of the means by which class relations are strengthened and reinforced by the legal order. On the other hand, not taking class differences into account could be viewed as a way of ignoring and/or denying the class differences that do exist. Although punishment would no longer vary by class, crime would continue to vary by class. In this respect Mandel's reform proposal has its advantages, but it is limited. It would only take us part way toward the development of a 'jurisprudence of insurgency.' Such a reform is not insurgent to the extent that it fails to call into question class relations.

Other writers have focused their attention on the content of law. While the criminal law defines certain acts as 'socially injurious' or 'harmful,' it does not tend to define other acts — which are potentially more serious and harmful — as criminal and hence worthy of severe sanctions. For instance, violence against individuals occurs regularly in the workplace of capitalist societies. This typically takes the form of unsafe or hazardous working conditions, exposure to carcinogenic substances and the like. The result has been the loss of life and health for a substantial number of workers. Yet, while such occurrences meet the requirements normally associated with crime (for example, the intentional failure to provide safety equipment or the flagrant violation of safety regulations by owners in order to cut costs and increase profits), they are seldom defined or sanctioned as such. Reiman, therefore, has suggested that the criminal law be redrawn to more accurately reflect the real dangers that individuals pose to society:

> Avoidable acts where the actor had reason to know that his or her acts were likely to lead to someone's death should be counted as forms of murder. Avoidable acts where the actor had reason to believe that his or her acts were likely to lead to someone's injury should be counted as forms of assault and battery. Acts that illegitimately deprive people of their money or possessions should be treated as forms of theft regardless of the color of the thief's collar. Crime in the suites should be prosecuted and punished as vigorously as crime in the streets.

Glasbeek and Rowland have taken this issue one step further. They suggest that there already exist provisions in the criminal law which, although not initially designed for the purpose, could be applied to employer violations of workplace health and safety. This approach is essentially one which advocates the use of criminal law as a vehicle for highlighting the class conflicts inherent in the productive process. By criminalizing employer practices which result in worker injury and death, the severity of the problem would be reinforced. In effect, the strategy proposed by Glasbeek and Rowland is one which aims at using the assumptions of the governing class to the advantage of the working class. To quote the authors:

> Because of the assumptions of the liberal state, the ideology of law requires it to claim that it punishes behaviour which has been judged unacceptable by society no matter who the perpetrator of the offensive behaviour is. It will be interesting to see how the administrators of the legal justice system respond when it is argued that entrepreneurs offend against the criminal process in much the same way as do robbers of private property and people.

In this respect, such a reform strategy would advance the development of a jurisprudence of insurgency in that it endeavours to push the rule of law to its full limit and extent. Defining the violence which occurs in the workplace of capitalist societies as criminal would have the potential of not only holding employers more accountable for their actions but raising the consciousness of workers as well.

On another level a jurisprudence of insurgency must also be capable of addressing the *manner* in which legal issues are handled by the courts. To elaborate, the law adheres to the principle of 'blind justice.' In so doing, it responds not to the "why" of an act, but to whether or not the act was committed. The race, class or sex of the accused is deemed irrelevant, as the primary criterion for judging cases is the empirical question of whether a formally proscribed act was committed. In short, the issue becomes a matter of "legally relevant facts" and, in the process of resolving this issue, the case is both *individualized* and *depoliticized*. As Grau explains:

> Cases are tried only between legal parties with defined legal interests that conflict over narrowly drawn legal issues. Collective needs are denied. The specificity of the rights and the narrowness of the legal issues combine to preclude the introduction of broader, though relevant, social questions. This restriction effectively depoliticizes the case.

This feature of the legal order contributes to one of the main legitimizing effects of the rule of law, that is, the idea that society is composed, almost exclusively, of individuals and not groups, aggregates or classes. Equally significant is the related belief that legal struggles and political struggles are separate and distinct activities. We would argue, therefore, that a jurisprudence of insurgency must alter this artificial distinction between legal and political issues. This will encompass a two-sided dialectical process. The one side involves attempting to bring the collective nature of the problem into the legal arena while the other side involves broadening the definition of the situation to encompass the political nature of the problem.

"Collectivizing" and "Politicizing" Legal Battles

One way in which the law is being pushed to deal with problems that are more than individual concerns is the strategic use of law by groups to address collective problems. Historically, the labour movement was one of the first to view the problems of workers as a condition common to all individuals whose work placed them in a subordinated position to capital. Because of the blatant nature of this subordination and the fact that workers could readily interact with other co-workers who were experiencing the same consequences of subordination, craft workers were quicker than other groups to approach their problems as collective in nature.

Before describing how some collectivities are currently attempting to use the law and assessing the insurgent nature of these efforts, it is important to note the dynamic interplay that appears to exist between groups defining their problems as collective problems and the concomitant recognition of the political nature of their problems. The consistency with which groups redefine their problems as political issues suggests that politicization is a typical — if not inevitable — consequence of recognizing the collective nature of the problem. By the very act of sharing their problem with others in a similar condition, people come to realize that approaching the problem as a narrow legal issue is unrealistic and often ineffective.

Of greater significance, however, is the tendency for groups not to rely solely on the courts to resolve their problems. By recognizing the political nature of their problems, activist groups also attempt to put pressure directly on the state by engaging in legislative and lobbying activities, which has traditionally been the almost exclusive domain of the major economic interests in society. The use of lobbying by farmworkers, tenants, environmental groups, women, Indians, the handicapped and the elderly is an indication of the extent to which collectivities are broadening the scope of their struggles beyond the traditional locus of the courts.

Although the lobbying efforts of the above groups may not be successful, they are an indication of how the groups view their difficulties as political problems and not simply legal problems. Billings describes this difference in her assessment on the use of advocacy by women's organizations:

> More and more, therefore, lobbying ... has become a familiar tool of the women's movement. Although largely unproductive in proportion to the amount of energy [expended], *lobbying has at least familiarized women with the corridors of power*, created networks across the country and ... created lengthy policy agendas that are agreed to nation-wide as the action priorities.

Although we will argue that the strategies utilized by some groups are more "insurgent" than other strategies, it is important to recognize that the very act of subordinate groups approaching the law as a collective is of value to the extent that it results in politicizing the manner in which the problem is defined.

Collectivities Using the Law

There appears to be a growing awareness among activist groups of the limitations and constraints of approaching the law as individuals. One way in which groups have attempted to increase their power in using the law is to develop strategies that increase the chances that cases heard before the courts represent the collective interests of the group (given the structural limitation that these collective interests must be fought on an individual basis since collectivities are not recognized as legal actors). Some of these strategies continue to use the courts as the arena for battle but expand the techniques by which groups gain access to the courts. The methods used include class action suits, test cases, judicial reviews, standing as *amicus curiae* and private prosecutions.

There are a number of current examples of individuals in Canada forming groups with the sole purpose of fighting legal issues from a collective rather than an individual base. One of the most recent examples of this is the organization of women fighting for a range of issues that address the many consequences of the systemic subordination of women in capitalist society. These issues include affirmative action, equal pay for work of equal value, the handling of sexual offenses by the criminal justice system and the way in which wife battering is dealt with by the police and the courts. One of the consequences of women defining the legal battle as a collective battle is the shift in strategies that will increase the ability of women to influence the types of cases that should be emphasized in the legal arena. A report by the Canadian Advisory Council on the Status of Women, for example, suggests taking a systematic approach to litigation that would further the collective interests of women. The approach would involve the following four steps:

1. defining a goal in terms of the desired principle of law to be established;
2. plotting how the principle of law can be established from case to case in incremental, logical and clear steps;
3. selecting winnable cases suitable for each stage taken to achieve the goal;
4. consolidating wins at each stage by bringing similar cases to create a cluster of cases in support of the principle established.

It is true that some of the above issues (such as affirmative action) simply strive for women to gain a larger piece of the pie within the existing system. Nonetheless, their importance is in the fact that the state is being asked to recognize that it

(iv) The Role of Law in Social Transformation: Is a Jurisprudence of Insurgency Possible?

is *not* the problem of a few individuals but a condition of a large segment of the population that has been adversely affected by the economic system. This demand for the recognition of problems as more than individual problems is also evident in the development of anti-poverty organizations, Indian groups fighting for aboriginal land claims and victims' groups demanding greater participation in the criminal justice system. The presumption that legal battles, particularly those in the area of civil law, are exclusively conflicts between individuals and the state or individuals against corporations is becoming less and less tenable.

Although the above strategies used by groups in approaching the law have a number of advantages over traditional approaches, the fact that the law forces these groups to fight their battles through cases of specific individuals in court limits the ability to use the law to redress collective problems. As long as the state is allowed to approach problems of inequality on an individual, case by case basis, there is little likelihood of the law being an effective tool for redressing the collective problems of subordinate groups.

Collective Rights

We would argue that one way in which the law could be used to promote substantive change is to have collectivities recognized as legal actors in society. In other words, to establish the legal principle that, in addition to individual rights in law, there are or should be collective rights that would acknowledge the existence of subordinate groups and provide them, analogically, with the same rights and freedoms that individuals currently have, in principle if not in practice. The recognition of collective rights enables groups to move away from the narrowly defined manner in which current legal ideology defines conflicts in society.

One subject which immediately comes to mind when discussing collective rights is the *Canadian Charter of Rights and Freedoms*. The passage of the *Constitution Act, 1982* has been lauded by some commentators as a means of providing the legal rights and guarantees that would mitigate against the discrimination of minorities in Canada. However, as Rush has argued, while the *Charter* protects individual rights, collective rights are either ill-protected or disregarded altogether. Rush suggests two ways in which collective rights can be perceived constitutionally:

> First, collective rights are those rights which accrue to individuals because of their placement or membership in an identifiable group. In this sense, the realization of the right for each individual depends on its realisation for everyone in the group. These are the rights of cultural communities, ethnic and minority groups.... Second, collective rights are also rights which accrue to groups as groups. These include: the right of Indian people to title to and jurisdiction over their aboriginal land; and the right of women to affirmative action programmes in the workplace.

Following this, Rush notes that "working class rights," full aboriginal rights and the rights of women have not been recognized. In this regard, we would argue, alongside Rush, that continued pressure from working people, women, and ethnic and minority groups for greater recognition of collective rights in the *Charter* is needed.

It should be noted that not every instance of the demand for, or recognition of, collective rights represents explicit insurgent activity. For example, the current legislation in Canada regarding hate literature gives groups the legal ability to prohibit the broadcast or publication of material that has the express purpose of producing hatred toward the group. It is the collective analogy to the law of libel that affords an individual the right to protection from malicious material. While this law recognizes the existence of groups as legal actors, there is nothing within the law that directly addresses the relationship of groups to the state or to the economic base of the system. Similarly, what has historically been recognized as the collective right of management to determine the conditions of work, rates of productivity and the like would obviously fall outside the boundaries of a jurisprudence of insurgency. What this highlights is the need to question "collective right to what?" and establish the criteria and principles on which collective rights should be based.

Legal Recognition of Structural Inequality

To what extent is the demand for collective rights and the politicization of collectivities in their legal struggles indicative of a jurisprudence of insurgency? We would argue that, in addition to the obvious value of individuals no longer viewing their problems as isolated, non-political problems, there has been limited success by collectivities in demanding that the legal system *not* approach all citizens as equals. That is, groups are contending that it is unjust to start from the premise that all individuals are equal legally.

The current emphasis on affirmative action programs by the government could be interpreted as a recognition by the state that there is *structural* and *systemic* inequality in capitalist society. Women, minority groups, the handicapped and other groups who have been at the economic margins have been successful in getting the state at least to acknowledge the problem (even if the remedies to the problem have not been forthcoming). In a similar manner, the current efforts to establish the principle of equal-pay-for-work-of-equal-value is an attempt to pressure the government to acknowledge the structural inequality that has resulted from a segmented labour market.

Both affirmative action and the principle of equal-pay-for-work-of-equal-value are *potentially* insurgent because they use a contradiction within legal ideology to push the law and the state past the limits established by the legal system. By groups bringing public attention to the inconsistency that the law is premised on all citizens being equal, yet large segments of the society have been placed in a position of structural inequality, the state is placed in a position of either admitting that all citizens are not equal or making adjustments to provide greater equality. Although the state may attempt to coopt movement toward greater equality, the public focus on the contradiction requires that the state take some form of ameliorative action.

CONCLUSION

The purpose of this paper has been to open up debate on and interest in the role of law in social transformation. If one accepts that a socialist society is not going to emerge in a full-blown manner, then one must assess how the existing system — including law — can be used to push capitalist society along the path toward socialism. The jurisprudence of insurgency is based on the idea that to abandon law as an agent of change is to negate one method that can be used to challenge the present system. The insurgent role of law is to identify the existing contradictions within legal ideology and to use those contradictions to pit that ideology against itself.

Although it has been argued in this paper that the area of collective rights is one avenue that has the potential of bringing the issue of systemic inequality to the forefront, it must also be admitted that the demand for collective rights has the potential of producing divisions within the working class. These divisions are most likely to occur where some segments of the working class perceive a threat from the collective rights won by other segments of that class. A current example of this is affirmative action policy and the negative reaction to this initiative by individuals who do not fit into one of the target groups identified in the policy. The nature of this conflict is often expressed in the form of collective rights versus individual rights. While there will undoubtedly be instances where collective and individual rights will come into conflict, one should also note that capitalists have in the past facilitated this view of the inherent incompatibility of collective rights and individual rights to suit their own interests.

It must also be admitted that there is a danger in groups using the law in the attempt to achieve their aims. Chief among these dangers is the likelihood that groups will start to define their struggles as ones to be fought exclusively within the legal arena. The consequence of this is that a loss in the courts is seen as the end of the struggle. Several authors have written on the difficulties encountered when a group places all of its energies in legal struggles. In fact, Glasbeek has taken the position that groups should avoid using the *Charter* as a political tool. While recognizing the difficulties in using law in a progressive manner, we would continue to argue, for the reasons stated earlier, that the law should not be abandoned as an arena for social struggle.

Finally, a jurisprudence of insurgency has implications for the role that social scientists and legal practitioners play in legal struggles. For the social scientist, perhaps the most important role is to perform the task originally explicated by C. Wright Mills: to demonstrate the linkage between private troubles and public issues. Applying Mills's dictum to the area of law, the task of the social scientist is to show the commonality of individuals' legal problems and the commonality of interests individuals have in collectively addressing these problems.

For the legal practitioner, the traditional approach to the practice of law and the lawyer-client relationship would be inadequate in developing collective struggles in law. In an article written on the subject of poverty law, Wexler describes the inadequacies of approaching social problems from a narrow legal perspective and suggests that conventional legal training does not equip lawyers for the problems that are systemic in nature:

> Traditional practice hurts poor people by isolating them from each other, and fails to meet their need for a lawyer by completely misunderstanding that need. Poor people have few individual legal problems in the traditional sense; their problems are the product of poverty, and are common to all poor people.... In this setting

the object of practicing poverty law must be to organize poor people, rather than to solve their legal problems. The proper job for a poor people's lawyer is helping poor people to organize themselves to change things so that either no one is poor or (less radically) so that poverty does not entail misery.

By defining legal problems in a larger economic and social context, the lawyer is more likely to adopt an approach to litigation and other legal activities that would best benefit the group. Just as importantly, a lawyer who views the problem in the above manner will, one hopes, also see the value of other kinds of insurgent activities that fall outside of the traditional boundaries of adversarial law, such as confrontations, rent strikes, boycotts and other actions that, while not always legal, can produce effective results for economically subordinate groups.

(v) Structure: The Mosaic of Dominion

Samuel Bowles and Herbert Gintis

Power may be wielded in numerous ways. Historically, armed force has been a central pillar of power, as liberal theory rightly stresses. But the arsenal of domination goes beyond the gun. Control of the tools with which we produce our livelihood and the words that give our lives and loyalties their meanings have been no less central to the exercise of power.

Debates among Marxian and liberal theorists concerning the roots of domination have tended to adopt an impoverished conception of power. The liberal concern with the despotic state is matched in its narrowness by the Marxian concern with class domination. Each ignores the undeniable insights of the other; both give scant theoretical attention to forms of power that cannot be reduced to either state despotism and class. The most ubiquitous of these excluded forms of power is the domination of women by men.

Equally important, the grand debates between the liberal and Marxian political traditions skirt a central concern of democratic theory, the relationship between power and freedom. Democracy promises the collective accountability of power, but it promises another, more constructive concept as well; namely, the ability of people to effectively carry out their individual and common projects unencumbered by arbitrary constraint. For the liberal, this positive side of power — agency — is rendered minimally, as political liberty and the freedom to contract with whomever one pleases. Both of these liberal forms of freedom represent the absence of constraint rather than personal or collective empowerment. They are, in Isiah Berlin's apt terminology, "negative freedoms." For the classical Marxist, agency is the ability of an emerging class to carry out a historic project dictated by the onward march of the productive forces of society. Neither the liberal nor the Marxian definition encompasses the vision of people and of a people free to be the architects of their own personal and social histories.

We will address the problems raised for democratic theory by these partial conceptions of power in this chapter and in chapter 5, which considers the question of the individual and agency. Here we will develop a conception of power, the structures of social domination, and the resistance to domination capable of understanding the historical dynamics of diverse forms of power — patriarchal, state, class, or other. We will analyze the reproduction of patriarchal domination both as a central issue of democracy in its own right and as an illustration of our approach.

. . . .

The underlying logic of our argument contrasts in two important ways with dominant conceptions in social theory. First, though we affirm that historical

---

From *Democracy and Capitalism* by Samuel Bowles and Herbert Gintis (New York: Basic Books Inc., 1987) at 92–98. Notes omitted. Copyright © 1986 by Basic Books, Inc. Reproduced by permission of Basic Books, a member of Perseus Books, L.L.C.

change is structured, systematic, and hence understandable in more than simply empirical terms, we reject the notion that either stability or change obeys a single logic, whether of enlightenment, modernization, or the advance of productive capacities. Underlying this denial is our second fundamental commitment, a rejection of the concept of power as unitary; it is the notion that power emanates from a single source in society that provides the bedrock of what might be called the unitary conception of history.

We believe that an alternative conception of power, social structure, and history can make better sense of the historical clash of rights in liberal democratic capitalism and the political nature of the economy. The next two sections develop such a conception of power, in terms of the following five propositions.

First, power is heterogeneous, wielding a variety of weapons, yielding to a host of counterpressures, and obeying no single logic. Here we focus on the distinct forms of domination and solidarity based on class, state, and gender.

Second, power is not an amorphous constraint on action but rather a structure of rules empowering and restraining actors in varying degrees. These distinct sets of rules may be embodied in concrete institutions (for example, the World Bank), in linguistic convention (as in the generic term *man*), in unwritten custom (for example, primogeniture), in legal practice (as in the formal recognition of collective bargaining for wages), and, as we have seen, in more general conceptions of property and personal rights.

Third, the perpetuation of any power structure is generally problematic. Further, a structure of power is secured or toppled not only by history-making collective struggles, but more prosaically by a complex society-wide web of everyday individual action and compliance.

Fourth, distinct structures of power — be they the liberal democratic state, the patriarchal family, the capitalist economy, or other — are not merely juxtaposed, they are bound together in a common process of social reproduction. Each one may contribute to the survival of another; or they may foster mutually corrosive and subversive impulses.

And fifth, because people's lives are generally governed by more than one distinct power structure — for example one may be a worker, a wife, and a citizen — we experience power as heterogeneous, and are often able to bring the experiences within one system of power to bear in the pursuit of our projects within another. The clash of rights, based on impressive ability of elites and democratic movements alike to extend rights from one sphere of society to others, is the most important historical example of this transportation of practices from one social realm to another.

We refer to our approach as a historical-structural model of power. As we deny the usefulness of a general theory of power and its reproduction, we will seek to develop these five propositions in a particular historical setting; that is, the liberal capitalist nations of Europe and North America over the past two centuries.

A Political Conception of Family, State, and Economy

It has become fashionable, in reacting against the traditional unitary conception of power, to profess a richly textured alternative notion — an idea of power as likely to be illuminated by the study of words and symbols as of armaments and property. Michel Foucault, for instance, writes:

> The analysis made in terms of power, must not assume that the sovereignty of the state, the form of the law or the overall unity of a domination are given at the outset.... Power is everywhere....

This acute and welcome sensitivity to the ubiquity of power, however, can easily slip into treating power *per se* as domination, and replacing a critique of domination with a diffuse critique of authority of no particular use to democratic social movements. Thus Thomas Wartenberg notes, in a perceptive analysis of Foucault's attempt at deconstructing power, that

> at the political level, this problem asserts itself in Foucault's failure to distinguish different types of repressive societies.... Though all social systems do exist by means of a structuring of human beings to meet the needs of that system, we need to have a way to talk about how much pain such structuring inflicts upon the creatures for whom it exists.

We also need, we might add, a way to talk about the *structure* of power in order to assess its *accountability*.

Our conception of power is at once a theory of domination and a theory of structural change flowing from collective resistance to domination. It is at the same time a structural theory and a theory of social action. Marx, in criticizing Ludwig Feuerbach, lamented the fact that materialist thought tended to denigrate action in favor of structure: "Hence it happened that the active side, in contradistinction to materialism, was developed by the idealism."

(v) Structure: The Mosaic of Dominion

Analogously, structural theories of power often support a conception either of unquestioned, monolithic, uncontested domination or of the mechanistic inevitability of the collapse of domination.† The commonplace observation that structures do not reproduce or destroy themselves but are perpetuated or overturned by *what people do* finds no place in most structural theories. The active side of power is more fully developed by theories of choice.

Theories of choice, however — for reasons we will address in the next chapter — generally fail to provide an adequate account of the forms of collective action central to an active and historical conception of power. By developing the relationship between domination and solidarity, we seek to avoid both the individualism of choice theories and the presumption of a pregiven logic of either stability or crisis in structural theories. More positively, we will embrace the fundamental tenet of structural theories — that individual action is highly regulated — in a framework that insists that the historical dynamics of the structures regulating choice are themselves the result, however indirect and unintended, of individual action.

Vertical relationships of superior to subordinate, of employer to worker, of man to woman, of despot to subject, of white to black, provide the raw materials with which people construct the corresponding horizontal structures of social bonding — class consciousness, democratic nationalism, racial unity, and the like. (This rudimentary statement of the conditions of collective action simply generalizes Marx's insight that the structure of exploitation might provide the conditions for the unification of the exploited. We will turn to this issue in some detail in chapter 6.) These structures of social bonding allow people to forge from their individual experiences of oppression (and those of other people) an ensemble of cultural and organizational tools upon which collective action may be based.

The active side of power surely includes the exercise of domination by the powerful and the complicity of the oppressed in their oppression. But it also includes revolutionary collective action: forging communicative and organizational tools of bonding from the cacophony of discourses to which the mosaic of domination gives rise, and putting these tools to use in transforming structures of power.

The clash of rights in liberal democratic capitalism, in particular, has seen both the collective action of the dispossessed in pitting personal rights against the privileges of wealth, race, and gender as well as the counterstrategies of the privileged in shoring up patriarchal rights, property rights, and "skin privilege."

Recognition of the heterogeneity of power invites a more searching analysis of the way in which distinct spheres of social life regulate social action in such a manner as to produce systems of domination *and* the possibility of their elimination.

Power is the capacity to render social action effective. It is coextensive with neither the state, nor with physical force, nor with face-to-face command. Power may be exercised through the ability to overcome the resistance of others — as in Max Weber's conception — but it may equally be exercised through the ability to avoid resistance, either through control over which issues become contestable or through influence over others' wants, sentiments, desires, or, more generally, objectives.

. . . .

We focus on three general forms of the asymmetrical exercise of power: domination through the monopoly of the means of coercion, through the exercise of property rights, and through the operation of gender-based privilege. These are certainly not the only forms of domination observed in modern society. Race, ethnicity, religion, language, and region, among others, have served as major bases of social oppression and *loci* of bitter conflict. We focus on these three forms of domination not because other forms are less general, affecting particular liberal democratic capitalist societies in widely differing degrees and in quite distinct manners.

Each of these three forms of domination may be considered to be a means of regulating social action. Thus, in three distinct ways, action is structured by a specific set of rules of the game: (a) the forms and rewards of participation of individuals in a practice are socially regulated; (b) the range of feasible alternative forms of practice are socially delimited; and (c) the potential effectiveness of distinct types of practice are socially mediated.

(vi) Toward a Political Economy of Law

Amy Bartholomew and Susan Boyd

Perhaps the most fundamental and problematic basis for the ideological aspect of law in organizing consent, legitimating oppressive social and material relations, and fragmenting collective endeavours emanates from the construction of "free" and "equal" subjects through juridical categories. Central premises of law in liberal democratic capitalism are that individuals are "free" in the economic realm, insofar as they may strike their own bargains and dispose of their labour and property "freely," and free from the juridical inequality and dependence present in pre-capitalist modes of production. The ideological importance of these premises is found in the way they may obscure and justify unequal and oppressive class, gender, and other relations. As many commentators note, "economic freedom" within capitalism is a particularly cramped notion of freedom. Moreover, as both Leo Panitch and Ellen Meiksins Wood have emphasized, because classes are constituted by the relations of production rather than directly by the state and law, the coercion that obtains within capitalist systems tends to be obscured.

Formal juridical freedom and equality may thus obscure the fact that capitalist relations of production are neither free nor equal. By treating unequally situated individuals and groups as if they were equal at least some of the time, formal juridical equality also perpetuates unequal relations between classes, sexes, and races more directly. Rights are mediated by social, historical, political, and economic contexts which may be "invisible" to the law, a point illustrated by reference to struggles for formal equality rights. For instance, although obtaining the right to own property in the name of formal juridical equality with men was a significant victory for married women, other material and ideological constraints limited access by women to waged labour and the ability to acquire property in their own right. Similarly, capital and labour bargain collectively under conditions of structural inequality that include capital's greater material resources, greater "organizational and ideological resources," and "greater access to the state." Yet, in crucial respects, capital and labour are treated in collective bargaining law as if they meet on an equal footing. Those who are "more equal" in reality are thereby favoured by the "neutrality" of law implicit in the concept of formal juridical equality, thus reinforcing the "net transfer" of power from those who do not own and control the means of production to those who do.

Further, the discretion present in the law, operating against the backdrop of the presumed universal, neutral application of the law to "free and equal" individuals, simultaneously permits disparate and unequal treatment. As Mandel points out, research into the invocation of criminal sanctions by courts demonstrates that "criminal law is applied in anything but an equal manner." In labour law, the discretionary imposition of penalties by courts may be, and often is, particularly harsh when dealing with labour, as in the jailing of Jean-Claude Parrot in the last decade for refusing to order his workers back to work and the recent jailing of Newfoundland labour leaders. The symbolic effects of such harsh example-setting should not be underestimated.

The juridical concepts of free and equal individuals are extended in capitalist democracies to the "interpellation" of people as free and equal citizens. Individual citizenship rights tend to both disarticulate classes and to rearticulate individual citizenship interests as the "national interest." In one fell swoop, classes are thereby fractured at the political level insofar as liberal democracies typically represent citizens, rather than classes, in the state. And political parties tend — at least in Canadian liberal democracy — to represent and articulate the "national interest," while the "national interest" represents pre-eminently the interests of capital. Hence, while subordinate classes may be disorganized by the categories of "free and equal," the capitalist class is brought together and represented broadly as if its interests truly expressed the common good. Thus, despite the fact that the franchise constituted a genuine victory for subordinate classes, oppressed races, and women, the exclusiveness of this mode of representation — the absence of class representation mechanisms, workplace democracy, and the like — may curtail genuine participatory possibilities.

From W. Clement and G. Williams, eds., *The New Canadian Political Economy* (Kingston: McGill-Queen's University Press, 1989) 212 at 229–33. Notes omitted. Reproduced by permission of the publisher.

Predicated on the core concepts of "free" and "equal" individuals, and contingent on historical resistances and struggles, is the constitution of state subjects as bearing other, predominantly individual-based civil liberties and rights in liberal democracies. The presumed atomizing consequences of these configurations are often commented on in the literature. However, the law does not only atomize. Vera Chouinard has provided an important corrective in the Canadian literature by arguing that historical and concrete class antagonisms and struggles may prey on systemic contradictions in particular conjunctures, thus creating possibilities for struggles to resist the logic of atomization. Chouinard indicates that concrete struggles may achieve both legal restrictions on the "degree and manner" of subjection to the logic of production and legal recognition as collectivities. She further argues that precisely to the extent that struggles achieve collectivized class-specific rights and recognition, class capacities may thereby be enhanced.

It seems clear that political struggles often revolve around rights claims in liberal democracies partly because of the cultural and historical commitment to at least some rights in such societies. But the pre-eminence of formal juridical equality may facilitate the appropriation of rights discourse by any political group, progressive or otherwise. Jenson has argued, for example, that instead of the abortion issue being seen as a debate between women and men as groups divided by sex, women's "right" to choose abortion has been pitted against pro-life arguments for foetal rights, thereby obscuring the gendered nature of the issue: "In such a discourse, women disappear as a group and reappear as individuals with needs which can only be assessed against those of all other persons, including foetuses." These sorts of struggles are implicitly, if not explicitly, premised on formal juridical equality — positing equality of "access" to the enormously important claim to "right."

The concepts of atomization, freedom, formal legal equality, individual civil liberties, and political and citizenship rights may currently constitute the most complex and pressing "'problem of legality' in historical materialism." The concepts of "free" and "equal" legal subjects do appear to fracture the subordinate classes, and the "centrality of a private isolated, autonomous, egoistic legal subject possessed above all of a freewill" *may* "enforce ... and legitimate ... oppressive class relations." At the same time, insofar as the ideological role of law requires some kernel of truth to its claims, individual civil liberties may help protect us against at least the most direct and obvious state coercion and intrusions — a not unimportant point in the era of Thatcher, Reagan, and Vander Zalm. Moreover, citizenship and political rights, as limited as they are in Canada, are valuable and were bestowed on us by neither a beneficent nor a cunning state, but rather were won through struggle. And the importance to disadvantaged groups of legal instruments acquired through struggles for formal legal equality should not be underestimated.

Much work in political economy of law in Canada does not adequately address these important and complex contradictions and problems. Indeed, an unmitigated hostility is displayed toward individual rights, most especially in the work emanating from legally trained scholars. Glasbeek and Mandel, for example, undervalue individual constitutional rights, while some work in administrative law also denigrates the importance of individual claims against the state. These approaches fail to seriously investigate the admittedly problematic but potentially emancipatory status of the individual legal subject endowed with free will and deserving of respect. An unexplored assumption that notions of "autonomy" and "community" are necessarily antithetical also abounds in both the work of Glasbeek and Mandel and in the critical legal studies-inspired work of Hutchinson and Monahan. Hutchinson and Monahan claim, in fact, that "rights-based theories have corrosive implications for communal aspirations."

The complexity of formal legal equality, the importance of civil and political rights against and within the capitalist state, and notions of individualism and citizenship must be explored much more seriously in a developed political economy of law. This task does not require us to concede significant ground to liberal approaches to law. It means simply refusing to throw the baby out with the bathwater. Ian Taylor has aptly criticized those who imply that we can simply take notice of the bourgeois form of law and then go home:

> The danger ... is that they frequently present law and legal institutions as an impenetrable and secure element in the apparatus of class domination, and that thereby they discourage the use of legal interventions as a useful move in political struggles. To say this is not, of course, to deny that one of the achievements of bourgeois law *is* to displace the *class* struggles that are constantly occurring in capitalist societies over commodities into disputes between *individual legal subjects* ... legal discourse is a mystification of the true character of social relations in a propertied, unequal society, but it is none the less an impor-

tant (imperfect) instrument in the defence of the liberties of the classes and the sexes.

We would add that the new political economy of law could do worse than to recall the work of some of the "old" political economists, including that of Macpherson and F.R. Scott in their defence of "liberties." Finally, work such as Chouinard's, which begins to theorize how the construction of legal subjects and rights can be challenged, how class-specific, collective rights may be secured in particular capitalist conjunctures, and how collective constructions may enhance the potential for transformative politics, constitutes an important challenge for the new Canadian political economy. While the questions surrounding appropriate forms of socialist legality have not even been broached in the Canadian literature, commentators have begun to consider the nature of collective and "activist" rights and progressive rights strategies. Even this work, however, is all too sparse and limited in Canada.

. . . .

Law, legal institutions, and rights represent both spaces and tensions, contradictions and possibilities, limitations and potential. We must, therefore, be cognizant of the ways in which law and legal institutions may contribute to the reconstitution and reproduction of existing relations of power. We must simultaneously begin to explore seriously what it means to say that law is embedded within struggle and is an arena of struggle itself; how and to what extent the discourse of rights and the forms of law may contribute to or detract from our struggles; how law, legal institutions, and rights may be used in strategic ways while minimizing the potentially demobilizing and integrative effects of participating within legal forms and legal arenas. If the new Canadian political economy meets these challenges, we will be that much better equipped to assess which strategies advance transformative and socialist politics.

(vii) The Statistical Protection of Minorities: Affirmative Action Policy in Canada

Rainer Knopff

INTRODUCTION

The age of affirmative action in Canada is upon us. It is fast becoming one of the leading policy responses to the political claims of Canadian women and minorities. In June of 1983, Treasury Board President Herb Gray "announced that an affirmative action program, under the direction of the Treasury Board, is being implemented across the Public Service of Canada." Many provincial governments have similar programs, as do a number of municipalities. While these public sector programs are mandatory, affirmative action in the private sector remains largely voluntary. Governments are actively promoting private sector affirmative action, however. In 1979 the Affirmative Action Directorate of the Canada Employment and Immigration Commission (CEIC) was established to act as a consultant to private industry in the creation and implementation of affirmative [action] programs; it does this for businesses under both federal and provincial jurisdiction. Some of the provincial human rights commissions have been doing the same thing. The response to these initiatives has not been overwhelming: from 1979 to 1983 only 49 of the 1130 firms approached by CEIC entered into agreements to establish affirmative action programs, a fact that led the Special House of Commons Committee on Visible Minorities to recommend the imposition of mandatory affirmative action in five years "if insufficient progress is detected under voluntary programs." (Daudlin, 1984:35)

The first affirmative action program in Canada, although it was not then known by that name, was

---

From N. Neville and A. Kornberg, eds., *Minorities and the Canadian State* (Oakville: Mosaic Press, 1985) 87 at 87–90. Notes omitted. Reproduced by permission.

the federal government's effort, beginning in the late 1960s, to increase the proportion of Francophones in the public service. The "target groups" benefitting from the most recent wave of affirmative action are women, indigenous people, the handicapped and blacks (in Nova Scotia). In March of 1984 the Commons Committee on Visible Minorities recommended extension of the policy to racial minorities in general.

In light of these developments, affirmative action becomes an important subject for a volume on minorities in Canada. Since the policy, in most of its current applications, has been borrowed somewhat uncritically from the United States, it is especially important for Canadians to assess its theoretical and practical validity.

. . . .

Affirmative Action and Systemic Discrimination

Advocates of affirmative action typically describe its purpose as the achievement of a more proportional representation of groups than currently exists. According to one formulation,

> Affirmative Action is a comprehensive planning process designed to ensure not only an equality of opportunity but also an equality of results. Its primary objective is to ensure the Canadian workforce is an accurate reflection of the composition of the Canadian population given the availability of required skills. (Phillips, 1981:2)

Depending on how one defines discrimination, this policy can be understood either as a remedial response to discrimination or as something separate from and additional to an anti-discrimination policy. In the early days of anti-discrimination legislation, when it was generally thought that the legal prohibition extended only to direct and intentional discrimination "because of" an individual's group affiliation, affirmative action was understood in the latter sense. Since not all group underrepresentation could be attributed to direct discrimination, the prohibition of such discrimination could be expected to have a less than adequate impact on the problem of disproportionality. A policy designed to bring about proportional representation had therefore to be understood as overcoming factors other than legally prohibited discrimination, not as a remedy to such discrimination. It followed that the enforcers of anti-discrimination legislation had no authority to compel affirmative action; at best, they could recommend voluntary implementation. Peter Robertson, now a consultant to CEIC, recalls that this was the understanding with which he began his career in the enforcement of anti-discrimination legislation. Upon his appointment as Executive Director of the Missouri Human Rights Commission, he was briefed by a group of experts, one of whom told him, "If *all* you do is remedy discrimination, you will fail. The wave of the future is *affirmative action*." Says Robertson,

> Thus, I started out in this field with the idea that affirmative action was entirely different from remedying discrimination and that it was really a sort of quasi-charitable activity which I would ask employers to engage in — out of the kindness of their hearts; but which I could not insist that they implement to comply with the law. (Robertson, 1980:4)

The second way of understanding affirmative action — as a remedy for discrimination — requires an expanded definition of discrimination. One must include in the concept those factors other than direct intentional discrimination that contribute to the underrepresentation affirmative action is designed to overcome. Proponents of affirmative action argue that such a transformation of the definition is logically required by the purpose to which anti-discrimination policy is directed. In this view, the legislation was enacted precisely to bring about greater proportionality, and the discrimination it prohibits must therefore be defined in a manner adequate to this end. Again, Peter Robertson summarizes this thinking:

> ...when we in the U.S. initially confronted the different unemployment rates, occupational distribution, and disparate income levels of minorities and women we attempted to change the situation by making it illegal to discriminate. When we discovered that eliminating discrimination (as it was then defined) was having no impact on the problem we began to talk about affirmative action and to perceive that action as something above and beyond eliminating discrimination. [However] that failure to change the underlying facts which had confronted Congress was not a failure of the anti-discrimination legislation but was, instead, a failure to understand the real nature of discrimination. It was only when we began to perceive discrimination in a totally different fashion that we began to have a real impact on the problem ... on the facts. (Robertson, 1980:4–5)

The main way in which the concept of discrimination was expanded was by including in it neutral rules, procedures or requirements that are not implemented in order to exclude members of a group —

and thus escape a prohibition of direct, intentional discrimination — but that have an "adverse impact" on the group nevertheless. A common example is a height and weight requirement for police work, which, while neutral on its face, excludes many more women than men, thereby contributing to the underrepresentation of women in the police force. In Canada such barriers have come to be known as "systemic discrimination." Other, less common labels include "adverse effect discrimination," "indirect discrimination," and "constructive discrimination." Affirmative action, understood as a policy of increasing the proportional representation of groups, is generally described as a response to this kind of discrimination. One CEIC report, for example, defines affirmative action as "a comprehensive result-oriented plan adopted by an employer as a remedy for employment discrimination with special emphasis on systemic discrimination." (CEIC, 1979:1) Another states that

> The affirmative action approach to the problem of inequity and inefficient utilization of target group workers is based on the concept of systemic discrimination. That is, this approach identifies discrimination in the workplace in terms of the impact of employment practices on the employment of target group members. (CEIC, 1982:41)

The prohibition of systemic discrimination is said to make it possible to conceive of affirmative action not only as a policy response to underrepresentation, but also, in appropriate circumstances, as a legal, and hence obligatory, remedy.

(viii) Sex Equality Litigation

Gwen Brodsky and Shelagh Day

Three Years Later

Women have invested hard work and important hopes in Canada's new Constitution and the guarantees of equality in the *Charter of Rights and Freedoms*. Now that the equality guarantees have been in effect for more than three years, some basic questions can be asked and answered. Are women using the Charter? How are the courts interpreting the equality guarantees? Are the guarantees helping women? What factors will determine whether women are helped by the Charter in the long run?

To answer these questions and many others, the authors of this study collected and analysed the 591 reported and unreported decisions handed down by courts at all levels during the first three years that section 15 of the Charter was in effect. Information about the decisions was consolidated in a computerized database. This has made it possible to identify patterns in the cases and to provide statistics about who is using the equality guarantees, and to what ends. By focussing particularly on the cases in which sex equality arguments were made, while considering *all* the decisions handed down, this study sets women's sex equality litigation in its full context.

The news is not good. Women are initiating few cases, and men are using the Charter to strike back at women's hard-won protections and benefits. At the time of writing, the Supreme Court of Canada had not delivered its first judgement concerning the equality guarantees. But the theories of equality and interpretive tests that, to date, have been applied by other courts in Canada will not improve women's condition.

This means that there is much more work to be done. The barriers to women's access to the courts must be removed, and interpretations of equality which are meaningful to women must be advanced more often in the courts. In addition, women must be actively concerned about judicial appointments as well as the education of lawyers and judges.

Recently some commentators have questioned the wisdom of investing work and hope in the Charter. These critics of entrenched rights argue that disadvantaged groups should not look to the courts for

---

Her Majesty the Queen in Right of Canada. All rights reserved. Source: *Canadian Charter Equality Rights for Women: One Step Forward or Two Steps Back* at 3–4, 49–50, 56, 59–67. Notes omitted. ISBN 0-6662-17011-3, Cat. No. LW31/1989E, Status of Women Canada. Reproduced with the permission of the Minister of Public Works and Government Services Canada, 2004.

assistance with their equality problems because the courts are, by nature, undemocratic and elitist. By and large, judges are white, middle-aged, middle-class men with no direct experience of disadvantage. And the courts, it has been argued, are not known to be agents of change. These commentators contend that women and other disadvantaged groups would be wiser to put their efforts into the democratic system, trying to change conditions of disadvantage through political rather than legal means.

This position is not without justification. Indeed, this study appears to support the views of these critics to the extent that its findings give reason for concern about the efficacy of seeking redress for equality problems in the courts.

However, women have not chosen the courts as the sole forum in which to seek advancement of their equality. Women are pressing governments actively and continually for improvements in laws and programs. Nor can women conclude from their experience that governments provide a better forum for their concerns; after all, governments, like the courts, are unrepresentative and too often unresponsive to women's needs. Because women's disadvantage is so entrenched, women do not have the luxury of choosing one forum over the other. The full support of both governments and the courts is needed for women to take their rightful place in Canadian society. Women must press for changes in both arenas.

It is our hope that the information provided in this study will draw new attention to the importance of access to the courts and of interpretations of equality that will positively affect the lives of women in Canada. If the Charter's guarantees are to be meaningful, governments must make them truly accessible to women and other disadvantaged groups; they cannot be available only to the rich. Also, governments must argue *for* women's interests in court, not against them. For their part, courts must be willing to listen, learn, and give the law its full effect.

The entrenchment of newly framed equality guarantees in the Constitution should be a positive step towards addressing the real conditions of inequality in Canada. However, if this positive step forward is to be taken, equality litigation cannot proceed as it has begun. A question is posed inescapably by the information revealed in this study: How real is Canada's commitment to equality for women?

. . . .

Three years of constitutional equality litigation in Canada have produced a body of 591 decisions. Of these 591 decisions, 52 are concerned with sex as a ground of discrimination. The number drops to 44 when appeals and other additional proceedings related to any one case are discounted. This means that, in less than 10 per cent of the equality rights decisions, a challenge has been made on the basis that a rule or practice infringes the sex equality guarantee of section 15 of the Charter. This percentage of sex equality challenges is small, considering the interest women have shown in Charter litigation, the range of inequalities they experience, and the fact that women make up a majority of Canada's population.

The fact that the number of challenges is small would be less important if the challenges were ones that significantly promoted the equality of women. However, this is not the case. Ironically, women's sex equality challenges are significantly underrepresented among the sex equality decisions. Only nine of the sex equality challenges were made by or on behalf of women. The other 35 challenges were made by or on behalf of men. If men's "fetal rights" challenges to women's reproductive autonomy and men's challenges to sexual assault legislation (based on age equality, freedom of expression, liberty, and fair trial rights) were added to the tally, the picture would look even worse. (The 44 sex equality decisions are listed and categorized in Appendix C.)

To analyse the sex equality challenges we begin by describing the women's challenges and then we examine the cases in which the sex equality guarantee has been invoked to further the interests of men. The purpose of this overview is to show what types of claims are being brought by women and men and their outcomes. We also hope to familiarize readers with the facts of cases that now form part of Canada's Charter sex equality jurisprudence and to introduce certain interpretive issues.

The chapter concludes with an examination of selected cases that illustrate trends in the equality rights arguments being advanced by litigants.

The Women's Challenges

Women's sex equality challenges have been divided evenly between the areas of family law, employment law, and personal injury law, with a smattering of challenges in the areas of human rights law, prison law, and laws concerning women's reproductive autonomy. To date, most of women's sex equality challenges have been directed at long-standing rules and practices that are overtly discriminatory.

The women's challenges have generally been made in the context of civil litigation initiated by them, such as maintenance proceedings or a human rights complaint. However, the initiator of a legal case and the party that raises the Charter challenge are not necessarily one and the same person. Therefore, some clarification of terminology is required. When we refer to "women's cases", we mean cases in which sex equality challenges have been raised to further women's interests, regardless of who commenced the litigation. Accordingly, *Wallace* and *Morgentaler*, both criminal cases, are included in the women's challenges. Correspondingly, when we refer to "men's cases" we mean cases in which sex equality challenges have been raised to further men's interests, regardless of who commenced the litigation. So, for example, a host of other criminal cases, mainly concerning sexual assault, are included in the men's challenges because, even though the cases were initiated by Attorneys General, these are cases in which the Charter has been invoked by men to further their interests in maintaining power over women.

The results of the women's cases have been mixed. The success rate of the women's initiatives stands at about 50 per cent, lower if one takes into account cases of marital status discrimination, lesbian rights cases, and lower court decisions that were reversed on appeal. However, because the number of women's cases is so small, this percentage may not be a reliable indication of the success rate of women's challenges over the longer term.

. . . .

Men's Use of the Equality Guarantee

Earlier, we said that approximately half of women's sex equality challenges had met with success. The success rate for men's challenges is somewhat lower. However, because there are more men's sex equality challenges (in fact, there were more than three times as many), men's successes have been more than double those of women. Men have succeeded in 13 challenges in the areas of family, employment, prison, and criminal law. The greatest concentration of men's sex equality challenges is in the area of criminal law, with family law challenges in second place....

. . . .

Placing Men's Sex Equality Litigation in a Social Context

Looking at the body of men's cases as a whole, it is apparent that men are using the Charter's guarantees to strike back at certain of the law reforms that women fought for in the 1960s and 1970s. There may be some exceptions, but this is definitely the pattern. Their efforts do not appear to be co-ordinated or part of any conscious political strategy — indeed, there are few signs that men are even aware of a broad social context for their sex equality challenges. However, most often, the targets of men applicants in sex equality cases are legislative protections and benefits that women have acquired in the last ten or twenty years as a result of intensive lobbying efforts. As the decided cases show, these protections and benefits include recent legislation concerning sexual assault, welfare benefits for single mothers, and unemployment insurance pregnancy benefits.

Whereas most women's challenges have been made in cases initiated by them, the pattern in the men's cases is quite different. Men's sex equality challenges have been made most often in the context of litigation in which they are on the defensive, either as accused persons in criminal cases or as respondents in civil cases. Some cases convey an impression that sex equality arguments are being made without a great deal of forethought, quite often in combination with other arguments, simply to help extricate men from uncomfortable legal predicaments.

The family law case of *Hommel v. Hommel* provides a good illustration. Mr. Hommel sought to reduce a monthly maintenance order for his former wife, Ms. Hommel, and their three children, contending that she had a "duty" to accept a marriage offer she had received from another man and, further, that she was keeping his maintenance payments artificially high by staying at home to care for the children rather than going out to work. The Nova Scotia Supreme Court noted that even though Ms. Hommel was caring for the three children of the marriage, the youngest of whom was under six years, Mr. Hommel took particular exception to her caring for a fourth "illegitimate" child who was not his. Mr. Hommel's Charter argument, which the Court rejected, was that he was being discriminated against because if he fathered another child, the courts would not consider the resulting added financial burden to him. This was plainly wrong, because the Court would have been required to consider a change in his ability to pay maintenance. The application for a reduction in maintenance was denied, and the Court had this to say about the equality argument:

> Counsel should not be quick to allege discrimination merely because a judicial determination does not favour counsel's client.

Some may imagine that litigation to secure more benefits for men also may assist women. This is the implication of a statement by Shalom Schachter quoted in a major article in *The Lawyers Weekly* following the Federal Court decision on his successful challenge to unemployment insurance pregnancy benefits:

> "I see this case as sort of opening the doors of fathers' consciousness that it is possible for them, it's appropriate for them [to care for their children]," he told *The Lawyers Weekly*. (words in square brackets added by *The Lawyers Weekly*)
>
> One reason Mr. Schachter took on the government was his firm conviction that men must play a greater role in child-rearing if women are to achieve their full potential in the workplace.
>
> "I felt it was ridiculous to expect women to take full advantage of the great opportunities outside the home if they then had to return to the house afterwards and shoulder all of the household responsibilities," he explained.
>
> "I see fathers taking a greater share of household responsibilities as being an assist to women."

We do not take issue with Mr. Schachter's social objectives. Increased public financial support for all parents has long been a goal of the Canadian feminist movement. The problem with the *Schachter* case is not its goal but the means of pursuing the goal. There is every reason to think that litigation of this sort, initiated by men, seriously endangers the minimal and fragile recognition that women's interests have received in the legislative arena. Indeed, Schachter proposed as a possible solution that biological fathers should be entitled to a share of the biological mother's pregnancy benefits. The Attorney General for Canada argued, moreover, that if any of the benefits provisions violated section 15, the Court should strike them down. Only the Women's Legal Education and Action Fund (LEAF), an intervenor in the case, argued consistently against reducing or eliminating pregnancy benefits.

The possibility that a court could strike down or reduce pregnancy benefits in response to the *Schachter* challenge was and still is a very real risk. Nobody could have predicted with confidence that Justice Strayer would extend the legislation as he did. There are numerous Charter precedents in which courts have specifically stated that the courts cannot fill in "legislative lacunae". Fortunately, Justice Strayer of the Trial Division of the Federal Court accepted the arguments of the intervenor (LEAF) and did, in fact, both protect pregnancy benefits and expand parental benefits for biological mothers and fathers. It is notable that, in *Schachter*, Justice Strayer not only accepted the arguments of the intervenor, but also explicitly acknowledged the assistance that the intervenor had provided, saying, "Through its counsel it played a very helpful role during these proceedings."

The outcome of *Schachter* in the Federal Court Trial Division creates an initial impression that the case has made a positive contribution to women's equality. However, it is far from clear that this will be the final result. The battle to protect pregnancy benefits has probably just begun. The federal government is appealing the Federal Court decision, and Justice Strayer's judgement is suspended, pending the outcome of the appeal.

Given the fact that women are initiating few challenges and men are attacking women's hard-won protections and benefits, the ability to intervene in cases initiated by men is extremely important. In the cases where men are attacking women's protections, the respondents are rarely women. The parties are usually a male applicant or male accused and one or more governments. Women require intervenor status in these circumstances in order to provide women's perspective on the equality issues that directly affect them and to defend the protections they have acquired. There is a great deal to say about women's inequality, little of which has ever been heard in Canadian courts.

Equality Concepts Advanced by Litigants

The underrepresentation of women in sex equality litigation is reflected in the equality concepts being advanced in the courts. In a majority of cases, these equality rights concepts are not in the best interests of women. The theory of equality consistently advanced by male applicants' lawyers is that men have the right to be treated the same as women. This formal equality theory is relied upon repeatedly, even in the face of the most obvious sex-based differences.

For example, in the case of *Re Getty and Crow*, an estates case concerning title to land, a lawyer representing an elderly man was required to persuade the court that his client would probably not have any more children. The man wanted to sell his land but there was a question about whether he might become a father to children who would have claims against the land. The lawyer sought to rely on an evidentiary presumption that women of an advanced age are incapable of having children. The client being male and the presumption applying only to females, the lawyer argued that his client was being discriminated against. He contended that section 15 of the Charter means that the presumption about childbearing capacities should be applied identically to men and women, notwithstanding biological differences between men and women.

In the *Re Getty and Crow* example, the concept of formal equality, or same treatment, is at odds with the biological differences between men and women. Whereas reproductive senescence in women is absolute once menstruation ceases, men's loss of reproductive capacity is relatively gradual, and sperm production can occur in men of very advanced years. However, not even in *Re Getty and Crow*, where one might have seen the absurdity of pretending that men and women are identical, did the Court say that it rejected the equality rights model put forward on behalf of the applicant. What District Court Judge Clements said was that he did not have to decide the "vexing problem" of the application of the Charter to men's and women's reproductive capacities.

The argument that equality requires the courts to ignore differences between men and women is prevalent not just in cases involving biological differences between men and women, but also in cases concerning facets of life in which women are socially or economically disadvantaged relative to men. These are the cases in which judicial endorsement of formal equality has its most devastating effects on women because the courts' decisions stand to legitimize real inequality.

For example, in the *Vincer* case, it was contended on behalf of the male applicant, who was a separated father with joint custody of his children, that the provisions of and regulations under the *Family Allowance Act* discriminate against men because they require that the family allowance cheque be paid to the mother, unless the father has sole custody of the children. In the Federal Court of Appeal, a central argument advanced on behalf of David Vincer was that "the mere fact" that a piece of legislation makes a distinction based on sex constitutes an "unreasonable classification". This argument was reinforced by reference to section 28 which states:

> **28.** Notwithstanding anything in this Charter, the rights and freedoms referred to in it are guaranteed equally to male and female persons.

On behalf of Vincer, it was contended that section 28 strengthens men's claim to be treated the same as women.

Although it is well documented that the negative financial consequences of marriage breakdown are experienced by women primarily, and that the financial position of divorced and separated men often improves, only one judge out of three indicated that he rejected the equality model put forward by the applicant. Justice Pratte noted that the legislation makes a distinction between men and women but said that the distinction is fully justified by the obvious disparity of income between husbands and wives. Justice Marceau and Stone offered no comment on the merits of the case.

The contention that section 28 requires courts to ignore the realities of women's inequality is a cruel twist on the use for which section 28 was intended. Although it may be noted that its gender-neutral wording belies its purpose (as outlined in the previous two chapters), section 28 was included by the Charter's drafters in response to women's lobby for its inclusion in the Charter. Women wanted to reinforce the section 15 promise of assistance to women in overcoming their position of disadvantage in society.

Unfortunately, Attorneys General have not shown themselves to be vigorous advocates for women's rights either, and often they are no better than advocates for men, in terms of the arguments they place before the courts. In most cases, Attorneys General assume the responsibility for defending impugned legislation. The characteristic posture of the Attorneys General is to defend challenged legislation, even if it is legislation that impinges on the Charter rights of women. There is no shortage of reports concerning cases in which Attorneys General have defended legislation that threatens women's interests.

For example, the party defending the abortion provisions of the *Criminal Code*, in the case of *Morgentaler*, was the Attorney General for Ontario. The government's position on the abortion question was opposed to women's equality. The interpretive arguments put forward in that case by the government lawyers were actually hostile to women's interests. Morgentaler's counsel argued that section 251 of the Code violated women's right to equal benefit of the law. Counsel for the Attorney General for Ontario attacked the sex equality arguments saying:

> ...for section 251 to be decreed invalid as discriminatory on the basis of sex, it would have to be established that a man seeking an abortion would be required to comply with section 251. Clearly this is an impossibility, and therefore sec-

tion 251 by its very nature cannot be attacked as discriminatory on the basis of sex, *per se*.

This argument that women's experiences are inconsequential unless comparable to an experience known to men is a corollary of the requirement that like be treated alike. It is a mirror image of the arguments put forward by the applicant in *Vincer*. Whereas in *Vincer* it was argued that equality requires that courts pretend that there are no differences between men and women, in *Morgentaler* it was contended by government that the differences can be so significant that no comparison is possible.

Williams v. Haugen is another case in which government lawyers argued that if there is no male group available for comparison, the distinction in question cannot possibly constitute discrimination. In *Williams*, the Saskatchewan Department of Justice argued that a one-year limitation period for women's child support claims could not discriminate on the basis of sex because the entire legislative scheme applied to women only.

Although the Attorneys General usually defend challenged legislation, they are apt to do so in a way that either ignores or undermines the substantive equality content of section 15. The position of most Attorneys General is that section 15 is essentially a guarantee of procedural equality. Counsel for Attorneys General frequently urge the courts to reaffirm a doctrine of judicial deference articulated by the Supreme Court of Canada in relation to the *Canadian Bill of Rights*. With the possible exception of the Attorney General of Ontario, Attorneys General in Canada do not accept the concept that the Charter imposes positive obligations on governments to assist disadvantaged groups in achieving equality. It should come as no surprise, therefore, that counsel for Attorneys General do not support the remedy of extension in equality cases involving under-inclusive benefits programs. The example of the *Schachter* case has already been mentioned.

In *Schachter*, although the Attorney General for Canada defended the two-part pregnancy and parental benefits scheme, he submitted that, if the Court found the scheme unconstitutional, it should strike down parental benefits. The position of the Attorney General for Canada then was that it would rather see adoptive parents' benefits eliminated than see parental benefits extended to biological parents.

Attorneys General are not even consistently strong advocates for the legislation of their own legislatures or parliament. For example, counsel for Attorneys General typically do not put forward constitutional sex equality arguments to defend law promulgated because of women's political actions. The case of *Canadian Newspapers Co. v. A.G. Canada* is illustrative.

In *Canadian Newspapers*, the company asserted the right to publish the name of a sexual assault victim, against her will. Section 442(3) of the *Criminal Code* protects sexual assault victims against involuntary publication of their names. The newspaper company applied under section 24 of the Charter for an order declaring that section 442(3) of the *Criminal Code* violates the freedom of the press guaranteed in section 2(b) of the Charter. Justice Osborne of the Supreme Court of Ontario upheld the provision under section 1 of the Charter, as a reasonable limit on freedom of the press.

Canadian Newspapers Co. appealed to the Ontario Court of Appeal, adding fair trial rights to its cache of legal arguments. The government lawyers who defended the legislation did not even mention the right of women to freedom from sexual assault or freedom to speak about sexual assault without fear of forced publication of their names. Instead, the legislation was defended solely under section 1 of the Charter as a reasonable limit, intended to facilitate the reporting of crime. In the result, the Ontario Court of Appeal weakened section 442(3), giving courts discretion to deny victims' requests for protection under section 442(3).

It was not until the Supreme Court of Canada level that the importance of section 442(3) for women's rights as distinct from government rights became a part of the case. On October 26, 1987, a coalition of feminist and community service organizations was granted leave to intervene in the case to argue the sex equality issues.

To ears that have not heard women talk about the experience of sexual assault or the fear of being sexually assaulted, the goal of facilitating the reporting of crime (by publishing the names of sexual assault victims) can sound as though it is the same thing as the goal of women's equality, making women's equality arguments redundant. But there is a difference. The following excerpts from the intervenor's *factum* illustrate concretely that difference:

> 32. Victims of sexual assault are, overwhelmingly, women; perpetrators of sexual assault are, overwhelmingly, men. Sexual violation of women by men is both an indication and a practice of inequality between the sexes, specifically of the low status of women relative to men.
>
> 33. Only a fraction of rapes are reported. Only a fraction of reported rapes are prosecuted. Only a fraction of prosecuted rapes result in convictions. Rape sentences are often short. Most rap-

ists, therefore, continue to live in society either undetected or unpunished and unrehabilitated.

34. In sum, victims of sex crimes, largely women, are comparatively disadvantaged relative to the perpetrators of sex crimes, largely men. A systemic situation of inequality between the sexes thus exists in the social practice of sexual violence, the victims of which are women and in the operation of the criminal justice system, which *de jure* outlaws sexual violence but *de facto* permits men to engage in it on a wide scale.

Seaboyer is another case where constitutional sex equality arguments could have been made by the Attorneys General but were not. In that case, two male accused challenged section 246(6) of the *Criminal Code* on the basis that it violated their rights to a fair trial. Section 246(6) limits the ability of the defence to canvas the past sexual history of a sexual assault victim with anyone other than the accused. Like the provision protecting sexual assault victims against involuntary publication of their names, section 246(6) is a protection for which women's groups lobbied to improve the treatment of women who report sexual assault. Despite this, counsel for the Attorneys General in that case made no reference to the competing constitutional sex equality rights of women.

Further, in the *Borowski* "fetal rights" challenge, the Attorney General for Canada neglected even to mention in its *factum* the negative implications that Borowski's position poses for women's section 15 sex equality rights.

Some of the factums filed by counsel for Attorneys General convey an impression that counsel may not understand that women's inequality problem is not that they are different from men, but that they are disadvantaged relative to men. In *Reference Re Family Benefits Act*, counsel for the Attorney General of Nova Scotia attempted to defend legislation that benefits women, but relied on the same formal equality arguments that are used to undermine women's claims to access to male privileges: "women are differently situated", and therefore can be treated differently. Instead of rejecting the formal model of equality and concentrating on the amelioration of disadvantage as a Charter goal, the Attorney General's counsel supported it in order to justify the benefits for single mothers.

In *Reference Re Family Benefits Act*, Counsel's authority for the proposition that persons who are differently situated may be treated differently was the decision of the Ontario Court of Appeal in *R. v. Swain*. In *Swain*, the finding that mentally disordered accused persons are "differently situated" from other accused persons operated as a blanket justification for the automatic incarceration of mentally disordered accused persons. The *Swain* case is inimical to the rights of persons with mental disabilities, a group that includes women. It is also a threat to women as women. What women have in common with other equality-seekers is disadvantage, not difference, and it is because of their disadvantage that women and other equality-seekers need legal advocates who can direct the attention of judges to the concept of disadvantage and away from the concept of difference.

Evidence of women's disadvantage from counsel representing Attorneys General in cases involving challenges to laws that benefit or protect women is typically very sparse. This is particularly striking in the case where section 146 of the *Criminal Code*, which prohibited sexual intercourse with a girl under 14 years of age (statutory rape), was challenged by the accused. For example, in *Lucas*, the Court commented on the lack of evidence from the Crown, saying that no psychological or sociological evidence had been presented to demonstrate the differences "if any" in the sexuality of young teenagers that would justify a different protection for females than males. The Court declared the offence of statutory rape unconstitutional and dismissed the charges against the accused. This decision was overturned on appeal on the grounds that section 15 could not be used because the charges were laid prior to its coming into force.

It must be acknowledged that, in some cases, women's rights advocates have also advanced formal equality arguments, saying that men and women should be treated the same. For example, in *Shewchuk*, a coalition of intervenors, including the West Coast Women's Legal Education and Action Fund, supported the view that special treatment of single mothers was unwarranted and argued in favour of extending the benefit in question to single fathers. Presented with the risk of losing the special programs completely — and the reality of extremely few precedents to support alternatives to formal equality — it is not surprising that women have tried to make the best of formal equality arguments.

However, feminist organizations are attempting increasingly to present substantive equality arguments to the courts and to provide judges with information concerning the realities of women's inequality. One example is the women-run defence in the *Federation of Women Teachers* case. The defence in this case consisted of in-depth argument and extensive expert evidence concerning the unequal position of women teachers in the teaching profession and of women in the work force generally. It also documented the silence of the men's federation concerning discrimination against women teachers, the improvements in conditions for women teachers brought about by the women teachers' federation, the historical failure of mixed organizations to recognize and represent women's interests, the capacity of women's organizations to address women's distinctive priorities effectively, the positive recognition that women's advocacy groups have achieved in other societies such as Norway, Sweden, Denmark, and the United States, and the inability of the same-treatment model of equality to rectify existing social imbalances among groups.

The defence in the *Federation of Women Teachers* case was not conducted by counsel for Attorneys General and demonstrated a very different appearance from those cases conducted by them. The *factum* and the evidence were developed over a two-year period by a team of privately retained feminist lawyers and scholars. The resources and role of women advocates in this case were exceptional. Unfortunately, as a rule, women's organizations have neither the resources nor the standing to be the primary parties in sex equality challenges.

Conclusion

Women have initiated very little sex equality litigation. Men have initiated more than three times as many sex equality challenges as women have. Many of the men's challenges are to legislated protections and benefits such as rape law reforms and unemployment insurance pregnancy benefits, which women fought for in the political arena. To defend their few hard-won gains against men's equality challenges, and to establish a voice for women in the courts, women have been forced to seek the courts' leave to participate in equality litigation as intervenors.

In order to better assess the impact of sex equality litigation, Chapter Four will provide a closer look at the judges' decisions to determine what equality concepts are being adopted by the courts in sex equality cases, and how other important interpretive issues are being resolved.

(ix) Ardour in the Court: The Charter has done less to enhance your rights than to increase the policy-making power of judges

Rainer Knopff and F.L. Morton

In 1992, former chief justice Antonio Lamer described the adoption of the Charter of Rights as "a revolution on the scale of the introduction of the metric system, the great medical discoveries of Louis Pasteur, and the invention of penicillin and the laser." Five years later, Mr. Lamer thanked "God for the Charter," adding that people "just don't have these rights." Life without the Charter, presumably, would be as bad as life before antibiotics.

We agree that the Charter has wrought a revolution but, contrary to the penicillin analogy, its effect hasn't been akin to saving and improving the lives of untold millions. Can anyone who remembers pre-1982 Canada seriously believe that the Charter has enriched and improved our lives to that extent?

Do we have dramatically improved freedom of speech? Well, okay, we are freer to collect kiddie porn.

Is freedom of religion much better protected? Maybe, but mainly in the sense of more freedom from religion, especially Christianity, which is increasingly seen as disqualifying any policy position with which it is associated.

Are we significantly less likely to convict the innocent? Probably not, though we may be more likely to let the guilty go free.

From *The Globe and Mail* (7 April 2000) A17. Reproduced by permission of the authors.

Are we more equal? Not if one is to believe equality rights advocates, who never tire of pointing out growing disparities.

The pre-Charter world was far from perfect, but it was hardly the Dark Age implied by Mr. Lamer's revolutionary rhetoric. Nor is the post-Charter world remarkably better. There have been changes, but inflationary "rights talk" notwithstanding, they have mainly been shifts in the policy balance on matters of ongoing reasonable disagreement.

The Charter's main revolutionary effect has not been to improve society but to enhance the political and policy influence of judges, to give them more power over the matters of reasonable disagreement that legislatures used to settle.

The judges themselves have admitted as much. Mr. Lamer, for example, has "no doubt" that the judiciary has been "drawn into the political arena to a degree unknown prior to 1982," and that it is often called upon "to make what used to be a political call." Similarly, the late Justice John Sopinka admitted that in "deciding a Charter case, the court is in a sense legislating." When York University's Ian Greene and several colleagues interviewed many of Canada's appellate court judges, virtually all of them admitted to a new lawmaking role. Earlier this week, Chief Justice Beverley McLachlin associated a "litigation explosion" with the advent of the Charter of Rights, indicating just how extensive the new policymaking role has become.

When so-called "court bashers" challenge this transfer of political power to unelected officials, the judges often reverse course insisting that there is no revolution after all. Judges have always enjoyed a degree of policymaking discretion, they contend, and have exercised that discretion in applying the constitutional law of federalism. The Charter, far from effecting a revolutionary change, now appears as just a minor extension of well-established practice.

Unfortunately, this dodge doesn't work. While it is certainly true that federalism jurisprudence also involves judicial policymaking, deciding under the Charter whether government as such may (or must) do something goes far beyond deciding which government may do it. As Ian Hunter has aptly put it, "It may be true that elephants and chipmunks are both mammals, but to fail to acknowledge the difference between them is wilful deception."

Another response to the court bashers is to claim that judges are merely discharging duties imposed on them by the Canadian people when the Charter was democratically adopted. They are simply applying the Charter. However, this legalistic view of judging cannot be reconciled with whatever meaning the judges choose. "We have lots of discretion," Justice Claire L'Heureux-Dubé told the Canadian Bar Association last August. "So put yourself in where there is nothing else to go on." In other words, judges drive the Charter, not vice versa.

Judges do not drive the Charter alone, however. When Justice L'Heureux-Dubé admits to putting herself into the Charter, she is following the lead of countless activist commentators who insist, for example, that "the shaping of the Charter will be an intensely political process, far more responsive to public pressure than to constitutional law," or that litigating "law reform is part of an ideological battle." Groups such as LEAF (the Legal Education and Action Fund) have mounted fully self-conscious campaigns of "influencing the influencers," by "flooding the law reviews" with advice on just how judges should put themselves into the Charter.

Without the constant barrage of such activist scholarship, Justice L'Heureux-Dubé's unabashed put-yourself-in statement would be inconceivable, as would her remark in another speech that she is an "equality person" who will "do any thing I can to achieve it [equality]." Anything? Judges from earlier eras would never have so blatantly treated law as the vehicle for a political agenda.

Like the Charter itself, in other words, judges are as much a means as a cause of the Charter revolution. While judges are in the vanguard of the revolution, they are being pushed as much as they lead. They are being pushed by what we call the "Court Party," a loose constellation of interests that assiduously promote judicial power because they stand to benefit from it.

Today's Court Party, we contend, is a party of elites. It is dominated by the chattering classes. The Charter revolution it promotes is a revolution from the top, part of what Christopher Lasch — turning Ortega y Gassett on his head — has christened the "revolt of the elites."

Despite the rhetorical evasions, the revolution in judicial power is now widely conceded — even, as we have seen, by judges in their more candid moments. The Charter itself, however, is not so much the cause of the revolution as the means through which it is carried out. The Declaration of Independence did not cause the American Revolution, nor the Declaration of the Rights of Man the French Revolution. A revolution cannot occur without leaders and the support of interested classes. The Charter Revolution and the Court Party explains the political economy and sociology of the Charter revolution.

(x) The Case for a Strong Court: The judiciary is accountable to the public interest, not public opinion

Judge Rosalie Abella

Democracy is not — and never was — just about the wishes of the majority. What pumps oxygen no less forcefully through vibrant democratic veins is the protection of rights, through the courts, notwithstanding the wishes of the majority. It is this second, crucial aspect of democratic values that has been submerged by the [recent] swirling discourse [about the role of judges in enforcing rights].

I think it is fair to say that until 1981, when the Charter was donated to the British North America Act by the federal government, no one ever accused the Canadian judiciary of aggressive rights protection. In fact, many of us, reared on the constitutional diet of division-of-powers jurisprudence, looked wistfully at the wide selection on the constitutional menu available to American judges. With rare exceptions, the Canadian Supreme Court not only shared the apparent inhibitions of its American and British counterparts about welcoming rights into the judicial fold, they remained reluctant at least a generation longer.

By the time I graduated from law school in 1970, the perception was that the Supreme Court was the place that decided constitutional issues such as whether Persons in the British North [America] Act included women and whether egg marketing boards were a provincial or a federal undertaking.

Then, in 1978, just before we got a Charter, the Supreme Court in Rathwell v. Rathwell reversed a decision it had made only five years earlier in Murdoch v. Murdoch, thereby rewriting the archaic matrimonial property regime we had been subject to for over 100 years. No longer equitable, said the court. Time to adjust to a new appreciation about the role played by husbands and wives in a marriage. Time, in short, to create a new social contract. The public cheered. The media cheered. Within months, practically every province had amended its family property laws accordingly.

Then we got the Charter of Rights and Freedoms. To the Constitution's division of powers, it added rights: civil rights, such as the freedoms of religion, association and expression; the right to counsel; and the right to security of a person. And human rights, such as equality, linguistic rights, aboriginal rights and multiculturalism. What Canada got with the Charter was a dramatic package of guaranteed rights, subject only to those reasonable limits that were demonstrably justified in a free and democratic society; a package assembled by the legislature, which in turn, it bears repeating, assigned to the courts the duty to decide whether its laws, policies or practices met the constitutional standards set out in the Charter.

In the first decade of Charter adjudication, the Supreme Court was energetic. It struck down Sabbatarian and sign laws, said equality meant more than treating people the same, and decriminalized abortion. It ventured fearlessly into the overgrown fields of the law and cut a wide path for other courts to follow. Again the public cheered. Even the media cheered. It was clear that the 1960s and 1970s had generated a public thirst for rights protection, and Charter adjudication in the Supreme Court in the 1980s was beginning to quench that thirst.

With the arrival of the 1990s, a few abrupt voices were heard to challenge the Supreme Court, voices in large part belonging to those whose psychological security or territorial hegemony were at risk from the Charter's reach. As the decade advanced, so did the courage and insistence of these New Inhibitors, most of whom appeared to congregate at one end of the ideological spectrum. While their articulated target was the Supreme Court of Canada, their real target was the way the Charter was transforming their traditional expectations and entitlements.

They made their arguments skillfully. In essence, they turned the good news of constitutionalized rights, the mark of a secure and mature democracy, into the bad news of judicial autocracy, the mark of a debilitated and devalued legislature. They called

---

This is an excerpt from a lecture delivered at a Constitutional Law Conference on April 7, 2000 at Osgoode Hall Law School. Reproduced by permission of the author.

minorities seeking the right to be free from discrimination "special interest groups seeking to jump the queue." They called efforts to reverse discrimination "reverse discrimination."

They pretended that concepts or words in the Charter such as freedom, equality and justice had no pre-existing political aspect and bemoaned the politicization of the judiciary. They trumpeted the rights of the majority and ignored the fact that minorities are people who want rights, too. They said courts should only interpret, not make law, thereby ignoring the entire history of common law. They called advocates for equality, human rights, and the Charter "biased" and defenders of the status quo "impartial." They urged the courts to defer to legislation, unless, ironically, they disagreed with the legislation. They said judges are not accountable because they are not elected, yet held them to negative account for every expanded right. They claimed a monopoly on truth, frequently used invectives to assert it, then accused their detractors of personalizing the debate.

The essence of their message was that there is an anti-democratic, socially hazardous turbulence in the air, most notably during judicial flights. And while it is a message that has every right to be heard, it is not the whole story. The whole story is that the Charter does not represent heterodoxy about democracy, but rather its finest manifestation. People elect legislators who enact the laws they think the majority of their constituents want them to enact, and appoint judges who are expected to be independent from those legislators and impartial in determining whether the legislature's actions meet constitutional standards.

When legislatures elected by majorities enact laws such as the Charter, the majority is presumed to agree with that legislature's decision to entrench rights and extend a constitutionally guaranteed invitation to the courts to intervene when legislative conduct is not demonstrably justified in a democratic society.

In enforcing the Charter, therefore, the courts are not trespassing on legislative authority, they are fulfilling their assigned democratic duty to prevent legislative trespass on constitutional rights.

While all branches of government are responsible for the delivery of justice, they respond to different imperatives. Legislators, our elected proxies, consult constituents, fellow parliamentarians, and available research until the public's opinions are sufficiently digestible to be swallowed by a parliamentary majority. And if they cannot be made sufficiently palatable, they are starved for want of political nourishment.

This is the dilemma all legislators face — they are elected to implement the public will, the public will is often difficult to ascertain or implement, and they are therefore left to implement only those constituency concerns that can survive the gauntlet of the prevailing partisan ideology. At the end of any given parliamentary session, many public concerns lay scattered of necessity on the cutting-room floor, awaiting either wider public endorsement or a newly elected partisan ideology.

The judiciary has a different relationship with the public. It is accountable less to the public's opinions and more to the public interest. It discharges that accountability by being principled, independent, and impartial. Of all the public institutions responsible for delivering justice, the judiciary is the only one for whom justice is the exclusive mandate. This means that while legislatures respond of necessity to the urgings of the public, however we define it, judges, on the other hand, serve only justice. As Lillian Hellman once said: "I will not cut my conscience to fit this year's fashions."

This means that the occasional judgment will collide with some public expectations, which will, inevitably, create controversy. But judgments that are controversial are not thereby illegitimate or undemocratic; they are, in fact, democracy at work.

This defence of constitutional rights does not mean that there are no outstanding issues. There are several to discuss: public information about who judges are and how they are appointed; the interrelationship between courts and legislatures, including the reminder that the notwithstanding clause gives legislatures the final say; when to read in corrective words to effect constitutional compliance and when to leave corrective compliance to the legislature; the tension between those who think the rights stage is overpopulated and those who are in the wings waiting to join the cast; whether labels such as progressive, conservative, activist, restraint, or politicization really contribute to a thoughtful analysis of judicial behaviour; whether the search for consensus is replacing compassion and courage as the defining justice objective and, as a corollary whether the proposition that entitlement should be a matter of timing can ever be consistent with the fact that rights are guaranteed now.

All of these are issues that we are, and should be, talking about. It is a conversation I hope we will keep constructive, rigorous, and continuous.